# DIMENSIONS OF PSYCHOLOGY

Introductory Readings

# DIMENSIONS
# of PSYCHOLOGY

## Introductory Readings

*Edited by*

**GALE B. BISHOP**
University of Albuquerque

**WINFRED F. HILL**
Northwestern University

**J. B. Lippincott Company**
Philadelphia   New York   Toronto

ISBN 0-397-47210-2

Library of Congress
Catalog Card Number:
79-155877

Printed in the
United States of America

Cover and interior design by Robert J. Perry

# ACKNOWLEDGMENTS

1 WILLIAM D. HITT: *Two Models of Man*
Reprinted from *American Psychologist,* volume 24 (1969), pages 651–658, by permission of the American Psychological Association.

2 EDWIN G. BORING: *Cognitive Dissonance: Its Use in Science*
Reprinted from *Science,* volume 145, pages 680–685 (August 14, 1964). Copyright 1964 by the American Association for the Advancement of Science.

3 MARK R. ROSENZWEIG: *Environmental Complexity, Cerebral Change, and Behavior*
Reprinted from *American Psychologist,* volume 21 (1966), pages 321–332, by permission of the American Psychological Association.

4 ROBERT B. LOCKARD: *The Albino Rat: A Defensible Choice or a Bad Habit?*
Reprinted from *American Psychologist,* volume 24 (1969), pages 734–742, by permission of the American Psychological Association.

5 DONALD D. JENSEN: *Paramecia, Planaria, and Pseudo-Learning*
Reprinted from *Animal Behaviour Supplement,* 1965, pages 9–20, by permission of Baillière, Tindall & Cassell Ltd.

6 O. L. GERICKE: *Practical Use of Operant Conditioning Procedures in a Mental Hospital*
Reprinted from *Psychiatric Studies and Projects,* volume 3 (1965), number 5, pages 2–10, by permission of the American Psychiatric Association.

7 O. IVAR LOVAAS, BENSON SCHAEFFER, AND JAMES Q. SIMMONS: *Building Social Behavior in Autistic Children by Use of Electric Shock*
Reprinted from the *Journal of Experimental Research in Personality,* volume 1 (1965), pages 99–109. Copyright © Academic Press.

8 LEON FESTINGER: *The Psychological Effects of Insufficient Rewards*
Reprinted from *American Psychologist,* volume 16 (1961), pages 1–11, by permission of the American Psychological Association.

9 J. McV. HUNT: *Experience and the Development of Motivation: Some Reinterpretations*
Reprinted from *Child Development,* volume 31 (1960), pages 489–504, by permission of the Society for Research in Child Development, Inc.

10 ROBERT G. HEATH: *Electrical Self-Stimulation of the Brain in Man*
Reprinted from *American Journal of Psychiatry,* volume 120 (1963), pages 571–577. Copyright, 1963, the American Psychiatric Association.

11 J. P. SCOTT: *Critical Periods in Behavioral Development*
Reprinted from *Science,* volume 138, pages 949–958 (November 30, 1962). Copyright 1962 by the American Association for the Advancement of Science.

41  ELI A. RUBINSTEIN: *Paradoxes of Student Protests*
       Reprinted from *American Psychologist,* volume 24 (1969), pages 133–141,
       by permission of the American Psychological Association.

42  JIMMIE SHERMAN: *From the Ashes: A Personal Reaction to the Revolt of
    Watts*
       Reprinted from *The Antioch Review,* volume 27, number 3 (Fall, 1967), by
       permission of the editors.

43  S. B. SELLS: *Ecology and the Science of Psychology*
       Reprinted from *Multivariate Behavioral Research,* volume 1 (1966), pages
       131–144, by kind permission of the Society of Multivariate Experimental
       Psychology, Inc., publishers, and of Professor S. B. Sells, author.

44  LEONARD KRASNER: *The Behavioral Scientist and Social Responsibility:
    No Place to Hide*
       Reprinted from the *Journal of Social Issues,* volume 21, number 2,
       pages 9–30.

# CONTENTS

# PREFACE

The student is the purpose of this book of readings, and it is totally what the student makes it. As editors it is our hope that this collection of readings will convey something of the wonder and scope of what psychology is today and can be tomorrow. The literature of psychology is vast, and no finite collection of readings can hope to sample any but a tiny portion of its variety. It is up to the student to use such a collection to his own best advantage, as a guide to further reading in areas of his interest.

In order to give the student some idea of the breadth of psychological thinking, it is necessary to limit the number of readings in each area. Each article is meant to serve as a starting point for a line of thought. The introductory notes represent our own thoughts about its meaning and implications. But the student must understand that the notes can reflect only general lines of our thinking. These need to be elaborated in the student's thought, with the help of his teachers and general textbook. At the beginning of each article, we have provided questions which are meant to stimulate thought and discussion.

Although this book was written as a complement to *Psychology: Principles and Problems* by Winfred Hill, it can be utilized to fit the needs of any introductory psychology class.

Each article in this book of readings may be taken at many different levels: as an example of research methodology or theoretical framework, as a starting point for the relevance of the work to our day-by-day life, or in relation to the other sciences and arts. Above all, however, the full utilization of this collection depends on the student's involvement with the material of each article and his willingness to give it careful thought and review.

Some technical articles have been included as well as articles representing the layman's point of view. Although the range of articles is from theoretical to practical, no article should be beyond the scope of the student of introductory psychology.

We would like to express our gratitude to those people who have helped in the preparation of this book of readings. Our thanks go to the authors and publishers who kindly granted permission to reprint their work. And our special thanks to our friends and associates for their personal help.

GALE B. BISHOP
WINFRED F. HILL

January, 1972

# PART 1

# The Science of Behavior

# READING 1

# Two Models of Man

**WILLIAM D. HITT**
**Battelle Memorial Institute, Columbus, Ohio**

The first article in this book discusses the contrasting ways in which behaviorism and phenomenology describe man. It is interesting to see how these models are reflected in different areas of psychology. After discussing these contrasting models, Hitt suggests that a combination of the ideas of both behaviorism and phenomenology could be both useful and appropriate.

## QUESTIONS

1. How do the two models of man lead to different kinds of investigation?
2. Which model of man is most in accord with your own ideas? Pick one model and support its validity.
3. What does Hitt mean when he asks: "Would it be reasonable to view man as both a dependent variable and an independent variable?"

A symposium sponsored by the Division of Philosophical Psychology of the American Psychological Association clearly pointed up the cleavage in contemporary theoretical and philosophical psychology. The symposium was held at Rice University to mark the inception of the Division of Philosophical Psychology as a new division of the APA. Participants included Sigmund Koch, R. B. MacLeod, B. F. Skinner, Carl R. Rogers, Norman Malcolm, and Michael

Presented at the meeting of the American Psychological Association, San Francisco, August 1968.

Scriven. The presentations and associated discussions were organized in the book: *Behaviorism and Phenomenology: Contrasting Bases for Modern Psychology* (Edited by T. W. Wann, 1964).

## THE ARGUMENT

As indicated in the title of the book, the main argument of the symposium dealt with phenomenology versus behaviorism. This argument also could be described as one between existential psychology and behavioristic psychology. The presentations dealt with two distinct models of man and the scientific methodology associated with each model. The discussions following each presentation may be described as aggressive, hostile, and rather emotional; they would suggest that there is little likelihood of a reconciliation between the two schools of thought represented at the symposium.

To illustrate the nature of the argument, some of the statements made by the participants are presented below.

## IN SUPPORT OF BEHAVIORISM
### Skinner (1964):
An adequate science of behavior must consider events taking place within the skin of the organism, not as physiological mediators of behavior, but as part of behavior itself. It can deal with these events without assuming that they have any special nature or must be known in any special way. . . . Public and private events have the same kinds of physical dimensions [p. 84].

### Malcolm (1964):
Behaviorism is right in insisting that there must be some sort of conceptual tie between the language of mental phenomena and outward circumstances and behavior. If there were not, we could not understand other people, nor could we understand ourselves [p. 152].

## ATTACKS ON BEHAVIORISM
### Koch (1964):
Behaviorism has been given a hearing for fifty years. I think this generous. I shall urge that it is essentially a role-playing position which has outlived whatever usefulness its role might once have had [p. 6].

### Rogers (1964):
It is quite unfortunate that we have permitted the world of psychological science to be narrowed to behavior observed, sounds emitted, marks scratched on paper, and the like [p. 118].

## IN SUPPORT OF PHENOMENOLOGY
### MacLeod (1964):
I am . . . insisting that what, in the old, prescientific days, we used to call "consciousness" still can and should be studied. Whether or not this kind of study may be called a science depends on our definition of the term. To be a scientist, in my opinion, is to have boundless curiosity tempered by discipline [p. 71].

### Rogers (1964):
The inner world of the individual appears to have more significant influence upon his behavior than does the external environmental stimulus [p. 125].

## ATTACKS ON PHENOMENOLOGY
### Malcolm (1964):
I believe that Wittgenstein has proved this line of thinking (introspectionism) to be disastrous. It leads to the conclusion that we do not and cannot understand each other's psychological language, which is a form of solipsism[1] [p. 148].

### Skinner (1964):
Mentalistic or psychic explanations of human behavior almost certainly originated in primitive animism [p. 79]. . . . I am a radical behaviorist simply in the sense that I find no place in the formulation for anything which is mental [p. 106].

This appears to be the heart of the argument:

The behaviorist views man as a passive organism governed by external stimuli. Man can be manipulated through proper control of these stimuli. Moreover, the laws that govern man are essentially the same as the laws that govern all natural phenomena of the world; hence, it is assumed that the scientific method used by the physical scientist is equally appropriate to the study of man.

The phenomenologist views man as the *source* of acts; he is free to choose in each situation. The essence of man is *inside* of man; he is controlled by his own consciousness. The most appropriate methodology for the study of man is phenomenology, which begins with the world of experience.

These two models of man have been proposed and discussed for many years by philosophers and psychologists alike. Versions of these models may be seen in the contrasting views of Locke and Leibnitz (see Allport, 1955), Marx and Kierkegaard, Wittgenstein and Sartre, and, currently, Skinner and Rogers. Were he living today, William James probably would characterize Locke, Marx, Wittgenstein, and Skinner as "tough-minded," while Leibnitz, Kierke-

---

[1] Solipsism is defined as the theory that only the self exists, or can be proven to exist.

gaard, Sartre, and Rogers would be viewed as "tender-minded." Traditionally, the argument has been one model versus the other. It essentially has been a black-and-white argument.

The purpose of this article is to analyze the argument between the behaviorist and the phenomenologist. This analysis is carried out by presenting and discussing two different models of man.

## CONTRASTING VIEWS OF MAN

The two models of man are presented in terms of these contrasting views:

1. Man can be described meaningfully in terms of his behavior; or man can be described meaningfully in terms of his consciousness.

2. Man is predictable; or man is unpredictable.

3. Man is an information transmitter; or man is an information generator.

4. Man lives in an objective world; or man lives in a subjective world.

5. Man is a rational being; or man is an arational being.

6. One man is like other men; or each man is unique.

7. Man can be described meaningfully in absolute terms; or man can be described meaningfully in relative terms.

8. Human characteristics can be investigated independently of one another; or man must be studied as a whole.

9. Man is a reality; or man is a potentiality.

10. Man is knowable in scientific terms; or man is more than we can ever know about him.

Each of these attributes is discussed below.

## SUPPORT FOR BOTH MODELS

The evidence offered below in support of each of the two models of man is both empirical and analytical. Perhaps some of the evidence is intuitive, but it at least seems logical to the author of this article.

## MAN CAN BE DESCRIBED MEANINGFULLY IN TERMS OF HIS BEHAVIOR; OR MAN CAN BE DESCRIBED MEANINGFULLY IN TERMS OF HIS CONSCIOUSNESS

According to John B. Watson, the founder of American behaviorism, the behavior of man and animals was the only proper study for psychology. Watson strongly advocated that

Psychology is to be the science, not of consciousness, but of behavior. . . . It is to cover both human and animal behavior, the simpler animal behavior being indeed more fundamental than the more complex behavior of man. . . . It is to rely wholly on objective data, introspection being discarded [Woodworth & Sheehan, 1964, p. 113].

Behaviorism has had an interesting, and indeed productive, development since the time of Watson's original manifesto. Tolman, Hull, and a number of other psychologists have been important figures in this development. Today, Skinner is the leading behaviorist in the field of psychology. Skinner (1957) deals with both overt and covert behavior, for example, he states that "thought is simply *behavior*—verbal or nonverbal, covert or overt [p. 449]."

As a counterargument to placing all emphasis on behavior, Karl Jaspers, an existential psychologist and philosopher, points up the importance of consciousness or self-awareness. According to Jaspers (1963), consciousness has four formal characteristics: (*a*) the feeling of activity—an awareness of being active; (*b*) an awareness of unity; (*c*) awareness of identity; and (*d*) awareness of the self as distinct from an outer world and all that is not the self (p. 121). Jaspers (1957) stresses that "Man not only exists but knows that he exists [p. 4]."

It is apparent from this argument that psychologists over the years have been dealing with two different aspects of man—on the one hand, his actions, and on the other, his self-awareness. It seems reasonable that man could be described in terms of either his behavior *or* his consciousness or both. Indeed, behavior is more accessible to scientific treatment, but the systematic study of consciousness might well give the psychologist additional understanding of man.

## MAN IS PREDICTABLE; OR MAN IS UNPREDICTABLE

Understanding, prediction, and control are considered to be the three objectives of science. Prediction and control are sometimes viewed as evidence of the scientist's understanding of the phenomenon under study. The objective of prediction rests on the assumption of determinism, the doctrine that all events have sufficient causes. Psychological science has traditionally accepted the objective of predicting human behavior and the associated doctrine of determinism.

Indeed, there have been some notable successes in predicting human behavior. Recent predictions of the number of fatalities resulting from automobile accidents on a given weekend, for example, have been within 5–10% of the actual fatalities. College administrators can predict fairly accurately the number of dropouts between the freshman and sophomore years. Further, a psychometrician can readily predict with a high degree of accuracy the distribution of scores resulting from an achievement test administered to a large sample of high school students. As another example, the mean reaction time to an auditory stimulus can be predicted rather accurately for a large group of subjects. All of these examples lend support to the doctrine of determinism.

There also have been some notable failures in attempts to predict human behavior. For example, the therapist has had little success in predicting the effectiveness of a given form of therapy applied to a given patient. Similarly, the guidance counselor has had relatively little success in predicting the occupation to be chosen by individual high school students. Such failures in predicting human behavior sometimes prompt one to question the basic assumption of determinism.

To illustrate the complexity associated with predicting the behavior of man—as contrasted with that of other complex systems—consider the following illustration. Suppose that a research psychologist has made a detailed study of a given human subject. He now tells the subject that he predicts that he will choose Alternative A rather than Alternative B under such and such conditions at some future point in time. Now, with this limited amount of information, what do you predict the subject will do?

The evidence suggests that there is support for both sides of this issue. It is difficult to argue with the deterministic doctrine that there are sufficient causes for human actions. Yet these causes may be unknown to either the observer or the subject himself. Thus, we must conclude that man is both predictable and unpredictable.

## MAN IS AN INFORMATION TRANSMITTER; OR MAN IS AN INFORMATION GENERATOR

The information theorists and cyberneticists have formulated a model of man as an information transmitter. W. Ross Ashby (1961), the cyberneticist, has proposed a basic postulate that says that man is just as intelligent as the amount of information fed into him.

Intelligence, whether of man or machine, is absolutely bounded. And what we can build into our machine is similarly bounded. The amount of intelligence we can get into a machine is absolutely bounded by the quantity of information that is put into it. We can get out of a machine as much intelligence as we like, if and only if we insure that at least the corresponding quantity of information gets into it [p. 280].

Ashby believes that we could be much more scientific in our study of man if we would accept this basic postulate and give up the idea that man, in some mysterious manner, generates or creates new information over and above that which is fed into him.

The information-transmitting model of man is indeed very compelling. It promises considerable rigor and precision; it is compatible with both empiricism and stimulus-response theory; and it allows the behavioral scientist to build on past accomplishments in the fields of cybernetics, systems science, and mechanics.

But, alas, man does not want to be hemmed in by the information-transmitting model. Man asks questions that were never before asked; he identifies problems that were never before mentioned; he generates new ideas and theories; he formulates new courses of action; and he even formulates new models of man. Now to say that all of these human activities are merely a regrouping or recombining of existing elements is an oversimplification, a trivialization of human activity. Further, the assumption that all information has actually been in existence but hidden since the days of prehistoric man is not intuitively satisfying.

Considering the evidence in support of man both as an information transmitter and as an information generator, would it be reasonable to view man as both a *dependent* variable and an *independent* variable?

## MAN LIVES IN AN OBJECTIVE WORLD; OR MAN LIVES IN A SUBJECTIVE WORLD

Man lives in an objective world. This is the world of facts and data. This is a reliable world; we agree that this or that event actually occurred. This is a tangible world; we agree that this or that object is actually present. This is the general world that is common to all.

But man also lives in a subjective world. This is the individual's private world. The individual's feelings, emotions, and perceptions are very personal; he attempts to describe them in words but feels that he can never do complete justice to them.

In making this comparison between the objective world and subjective world, it is important to distinguish between two types of knowledge. We can know *about* something, or we can personally *experience* something. These two forms of knowledge are not the same.

We conclude that man is both object and subject. He is visible and tangible to others, yet he is that which thinks, feels, and perceives. The world looks at man, and he looks out at the world.

Are both the objective world and the subjective world available to the methods of science? Empiricism in general and the experimental method in particular can be applied to the objective world; phenomenology can be applied to the subjective world. In his efforts to understand man, perhaps the psychologist should attempt to understand both worlds.

## MAN IS A RATIONAL BEING; OR MAN IS AN ARATIONAL BEING

Man is sometimes referred to as a rational animal. He is intelligent; he exercises reason; he uses logic; and he argues from a scientific standpoint. Indeed, man is considered by man to be the *only* rational animal.

An individual's action or behavior, of course, is sometimes considered irrational. This is the opposite of rational. The irrational person defies the laws of reason; he contradicts that which is considered rational by some particular community of people.

But man also is arational. This characteristic transcends the rational-irrational continuum; it essentially constitutes another dimension of man's life. As an example of man being arational in his life, he makes a total commitment for a way of life. This commitment may be for a given faith, a religion, a philosophy, a vocation, or something else. It may be that any analysis of this decision would reveal that it was neither rational nor irrational—it merely was.

Man's actions are guided by both empirical knowledge and value judgment. Empirical knowledge belongs to the rational world, whereas value judgment often belongs to the arational world. According to Jaspers (1967): "An empirical science cannot teach anybody what he ought to do, but only what he can do to reach his ends by statable means [p. 60]."

To achieve greater understanding of man, it would seem essential that the psychologist investigate man's arational world as well as his rational world.

## ONE MAN IS LIKE OTHER MEN; OR EACH MAN IS UNIQUE

A major goal of science is to develop general laws to describe, explain, and predict phenomena of the world. These laws are frequently based upon the study of one sample of objects or events and are then expected to be valid for a different sample of objects or events. It then follows that a major goal of psychology is to formulate general laws of man. In fact, without the possibility of developing general laws of human behavior, can psychology even be considered a science?

There is a considerable amount of evidence to support the possibility of developing general laws of human behavior. For example, the results of the reaction-time experiments have held up very well over the decades. Moreover, the many conditioning experiments conducted over the past several decades—either classical or operant—certainly suggest that man is governed by general laws applicable to all. Further, the cultural anthropologist and social psychologist have clearly pointed up the similarity of people in a given culture, suggesting that they might be taken from the same mold.

On the other hand, there is considerable evidence to support the concept of individual uniqueness. For example, there are thousands of possible gene combinations and thousands of different environmental determinants, all of which bring about millions of different personalities. Further, it is apparent that no two people ever live in exactly the same environment. As someone once said about two brothers living in the same house, with the same parents, and with the same diet: "Only one of the boys has an older brother." Then, too, we might reflect on a statement made by William James (1925): "An unlearned carpenter of

my acquaintance once said in my hearing: 'There is very little difference between one man and another; but what little there is, is very important' [pp. 242–243]."

Our conclusion from this brief analysis is that the evidence appears to support both models of man: (*a*) that he is governed by general laws that apply to all of mankind, and (*b*) that each individual is unique in a nontrivial way.

## MAN CAN BE DESCRIBED MEANINGFULLY IN ABSOLUTE TERMS; OR MAN CAN BE DESCRIBED MEANINGFULLY IN RELATIVE TERMS

If we believe that man can be described in absolute terms, we view such descriptions as being free from restriction or limitation. They are independent of arbitrary standards. Contrariwise, if we believe that man can be described in relative terms, we see him as existing or having his specific nature only by relation to something else. His actions are not absolute or independent.

If the concept of absoluteness is supported, we must accept the idea of general laws for all of mankind, and we also must accept the related idea that man is governed by irrefutable natural laws. On the other hand, if the concept of relativism is supported, we probably can have no general laws of man; we must realize that everything is contingent upon something else; and we can be certain of nothing.

It would appear that there is evidence to support the concept of absoluteness in psychology. The basic psychophysical laws, for example, might be characterized as irrefutable natural laws. Similarly, the basic laws of conditioning seem to be free from restriction or limitation. This evidence might lead us to conclude that man can be described in absolute terms.

But before we can become smug with this false sense of security, the relativist poses some challenging questions. For example: What is considered intelligent behavior? What is normal behavior? What is an aggressive personality? What is an over-achiever? At best, it would seem that we could answer such questions only in relative terms. The answers would be contingent on some set of arbitrary standards.

What can we conclude? Perhaps man can be described meaningfully in either absolute terms or relative terms, depending on what aspect of man is being described.

## HUMAN CHARACTERISTICS CAN BE INVESTIGATED INDEPENDENTLY OF ONE ANOTHER; OR MUST BE STUDIED AS A WHOLE

The question here is: Can man be understood by analyzing each attribute independently of the rest, or must man be studied as a whole in order to be understood? Another way of phrasing the question is: Can we take an additive approach to the study of man, or is a holistic or Gestalt approach required?

There is some evidence to support an additive approach to the study of man. Consider the following areas of research: psychophysics, physiological psychology, motor skills, classical and operant conditioning, and sensation. All of these areas have produced useful results from experimentation involving the manipulation of a single independent variable and measuring the concomitant effects on a single dependent variable. Useful results have been produced by investigating a single characteristic independently of other characteristics.

Other areas of research, however, point up the value of a holistic point of view. Research in the area of perception, for example, has demonstrated the effect of individual motivation on perception. Similarly, studies of human learning have shown the great importance of motivation and intelligence on learning behavior. Further, as one more example, research in the area of psychotherapy has revealed that the relation between the personality of the therapist and that of the patient has a significant influence on the effectiveness of the ther-

apy. All of these examples illustrate the importance of the interactions and interdependencies of the many variables operating in any given situation.

Support for a holistic view of man is seen in the works of Polanyi and Tielhard de Chardin, to mention only two. Polanyi (1963) gives this example: "Take a watch to pieces and examine, however carefully, its separate parts in turn, and you will never come across the principles by which a watch keeps time [p. 47]." Tielhard de Chardin (1961) says:

In its construction, it is true, every organism is always and inevitably reducible into its component parts. But it by no means follows that the sum of the parts is the same as the whole, or that, in the whole, some specifically new value may not emerge [p. 110].

What can be concluded from this discussion? First, it would seem that a detailed analysis of man is essential for a systematic understanding. Yet, synthesis also is required in order to understand the many interactions and interdependencies. We can conclude that the most effective strategy for the behavioral scientist might be that used by the systems analyst—a working back and forth between analysis and synthesis.

## MAN IS A REALITY; OR MAN IS A POTENTIALITY

Is man a reality? If so, he exists as fact; he is actual; he has objective existence. Or is man a potentiality? If so, he represents possibility rather than actuality; he is capable of being or becoming. The question here is: Can we study man as an actually existing entity—as we would study any other complex system—or must we view man as a completely dynamic entity, one that is constantly emerging or becoming?

There is support for the view of man as an actuality. The numerous results from the many years of research in the area of experimental psychology, for example, suggest that man is definable and measurable, and is capable of being investigated as an actually existing complex system. Further, the many current studies in the area of cybernetics, which point up similarities between man and machine, lend credence to the concept of man as an existing system.

There also is evidence to support the view of man as a potentiality. For example, case studies have revealed that long-term criminals have experienced religious conversions and then completely changed their way of life. Further, complete personality transformations have resulted from psychoanalysis and electroshock therapy. Indeed, man is changeable, and any given individual can become something quite different from what he was in the past.

Maslow (1961) has stressed the importance of human potentiality:

I think it fair to say that no theory of psychology will ever be complete that does not centrally incorporate the concept that man has his future within him, dynamically active at this present moment [p. 59].

What can we conclude? Only that man is both a reality and a potentiality. He represents objective existence, yet he can move toward any one of many different future states that are essentially unpredictable.

### MAN IS KNOWABLE IN SCIENTIFIC TERMS; OR MAN IS MORE THAN WE CAN EVER KNOW ABOUT HIM

This final issue is basic to the entire study of man, and is closely tied to all the previous issues discussed. Is man knowable in scientific terms, or is man more than we can ever know about him?

There are many centuries of evidence to support the idea that man is scientifically knowable. Aristotle, for example, applied the same logic to his study of man as he did to other phenomena in the world. Further, volumes of data resulting from psychological experiments since the time of Wundt's founding of the first experimental psychology laboratory in 1879 indicate that man is scientifically knowable. Then, too, the many laboratory experiments and field studies recently conducted by the different disciplines included in the behavioral and social sciences certainly suggest that man is scientifically knowable.

Yet, there also is support for the idea that man is more than we can ever know about him. Man has continued to transcend himself over the past million or so years, as demonstrated by the theory of evolution. Further, on logical grounds, it can be demonstrated that man becomes something different every time he gains new knowledge about himself, which would suggest that man is truly an "open system."

It is apparent that we know very little about man. William James (1956) says: "Our science is a drop, our ignorance a sea [p. 54]." Erich Fromm (1956) believes that "Even if we knew a thousand times more of ourselves, we would never reach bottom [p. 31]."

What can we conclude? We must conclude that man is scientifically knowable— at least to a point. Yet there is no evidence to support the idea that man is—or ever will be—*completely* knowable.

### CONCLUSIONS

This paper has presented two models of man:

- The behavioristic model: Man can be described meaningfully in terms of his behavior; he is predictable; he is an information transmitter; he lives in an objective world; he is rational; he has traits in common with other men; he may be described in absolute terms; his characteristics can be studied independently of one another; he is a reality; and he is knowable in scientific terms.

- The phenomenological model: Man can be described meaningfully in terms of his consciousness; he is unpredictable; he is an information generator; he lives in a subjective world; he is arational; he is unique alongside millions of other unique personalities; he can be described in relative terms; he must be studied in a holistic manner; he is a potentiality; and he is more than we can ever know about him.

This analysis of behaviorism and phenomenology leads to these conclusions:

1. The acceptance of either the behavioristic model or a phenomenological model has important implications in the everyday world. The choice of one versus the other could greatly influence human activities (either behavior or awareness) in such areas as education, psychiatry, theology, behavioral science, law, politics, marketing, advertising, and even parenthood. Thus, this ongoing debate is not just an academic exercise.

2. There appears to be truth in both views of man. The evidence that has been presented lends credence to both the behavioristic model and the phenomenological model. Indeed, it would be premature for psychology to accept either model as the final model.

3. A given behavioral scientist may find that both models are useful, depending upon the problem under study. The phenomenological model, for example, might be quite appropriate for the investigation of the creative process in scientists. On the other hand, the behavioristic model might be very useful in the study of environmental factors that motivate a given population of subjects to behave in a certain manner.

4. Finally, we must conclude that the behaviorist and the phenomenologist should listen to each other. Both, as scientists, should be willing to listen to opposing points of view. Each should endeavor to understand what the other is trying to say. It would appear that a dialogue is in order.

## REFERENCES

Allport, G. W. 1955. *Becoming: Basic considerations for a psychology of personality.* New Haven: Yale University Press.

Ashby, W. R. 1961. What is an intelligent machine? *Proceedings of the Western Joint Computer Conference* 19:275–280.

de Chardin, P. T. 1961. *The phenomenon of man.* New York: Harper & Row (Harper Torchbook Edition).

Fromm, E. 1956. *The art of loving.* New York: Harper & Row.

James, W. 1956 (originally published 1896). *The will to believe and other essays on popular philosophy.* New York: Dover.

James, W. 1925 (originally published 1897). The individual and society. In *The philosophy of William James.* New York: Modern Library.

Jaspers, K. 1957 (originally published in Germany, 1931). *Man in the modern age.* New York: Doubleday.

Jaspers, K. 1963. *General psychopathology.* Manchester, England: Manchester University Press; Chicago: University of Chicago Press.

Jaspers, K. 1967. *Philosophy is for everyman.* New York: Harcourt, Brace & World.

Koch, S. 1964. Psychology and emerging conceptions of knowledge as unitary. In *Behaviorism and phenomenology: Contrasting bases for modern psychology,* ed. T. W. Wann. Chicago: University of Chicago Press.

MacLeod, R. B. 1964. Phenomenology: A challenge to experimental psychology. In *Behaviorism and phenomenology: Contrasting bases for modern psychology,* ed. T. W. Wann. Chicago: University of Chicago Press.

Malcolm, N. 1964. Behaviorism as a philosophy of psychology. In *Behaviorism and phenomenology: Contrasting bases for modern psychology,* ed. T. W. Wann. Chicago: University of Chicago Press.

Maslow, A. H. 1961. Existential psychology—What's in it for us? In *Existential psychology,* ed. R. May. New York: Random House.

Polanyi, M. 1963. *The study of man.* Chicago: University of Chicago Press (First Phoenix Edition).

Rogers, C. R. 1964. Toward a science of the person. In *Behaviorism and phenomenology: Contrasting bases for modern psychology,* ed. T. W. Wann. Chicago: University of Chicago Press.

Skinner, B. F. 1957. *Verbal behavior.* New York: Appleton-Century-Crofts.

Skinner, B. F. 1964. Behaviorism at fifty. In *Behaviorism and phenomenology: Contrasting bases for modern psychology,* ed. T. W. Wann. Chicago: University of Chicago Press.

Wann, T. W., ed. 1964. *Behaviorism and phenomenology: Contrasting bases for modern psychology.* Chicago: University of Chicago Press.

Woodworth, R. S., and Sheehan, M. R. 1964. *Contemporary schools of psychology.* New York: Ronald Press.

# READING 2

# Cognitive Dissonance: Its Use in Science

**EDWIN G. BORING**

E. G. Boring is examining the process which leads to scientific innovation. He suggests that the development of science is a gradual and continuous process. He notes that scientists often hold inconsistent or dissonant views, and that when the scientist becomes aware of this dissonance, the ultimate resolution often leads to scientific innovation.

## QUESTIONS

1. Why is cognitive dissonance important to intellectual and/or scientific progress?
2. Define and describe the *Zeitgeist* of today. How does the *Zeitgeist* influence psychology?
3. Give an example of cognitive dissonance from your personal experience. Which of Festinger's methods do you use to resolve the dissonance?

The term *cognitive dissonance* has been used by Leon Festinger *(1)* to indicate the existence of incompatible beliefs or attitudes held simultaneously by a human being, and in this respect scientists turn out to be human. The dissonance may be unconscious, and indeed it usually begins in that way. Some event, however, may make

Dr. Boring was Edgar Pierce Professor of Psychology Emeritus at Harvard University. This article is a condensation of a lecture that was given at various stages of its evolution and under different titles at George Peabody College, Brandeis University, Springfield College, and finally as the Shepard lecture at the University of Michigan.

you conscious of the incompatibility, and then there you are, convicted, to your own knowledge, of rank inconsistency—convicted because the culture still insists, long years after the age of reason, that it is reason which yields truth and that contradiction is rationally insupportable. You like to smoke and do, and yet recent events convince you that smoking carries a hazard of lung cancer. You accept both the Christian ethic that the meek should inherit the earth but also the ethic of chivalry that sullied honor must be avenged. How can you manage then to give rationalism its due? Festinger says that (i) you change your behavior (stop smoking) or (ii) you change your cognition (pooh-pooh the scare about cancer) or (iii) you suppress or ignore the dissonance (forget that Jesus condemned war) or (iv) you do something in between, like rationalizing, distorting the cognition. But science? Is not science the inexorably rational enterprise? Does it ever condone dishonesty? Does it not oust dissonance just as soon as it becomes aware of it? Let us see.

## THE GEISTER

There is a new history—or at least Count Tolstoy (2) said there is, 95 years ago—one that looks below men's ready consciousness to deeper forces that control their acts and opinions. One of these forces is the current of credence, the stream of change in what the culture carries as the truth at any particular time, or at least as the generally accepted opinion. Goethe called this influence the *Zeitgeist* (3), and recently the term has come into more common use as the new Tolstoyans see how the climate of opinion affects thought and action, now this way and then presently otherwise.

The paradigms of science—that is T. S. Kuhn's word (4) for the fundamental hypotheses—are in the *Zeitgeist*—in biology, for example, special creation once and then natural selection later. Scientific revolutions change the *Zeitgeist* — the big changes, Ptolemy to Copernicus; the little ones, Galton to rediscovered Mendel. The *Zeitgeist* is also the most plagiarized source of information and attitude, but then of course ideas have to come from somewhere. Surely the age-old belief that the "originality" of genius is a kind of intellectual spontaneous generation, surely that faith in the existence of uncaused thinking is passing.

The *Zeitgeist* can, of course, be conscious or unconscious. Goethe believed in it as unconscious, quite possibly because he thought of its effect upon the thinking of genius as insidious, for it is always there, often secretly sapping the defenses of originality.

Time is not the only parameter in respect of which these insidious forces change. There are several other well known *Geister*, if I may try to enhance attention by continuing to use these not very lovely Teutonisms. There are *Ortgeister*, the national habits of thinking. The psychologists know how much better subjective introspection still fares in Germany than under the dialectical materialism of the Soviets. Certainly the political climate of opinion is not quite the same in Alabama as in Maine, nor was the difference the same in 1960 as it was in 1860. The *Fachgeister* in science are the intellectual forces that differ between schools—a century ago between the vitalists and the mechanists. These prejudices shade over into the individual preferences, which might be called *Eigengeister* — Johannes Müller and Helmholtz, Louis Agassiz and any good Darwinian or Darwin himself. It is a convenient vocabulary if one does not take it too seriously.

## OCCASIONS FOR DISSONANCE

Festinger notes that any serious decision, made to resolve a doubt when no additional evidence becomes available, creates dissonance. The 50—50 decision as you review the evidence under the necessity for making a choice, may change to 60—40, and then you act—you may have to—on the 60, knowing well that there still exists a good argument in back of the 40. With the choice made, the healthy person forgets about the weaker alternative and, if the consequence proves the result of the choice to have been wrong, still a mature mind maintains: "But the choice itself was right even though the result was unwanted; all I had to go on was the 60—40, and 60 is more than 40." The business of living is coping—says Karl Menninger (5), ably supported by Samuel Butler (6)—and the refusal to worry over a persistent cognitive dissonance is a symptom of effective living.

Now let me place in the record seven instances of occasions on which the scientist proceeds in the face of cognitive dissonance, sometimes aware of what he is doing, sometimes not, sometimes suppressing into unawareness a rejected alternative, sometimes, on the other hand, consciously achieving resolution of his dilemma by changing his opinion. My argument is that the investigator is often made more effective by his pushing the contradiction aside and his going on with whatever business he has in hand. His refusal to worry is not immoral. He had chosen a prescribed universe in which to work and it is best that he carry through to whatever goal he had in mind, letting others (and most especially posterity) judge whether he shut his mind to the wrong things.

## PARADIGMS

A paradigm is a fundamental hypothesis or model in respect of which scientific thinking occurs. A change in an important paradigm constitutes a scientific revolution (4). Everybody knows about the great instances: the geocentric system of Ptolemy versus the heliocentric system of Copernicus; the pendulum as a constrained falling body for Aristotle versus the pendulum as a freely moving body for Galileo; Newton's addition of attraction as a characteristic of all matter; special creation versus natural selection. A moot revolution is still in progress, a gift of Descartes to psychology: the dualism of mind and matter versus the physicalism of both mind and matter as demanded by modern positivism.

A paradigm is a way of perceiving nature, and, as in all perception, the shift from one hypothesis to another is all-or-none. There are no intermediates. That camel in the field suddenly is seen for what it is, a pile of stones. The textbooks of psychology give ambiguous figures to illustrate this point—the duck-rabbit which is perceived as one or the other but never as

both together, or the old-lady-and-the-young-lady, which alternates, the ribbon on the young lady's neck shifting instantly to become the old lady's mouth, and so with the other features. The change is abrupt. In the thinking of an individual it must at any moment be sudden, from the duck to the rabbit, from special creation to natural selection.

The cognitive change between these alternatives of a paradigmatic dissonance is sudden, but the historical change is slow, both in the body of scientific belief and usually in the individual's thought. There is no contradiction here. It was a long time from Copernicus to Galileo, and the general understanding and acceptance of the heliocentric theory took even longer as learned belief edged over toward the new view. The gradual change is measured by an opinion poll, as it were. Darwin spent many years weighing the alternatives for evolution in his mind.

A scientific theory is a policy, said J. J. Thomson (7), and when a revolution is on—as it is just now in respect of the dualism of mind and matter—choice of a preferable faith is hard. Eventually the victorious new belief drops down into the stream of the *Zeitgeist* and is carried along, unconsciously, for the most part, and fundamental to the thinking of most wise men until something new happens. These paradigms are, however, faiths, the consequences of decisions. The policy that resolved the dissonance has merely pragmatic truth-value in that it works best, at least for the time being. Relativity theory made both the heliocentric theory and Newtonian mechanics less sure.

## EPONYMS

The conventional view of the history of science is that science advances gradually by the hard work of many investigators but that its course involves sudden spurts when someone, who is eventually to become known as a "Great Man," has a revolutionary insight or makes a crucial discovery which changes the speed or direction of progress in scientific endeavor. If the change is radical enough, the Great Man, after he has been recognized as great on account of his contribution, has his name put down upon the discovery or the theory or the resultant school of thinking and thus becomes an Eponym. Aristotelian thinking, the Copernican theory, Newtonian mechanics, Cartesian dualism, the Darwinian epoch, and Mendelian inheritance are all examples of eponymous thinking.

Even while we admit that some men make habitually greater contributions to knowledge than others and note that feeble-mindedness has done little to advance science, careful consideration must lead to the conclusion that eponymity is mostly a delusion—the Great-Man theory of history, as it used to be called when William James (8) and Herbert Spencer (9) were disagreeing about its validity. The course of science is gradual and continuous, as the occurrence of multiples in discovery and invention proves, for almost always the "great discovery" has already been anticipated—perhaps less assuredly or else with inadequate publication. Multiple discovery is, however, the rule, and often discoveries are practically simultaneous, as the evolving *Zeitgeist* finds itself at a given stage realized through more agents than one (10). Lancelot Whyte thinks that it takes about 200 years for the maturation of a new paradigm—at any rate he traces the gradual acceptance of Freud's paradigm of the unconscious from 1695 to 1895, when Freud provided a previously weak belief with enough stamina for it to stand alone (11), believed by a minority of intelligent minds —and then later by a majority.

Why does eponymity occur? In part because men are hero-worshippers. We hear enough about the conflicts that arise because human aggression makes too many men want to lead, but not very much about followership, the human need for heroes

(12). History does, moreover, need help to be understood. It is too multifarious for man with his limited spans of attention and memory to carry in his mind. Eponymity performs the service of packaging history for handling, just as science itself is said to exist to promote economy of thinking.

For the most part the scientist and the historian of science simply suppress the unpleasant part of this cognitive dissonance. They need their beloved heroes and also their packages. Especially does the ambitious investigator on his way to recognition stand in need of his Eponyms, for his fantasies run toward eponymity for himself and he can hardly bear to reduce himself to being a mere agent of the *Zeitgeist*.

## FREEDOM AND DETERMINISM

In the antithesis between freedom and determinism we see what is perhaps the best known instance of cognitive dissonance that the scientist encounters. Determinism is a paradigm which science has long accepted. Laplace held that if you could know absolutely all about the universe at some instant, then you could casually extrapolate to all its past and all its future (13). Of late the principles of uncertainty and complementarity have led physicists to doubt the universal usefulness of causality in particle physics, where statistical laws hold and a particular event is sometimes indeterminate. The difficulty here is operational: if you cannot observe the position and momentum of an electron synchronously, does the one not exist whenever the other does, or do both exist at once although only one, either one, but not both, can be observed at one time? Can what is not observable exist? P. W. Bridgman said not (14), but this difficulty does not affect the fact that, in general, science asserts that causality and thus determinism are essentials of the orderliness of nature.

So in science the paradigm of determinism works well. It is a good policy for science. It is, however, dissonant with practical policies of living, and for 99 percent of his life the scientist is a human being, not only outside the laboratory but in his conduct of experimentation and in all his relations with people. Any social occasion that implies his own duty or responsibility is founded upon the paradigm of freedom. All morality and altruism and affection, as well as hatred and opposition, imply freedom. Language is shot through and through with the implication that men are free to choose. If ever a policy was justified by almost universal use, it is the theory that man is free to choose. He is even free to choose his paradigms, free to believe in freedom or free to believe he is not free.

The resolution of this dissonance which Kant even listed among the antinomies (15), becomes clear, however, once we accept the doctrine of paradigms. The scientist chooses the paradigm of determinism when he designs his experiment, when he theorizes, when he is thinking scientifically. As a practical man he needs to believe in his freedom and usually in the freedom of others, unless he is being a psychologist, when he may examine the behavior of a subject in respect of the conditions that determine it. It may be said that determinism is the broader and more positive paradigm, for its complement, freedom, is negative, consisting in a preference for ignorance. To believe that the "originality" of a Great Man is caused, as Herbert Spencer did (9), is to refuse to be content with ignorance, even when the causes cannot be actually discovered. To believe with William James that human dignity must be preserved by wresting some fraction of human behavior from the shackles of causality is to gain contentment without even a struggle to penetrate ignorance (8). The paradigm that asserts freedom is a negative paradigm.

In my thinking freedom is a preference for certain kinds of ignorance, but it has its scientific uses. It frees the investigator—as well as the historian—to think of effects and not to waste time worrying about causes which, if they exist, may still remain inscrutable by any means of observation available.

## MULTIPLES

The chief argument for the existence of the *Zeitgeist* and for the gradualness and continuity of the progress of science is the occurrence of multiples in discovery and invention (16). Discovery and new insight tend to be independent but synchronous in the minds of unassociated contemporaries. The great discovery or insight almost always turns out to have had a long history of somewhat less specific or at any rate less well publicized anticipations, a history extending through many decades or even a couple of centuries. Robert K. Merton gives us a convincing explication of this view, but by no means claims to be its discoverer, for he shows how this theory of multiples is itself a theory confirmed by its own history, and he lists more than a score of rediscoveries or reaffirmations of the theory between 1828 and 1922 (17). It was in 1922 that Ogburn and Thomas published their list of 148 multiples, mostly doublets (18). Merton with Elinor Barber has, however, studied intensively 264 multiple discoveries, finding 179 of them to be doublets, 51 triplets, and so on up to two discoveries, each of which was made independently nine times!

With multiples so common, a long list would be inappropriate here. Let me mention a few of the better known instances so that the reader will recall their nature. Napier and Briggs each independently invented logarithms in 1614. Newton and Leibniz warred over which of them was first in the invention of the calculus. Charles Bell in 1811 and François Magendie in 1822 independently discovered the law of spinal nerve roots, and Bell also in 1811 and Johannes Müller in 1826 formulated the doctrine of specific nerve energies which had, in a sense, been anticipated by John

Locke. Adams and Leverrier discovered Neptune within a few days of each other in 1845 because the obvious thing to do then was to predict another planet from a study of the perturbations of Uranus. Helmholtz in 1852 found himself anticipated by Thomas Young in 1801 on color theory and gave him full credit. The most famous case may be Alfred Russel Wallace's independent formulation in 1858 of what was also Charles Darwin's theory of natural selection.

But, if multiples are the rule, why must Merton be at such pains to demonstrate what is being perpetually rediscovered? Because the rule establishes a major cognitive dissonance in the thinking of scientists. Merton has even written a paper on the resistance of scientists to a belief in multiples (19). The fact of multiples threatens the scientist's priority of discovery and thus his most carefully nurtured ambition, the demonstration of his own originality. The existence of multiples means that "originality" is at least in part externally determined and threatens the individual uniqueness. That is a threat to his identity, one that he cannot very well accept, and indeed it is a question whether the scientist's failure to orient his thinking with respect to this conclusion interferes very much with the quality and quantity of his contribution. His achievement may even be greater if he has enough channel vision to keep his eye on the main undertaking and so avoid distraction.

## EGOISM

Egoism is where the *Fachgeister* and the *Eigengeister* come in. The most prevalent generator of cognitive dissonance is surely egoism. In science the persistent dissonance-inducing dilemma is between pride and objectivity, a conflict so common that it has been called the scientist's motivational predicament. Important theories, marked for death by the discovery of contradictory evidence, seldom die before their

authors, commented Max Planck (20), but why does not an author abandon his theory instead of turning traitor to science and retarding its advance? Because a theory which has built up its author's image of himself has become part of him. To abandon it would be suicidal or at least an act of self-mutilation. It is better to live with this fresh dissonance, suppressing new evidence from cognizance as far as possible.

Seldom over the ages has scientific controversy been impartial and judicious, with the energies of both parties concerned only with getting at the truth (21), but this is not the place for an anthology of these quarrels, in which I assure you each antagonist defends and does not condemn himself. Let me provide just one illustration of a quarrel between two eminent German psychologists in the early 1890's over the question whether a perceived tonal interval is bisected psychologically by the arithmetic or by the geometric mean of its tonal stimuli. Wilhelm Wundt, the more vehement, was so angry that he said he "would speak without anger," hoping that his antagonist, Carl Stumpf, would learn to be more just to others and more severe toward himself (22). Stumpf, less vigorous and saying that he meant to be calm, nevertheless spoke of Wundt's "mixture of untrue assertions, confusions, mutilations of the course of my thought, obscure imputations and negligences, infirm evasions, fallacies of every kind, and frequent assurances of the incapacity and ignorance of his adversary" (23). When the pot calls the kettle black we are in the presence of dissonance.

Any reader of Kepler's biography will wonder how the three great planetary laws could have emerged from so inconsonant a mind, in which mysticism was mixed up with a passion for accurate observation, which perceived as one of its great intellectual achievements the spacing of the six planets in the solar system as related to the shape of the five regular geometrical solids, a mind which took astrology seriously, and which experienced ecstasy over both its true and false successes *(24)*. There is, however, a lesson to be learned from emergence of great discovery from the many dissonances of Kepler's mind: enthusiasm that promotes indefatigability can sometimes achieve more than a complacent intellectual integration. Dissonance need not be lethal when the drive toward a goal remains fixed in spite of potential distractions. It is indeed a fact that potential distraction may sometimes spur attention to higher levels *(25)*, and it would sometimes seem to be true that people who complain about distracting noise are really complaining because the noise keeps them on the *qui vive* so that, being unable to relax, they discover themselves in possession of new achievement *(26)*.

The dissonance due to egoism gets resolved in science by a division of energies: the egoist furnishes the drive needed for research and a reviewer or commentator provides the objectivity that cuts the claim down to size. Sometimes objectivity is reserved for the insights of posterity; yet in other instances the dual role may be played alternately by the same person, now the fanatic but subsequently his own critic. Science cannot do without the drive, dissonance or no dissonance. Nowadays there is some evidence that this dissonance of egoism is being reduced by the explosion of science which forms investigators into teams and produces papers with multiple authors *(27, 28)*. In spite of loyalty and group pride, a *nos* has less selfhood to defend than does an *ego*.

## AMBIVALENCE

Once again Merton supplies us with an idea and information about it. Scientists seem to hold many incompatible values simultaneously. Merton lists nine such instances and a half dozen of them I paraphrase here, with some of Merton's careful qualifications pruned off for the sake of simplicity *(29)*.

a. Publish promptly
   BUT not prematurely;
b. Remain receptive to new ideas
   BUT resist intellectual fads;
c. Be erudite
   BUT do not sacrifice research to reading;
d. Teach the young researcher
   BUT do not sacrifice research to teaching;
e. Attend to details
   BUT ignore inconsequentials;
f. Accept tutelage from the wise
   BUT maintain your own independence.

Certainly these dissonances of counsel are not dangerous. They have the effect of warning the neophyte that wisdom is not to be had by simple guides but that success is for him who learns to sail a course safely between these buoys.

Merton's interest in ambivalence is centered chiefly on scientists' desire for priority, a dissonance between the pride of creation and the humility of the dedicated objectivist. Scientific morality teaches that it is the contribution that counts, not who makes it, and often the fanatical investigator accepts this view explicitly in print, pointing with pride to his modesty, as it were. Merton, however, gives it as "a rule-of-thumb" that "whenever the biography or autobiography of a scientist announces that he had little or no concern with priority of discovery, there is a reasonably good chance that, not many pages later in the book, we shall find him deeply embroiled in one or another battle over priority" *(30)*. Merton goes on to cite his instances, not the least of whom is Freud, whose dissonance about priority he deploys at length.

In these dissonances there is nothing new to us. They are the case of Abraham and Isaac. To sacrifice one's very own brain child by welcoming a prior multiple is the supreme test, one that no father of an idea can easily undertake.

## PERSONAL BIAS

Individual differences in values and attitudes are familiar subject matter for the psychology of personality, and the cybernetic interaction of dissents is one of the most important social dynamics for the advance of intellectual civilization. To conclude our list with personal bias as an important cause of dissonance is merely to assert again how important cognitive dissonance is in the welter of intellectual progress. Though it may be a hindrance to a little thought, it belongs in the matrix from which the big thoughts eventually emerge.

A good example of the prevalence of attitudinal dissonance is the phenomenon known as love—plain everyday heterosexual love. Your lady fair is your great delusion, so important that even courts of law recognize the essentiality of this personal bias in the social fabric and do not require one spouse to testify against the other, though justice be thereby refused.

Loyalty creates dissonance, loyalty to a school or a principle, carried often by the *Fachgeist*. Hatred creates dissonance, and the literature of controversy—the bitter controversies—carries those examples. There is no need to stress the obvious, and we can leave the bitter dissonances to the journals where the polemics can be found. Let me rather give here the record of two pleasant dissonances, published sentiment by two of psychology's eponyms on the occasion of the death of an admired colleague.

Chauncey Wright, a clear intellect who lived a life of brilliant thinking, and who evolved for the most part from conversational bouts with other top-notch minds in the periphery of Cambridge, Massachusetts, in the 1860's and early 1870's, was one of the forebears of pragmatism, for he stimulated C. S. Peirce, William James, Oliver Wendell Holmes, Jr., and others, and they met constantly for conversation in what Peirce called the Metaphysical Club. Wright talked but did not publish. His influence was personal, and he died suddenly of a stroke in 1875 when only 45 years old. Of him William James then wrote (31):

If power and analytic intellect pure and simple could suffice, the name of Chauncey Wright would assuredly be as famous as it is now obscure, for he was not merely the great mind of a village—if Cambridge will pardon the expression—but either in London or Berlin he would, with equal ease, have taken the place of master which he held with us. The reason why he is gone now without leaving any work which his friends can consider as a fair expression of his genius, is that his shyness, his want of ambition, and to a certain degree his indolence, were almost as exceptional as his power of thought. Had he, in early life, resolved to concentrate these and make himself a physicist, for example, there is no question but that he would have ranked today among the first few living names.

How could James know, how does anyone ever know, that a man with a change of personality would have been great, that by speculation one can say what change of conditions would transform the impossible into the actual? This was a loyal statement for him who defended the dignity of man against Herbert Spencer, although not for the writer of a textbook in which "every sentence had to be forged in the teeth of irreducible and stubborn fact." We may appreciate James's loyalty and note the dissonance.

Hermann Ebbinghaus, the German originator of the experimental psychology of memory who made a brilliant start and then left the field for others to develop, a lucid writer of a systematic textbook who completed the first volume but not the second, and an influential personality for over 20 years in the scene of German psychology, died in 1909 a few months before he was due to speak at the vigentennium of Clark University at which Freud and the other psychoanalysts first made their appearance in America. E. B. Titchener, the erudite, German-trained Briton, who was protector of the German mentalistic tradition in America, said in his address on this occasion (32):

When the cable brought the bare news, last February, that Ebbinghaus was dead, just a month after the celebration of his fifty-ninth birthday, the feeling that took precedence even of personal sorrow was the wonder what experimental psychology would do without him. . . . What characterized him was, first, an instinctive grasp of the scientific aspect of a problem . . . ; secondly, a perfect clarity of thought and language . . . ; and thirdly, an easy mastery of the facts. I say mastery, but the truth requires a stronger word. There was about Ebbinghaus a sort of masterfulness; he never did violence to facts, but he marshalled them; he made them stand and deliver; he took from them, as of right, all that they contained; and with the tribute thus extracted he built up his theories and his system.

Titchener, graceful master of the English idiom, was of tougher fiber than James. You would hardly have expected this panegyric from him, and yet there it is as he was led away from facts to romance by his loyalty to an ideal. Ebbinghaus has remained "great" because he was the eponym for the experimental psychology of memory and learning, but psychology got along as well without him as it has without every other great figure that has passed on. History takes care of itself pretty well, and progress is not always aided by the longevity of eponyms.

## THE ECONOMY OF DISSONANCE

It is obvious that operating in the face of dissonance in belief and attitude is a characteristic of man, whereas the culture demands that man deplore that fact and that he strive always for his own consistency. It is interesting to speculate what life would be like if men could be computerized, each with an enormous permanent memory which could be almost instantly scanned before a new thought was added to the wholly consistent inventory of accepted truth. Frustration would be reduced, controversy eliminated, complacency magnified, and progress might be speeded up enormously, if complacency did not slow it down. As it is, man must be content to accept very considerable limitations in the range of his apperception and in the adequacy with which he can scan the traces of his past experience. He enlarges his range of thinking by the use of symbolism, letting a symbol stand for a complex, and another symbol for a higher complex of symbols. That is why language places man intellectually above the animals, and why mathe-

matics is such a powerful tool in the extension of thinking. But beyond such means man has to make do, living with his dissonances because his brain does not give him the power to unify the universe of his thoughts. We have seen how he adjusts to dissonance: he remains unaware of it until the discrepancy forces itself upon him; then he may alter his belief and action, or he may suppress from ready cognizance one-half of the contradiction, or he may by rationalization rack the incompatibility into the conformity of a false resolution.

Is it the conclusion of this article then that scientists are human? No, the article says more than that. It is its conclusion that the major dissonance in science between the goal of consistency and the fact of persistent inconsistency is not, as a practical matter, resolvable. Dissonance is seen to become useful when it is understood as freedom for concentration on a limited enterprise, freedom to ignore the remotely relevant because apperception, limited always by its channel vision, sees for the time being only the main goal. The investigator may sometimes shake himself free of his concentration and criticize more generally the significance of his enterprise, and there are also other critics who will do it for him. At any rate, though scientific progress may be hindered by dissonance, it is not necessarily blocked, for there is always waiting off in the future that most objective of critics, posterity, as well as posterity's posterity.

## REFERENCES

1. Festinger, L. 1957. *A theory of cognitive dissonance.* Stanford: Stanford University Press.

2. Tolstoy, L. 1942 (originally published 1869). *War and peace.* New York: Simon & Schuster. Bk. 9, sec. 1; bk. 10, sec. 1; bk. 11, sec. 1; bk. 13, sec. 11; 1st epilogue, sec. 1; 2d epilogue, appendix.

3. Goethe, J. W. v. 1827. Homer noch einmal. Reprinted in *Goethes sämtliche Werke* (Berlin: Cotta, 1902), vol. 38, p. 78.

4. Kuhn, T. S. 1962. *The structure of scientific revolutions.* Chicago: University of Chicago Press.

5. Menninger, K.; Mayman, M.; and Pruyser, P. 1963. *The vital balance: The life process in mental health and illness.* New York: Viking. Chap. 7.

6. Butler, S. 1901. *The way of all flesh.* New York: Modern Library. Chap. 69, paragraph 25.

7. Thomson, J. J. 1907. *The corpuscular theory of matter.* New York: Scribner. Pp. 1 f.

8. James, W. 1880. Great men, great thoughts, and the environment. *Atlantic Monthly* 46:441. Reprinted in *The will to believe* (New York: Longmans, Green, 1897), pp. 216–254.

9. Spencer, H. 1873. *The study of sociology.* London: Paul. Chaps. 2–3.

10. Boring, E. G. 1963. Eponym as placebo. *History, psychology, and science.* New York: Wiley. Pp. 5–25.

11. Whyte, L. L. 1960. *The unconscious before Freud.* New York: Basic Books.

12. Carlyle, T. 1840. *On heroes, hero worship, and the heroic in history.* London: Chapman and Hall.

13. de Laplace, P. S. 1808 (originally published 1796). *Exposition du système de monde.* 3d ed. Paris: Courcier.

14. Bridgman, P. W. 1927. *The logic of modern physics.* New York: Macmillan.

15. Watson, J. 1901. *Selections from Kant.* Edinburgh: Maclehose. Pp. 155–194.

16. Boring, E. G. 1950. Great men and scientific progress. *Proceedings of the American Philosophical Society* 94:339. Reprinted in (10), pp. 29–49. 1955. Dual role of the *Zeitgeist* in scientific creativity. *Scientific Monthly* 80:101. Reprinted in *Psychologist at large* (New York: Basic Books, 1961), pp. 325–337.

17. Merton, R. K. 1961. Singletons and multiples in scientific discovery: A chapter in the sociology of science. *Proceedings of the American Philosophical Society* 105:470.

18. Ogburn, W. F., and Thomas, Dorothy. 1922. Are inventions inevitable? *Political Science Quarterly* 37:83.

19. Merton, R. K. 1963. Resistance to the systematic study of multiple discoveries in science. *European Journal of Sociology* 4:237.

20. Planck, M. 1949. *Scientific autobiography and other papers.* Trans. New York: Philosophical Library. Pp. 33 f.

21. Boring, E. G. 1929. The psychology of controversy. *Psychological Review* 36:97. Reprinted in (10), pp. 67–84.

22. Wundt, W. 1892. Auch ein Schlusswort. *Philosophische Studien* 7:633.

23. Stumpf, C. 1891. Mein Schlusswort gegen Wundt. *Zeitschrift für Psychologie* 2:438.

24. Koestler, A. 1960. *The watershed: A biography of Johannes Kepler.* Garden City, N.Y.: Anchor Books.

25. Tinker, M. A. 1922. A study of the relation of distracted motor performance to performance in an intelligence test. *American Journal of Psychology* 33:578.

26. Boring, E. G. 1945. *Psychology for the armed services.* Washington, D.C., Infantry Journal. P. 119.

27. Holton, G. 1962. Scientific research and scholarship. *Daedalus* 91:362–399, esp. 371–375.

28. See also Merton (19), esp. pp. 278 f.

29. Merton, R. K. 1963. The ambivalence of scientists. *Bulletin of Johns Hopkins Hospital* 112:77.

30. See also Merton (19), esp. pp. 252–258.

31. James, W. 1875. Chauncey Wright. *The Nation* 21:194. Reprinted in E. H. Madden, *Chauncey Wright and the foundations of pragmatism* (Seattle: University of Washington Press, 1963), pp. 143–146.

32. Titchener, E. B. 1910. The past decade in experimental psychology. *American Journal of Psychology* 21:404–421, esp. 405.

# READING 3

# Environmental Complexity, Cerebral Change, and Behavior

**MARK R. ROSENZWEIG**
**University of California, Berkeley**

The relationship between heredity and environment in intellectual development has been an issue in psychology for many years. Contemporary psychologists stress the interaction of these two influences. That learning is dependent upon biological maturation is not a new concept; Mark Rosenzweig provides us with data which indicate that the inverse is also true: experience influences the rate and/or extent of biological growth.

## QUESTIONS

1. Is the rat a good choice of subject for this research? Can the results be generalized to apply not only to other strains of rats, but to other species?
2. What is the relationship between this type of research and the social action programs such as Project Head Start?
3. Is it a valid criticism to say the IC group was retarded by its environment? Can you suggest other interpretations for the results of this study?

Relating brain processes to behavior in animals is the subject of this paper. Addressing an audience not from my own special field reminds me of the animal psychologist who presented a paper at a psychoanalytic meeting. At the end of the paper, one of the psychoanalysts grumbled, "We knew all this already." "Yes," a colleague placated him, "but we didn't know that it was true of *rats!*" In my own case, I hope that you will neither reject this re-

Abbreviated version of an address given to the Division of Developmental Psychology at American Psychological Association, Chicago, September 1965. This research has been supported by grants or contracts from the National Institute of Mental Health, United States Public Health Service; the Surgeon General's Office; and the National Aeronautics and Space Agency. It has also received support from the United States Atomic Energy Commission.

search as irrelevant to your own nor, on the other hand, apply it uncritically to work in human behavior and development. Therefore, after presenting the main findings, I will want to discuss with you the possible significance of such work for the study of human behavior.

The research has been done by a team in which Edward L. Bennett, a biochemist, David Krech, a psychologist, and I have collaborated for a dozen years. More recently we have been joined by Marian C. Diamond, a neuroanatomist. The overall scope of our program concerns both hereditary and environmental factors that have been demonstrated to affect learning ability. We have been attempting to determine whether they do so by affecting the anatomy and chemistry of the brain. Today I will concentrate on these questions: Can differential experience modify the brain in measurable anatomical and chemical terms? If so, can these cerebral changes be related to the effects of experience on learning ability?

The suggestion that thinking might induce growth of the brain is an old one, dating back at least to the late eighteenth century (Sömmering, 1791). In the early nineteenth century, the phrenologist Spurzheim (1815) held it highly probable that "the organs [of the brain] increase by exercise." Showing more caution than usual, Spurzheim added, "In order, however, to be able to answer this question positively, we ought to observe the same persons when exercised and when not exercised; or at least observe many persons who are, and many others who are not, exercised during all periods of life [pp. 554–555]." This idea has recurred from time to time; essentially the same research proposal was made a century and a half later by the anatomist, J. Z. Young (1964, p. 272).

## EXPERIMENTAL PROGRAM
### PROCEDURES

In our research on this question starting in 1958, we followed essentially the design suggested by Spurzheim. However, we benefited from many intervening investigations demonstrating that the brain is relatively stable and not likely to show large changes—a fact of which Sömmering (1785) was already aware. Because the cerebral effects that we hoped to induce might be small at best, we employed procedures that we hoped would *maximize* these effects of experience and that would *minimize* variability from extraneous sources.

In an attempt to maximize the effects of differential experience on the brain, we decided to set up two markedly different experimental situations, to put the rats in one or the other at an early age when their brains might be most plastic, and to maintain the animals in these situations for a prolonged period. Animals are therefore assigned at weaning (about 25 days of age) and kept for 80 days in either an enriched environment — environmental complexity and training (ECT)—or in an impoverished condition (IC). These conditions have been described in some detail elsewhere (Krech, Rosenzweig, and Bennett, 1960), so only a summary description will be given here. In the enriched situation the animals are housed in groups of 10 to 12 in a large cage that is provided with "toys" such as ladders, wheels, boxes, platforms, etc. The toys are selected each day from a larger group. To enrich the rats' experience further, we give them a daily half-hour exploratory session in groups of 5 or 6. This takes place in a 3- by 3-foot field with a pattern of barriers that is changed daily. Rat pups are as playful and as amusing to watch as kittens in these situations. After about 30 days in this permissive free play environment, some formal training is given in a series of mazes. In the home cage they have food and water ad lib. Thus these animals are stimulated by their cagemates, by their complex environment and by trials in several apparatuses.

Each ECT animal has a littermate assigned to the impoverished condition. Here animals live in individual cages with solid side walls, so that an animal cannot see or touch another. These cages are placed in a separate, quiet, dimly lighted room, while the ECT cages are in a large, brightly lighted room with considerable incidental activity. The IC rats have food and water ad lib and, like their ECT brothers, they are weighed about once a week. In some experiments there is also an intermediate

### TABLE 1

Effects of Enriched (ECT) and Impoverished (IC) Conditions on Brain Weights of 130 Littermate Pairs of $S_1$ Rats Run from 25 to 105 Days of Age

|  | Total cortex | | Rest of brain | |
|---|---|---|---|---|
|  | M | SD | M | SD |
| ECT | 698 | 31 | 939 | 39 |
| IC | 671 | 30 | 952 | 40 |
| No. pairs | | | | |
| ECT>IC[a] | 101/130 | | 54/130 | |
| ECT/IC[b] | 1.040 | | .987 | |
| p[c] | <.001 | | <.01 | |

[a] Number of littermate pairs in which the ECT value exceeds the IC value.
[b] The value for each ECT animal was divided by that of its IC littermate, and the mean of these ratios was then calculated.
[c] Determined by analyses of variance.

group in which animals are kept under standard-colony (SC) conditions, three to a cage and without any special handling or training.

In order to minimize variability from extraneous sources, we have consistently observed the following precautions: In any given experiment, animals of only one strain, age, and sex are used. (In most cases, they are males.) All comparisons are made between littermates. The littermates are assigned randomly between the experimental conditions, so that no initial bias can enter. All brain analyses are carried out under code numbers that do not reveal the experimental treatment, so that no analytical bias can affect the results.

At the end of the behavioral phase of an experiment, the brains are removed and, in most cases, divided by gross dissection into five samples (see Figure 1 in Rosenzweig, Krech, Bennett, and Diamond, 1962). With

WEIGHT DIFFERENCES IN TOTAL CORTEX

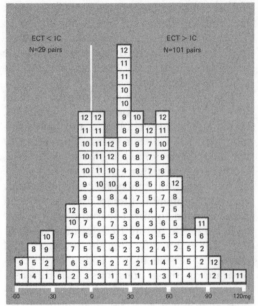

**Figure 1.** Differences in cortical weight between the enriched-experience (ECT) and impoverished (IC) members of 130 littermate pairs of $S_1$ rats. (Each square represents the weight difference, in milligrams, between the members of a pair. The data came from 12 successive experiments, and the number in each square is the number of the experiment. In each of the experiments, most of the cases will be seen to lie on the right-hand side; i.e., the ECT animal has greater weight of total cortex than does its IC brother.)

the aid of a small calibrated plastic T square, a sample of the visual cortex is first circumscribed and then peeled off from the underlying white matter. Next, a sample of the somesthetic cortex is removed. The third sample is the remaining dorsal cortex. (In the rat, cortex can be separated from the white matter much more readily and accurately than is the case in the cat or dog or primate.) The fourth sample includes ventral cortex and associated tissues such as the hippocampus, the amygdaloid nuclei, and the corpus callosum; by weight, it is about two-thirds hippocampus. The fifth and final sample consists of all the rest of the brain after the cortex and associated tissues have been removed. This final sample includes not only the core of the cerebral hemispheres, but also the olfactory bulbs, the midbrain, the cerebellum, and the medulla.

## RESULTS

**Anatomical effects.** Our first attempts were to measure effects of experience on brain chemistry. Brain anatomy was disregarded, since we had inherited the dogma of absolute stability of brain weight. Fortunately, we had to record the weights of our brain samples in order to measure chemical activity per unit of tissue weight. After about 2 years of contemplating the chemical effects, we finally realized that the weights of the brain samples were also being altered by the environmental manipulations (Rosenzweig et al., 1962). It will be simpler to present the weight effects first.

The results demonstrate that the ECT rats consistently develop greater weight of cerebral cortex than do their impoverished littermates, as Table 1 shows. Here all four cortical samples are pooled into total cortex for simplicity of exposition. This table is based on 130 littermate pairs of male rats of the $S_1$ strain; they were run in 12 experiments conducted over a 5-year period. Overall, the cortex of the enriched rats weighs 4% more than that of the restricted rats ($p < .001$), and four-fifths of the pairs show a difference in this direction. The standard deviation is small, being only about 4% of the mean. The rest of the brain does not show the gain in weight with experience that is characteristic of the cortex. Several other strains of rats have also been used in such experiments, and they have yielded similar results. It is worth noting that we probably would not have noticed any effect if we had not analyzed separately the cortex and the rest of the brain.

Now, let us look at a distribution of weight differences between littermates (Figure 1). Each square represents the difference in cortical weight between the two

**TABLE 2**

Effects of ECT and IC in Weights (Milligrams) of Four Cortical Tissue Samples of 130 Littermate Pairs of $S_1$ Rats Run from 25 to 105 Days of Age

| | Visual | | So-mesthetic | | Remaining dorsal | | Ventral | |
|---|---|---|---|---|---|---|---|---|
| | M | SD | M | SD | M | SD | M | SD |
| ECT | 65.0 | 4.2 | 51.2 | 3.1 | 282.1 | 17.0 | 299.3 | 22.7 |
| IC | 61.3 | 4.6 | 50.3 | 3.1 | 269.2 | 15.6 | 290.0 | 22.7 |
| No. pairs ECT>IC | 97/130 | | 78/130 | | 96/130 | | 84/130 | |
| ECT/IC | 1.061 | | 1.019 | | 1.048 | | 1.032 | |
| p | <.001 | | <.05 | | <.001 | | <.001 | |

DIFFERENCES IN WEIGHT RATIOS, TOTAL CORTEX/REST OF BRAIN

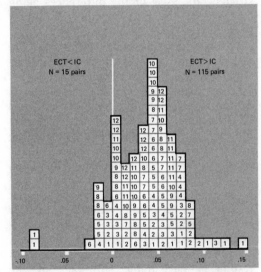

**Figure 2.** Differences between ECT and IC littermates in the ratio of weight of total cortex to weight of the rest of the brain. (Each square represents the differences in this ratio between the two members of a pair. The data are based on the same animals as in Figure 1. The numbers inside the squares indicate in which of the 12 replication experiments a pair of animals was run.)

members of a littermate pair. It is clear that the mean difference cannot be attributed to some aberrant animals but rather that the entire distribution has been shifted to one side by the experimental treatment.

Although the ECT animals are greater in cortical weight, they are about 7% less in body weight than the IC animals. If we were to express brain weight in terms of body weight or to correct for differences in body weight, this would enlarge the effects that we have reported. As Sömmering (1778) noted long ago, body weight can fluctuate rather widely due to many factors, and he suggested expressing the weight of one part of the brain in terms of another part. If we take the ratio of weight of total cortex to that of the rest of the brain, we obtain the results shown in Figure 2. Here we see that the cortical/ subcortical weight ratio is consistently greater for the enriched than for the restricted rats, 90% of the differences being in favor of the ECT member of a pair ($p < .001$).

Not only does the cortex differ from the rest of the brain in its response to differential experience, but the regions of the cortex do not participate equally, as Table 2 demonstrates. With our standard ECT and IC situations, the occipital region shows the largest changes in weight, amounting to 6% ($p < .001$). The nearby somesthetic region shows the smallest differences, amounting to 2% ($p < .05$). Further experiments that we have done indicate that it is possible to modify selectively one or another region of the cortex, depending upon the particular program of enrichment used. For example, raising rats in the dark results in measurable shrinkage of the visual cortex. If the environment is complex, the dark-raised rats develop heavier somesthetic areas than light-raised littermates. Thus the effects are opposite in the visual and somesthetic regions. Time will

not allow us to consider these specific regional effects further here, although I will later make a suggestion for human research based upon them.

The greater weight of the cortex of the stimulated rats reflects greater thickness of cortex, as we found in independent experiments. In these experiments we made anatomical sections of the brains, rather than consuming the tissue for chemical analyses. Depth has been measured in a standard part of the occipital area. The results of four experiments (Table 3) demonstrate that the cerebral cortex becomes significantly thicker in the ECT rats than in their IC littermates. The outermost layer of the cortex shows no change, so it has been excluded from these data. For the remaining layers, the overall effect amounts to 6% ($p < .001$). Preliminary measures indicate that the hippocampus also becomes thicker as a consequence of enriched experience. So the whole gray bark of the brain grows thicker with enriched experience.

In one experiment (Diamond, Krech, and Rosenzweig, 1964) we measured the diameter of capillaries in the cortex, and we found the average diameter to be greater in the ECT animals than in their IC littermates. Other investigators have found that with acclimatization to high altitude, the cortical capillaries of the rat increase in diameter (Opitz, 1951). Apparently, then, the anatomy of the cerebral vasculature can respond adaptively to increased demand.

**TABLE 3**

Depths ($\mu$) of Visual Cortex from ECT and IC Rats (Excluding Layer I)

| Experiment | N (pairs) | ECT | | IC | | ECT/IC | p | No. pairs ECT/IC |
|---|---|---|---|---|---|---|---|---|
| | | M | SD | M | SD | | | |
| Frozen sections (25 $\mu$) | | | | | | | | |
| I | 11 | 1,332 | 56 | 1,271 | 73 | 1.048 | <.01 | 9/11 |
| II | 9 | 1,404 | 87 | 1,298 | 81 | 1.082 | <.001 | 9/9 |
| I & II | 20 | 1,364 | 72 | 1,284 | 76 | 1.062 | <.001 | 18/20 |
| Celloidin sections (10 $\mu$) | | | | | | | | |
| III | 12 | 813 | 35 | 779 | 38 | 1.044 | <.05 | 11/12 |
| IV | 9 | 844 | 35 | 772 | 36 | 1.093 | <.001 | 9/9 |
| III & IV | 21 | 826 | 38 | 776 | 35 | 1.064 | <.001 | 20/21 |

Biochemical effects. Much of our biochemical work has concerned the enzyme acetylcholinesterase (AChE). This enzyme is important at those central synapses where acetylcholine is the chemical transmitter that conveys messages from one neuron to the next. Enzymes are measured in terms of their activity; one can consider either the total activity in a sample or the activity per unit of weight of the sample. The total activity of AChE is found to increase slightly but consistently in the ECT animals, both in the cortex and in the rest of the brain (Table 4). In the cortex, this increase in enzymatic activity is less than the increase in tissue weight, so the activity per unit weight decreases in the ECT animals.

#### TABLE 4

Effects of ECT and IC on Total AChE Activity in 130 Littermate Pairs of $S_1$ Rats Run from 25 to 105 Days of Age

|  | Total cortex | | Rest of brain | |
|---|---|---|---|---|
|  | M | SD | M | SD |
| ECT | 6,358 | 392 | 18,734 | 938 |
| IC | 6,231 | 323 | 18,475 | 977 |
| No. pairs | | | | |
| ECT > IC | 81/128 | | 82/130 | |
| ECT/IC | 1.020 | | 1.014 | |
| p | <.001 | | <.01 | |

Note.—Activity measured in terms of m$\mu$moles acetylthiocholine hydrolyzed/min.

Now there are other enzymes in the brain that can also act on acetylcholine, although less specifically than does AChE. These other enzymes are known collectively as cholinesterase (ChE). In the rat, there is relatively little ChE activity, but we wanted to be certain that the effects we were measuring could not be attributed to ChE. Therefore, we measured ChE activity independently. These measures confirmed our previously reported AChE effects, since there is too little ChE activity to affect the AChE values. Unexpectedly, these new measures also showed that ChE activity was being modified by differential experi-

ence and according to its own pattern (Table 5). Total ChE activity is up by 8% in the cortex of the ECT rats, while showing no change in the rest of the brain.

Let us summarize these effects by showing results for 88 littermate pairs of $S_1$ rats for whom we have both enzymatic measures (Figure 3). Note that at the cortex, tissue weight and the total activity of both enzymes increase significantly, but with

#### TABLE 5

Effects of ECT and IC on Total ChE Activity in 89 Littermate Pairs of $S_1$ Rats Run from 25 to 105 Days of Age

|  | Total cortex | | Rest of brain | |
|---|---|---|---|---|
|  | M | SD | M | SD |
| ECT | 231 | 13 | 551 | 27 |
| IC | 214 | 14 | 552 | 25 |
| No. pairs | | | | |
| ECT > IC | 80/88 | | 41/88 | |
| ECT/IC | 1.078 | | 0.998 | |
| p | <.001 | | NS | |

Note.—Activity measured in terms of m$\mu$moles butyrylthiocholine hydrolyzed/min.

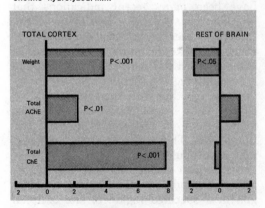

PERCENTAGE DIFFERENCES, ECT MINUS IC BASED ON 88 LITTERMATE PAIRS OF $S_1$ RATS

**Figure 3.** Percentage differences between ECT and IC littermates in tissue weight, total activity of AChE and of ChE. (The data were obtained from 88 littermate pairs of $S_1$ rats. Results are shown separately for total cortex and for the rest of the brain. In the cortex, total activity of AChE is seen to increase significantly but by a lesser percentage than does tissue weight; total activity of ChE increases by a greater percentage than does weight.)

the percentage change in AChE lagging beyond that in tissue weight, while the percentage change in ChE surpasses the change in weight. Note also that, on these measures at least, the cortex is clearly more responsive to the environmental influences than is the rest of the brain.

In other experiments we have taken further chemical measures. These have included total protein, the enzyme hexokinase, and RNA. In all these further regards, the chemical measures per unit of tissue weight are unchanged. That is to say, the cortex added as a consequence of enriched experience is normal in these respects and is unusual only in the relative activities of AChE and ChE.

In seeking to understand what these enzymatic changes might mean, it occurred to us that neurons contain chiefly AChE, while the glial cells contain chiefly the less specific enzyme ChE. The glia had long been regarded simply as structural members, supporting the neurons, but there have been many recent indications that glia may play an active role in the brain. It has also been known that the number of nerve cells, like the number of muscle cells, is fixed at birth or soon thereafter, but glia may multiply. We therefore sought to determine whether the increased bulk of cortex as a consequence of experience might be due, in part at least, to proliferation of glia. This sent us back to anatomy, now at a cellular level.

Histological results. To test this possibility, we made counts of neurons and of glia in a specified region of the occipital cortex. In order to obtain a satisfactory degree of reliability in such counts, we devised a procedure in which photographic enlargements were made of the anatomical slides, and two anatomists made independent counts. The results of these cell counts in two experiments are given in Table 6. The number of neurons within the region measured shows a slight decrease for the ECT rats. Presumably this decrease in packing density occurs because the number of neurons is fixed, and they are forced somewhat further apart as the cortex expands.

**TABLE 6**

Effects of ECT and IC on Neural and Glial Counts in 17 Littermate Pairs of S$_1$ Rats Run from 25 to 105 Days of Age
(Visual Cortex)

|  | M no. neurons | M no. glia | M glia/neuron ratio |
|---|---|---|---|
| ECT | 485.8 | 185.4 | .385 |
| IC | 500.6 | 162.8 | .332 |
| No. pairs |  |  |  |
| ECT > IC | 6/17 | 13/17 | 12/17 |
| ECT/IC | .970 | 1.139 | 1.160 |
| p | NS | <.01 | <.02 |

The glia, on the contrary, increase significantly in number, and the ratio of glia to neurons then also increases. Both our chemical and anatomical findings therefore demonstrate that one response of the brain to heightened environmental demands is a proliferation of glia. This conclusion has recently been supported by Altman and Das (1964), using a different measure of glial proliferation.

What the increase in the number of glia cells means in the functioning of the brain is not clear, since the role of the glia is a subject of active research and controversy. Here are two possibilities, among many that could be advanced: If the glia help to nourish the neurons, as has been suggested, then increasing the functional load on the neurons may raise their metabolic turnover and thus require more glial support. Again, it is possible that the branches of the neurons ramify more completely during learning. (We are attempting to test this in some experiments in progress.) Since the glia form the sheaths around neural processes, more branching may require more glia.

Control experiments. Granting that the brain adapts anatomically and chemically to the differential environments, we still need to determine to what extent various features of the environments are responsible for the effects. Is it possible, for example, that unintended features have played an important role? And if the effects *are* due to complexity of experience, what relative weights should be attached to the social grouping, to the varied cage environment, and to the formal training?

We have done some experiments to test possible effects of differential amounts of locomotion and of handling.[1] The ECT animals are handled every day and they engage in more locomotor activity than do their IC brothers. The results indicate that neither handling nor differential locomotion nor a combination of the two is responsible for the effects we have reported.

The possibility that our effects are due to isolation stress rather than to enrichment of experience must also be considered. The difference in cortical weight, for example, might be caused either by an *increase* in the ECT group, or by a *decrease* in the IC group, or by a combination of both effects. There are reports in the literature that isolated rats become aggressive and less healthy than animals kept in groups. Rats of our strains do not become aggressive in isolation; you can still pick them up easily with bare hands after they have endured months of isolation. Nor do they show poor health; they actually gain somewhat more weight than their ECT littermates. Nevertheless, the cerebral effects might be due principally to isolation. To test this, we employed a colony comparison group in some experiments. The brain values of these SC rats were found to be intermediate between those of their ECT and IC littermates, just as their environment was intermediate. But the SC values were generally closer to those of the isolated rats, indicating that isolation is less important than environmental complexity in producing the

differences we have seen between ECT and IC groups.

In further experiments we have intensified the environmental impoverishment and have produced still greater cerebral differences from the ECT animals. These experiments with more stringent impoverishment were carried out in the Space Sciences Laboratory of the University of California. Each isolation cage was suspended in an individual box lined with fiberglass, and the boxes were placed in a sound-insulated room. Figure 4 gives

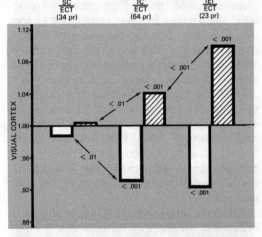

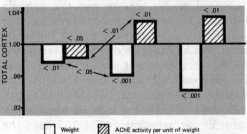

**Figure 4.** Cerebral measures from (ECT) rats are compared with those of littermates in three different conditions—standard colony (SC), our usual impoverished condition (IC), and isolation in extreme impoverishment (IEI). (Values in the upper part of the figure are for the visual sample, the part of the cortex that is most responsive to differential experience, while the lower part of the figure gives results for total cortex. As the environmental differences become greater, going from left to right in the figure, the resultant cerebral differences become greater.)

---

[1] For indications that handling can affect certain physiological variables and physical development, see chapters by Levine, Schaeffer, Casler, and Maier in Newton and Levine (1966).

values of weight and of AChE activity per unit of weight for visual cortex and for total cortex. It demonstrates that the animals isolated in extreme impoverishment (IEI) differ more from ECT littermates than do the animals in our usual IC condition; the animals in the SC condition differ least of all from their ECT littermates. Thus, the greater the difference in environments, the greater the resultant differences in brain anatomy and chemistry.

One of our graduate students, Robert Slagle, is now trying to unravel some of the complexities of the ECT program to decide what the various features contribute to the overall results. It is too early to give definitive results, but here are some preliminary indications: Simply putting the animals in groups of 12 in a large cage accounts for part of the cerebral effects, and equipping the cage with toys adds more. The inclusion of two training trials a day in various mazes adds relatively little. Whether intensified formal training without group living will produce brain growth is the subject of further experiments, both in progress and projected.

**Effects in adult animals.** One of the procedures in all the experiments that I have described so far was to put the animals into the differential situations rather young —at weaning—when their brains might be most plastic. More recently we have tested to see whether or not similar results could be obtained with adult rats. For this purpose we kept rats under SC conditions until 105 days of age—the age of sacrifice in most of our experiments. At 105 days the rat has been sexually mature for over a month, and brain growth, which never completely ceases in the rat, has leveled off. Figure 5 shows brain weights of rats sacrificed at three ages—25 days, at weaning; 105 days, after spending 80 days in one of the three environments; 185 days, after spending their last 80 days in one of the three environments. These anatomical results, and the chemical results as well, indi-

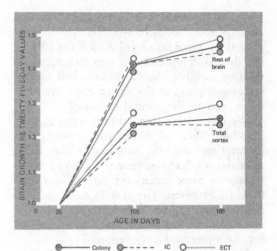

**Figure 5.** Growth of total cortex and of the rest of the brain is shown in relation to weight values at 25 days of age. (Keeping rats from 25 to 105 days under three different conditions —ECT, SC, or isolated (IC)—leads to differences in cortical weights but not in weight of the rest of the brain. Taking animals that have been in the SC condition until 105 days and then dividing them among the three conditions also leads to differences in cortical weight— and to some degree in weight of the rest of the brain as well. Thus, the adult rat brain appears capable of adaptive growth.)

cate that the cortex of the adult rat brain is as capable of adaptive growth as is the cortex of the young animal. If these cerebral changes reflect learning and storage of memory, these results may be encouraging to those of us who are gray around the edges.

**Extensions and confirmatory findings.** Our first announcements of measurable changes in the brain as consequences of experience met with the expected scientific skepticism. Could the results be replicated? Could they be produced in other laboratories?

By now we have shown that the results are obtained consistently in experiment after experiment during 5 years in our laboratory, and with all the strains of rats that we have tried. I even assigned this as a class laboratory last spring, using a strain we had not tried previously, Long-Evans rats. The class obtained clear-cut results.

This research has also been extended to mice in recent experiments done by Jean Moller, a graduate student of McGill University working at the University of California under my supervision. Two inbred strains of mice, the A and the C57, were employed. Both showed patterns of effects rather like rats in that they yielded significant results in total cortex and little or no effect in the rest of the brain. Again, there were significant increases in cortical weight and in total AChE and ChE. The increase in total AChE activity with enriched experience fell below the increase in weight; total ChE activity increased significantly, although it did not surpass the increase in weight.

Other laboratories have also begun to report results that confirm or extend our own. I have already mentioned that Altman and Das (1964) reported glial proliferation in the rat as a consequence of ECT; they also found an increase in cortical depth. Workers at the University of California, Los Angeles—Geller, Yuwiler, and Zolman (1965)—have found increased weight of brain and certain chemical changes as a consequence of enriched experience. A doctoral thesis by Bryan (1965) at Utah also reports the increase in cortical weight but no clear change in RNA per unit of weight. Pryor, Otis, and Uyeno (1965) at Stanford Research Institute have found increases in brain weight and some changes in AChE and ChE activities with electrical stimulation of the brain. Other laboratories have informed us of work in progress on cerebral changes with experience, so that this appears to be a growing area of study. We hope to help attract more workers to the field so that it may be cultivated intensively.

Relations between cerebral changes and learning ability. One more type of experimental result should be mentioned before we consider the implications of this research for the study of human behavior. This last line of research is concerned with the following problem: Are the cerebral changes actually related to effects of experience on learning ability? We do not yet have a definitive answer, but we do have some evidence indicating that the brain changes run in parallel with changes in problem-solving ability.

In 1962, we reported a study (Krech, Rosenzweig, & Bennett, 1962) in which rats were raised for 1 month in either ECT or IC environments and then were tested on a reversal discrimination problem. The tester had not participated in the earlier treatment of the animals nor was he informed which rats came from which situation. In error scores on the first rather simple light-dark discrimination problem, the groups did not differ. This is important because it has been suggested that isolated animals have an unsatiated exploratory tendency which leads them to make apparent errors when they are only finding out about the world. Perhaps because of our prolonged pretraining, no such effect appeared. But when the rats had to reverse cues and the problems became more difficult, the previously isolated group became relatively worse and worse in its performance. The difference in favor of the ECT animals on all reversal problems was significant at the .01 level. This experiment has since been replicated with rats of both the $S_1$ and $S_3$ lines, and the original effect has been confirmed in each experiment.

Other experiments are being done to determine whether the cerebral changes and the changes in ability go together regularly or whether they can be split apart. To date, the results have not forced us to abandon our initial hypothesis that changes in the brain induced by experience underlie the changes in learning ability brought about by experience.

## IMPLICATIONS OF ANIMAL RESEARCH FOR HUMAN STUDIES

Now that you have seen that enriched experience leads to anatomical and chemical changes in the brains of rats and mice, what relevance may this or other animal research have for the study of human behavior? I would like to discuss three ways in which animal research may contribute. And I would also like to point out a few limitations that should be kept in mind.

## CONTRIBUTIONS OF ANIMAL RESEARCH

**Extrapolating from animal to man.** First, animal experiments and especially a comparative approach may allow extrapolation to human behavior where direct experiments with humans are not possible. To take an example close at hand, we have seen that the hypothesis of growth of the brain with use was originated in the eighteenth century with regard to the human brain. During the nineteenth century much research was conducted on this problem, but by the end of the century it was recognized that the results were inconclusive. It simply was not possible to secure brains of matched samples of men where everything except the exercise of the brain has been kept constant. Now, suppose (as we hope) that we can extend our experiments on rodents to carnivores and to primates, and that cerebral differences as a consequence of experience are found throughout the series. (A conceivable finding is that the differences will increase in magnitude as we examine animals capable of more and more complex behavior.) It should then be possible to extrapolate from this animal series to the human brain.

As another example, Harold Jones (1954) stated in the *Handbook of Child Psychology* in both 1946 and 1954 that studies to test whether early training increases the IQ remained inconclusive. Jones pointed out a number of design requirements for adequate research in this area. The first of his several points was this: "The experimental and the control group should consist of matched pairs from the same population, one member of each pair being assigned at random to the experimental procedure [p. 679]." He showed why attempting to

match pairs after the fact is unlikely to be successful.

Well-designed animal experiments on effects of early training are feasible, and in fact they are being performed in increasing numbers. (See chapters and references in Newton & Levine, 1966.) Donald Hebb foresaw this in 1954 (just when Harold Jones was pointing out the deficiencies of the human studies). Hebb (1954) wrote,

Failing the possibility of radical rearing experiments with human children, it seems that comparative study offers a solid line of advance in this field. Studies of . . . a number of species will provide some basis for tentative extrapolation of the curves of phylogenetic development through chimpanzee to man, where the ideas thus arrived at can be tested for their value in clarifying clinical and naturalistic observations [p. 534].

**Providing perspectives for study of human behavior.** The second value of animal studies is that they may provide new or broader perspectives in which to place and understand human behavior. Thus Ford and Beach (1951) in their book, *Patterns of Sexual Behavior*, set up a threefold frame of reference to assist in understanding human sexual behavior. One perspective is cross-cultural; the second is evolutionary or zoological, involving comparisons between human beings and lower animals; the third perspective is physiological, and this of course also draws upon animal studies. In the perspective of comparative psychology, Ford and Beach consider many aspects of man's sexual behavior to be part of a common mammalian pattern. On the other hand, they relate his unique degree of dependence upon learning and experience to the evolution of his large and complex cerebral cortex.

In considering effects of early experience on human development, both cross-cultural and animal studies may provide clues to understanding. For example, Jones (1954) reviewed several studies indicating that the firstborn is more likely to be gifted or eminent than are his siblings. Jones felt that there was no satisfactory interpretation for these findings. Subsequent studies have yielded these further findings (Hunt, 1961, p. 341 ff.): Twins on the average have IQs several points lower than singletons. Pairs of siblings spaced further apart in age do better on intelligence tests than those born closer together. One way of interpreting all of these findings is to hypothesize with Hunt that siblings born close together do not get all the adult attention and stimulation they need for full development. Support for this hypothesis comes from cross-cultural studies on African children who receive a great deal of attention and stimulation until weaning and whose intellectual and motor development to that point is well in advance of European children (Geber, 1958).

Geber describes the Ugandan mother's care of the child in this way:

Before the child is weaned, the mother's whole interest is centred on him. She never leaves him, carries him on her back—often in skin-to-skin contact—wherever she goes, sleeps with him, feeds him on demand at all hours of the day and night, forbids him nothing, and never chides him. . . . He is, moreover, continually being stimulated by seeing her at her various occupations and hearing her interminable conversations, and because he is always with her, his world is relatively extensive. He is also the centre of interest for neighbours and visitors . . . [p. 194].

Weaning in Uganda is usually abrupt and severe, and most children tested after weaning no longer show the earlier precocity. "On the other hand, children for whom weaning had not caused a sudden break in the way of life retained their liveliness after weaning, and developed without interruption [p. 195]."

One further point from Geber's paper strengthens the interpretation that early stimulation is the main cause of the precocious development of Ugandan children: "A few children . . . were being brought up in the European way, passing most of their lives in their cots and fed at regular intervals. . . . They did not show similar precoc-

ity after the first month, and later were inclined to be quiet or subdued [pp. 194–195]."

Further support comes from animal studies of the last 15 years showing that the greater the richness and variety of experience the subject receives, the more does its learning ability increase. You saw some examples of this from our own research reported above.

Now let us speculate somewhat broadly. Suppose it could be demonstrated that for full development of their potential our children need more adult care than they now receive. Does anyone suppose that American mothers could be persuaded to adopt the early Ugandan pattern and to sustain this degree of care and attention throughout childhood? Is this degree of adult tutelage possible when over half our population is under 20 years of age? Or are we on our way to a society where the child graduates from aircrib to neighborhood play group to teen-age society, almost untouched by adult hands? Challenging most current prophets, the biophysicist John R. Platt (1965) argues that in population and in many other characteristics of society we are already "past the middle of the S-curve" of expansion. He pictures a future steady-state population with "just as many people at age 40 or at age 60 as at age 10. And if they all live to about 80, as it now seems they might, then half of them will be over 40 and only one-fifth of them will be children under 15 [p. 611]." Platt suggests that such a society could use its "great excess of adult-power, prosperous and leisured, to make the richest education for children that the world has ever known [p. 611]." Coming back to the present, there would seem to be a great deal of research necessary with both human and animal subjects, to provide a comprehensive picture of how capacity develops with training and of how available instructional time can be spent most effectively.

Suggesting new hypotheses about human

behavior. Since human learning is distinctively verbal, there is great potential in research on the effects of encouraging early verbal development. Specifically, I would like to suggest using the Human Relations Area Files to compare intellectual development in those cultures where adults speak a great deal to infants and expect children to speak early and in those cultures where adults neither speak much to infants nor expect them to speak before the age of 3 or 4.

This brings me to the last value of animal research that I would like to discuss: It may prompt investigators to make new observations or to formulate hypotheses about human behavior that would not otherwise have occurred to them. Let me give two examples, one potential and the other actual.

For the potential example let us refer back to two points mentioned earlier: First is the difficulty of studying brain growth as a consequence of experience in human beings. Second are the animal studies indicating that differential growth of cortical regions can be induced by specific programs of experience. The reason for giving up human studies was that it was not possible to obtain adequate controls. To meet this requirement, it may be possible, following the animal model, to use the individual as his own control by measuring differential development of various regions of the brain as a function of differential experience. In one of the first numbers of the *American Journal of Psychology*, Donaldson (1892) did in fact consider in this way the brain of the blind deaf-mute, Laura Bridgman. He reported from postmortem examination a somewhat deficient development of the cortical areas representing the lacking senses, coupled with essentially normal development of the area representing the skin senses. To my knowledge, there has not been a systematic compilation of human data concerning relative development of cortical areas in relation to sensory impair-

ment or to heightened experience. Our recent animal studies suggest that this might be a valuable line of research to pursue.

Now for an actual example in which animal research has prompted investigators to make new observations and to formulate a novel hypothesis about human development. This example is found in the recent paper, "Infantile Stimulation and Adult Stature of Human Males," by Landauer and Whiting (1964). Here is part of their summary:

We have reviewed some recent studies that have shown that rats and mice stimulated during an early period of life attain greater size at adulthood. We have indicated that there are plausible explanations for this effect involving changes in functioning of the adrenal-pituitary system. In exploring whether these results could be generalized to humans, we found that for two independent cross-cultural samples, in societies where the heads or limbs of infants were repeatedly molded or stretched, or where their ears, noses, or lips were pierced, where they were circumsized, vaccinated, inoculated, or had tribal marks cut or burned in their skin, the mean adult male stature was over two inches greater than in societies where these customs were not practiced. The effects of these practices appear to be independent of several other factors known to be associated with increased stature [p. 1018].

Landauer and Whiting do not claim that their data give conclusive evidence that infantile stress enhances growth. Nevertheless, they point out that their hypothesis is given strong support by the fact that the correlation they found

for humans corresponds to an experimentally demonstrated effect in laboratory mammals, and the type of phenomenon—endocrine control of growth—is one in which interspecies generality is common. Therefore, [they conclude] it seems to us that the inference from our data of a causal relation between infant experience and human growth is sufficiently plausible to warrant serious consideration [p. 1018].

## SOME LIMITATIONS

This last example can be used to make a transition to some of the limitations of extrapolating from animals to human beings. It should be clear that each species of animal starts at its own level of development and displays its own rate and sequence of development. The rat, for example, is born in a very immature state compared to the human. Rapid changes in its brain chemistry occur during the first 2 weeks after birth, and these are analogous to changes that occur before birth in the human baby. In the rat the first 10 days seems to be the "critical period" for inducing alterations in the pituitary-adrenal axis and in growth. The human baby at an analogous period of its cerebral development is still safely in the womb. Thus it is not clear that the first 2 years of human life—chosen by Landauer and Whiting to be the equivalent of the preweaning period in rats and mice—is physiologically equivalent to the critical period for inducing growth in the rat. It is quite possible that this discrepancy, if it is real, may point the way to some factor other than the pituitary-adrenal system as being responsible for the growth effect in humans. To take another example, the fact that in the rat we can induce brain growth in the adult as readily as in the young animal by giving enriched experience, does not necessarily indicate that this will be true of people. A series of comparative studies will be necessary before we can tell whether higher mammals show a critical period for brain development as a function of experience.

Now for a final word of optimism about this long-range enterprise of animal and human studies of growth and behavior. Long ago men were reminded of their limitations in these words: "Which of you by taking thought can add one cubit unto his stature?" This admonition retains its force, and it appears that rather drastic action is required to add even two inches to human stature. Yet I hope that the research that we have been considering may eventually add, not cubits to stature, but cubic centimeters to human brains.

## REFERENCES

Altman, J., and Das, G. D. 1964. Autoradiographic examination of the effects of enriched environment on the rate of glial multiplication in the adult rat brain. *Nature* 204:1161–1163.

Bryan, R. N. 1965. Brain RNA metabolism in differential experience. Unpublished doctoral dissertation, University of Utah.

Diamond, M. C.; Krech, D.; and Rosenzweig, M. R. 1964. The effects of an enriched environment on the histology of the rat cerebral cortex. *Journal of Comparative Neurology* 123:111–119.

Donaldson, H. H. 1892. Anatomical observations of the brain and several sense-organs of the blind deaf-mute; Laura Dewey Bridgman. *American Journal of Psychology* 4:247–294.

Ford, C. S., and Beach, F. A. 1951. *Patterns of sexual behavior.* New York: Harper.

Geber, M. 1958. The psychomotor development of African children in the first year, and the influence of maternal behavior. *Journal of Social Psychology* 47:185–195.

Geller, E.; Yuwiler, A.; and Zolman, J. 1965. Effects of environmental complexity and training on constituents of brain and liver. Paper read at International Neurochemical Conference, Oxford.

Hebb, D. O., and Thompson, W. R. 1954. The social significance of animal studies. In *Handbook of social psychology*, ed. G. Lindzey, pp. 532–561. Cambridge, Mass.: Addison-Wesley.

Hunt, J. McV. 1961. *Intelligence and experience.* New York: Ronald Press.

Jones, H. E. 1954. The environment and mental development. In *Handbook of child psychology*, ed. L. Carmichael, chap. 10. New York: Wiley.

Krech, D.; Rosenzweig, M. R.; and Bennett, E. L. 1960. Effects of environmental complexity and training on brain chemistry. *Journal of Comparative and Physiological Psychology* 53:509–519.

Krech, D.; Rosenzweig, M. R.; and Bennett, E. L. 1962. Relations between brain chemistry and problem-solving among rats raised in enriched and impoverished environments. *Journal of Comparative and Physiological Psychology* 55:801–807.

Landauer, T. K., and Whiting, J. W. M. 1964. Infantile stimulation and adult stature of human males. *American Anthropologist* 66:1007–1028.

Newton, G., and Levine, S., eds. 1968. *Early experience and behavior: The psychobiology of development.* Springfield, Ill.: Charles C. Thomas.

Opitz, E. 1951. Increased vascularization of the tissue due to acclimatization to higher altitudes and its significance for oxygen transport. *Experimental Medicine and Surgery* 9:389–403.

Platt, J. R. 1965. The step to man. *Science* 149:607–613.

Pryor, G. T.; Otis, L. S.; and Uyeno, E. 1965. Effects of nonspecific stimulation on behavior, brain chemistry, and brain weight. Paper read at Western Psychological Association, Honolulu.

Rosenzweig, M. R.; Krech, D.; Bennett, E. L.; and Diamond, M. C. 1962. Effects of environmental complexity and training on brain chemistry and anatomy: A replication and extension.

*Journal of Comparative and Physiological Psychology* 55:429–437.

Sömmering, S. T. 1778. *De basis encephali.* Gottingen.

Sömmering, S. T. 1785. *Ueber die Korperliche Verschiedenheit des Negers von Europaer.* Frankfurt am Mainz. Extracts given as an appendix in C. White, *An account of the regular gradation in man and in different animals and vegetables* (London, 1799).

Sömmering, S. T. 1791. *Von Baue des menschlichen Koerpers.* Vol. 5, pt. 1. Frankfurt am Mainz: Barrentropp & Wenner.

Spurzheim, J. G. 1815. *The physiognomical system of Drs. Gall and Spurzheim.* London: Baldwin, Cradock & Joy.

Young, J. Z. 1964. *A model of the brain.* Oxford: Clarendon Press.

# READING 4
# The Albino Rat: A Defensible Choice or a Bad Habit?

**ROBERT B. LOCKARD**
**University of Washington**

In view of the amount of research that has used the albino rat as a subject, Lockard presents some very valid questions. He suggests that the present strain of laboratory rats has evolved away from the original strains and questions the general validity of the results of some studies. After presenting his criticisms, Lockard suggests either a change of animal or the use of inbred rat strains whose genetic background would be clearly defined.

## QUESTIONS

1. Was learning "an adaptive mechanism conferring a reproductive advantage"? Has learning evolved? Is learning a collection of evolved functions?
2. In light of Lockard's comments, how valid are the results of the voluminous rat research conducted during this century? How meaningful are the results? Have psychologists created an artificial system with the use of the rat?
3. How would you refute Lockard's criticisms? Present as many arguments as you can. Demonstrate how his criticisms do not invalidate the research which has used albino rats as subjects.

The albino rat obviously occupies a prominent role in psychology: theories are tested upon it, students are trained with it, and generalizations are based upon it. If the albino rat had come into fashion as the consequence of deliberate and complete consideration of its merits in relation to

The preparation of this paper was greatly aided by Grant GB-5895 from the National Science Foundation.

scientific criteria, we could merely review periodically the wisdom of the choice and relax in the interim, secure in the belief that millions of man-hours and dollars were not being invested on a poorly chosen animal. However, the albino rat, which I shall call *albinus*, occupied the laboratory largely as the result of a chance chain of circumstances, described later. Though accidental, its dominance of laboratories, articles, and theories of the behavior of organisms has become a fact. Thus we are faced with a most serious problem, for if *albinus* is unsuitable or unique or misleading, so are many of the products of psychology. Just as any science scrutinizes its tools and methods for flaws which might affect its findings, it is time we had an analytical examination of our *albinus* and asked what it is and where it is leading or misleading us.

The albino rat, *Rattus norvegicus* var. *albinus,* is a domesticated variant of the Norway rat, *Rattus norvegicus,* also called the brown rat. To understand to what extent *albinus* is representative of "animals," whether it is a freak or a good sample from which to generalize, it is necessary to understand the relationship to the wild Norway, the Norway itself, and the known and probable effects of domestication.

## FROM ASIA TO THE LABORATORY

The Norway rat is a native of eastern Asia (Walker, 1964, p. 904), normally inhabiting stream banks and other watery places. Great migrations probably occurred in ancient times, for there are descriptions of them "Making periodical visits in infinite multitudes to the countries bordering the Caspian Sea and swimming boldly over the rivers holding by one another's tails [Barrett-Hamilton & Hinton, 1916, p. 608]." "Rats" in the sense of pests entering human dwellings were unknown in Europe until the time of the Crusades (1095, 1147, and 1191), when the black rat, *Rattus rattus,* a south Asian rat, was introduced by returning caravans. *Rattus rattus* was probably the rat of the Pied Piper, though no other German records of *rattus* occur until later. It quickly spread throughout Europe, became a formidable pest, and indirectly killed a quarter of the population with typhus and the black plague, which is transmitted to humans by rat fleas. Rat-borne disease has altered human destiny more than the doings of any single human

famous in our histories (Zinsser, 1935). *Rattus rattus* became known as "the common rat" and gained worldwide distribution aboard ships of the early explorers. However, in about 1727, which was a "mouse year" in the Caspian region, hordes of *norvegicus* crossed the Volga and migrated westward. There may have been slightly earlier migrations, for a visit of the Russian fleet probably transported *norvegicus* to Copenhagen in 1716, and *norvegicus* may have been aboard the ship which transported the House of Hanover from Germany to England in 1714, giving rise to the eighteenth century political name, "Hanoverian rat." Early *norvegicus* colonies were established by Russian ships and wrecks in the Baltic regions; meanwhile, *norvegicus* dispersed overland, reaching Paris and most of low-altitude Europe by about 1750 and Switzerland by 1809. *Rattus norvegicus* also traveled by ship, reaching Greenland about 1780, eastern United States in 1775, and our Pacific coast about 1851.

In the later 1700s records of royal rat catchers often showed *Rattus rattus* and *Rattus norvegicus* inhabiting the same buildings, with *rattus* in the rafters, walls, and thatched roofs in accordance with its arboreal habits, and *norvegicus* in the basements and sewers. Rather quickly, however, the heavier and more pugnacious *norvegicus* displaced *rattus* throughout most of Europe and in northern latitudes connected by trade routes. *Rattus rattus* dwindled to isolated colonies except in warm climates, where *norvegicus* often seems unable to displace the established *rattus.* Though *norvegicus* became the dominant pest associated with man in a parasitic fashion, it also survives well in the wild in certain California valleys and on most islands, some of which have been devasted by the omnivorous *norvegicus,* which eats bird's eggs, most vegetation, and can even survive by eating marine debris after turning an island into a sterile rock.

Albino forms of *norvegicus* were noted in England in 1822 and 1858, and doubtlessly occurred elsewhere. From 1800 to 1870 rats were trapped and held in large numbers for the sport of rat baiting, popular in England and France. Up to 200 rats were put in a pit and a terrier freed among them, spectators betting upon the time taken to kill the last rat. Richter (1954) discussed records indicating that albinos were removed from the collections and kept for breeding and show purposes. The precise time and place of the origin of albino varieties is unknown, as is the question of single or multiple origin, but it is very likely that the first laboratory albinos came from the collections of animal fanciers. According to Richter (1954, 1959), the first laboratory use of albino rats was by Philipeaux (1856) in Paris. Rats were first used in breeding experiments by Crampe (1877–1885). H. H. Donaldson, a noted authority on rats, began using them in 1893 at the University of Chicago. The first psychological research with rats was by Steward (1898), Kline (1899), and Small (1900); see Miles (1930). Donaldson's colony at Chicago seems the basis for the influential experiments of Watson in 1903 and 1907, and the 1908 study of orientation in the maze by Carr and Watson. Donaldson's *The Rat*, published in 1915 and revised in 1924, emphasized certain physiological similarities between rat and man and repeatedly stressed a formula for supposedly equating age between the two species. Donaldson's book and his colony, which was the basis of the stock at the Wistar Institute, were extremely influential for the widespread adoption of the rat in medical research. Although the Wistar Institute is now out of the rat business, a number of commercial suppliers now maintain colonies.

## THE EFFECTS OF DOMESTICATION

The first laboratory albinos were probably not a representative sample of *nor-*vegicus. It is well known that trapping is not a random process, and Boice (1966) has pointed out that hungry, timid, small, scared low social status *norvegicus* are the most likely to enter traps. The subsequent selection of "sports"—albinos and piebalds—from the rat pens introduced an additional bias, making the very start of the laboratory stock a somewhat unique group.

Later analysis of Crampe's breeding experiments of about 1880 showed that an albino female mated with a wild male transmitted to her offspring three mutant genes: c (albino), a (nonagouti), and h (hooded). When albino rats were brought from Europe by Donaldson and others about the turn of the century, they proved to be homozygous for these same three mutant genes. Some albinos supplied to W. E. Castle by H. H. Donaldson in 1903 were of this triple recessive type (Castle, 1947). The nonagouti, or black mutation, is accompanied by gentler behavior, and when these were mated with double recessive hooded rats and the offspring crossed with albinos, some homozygous triple recessives (cc, aa, hh) resulted. Most of today's albino rats are black and hooded, although the coat color cannot be expressed because of albinism, itself unrelated to tameness. Today's pigmented laboratory rats, like the hooded, do not differ much from *albinus* and will be lumped under that name.

In 1906, Donaldson transferred his albino colony to the Wistar Institute. Helen King became associated with him in a re-enactment of the domestication of the wild *norvegicus* under controlled conditions. She published two extensive reports, the first in 1929 (King & Donaldson, 1929) after 10 generations of captive *norvegicus* and the second in 1939 (King, 1939) after 25 generations. Albinos were similarly bred and used as controls. The initial differences between captive *norvegicus* and the albinos were appreciable:

The wild Norway are more excitable and much more savage. They gnaw their cages. The body weight is less for a given body length, hence it is a slighter animal. The skeleton is relatively heavier, also the suprarenals (both sexes) and the testes and ovaries. The thyroid is of like weight, but the hypophysis distinctly lighter in both sexes. On the other hand, the brain and spinal cord are both heavier than in the Albino [King & Donaldson, 1929, p. 7].

Across 25 generations in captivity, the captive *norvegicus* changed. They became fatter, like *albinus*. Growth was accelerated, finally averaging 20% heavier than the first generation. The brain, thyroid, and suprarenals decreased in weight. The average length of reproductive period became 8 months longer than at first. Fertility increased; Generation 1 had an average of 3.5 litters, whereas Generation 19 produced an average of 10.18 litters each. Even by the end of 10 generations in captivity the behavior had changed remarkably:

They had lost much of their viciousness and their fear of man; females rarely killed the young returned to the nest after being handled with bare hands; their nervous tension was distinctly less than that in animals of the earlier generations . . .; they made but little effort to escape when the door of the cage was opened or when the cage was cleaned. Rats of the later generations had not, however, overcome their aversion to the presence of strange individuals, and such intruders were killed as promptly as in the earlier generations [King & Donaldson, 1929, p. 67].

While an animal species is often thought of as a "type," such as the type specimen in a museum, a more fertile approach has been to consider individual animals as the morphological results of a sample of genes from the gene pool of the population. The animal is "made" from the genes in the sample. In this view, species differ not because they have different coat colors or types of teeth, but because the two gene pools differ. Rat and lizard gene pools probably contain a few, but just a few, of the same genes. *Rattus rattus* and *Rattus norvegicus* share a large number of genes, but not enough to produce viable fetuses. *Rattus norvegicus* and *albinus* have somewhat different gene pools and hence are somewhat

different animals. But how different, and in what ways? Fortunately, the issue at hand is not the impossible task of a complete genetic analysis, but is an estimate of how unique *albinus* has become in matters of behavior and related sensory, endocrine, and nervous system function. A complete review would be lengthy indeed, but the following brief examples assembled from the writings of Richter, Robinson, and Barnett (except where noted) serve to illustrate how some of the known differences are expressed.

Wild or $F_1$ captive Norways have a complex social organization in which a number of specific behavioral displays operate. Tolman (1958, p. 229) once remarked that rats have little social life, partly true for *albinus*, which has lost a number of stereotyped behaviors. The "threat posture" is absent, and the "amicable" display of "crawling under" is gone. Fighting behavior in *albinus* is incomplete, immature, and rather harmless in character, resembling play. Placed together in a chamber and shocked, *norvegicus* pairs fight savagely while many *albinus* varieties do not. Intruders are killed by *norvegicus* but merely sniffed by *albinus*. Wild types show flight from man and violent struggling, attack, vocalization, and sometimes death when held; *albinus* has the remnant behavior of "backing away." Vocalization in *norvegicus* is common, with a fundamental of 400 cycles per second and other components at 200 and 4,400 cycles per second; albino mutants of wild *norvegicus* vocalized with a fairly pure fundamental of 2,800 cycles per second, and today's *albinus* is almost silent. Fits and convulsions in treadmills (Griffiths, 1956) and other situations common in various *albinus* strains are almost unknown in *norvegicus*. Activity during food deprivation is much greater in *norvegicus* than *albinus*. The killing of mice (which normally compete with rats within the habitat) was investigated by Karli (1956), who found that mice were killed by 70% of *norvegicus* but only by 12% of *albinus* types. Boice (1966) has noted a number of interesting differences: *norvegicus* mothers kept cleaner nests than *albinus*, removing fecal bolli to the front of the cage. When originally trapped, the wild *norvegicus* were obviously "agitated" but showed absolutely no defecation, a response common in *albinus* and allegedly indicative of "emotion." When watered, Boice's deprived $F_1$ *norvegicus* paused several times before approaching the water tube, then drank from a sideways posture; *albinus* waited at the watering place and drank head-on, without pauses. The "new object response" or neophobia of *norvegicus* is quite marked, leading to avoidance behavior, delays in feeding, "shyness," and reduction in food intake. This behavior is absent in *albinus*, which may briefly investigate, but "this has nothing in common with avoidance behavior in wild rats [Barnett, 1958]."

The endocrine system of *albinus* differs markedly from *norvegicus*, possibly qualitatively, in that the enlarged *albinus* pituitary may now perform substitute functions formerly sustained by the now diminutive adrenals, which may weigh $\frac{1}{10}$ as much as those of *norvegicus*. Albinos also have smaller preputials, liver, spleen, heart, kidneys, and brain; however, albinos have larger pituitaries, thymus, thyroid, parathyroids, and Peyer's patches. The substantial departure of the brain and endocrine system of *albinus* led Keeler (1947) to characterize *albinus* as hypoglandular. Robinson (1965) summarized the Keeler thesis:

The Wistar albino is to a great extent a quiet and tractable rat because of (1) a small brain which could interfere with alertness, (2) diminutive olfactory bulbs which could reduce much of the disturbing stimuli of the laboratory environment and (3) the reduced size of the adrenal glands which could have a depressing effect on violent reaction [p. 188].

The above collection of differences is but some fraction of the total, for only a few research efforts have aimed directly at the topic. However, the incomplete picture may be sketched in because the process of domestication, more properly called laboratorization in this case (Robinson, 1965, p. 417), is well understood in terms of its general outlines (Castle, 1947; Hale, 1962; Richter, 1954; Spurway, 1955). The phylogenetically established behaviors essential to survival in the wild are no longer kept intact in peak condition. Many, such as attack and flight from big species like man, intraspecific aggression, and strong pair bonds, are maladaptive in the new environment and are vigorously selected against. Phenotypes with these traits leave few progeny, and the genes responsible for the behavior decline in frequency and may vanish from the population. A great number of other genetically determined properties are subject to either low or neutral selection pressure; they are not disadvantageous, just unnecessary. There is little apparent reproductive advantage to keen sensory function, predator recognition, dietary preferences, digestive efficiency, heat-conserving nests, complicated burrows, or accurate behavioral periodicities. These sorts of functions, or characters, would more or less persist, but with greatly increased variability. Mutations affecting them would be preserved and accumulate in the gene pool. The net results would fall along a spectrum from complete loss of the function through degenerate, incomplete, or inappropriate expression to apparent intactness, depending upon the specific case. On the other hand, the new environment is not merely a route to tame degeneracy; it makes various positive demands, vigorously selecting for genes favoring survival and differential reproduction in captivity, the new "natural habitat." Examples of the sorts of traits favored might be intraspecific "amiability," immediate acceptance of strangers, large litters, long reproductive period, year-round fertility, reduced mobility, tolerance of loud sounds and handling by humans, and possibly even such specific items as the ability to extricate feet stuck in ½-inch wire mesh.

The overall result of the complex of genetic changes during domestication is like speciation; a new species forms, rapidly or slowly, depending upon severity of selection pressure, and resembles the wild parent species less and less with time. The greater the number of captive generations, the more different the new habitat; and the less the influx of the wild genotype, the less will be the overall resemblance to the wild form, as in cattle and dogs. The chihuahua, great dane, and poodle are largely the products of man, while their ancestors, wolf or jackal, are products of nature. The new habitat of *albinus* differs more from the wild one than the barnyards and pastures of most other domesticated animals differ from previous conditions; hence, one may expect *albinus* to be in the process of becoming one of the more extreme domestic animals, least related to its ancestors.

To complicate matters, there is not just one *albinus* population nor habitat; there are distinct colonies with little or no gene exchange and different selection pressures within each colony. Not only do nondeliberate practices alter the gene pool, but each breeder engages in unique practices based upon a mixture of folklore, science, and business economics. A casual glimpse leaves one with the impression of a stable "inbred" strain "just like" the famous parent stock; but commercial breeders select for what they think their customers fancy, such as resistance to respiratory disease. They also select for profit, such as countering the usual tendency of domestic animals to weigh more than wild by selecting small rats, for rats sell by the unit but eat by the pound. Breeding advertised as "random" is probably not, except where geneticists give the orders, and strains called "inbred" may be just as genetically heterogeneous as wild populations:

a population, long inbred, raised under laboratory conditions and homogeneous with respect to age, has a variability entirely comparable to a population existing under natural conditions, genetically diverse, and [with] a somewhat less uniform age distribution [Bader, 1956, quoted by Robinson, 1965, p. 440].

The rat types most popular with psychologists are neither genetically homogeneous, time-stable in genotype, nor genetically "understood." Robinson (1965), for example, stated:

the strain appellations Long-Evans, Osborne-Mendel, Slonaker, Sprague-Dawley and Wistar, to name a few of the more well-known designations in common usage, have little genetic meaning. The names indicate remote origin more than anything else, yet rats of these descriptions are employed extensively in laboratories. There is nothing wrong in this, of course, provided the designation does not inadvertently obscure the genetic diversity inherent in the rats of the various colonies. Abundant evidence of such diversity has been presented in the foregoing chapters [p. 675].

In summary, *albinus* is not one rat, but many, depending upon the source. Types popular with psychologists are heterogeneous, with wide individual differences, in contrast to recognized strains designated by combinations of capital letters and numbers. The statistical properties of a colony's gene pool change with time, making last decade's data out of date—from animals no longer existent. And *albinus* is not *norvegicus*; it is rapidly evolving, and it is only a matter of time until it is recognized as a separate species. It is hardly a random sample from the population of "organisms"; it is more like a commercial product.

## WHAT ABOUT NORVEGICUS?

By now, some readers will have been persuaded that *albinus* is unsuitable for their purposes and will be considering *norvegicus*. There are, however, a number of reasons that might persuade one differently. First, the anthropocentrically inclined will find that rodents are rather separated evolutionarily from primates, the latter having arisen from protoinsectivores (Davis & Golley, 1963, p. 129). Moles and shrews would be a bit closer. Second, murid rodents (Old World rats and mice, 100 genera, of which *Rattus* is one genus, with about 570 named forms) did not emerge until late Miocene, about 15 million years ago (Walker, 1964, pp. 869, 903). Rodents themselves evolved in Paleocene times, about 60 million years ago; thus murid rodents are newcomers. They are not some sort of preserved form of ancestral stock from which many other animals and their behavior evolved. One of the earliest known rodents, *Paramys*, was like a large squirrel (Colbert, 1955, p. 295). The oldest known group of living rodents is *Aplodontia*, called Sewellels or "Mountain Beavers," inhabiting the Northwest (Walker, 1964, p. 668). Third, rodents in general and *norvegicus* in particular are not "general" forms of animal, but are specialized:

It [*norvegicus*] has acquired accordingly a stouter and heavier body, a shorter tail, and its structure, in many points, has suffered modifications adapting it for burrowing, swimming, and the other activities incidental to its peculiar mode of living [Barrett-Hamilton & Hinton, 1916, p. 612].

Fourth, since *norvegicus* so very recently spread throughout the world from its eastern Asia habitat it is axiomatic that it is rapidly speciating. It may be that no other undomesticated mammal is undergoing such rapid genetic change in various newly inhabited regions. Thus data from captive *norvegicus* would be like a still snapshot of a moving process, an interesting document in the history of its change. Certain zoologists specifically interested in the process of domestication and speciation have deliberately chosen *norvegicus* because of its unique history; but the very properties which make the rat valuable to them should serve as a warning to others wishing a preparation with temporal stability, unspecialized, with an evolutionary position allowing some generalization to subsequent animal groups.

## THE PSYCHOLOGIST AND THE RAT

For sake of convenience I would like to distinguish two kinds of rat research: that involving learning and motivation and that concerned with what might be called the natural functions, such as sexual and maternal behavior; social behavior including dominance, displays, aggression, etc.; hoarding; diet selection and feeding behavior; sensory and physiological function; and so on. Learning will be discussed later; for the moment, consider the wisdom of studying some natural function in *albinus*.

For the biologist it would be automatic to presume that all structures and stable functions resulted from developmental processes coded in the genome of the individual, the "genetic instructions" themselves phylogenetically established by natural selection. The structures and functions are kept intact because "bad" genes causing unintactness are eliminated. The mechanisms of behavior resulting from this process are simply not going to remain unimpaired during the genetic change of domestication (see Lorenz, 1965, p. 99). Therefore, *albinus* is an indefensible choice not only in the realm of species-typical behaviors, but also for dietary and taste preferences (*albinus* may now eat whatever does not bite back), motivational mechanisms, and so on. Even in matters of growth, reproduction, endocrinology, nervous and sensory systems, disease, and drug response, the numerous instances of differences between strains, and between wild and domesticated rats, should convince any investigator that *albinus* is not the place to start looking for mechanisms nature has produced nor for analyzing how they work. It is at least a waste of time, if not outright folly, to experiment upon the degenerate remains of what is available intact in other animals. Psychology has enough embarrassing incidents such as "studying" antipredator responses to hawk shapes by domestic white leghorn chickens. Commercial pharmaceutical and other biological research using domestic forms is not undertaken with the blithe assumption that a given function is representative; the matter is carefully checked, and animals become characterized as "good for" one function and "atypical" for another.

If one rules out *albinus* because it is a poor carrier of phylogenetically acquired natural mechanisms, one is left with the problem of its suitability for the study of learning. Obviously *albinus* learns; why not use this tame convenient animal at least as a test run, to see if we can analyze how its learning process works? Its degenerate sensory, emotional, and natural behavior systems are not matters of concern, and are even assets in the laboratory, making it manageable and easily recaptured. Besides, a shift to other species would disconnect psychology from the vast literature and experience with *albinus*, undoing half a century of accumulated work.

There can be no doubt that differences between strains and between wild and domesticated rats have been found in a wide variety of learning situations; these have been reviewed by Robinson (1965, pp. 508–569). Psychologists, however, perhaps as a result of familiarity with the sequence stemming from Tryon's work, seem to dismiss the possibility of genetically determined differences in learning itself in favor of the belief that the differences are due to "emotional factors," mere physical differences, or sometimes to "parameters" or "constants" in equations. In addition, there seems to be the assumption that learning is a monolithic uniprocess, not a name for a collection of processes; that it is a completely general mechanism, not related to the animal's adaptive requirements; that the mechanism operates in the same qualitative way in whatever animal it is found, with "slow learners" or primitive forms manifesting a mere "rate parameter" difference; and that despite the degeneration of sensory input mechanisms, central mechanisms, and motor output, "the learning mechanism" has remained intact in *albinus*.

Many animals had "the learning process," and *albinus* was the most convenient carrier, though itself superfluous.

A biological approach to learning supports quite a different set of views. To begin with, learning is not inherent in the physical world like gravitation; it occurs in organisms. For perhaps two billion years the Earth had no organisms, and no learning. Life appeared in the form of some self-reproducing molecule or aggregate; it diversified and proliferated over some two to three billion years, producing new adaptations to the environment during evolution. The first fish occurred about .3 billion years ago, then amphibians, then reptiles about .185 billion years ago. Some reptiles evolved mammalianlike adaptations, and then mammals appeared .06 billion years ago, occupying about the last 2% of life's history on earth. The unicellular life forms, and those which fermented or photosynthesized for a living, were not endowed with a full-blown learning mechanism. Learning evolved at some stage in evolution; it was an adaptive mechanism conferring a reproductive advantage. Those genes allowing it were reproduced in greater numbers each generation, finally typifying the first species able to profit in some way from experience. Just as the first photoreceptor was a simple thing countless evolutionary developments short of the vertebrate eye, the first learning mechanism was doubtlessly primitive. What it could do is yet unknown; perhaps it could briefly store a little sensory information or facilitate a motor neuron, but certainly it could not handle the Hampton Court maze. Like other structures and functions which evolved, learning no doubt responded to selection pressure like any other survival function, increasing in complexity and storage capacity by accumulating whatever fresh additions, novelties, and extensions increased the probability of reproduction.

Thus it is more probable that learning in mammals is a collection of evolved functions, not a monolithic uniprocess. It is probably not a completely general process qualitatively the same in rat, octopus, and bee, but strongly reflects idiosyncrasies of the adaptive requirements. It is also the case that functions of superficial resemblance actually evolved independently on different occasions; they occur in qualitatively different ways, such as flying in reptiles, birds, mammals, and insects. It is quite possible that learning independently evolved a number of times, creating superficial similarities but quite different underlying mechanisms, analogous but not homologous.

Perhaps the rat's most complex phenomenon is learning, as it involves the way the central nervous system regulates behavior. Because domestication allows an increase in genetic diversity and the accumulation of random mutations, these stand every chance of debilitating, gene by gene, the learning phenomenon. "The more complicated an adapted process, the less chance that a random change will improve its adaptedness [Lorenz, 1965, p. 12]." Furthermore, if learning in the rat is a collection of processes instead of a uniprocess, certain "items" in the collection will be lost, then more, as domestication proceeds. With selection pressure no longer keeping the functions intact, its parts will disintegrate in whatever sequence the supporting biology fails. "Shelter, food, and mates are provided without the individual making a move to fend for himself. Even an 'idiot' rat could flourish in such an environment [Robinson, 1965, p. 514]." If a uniprocess began to fail, it should remain qualitatively the same while declining in some quantitative index. But if a multiprocess disintegrated, not only would it change qualitatively, but different individuals—being random samples from a diverse gene pool—would be qualitatively different. Thus a group of albinus would produce appreciable variance in certain tasks—unnecessary variance, in fact, when viewed against another

animal in a more intact state. Also, when a function begins to atrophy, it is probable that certain of its components fail first, being the most "difficult" to maintain by natural selection. Therefore, even if rat learning were completely analyzed, the result might be quite incomplete, lacking in aspects normally occurring in animals and providing an inaccurate and incomplete picture. The learning theorist using albinus must either claim disinterest in generality or admit subscription to the theory that the learning processes of albinus are not much different from those of "mammals in general." This theory would seem quite difficult to support.

One cannot prove that albinus is unsuitable for learning research; the facts necessary for this presume the complete comparative analysis of learning which the very concentration on albinus delays. Also, facts alone would probably not be enough, for albinus is so entrenched in its cozy new habitat that it has influential members of the host species emotionally committed to its continued welfare. One may, however, weigh the risks inherent in developing a natural science around an unnatural animal, one which was produced in its present form by the laboratorization process absolutely unique in natural history. The present albinus never before existed and will never again exist; the laboratory rats of next century will be quite different. One can imagine a sort of "schmoo" in a germ-free environment, surrounded by life-support systems and fitted with prosthetic devices, attended by technicians and still studied by scientists; its riddles of "the learning process" still unsolved, for continued survival in the new habitat favors a baffling learning process, one which is composed of pieces no longer harmoniously interlocking and which changes in time rapidly enough to make past findings discrepant, all the while producing enough variability to keep the entire enterprise confused.

## ALTERNATIVES TO *ALBINUS*

1. Inbred rat strains meeting the definitions and recommendations of competent committees and of recognized genetic nomenclature could be used in place of popular types with "little genetic meaning." A table of 57 such rat strains is given in Robinson (1965, pp. 672–675), and the commercial availability of some of these and numerous inbred mouse strains is covered in the publication *Laboratory Animals: Part II. Animals for Research* (revised August 1966). . . . Use of inbred rat or mouse strains would be a concession to the rat habit having the virtue of reducing intraexperiment variability, clearly defining the animal, drawing from a population of genetic meaning and knowledge, and having a rate of genetic change less than that of commercial animals. The collection of problems associated with domestication would remain, as would those of phyletic position.

2. Similarly, the American Psychological Association could establish a special strain for laboratory studies of behavior, maintaining a complicated breeding system which preserved tameness, while maintaining a constant influx of genes from the wild type. Rigidly maintained procedures could eliminate temporal change and many of the problems of domestication, leaving principally the problems of phyletic position and lack of generality of findings.

3. Simpler forms abundant in nature, such as earthworms, fish, or frogs would overcome most of the *albinus* problems mentioned, as well as provide the distinct possibility that simpler forms have simpler mechanisms more likely to yield to analysis than complex ones.

4. For those rat runners who are really educational psychologists in disguise and who would like results broadly applicable to "higher mammals," principally humans, an animal in a better ancestral position than the offshoot rat should be selected. One possibility is the Solenodon, a primitive insectivore thought to resemble the basic stock from which a number of mammalian lines, including primates, evolved. An even more impressive candidate is the Tupaia (oriental tree shrew), a sort of living fossil transitional between insectivores and primates, from which the prosimians most probably evolved. It is a primitive placental, one of the most generalized of all living mammals. The Tupaia is diurnal, thus more suited for human daytime research habits than nocturnal animals. It is easily tamed and breeds throughout the year. (See Colbert, 1955, and index of Walker, 1964.) *Laboratory Animals*, mentioned above, lists five suppliers.

5. The approaches mentioned above presume the current strategy of focusing resources upon a single animal. Regardless of the species chosen, this approach risks mistaking the particular for the general. Beach (1950) has eloquently argued the case that concentration upon *albinus* provides too narrow a view of behavior, leading to a science of "rat learning" and neglecting most other behaviors. Behavioral science presumably aims to analyze and understand *all* behaviors of anything that behaves, taking a truly broad and scientific approach to the vast array of phenomena about us. Within this framework one's thinking changes from "What learning problem shall I study with *albinus*?" to "What problem in behavior is the most interesting and potentially significant, and which animal is best for its study?" Instead of thinking of various animals as "laboratory difficulties," one may view them as natural preparations; there are squirrels with all-cone retinas, mammals with no corpus callosum, nocturnal animals, diurnal animals, animals which imprint and those which do not, fish with electric organs, raccoons with overdeveloped "hand areas" in the cortex, animals which stay still when hungry, animals with built-in stellar charts, bug detectors, mouse detectors, animals which can learn one thing but not another, and so on and

on. These and many more natural preparations, achieved without surgery, are literally awaiting research; fewer than 1% of all species have a single behavioral paper. There is a best animal for every problem.

Chemistry made advances after the "practical" effort to transmute lead into gold was abandoned in favor of scientific curiosity of much broader scope, and we would be astonished if astronomers studied only Earth and applied false generalizations to the rest of the universe. Future historians of psychology may devote a few paragraphs to the *albinus* era, noting that progress was made only after getting some perspective and generality into the field by comparing results from different species, and avoiding atypical findings by abandoning unnatural animals.

## REFERENCES

Barnett, S. A. 1958. Experiments on "neophobia" in wild and laboratory rats. *British Journal of Psychology* 49:195–201.

Barrett-Hamilton, G. E. H., and Hinton, M. A. L. 1916. *A history of British mammals*. London: Gurney & Jackson.

Beach, F. A. 1950. The snark was a boojum. *American Psychologist* 5:115–124.

Boice, R. 1966. The problem of domestication in the laboratory rat and a comparison of partially reinforced "discriminatory" and anticipatory licking in domestic and wild strains of *Rattus norvegicus*. Unpublished doctoral dissertation, Michigan State University.

Carr, H. A., and Watson, J. B. 1908. Orientation in the white rat. *Journal of Comparative Neurology and Psychology* 18:27–44.

Castle, W. E. 1947. The domestication of the rat. *Proceedings of the National Academy of Science* 33:109–117.

Colbert, E. H. 1955. *Evolution of the vertebrates*. New York: Wiley.

Crampe, H. 1877. Kreuzungen zwischen Wanderraten verschiedener Farbe. *Landwirthschaftliche Jahrbücher* 6:385–395.

Davis, D. E., and Golley, F. B. 1963. *Principles in mammology*. New York: Reinhold.

Donaldson, H. H. 1924. *The rat: Data and reference tables*. Rev. ed. Philadelphia: Wistar Institute Memoir no. 6.

Griffiths, W. J. 1956. Diet selections of rats subjected to stress. *Annals of the New York Academy of Science* 67:1–10.

Hale, E. B. 1962. Domestication and the evolution of behaviour. In *The behaviour of domestic animals*, ed. E. S. E. Hafez. London: Bailliere, Tindall & Cox.

Karli, P. 1956. The Norway rat's killing response to the white mouse: An experimental analysis. *Behaviour* 10:81–103.

Keeler, C. E. 1947. Modification of brain and endocrine glands, as an explanation of altered behavior trends, in coat character mutant strains of the Norway rat. *Journal of the Tennessee Academy of Science* 22:202–209.

King, H. D. 1939. Life processes in gray Norway rats during fourteen years in captivity. *American Anatomical Memoirs*, no. 17.

King, H. D., and Donaldson, H. H. 1929. Life processes and size of the body and organs of the gray Norway rat during ten generations in captivity. *American Anatomical Memoirs*, no. 14.

Kline, L. W. 1899. Methods in animal psychology. *American Journal of Psychology* 10:256–279.

Lorenz, K. 1965. *Evolution and modification of behavior*. Chicago: University of Chicago Press.

Miles, W. R. 1930. On the history of research with rats and mazes. *Journal of General Psychology* 3:324–337.

Philipeaux, J. M. 1856. Note sur l'extirpation des capsules survénales chez les rats albinos (*Mus rattus*). *Comptes Rendus de la Academie des Sciences* (Paris), 43:904–906.

Richter, C. P. 1954. The effects of domestication and selection on the behavior of the Norway rat. *Journal of the National Cancer Institute* 15:727–738.

Richter, C. P. 1959. Rats, man, and the welfare state. *American Psychologist* 14:18–28.

Robinson, R. 1965. *Genetics of the Norway rat*. Oxford: Pergamon Press.

Small, W. S. 1900. An experimental study of the mental processes of the rat. *American Journal of Psychology* 11:133–165.

Spurway, H. 1955. The causes of domestication: An attempt to integrate some ideas of Konrad Lorenz with evolution theory. *Journal of Genetics* 53:325–362.

Steward, C. C. 1898. Variations in daily activity produced by alcohol and by changes in barometric pressure and diet, with a description of recording methods. *American Journal of Physiology* 1:40–56.

Tolman, E. C. 1958. *Behavior and psychological man*. Berkeley: University of California Press.

Walker, E. P. 1964. *Mammals of the world*. Baltimore: Johns Hopkins Press.

Watson, J. B. 1903. Animal education. *Contributions of the Psychology Laboratory of the University of Chicago* 4:5–122.

Watson, J. B. 1907. Kinaesthetic and organic sensations: Their role in the reactions of the white rat. *Psychological Review Monographs* 8:2, whole no. 33.

Zinsser, H. 1935. *Rats, lice, and history*. Boston: Little, Brown.

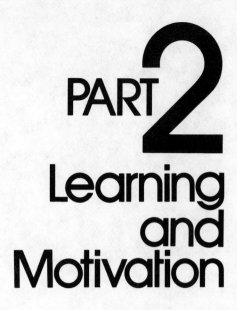

# PART 2
# Learning and Motivation

# READING 5

# Paramecia, Planaria, and Pseudo-Learning

**DONALD D. JENSEN**
**University of Nebraska**
**Lincoln, Nebraska**

Jensen presents a critical review of the literature on learning in paramecia and planaria. He gives several examples of experiments which did not include proper controls, delineates the confounding variables, cautions against the uncritical use of demonstrational research, and suggests that such experiments are perhaps more properly concerned with the behavior of planaria than with learning in mammals.

**QUESTIONS**

1. What are the problems associated with demonstrational research?
2. Design an experiment which you think would determine whether learning can occur in paramecia or planaria. Keep in mind the methodological considerations pointed out by Jensen.
3. What is pseudo-learning? How does it differ from learning?

I trust that all of our British hosts and most of us foreign guests are familiar with the legend of the Holy Grail—that the platter or goblet used at the Last Supper had survived and had been brought to England. According to the legend the knights of King Arthur's court went singly in quest of the Holy Grail, but only one who possessed special virtue was fated to find it. Today we are reconciled with the less romantic view that there may never have been a Holy Grail, and thus you and I no longer seek it, but it seems likely that some of us have been involved in a similar quest—in a search for something that may not exist, in a search for learning in lower organisms.

I started on my own quest for learning in lower organisms as a graduate student. Intrigued by the possibility of studying learning in a single cell, i.e. within a protozoan, I began to read about and to observe para- that others had searched before; a number of times in the last 50 years, learning in paramecia has been reported, only to be later refuted by the discovery of errors in design or interpretation. This pattern of demonstration and refutation has been repeated at least four times.

The first case began with the work of Smith (1908) who concluded that paramecia were introduced into constricting the frequency and efficiency of already present reactions to situations by practice, but could not learn associatively. The paramecia. In the literature there was evidence capillary tubes (Figure 1); Smith observed

**Figure 1.** Behavior of paramecia in a constricting tube. Smith (1908) and Day & Bentley (1911).

that the time between completed turns in the tube decreased as a function of time in the tube.

Day & Bentley (1911) confirmed and extended Smith's observation of decreased time between turns in a constricting tube, demonstrating as well that this decrease in time per successful reversal was accompanied by a decrease in the average number of partial or attempted reversals per completed reversal and that the increase in facility of turning was evident if paramecia were reintroduced into the situation after 30 minutes in a watch glass of culture medium.

Both Smith (1908) and Day & Bentley (1911) failed to use control groups of any kind; their findings were criticized on this account by Buytendijk (1919) who repeated these experiments and concluded that the results were due not to learning, but to the fact that paramecia, when subjected to much mechanical stimulation, lose "tonus", that is, become limp and flexible. Buytendijk found that paramecia treated with chloroform became flexible enough to turn easily within the capillary tube, a result which suggests that purely physical effects were involved.

This first example of demonstration and

refutation of learning in paramecia involved *confounding of variables*, that is, failure to dissociate the variables of practice in a task and of mechanical stimulation and then a confusion of the effects of the uncontrolled variable of mechanical stimulation with the effects of the independent variable of practice. Buytendijk's research suggested that here was a case of pseudo-learning—a case of misidentification of an effect as learning when the variables that are important in producing the effect and/or the characteristics of the effect are different than those typical of learning.

After classical conditioning techniques became widely known in the thirties, paramecia were subjected to a number of situations in which light was paired with a noxious stimulus.

Bramstedt (1935) reported conditioned responses in paramecia in this type of situation (Figure 2). Bramstedt placed a slide with a flat drop of culture medium on a crystallizer filled with water and divided into two halves, one of which contained water at 15°C., the other at 42°C. The cooler half was dark, the warm one strongly lit. Under these conditions a single paramecium swimming in the drop remained practically exclusively in the cooler half and to every contact with the boundary between the two temperatures responded with an avoiding reaction. After 90 min-

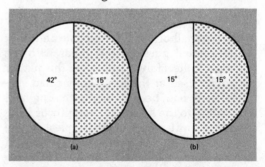

**Figure 2.** Association of light and heat. For 90 minutes the lighted half of a drop was heated to 42° (Figure 2a), then both halves were allowed to revert to 15° (Figure 2b). The darker half of the drop is stippled.

utes both halves of the crystallizer beneath the drop were filled with water at the same temperature of 15°C. Nevertheless, the paramecium continued to stay in the darkened area and to respond with an avoiding reaction when entering the lighted region. Light was not absolutely avoided, but the subject stayed more in the dark half than in the lighted half. After some 15 minutes, the reaction ceased and the subjects swam indifferently in the whole drop. Alverdes (1937) confirmed Bramstedt's conclusion that learning was involved.

Grabowski (1939) and others disagreed with Bramstedt's conclusion that learning was involved. The fact that after some time there develops a negative reaction toward the lighted half of the drop remains true, but chemical changes produced by the experimental procedure of heating and not learning were used to explain the result. Grabowski observed that after the temperatures of the two halves had been equated, the subject gradually made excursions further and further into the lighted half of the drop and concluded that the paramecium avoids, not the boundry between the light and darkness, but some other boundary which is initially identical with the boundary of light and which gradually shifts into the lighted half. Heating one half of the drop to 42°C. causes bubbles of gas to escape from the water, the solubility of gas being diminished with increasing temperature. As a consequence the two halves of the drop differed not only in light conditions, but in gas content as well. Jennings (1906) had long before shown that the presence of dissolved gases, particularly carbon dioxide, is important to the behaviour of paramecia and that differences in concentrations of such chemical agents could stimulate avoiding reactions.

To test the effect of the uncontrolled variable of gas content, Grabowski heated one half of a drop for 90 minutes and then equated the temperature of the two halves. Only then did he put a paramecium into the drop. The paramecium began immediately to "react negatively toward light", remaining mainly in the previously heated part. It seems obvious that the water, not the paramecium, had been altered by the experimental procedure.

In this second case of demonstration and refutation, chemical effects were confounded with the effects of training. In addition, data not in keeping with the claim of learning were not considered and an alternative explanation offered by earlier work was ignored. Here was another instance of pseudo-learning.

The third case of demonstration and refutation began with work of Soest (1937) who used a different experimental procedure, following a light stimulus by electric shock (Figure 3). Whenever the paramecium swam into the lighted half of the drop,

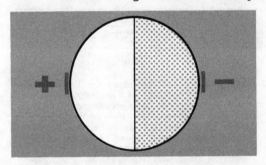

**Figure 3.** Association of light and shock. The cathode (−) and the anode (+) are shown; the darker half of the drop is stippled. After Soest (1937).

it received a series of electric shocks until it turned back. Eventually the paramecium began to make avoiding reactions prior to entering the lighted half and stayed almost exclusively in the darker half where no shocks had been given. Soest's procedures, however, had certain difficulties. Soest placed the cathode in the darker half of the drop; since paramecia are galvano-tropic and swim toward the cathode of a direct current, the shocks turned the animals back toward the cathode and into the darker half; when Soest attempted to train paramecia to avoid the darker half, the shocks delivered with the cathode in the darker half carried the animals further into the darker half and training was unsuccessful. The successful experiments were interpreted as evidence of classical conditioning to light CS by shock US.

Soest's method was refined by Wawrzynczyk (1938) who placed a paramecium in a capillary tube between two electrodes (Figure 4). The experiment began

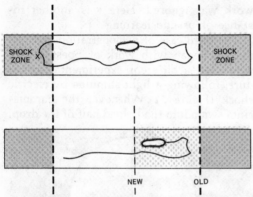

**Figure 4.** Refined technique for light-shock pairing. A central zone of a capillary tube was surrounded by two differently-lit zones (here stippled) in which shocks were administered to drive the paramecium back into the central zone. One shock is shown delivered at X, eliciting an avoiding reaction and a reversal of direction. Dembowski (1950) showed that spontaneous reversals that occurred were not affected by changing the light boundary as in the lower portion of the figure.

with the animal in a central zone which was bounded on either end by areas illuminated differently than the central zone. Whenever the animal swam out of the central zone, it was shocked with the cathode behind it so that it turned back toward and returned to the central zone. Eventually the paramecium would turn back before it reached the light boundary and before it was shocked. Wawrzynczyk claimed conditioning to light. Dembrowski (1950) repeated this study and performed the simple control of moving the light boundary after the paramecium had begun to turn without

being shocked (Figure 5). When this was done the animal was uninfluenced by the light but continued to turn about where it had do so before. Dembrowski surmised that metabolic traces given off by the animal persisted and influenced the behaviour of the animal. This conclusion was confirmed by Jensen (1955).

Again in this case of demonstration and refutation, confounding was involved—confusing effects of self-produced metabolic traces with effects of training. Again, peculiarities of the data had to be overlooked for the data to be interpreted as evidence of conditioning. The animals reversed before and not after they reached the differently lighted zone; they frequently showed repeated reversals at one end of the tube but not at the other; Wawrzynczyk found that subtle differences in light intensity or wave length made just as effective CSs as gross differences of light and dark, even though paramecia have no organs of light reception and normally make no responses to light. The whole pattern of data did not fit the concept of conditioning, and one selected aspect of the data was emphasized in claiming conditioning. And again, there was neglect of previous work on the behaviour of paramecia. As previously mentioned, Jennings in 1906 had identified a self-produced metabolic trace, carbon dioxide, which could have produced exactly the behaviour observed. Here was a third case of pseudo-learning.

These 3 cases of pseudo-learning impressed me greatly. The more I studied, the less certain did it seem that learning was waiting to be discovered and the more likely that other reports of learning in paramecia were also cases of pseudo-learning, produced by unknown or overlooked factors. With that suspicion I examined a demonstration that had not previously been refuted. Gelber (1952) claimed to have demonstrated instrumental learning in paramecia for food reward. A silver needle which was periodically coated with food bacteria was repeatedly inserted into a drop of culture medium which contained around 100 paramecia (Figure 5). It was presumed

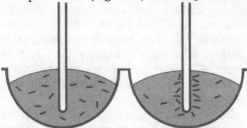

Figure 5. Association of food bacteria with a platinum needle. Gelber (1952) repeatedly inserted a needle that was coated with bacteria into a depression containing about 0•3 ml. of culture fluid and 100 paramecia. At first, as in Figure 5a, there was no tendency for paramecia to collect at the needle. Later, as in Figure 5b, the animals collected on or near the needle even after all bacteria were removed from the needle.

that the paramecia would learn to approach and attach to the needle for food reward. Later the needle, now cleaned of any food bacteria, was lowered into the pool, and the paramecia flocked around it. This study had several control groups, one which received training without bacterial reinforcement and one which received neither training with the needle nor bacterial reinforcement. Behavioural modification by reinforcement was claimed and the study was widely interpreted as having demonstrated instrumental learning in protozoa. As we look at this design we can see that one cell is empty (Figure 6) and that presence of bacteria and the training procedure were confounded. I (1957) and Katz & Deterline (1958) filled that cell. It was established that the reinforcement procedure used created a zone of bacteria-rich fluid in the centre of the pool (Figure 7) and that the addition of food bacteria by any means that would create such a central zone of bac-

|  | Bacteria | No Bacteria |
| --- | --- | --- |
| Training | Reinforced | Unreinforced |
| No Training |  | Control |

Figure 6. Experimental design of Gelber (1952).

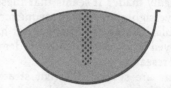

Figure 7. The effects of the reinforcement procedure of inserting a bacteria-coated needle. The bacteria-rich zone is stippled.

teria-rich fluid into which the clean needle could be lowered would produce the observed effect. Once again the culture and not the animals had been conditioned. Once again confounding was involved, this time of bacteria left in the fluid with the reinforcement training. Again the whole pattern of data was not considered. Katz & Deterline (1958) noted eccentric gatherings, changes in activity, and drastic effects of stirring the fluid, all of which are not consistent with the concept of learning that was suggested in Gelber's work. And again other research on the behaviour of the organism studied was not considered. Jennings had described the behavioural capabilities of paramecia as largely limited to stereotyped avoiding reactions or phobotaxes; he had found no evidence of the direct approach type of response presumed in this experiment. Further, he found no evidence of sensory capabilities of the sort required for the behaviour reported. And finally, Jennings had described the effect of bacteria-rich-zones on the behaviour of paramecia. Major conclusions reached by Jennings were ignored by this research and its refutation followed as soon as other investigators considered the research in light of the earlier work of Jennings. For the fourth time further investigation indicated pseudo-learning.

One case of pseudo-learning made me cautious, 2 cases made me concerned, 3 cases made me critical, and there were 4 cases. Four times variables were confounded, data overlooked, alternative hypotheses ignored. Why were these errors repeatedly made? It seems that these errors and oversights are the consequence of the particular strategy of inquiry that has been employed—the consequence of demonstrational research.

There are several different strategies of inquiry that one can employ. At the one extreme one can be a mystic, ignoring data and accepting the teachings of tradition or the inner voice of revelation. For such a person, whether he be a believer who accepts or a sceptic who doubts, data is unimportant; faith is enough. I trust there are few mystics among us today. At the other extreme one can be a scientific investigator, one who uses data to develop theory. Data are used to test theory, to force and guide its revision; theory is used to predict data and to encourage its gathering. The investigator accepts the theory only as a working hypothesis which is to be used, tested, doubted, and improved under the impact of unexpected data.

There is a strategy that is intermediate to those of the mystic and the investigator. This is the strategy of the demonstrationist and of some of the research we have discussed. Demonstrations are searches for data which conform to and confirm a predetermined theory. The theory itself is not seriously in question; it provokes the gathering of data, but the data are used, not to force revision of the theory, but to argue for the theory.

The strategy of demonstration is all too common in practical affairs. The salesman talks only about the virtues of his product; the lawyer presents the evidence for his client alone. The question is whether this strategy is acceptable in science. The inefficiency of demonstration is shown in 4 instances we've reviewed; much energy was expended with little useful return, except perhaps in number of publications for participants. More important than inefficiency is the confusion and mythology that can be created by demonstrational research. While demonstrations are unrefuted, they persist to misguide and misinform the reader who seldom realizes that "caveat lector"—let the reader beware. For such reasons demonstration, i.e. "making a case for a hypothesis," is not usually an acceptable strategy of inquiry in biology. Sir Gavin de Beer (1964) succinctly expressed the standard view in a phrase: "special pleading masquerading as science."

But if special pleading is unacceptable, why were these cases of special pleading for learning in paramecia not rejected immediately? At least part of the matter is the unfamiliarity of the organisms involved, but much of the matter is probably the ease with which demonstration and investigation may be confused. Both techniques do make use of data and the resemblance between them is increased by the manner in which scientists often report their findings and conclusions.

In scientific papers predictions are made and data confirming the predictions are reported. This mode of presentation is dramatic, forceful, and concise; it has become standard. Unfortunately this organization does *not* reflect the nature of the scientific investigations. Scientists from Einstein to Medawar have emphasized that the logic of scientific investigation is much different, that theory is developed and evolved in the process of gathering and/or analyzing data, that data and theory interact in a cyclical, iterative process which has as its essential features disconfirmation rather than confirmation of theory and revision rather than acceptance (Popper, 1959). The scientific paper does not ordinarily reflect the processes of disconfirmation and revision; instead it presents the revised theory and the new data for which it accounts; in other words the ordinary scientific paper is demonstrational in organization. This allows demonstration to mimic investigation most easily, since the investigator writes and the demonstrationist works in the same way—predict and confirm.

The resemblance between the organization of the scientific paper and the logic of demonstrational research is not the only additional reason that demonstrations of learning in paramecia were widely accepted. Not all scientists are automatically rejecting of special pleading. Maier (1960) suggested as much in stating the satirical principle that "if the facts do not conform to the theory, they must be disposed of." Maier detected the defence of theory and neglect of data that has occurred in much psychological research. Solomon (1964) more recently made a similar observation in noting that most psychological research on punishment and conflict has been theory-oriented, i.e. demonstrational, and that data-oriented theories of punishment have only recently been developed. Many of the classic experiments in introductory psychology texts are openly demonstrational (i.e. work on learned drive, displaced aggression, superstition, imitation, and learned social behaviour in rats).

It may be that demonstrations once were appropriate as pedagogic devices to introduce and promulgate behaviouristic views in psychology, but there seems no justification for special pleading in the area of invertebrate behaviour, here where behaviouristic views were first developed (Jensen, 1962) and now when behaviourism is the standard approach.

We've seen that research on learning in paramecia led to pseudo-learning through errors and special pleading. Now let us examine some of the research on learning in planaria and see if the same pattern holds, if here too we find errors, special pleading, and pseudo-learning.

The first of the recent articles appeared in 1955 by Thompson & McConnell. This article is of considerable importance because a number of other studies have omitted control groups on the basis of its results. The design of this study (Figure 8) involved 4 groups which differed in training conditions. One group received CS of light paired with a US of shock, one received only light, one received only shock, and one received neither light nor shock. This design controls for the simple effect of light presentation and the simple effect of shock presentation, but not for the effect of both (Jensen, 1961). Close temporal association of light and shock, as in typical conditioning, is here confounded with joint presence of both light and shock. This confounding is evident when we consider that there are many ways of giving both light and shock; for example they can occur at random intervals, they can alternate, or they can be closely associated as in typical conditioning experiments. The design used by Thompson & McConnell does not control for the possible importance of having the stimuli in general temporal association as contrasted with the importance of pairing them as in mammalian conditioning. To do this one can use another design, such as that employed by Baxter & Kimmel (1963).

A second type of confounding was involved also, since not all 4 groups were tested in the same way. The group that

| GROUP | 150 TRAINING TRIALS OF: | DATA OBTAINED ON: |
|-------|-------------------------|-------------------|
| E | Light and shock paired | First 2 seconds of light in training trial. |
| LC | Light only | First 2 seconds of light in training trial. |
| SC | Shock only | 30 special test trials |
| RC | Neither light nor shock | Mock trials (2 seconds without light) |

**Figure 8.** Experimental design of Thompson & McConnell (1955).

received the light followed by shock and the group that received only the light were observed during the first 2 seconds of light presentation, and responses were recorded. In contrast with this, the group that received neither light nor shock during training was simply observed during 2-second periods corresponding to the times the light was presented to the 2 groups receiving the light. The group that received training with shock but without light was tested in still another way. Test trials were used for this group; light was presented unpaired with shock after every fifth shock trial. Only 30 observations were available for animals of this group while 150 observations were available for the other 3 groups.

The data for the 3 groups were presented graphically (Figure 9). The greater number of responses in the group receiving paired light and shock and the increase in this number over trials were used as evidence of learning. There seems no doubt about the reality of the superior responsiveness of the group trained with paired light and shock relative to the groups trained with light only and neither light nor shock. But what about the performance of the light-shock group in comparison with the group trained with shock alone? The comparison of these 2 groups was never made directly. Instead separate tables were presented in which the number of responses on various blocks of trials were given. In analysing these tables it was pointed out that the group trained with light and shock showed a reliable increase over trials while the group trained with shock alone did not. The obvious comparison, the comparison between amount of responding to light stimuli, was never made. To be sure, one can make it oneself. One sees from the tables that the group trained with light and shock averaged 13·8 responses in the first block of trials and 21·6 on the last block: meanwhile the group trained with shock alone averaged only 5·6 responses on the first block of trials and only 4·6 on the last

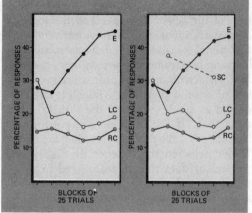

**Figure 9.** Percentage of responses for the Experimental (E), Light Control (LC), Response Control (RC), and Shock Control (SC) groups. The left graph presents the data as did Thompson & McConnell (1955); the right graph presents the data so as to facilitate comparison of Shock Control (SC) and the other groups.

block. At first glance this comparison seems most favourable to the hypothesis but careful examination discloses that the figures of 13·8 and 21·6 are for blocks of 50 trials while the figures 5·6 and 4·6 are for blocks of 15. If we make these figures comparable by translating them into percentages, we find that the group trained only with shock was initially more responsive than any other and only later becomes less responsive than the group trained with paired light and shock (Figure 9).

One cannot help but wonder why percentages were not computed, why trends were compared instead of absolute levels of performance, and why the fact that the group trained with shock alone was initially superior to all others was hidden. "Caveat lector" is hardly an overstatement when the reader must watch for changing numbers of trials in blocks and must compute his own percentages to make the most relevant comparison. If one does not ignore the level of performance of the group trained with shock only, one cannot easily interpret the data in this experiment as evidence for learning. The major effect in the experiment is the difference between groups which are shocked and those which are not. Shock, not association of light and shock, would appear to be the important variable. Precise comparison between the 2 groups receiving shocks would not seem justified since only 1 of the 2 groups received test trials and since total number of light presentations is confounded with difference in training procedure.

The experiment reported by Baxter & Kimmel (1963) is perhaps the best available to indicate the effect of association unconfounded with the effect of shock presentation. The experiment was a $2 \times 2 \times 2$ factorial design, comparing paired presentation with alternation of light and shock, comparing two different shock intensities, and comparing two different light intensities. Baxter & Kimmel found that the paired groups were superior to the alternation groups during acquisition training; if one considered only these data one might conclude that learning was demonstrated. But this design allows subtle confounding: when CS and US alternate, the time from the occurrence of the shock US to the occurrence of the following light CS is much shorter than when the US closely follows the CS. To protect against this confounding, one can use groups which are matched in time since shock US, or one can observe the behaviour during extinction when no shock is being given. Baxter & Kimmel did the latter and found that the differences present during acquisitions were completely absent in extinction. When the association and alternation groups no longer differed in time from shock to light, their behaviour was equivalent, even though on previous days one group had received 250 paired presentations and the other had received 250 unpaired presentations. In contrast the variables of CS and US intensity were important during both acquisition and extinction. James & Halas (1964) also reported no differences between groups during extinction.

It would appear that the recent work on classical conditioning in planaria is another instance of pseudo-learning based upon confounding, ignoring certain aspects of the data, and special pleading. Regarding this possibility, some advice that Dr. McConnell offered in the March 1964 issue of the *Worm Runner's Digest* is relevant. He commented that "we have over the years, received many letters from individuals who have attempted to train planarians and who have encountered difficulties. They write to us asking for the magic formula. Sadly enough, we don't have much magic to offer anyone, save for an admonition to keep at it, keep changing the experimental situation until the right conditions are hit upon."

This advice may provide magic enough. It says to use data only to confirm theory. It says to vary conditions until the data fit the theory that planaria learn. It says to change procedures until one is successful and it ignores the possibility that with patience and time one will happen upon an experimental procedure which involves just the right confounding to produce pseudo-learning. Continued manufacture of instances of pseudo-learning seems rather likely if the advice offered in the *Worm Runner's Digest* is followed.

We have found evidence of confounding, special pleading, and pseudo-learning in work on both paramecia and planaria. In paramecia we were able to specify rather precisely the mechanism other than learning that was influencing the behaviour of the animal. We noted, you will recall, that in Bramstedt's situation avoiding reactions were produced by chemical gradients produced by heat and in Wawrzynczyk's situation avoiding reactions were produced by metabolic traces left by the paramecium itself. Information necessary to specify these mechanisms of pseudo-learning derived from the work of H. S. Jennings whose investigations focussed, not on a particular topic, but on the general behaviour of the animal type. The difference

| | Man | Ape | Dog | Rat | Planaria | Paramecia | Euglena | Etc. |
|---|---|---|---|---|---|---|---|---|
| Stimulation Light | | | | | | | | |
| Sound | | | | | | | | |
| Touch | | | | | | | | |
| Habituation | | | | | | | | |
| Motivation | | | | | | | | |
| Associative Learning | | | | | | | | |
| Emotion | | | | | | | | |
| Etc. | | | | | | | | |

**Figure 10.** The organization of information for the comparative study of behaviour.

between research focussed upon a topic and upon an animal type deserves emphasis (Figure 10). One can organise information about behaviour in two independent ways, by topic and by animal type. The field of comparative behaviour can be represented as a matrix of cubbyholes in which information is filed along a column of topics and along a row of animal types. Comparative psychologists usually study across a row, comparing effects of light, for example, in a number of forms. One can also work as does an ethologist and study up and down a column, and thereby study the entire behavioural organization of the particular animal form, and one can do as did Maier & Schneirla (1935) and compare entire behavioural organizations of different animal groups.

An investigator interested in a particular cell of this matrix, such as the cell corresponding to learning in paramecia, has much to gain from study of his topic in all species and just as much to gain from study of all topics of his species. If an investigator does not know previous work with the concept, he can misapply the concept as did Hovey (1929); if the investigator does not know previous work with the animal, he can overlook and unintentionally confound variables and thereby misinterpret his results. In a similar way investigations of general problems of the behaviour of a

species may elucidate previously unexplained aspects of data. For example, the effects of a variety of independent variables on the behaviour of paramecia were studied and an attempt was made to develop a physiological theory of behavioural organization of the paramecium (Jensen, 1959). This more general investigation provided explanation for what had been interpreted by Gelber as a directed approach and immediate attachment to the food-baited wire. It was observed that animals taken from a culture poor in bacteria and then placed in a culture rich in bacteria showed a drastic change in behaviour, increasing their aboral turning tendency and their tendency to attach to any object which was contacted. This non-specific change had been interpreted by Gelber as a directed approach and attachment to the needle.

Let us now discuss the work that has been done on the general behavioural organization of planaria for the purpose of considering the possible confoundings and misinterpretations involved in pseudo-learning in planaria. The major relevant work is a 200-page monograph by Pearl (1903) which is extensively cited in Jennings (1906). Pearl described the basic behaviours of planaria and investigated the influence of a number of stimuli and other variables. His investigation led him to the view that all stimuli except electric shock produce 2 basic responses, one of which is a small magnitude turn toward a weak stimulus (positive reaction) and the other of which is a large magnitude turn from or contraction to a strong stimulus (negative reaction). Schneirla (1959) recently discussed this type of approach-withdrawal system and analyzed a number of behavioural problems in a wide variety of organisms in terms of approach to mild and withdrawal from strong stimuli. Pearl (1903) noted that repeated strong stimulation decreased the number of positive reactions and increased the number of negative reactions given to any particular stimulus. By this principle electric shock would be expected to increase the number of large magnitude, negative reactions to light of an appropriate brightness and the results obtained by Thompson & McConnell and by Baxter & Kimmel become explicable as alteration in responsivity to one stimulus by strong stimulation with another. This is usually termed pseudo-conditioning. This explanation is consistent with the lack of importance of association, the importance of CS and US intensities (Baxter & Kimmel, 1963) the absence of differences between groups during extinction (Baxter & Kimmel, 1963; James & Halas, 1964), and the fact that light and shock both tend in planaria to produce behaviours that are qualitatively similar (Halas, James & Stone, 1961; Halas, James & Knutson, 1962).

There are a number of other recent demonstrations of learning and related phenomena in planaria. Best & Rubinstein (1962a) reported maze learning and Best & Rubinstein (1962b) reported inhibition of feeding in unfamiliar surroundings. Lee (1963) reported operant conditioning and Griffard & Peirce (1964) reported learned discrimination. All these seem open to criticisms similar to those made earlier. In the feeding experiments familiarity and number of times the animal is transferred

are confounded (Davenport, 1962; Dufort, 1962). The maze experiments had light as a cue. According to Pearl (1903), light could produce turning toward or away from the light, depending upon other factors which influence whether the positive or negative reaction is given; this explanation is consistent with the findings by Best & Rubinstein (1962a) that periods of rejection occur.

Lee's experiment can be explained by still another influence discussed by Pearl (1903). Pearl noted that planaria "seem to be incapable of continuing movement more than a certain, not very great, length of time. Then a period of rest must intervene. Thus one may see a specimen which has been moving about come to rest, and after a length of time, varying from a comparatively few minutes to several hours, it will start into spontaneous movements again, and repeat the whole cycle over and over. If one stirs up a specimen, and sets it into activity again just as soon as it comes to rest, the periods of spontaneous activity will become progressively shorter, until finally the worm will only move a very short distance before coming to rest again (Pearl, 1903, p. 533)." Pearl also noted that probably the most important cause of the onset of rest in planaria of appropriate physiological state is the intensity of light. Animals entering areas of decreased light intensity are likely to cease locomotion and come to rest (p. 564).

In Lee's free operant situation (Figure 11) both the experimental and control animals were stimulated by intense overhead light until the experimental animal interrupted the weak light beam coming up at one point on the perimeter of a circular experimental chamber. Whenever this occurred, the overhead light was extinguished for 15 minutes. What behavioural effect would this stimulus change be expected to have? The experimental procedure in question undoubtedly stimulated the planaria repeatedly and accordingly would be expected to produce a general readiness to come to rest soon after the overhead light was extinguished. The temporal patterns of light stimulation administered to the pairs of experimental and control animals were exactly the same, but where the control and experimental animals were when the overhead light was extinguished differed markedly. When the overhead light was extinguished the control animals could be anywhere, but by virtue of the reinforcement contingency the experimental animals

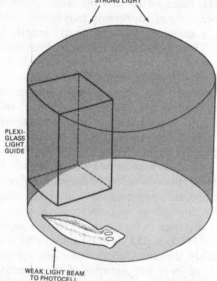

STRONG LIGHT

PLEXI-GLASS LIGHT GUIDE

WEAK LIGHT BEAM TO PHOTOCELL

**Figure 11.** Operant conditioning chamber for planaria. After Lee (1963).

were invariably near the light beam. If the planaria would occasionally remain at rest for the 15 minutes that the overhead light remained out, the experimental subjects would be found to be in the immediate vicinity of the light beam when the overhead light again came on. As a result the experimental subjects would be more likely to interrupt the central light beam than would the control subjects whose presence near the central beam is not so insured. "Extinction" would be expected whenever the removal of the response contingency removes the selective influence on position of the experimental subjects.

Still other influences, in addition to those just outlined, are probably operative in this situation. The persistent circling described probably results from thigmotactic reactions; greater frequency of turning under conditions of strong light would be expected (Ullyott, 1936); the frequent contact with the sides of the chamber produced by the persistent circling may tend to mask or inhibit the turning tendencies induced by light; control subjects may spend more time resting on the sides of the chamber or against the plexiglass light guide. Regardless of these further complexities it seems likely that the reinforcement procedure utilized in the experiment in question influenced the behaviour of planaria by selectively influencing the position rather than the behavioural tendencies of the planaria. We probably have another case of pseudo-learning.

The discrimination experiment by Griffard & Peirce (1964) is reported so briefly that it is difficult to evaluate, but general comments can be made on the basis of the use of DC shock to produce left and right turns. Pearl (1903) concluded that shock causes contraction of muscular elements whose long axes are parallel to the direction of current flow, that the portion of the body nearest the anode contracts, that the anterior of an animal which is not oriented directly toward either pole bends toward the cathode, and that DC quickly paralyzes the planaria. Pearl (1903, p. 694) concluded that "in the case of these lower organisms the current does not cause the reaction in any way comparable to that in which a mechanical stimulus causes a reaction." The effect of DC current appears to be equivalent to stimulating muscles directly rather than via the nervous system, a procedure which in mammals does not produce learning (Kimble, 1961, p. 7). DC current does, of course, have profound effects on all parts of an organism, and some of these effects may be confounded with "correctness", which in this experiment never reaches particularly high levels.

The anomalous nature of shock can hardly be overemphasized. Barnes & Katzung (1963) reported that animals trained as by Thompson & McConnell differed drastically in their responsiveness to light, depending upon the polarity of the shock administered. Strong shocks appear to produce heavy glandular secretion from the marginal glands of planaria; the animals tend to remain adhered to the substrata following such shocks and the amount and location of the portion adhering seem to be a function of shock polarity. Obviously investigation of the various effects of shock on the general behaviour of planaria seem necessary before studies involving the use of shock can be well understood and usefully interpreted. The recent work by van Deventer & Ratner (1964), which disclosed the importance of such variables as temperature, shape of trough, and size of planarian, is an example of the type of investigation which is necessary to provide the background of data which facilitates meaningful interpretation of other experiments. Similar empirical investigations are in order on the effects of shock; only then can the work by Griffard & Peirce be evaluated.

Some of us have quested for learning in paramecia and in planaria and we have found only pseudo-learning. A knight of King Arthur's court who returned from an unsuccessful quest might find solace in the fact that he had learned much about the local geography. We also could maintain that we had learned much from our fruitless quest. But let us recognize that we have learned little about paramecia and planaria. We have learned mainly about the dangers of confounding and special pleading and about the futility of seeking to demonstrate particular phenomena or topics in lower organisms without considering with greatest care the general behavioural organization of the organism. Just as we learn more geography by intentional mapping than by questing after the Holy Grail, so we learn more about behaviour of invertebrates by investigating their taxon-specific behavioural organization than by seeking to demonstrate in them phenomena observed originally in higher animals.

## SUMMARY

Studies on learning in paramecia were critically reviewed. Experiments have repeatedly been misinterpreted through failure to consider adequately either previous relevant research, the confounding of variables, or the whole pattern of data available. These misinterpretations and methodological errors appear to be consequences of the demonstrational approach involved in the research in question: data has been sought for pre-established hypotheses and special pleading has occurred. Studies on conditioning in planaria were then considered and again demonstrational approaches, special pleading, misinterpretations, and methodological errors were to be found. There appears to be little justification for the view that paramecia and planaria learn.

## ADDENDUM

After this paper was delivered Brown (1964) reported an extensive series of experiments with planaria in which it was observed that association was not necessary, that training with shock eliminated response decrement attributable to light adaptation, and that individual performance of worms was exceedingly variable during extended training. Brown concluded that sensitization by shock and not classical conditioning was involved in the experiments pairing light with shock. His data also indicated the importance of a wide variety of variables (i.e. light intensity, body length, part of body from which a regenerating animal is derived, time allowed for regeneration, etc.) to the reactiveness of the planaria. Brown's work is an example of investigational rather than demonstrational research with planaria.

Even more recently Hartry, Keith-Lee & Morton (1964) report an experiment in which effects of cannibalism of differently trained planaria by differently treated planaria were studied; their results were consistent with a pseudo-learning interpretation.

## REFERENCES

Alverdes, F. 1937. Das Lernvermögen der einzelligen Tiere. *Tierpsychologie* 1:35–38.

Barnes, C. D., and Katzung, B. G. 1963. Stimulus polarity and conditioning in planaria. *Science* 141:728–730.

Baxter, R., and Kimmel, H. D. 1963. Conditioning and extinction in the planarian. *American Journal of Psychology* 73:618–622.

Best, J. B., and Rubinstein, I. 1962a. Maze learning and associated behavior in planaria. *Journal of Comparative and Physiological Psychology* 55:560–566.

Best, J. B., and Rubenstein, I. 1962b. Environmental familiarity and feeding in a planarian. *Science* 135:916–918.

Bramstedt, F. 1935. Dressversuche mit *Paramecium caudatum* und *Stylonychia mytilus*. *Zeitschrift für Vergleichende Physiologie* 22:490–516.

Brown, H. M. 1964. Experimental procedures and state of nucleic acids as factors contributing to "learning" phenomena in planaria. Unpublished Ph.D. thesis, University of Utah.

Buytendijk, F. J. 1919. Acquisition d'habitudes par des êtres unicellulaires. *Archives Néerlandaises de Physiologie de l'Homme et des Animaux* 3:455–467.

Davenport, D. 1962. Letter. *Science* 137:452–453.

Day, Lucy, and Bentley, M. 1911. A note on learning in *Paramecium*. *Journal of Animal Behavior* 1:67–73.

de Beer, G. 1964. *Charles Darwin*. Garden City: Doubleday & Co.

Dembowski, J. 1950. On conditioned reactions of *Paramecium caudatum* towards light. *Acta Biologiae Experimentalis* 15:5–17.

Dufort, R. H. 1962. Letter. *Science* 138:400–401.

Gelber, B. 1952. Investigations of the behavior of *Paramecium aurelia*, I: Modification of behavior after training with reinforcement. *Journal of Comparative and Physiological Psychology* 45:58–65.

Grabowski, U. 1939. Experimentelle Untersuchungen über das angebliche Lernvermögen von *Paramecium. Zeitschrift für Tierpsychologie* 2:265–282.

Griffard, C. D., and Peirce, J. T. 1964. Conditioned discrimination in the planarian. *Science* 144:1472–1473.

Halas, E. S.; James, R. L.; and Knutson, C. S. 1962. An attempt at classical conditioning in the planarian. *Journal of Comparative and Physiological Psychology* 55:969–971.

Halas, E. S.; James, R. L.; and Stone, L. A. 1961. Types of responses elicited in planaria by light. *Journal of Comparative and Physiological Psychology* 54:302–305.

Hartry, A. L.; Keith-Lee, P.; and Morton, W. D. 1964. Planaria: Memory transfer through cannibalism re-examined. *Science* 146:274–275.

Hovey, H. B. 1929. Associative hysteresis in marine flatworms. *Physiological Zoölogy* 1:322–333.

James, R. L., and Halas, E. S. 1964. No difference in extinction behavior in planaria following various types and amounts of training. *Psychological Record* 14:1–11.

Jennings, H. S. 1906. *Behavior of the lower organisms*. New York: Columbia University Press.

Jensen, D. D. 1955. A critical examination of learning in paramecia. Unpublished M.A. thesis, University of Nebraska.

Jensen, D. D. 1957. Experiments on "learning" in paramecia. *Science* 125:191–192.

Jensen, D. D. 1959. A theory of the behavior of *Paramecium aurelia* and behavioral effects of feeding, fission, and ultraviolet microbeam irradiation. *Behaviour* 15:82–122.

Jensen, D. D. 1961. Operationism and the question "Is this behavior learned or innate?" *Behaviour* 17:1–8.

Jensen, D. D. 1962. Foreword to H. S. Jennings, *Behavior of the lower organisms*. Bloomington: Indiana University Press.

Katz, M. S., and Deterline, W. A. 1958. Apparent learning in the paramecium. *Journal of Comparative and Physiological Psychology* 51:243–247.

Kimble, G. A. 1961. *Hilgard and Marquis' conditioning and learning*. 2d ed. New York: Appleton-Century-Crofts.

Lee, R. M. 1963. Conditioning of a free operant response in planaria. *Science* 139:1048–1049.

Maier, N. R. F. 1960. Maier's law. *American Psychologist* 15:208–212.

Maier, N. R. F., and Schneirla, T. C. 1935. *Principles of animal psychology*. New York: McGraw-Hill.

Pearl, R. 1903. The movements and reactions of fresh water planaria. *Quarterly Journal of Microscopical Science* 46:509–714.

Popper, K. R. 1959. *The logic of scientific discovery*. New York: Basic Books.

Schneirla, T. C. 1959. An evolutionary and developmental theory of biphasic processes underlying approach and withdrawal. In *Nebraska symposium on motivation*, ed. M. R. Jones. Lincoln: University of Nebraska Press.

Smith, S. 1908. The limits of educability of *Paramecium. Journal of Comparative and Physiological Psychology* 18:499–510.

Soest, H. 1937. Dressurversuche mit Ciliaten und Rhabdocoelen Turbellarien. *Zeitschrift für Vergleichende Physiologie* 24:720–748.

Solomon, R. L. 1964. Punishment. *American Psychologist* 19:239–253.

Thompson, R., and McConnell, J. 1955. Classical conditioning in the planarian, *Dugesia dorotocephala. Journal of Comparative and Physiological Psychology* 52:1–5.

Ullyott, P. 1936. The behaviour of *Dendrocoelum lacteum*. I — Responses at light-and-dark boundaries. II — Responses in non-directional gradients. *Journal of Experimental Biology* 13:253–278.

Van Deventer, J. M., and Ratner, S. C. 1964. Variables affecting the frequency of response of planaria to light. *Journal of Comparative and Physiological Psychology* 57:407–411.

Wawrzynczyk, S. 1938. Die Reaktionen von *Paramaecium caudatum* auf Lichtreize. *Trav. Soc. Sci. Wilno*, XII. Cited by Dembowski (1950).

# READING 6

# Practical Use of Operant Conditioning Procedures in a Mental Hospital

O. L. GERICKE, M.D.

The application of learning research to other areas of psychology has increased in recent years. The following article is representative of the research done in behavior therapy. Gericke demonstrates how behavior therapy can be used in a mental hospital: desired behavior is selectively reinforced using the principles of partial reinforcement and shaping; reinforcement is withheld from undesired behavior.

**QUESTIONS**

1. Discuss the ways that operant conditioning procedures are used in child-rearing practices, education, advertisement, et cetera.
2. Is the use of operant conditioning procedures in mental hospitals practical? Could these procedures be used in all of our correctional institutions? Discuss.
3. Do you think the behavioral changes brought about by this study are permanent? What would happen to this behavior if the reinforcement was removed? Apply the laws of learning to this situation.

During the last dozen years or so a field of research has opened that is variously called operant conditioning, behavioral engineering, or behavioral science.

To date, the most impressive findings in this field have been largely confined to the laboratory. This is unfortunate, because the very things that the behavioral scientist

Dr. Gericke is superintendent of the Patton (Calif.) State Hospital.

The author is indebted to the following members of the hospital staff, without whose constructive help and enthusiasm the project would not have been possible: V. G. Arcadi, M.D., senior psychiatrist; Dovie Farish, R.N., senior psychiatric nurse (unit supervisor); Norma Fullgrabe, R.N., senior psychiatric nurse (unit supervisor); Mary Jo Harrell, ACSW, psychiatric social worker; Wesley Ishikawa, ACSW, chief of social service; H. H. Schaefer, Ph.D., research psychologist; Joseph F. Williams, ACSW, psychiatric social worker; and Doreen Wysocki, R.N., assistant superintendent of nursing services.

can demonstrate as workable are of the utmost interest to the staff of a mental institution. By using well-described techniques, or schedules of reinforcement as they are more appropriately technically called, the behavioral scientist can strengthen existing behaviors, shape new behaviors, and teach discrimination of a subtlety which could only with difficulty be achieved through verbal communication.

To appreciate fully the applicability of behavioral science techniques to a mental institution, we must recognize that a patient is not always admitted to an institution because he suffers from schizophrenia, anxiety, paranoia, or neurosis, but frequently because he behaves in a way that is not acceptable to the community in which he lives. After he is admitted to the institution, the behavior he displays is labeled in accordance with the findings of a psychiatric examination. There is no denying that such a label is useful as a shorthand method to describe the patient's difficulties, as well as a guide to determine what should be done with him. The situation here is not entirely different from that prevailing elsewhere in medicine: a patient is seldom admitted to a hospital because he has measles; rather he is brought to the attention of a physician because there are red splotches on his skin. Examination reveals that there is a certain virus present, and the disease is identified. That the community, parents, or friends who petition for commitment of a psychiatric patient often prejudge the issue does not detract from the point that is made here.

No analogy is perfect, and this one is no exception. When the patient who has splotches on his skin is examined, it is possible to look for, and sometimes to find, a virus that allows identification of the disease with which he is afflicted. In mental disorders it is, however, by no means as easy to identify the precipitating factor or organic dysfunction that causes the difficulty. In fact, one might speculate whether unconscious transfer of the medical analogy causes us in all instances to regard faulty behavior or thinking as a symptom of some underlying disorder. At the moment, aside from some well-understood organic disorders and some identifiable genes, very little is known about the extent to which anxiety, depression, and other inferred mental states really cause the behavior for which a patient is committed to a mental institution. Hence the behavioral scientist, who deals with behavior pure and simple, is perhaps not really concerned with dynamics as he extends his activities to include the mental patient.

A survey of the very few instances where behavioral science techniques have been used in mental institutions offers striking evidence of their efficacy. B. F. Skinner (12), Ogden R. Lindsley (9,10), and Martha T. Mednick (11) obtained purely behavioral data from psychotics from Metropolitan State Hospital in Waltham, Massachusetts. They used food, cigarettes, money, candy, and pictures of various sorts to reinforce behaviors they wanted to strengthen. They showed that by manipulating the occurrence of these events or objects they could control the frequency and the conditions under which behaviors occurred as completely as they wished.

Ferster and DeMyer (6,7) at the University of Indiana Medical Center in Indianapolis worked exclusively with autistic children. They used toys and food as reinforcers and succeeded in establishing new or re-establishing lost behaviors that had hitherto been impossible to obtain. The children learned to count, to talk, to react to their social environment; in short, they lost their autism without the scientist making any reference to or manipulation of inferred pathological causes of the absence of these behaviors.

Ayllon (1,2,3,4) and his co-workers at Saskatchewan Hospital trained nurses on a closed ward to selectively reinforce specific behaviors by individual patients, and remarkable results were obtained.

Azrin (5,8) at Anna (Ill.) State Hospital applied operant techniques to patients on a closed ward to achieve a variety of changes in their behavior.

There are perhaps two reasons why there has not been more widespread use of operant conditioning techniques. On the one hand, the behavioral scientist might feel that he does not know enough at this time to be able to apply his findings immediately to practical situations. Moreover, he is seldom in direct contact with clinical work. The behavioral scientists mentioned above did most of their initial work with rats, pigeons, and other lower animals. Each happened to be located at or near a mental hospital and found that for one reason or another the staff was interested in clinical application of what he was doing. It is evident that the science of behavior as we conceive of it here is so young that its findings have not yet been widely disseminated outside the field itself.

Yet there is no reason why some of the techniques should not be applied on a broader scale. At Patton State Hospital we felt that it would be valuable to try out behavioral techniques to explore their degree of usefulness in a variety of specific situations. We therefore began a project aimed at exploring the effectiveness of behavioral control methods with a group of men and women patients on open units.

Patton has a patient population of more than 4000, including mentally ill and retarded patients, patients with neurological disorders, and a large percentage of geriatric patients. There are some 60 individual buildings, called "units," each housing from 50 to 100 patients. Our intention was to utilize the nursing staff of some of the units to shape and control the behavior of patients.

To give the experiment in operant conditioning a fair chance, we started out with a newly composed staff of well-experienced nurses and psychiatric technicians on units with patients who, before the project, had been in other units in the hospital. We limited ourselves to two units, one for women and one for men. We were so impressed with the simplicity of the operant conditioning technique that we did not feel we should, at this stage, ask for additional funds or supplement the established nursing staff ratio. This meant that for each unit we would work with the regular staff of 10 nurses or psychiatric technicians, who provided 24-hour coverage.

As the first step in implementing the program, we gave a series of lectures to the newly formed staffs on the underlying theory of operant conditioning. It was clear that the nursing staff's role in this program would require a change in their attitudes. Rather than carrying out orders to the letter, nurses would now be required to understand their underlying rationale. To make a decision on the spot, as when reinforcing a patient's behavior, the nurse had to have more responsibility and authority than she had had in the past. How well experienced nurses could adapt to this new role was one of the questions we attempted to answer.

Following each lecture we conducted a lengthy discussion session. During these sessions the general plan of the program, as well as the specific procedures that were to be employed, took shape, and we tried to ascertain precisely with what behavioral problems we should primarily concern ourselves. We were in a sense training the nursing staff to become "behavioral engineers," a term coined by Ayllon (4), who first experimented with these procedures at Saskatchewan Hospital.

Much of what we taught the nursing staff ran counter to what they considered their normal function. We told them that while they should be of service to patients, such service should not be given indiscriminately. We also told them that patients should, of course, be made comfortable, but degree of comfort should be contingent upon specific desired behavior on the part of the patient. To operate in this way called for the nurse to make decisions rather than to follow solidly established rules. She had to weigh the desirability of specific behaviors in specific cases within the context of each patient's prescribed treatment plan.

Nurses are generally used to following explicit instructions in dealing with patients. In our program directions are still given, but they are much more general. We say, for example, that a certain patient should change his patterns of interactions with other patients by talking more to others. We further specify that such a change in behavior should be reached by successive stages through selectively reinforcing responses that promise to lead eventually to increased interaction between this patient and his fellow patients. When to reinforce and by what means necessarily had to be left to the staff member who undertook to carry out this order. The need to make a quick decision about what to do with a patient is quite a new experience for a nurse. Yet the staff members we had selected were so challenged to actually enter the therapeutic process that almost from the start their enthusiasm was most gratifying.

The over-all plan as to what operant conditioning procedures were to be used was determined entirely by practical considerations. We knew that with only 10 nurses or psychiatric technicians per unit (and usually fewer than 5 of these on duty) it would be impossible to give close attention to more than 10 or 15 patients. Yet each unit contained at least 70 and sometimes as many as 90 patients. Consequently, we decided to have three groups of patients on each unit: an orientation group of approximately 60 per cent of the total unit population, a therapy group of approximately 20 per cent, and a "ready to leave" group of another 20 per cent. The staff

would work intensively only with the therapy group. They were to obtain behavioral baselines from patients in the orientation group. The habits, idiosyncrasies, and details of behavior of these patients were to be noted as time allowed, but no action was to be taken on this information until a patient was transferred into the therapy group. Each nurse was to be responsible for two or three patients in the therapy group, for three times as many patients in the orientation group. At first there were, of course, no patients in the "ready to leave" group, but when a patient entered it following successful therapy, the nurse who had previously engineered his behavior would continue to work with him until he left the hospital. Other forms of group therapy and, of course, individual supervision of medication through the unit physician continued concurrently with the program.

The next step was to list the reinforcers available to us. The food the patient eats, the bed he sleeps on, the minor privileges he enjoys on the unit, such as watching TV or being permitted to go to the cafeteria, were obvious variables that we felt we could use within limits to control the behavior of patients. In order to have some versatility in granting these primary reinforcers, we decided to introduce tokens (poker chips) into the program. Patients could exchange these tokens for desired minor privileges.

We then drew up a list of the desirable behaviors that we expected to influence through these reinforcers. We required each member of the nursing staff to make up his list independently. Making this list gave individuals much insight into the purposes of our plan. The immediate behaviors listed were "getting to the dining room on time," "maintaining personal hygiene" (these are open units and the patients are expected to be able to perform adequately in these respects), "performing simple household duties on the unit," and, as appropriate, "seeking off-the-unit jobs in the patient laundry, the kitchen, the cafeteria, the grounds crew, or in offices within the hospital."

The staff quickly grasped that such global statements of goals are of little value to the behavioral engineer. Personal hygiene means many things to many people. We demonstrated that to make this term meaningful we must be more specific. For "personal hygiene" we arrived at the following list: a) no desquamatus between the toes, b) no dirt on the instep or heels of the feet, c) no dirt on legs and knees, d) no evidence of body odor, e) no residue in the naval, f) clean hands and fingernails, g) neat and recent shave (or neatly trimmed beard) for the men, h) nicely combed hair, and i) a daily change of underwear. A separate list for the women included appropriate use of cosmetics.

It became overwhelmingly evident that although there might be disagreement about poorly defined global goals, the items on the detailed list could be agreed upon without much difficulty and, most important for our purposes, could be selectively reinforced. Everyone understood that this was quite different from demanding "adequate personal hygiene," which society at large reinforces, but which it does little to shape selectively.

An important feature of the program was structuring the unit environment to make living in the orientation group sufficiently undesirable to motivate patients to move into the therapy group. We adhered, of course, to the minimal requirements that human dignity and common sense demand, but whereas the therapy group could watch television, visit the cafeteria (some distance away from the unit), and go to social functions, dances, and movies, the orientation group enjoyed none of these privileges. Furthermore, the therapy group enjoyed the most desirable dormitories or single rooms, equipped with night stands, curtains, and attractive bedspreads. The orientation group slept in community rooms equipped with plain beds, no bedspreads, and a "bed sack" commonly in use throughout the hospital for storing personal belongings. In the dining rooms, the therapy group could sit at tables for four, covered with a tablecloth and set with attractive china, stainless steel flatware, and flowers. The patients in the orientation group sat at a long, bare table, and their meals were served out of picnic trays. The quantity and quality of meals for both groups were, of course, the same.

As a routine procedure the staff had daily meetings during which individual problems could be discussed, and procedures considered for use with individual patients.

The last step was to screen patients for admission to the program. To be admitted to the units, patients must have been hospitalized for more than six months, have no brain damage, and be able to function on an open unit. There were no other restrictions.

Because we knew that our procedures were likely to elicit strong letters of concern from relatives, we designated the units' social worker as director of the project and asked him to explain to relatives, when necessary, the basic principles underlying the operant conditioning program.

Finally came the day when the program officially started. The patients received their first tokens for answering "pill call" and for doing various chores around the unit. The nurses went to some length to invent small jobs for the patients because the main purpose of this day was to establish the tokens as behavior reinforcers.

At lunchtime the patients were admitted to the dining room only if they could pay for their entry with a token. A small number only had been selected for the therapy group, and they were told that they had to pay more tokens to eat at the specially designated tables. Some patients did not have enough tokens, and they were told that although they could easily earn enough in the course of a day, since they unfortunately did not yet have enough tokens to pay for this privilege, they would have to sit with the orientation group patients at the long bare table. Some patients, even though they had earned a token in the course of the morning, thought the hospital staff had no right to charge for entering the dining room. These patients, we well understood, were merely trying to find out how serious we were. The staff stuck to the rules, especially when they noticed that those who missed a meal could easily afford to do so because they were overweight. No male patient missed his meal.

During this first day patients began to ask for jobs, such as emptying wastebaskets, rearranging chairs, setting the table and helping in the kitchen, to earn tokens. It became obvious that there could be no general rule about how many tokens a patient could earn for a given job. Some worked so much that, if a standard rule had been enforced, they would have earned as many as 50 tokens in one day. Therefore we simply increased the number of responses needed to earn one token. This procedure is called a variable ratio schedule. The patient never knows exactly when or how much he is getting paid. Because of that, he increases his responses. Doing more instead of less under a variable ratio schedule is a somewhat unexpected empirical finding of behavioral scientists. Yet, on reflection, we can see that much of our own daily behavior is reinforced on a variable ratio. We know that after continuous reinforcement—a reward for each response —the response ceases very swiftly. (This is called extinction by behavioral scientists.) A good example is the continuous reinforcement we receive when we deposit a coin into a postal meter to obtain a stamp. For every coin we deposit we obtain one stamp. If for some reason the machine breaks down, extinction (the cessation of

our response) would be swift. At most we would deposit one more coin into the machine to try it out. The situation is different when we are responding to a variable ratio schedule as, for example, with a gambling machine. If such a machine is cold and does not pay off, the gambler continues to throw in coins for a long time before his responses are finally extinguished.

Since our long-term goal is to wean the patients away from the artificial support of token reinforcement, we welcomed every opportunity to introduce a variable ratio reinforcement; we replaced tokens by other types of reinforcement, such as friendly praise from the nurse to a patient for doing a job well.

One of the most impressive over-all results of the program was that we could reach patients who had heretofore remained passive. They felt that all of a sudden something was expected of them and someone was taking them seriously. Some rebelled against the system. (While such rebellion is obviously not a desirable response to any therapeutic technique, it is better to have a patient react even negatively than not to react at all.) Many rebelled by being absent without leave from the unit. We dealt with this problem by assigning baby-sitters (who were patients themselves and earned one token an hour for this job) to patients who left the unit without authorization. The term "baby-sitter" was used deliberately to imply that absentees were acting childishly. No patient required a baby-sitter for more than four days, although at various times we had as many as eight baby-sitters assigned.

Some patients did not earn enough tokens even for the plainest beds on the unit. Theoretically these patients should sleep on the floor or on cots. We felt that if the secondary reinforcers, the tokens, were to have any value at all, we would have to tie them strongly to such primary reinforcers as food and a place to sleep. We knew from previous experience that none of the patients would have to go without meals or without a bed for any length of time. However, we were mindful of possible public criticism of a hospital procedure that might appear to deprive patients of basic rights.

In the light of this consideration, we agreed that no patient would be denied adequate sleeping facilities or a meal if he was not able to "pay" for these services with a token. At that time we also drafted a statement to ourselves to clarify our own thinking:

"The basic premise on which operant conditioning procedures rest is that there are reinforcers which, as a consequence of some behavior, will strengthen or weaken that behavior. The details are that the removal of a negative reinforcer will strengthen the behavior which removed it; appearance of a positive reinforcer will strengthen the behavior which brought it about. Thus, both negative reinforcers and positive reinforcers can be used to bring about reinforcement of a behavior. Withholding of a positive reinforcer constitutes extinction or weakening a behavior. The granting of a negative reinforcer as a consequence of some behavior constitutes punishment and does not have the same result, i.e., a weakening or extinction of that behavior. What happens in that case is that the behavior in question is *temporarily* suppressed, only to emerge more strongly when the aversive consequences no longer follow. Hence, while there are negative and positive reinforcers, it is not correct to speak of negative and positive reinforcement. To change a behavior *permanently*, to strengthen or to weaken it, it is necessary to employ the procedures of reinforcement or extinction but not procedures of punishment.

"There are some reinforcers which are very general, such as food, water and a place to sleep. Interestingly, these reinforcers play a relatively minor role in our daily lives. Much more important to all of us are such conditioned reinforcers as social approval, praise, money in all its forms, social privileges, and so on. A particularly useful conditioned general reinforcer for the operant conditioning project are tokens. These tokens would have, however, no reinforcing value if they were not paired with primary reinforcers, that is to say, if they had not acquired the status of being conditioned reinforcers. It was on the basis of such deliberations that we originally planned making a patient's meals and bed ('room and board') contingent on the presence of carefully selected behaviors. The patient would earn tokens by having these types of behavior and 'buy' his room and board, as it were, with the token.

"In general the tokens have now been established successfully as conditioned reinforcers. From now on the tokens will be made to maintain their reinforcing status by careful manipulation of social prestige privileges (often of very minor apparent nature) which exceed minimum services to which the patient ethically, or by law, is entitled. Thus, a meal served from handsome china, on a tablecloth decked with tasteful silverware, is more reinforcing than one served from a stainless steel mess tray. A bed in a room with drapes, bed stands, and minor conveniences is more desirable than a bed in an otherwise barren room."

As it developed, the final solution of the sleeping question was to provide military cots, which conformed entirely to minimum standards but were sufficiently disliked by the patients to motivate them to respond to our therapy program.

As anyone who has slept on such cots knows, they are not uncomfortable. But in comparison with a full-sized bed that could be obtained with tokens earned by socially acceptable behavior, the cots achieved the purpose of reinforcing such behavior.

On the men's unit from the beginning the main source of token income was passing inspection for personal cleanliness. Two technicians shared the task of carrying out the inspection. The effect was that the men patients quickly learned that in order to be somebody on this unit, they merely had to do regularly a few things which they did (or knew they should do) anyway, such as bathing and shaving. All the coaxing, admonishing, and helping that had heretofore required much of the nurses' time was now no longer necessary.

One of the most gratifying aspects of the project was the personal interest the nursing staff took in working with individual patients. There was, for example, the patient named Susan, who for months had sat seclusively in a corner by herself. The token system had moved her slightly. She began to earn enough tokens for her bed and meals, but beyond that did nothing much. Susan is a 26-year-old Mexican girl, the youngest of four children. Her mother and father are still living, although they are not physically well. Susan was educated formally to the third grade and quit school because she disliked one of her teachers. She preferred to stay at home. As a teen-age girl she had occasionally worked as a housekeeper and baby-sitter. She was married nine years ago, when she was 17. After her marriage she stayed home as a housewife.

About a year later her husband noticed that her behavior became odd, while she was going to a gynecologist for treatment of a female disorder. She became increasingly nervous, tore her clothing, and threw things. She also expressed paranoid ideation and had many somatic complaints. Over the years she began a sequence of periods during which she was hospitalized and then discharged again to return to her husband.

Every time she returned to the hospital she seemed more depressed. The nursing staff noticed that milk was the only nourishment she would take and that she would dress only in white or light-colored clothing. The nurse assigned to her mentioned this preference, and we decided to use white clothing as a positive reinforcer for acceptable behavior. When Susan's white dress was taken away from her, and institution dark olive-drab clothing substituted, she reacted for the first time in the course of her current hospitalization: she tore the institution dress, sat on her bed, and refused to dress. The nurses left her and waited to see what would happen next. After about two hours, Susan called the nurse and asked for a needle and thread to fix the dress that she had ripped. The nurse complied and immediately gave her a white scarf to wear with her dark dress.

The resulting change in Susan's behavior was dramatic. After she had mended the clothing, she asked for odd jobs in the kitchen. Each time she completed a task, she received a token and some of her white clothing back. During the next few days she earned the right to get all her clothing back. She added white ice cream and mashed potatoes to her diet, after being satiated by increasing portions of milk daily. The next goal of the staff was to condition her to wearing dark clothing and to eating foods that were not white.

During discussions between the charge nurse and Susan, it emerged very clearly that the color white was an irrationally powerful control stimulus for Susan. She associated white with purity, goodness, and the worth of life. Black and dark colors symbolized the devil, sin, and everything undesirable. She felt that God had punished her by giving her black hair and that she would have to bear this burden. Her first reaction to the milk satiation program was to gorge herself with milk. After a few days the nurse began to charge extra tokens for extra glasses of milk but not for other food. Since Susan, until then, had not earned sufficient tokens to stay with the program, one of two things was expected to happen. She would either have to work more and interact more with patients (a behavior that was, of course, sought for her) or she would have to choose other foods that would cost her no tokens. The second alternative happened. Susan began to eat bacon and toast for breakfast. Although Susan's troubles were not over, some communication had been established between this withdrawn girl and the nursing staff.

It is interesting to read the report that the charge nurse of the women's unit wrote at the end of the first month of the program: "The project goes extremely well. We no longer have to call individuals for meals or coax them to go into the dining room. This used to require considerable time. Patients are taking the responsibility now of getting to the dining room on time. It sometimes seems to us today that this came about automatically with the use of tokens. Other by-products are that at meal-times the general atmosphere seems more relaxed. There is no longer the mad rush to eat and get out. Patients get up without being called. Many of the patients we had to look out for in the beginning are now looking out for themselves. We hope this will continue. The night technician no longer has to go from bed to bed, calling the patients to get up for breakfast, get dressed for breakfast, and so on. She merely turns on the light and in three minutes goes back, and the patients who are up get their tokens. The ones who are not up get nothing. Very few are not up by then.

"We have a much larger percentage of patients turning up for breakfast now than we did before the program. In the beginning our plans were to more or less ignore the orientation group. But the orientation patients refuse to be ignored, and they are getting as much attention as any other patients. I feel that the visibility of progress is also much more evident in the orientation group than it is with those in the therapy group. The patients in the orientation group very much dislike eating at the big community table and from the mess dishes. This is, of course, exactly what we wanted, and it provides excellent motivation for them to try to get into the therapy groups. I have known some of the patients for five years, and for the first time I am seeing real progress made with them. I feel quite encouraged with our program, and we are learning as we go along. We understand fully now that we must reinforce good behavior when it occurs. Reinforcement is not as effective if it is given [too long] after the behavior has occurred. All the staff are extremely enthusiastic and feel that their own thinking is tremendously stimulated by what they are learning in this project."

Although the problems are different on the men's unit, the results are the same. Perhaps the most striking difference on the men's unit is that the men are undoubtedly now the cleanest group of men on an open unit anywhere in the hospital. There is none of the stale odor frequently encountered when large numbers of men live in one unit. Everyone wears neatly pressed clothes and is shaved and well scrubbed.

The creation of special schedules of reinforcement for individual patients is practiced on the men's unit, too. The following is an example:

Cecil is a 61-year-old single patient who has been at Patton State Hospital since 1930. He was brought to staff attention for placement on the men's open unit because he required no medication, displayed no psychotic symptoms, and had been known for many years as a dependable worker in the print shop. But he had come to accept being in the hospital as a normal way of life.

Cecil is a mild-mannered, apologetic, white-haired, balding man. He is considered a loner in his relations to other patients and his distant relatives. In accepting this patient in the program, we surmised that transferring him to a less comfortable setting in an environment that offered choice and competition might trigger some change in his attitude and perhaps renew his interest in the world outside. We also assumed that the change to a new unit would be difficult and upsetting to this patient.

After experiencing the new life for a short time, Cecil sought the social worker and expressed an interest in seeing downtown Los Angeles again. He also asked for an interview with the unit physician, with whom he discussed his problems of his situation. He said that he had been worried about the change in units, but found the new procedure something he could cope with.

After only three weeks in the orientation group, Cecil was accepted in the therapy group. This step, the physician had told him, was necessary if he was to visit his brother in Los Angeles. Two interviews with staff members from social service preceded this planned visit. During these interviews he said that if he could keep up with the young fellows on the unit under the therapy program, he could probably make it on the outside. "I felt pushed around," he said, "but now they promoted me, and I have no one to thank for that but myself." This increase in self-confidence was striking compared to the stolid and indifferent attitude Cecil had shown before entering the program.

The five-day visit was a complete success. In the course of it Cecil made tentative plans to live at his brother's house with the brother's family, who are happy at the thought of having their uncle back. Presently, plans are being made for Cecil to receive funds from the aid to the totally disabled program when he is discharged. In view of his 34 years of hospitalization and because of his age it will be difficult, although not impossible, for him to obtain remunerative employment.

Another patient, Rudy, has no family, and his only friend is a male volunteer who visited him regularly for the last eight years. This volunteer expressed his amazement at the change the program has brought about in Rudy. "Christmas meant something to him for the first time since I have known him," he told us after visiting Rudy. He felt that Rudy had become a person, that he responded with feeling to his questions, that, in short, he was a new man.

In these cases, we know exactly what variables we manipulated to bring about the changes. These and other instances give us great confidence in the unorthodox techniques we are now using, and we point to them whenever we are called upon to explain and justify a therapy that requires the patient to pay for what he used to regard as his due.

Not the least benefit of a program involving behavioral science techniques is that everyone involved is often forced to ask, "Why am I doing what I do, and how does it affect the patient's behavior?" Ever since mental hospitals came into being, the great leaders in psychiatry have asked this question. But in the course of time, as routine and habit make it easy to move along the path of least resistance, perhaps many of us do not really question as seriously as we should our roles in the recovery of patients. Some even defend the view that technicians and nurses should never ask questions. To be sure, there are situations in life, such as with the military, where the success of an operation depends on a person's ability, not to reason *why*, but to *do*, if necessary without understanding. But such situations hardly apply to the problems we face in the mental institution. Operant procedures rest primarily on the analysis of behavior and, thus, on questioning our own responses.

With the complexity of human behavior it is, however, no task for one single person to explore all the reinforcers, all the control stimuli, and all response contingencies even for a single patient. A team is needed to provide baselines of the be-

havioral repertory of the patient, to structure the physical environment, and to
arrange schedules of reinforcement that
lead to acceptable behavior and to recovery. Nurses and psychiatric technicians
are a vital part of this team.

In initiating this project we questioned
whether behavioral techniques are practical
and useful in a mental hospital. We are
now satisfied that this question has been
affirmatively answered. As our knowledge
increases, we are beginning to ask to what
degree these techniques can be applied to
deal with individual problems and, in particular, how *permanently* we can change a
pattern of behavior. The discharged patient
usually returns to an environment that is
not very different from that which pre-
vailed when his difficulties began. This environment is not under our control. Our
job must be to prepare the patient to cope
with this environment. Will behavioral
techniques enable us to do this? We shall
try to provide empirical answers to this
question by continuing and expanding our
project.

## REFERENCES

1. Ayllon, T. 1963. Intensive treatment of psychotic behaviour by stimulus satiation and
   food reinforcement. *Behaviour Research and
   Therapy* 1:53–61.

2. Ayllon, T., and Haughton, E. 1962. Control
   of the behavior of schizophrenic patients by
   food. *Journal of the Experimental Analysis of
   Behavior* 5:343–352.

3. Ayllon, T.; Haughton, E.; and Osmond, H. O.
   1964. Chronic Anorexia: A behavior problem.
   *Canadian Psychiatric Association Journal*
   9:147–154.

4. Ayllon, T., and Michael, J. 1959. The psychiatric nurse as a behavioral engineer. *Journal of the Experimental Analysis of Behavior*
   2:323–334.

5. Azrin, N. H.; Holz, W.; Ulrich, R.; and Gol-
   diamond, I. 1961. The control of the content
   of conversation through reinforcement. *Journal of the Experimental Analysis of Behavior*
   4:25–30.

6. Ferster, C. B., and DeMyer, M. K. 1962. A
   method for the experimental analysis of the
   behavior of autistic children. *American Journal
   of Orthopsychiatry* 32:89–98.

7. Ferster, C. B., and DeMyer, M. K. 1961. The
   development of performances in autistic children in an automatically controlled environment. *Journal of Chronic Diseases* 13:312–345.

8. Hutchinson, R. R., and Azrin, N. H. 1961.
   Conditioning of mental hospital patients to
   fixed-ratio schedules of reinforcement. *Journal of the Experimental Analysis of Behavior*
   4:87–95.

9. Lindsley, O. R. 1960. Characteristics of the
   behavior of chronic psychotics as revealed by
   free-operant conditioning methods. *Diseases
   of the Nervous System* 21:3–15.

10. Lindsley, O. R. 1956. Operant conditioning
    methods applied to research in chronic schizo-
    phrenia. *Psychiatric Research Reports of the
    American Psychiatric Association* 5:118–139.

11. Mednick, M. T., and Lindsley, O. R. 1958.
    Some clinical correlates of operant behavior.
    *Journal of Abnormal and Social Psychology*
    57:13–16.

12. Skinner, B. F.; Solomon, H. C.; and Lindsley,
    O. R. 1956. Technical Report no. 2, ONR
    Contract N5-ori-07662, Metropolitan State
    Hospital, Waltham, Mass. Section: "The re-
    inforcement of cooperation between children."
    *Journal of Abnormal and Social Psychology*
    52:100–102.

# READING 7

# Building Social Behavior in Autistic Children by Use of Electric Shock

**O. IVAR LOVAAS**
**BENSON SCHAEFFER**
**JAMES Q. SIMMONS**
**University of California, Los Angeles**

Lovaas, Schaeffer, and Simmons present a case for the use of electric shock in controlling behavior. This idea appears abhorrent at first glance, but, as the authors explain, the children involved were facing a life of institutional care unless their behavior could be modified. In conjunction with the ethical considerations of this research is the question of whether this is a case of symptomatic treatment and control, or of actually eliminating the cause of the behavior. Many argue that unless the cause of deviant behavior is found and treated, treatment of the symptoms is useless: new symptoms will appear as the old symptoms are treated. The methods used in this study are also illustrative of escape conditioning procedures.

**QUESTIONS**
1. Do you have objections to the use of electric shock in this experiment? Do you think the use of physical punishment or pain is ever justified in experimental research? Discuss.
2. Do you think autistic children would respond to the operant conditioning procedures used by Gericke?
3. Discuss the methodology of the three studies presented. How well do they reflect the information derived from animal research in the same area?

Psychological or physical pain is perhaps as characteristic in human relationships as is pleasure. The extensive presence of pain in everyday life may suggest that it is necessary for the establishment and maintenance of normal human interactions.

Despite the pervasiveness of pain in daily functioning, and its possible necessity for maintaining some behaviors, psychology and related professions have shied away from, and often condemned, the use of pain for therapeutic purposes. We agree with Solomon (1964) that such objections to the use of pain have a moral rather than a scientific basis. Recent research, as reviewed by Solomon, indicated that the scientific premises offered by psychologists for the rejection of punishment are not tenable. Rather, punishment can be a very useful tool for effecting behavior change.

There are three ways pain can be used therapeutically. First, it can be used directly as punishment, i.e., it can be presented contingent upon certain undesirable behaviors, so as to suppress them. This is perhaps the most obvious use of pain. Second, pain can be removed or withheld contingent upon certain behaviors. That is, certain behaviors can be established and maintained because they terminate pain, or avoid it altogether. Escape and avoidance learning exemplify this. The third way in which pain can be used is the least well known, and perhaps the most intriguing. Any stimulus which is associated with or discriminative of pain reduction acquires *positive* reinforcing (rewarding) properties (Bijou and Baer, 1961), i.e., an organism will work to "obtain" those stimuli which have been associated with pain reduction. The action of such stimuli is analogous to that of stimuli whose positive reinforcing properties derive from primary positive reinforcers.

These three aspects of the use of pain can be illustrated by observations on parent-child relationships. The first two are ob-

This study was supported by a grant from the National Institute of Health (HD 00938). The authors express their gratitude to Professor Donald M. Baer of the University of Washington for his help in the design and report of these studies. They are also indebted to Gilbert Freitag, M. I. Kinder, and B. D. Rubenstein for their assistance in carrying out Study 1. Finally, we acknowledge the cooperation of the Staff at the Children's Unit, Department of Child Psychiatry, Neuropsychiatric Institute, U.C.L.A. The substance of these studies was presented in a paper to the American Psychological Association, September, 1964, Los Angeles.

vious; a parent will punish his child to suppress specific behaviors, and his child will learn to behave so as to escape or avoid punishment. The third aspect of the use of pain is more subtle, but more typical. In this case, a parent "rescues" his child from discomfort. In reinforcement, theory terms, the parent becomes discriminative for the reduction or removal of negative reinforcers or noxious stimuli. During the first year of life many of the interactions a parent has with his children may be of this nature. An infant will fuss, cry, and give signs indicative of pain or distress many times during the day, whereupon most parents will pick him up and attempt to remove the discomfort. Such situations must contribute a basis for subsequent meaningful relationships between people; individuals are seen as important to each other if they have faced and worked through a stressful experience together. It may well be that much of a child's love for his parents develops in situations which pair parents with stress reductions. Later in life, the normal child does turn to his parent when he is frightened or hurt by nightmares, by threat of punishment from his peers, by fears of failure in school, and so on.

In view of these considerations, it was considered appropriate to investigate the usefulness of pain in modifying the behaviors of autistic children. Autistic children were selected for two reasons: (1) because they show no improvement with conventional psychiatric treatment; and (2) because they are largely unresponsive to everyday interpersonal events.

In the present study, pain was induced by means of an electrified grid on the floor upon which the children stood. The shock was turned on immediately following pathological behaviors. It was turned off or withheld when the children came to the adults who were present. Thus, these adults "saved" the children from a dangerous situation, they were the only "safe" objects in a painful environment.

## STUDY 1

The objectives of Study 1 were (1) to train the children to avoid electric shock by coming to E when so requested; (2) to follow the onset of self-stimulatory and tantrum behaviors by electric shock so as to decrease their frequency; and (3) to pair the word "no" with electric shock and test its acquisition of behavior-suppressing properties.

### METHOD

Subjects. The studies were carried out on two identical twins. They were five-years old when the study was initiated and were diagnosed as schizophrenics. They evidenced no social responsiveness; they did not respond in any manner to speech, nor did they speak; they did not recognize each other or recognize adults even after isolation from people; they were not toilet trained; their handling of physical objects (toys, etc.) was inappropriate and stereotyped, being restricted to "fiddling" and spinning. They were greatly involved in self-stimulatory behavior, spending 70 to 80 per cent of their day rocking, fondling themselves, and moving hands and arms in repetitive, stereotyped manners. They engaged in a fair amount of tantrum behaviors, such as screaming, throwing objects, and hitting themselves.

It is important to note, in view of the moral and ethical reasons which might preclude the use of electric shock, that their future was certain institutionalization. They had been intensively treated in a residential setting by conventional psychiatric techniques for one year prior to the present study without any observable modification in their behaviors. This failure in treatment is consistent with reports of other similar efforts with such children (Eisenberg, 1957; Brown, 1960), which have suggested that if a schizophrenic child does not have language and does not play appropriately with physical objects by the age of three to five, then he will not improve, despite traditional psychiatric treatment, including psychotherapy, of the child and/or his family.

Apparatus. The research was conducted in a 12 × 12-foot experimental room with an adjoining observation room connected by one-way mirrors and sound equipment. The floor of the experimental room was covered by one-half inch wide metal tapes with adhesive backing (Scotch Tape). They were laid one-half inch apart so that when the child stepped on the floor he would be in contact with at least two strips, thereby closing the circuit and receiving an electric shock. A six-volt battery was wired to the strips of tape via a Harvard Inductorium. The shock was set at a level at which each of three Es standing barefoot on the floor agreed that it was definitely painful and frightening.

The Ss' behavior and the experimental events were recorded on an Esterline Angus pen recorder by procedures more fully described in an earlier paper (Lovaas et al., 1965). The observer could reliably record both frequency and duration of several behaviors simultaneously on a panel of pushbuttons. A given observer recorded at randomly selected periods.

Pre-shock Sessions. The Ss were placed barefoot in the experimental room with two Es, but were not shocked. There were two such pre-experimental sessions, each lasting for about 20 minutes. The Es would invite the Ss to "come here" about five times a minute, giving a total of approximately 100 trials per session. The observers recorded the amount of physical contact (defined as S's touching E with his hands), self-stimulatory and tantrum behavior, the verbal command "come here," and positive responses to the command (coming to within one foot of E within five seconds).

First Shock Sessions. The two pre-experimental sessions were followed by three shock sessions distributed over three consecutive days during which Ss were trained, in an escape-avoidance paradigm, to avoid shock by responding to E's verbal command according to the pre-established criterion. In the escape phase of the training, consisting of fifty trials, the two Es faced each other, about three feet apart, with S standing (held, if necessary) between them so that he faced one of the Es, who would lean forward, stretch his arms out, and say "come here." At the same time shock was turned on and remained on until S moved in the direction of this E, or, if S had not moved within three seconds, until the second E pushed S in the direction of the inviting E. Either type of movement of S toward the inviting E immediately terminated the shock. The S had to walk alternately from one E to the other.

In the avoidance sessions which followed, shock was withheld provided S approached E within five seconds. If S did not start his approach to the inviting E within five seconds, or if he was not within one foot of E within seven seconds, the shock was turned on and the escape procedure was reinstated for that trial.

During these avoidance sessions Es gradually increased their distance from each other until they were standing at opposite sides of the room. At the same time they gradually decreased the number of cues signaling S to approach them. In the final trials, Es merely emitted the command "come here," without turning toward or otherwise signaling S.

Shock was also turned on if S at any time engaged in self-stimulatory and/or tantrum behaviors. Whenever possible, shock was administered at the onset of such behaviors. Shock was never given except on the feet; no shock was given if S touched the floor with other parts of his body. In order to keep S on his feet, shock was given for any behavior which might have enabled him to avoid shock, such as beginning to sit down, moving toward the window to climb on its ledge, etc.

Extinction Sessions. The three shock sessions were distributed over a ten-month period. These sessions were the same as those in the previous sessions, except that shock and the command "no" were never delivered during this period.

The Second Shock Sessions. Three additional sessions terminated Study 1. In the first of these, S was brought into the experimental room and given a two-second shock not contingent upon any behavior of S or E. This was the only shock given. In all other respects these final sessions were similar to the preceding extinction sessions.

Procedure for Establishing and Testing "No" as a Secondary Negative Reinforcer. During the first shock sessions, shock had been delivered contingent upon self-stimulatory and/or tantrum behaviors. Simultaneous with the onset of shock Es would say "no," thereby pairing the word "no" and shock. The test for any suppressing power which the word "no" had acquired during these pairings was carried out in the following manner. Prior to the shock sessions, Ss were trained to press a lever (wired to a cumulative recorder) for M & M candy on a fixed ratio 20 schedule. The sessions lasted for ten minutes daily. A stable rate of lever-pressing was achieved by the twelfth session, at which Es tested the word "no" for suppressing effects on the lever-pressing rate. The E delivered the "no" contingent upon lever-pressing toward the middle of each session, during three sessions *prior* to the shock sessions, and during three sessions *subsequent* to the shock sessions, i.e., after "no" had been paired with shock.

## RESULTS AND DISCUSSION

Figure 1 gives the proportion of time Ss responded to Es' commands (proportion of Rs to $S^D$s). As can be seen, in the two pre-shock sessions Ss did not respond to Es' commands. During the first three shock sessions (Shock I), Ss learned to respond to Es' requests within the prescribed time interval and thus avoided shock. This changed responsiveness of Ss to Es' requests was maintained for the subsequent

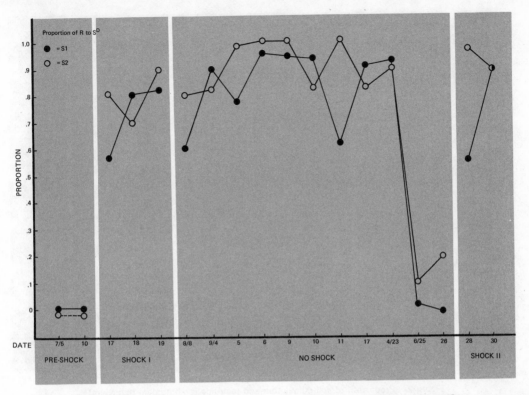

**Figure 1.** Proportion of time Ss responded to E's commands—proportion of Rs to $S^D$s.

nine months (no shock sessions). There was a relatively sudden decrease in Ss' responsiveness after nine months, i.e., the social behavior of coming to E extinguished. One non-contingent shock, however, immediately reinstated the social responsiveness (Shock II), suggesting that Ss responded to it as a discriminative stimulus for social behavior.

The data on Ss' pathological behaviors (self-stimulation and tantrums) and other social behaviors (physical contacts) are presented in Figure 2. Prior to shock pathological behaviors occurred 65-85 per cent of the time; physical contacts were absent. Shock I suppressed the pathological behaviors immediately, and they remained suppressed during the following eleven months. In addition, social behaviors replaced the pathological behaviors. This

change was very durable (ten to eleven months), but did eventually extinguish. One non-contingent shock reinstated the social responsiveness and suppressed the pathological behaviors.

The data on the acquisition of "no" as a negative reinforcer are presented in Figure 3. The records of bar-pressing for candy are presented as cumulative curves. The word "no" was presented contingent upon a bar-pressing response three sessions before and three sessions subsequent to shock, i.e., before and after the pairing of "no" with shock. The cumulative curves of the session immediately preceding and the session following shock to S1 is presented. The curves for the other sessions, both for S1 and S2, show the same effects. It is apparent upon inspection of Figure 3 that the word "no" had no effect upon S1's performance prior to

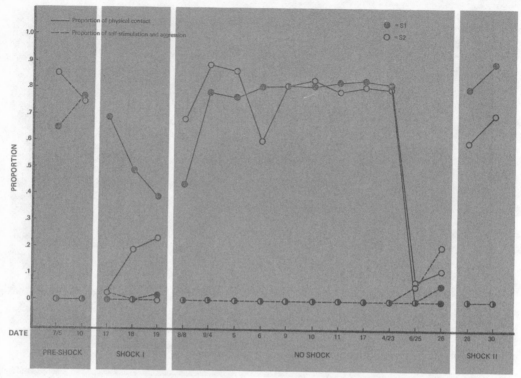

**Figure 2.**  Proportion of self-stimulation and tantrums (pathological behaviors)
and physical contact (social behavior).

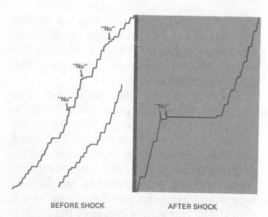

**Figure 3.**  Lever-pressing for candy as cumulative response curves: effect of "no" on
lever-pressings by S1 before and after "no" was
paired with shock.

its pairing with shock, but that after such
pairing it suppressed the bar-pressing
response.

Observations of Ss' behaviors in the experimental room indicated that the shock
training had a generalized effect; it altered
several behaviors which were not recorded.
Some of these changes took place within
minutes after the Ss had been introduced to
shock. In particular, they seemed more
alert, affectionate, and seeking of E's company. And surprisingly, during successful
shock avoidance they appeared happy.
These alterations in behavior were only
partially generalized to the environment
outside the experimental room. The changes
in behaviors outside were most noticeable
during the first fourteen days of the shock
training, after which Ss apparently discriminated between situations in which
they would be shocked and those in which
they would not. According to their nurse's
notes, certain behaviors, such as Ss' responsiveness to "come here" and "no" were

maintained for several months, while others, such as physical contact, soon extinguished.

These observations formed the basis for the subsequent two studies. In Study 2 a more objective assessment of the changes in Ss' affectionate behavior toward adults was made, and a technique for extending these effects from the experimental room to the ward was explored. In Study 3 a test was made of any reinforcing power adults might have acquired as a function of their association with the termination of shock.

## STUDY 2

Study 2 involved two observations. One attempted to assess changes in S's affectionate behavior to E who invited them to kiss and hug him. The other observation was conducted by nurses who rated Ss on behavior change in seven areas (given below). Both observations incorporated measures of transfer of behavior changes to new situations brought about by the use of the remote control shock apparatus. Both observations were conducted immediately following the completion of Study 1.

The "Kiss and Hug" Observations. These observations consisted of six daily sessions. Three of the sessions (3, 5, and 6) are referred to as shock-relevant sessions. Sessions 3 and 5 were conducted in the experimental room where Ss had received shock during avoidance training. Three sessions (1, 2, and 4) are labeled control sessions. They took place in a room sufficiently different from the experimental room to minimize generalization of the shock effect. The last shock-relevant session (session 6) was conducted to test the changes produced by remotely controlled shock. This session was conducted in the same room as the previous control sessions. However, immediately preceding the session Ss received five shock-escape trials, similar to those of Study 1. The shock was delivered from a LeeLectronic Trainer.[1] The S wore the

[1]Lee Supply Co., Tucson, Arizona.

eight-ounce receiver (about the size of a cigarette pack) strapped on his back with a belt. Shock was delivered at "medium" level over two electrodes strapped to S's buttock.

In order to minimize the effects of a particular observer's recording bias, two observers alternated in recording S's behavior. Each observer recorded at least one shock session. The sessions lasted for six minutes each. Every five seconds E would face S, hold him by the waist with outstretched arms, bow his head toward S, and state "hug me" or "kiss me." The E would alternate his requests ("hug me," "kiss me") every minute. The observer recorded (1) embrace (S placing his arms around E's neck), (2) hug and kiss (S hugging E cheek to cheek or kissing him on the mouth), (3) active physical withdrawal by S from E when held by the waist, and (4) E's requests.

## RESULTS

Since Ss' behaviors on the test were virtually identical, their behaviors were averaged. The data are presented in Figure 4. During the control sessions (sessions 1, 2, and 4) the proportion of time that Ss embraced, or hugged and kissed E was extremely low. Rather, they withdrew from him. During the shock-relevant sessions (sessions 3, 5, and 6) Ss' behavior changed markedly toward increased affection. In a situation where they had received shock-avoidance training they responded with affection to E and did not withdraw from him. The fact that this affectionate behavior maintained itself in session 6 demonstrates that the remotely controlled shock can produce transfer of behavior change to a wide variety of situations.

Nurses' Ratings. The nurses' ratings were initiated at the completion of the "kiss and hug" sessions. Four nurses who were familiar with Ss but unfamiliar with the experiment, and did not know that shock

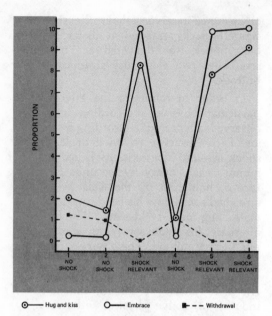

○─── Hug and kiss     ○─── Embrace     ■--- Withdrawal

**Figure 4.** Social reactions of Ss as a function of shock presentations. The "no shock" sessions (1,2,4) were run in a room where Ss had not been shocked. ["Shock" sessions (3, 5) were conducted in a room in which Ss had received shock-avoidance training. The last "shock" session (6) was conducted in the same room as the "no shock" sessions, but Ss had received remote controlled shock.]

had been used, were asked to complete a rating scale pertaining to seven behaviors: (1) dependency on adults, (2) responsiveness to adults, (3) affection seeking, (4) pathological behaviors, (5) happiness and contentment, (6) anxiety and fear, and (7) overall clinical improvement. The scale was comprised of nine points, with the midpoint indicating no change. The nurses were asked to indicate whether they considered S to have changed (increased or decreased) in any of these behaviors as compared to S's behaviors the preceding day or morning. The ratings were obtained under two conditions: (1) an experimental condition in which S, wearing the remote control unit on his belt underneath his clothing, was introduced to the nurses who "casually" interacted with him for ten minutes. S was not shocked while with the nurses, but

he had been given a one-second, non-contingent shock immediately prior to his interaction with the nurses; (2) a control condition, which was run in the same manner as the experimental condition, except that S had no shock prior to the ratings.

The nurses rated changes in Ss under both conditions. They were not counterbalanced. The ratings from the control conditions were subtracted from the ratings based on the experimental conditions. The difference shows an increase in the ratings of all behaviors following the shock treatment, except for pathological behaviors and happiness-contentment, which both decreased. Only the ratings on dependency and affection seeking behaviors increased more than one point.

## STUDY 3

Study 3 showed the degree to which the association of an adult with shock reduction (contingent upon an approach response of the children) would establish the adult as a positive secondary reinforcer for the children. Increased resistance to extinction of a lever-pressing response producing the sight of the adult was used to measure the acquired reinforcing power of the adult.

The study was conducted in two parts. The first part constituted a "pretraining" phase. During this period the children were trained to press a lever to receive M & Ms and simultaneously see E's face. Once this response was acquired, extinction of the response was begun by removing the candy reinforcement, S being exposed only to E's face. The second part of the study constituted a test of the reinforcing power E had acquired as a result of having been associated with shock reduction. This association occurred when, immediately preceding several of the extinction sessions of the lever-press, Ss were trained to come to E to escape shock. The change in rate of responding to obtain a view of E during these sessions was used as a measure of E's acquired reinforcing power.

## METHOD

Study 3 was initiated after the completion of Study 2. It was conducted in an enclosed cubicle, four feet square, in which $E$ and $S$ sat separated by a removable screen. A lever protruded from a box at $S$'s side. Lever-pressings were recorded on a cumulative recorder. An observer (O) looking through a one-way screen recorded the following behaviors of $S$ as they occurred: (1) vocalizations (any sound emitted by $S$), and (2) standing on the chair or ledge in the booth. The latter measures were taken in a manner similar to that described in Study 1. These additional measures were obtained in an attempt to check on the possibility that an eventual increase in lever-pressing for $E$ might be due to a conceivable "energizing" effect of shock, rather than to the secondary reinforcing power associated with shock reduction. This rationale will be discussed more fully below.

The first ten were labeled *pre-training* sessions. In each, a fifteen-minute acquisition preceded a twenty minute extinction of the lever-pressing response. During acquisition $S$ received a small piece of candy and a five-second exposure to $E$ (the screen was removed momentarily, placing $E$'s face within $S$'s view) on a fixed ratio 10 schedule. During extinction, $S$ received only the five-second exposure to $E$ on the same schedule as before. Both $S$s reached a stable rate of about 500 responses during the first acquisition session.

The ten pre-training sessions were followed for $S1$ by nine *experimental* sessions. In these experimental sessions $S$ never received candy. The sessions consisted only of a twenty-minute extinction period. An $S$'s performance during the last extinction session of pre-training, labeled Session 1 in Figure 5, served as a measure of the pre-experimental rate of lever-pressing. Electric shock was administered before the 2nd, 7th, and 9th experimental sessions, as follows: $S$ was placed facing $E$ in the room outside the cubicle. Shock was administered for two to four seconds, at which point $E$ would tell $S$ to "come here." $S$ would invariably approach $E$ and shock would be terminated. The $E$ would then comfort $S$ (fondle and stroke him) for one minute. This procedure was repeated four times. Immediately following this procedure, $S$ was placed within his cubicle. $E$ would repeat $S$'s name every five seconds. On the fixed ratio 10 schedule, the screen would open and $E$ would praise $S$ ("good boy") and stroke him.

The experimental treatment of $S2$ was identical to that of $S1$ with the following exceptions: (1) $S2$ received only seven experimental sessions; (2) shock preceded session 2, 6, and 8; (3) $E$ did not call $S2$'s name while he was in the cubicle; and (4) $E$ was only visually exposed to $S2$ ($E$ did not stroke or praise $S2$).

## RESULTS AND DISCUSSION

The $S$s' lever-pressing behavior is presented in Figure 5 as cumulative curves. The last extinction curve from the pre-training is labeled one. This curve gives the rate of lever-pressing in the last extinction session preceding $E$'s association with shock reduction. The upward moving hatchmarks on the curves show the occasions on which $E$ was visually presented to $S$. The heavy vertical lines labeled shock, show shock-escape training preceding sessions 2, 7, and 9 for $S1$, and sessions 2, 6, and 8 for $S2$.

There was a substantial increase in rate of lever-pressing accompanying shock-escape training for both $S$s. The curves also show the extinction of this response. The extinction is apparent in the falling rate between shock sessions (e.g., sessions 2 through 6 for $S1$ show a gradual decrease in rate of responding). A similar extinction is also manifested over the various shock sessions, i.e., the highest rate was observed after the first shock training, the next highest after the second shock training, and so on. The $S$s' performances were very systematic and orderly.

Data based on the two additional meas-

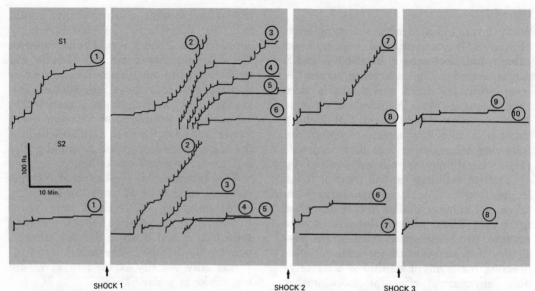

**Figure 5.** The Ss' lever-pressing behavior for E as function of E's association with shock reduction. [Curve labelled "1" is the last extinction curve from the pretraining. Shock preceded sessions 2, 7 and 9 for S1, and sessions 2, 6, and 8 for S2. The upward moving hatchmarks on the curves indicate occasions at which E was visually presented to S].

ures, vocalization and standing on the chair or ledge, are presented in Table 1. The entries in the column labeled O1 can be compared to those in column O2. These data indicate that there was a high degree of agreement between the two observers rating amount of vocalizations of Ss. The O2's ratings were based on tape recordings taken from Ss while in the booth. It was physically impossible to have a second O assess the reliability of O1's ratings of

climbing. However, because of the ease of recording such behavior it was judged unnecessary to check on its reliability. The agreement between Os on vocalizations was judged adequate for the purposes of this study.

If the increase in lever-pressing behavior was correlated with an increase in the two additional behaviors, then it might not be that shock-escape training had led to an increase in behavior toward people *per se*.

**Table 1**
Per Cent of Total Time Engaged in Vocalization and Climbing

| | | S1 | | | S2 | | |
|---|---|---|---|---|---|---|---|
| | | Vocal. | | Climb. | Vocal. | | Climb. |
| Session | Shock | 01 | 02 | 01 | 01 | 02 | 01 |
| 1 | | 49 | | 0 | 27 | | 96 |
| 2 | S1 and S2 | 19 | 19 | 0 | 27 | | 0 |
| 3 | | 47 | | 0 | 20 | | 20 |
| 4 | | 25 | | 32 | 23 | | 0 |
| 5 | | 18 | | 65 | 26 | 29 | 0 |
| 6 | S2 | 22 | 23 | 97 | 22 | | 0 |
| 7 | S1 | 22 | 23 | 33 | 23 | 23 | 0 |
| 8 | S2 | 22 | | 83 | 22 | | 0 |
| 9 | S1 | 11 | | 0 | | | |
| 10 | | 13 | | 75 | | | |

Rather, it might have led to an "arousal" of many behaviors, asocial as well as social. As Table 1 shows, the two additional measures showed no systematic relationship to the shock-escape sessions for S2. In the case of S1 there is some possibility of *suppression* of vocalization and climbing subsequent to shock-escape sessions (sessions 2, 7, and 9). It is unlikely, then, that shock-escape training involving other people can be viewed simply as activating many behaviors; rather, such training selectively raised behavior which yielded a social consequence.

Thus it is concluded that this increase in behavior toward E subsequent to shock-escape training came about because E was paired with shock reduction, thereby acquiring reinforcing powers. This conceptualization is consistent with the findings of Studies 1 and 2, both of which demonstrated an increase in social and affectionate behaviors. The findings are similar to those reported by Risley (1964) who observed an increase in acceptable social behavior (eye-to-eye contact) in an autistic child to whom E had administered electric shock for suppression of behaviors dangerous to the child. The data are also consistent with the results of studies by Mowrer and Aiken (1954) and Smith and Buchanen (1954) on animals which demonstrated that stimuli which are discriminative for shock reduction take on secondary positive reinforcing properties. It is to be noted, however, that the data from the studies reported here also fit a number of other conceptual frameworks.

An apparent limitation in these data pertains to the highly situational and often short-lived nature of the effects of shock. This had definite drawbacks when one considers the therapeutic implications of shock. It is considered, however, that the effects of shock can be made much more durable and general by making the situation in which shock is delivered less discriminable from situations in which it is not. The purpose of the present studies was to explore certain aspects of shock for possible therapeutic use. Therefore, only the minimal amount of shock considered necessary for observing reliable behavior changes was employed. It is quite possible that the children's responsiveness to adults would have been drastically reduced if shock had been employed too frequently. It is worth making the point explicitly: a certain use of shock can, as in these studies, contribute toward beneficial, even therapeutic, effects; but it does not at all follow that a more widespread use of the same techniques in each case will lead to even better outcomes. Indeed, the reverse may be true. Recent studies with schizophrenic children in our laboratory have shown, tentatively, that non-contingent shock facilitates performance of a well-learned task; however, such shock interferes with learning during early stages of the acquisition of new behaviors.

Certain more generalized effects of shock training, even though not recorded objectively, were noticed by Es and ward staff. First of all, Ss had to be trained (shaped) to come to E to escape shock. When shock was first presented to S2, for example, he remained immobile, even though adults were in the immediate vicinity (there was no way in which Ss could have "known" that Es presented the shock). This immobility when hurt is consistent with observations of Ss when they were hurt in the play-yard, e.g., by another child. But after Ss had been trained to avoid shock successfully in the experimental room, their nurses' notes state that Ss would come to the nurses when hurt in other settings.

Es had expected considerable expression of fear by Ss when they were shocked. Such fearful behavior was present only in the beginning of training. On the other hand, once Ss had been trained to avoid shock, they often smiled and laughed, and gave other signs of happiness or comfort. For example, they would "mold" or "cup" to E's body as small infants do with parents.

Such behaviors were unobserved prior to these experiments. Perhaps avoidance of pain generated contentment.

In their day-to-day living, extremely regressed schizophrenic children such as these Ss rarely show signs of fear or anxiety. The staff who dealt with these children in their usual environments expressed concern about the children's lack of worry or anxiety. There are probably several reasons why children such as these fail to demonstrate anxiety. It is possible that their social and emotional development has been so curtailed and limited that they are unaffected by the fear-eliciting situations acting upon a normal child. For example, they do not appear to be afraid of intellectual or social inadequacies, nor are they known to experience nightmares. Furthermore, by the age of three or four, like normal children, these children appear less bothered by physiological stimuli, and unlike the small infant, are rather free of physiological discomforts. Finally, when these children are brought to treatment, for example in a residential setting, there is much effort made to make their existence maximally comfortable.

If it is the case, as most writers on psychological treatment have stated, that the person's experience of discomfort is a basic condition for improvement, then perhaps the failure of severely retarded schizophrenic children to improve in treatment can be attributed partly to their failure to fulfill this hypothesized basic condition of anxiety or fear. This was one of the considerations which formed the basis for the present studies on electric shock. It is important to note that the choice of electric shock was made after several alternatives for the inducement of pain or fear were tested and found wanting. For example, in the early work with these children we employed loud noise. Even at noise levels well above 100 decibels we found that the children remained unperturbed particularly after the first two or three presentations.

It seems likely that the most therapeutic use of shock will not lie primarily in the suppression of specific responses or the shaping of behavior through escape-avoidance training. Rather, it would seem more efficient to use shock reduction as a way of establishing social reinforcers, i.e., as a way of making adults meaningful in the sense of becoming rewarding to the child. The failure of autistic children to acquire social reinforcers has been hypothesized as basic to their inadequate behavioral development (Ferster, 1961). Once social stimuli acquire reinforcing properties, one of the basic conditions for the acquisition of social behaviors has been met. A more complete argument supporting this thesis has been presented elsewhere (Lovaas et al., 1964). A basic question, then, is whether it is necessary to employ shock in accomplishing such an end or whether less drastic methods might not suffice. In a previous study (Lovaas et al., 1964) autistic children did acquire social reinforcers on the basis of food delivery. However, the necessary conditions for the acquisition of social reinforcers by the use of food were both time-consuming and laborious, and by no means as simple as the conditions which were necessary when we employed shock reduction.

## REFERENCES

Bijou, S. W., and Baer, D. M. 1961. *Child development: A systematic and empirical theory.* New York: Appleton-Century-Crofts.

Brown, Janet L. 1960. Prognosis from presenting symptoms of preschool children with atypical development. *American Journal of Orthopsychiatry* 30:382–390.

Eisenberg, L. 1957. The course of childhood schizophrenia. *American Medical Association Archives for Neurology and Psychiatry* 78:69–83.

Ferster, C. B. 1961. Positive reinforcement and behavioral deficits of autistic children. *Child Development* 32:437–456.

Lovaas, O. I.; Freitag, G.; Gold, V. J.; and Kassorla, I. C. 1965. A recording method and observations of behaviors of normal and autistic children in free play settings. *Journal of Experimental Child Psychology* 2:108–120.

Lovaas, O. I.; Freitag, G.; Kinder, M. I.; Rubenstein, D. B.; Schaeffer, B.; and Simmons, J. Q. 1964. Experimental studies in childhood schizophrenia—Establishment of social reinforcers. Paper delivered at Western Psychological Association, Portland.

Mowrer, O. H., and Aiken, E. G. 1954. Contiguity vs. drive-reduction in conditioned fear: Temporal variations in conditioned and unconditioned stimulus. *American Journal of Psychology* 67:26–38.

Risley, Todd. 1964. The effects and "side effects" of the use of punishment with an autistic child. Unpublished manuscript, Florida State University.

Smith, M. P., and Buchanen, G. 1954. Acquisition of secondary reward by cues associated with shock reduction. *Journal of Experimental Psychology* 48:123–126.

Solomon, R. L. 1964. Punishment. *American Psychologist* 19:239–253.

# READING 8

# The Psychological Effects of Insufficient Rewards

**LEON FESTINGER**
**Stanford University**

Festinger has applied a theory developed for humans (see the foregoing selection by Boring) to animal behavior. His views stress the principle of consistency in cognition. When an organism receives a reward which is inconsistent with its expectations, an extra preference for the reward is developed to maintain consistency. He suggests that the partial reward effect is a direct consequence of the process of dissonance reduction.

**QUESTIONS**
1. Do you agree with Festinger's explanation of the partial reinforcement effect?
2. Festinger states that the "major operational variable which will affect resistance to extinction is the total number of non-rewarded trials rather than the ratio of non-reward." Discuss this statement.
3. What is the effect of reward on learning and thinking; is reward the most important variable?

Some fields of Psychology have for many years been dominated by ideas concerning the importance of rewards in the establishment maintenance of behavior patterns. So dominant has this notion become, that some of our most ingenious theoretical thinking has been devoted to imagining the existence of rewards in order to explain behavior in situations where, plausibly, no rewards exist. It has been observed, for example, that under some circumstances an organism will persist in voluntarily engaging in behavior which is frustrating or painful. To account for such behavior it has, on occasion, been seriously proposed that the cessation of the frustration or pain is rewarding and thus reinforces the tendency to engage in the behavior.

I want to maintain that this type of explanation is not only unnecessary but also misleading. I certainly do *not* wish to say that rewards are unimportant, but I propose to show that the absence of reward or the existence of inadequate reward produces certain specific consequences which can account for a variety of phenomena which are difficult to deal with if we use our usual conceptions of the role of reward.

Before I proceed, I would like to say that most of the thinking and most of the experimental work which I will present are the result of collaboration between Douglas H. Lawrence and myself. Indeed, whatever you find interesting in what I say you may safely attribute primarily to him.

I will start my discussion in a rather roundabout manner with some remarks which concern themselves primarily with some aspects of the thinking processes of human beings. Human thinking is sometimes a strange mixture of "plausible" and "magical" processes. Let us examine more closely what I mean by this. For example, imagine that a person knows that some event is going to occur, and that the person can do something to prepare himself to cope more adequately with the impending event. Under such circumstances it is very reasonable (perhaps you might even want to use the word "rational") for the person to do whatever is necessary in preparation for the coming event. Human thinking, however, also works in reverse. Consider a person who goes to a lot of trouble to prepare himself for a future event which might possibly occur. Such a person will subsequently tend to persuade himself that the event is rather likely to occur. There is nothing very plausible or rational about this kind of mental process—rather, it has almost a magical quality about it. Let me illustrate this briefly by describing an experiment recently conducted by Ruby Yaryan.[1]

Under the pretext of investigating the manner in which students study for examinations, she asked subjects to study a list of arbitrary definitions of symbols in preparation for a possible test. Two conditions were experimentally created for the subjects. Half of the subjects were told that, if they actually took the test, this list of definitions of the symbols would be in their possession during the test, and so, all that was necessary in preparation was to familiarize themselves with the list. This was, essentially, an "easy preparation" condition. That is, not much effort was required of the subjects in advance preparation for the test.

The other half of the subjects were told that, if they actually took the test, they would *not* have the list of definitions with them and so it was necessary for them to memorize the symbols and their definitions in preparation for the test. It is clear that this constitutes a much more "effortful preparation" condition. Considerable effort was required of these subjects in advance preparation for the possible test.

It was carefully explained to each subject that not everyone would actually have to take the test. Specifically, they were told that only half of the people in the experiment *would* take the test. It was also carefully explained that the selection of who would, and who would not, have to take the test had already been made in consultation with their teachers (the subjects were all high school girls). Nothing that happened during the experiment would affect whether or not they took the test—this had already been decided in advance for each of them.

After they finished studying the list of definitions, they were asked a number of questions to preserve the fiction that the experiment was concerned with study habits. Each subject was also asked to indicate how likely she thought it was that she, personally, would have to actually take the test. The results show, quite clearly, that subjects in the effortful preparation condition, on the average, thought it was more likely that they would have to take the test than did subjects in the easy preparation condition. In other words, those who were experimentally induced to engage in a lot of preparatory effort, persuaded

---

[1] Yaryan, R. B., & Festinger, L. The effect of preparatory action on belief in the occurrence of possible future events. Unpublished paper.

themselves that the thing they were preparing for would actually occur.

The relevance of this experiment to the problem of the effects of inadequate rewards will become clearer in the following example which illustrates the same psychological process. Consider some person who is strongly attached to some goal. It is quite reasonable for this person to be willing to expend more effort, or to endure more pain, in order to reach the goal than he would be if he were less attracted. Once more, however, one finds the same process of reasoning in reverse. That is, if a person exerts a great deal of effort, or endures pain, in order to reach some ordinary objective, there is a strong tendency for him to persuade himself that the objective is especially desirable. An experiment conducted by Elliot Aronson and Judson Mills (1959) shows the effect quite nicely.

The subjects in the experiment by Aronson and Mills were college girls who volunteered to join small discussion groups. Each subject, when she appeared for the discussion group, was told that, instead of being put into a new group, she was being considered for inclusion in an ongoing group which had recently lost one of its members. However, the subject was told, because of the group's concern that the replacement be someone who would be able to discuss things freely and openly, the experimenter had agreed to test the replacement before admitting her to the group. Some subjects were then given a very brief and not painful test while others were given a rather extended and embarrassing test. The experimenter then, of course told each subject that she had done well and was admitted to the group. Thus, there were some subjects who had attained membership in the group easily and some subjects who had endured a painful experience in order to be admitted to the group.

The experimenter then explained to the subject that the discussion was carried on by means of an intercommunication sys-

tem, each girl being in a separate room. She was brought into her room which contained a microphone and earphones. The experimenter told her that the others had already started and perhaps it would be best for her not to participate in the discussion this time but just to listen. Next meeting, of course, she would participate fully. Speaking into the microphone the experimenter then went through the illusion of introducing her to the three other girls in the group. He then "disconnected" the microphone and gave the subject the earphones to wear. The subject then listened for about 25 minutes to a tape recording of a rather dull and halting discussion. All subjects, of course, heard exactly the same tape recording thinking they were listening to the actual live group discussion.

When the discussion was finished, the experimenter explained to the subject that, after each meeting, each of the girls filled out a "post-meeting reaction form." She was then given a questionnaire to complete which asked a variety of questions concerning how interesting she had found the discussion to be, how much she liked the other members of the group, and other similar questions. The results show, as anticipated, that those subjects who had gone through a painful procedure in order to be admitted to the group thought the discussion was more interesting and liked the other group members better than did those who had gained admission to the group easily. In other words, we see the same process operating here as we noted in the previous experiment. If someone is somehow induced to endure embarrassment in order to achieve something, she then persuades herself that what she has achieved is valuable.

In both of the examples which I have discussed (and one could present many more examples of similar nature) a situation has been produced where the organism has two pieces of information (or cognitions) which do not fit together. In the first example, these two pieces of information were: (a)

I have worked hard in preparation for an event. (b) The event is not too likely to occur. In the second example, the two cognitions which did not fit together were: (a) I have endured pain to attain an objective. (b) The objective is not very attractive. This kind of "nonfitting" relationship between two pieces of information may be termed a dissonant relation (Festinger, 1957). The reason, of course, that dissonance exists between these cognitions is that, psychologically, the obverse of one follows from the other. Psychologically, if an objective *is* very attractive, it follows that one would be willing to endure pain to attain it; or if the objective is *not* attractive, it follows that one does *not* endure pain to attain it. This specification of why a given relation between cognitions is dissonant also provides the clues to predicting specifically how the organism will react to the existence of the dissonance. Assuming that the organism will attempt to reduce the dissonance between the cognitions, there are obviously two major classes of ways in which this can be done. He can attempt to persuade himself that the pain which he endured was not really painful or he can attempt to persuade himself that the objective *is* very attractive.

I will not spend any more time than this in general theoretical discussion of the theory of dissonance and the reduction of dissonance. I hope that this small amount of general theoretical discussion will be enough to give context to the specific analysis of the psychological effects of insufficient rewards.

Let us consider in more detail what is suggested by the example of the experiment by Aronson and Mills and by the theory of cognitive dissonance. In that experiment the dissonance which was created was reduced by enhancing the value of the goal. This suggests that organisms may come to like and value things for which they have worked very hard or for which they have suffered. Looking at it from another aspect,

one might say that they may come to value activities for which they have been inadequately rewarded. At first glance this may seem to contradict a widely accepted notion in Psychology, namely, that organisms learn to like things for which they *have* been rewarded. In a sense it is contradictory, but not in the sense that it denies the operation of this widely assumed process. It does, however, state that another process also operates which is rather of an opposite character.

Let us analyze the situation with which we are concerned somewhat more carefully and more precisely. We are concerned with the dissonance between two possible cognitions. One of these is a cognition the organism has concerning his behavior, namely, I have voluntarily done something which, all other things being equal, I would avoid doing. The other is a cognition about the environment or about the result of his action, namely, the reward that has been obtained is inadequate. As we mentioned before, this dissonance can be reduced if the organism can persuade himself that he really likes the behavior in which he engaged or if he enhances for himself the value of what he has obtained as a result of his actions.

There is, of course, another way to reduce the dissonance, namely, for the organism to change his behavior. That is, having done something which resulted in an inadequate reward the organism can refuse to perform the action again. This means of reducing the dissonance is undoubtedly the one most frequently employed by organisms. If the organism obtains information which is dissonant with his behavior, he usually modifies his behavior so that it fits better what he knows concerning his environment. Here, however, I am going to consider only situations in which this means of reducing dissonance is not available to the organism. That is, I will consider only situations in which the organism is somehow tricked or seduced into continuing to engage in the activity in spite of the dissonance which is introduced. Under these circumstances we would expect one of the two previously mentioned dissonance reduction mechanisms to be used.

If one thinks for a while about the possible behavioral consequences of such a psychological process as we have described, an explanation suggests itself for the well known finding that resistance to extinction is greater after partial reward than after complete reward.

Before I explain this more adequately, I would like to digress for a moment. Since much of the research on the effects of partial reward has been done on rats, and since the experiments that Lawrence and I have done are also on rats, the question will inevitably arise as to whether or not I really think that rats have cognitions and that rats reduce dissonance the way humans do.

First for the matter of cognitions in rats: All that is meant by cognition is knowledge or information. It seems to me that one can assume that an organism has cognitions or information if one can observe some behavioral difference under different stimulus conditions. If the organism changes his behavior when the environment changes, then obviously he uses information about the environment and, equally obviously, can be said to have cognitions.

Now for the question of whether or not rats reduce dissonance as humans do: Although Lawrence keeps telling me that rats are smarter than humans, I suspect that the rat is a rather stupid organism and does not reduce dissonance nearly as effectively as the human being does. I suspect that the mechanisms available to the rat for dissonance reduction are very limited and that the amount of dissonance which gets effectively reduced is relatively small. Still, I suspect that they *do* reduce dissonance. At any rate, if we find that the theory of dissonance can make valid predictions for rat

behavior, this will be evidence that they do, indeed, reduce dissonance.

Now to return to the matter of the increased resistance to extinction following partial reward. Let us examine what occurs, psychologically, during a series of trials on which the behavior of an organism is only occasionally rewarded. Imagine a hungry animal who dashes frantically down some runway and into some so-called "goal box" only to find that there is nothing there. The cognition that he has obtained nothing is dissonant with the cognition that he has expended effort to reach the goal box. If this state of affairs were continually repeated, as we all know, the animal would reduce the dissonance by refusing to go to the goal box, that is, he would change his behavior. But, in a partial reward situation, the animal is tricked into continuing to run to the goal box because an appreciable number of times that he goes there he does find food. But, on each nonrewarded trial dissonance is introduced when the animal finds the goal box empty. The assumed process of dissonance reduction would lead us to expect that, gradually, the animal develops some extra preference either for the activity or for the goal box itself. A comparable animal that was rewarded every time he ran to the goal box would not develop any such extra preference.

Consider the situation, then, when extinction trials begin. In addition to realizing that food is no longer present, the partially rewarded animal also has to overcome his extra preference before he stops going to the goal box. We would thus expect "extinction" to take longer for a partially rewarded animal than for an animal that was always rewarded. The magnitude of the difference should be far greater than just the slight effect which would exist if the 100% animal discovers more rapidly that the situation has changed.

If this explanation is correct, then the greater resistance to extinction following partial reward is a direct consequence of the process of dissonance reduction. This, of course, immediately suggests an extension of this line of reasoning to situations other than those involving partial reward. *Any* procedure which introduces dissonance during the training trials should similarly be expected to increase resistance to extinction since the same kind of dissonance reduction process should operate.

Let us, however, try to be precise about what kinds of procedures would introduce dissonance for an organism during training trials in an experiment. It is, fortunately, possible to define this operationally in a precise manner. Let us imagine that we test an organism in a single choice situation. In the case of a rat, for example, this might be simply an apparatus where, from the starting point the animal can turn either right or left. Let us further imagine that the organism we are testing is quite hungry and that, whichever alternative he chooses, he obtains food. We can, then, vary one at a time a variety of factors to discover what the organism will ordinarily avoid doing. One would, of course, find many such factors which would lead the organism not to choose the alternative with which that factor is associated. Dissonance will be created for the organism if he is somehow tricked into consistently engaging in an activity involving such a factor.

This may sound very involved so let me try to say it again, this time, a bit less abstractly. Imagine that we test rats in a simple left-right choice apparatus and, no matter whether the animal goes left or right, he obtains food. But, imagine that, if he goes left, the animal must swim through water to get to the food but, if he goes right, there is simply a short run down an alley to the food. Let us further imagine that, under such circumstances, the animal will consistently choose to go to the right, that is, he will avoid swimming through water. Armed with this knowledge concerning the behavior of the rat we can then assert the following: if one puts a rat in a situation where we somehow trick the rat into consistently swimming through water, dissonance will have been created.

Remembering what we have already said about the ways in which dissonance can be reduced in this kind of situation (provided that we are successful in tricking the organism into continuing to engage in the activity) we would then arrive at the following statement: any condition which the animal will avoid in the above mentioned test situation will increase resistance to extinction in a nonchoice situation.

Let us look at some of the data which exist which are relevant to this statement. We know that if a hungry rat is put in a situation where he has a choice between a goal box where he is rewarded 100% of the time and a goal box where he is rewarded only part of the time, he will fairly consistently go to the place where he is rewarded 100% of the time. And, of course, we also know that where no choice is involved, partial reward increases resistance to extinction. But there are other variables or conditions which should increase resistance to extinction in a similar manner if our theoretical analysis is correct.

Consider the question of delay of reinforcement. Once more, thinking of our hypothetical test situation, we can be reasonably certain that a rat, if faced with a choice where one alternative led to immediate reward while the other alternative involved an appreciable delay before the rat was allowed to continue to the goal box to obtain food, the rat would rather consistently choose the alternative that led to immediate reward. We should then expect that, in a nonchoice situation, delay of reward should lead to greater resistance to extinction. Existing data show that this is indeed correct. Appreciable delay of reward does lead to greater resistance to extinction. I will briefly review some of the data which exist on delay of reward to give you some idea of the effect which is obtained.

The usual experiment that has been done

on extinction following delay of reinforcement compares one condition in which the rats encounter no enforced delay between starting down a runway and obtaining food in the goal box with other conditions in which, on some trials, the rats are detained in a delay chamber before being allowed to proceed to the food. The usual period of delay which has been used has been about 30 seconds. Crum, Brown, and Bitterman (1951) and Scott and Wike (1956) both find that a group of rats delayed on half the trials shows much greater resistance to extinction than a group which was never delayed. In another experiment, Wike and McNemara (1957) ran three groups which differed in the percentage (and of course, number) of trials on which they were delayed. They find that the larger the percentage or number of trials on which the animal experiences delay, the greater is the resistance to extinction. The same kind of result is obtained by Fehrer (1956) who compared rats who were delayed for 20 seconds on *every* trial with ones who were never delayed. She also finds that delay results in increased resistance to extinction.

Before we proceed to other matters, I would like to briefly raise a question concerning one kind of explanation that has frequently, in one form or another, been offered to account for increased resistance to extinction after partial reward. The basis of this kind of explanation, whether it be in terms of expectancy, or conditioning of cues, or any of a number of other varieties, rests in pointing out that there is more similarity between acquisition and extinction for partial reward conditions than for 100% reward conditions. I would like to point out that this type of explanation is clearly not very useful in explaining the increased resistance to extinction after delay of reward. From the point of view of the explanation I am here proposing, however, partial reward and delay of reward clearly involve the same psychological processes.

Let us go on now to examine the matter of work and effort. I am sure it is fairly obvious to all of you now what I want to say about work and effort. If we return to a consideration of our hypothetical test situation we know that, given a choice between an effortless path to food and a path requiring expenditure of effort, the hungry animal will choose the effortless path rather regularly. Hence, in accordance with our analysis concerning dissonance and dissonance reduction, we would expect the requirement of greater effort during acquisition to lead to increased resistance to extinction.

It is surprising that, in spite of the relative consistency of results among the studies which exist in the literature, the effect of effort during acquisition on resistance to extinction has not been generally noted. People have rather tended to note the finding that the greater the effort required during extinction, the faster does extinction occur. But the data are also clear with respect to the effect of effort during acquisition. They show quite clearly that, holding effort during extinction constant, the more effort required during acquisition, the more resistance there is to extinction. The data from one of the more adequately controlled experiments will suffice to illustrate the effect.

Aiken (1957) reports an experiment in which the animal was required to press a panel in order to gain access to food. Some rats were required to exert little effort while others were required to exert considerable effort during training. Half of the animals in each condition were extinguished with the low effort requirement and half with the high effort requirement. Holding effort during extinction constant, the results show clearly that the average number of trials to a criterion of extinction was considerably greater for the high effort acquisition condition than for the low effort acquisition condition. Other experiments in the literature also show this same effect if one examines the data carefully. It should once more be pointed out that any explanation of this effect which depends upon a notion of similarity between acquisition and extinction conditions is clearly inadequate.

One could list many other specific conditions which, analyzed in the same way, would be expected to increase resistance to extinction. I have chosen the three preceding ones to discuss because reasonably good data concerning them exist in the literature. Now, however, I would like to return to a more thorough consideration of the partial reward situation.

| REWARD SCHEDULE | Number of Unrewarded Trials | | | |
|---|---|---|---|---|
| | 0 | 16 | 27 | 72 |
| 33% | | 24 | 43 | 108 |
| 50% | | 31 | 54 | 144 |
| 67% | | 48 | | 216 |
| 100% | 0 54 216 | | | |

**Figure 1.** Total number of trials after preliminary training in partial reward experiment.

I have stated that, on nonrewarded trials in a partial reward situation, dissonance is introduced into the animal's cognition when he realizes that there is no food available. The amount of dissonance can, of course, vary in magnitude. It is important for us to consider the operational variables which will affect the total magnitude of dissonance which is introduced in this manner. This total magnitude of dissonance, of course, will determine how much dissonance reduction occurs through the development of extra preferences (always assuming that the animal does not change his behavior) and hence will determine the resistance to extinction.

In the past, it has generally been assumed that the major operational variable affecting resistance to extinction is the ratio of reward. That is, the smaller the proportion of rewarded trials, the greater the resistance to extinction. However, one might reason that since dissonance is created for

the animal on every nonrewarded trial, it seems plausible to suppose that the major operational variable which will affect the resistance to extinction is, rather, the sheer total number of nonrewarded trials which the animal has experienced rather than the ratio of nonreward. From the data in published experiments it is impossible to assess whether or not this is correct since these two variables are completely confounded in the literature. Experiments on partial reward have always held constant either the number of rewarded trials or else the total number of trials that the animal experiences. It is clear, of course, that when either of these quantities is held constant, the number of nonrewarded trials is perfectly correlated with the ratio of nonreward and so the effects cannot be separated.

It is possible, perhaps, to get some hunch about this, however, from examining the results of experiments which have used rather few training trials. If we are correct, these experiments should show very weak effects of partial reward on resistance to extinction. Sheffield (1949), for example, using a total of 30 trials (only 15 nonrewarded trials) found very small differences between extinction after partial and complete reward. Wilson, Weiss, and Amsel (1955) and also Lewis (1956), replicating the Sheffield experiment almost exactly, also find such small differences that it requires an analysis of covariance to make them appear significant. However, Weinstock (1954), using a similar apparatus, but employing 75 training trials, finds huge and unmistakable differences.

It is unnecessary to belabor the matter by quoting many studies here since it is all a matter of hunch and impression. In general, when one goes through the literature one gets the impression that the experiments which show small effects after partial reward have tended to employ rather few trials. But comparison of this kind between different experiments done by different experimenters is a very shabby business at best since the variation from experimenter to experimenter can be quite large for unknown reasons. The question seemed important enough, however, so that Lawrence and I thought it worthwhile to do a study which could answer the question. The study was carried out through the kind efforts of John Theios. I would like to describe it to you briefly.

The general design of the study is very simple and does not differ in any essential way from the usual study which has been done on the effects of partial reward. The major difference was that we were primarily concerned with seeing the effects of the absolute number of nonrewarded trials and with being able to separate these effects from the effects of ratio of reward. We employed four different conditions of "number of unrewarded trials." Some groups experienced 0 unrewarded trials; some groups of animals experienced a total of 16 unrewarded trials in the apparatus; still other groups experienced a moderate number of unrewarded trials, namely, 27; and finally some groups were run who experienced very many unrewarded trials, namely, 72.

Within these conditions, by varying the total number of trials, different conditions of ratio of reward were set up. Some animals were run with 33% reward, others with 50% reward, and still others with 67% reward. Of course, it was not possible to vary the ratio of reward for animals in the condition of 0 unrewarded trials but the animals were run for varying numbers of trials anyhow. Figure 1 shows the total design. The numbers in the cells indicate the total number of trials after preliminary training which the animals in that condition ran. During preliminary training, of course, all groups were rewarded 100% of the time. There were between 11 and 16 animals in each condition. It will be noted that we did not run a condition of 67% reward and 27 unrewarded trials. The reason for this is simple. We ran out of

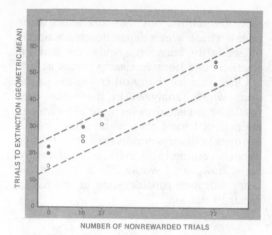

**Figure 2.** Number of trials to extinction after partial reward.

patience and decided this condition was not essential.

It will also be noted that three groups of 0 unrewarded trials were run so that the total number of trials brackets the entire range for the other groups.

Figure 2 shows the results of the experiment. Along the horizontal axis of the figure are indicated the various values of number of unrewarded trials which we employed and along the ordinate are the average number of trials to reach a criterion of extinction. Each circle on the figure represents the results for one of our experimental conditions. The empty circles represent the data for those with the fewest total number of trials. Thus, except for the 0 unrewarded trials conditions, these empty circles represent the data for the 33% reward conditions. Similarly, the dark circles represent the longest number of total trials and hence, for the partial reward groups, represent the 67% reward conditions.

It is clear from an examination of the figure that, holding constant the number of unrewarded trials, there were only slight differences among the different conditions of ratio of reward. On the other hand, the variable of total number of unrewarded trials has a large and significant effect. It would, indeed, seem that in these data the only variable affecting resistance to extinction after partial reward is the number of unrewarded trials. The results of the experiment are hence, quite consistent with the interpretations which we have made from the theory of dissonance.

These data are, of course, encouraging but certainly not conclusive. It would be nice to be able to have more direct evidence that nonreward tends to result in the development of extra preferences. From the point of view of obtaining such more direct evidence concerning the validity of our theoretical interpretation, the partial reward situation is not very adequate. For one thing, our theoretical analysis states that quite different processes occur, psychologically, on rewarded and on unrewarded trials. In a partial reward situation, however, the animal experiences both kinds of trials and, hence, an attempt to separate the effects of the two kinds of trials is bound to be indirect. And, of course, the possibility always exists that the increased resistance to extinction may depend upon some more or less complicated interaction between rewarded and unrewarded trials.

It would then be desirable to be able to compare pure conditions of reward and nonreward. That is, we could test the theory more adequately if we could compare the resistance to extinction of two groups of animals, one of which had always been rewarded in a given place, and the other of which had *never* been rewarded in that same place. This, of course, presents technical problems of how one manages to induce an animal to consistently go to a place where he never gets rewarded. This problem, however, can be solved by employing a variation of what is, essentially, a delay of reward experiment. With the very able assistance and hard work of Edward Uyeno we proceeded to do a series of such experiments in an attempt to get more direct validation of our theoretical derivations. I would like to describe

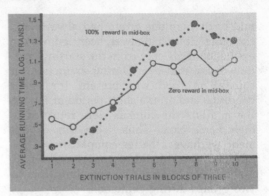

**Figure 3.** Running time during extinction in single mid-box experiment.

some of these experiments for you.

The apparatus we used was a runway with two boxes in addition to the starting box. The two boxes were, of course, quite easily distinguishable. We will refer to one of them as the end-box and to the other as the mid-box. From the starting place, the animal was to run through a section of alley to the mid-box and then through another section of alley to the end-box. One group of rats was fed on every trial in the mid-box and also fed on every trial in the end-box. We will refer to this group as the 100% reward condition. Another group of rats was never fed in the mid-box but, instead, was delayed there for the same amount of time that it took the other to eat its food. These animals then continued to the end-box where they were also fed on every trial. We will refer to this group as the 0% reward condition. The designations of 100% and 0% reward refer, of course, to the reward in the mid-box. Both groups were rewarded on every trial in the end-box and this, of course, is what induced the animals in the 0% reward condition to run consistently to a place where they were never rewarded.

The procedure which was employed in extinction was also somewhat different from the usual procedure in a delay of reward experiment. Because we were interested in comparing the two groups of animals in their willingness to go to the mid-box where one group had always, and the other group had never, been fed, we ran extinction trials only from the starting position to the mid-box. During extinction, of course, no food was present for either condition and after a short period of time in the mid-box the animals were returned to their home cage. Thus, from this experiment we have a better comparison of the effects of reward and of nonreward. Figure 3 shows the average running times for the two groups during extinction.

The figure shows the data for the first 30 extinction trials averaged in groups of 3 trials each. It is clear from the figure that there is a very marked difference between the two groups of animals. Those who were always fed in the mid-box start off running quite fast (reflecting their speed of running during acquisition) but slow down very rapidly. Those animals that were never fed in the mid-box start off more slowly (again reflecting their speed of running during acquisition) but they do not show as rapid a rate of extinction. Indeed, between the fourth and fifth blocks of trials the two curves cross over and thereafter the animals run considerably faster to a place where they have never been rewarded than they do to a place where they have always been rewarded.

One may certainly conclude from these data that increased resistance to extinction results from nonreward and that an explanation of the partial reward effect in terms of some interaction between reward and nonreward is not very tenable. Actually, in the experiment I have just described we ran a third group of animals which was rewarded 50% of the time in the mid-box and the results for these animals during extinction fall nicely midway between the two curves in Figure 3. The resistance to extinction of those who were never fed in the mid-box is greater than that of either of the other two groups of animals.

At the risk of being terribly repetitious, I would like to remind you at this point of the explanation I am offering for these data. Briefly, dissonance is introduced as a result of the insufficient reward or absence of reward. As long as the organism is prevented from changing his behavior, the dissonance tends to be reduced by developing some extra preference about something in the situation. The existence of this extra preference leads to the stronger inclination to continue running during extinction trials.

If this explanation is correct, however, one should be able to observe the effects of this extra preference even in a situation where all the motivation for food was removed. Indeed, it would seem that this would be a better test of this theoretical explanation. We consequently repeated the experiment I have just described to you with one modification. Three days were allowed to elapse between the end of acquisition and the beginning of extinction. During these 3 days food was always present in the cages so that by the time the extinction trials started the animals were quite well fed and not hungry. Food remained always available in their cages during the extinction period. In addition, during the 3 intervening days, each animal was placed for periods of time in the end-box without food being available there. In other words, there was an attempt to communicate to the animal that food was no longer available in the apparatus and anyhow the animals were not very motivated for food.

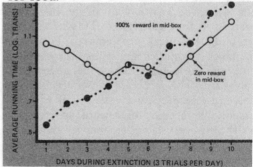

**Figure 4.** Running time while satiated during extinction in single mid-box experiment.

Extinction trials were, of course, run just from the starting box to the mid-box. Three trials were run each day and Figure 4 shows the results for the first 10 days of extinction. It is clear from an examination of the figure that the results are very similar to the previous results and are, in a sense, even stronger. Those animals who were always fed in the mid-box start off relatively fast and as extinction trials progress the curve shows steady and rather rapid increase in running time. In short, one obtains a familiar kind of extinction curve for these animals.

The group that was never fed in the mid-box, however, shows a very different pattern of behavior. They start off much more slowly than the other group but, for the first 4 days of extinction, they actually run faster than at the beginning. By the seventh day the two curves have crossed and thereafter the 0% reward group runs faster than the 100% reward group. It is also interesting to note that, for the 0% reward group, through the eighth day, one can see no evidence of any extinction having occurred at all. If one is inclined to do so, one can certainly see in these data some evidence that an extra preference of rather weak strength exists for the animals that were never rewarded in the mid-box.

We were sufficiently encouraged by these results so that we proceeded to perform what I, at least, regarded as a rather ambitious experiment. Before I describe the experiment, let me briefly explain the reasoning which lay behind it. It is plausible to suppose that the extra preference which the organism develops in order to reduce dissonance may be focused on any of a variety of things. Let me explain this by using the experiment I have just described as an illustration. Those animals who were never fed in the mid-box, and thus experienced dissonance, could have developed a liking for the activity of running down the alley to the mid-box, they could have developed a preference for some aspect of the

mid-box itself, or they could have developed a preference for any of the things they did or encountered subsequent to leaving the mid-box. Experimentally, of course, there was no control over this.

It occurred to us, in thinking about this, that if the dissonance were reduced, at least to some extent, by developing a preference for something about the *place* where the dissonance was introduced, then it would be possible to show the same effects in a very well controlled experiment. In other words, if the dissonance introduced by absence of reward were reduced, at least in part, by developing some liking for the place where they were not rewarded, then one could compare two groups of animals, both of which experienced the identical amount of dissonance, but who would be expected to develop preferences for different places.

To do this we used the same basic technique as in the previous two experiments I

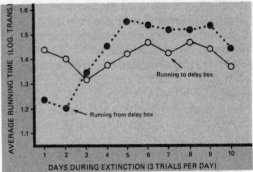

**Figure 5.** Running time while satiated during extinction in double mid-box experiment.

have described but with an important modification. Instead of one mid-box, two mid-boxes were used. From the starting box the animals went to Mid-box A, from there to Mid-box B, and from there to the end-box where all animals received food on every trial. Two groups of animals were run in this experiment. Group A was delayed in Mid-box A for a period of time and then was allowed to run directly through Mid-box B to the end-box. Group B was allowed to run directly through Mid-box A but was delayed for a period of time in Mid-box B before being allowed to go to the end-box. In other words, both groups of animals had identical experience. The only difference between the groups lay in the particular box in which they were delayed. (All three boxes were, of course, quite distinctive.) For the extinction trials the animals were satiated as in the preceding experiment. For the extinction trials, the animals were run only from Box A to Box B. That is, during extinction the animals were placed directly into Box A, the door was then opened, and when they ran to Box B were removed to their home cage.

Thus, Group A during extinction was running away from the place where they had been delayed, while Group B was running to the place where they had been delayed. If some extra preference had developed for the place where they had been delayed, we would expect Group B to show more resistance to extinction than Group A. In short, during extinction, Group B should behave like the 0% reward groups in the previous experiments. Group A, however, should behave during extinction more like the 100% reward animals in the preceding experiments.

Figure 5 shows the data for these two groups of animals for the first 10 days of extinction, three trials having been run on each day. The two curves in the figure must, by now, look very familiar to you. The same result is obtained as in the two previous experiments. The initial difference between the two groups again reflects their previous running speed in that section of the apparatus. During acquisition, Group B ran more hesitantly in the section between the two mid-boxes than did Group A. This difference, of course, still exists at the start of the extinction trials. Thereafter, however, Group A, which was running away from its delay box, rapidly increases its running time. Group B, which was running to its delay box, does not increase its time at

all and shows no evidence of any extinction during 30 trials. By the fourth day of extinction, the two curves have crossed and thereafter Group B consistently runs faster than Group A.

If one looks carefully at all the data, I think one finds reasonable evidence that insufficient reward does lead to the development of extra preference. This extra preference, at least in the white rat, seems to be of a rather mild nature, but the magnitude of the effect is quite sufficient to account for the increased resistance to extinction after partial reward or after delay of reward.

Let us then briefly examine the implications of these findings and of the theory of dissonance for our traditional conception of how reward functions. It seems clear that the inclination to engage in behavior after extrinsic rewards are removed is not so much a function of past rewards themselves. Rather, and paradoxically, such persistence in behavior is·increased by a history of nonrewards or inadequate rewards. I sometimes like to summarize all this by saying that rats and people come to love things for which they have suffered.

## REFERENCES

Aiken, E. G. 1957. The effort variable in the acquisition, extinction, and spontaneous recovery of an instrumental response. *Journal of Experimental Psychology* 53:47–51.

Aronson, E., and Mills, J. 1959. The effect of severity of initiation on liking for a group. *Journal of Abnormal and Social Psychology* 59:177–181.

Crum, J.; Brown, W. L.; and Bitterman, M. E. 1951. The effect of partial and delayed reinforcement on resistance to extinction. *American Journal of Psychology* 64:228–237.

Fehrer, E. 1956. Effects of amount of reinforcement and of pre- and postreinforcement delays on learning and extinction. *Journal of Experimental Psychology* 52:167–176.

Festinger, L. 1957. *A theory of cognitive dissonance.* Evanston, Ill.: Row, Peterson.

Lewis, D. J. 1956. Acquisition, extinction, and spontaneous recovery as a function of percentage of reinforcement and intertrial intervals. *Journal of Experimental Psychology* 51:45–53.

Scott, E. D., and Wike, E. L. 1956. The effect of partially delayed reinforcement and trial distribution on the extinction of an instrumental response. *American Journal of Psychology* 69:264–268.

Sheffield, V. F. 1949. Extinction as a function of partial reinforcement and distribution of practice. *Journal of Experimental Psychology* 39:511–526.

Weinstock, S. 1954. Resistance to extinction of a running response following partial reinforcement under widely spaced trials. *Journal of Comparative and Physiological Psychology* 47:318–322.

Wike, E. L., and McNemara, H. J. 1957. The effects of percentage of partially delayed reinforcement on the acquisition and extinction of an instrumental response. *Journal of Comparative and Physiological Psychology* 50:348–351.

Wilson, W.; Weiss, E. J.; and Amsel, A. 1955. Two tests of the Sheffield hypothesis concerning resistance to extinction, partial reinforcement, and distribution of practice. *Journal of Experimental Psychology* 50:51–60.

# READING 9

# Experience and the Development of Motivation: Some Reinterpretations

## J. McV. HUNT

Contemporary psychology views motivation and its development in new ways. In this article, some of the basic tenets of the dominant theory are questioned, and a new look at motivation and development is provided by Hunt. The article concludes with a look at motivation from the viewpoint of the incongruity-dissonance principle.

### QUESTIONS

1. Do you agree with Hunt's criticisms of the dominant theory? Explain.
2. Is all behavior motivated? Give an example of "unmotivated behavior."
3. Are words like *habit* and *drive* labels for real processes, or are they hypothetical constructs which we refer to as reality? (Is there such a thing as a habit or a drive?)

A recent issue of the *Saturday Evening Post* carried a cartoon that some of you may have noted. It depicts a boy entering his house, perhaps from school, where his

Reprinted from *Child Development* (1960), *31*, 489-504, by permission of the author and the Society of Research in Child Development, Inc.

Earlier versions of this paper were read at the Eleventh Annual Institute in Psychiatry and Neurology of the Veterans Administration Hospital at North Little Rock, Arkansas, 27 February 1959, and at colloquia of the Department of Psychiatry at the Medical School of Colorado. The paper was prepared in connection with a survey of the implications of the work in behavioral science for childrearing which has been supported by the Russell Sage Foundation.

father is sitting with his paper. The boy appears to be fixing his father with an accusing glare. The punch line reads, "Somebody goofed, I'm improperly motivated."

This cartoon depicts the vantage point from which I have been examining what we think we know about the relation between experience and motivation. When a child's behavior fails to fit the standards somebody in our society holds for him, it is pretty well agreed among us who are supposed to be experts on human nature that "somebody goofed." And that somebody is usually considered to be a parent.

The question is: what is the proper formula? If one examines the accruing evidence relevant to what has been the dominant conception of the experiential sources of motivation, one can hardly escape the conclusion that this conceptual scheme needs some revisions. If we based our child-rearing entirely on our dominant theory of motivational development, we would probably goof as often and as badly as run-of-the-mill parents.

Today I wish, first, to remind you of three of the most basic and general of the propositions in that theory of motivation which has been dominant for the past 30 to 40 years. These are propositions which, although stated in somewhat varied forms, have been shared by both psychoanalysts and academic behavior theorists. Secondly, I wish to cite evidence which calls these propositions into question, and thirdly, to suggest, tentatively, three new interpretative principles which appear to me to be congruent with a large number of facts and which have interesting implications.

Our conceptions of motivation have traditionally been concerned with three large questions: (a) Why does an organism or person become active? (b) Why does the organism or person to change his behavior another? and (c) How do you get the organism or person to change his behavior to something conceived to be more desirable or appropriate?

## THE DOMINANT THEORY

### DRIVE

According to our dominant theory, it is claimed, first of all, that "all behavior is motivated," and that the aim or function of every instinct, defense, action, or habit is to reduce or eliminate stimulation or excitation within the nervous system. It is not easy to state when this view was first presented. Signs of it appear in the seventh chapter of Freud's *Interpretation of Dreams*

(15) in 1900, and the idea is full-blown in his paper entitled *Instincts and Their Vicissitudes* (17) in 1915. The idea also appears in Woodworth's *Dynamic Psychology* (68), published in 1918, where the term *drive* was first introduced into the glossary of American psychology. The idea was full-blown in Dashiell's *Fundamentals of Objective Psychology* (11) in 1928.

Although Freud (17) believed that the source of motivation lay outside the domain of psychology in physiology, American psychologists, untroubled by such limits to their domain, have gone on to answer the first question concerning what motivates organisms to become active by saying that they are *driven*. Organisms have been conceived to be driven, first by those so-called primary inner stimuli which arise from homeostatic imbalances or needs. With no shame whatsoever, psychologists have long cited the evidence from the work of such physiologists as Claude Bernard (5) and his successors, and especially of Walter B. Cannon (10), and also of the psychologist Curt Richter (59) to document this answer. Organisms are driven, second, by various forms of intense and painful external stimulation. It has been assumed that these two forms of stimulation arouse an inner state of excitement which has usually been called *drive*.

It is also assumed, as the proposition that "all behavior is motivated" implies, that the organism would be inactive unless driven by either inner or outer stimuli. Freud (17) has been highly explicit about this assumption, and the assumption lies implicitly behind the notion of conditioned or learned drive in behavior theory and behind the traumatic notion of anxiety in psychoanalysis. It is obvious, of course, that animals and people are sometimes active when it is hard to see how either homeostatic drive or painful external stimulation could be operative. It is then assumed that some of the weak, innocuous stimuli present must have been associated in the past with either painful stimuli or homeostatic needs. In such a way the weak stimuli which are present must have acquired the capacity to arouse the drive, often now called anxiety by psychologists as well as psychoanalysts, and it is such acquired or conditioned drive that is conceived to activate the organism.

Such conditioned drive or anxiety has been well demonstrated in the laboratory. Before World War II, Miller (45, 46) at Yale showed that rats which had been repeatedly shocked in a white box would, when later returned to the white box, make an effort to escape. Moreover, in the course of these efforts, they could be got to learn new skills such as that of turning a wheel to open a door. Rats which had not been shocked in the white box made no such efforts to escape. In another demonstration, Solomon and Wynne (64) have shown that dogs which have experienced a tone or a buzzer paired a few times with a sub-tetanizing shock will run away from that tone or buzzer for hundreds of trials, with the average reaction time of starting continuing to decrease through 600 such trials. In my own work (31) rats fed irregularly in infancy ate more than their littermate controls and sometimes (32) hoarded food in adulthood after a period without food. Here, as I conceived it, the cues of hunger were conditioned to intense hunger excitement during the infantile experience. In adulthood the conditioned hunger drive facilitated the rate of eating and, sometimes hoarding.

Such work has demonstrated that this notion of conditioned drive or anxiety, which goes back to the work of Bechterev (2) and Watson and Raynor (67), has a solid basis in reality. But in what has been the dominant theory of motivation, as epitomized by Freud's (18) later traumatic theory of anxiety, and by the Hull (30) and Dollard-Miller (13, 47) theory of acquired drives, conditioning is conceived to be the only way in which an organism can become fearful of innocuous stimuli.

## HABIT

Habit has been the answer to the second question concerned with why an animal or person acts one way rather than another. The organism is controlled by the habits which have served to reduce drive in the past when that organism was in the presence of the inner and outer drive stimuli, and the cue stimuli impinging upon him at any given moment now. Under the term *habit*, I am including psychoanalytic modes, which have supposedly been fixated during infancy in the course of either too much gratification or too much frustration, and I am including also ego-defenses, or anxiety equivalents, and cathexes, as well as the instrumental responses and traits commonly investigated in psychological laboratories.

Changing behavior has been conceived to be a matter of motivating the organism with either punishment or homeostatic need to make the desired behavior which can then be reinforced by arranging for it to reduce the drive aroused by the punishment or the need. Although the conditions and conceptions of psychotherapy in the clinic differ considerably from the conditions and conceptions of the behavior theorist investigating learning in laboratory animals, in either case it is conceived that motivation is a necessity, and motivation means changing the emotional or drive conditions which are quite extrinsic to either the instrumental behavior or the congnitive, informational processes concerned.

This dominant theory has been a conceptual edifice of large dimensions and of considerable detail. It has provided a plausible account of both personality development and social motives. The experimental facts of homeostasis and of conditioned drive and fear are sound. Nevertheless, it has become more and more evident in the past 10 years that some of the basic assumptions of this dominant theoretical scheme and some of the explanatory extrapolations contradict facts and call for reinterpretation.

## REINTERPRETATIONS

### IS ALL BEHAVIOR MOTIVATED?

The first of the assumptions to be called into question is the one that *all behavior is motivated* and that *organisms become inactive unless stimulated* by homeostatic need or painful stimulation or conditional stimuli for these. A large variety of observations contradict this assumption and imply spontaneous molar activity. Beach (1) has reviewed the observations of play in the young to show that playful activities are most likely to occur when either young animals or children are homeostatically satisfied and also comfortably warm. The very occurrence of either homeostatic need or strong external stimulation stops play and turns the young animal or child to activities calculated to relieve such stimulation. Berlyne (3, 4) has shown that well-fed and watered rats will explore areas new to them if given only the opportunity. Montgomery (49) moreover, has shown that hunger and thirst tend to limit the exploratory behavior of rats rather than facilitate it, and Montgomery and Monkman (50), as well as others, have shown that conditioned fear inhibits exploration. Harlow, Harlow, and Meyer (23) have demonstrated that well-fed monkeys will learn to unassemble a three-device puzzle with no other drive and "no other reward than the privilege of unassembling it." In another study Harlow (20) found two well-fed and well-watered monkeys worked repeatedly at unassembling a six-device puzzle for 10 continuous hours, and they were still showing what he characterized as enthusiasm for their work on the tenth hour of testing. From his observations of the human child, moreover, Piaget (55) remarks repeatedly on the enthusiastic and repeated performance of such emerging skills as the release of a toy, sitting up, standing, etc.

Such evidences of spontaneous behavior,

which is unmotivated in the traditional sense, have led to the naming of such new motives as a curiosity drive by Berlyne (4), an exploratory drive by Montgomery (48), and exteroceptive and curiosity drives by Harlow (21). I would like to object that merely naming such drives explains nothing. If we continue, we shall be revisiting McDougall's (44) practice of postulating a separate drive for almost every variety of activity. Let us stop with noting that such observations do contradict our assumption that organisms will become inactive unless driven by homeostatic needs and painful stimuli, and give up this ancient Greek notion that living matter is inert substance to which motion must be imparted by extrinsic forces. We can then embrace the thermodynamic conception of living things as open systems of energy exchange which exhibit activity intrinsically and upon which stimuli have a modulating effect, but not an initiating effect.

This notion of activity being intrinsic in living tissue is receiving support from studies of organ systems as well as studies of molar organisms. The EEG, for example, shows that brain cells are continuously active (33, 58). In sleep the slow waves of large amplitude are taken to imply that large numbers of cells are firing synchronously, and the effect of waking and stimulation and exciting the brain-stem-reticular formation is to asynchronize this firing which shows in rapid waves of low magnitude (42).

Granit (19) points out that the spontaneous firing of retinal cells increases with dark adaptation and thereby functions to prevent the deafferentization of visual cortex with darkness. Twenty years ago, this spontaneous firing was considered, at worst, to be due to some failure of experimental control, or at best, noise in the channel of information. Recently, the Laceys (36) have found spontaneous fluctuations of sudomotor activity and cardiac activity which they also see as functioning in the control of the organism's relations with its environment. Especially intriguing is their notion that the carotid sinus mechanism functions as a feedback loop which participates in the directing of attention inward or outward by inhibiting or facilitating receptor inputs. But the point of mentioning these evidences of spontaneous activities of organ systems here is merely to help inter for good the notion that activity of living systems requires homeostatic need or painful external stimulation and to foster the idea that to live means to be active in some degree.

## REINFORCEMENT

This idea of activity being intrinsic in living organisms has implications for our conception of reinforcement. It makes it unnecessary to see all activity as a matter of either reducing or avoiding stimulation which is implied in the assumption organisms become inactive unless stimulated. This is a second fundamental assumption of the dominant theory which has been shared by psychoanalysts and behavior theorists alike.

On the one hand, there is still a place for drive reduction. It is clear that under conditions of homeostatic need and painful stimulation, and perhaps under circumstances when the conditions of stimulation are changing with too great rapidity, both animals and persons learn techniques and strategies leading to gratification or reduction in external stimulation. The evidence that led Thorndike to formulate the "law of effect" is as convincing as ever. Moreover, in association with reductions of homeostatic need, animals and men may also learn cathexes or emotional attachments. The facts referred to are those highly familiar in secondary reinforcement (30, 54).

On the other hand, the facts implying that organisms show spontaneous molar activity also imply that, when animals and human beings have been living under conditions of low and unchanging stimulation

for a time, increases of stimulation become reinforcing. Butler has shown that rhesus monkeys will learn quite complex discriminations with the only reward being a peek through a glass window (7) at the things in the next room or a few seconds of auditory experience (8). Berlyne (3) has shown that, the greater the variety of stimulation in an area which rats are permitted to explore, the longer they continue their explorations.

Especially important in this connection are the studies of human behavior under conditions of minimal variation in stimulation. I refer to the studies of perceptual isolation by Bexton, Heron, and Scott (6) at McGill and also the work of Lilly (41). At McGill, college students were paid 20 dollars a day to do nothing. They lay for 24 hours a day on a comfortable bed. The temperature was optional and constant. Eyes, ears, and hands were shielded to minimize stimulus variation. Few subjects could endure more than two or three days of such conditions. They developed a desire for variation which was almost overwhelming.

While interpreting such facts in terms of a multiple set of drives for curiosity, exploration, or stimulation will get us only to a redescription of them, Hebb's (26) notion of an optimal level of activation — and, I would like to add, stimulus variation below which *increases* are reinforcing and above which *decreases* are reinforcing — is an integrative conception of fair magnitude. Moreover, the drive-reduction principle of reinforcement may be seen to be but half of this more general curvilinear principle.

But this is probably not the whole story. It looks as if there were, natively, both positive and negative forms of exciting stimulation. Sheffield, Roby, and Campbell (61) have argued that the reinforcing effect of eating is not a matter of reduction of the hunger drive but rather a matter of the positive value of the consummatory act of eating. Moreover, Sheffield, Wulff, and Backer (62) have shown that male rats will learn mazes to get to females in heat even when they are allowed only intromission but not allowed to continue coitus to the point of drive-reducing ejaculation. From the fact that Davis (12) and his collaborators at Indiana have shown that showing pictures of nude women to college males increases excitement as shown by increased palmar conductance and the arrest of EEG-alpha, it is clear that such stimulation is exciting rather than excitement-reducing. Young (69) has long emphasized the importance of the hedonic quality of experience for reinforcement, and he has shown that speed of running in rat subjects increases with the concentration of sucrose in the incentive drink.

The suggestion that the two forms of excitation, one positive and one negative, are built into organisms comes also from the work of Olds and Milner (53). Electrical stimulation of the septal area is positively reinforcing, but electrical stimulation of the brain-stem reticular formation is negatively reinforcing. Perhaps, it is not without significance that the septal area is part of the old olfactory brain which has been considered to have an especially important part in the mediation of sexual and consummatory behavior in mammals. At any rate, it looks as though certain types of stimulation may be positively reinforcing even though they be intense and exciting. This may mean that the curvilinear principle may be limited in its domain to strong stimulation via the exteroceptors when homoeostatic needs are minimized.

The suggestion of innate, positive and negative exteroceptive stimulation comes secondly from recent work by Harlow (22). It has been customary to see an infant's cathexis or love for its mother developing as secondary reinforcement largely out of its feeding experiences. Freud (16), of course, contended that the pleasure from stimulation of the oral erogenous zone furnished the experiential basis for both pleasure-sucking and maternal attachment,

a contention which contradicted his most definitive formulations of drive theory (17). The fact that an infant must suck for its nourishment, according to libido theory (16, p. 587), merely guaranteed discovery of the pleasures of oral stimulation. Behavior theorists have seen both sucking and love of mother as forms of secondary reinforcement deriving from the fact that the child satisfies its hunger by means of sucking the mother's breasts (51, pp. 137 ff.). Harlow (22), however, has recently compared the degree of attachment of young monkeys to a wire mother-surrogate on which they nursed at a bottle with attachment to a padded and cloth-covered mother-surrogate on which they received nothing but the feel of softness. In terms of the amount of time spent on each of the two mother-surrogates, the monkeys showed more than 10 times the attachment to the soft-padded surrogate as to the wire surrogate. When various fear-evoking stimuli were presented to the baby monkeys in their cages, it was to the padded and cloth-covered surrogate that the frightened infant monkey turned, not to the wire surrogate on which it had been nursed. Harlow argues from these findings that it is the sensory quality of softness which gives the reinforcement. His study suggests moreover, that it is important to investigate the capacity for various kinds of stimuli for positive and negative reinforcement in the very young. Pratt (57) cites a monograph by Canestrini (9) on the sensory life of the newborn for an observation that certain stimuli are associated with decreases in the rate of the heart rate, and are therefore pleasant, while others are associated with increases in heart rate and are unpleasant.[1]

---

[1] An examination of Canestrini's (9) monograph shows that Pratt was mistaken in stating that Canestrini remarked upon decreases in heart rate being associated with pleasure, but some of his published kymograph records do indicate decreases in heart rate. It may well be that heart rate could serve as an indicator of the emotional value of various sensory inputs and these might be tested for their reinforcement values. I am indebted to Dr. William Gerler for reading this monograph carefully to check my own impression of Canestrini's text.

In view of the finding by Davis (12) and his collaborators that seeing a picture of a nude female results in reduction of the heart rate of male college students, it is possible that this physiological indicator may provide a technique for determining the direction of the reinforcing effect of stimuli in the newborn. At any rate, what is suggested is that McDougall's (44) old notion of natively positive and negative values for receptor inputs be reexamined.

## CONDITIONED FEAR AND ANXIETY

The third assumption that I wish to examine in the light of empirical evidence is the notion that fear and anxiety are *always* inculcated as a consequence of traumatic experiences of helplessness in the face of homeostatic need or painful external stimulation. Note that I am not denying that such conditioned fears do exist. I am only questioning the word *always* . . . are always inculcated as a consequence of traumatic experiences.

The first relevant studies go way back to the 1920's. Harold and Mary Cover Jones (34) attempted to test the claims of Watson (66) and Watson and Raynor (67) concerning conditioned fears. They exposed their subjects of various ages, ranging from early infancy to adult, to a large but sluggish and harmless bull-snake. Fear of the snake was exceedingly common among adults, teenagers, and latency-age children, but it was absent in children below three years of age. It began to appear among children older than 3 and was typical of children 6 and older. From the fact that the fear appeared at a younger age in those of higher intelligence than those of lower intelligence, the Joneses argued that fear of snakes is a response which comes automatically into the developing child's repertoire through maturation. This remains as an alternative hypothesis to that of conditioned fear.

A study by Frances Holmes (29), which is seldom cited, calls both of these interpretations into question. Holmes compared the fearfulness of the children of lower-class background who were attending a day nursery, with the fearfulness of children of upper-class background who were attending a private nursery school. She got her fear scores by indicating that the child could get some attractive toys with which to play by going into the dark room adjacent to the examining room, or by taking them off a chair situated beside that of a strange woman dressed in a large floppy black hat and a long gray coat, or by climbing along a plank some three feet off the floor. If the child started immediately for the toys, he got a score of one for that item. If he hesitated but ultimately went ahead on his own, he got a score of two. If he would go only if accompanied by the examiner, the score was three. If he refused to go at all, the score was four. There were seven such situations. The results show that the fear scores of the lower-class children averaged only about half the size of those for the upper-class children, and the fear scores for boys were lower than those for girls. Yet it would be the lower-class children who had experienced the more homeostatic need and painfully rough treatment than the upper-class children, and the boys had probably experienced more painful experiences than the little girls. That intelligence is not the factor is shown by the fact that the fear scores showed a correlation of only about +.2 with mental age, and the differences were still significant when intelligence was partialed out. Something besides either conditioned fear or the correlation between fear and intelligence is required to make these results comprehensible.

Recently, evidence even more contradictory to the notion of conditioned fears has been coming from the work of Seymour Levine. Levine, Chevalier, and Korchin (40) have compared the adult behavior of rats shocked and rats petted daily from birth to their 20th day with the adult behavior of rats left continuously in their nest with their mothers. When he started this work, Levine expected to find that the shocked animals would show traumatic effects of their shock experiences in heightened emotionality and damaged capacity to learn adaptive responses. On the contrary, the shocked animals, along with the handled animals gained weight faster than those left in the nest (37, 38, 39, 40). Byron Lindholm, working with the writer, has repeated and confirmed this finding. Moreover, Levine's shocked and handled animals both showed less emotionality than those left continuously in the nest with their mothers, i.e., less emotionality in the sense that they defecated and urinated less frequently when placed in a strange situation. Finally, the shocked and handled animals, which have appeared alike in all of these experiments, learned an avoidance response more rapidly and drank more readily after 18 hours without water than did the rats left in the nest with their mother.

Clearly these results on both human children and rats imply that fear and anxiety must sometimes have some other basis than that of being associated with painful stimulation. As many of you know, Hebb (24, 25) has formulated a radically different explanation of fear which may be termed either an incongruity or a dissonance theory.

The facts which suggested Hebb's conception came largely from observing chimpanzees being raised under controlled conditions at the Yerkes Laboratory. Fear, defined as withdrawal behavior in response to the appearance of some object, does not appear in young chimpanzees until they are approximately four months old. Then, the objects feared are familiar objects in unfamiliar guise. Fear of strangers is an example. This appears spontaneously to the first stranger seen, so it cannot be based on associating strangers with painful stimulation. Fear of strangers does not appear in chimpanzees—or in children, I might add—

who have always been exposed to a large number of persons. While the avoidance response is unlearned, the familiar, expected aspects of objects must be learned. The young animal must have established as residues of his experience cortical firing patterns (or cognitive structures—whichever term you like) from which new receptor inputs can be incongruous. Consider the kinds of objects regularly feared. They are, for instance, the familiar keeper or experimenter in strange clothes, the experimenter in a Halloween mask, a plaster cast of a chimpanzee head (which lacks, of course, the familiarly attached body), and anesthetized chimpanzee infant (from which the familiar patterns of motion are absent). On the other hand, objects which have never entered into the young chimpanzee's life may be strange without evoking withdrawal. In other words, the feared object is one which excites receptors in a fashion which is incongruous with the central, sequential pattern of neural firing which has accrued as a residue of the chimpanzee or human infant's past experience. Until the central pattern has been learned, incongruous stimulation is impossible.

Such a conception can well account for Holmes' findings that lower-class children are less fearful than higher-class children and that boys are less fearful than girls even though both lower-class children and boys of nursery school age are likely to have had the wider experience with the sorts of situations used by Holmes to evoke fear. It may well be that being shocked and handled provides a variety of experience which leaves the rat pups which have been subjected to it less disturbed by such things as open fields and 18 hours without water, but these effects may ultimately be found to be a matter of still another mechanism. It is too early to say.

Taking seriously this incongruity-dissonance conception of the genesis of fear leads to interesting reinterpretations of a great many of the motivational phenomena of child development. Consider these few. In considering separation anxiety, the incongruity principle makes it necessary to puzzle about how the absence of mother could be the conditional stimulus for the traumatizing and helpless distress that has been supposed to have occurred in her absence. In considering fear of the dark, it also becomes unnecessary to puzzle about how the absence of light stimulation could so widely have been associated with painful stimulation. Multiple mothering need not be seen as a traumatizing experience in the light of this conception, but rather as an inoculation against social shyness and fear. The timidity of the overprotected child and the social shyness of the rural mountain people get an explanation which has been difficult in terms of the theory of conditioned fear.

## MOTIVATION IN TERMS OF THE INCONGRUITY-DISSONANCE PRINCIPLE

This introduction of the incongruity-dissonance principle concludes the three reinterpretations I wish to present today, but I do wish to call your attention to the pervasive character of this incongruity-dissonance principle. It appears to have great explanation power which figures, in one guise or another, in several systematic theories besides that of Hebb, all of which have been characterized as nondynamic.

Hebb's (25) theorizing is physiological, at least in a verbal sense, in that he conceives the residues of past inputs to be stored in semiautonomous, reverberating cerebral circuits which he terms *cell assemblies*. These cell assemblies are the neural analogue of concepts, and they get sequentially integrated into what he calls *phase sequences*. The sequential organization in time provides for the subjective phenomenon of expectation. When markedly incongruous receptor inputs disrupt this sequential organization, behavior is changed and the process is felt as unpleasant emotion. Slight degrees of incongruity, which

can readily be accommodated, lend interest and may provide attractive problems, but the larger ones are repelling and perhaps even devastating.

Piaget (55, 56) utilizes very much the same incongruity notion to account for the development of intelligence and concepts in human children. In his system, the child comes at birth with certain sensory-motor coordinations which he terms *schemata*. Variation in stimulus situations call for adaptive *accommodations* or changes in these schemata, which changes are *assimilated* or stored as residues. Piaget also finds limited incongruities between central schemata and receptor inputs to be interesting and facilitative of growth, but incongruities which extend beyond the child's capacity for accommodation instigate withdrawal or fear and even terror. In Piaget's theory the child's gestalt-like conceptions of reality (space, time, and number) are schemata which develop through a continuous process of accommodations and assimilations and become fixed or static only when the child's schemata come to correspond so well with reality that no further accommodations are required. Here agreement among people is dictated by reality.

Helson (27, 28) has called the residues of immediate past experience in the typical psychophysical experiment an *adaptation level*. Both he and McClelland (43) have seen affective arousal to be a matter of the size of the discrepancy between receptor inputs and the adaptation level. Small discrepancies may be attractively pleasant, large ones repellingly unpleasant. As an example, some of you will readily recall having experienced the affective startle that comes when you have been set to pick up what you thought was a full pail, only to find it empty.

Festinger (14) has recently written a book entitled *A Theory of Cognitive Dissonance* in which he shows that a discrepancy between belief about a situation and perception of that situation acts like a drive.

The subject acts to reduce the *dissonance* by either withdrawing from the incredible situation or by changing his beliefs, and, not incidentally, he finds the dissonance highly unpleasant.

Rogers (60) has described the basis for anxiety as discrepancy between the "phenomenological field" and the perceived reality as represented by his two circles. Rogers' phenomenological field, however, is not the perceptually-given phenomenal field of such German phenomenologists as Delthei and Husserl. It is rather the inferred storehouse of the past experience and represented in the present by expectations, aspirations, self-concept, and the like. Thus, his conceptual scheme appears to fall within the domain of the incongruity-dissonance principle.

Kelly's (35) *Psychology of Personal Constructs* also makes central use of this principle. The term *personal constructs* refers to the ways in which individuals construe and anticipate events. These each person derives from the way in which he has experienced such events in the past. When a person's constructions fail to predict events, this is disturbing, even anxiety-producing, and it motivates some kind of change, but the change may take place in defenses against such change of constructs or in avoiding such events, or in the constructs themselves.

Perhaps, it is worth noting in closing that this incongruity-dissonance principle makes both motivation and reinforcements intrinsic to the organism's relations with its environment, intrinsic, if you will, to the organism's information-processing. It is as if the organism operated like an error-actuated, feedback system where the error is derived from discrepancy between receptor-inputs of the present and the residues of past experience which serve as the basis for anticipating the future. The dominant view of the past half century has seen both motivation and reinforcement as extrinsic to the information-processing. This has put a tremendous burden of responsibility for the management of affective motivation on parents, teachers, and all those in positions of authority and control. Visions of man completely controlled, as examplified by George Orwell's *1984*, are conceivable only by assuming that the extrinsic motivating forces of homeostatic need and painful stimulation are completely dominant. In this light the terror of the baby chimp at seeing his keeper in a Halloween mask and the irritation of the believer when his beliefs are disconfirmed are perhaps symbols of hope. They may justify Abraham Lincoln's well-known dictum that "you can fool some of the people all the time, and all the people some of the time, but you cannot fool all the people all the time."

To return to the cartoon of the lad who was improperly motivated: Perhaps the task of developing proper motivation is best seen, at least in nutshell form, as limiting the manipulation of extrinsic factors to that minimum of keeping homeostatic need and exteroceptive drive low, in favor of facilitating basic information-processing to maximize accurate anticipation of reality.

## REFERENCES

1. Beach, F. A. 1945. Current concepts of play in animals. *American Naturalist* 79:523–541.

2. Bechterev, V. M. 1913. *La psychologie objective*. Trans. by N. Kostyleff. Paris: Alcan.

3. Berlyne, D. E. 1950. Novelty and curiosity as determinants of exploratory behavior. *British Journal of Psychology* 41:68–80.

4. Berlyne, D. E. 1955. The arousal and satiation of perceptual curiosity in the rat. *Journal of Comparative and Physiological Psychology* 48:238–246.

5. Bernard, C. 1859. *Lecons sur les propriétés physiologiques et les alterations pathologiques des liquides de l'organisme*. 2 vols. Paris: Ballière.

6. Bexton, W. H.; Heron, W; and Scott, T. H. 1954. Effects of decreased variation in the sensory environment. *Canadian Journal of Psychology* 8:70–76.

7. Butler, R. A. 1953. Discrimination learning by rhesus monkeys to visual-exploration motivation. *Journal of Comparative and Physiological Psychology* 46:95–98.

8. Butler, R. A. 1957. Discrimination learning by rhesus monkeys to auditory incentives. *Journal of Comparative and Physiological Psychology* 50:239–241.

9. Canestrini, S. 1913. Uber das Sinnesleben des Neugebornen. In *Monographien aus dem Gesamtgebiete der Neurologie und Psychiatrie* (Heft 5), ed. A. Alzheimer and M. Lewandowsky. Berlin: Springer.

10. Cannon, W. B. 1915. *Bodily changes in pain, hunger, fear, and rage.* New York: Appleton-Century.

11. Dashiell, J. 1928. *Fundamentals of objective psychology.* Boston: Houghton Mifflin.

12. Davis, R. C., and Buchwald, A. M. 1957. An exploration of somatic response patterns: Stimulus and sex differences. *Journal of Comparative and Physiological Psychology* 50:44–52.

13. Dollard, J., and Miller, N. E. 1950. *Personality and psychotherapy.* New York: McGraw-Hill.

14. Festinger, L. 1957. *A theory of cognitive dissonance.* Evanston, Ill.: Row, Peterson.

15. Freud, S. 1938 (originally published 1900). The interpretation of dreams. In *The basic writings of Sigmund Freud,* trans. by A. A. Brill, pp. 179–548. New York: Modern Library.

16. Freud, S. 1938 (originally published 1905). Three contributions to the theory of sex. In *The basic writings of Sigmund Freud,* trans. by A. A. Brill, pp. 553–629. New York: Modern Library.

17. Freud, S. 1950 (originally published 1915). Instincts and their vicissitudes. In *Collected papers,* vol. 4, pp. 60–83. London: Hogarth.

18. Freud, S. 1936 (originally published 1926). *Inhibition, symptom, and anxiety.* Trans. by H. A. Bunker as *The problem of anxiety.* New York: Norton.

19. Granit, R. 1955. *Receptors and sensory perception.* New Haven: Yale University Press.

20. Harlow, H. F. 1950. Learning and satiation of response in intrinsically motivated complex puzzle performance by monkeys. *Journal of Comparative and Physiological Psychology* 43:289–294.

21. Harlow, H. F. 1953. Motivation as a factor in the acquisition of new responses. In *Current theory and research in motivation: A symposium,* pp. 24–49. Lincoln: University of Nebraska Press.

22. Harlow, H. F. 1958. The nature of love. *American Psychologist* 13:673–685.

23. Harlow, H. F.; Harlow, M. K.; and Meyer, D. R. 1950. Learning motivated by a manipulation drive. *Journal of Experimental Psychology* 40:228–234.

24. Hebb, D. O. 1946. On the nature of fear. *Psychological Review* 53:259–276.

25. Hebb, D. O. 1949. *The organization of behavior.* New York: Wiley.

26. Hebb, D. O. 1955. Drives and the CNS (conceptual nervous system). *Psychological Review* 62:243–254.

27. Helson, H. 1947. Adaptation-level as frame of reference for prediction of psycho-physical data. *American Journal of Psychology* 60:1–29.

28. Helson, H. 1948. Adaptation-level as a basis for a quantitative theory of frames of reference. *Psychological Review* 55:297–313.

29. Holmes, Frances B. 1935. An experimental study of the fears of young children. In A. T. Jersild and Frances B. Holmes, Children's fears, *Child Development Monographs* 20:167–296.

30. Hull, C. L. 1943. *Principles of behavior.* New York: Appleton-Century.

31. Hunt, J. McV. 1941. The effects of infant feeding-frustration upon adult hoarding in the albino rat. *Journal of Abnormal and Social Psychology* 36:338–360.

32. Hunt, J. McV.; Schlosberg, H.; Solomon, R. L.; and Stellar, E. 1947. Studies on the effects of infantile experience on adult behavior in rats: I. Effects of infantile feeding frustration on adult hoarding. *Journal of Comparative and Physiological Psychology* 40:291–304.

33. Jasper, H. H. 1937. Electrical signs of cortical activity. *Psychological Bulletin.* 34:411–481.

34. Jones, H. E., and Jones, Mary C. 1928. A study of fear. *Child Education* 5:136–143.

35. Kelly, G. A. 1955. *The psychology of personal constructs.* New York: Norton.

36. Lacey, J. I., and Lacey, Beatrice C. 1958. The relationship of resting autonomic activity to motor impulsivity. In *The brain and human behavior,* pp. 144–209. Baltimore: Williams & Wilkins.

37. Levine, S. 1957. Infantile experience and consummatory behavior in adulthood. *Journal of Comparative and Physiological Psychology* 50:609–612.

38. Levine, S. 1957. Infantile experience and resistance to physical stress. *Science* 126:405.

39. Levine, S. 1958. Noxious stimulation in infant and adult rats and consummatory behavior. *Journal of Comparative and Physiological Psychology* 51:230–233.

40. Levine, S.; Chevalier, J. A.; and Korchin, S. J. 1956. The effects of shock and handling in infancy on later avoidance learning. *Journal of Personality* 24:475–493.

41. Lilly, J. C. 1956. Mental effects of reduction of ordinary levels of physical stimuli on intact, healthy persons. *Psychiatric Research Reports* 5:1–9.

42. Lindsley, D. B. 1957. Psychophysiology and motivation. In *Nebraska symposium on motivation*, ed. M. R. Jones, pp. 44–105. Lincoln: University of Nebraska Press.

43. McClelland, D. C.; Atkinson, J. W.; Clark, R. A.; and Lowell, E. L. 1953. *The achievement motive.* New York: Appleton-Century-Crofts.

44. McDougall, W. 1915. *An introduction to social psychology.* Boston: Luce.

45. Miller, N. E. 1941. An experimental investigation of acquired drives. *Psychological Bulletin* 38:534–535.

46. Miller, N. E. 1948. Studies of fear as an acquirable drive: I. Fear as motivation and fear-reduction as reinforcement in the learning of new responses. *Journal of Experimental Psychology* 38:89–101.

47. Miller, N. E., and Dollard, J. 1941. *Social learning and imitation.* New Haven: Yale University Press.

48. Montgomery, K. C. 1951. The relation between exploratory behavior and spontaneous alternation in the white rat. *Journal of Comparative and Physiological Psychology* 44:582–589.

49. Montgomery, K. C. 1953. The effect of the hunger and thirst drives upon exploratory behavior. *Journal of Comparative and Physiological Psychology* 46:315–319.

50. Montgomery, K. C., and Monkman, J. A. 1955. The relation between fear and exploratory behavior. *Journal of Comparative and Physiological Psychology* 48:132–136.

51. Mussen, P. H., and Conger, J. J. 1956. *Child development and personality.* New York: Harper.

52. Olds, J. 1955. Physiological mechanisms of reward. In *Nebraska symposium on motivation*, ed. M. R. Jones, pp. 73–139. Lincoln: University of Nebraska Press.

53. Olds, J., and Milner, P. 1954. Positive reinforcement produced by electrical stimulation of septal area and other regions of the rat brain. *Journal of Comparative and Physiological Psychology* 47:419–427.

54. Pavlov, I. P. 1927. *Conditioned reflexes.* Trans. by G. V. Anrep. Oxford University Press.

55. Piaget, J. 1952. *The origins of intelligence in children.* New York: International Universities Press.

56. Piaget, J. 1954. *The construction of reality in the child.* Trans. by Margaret Cook. New York: Basic Books.

57. Pratt, K. C. 1954. The neonate. In *Manual of child psychology*, 2d ed., ed. L. Carmichael, pp. 215–291. New York: Wiley.

58. Prosser, C. L. 1934. Action potentials in the nervous system of the crayfish: I. Spontaneous impulses. *Journal of Cellular and Comparative Physiology* 4:185–209.

59. Richter, C. P. 1927. Animal behavior and internal drives. *Quarterly Review of Biology* 2:307–343.

60. Rogers, C. R. 1951. *Client-centered therapy.* Boston: Houghton Mifflin.

61. Sheffield, F. D.; Roby, T. B.; and Campbell, B. A. 1954. Drive reduction versus consummatory behavior as determinants of reinforcement. *Journal of Comparative and Physiological Psychology* 47:349–355.

62. Sheffield, F. D.; Wulff, J. J.; and Backer, R. 1951. Reward value of copulation without sex drive reduction. *Journal of Comparative and Physiological Psychology* 44:3–8.

63. Solomon, R. L., and Brush, Elinor S. 1956. Experimentally derived conceptions of anxiety and aversion. In *Nebraska symposium on motivation*, ed. M. R. Jones, pp. 212–305. Lincoln: University of Nebraska Press.

64. Solomon, R. L., and Wynne, L. C. 1953. Traumatic avoidance learning: Acquisition in normal dogs. *Psychological Monographs* 67, no. 4 (whole no. 354).

65. Thorndike, E. L. 1913. *Educational psychology.* Vol. I, *The original nature of man;* Vol. II, *The psychology of learning.* New York: Teachers College.

66. Watson, J. B. 1928. *Psychological care of the infant and child.* New York: Norton.

67. Watson, J. B., and Raynor, Rosalie. 1920. Conditional reactions. *Journal of Experimental Psychology* 3:1–4.

68. Woodworth, R. S. 1918. *Dynamic psychology.* New York: Columbia University Press.

69. Young, P. T. 1955. The role of hedonic processes in motivation. In *Nebraska symposium on motivation*, ed. M. R. Jones, pp. 193–237. Lincoln: University of Nebraska Press.

# READING 10

# Electrical Self-Stimulation of the Brain in Man

**ROBERT G. HEATH, M.D.**

Electrical self-stimulation is not new in psychology. Olds's (1958) study* on the rat has generated a great deal of research in this area. Only recently has this work been applied to the brain of man. Heath presents the study of two subjects who were able to stimulate their brains electrically. This study is interesting not only because of the behavioral changes in these men, but also because verbal reports were obtained.

## QUESTIONS

1. What implications does this study have for the future? Is it unreasonable to think brain stimulation might be used as a reinforcement for behavior for certain groups such as criminals or the mentally ill?
2. What are the ethical considerations of scientists working in this area?
3. Do you consider the results of this study valid? Do you have methodological criticisms? How would you interpret the results?

At a symposium concerning depth electrode studies in animals and man in New

---

*Olds, J. 1958. Self-stimulation of the brain. *Science* 127 (3294): 315–324.

Read at the 119th annual meeting of The American Psychiatric Association, St. Louis, Mo., May 6-10, 1963.

At the time of presentation, a 16 mm. sound film was shown demonstrating the effects of stimulation by the transistorized portable self-stimulator to a number of specific regions of the brain in Patients No. B-7 and No. B-10. The two subjects were interviewed to obtain subjective descriptions of the effects of stimulation.

Supported by funds provided by the Louisiana State Department of Hospitals.

Dr. Heath is with the Department of Psychiatry and Neurology, Tulane University School of Medicine, New Orleans, La.

Charles J. Fontana, Electroencephalographic Technologist, and Esther Blount, R.N., Research Nurse, Assistants.

Orleans in 1952, the Tulane investigators described (and illustrated with films of patients treated between 1950–1952) a pleasurable response with stimulation of specific regions of the brain (5). The pleasurable response to stimulation of some deep regions of the brain, first observed with electrical stimulation to the septal region, has proved a consistent finding in continuing studies (6, 7, 12). Since 1952 we have reported various aspects of the phenomenon including demonstration of relief of physical pain by stimulation to this pleasure-yielding area of the brain (11).

With the introduction of ingenious techniques for self-stimulation by Olds (14–17), the need to depend largely upon verbal reports of the subjective response was eliminated and it was possible to study apparent reward and aversive areas of the brain in animals. Subjective data, of course, were lacking in the animal studies.

During the last few years the Tulane researchers have incorporated and modified some animal intracranial self-stimulation (ICSS) methods for human investigation, permitting extension of the pleasurable phenomenon studies in man. An ICSS study recently published (3) was designed to explore human behavior under strict laboratory conditions of the type characteristically employed in animal studies. A study has also been described in which a patient was equipped with a small portable self-stimulator with 3 buttons, permitting delivery of electrical stimuli of fixed parameters to any one of 3 brain sites (8). The primary motivation in these studies, as in all depth electrode studies in man at Tulane, was therapeutic (5).

Study of reward areas in the brain of man, including use of induced reward for therapeutic purposes, is extensive and complex. This presentation will focus on a description of the subjective responses of two patients treated by the self-stimulation technique. Their reports provide information concerning the reasons for repeated ICSS—information that is not available from animal studies.

## MATERIAL AND METHODS

Two patients were used in the study. Patient No. B-7, age 28, with a diagnosis of narcolepsy and cataplexy, had failed to respond to conventional treatments. He had electrodes implanted by the method developed in our laboratory (1, 2) into 14 predetermined brain regions and fixed to remain in exact position for prolonged study. These small silver ball electrodes (most of those used in this study consisted of 3 leads each separated by 2 mm.) were placed into

the right anterior and posterior septal region, left anterior and posterior septal region, right anterior hypothalamus, midline mesencephalic tegmentum, left anterior and posterior hippocampus, left anterior and posterior caudate nucleus and over the right frontal cortex, right and left mid-temporal cortex, and left anterior temporal cortex.

Patient No. B-10, age 25, a psychomotor epileptic with episodic brief periods of impulsive behavior uncontrolled with the usual treatments, had 51 leads implanted into 17 brain sites: left and right centromedian, left caudate nucleus, right ventricle, left and right hippocampus, mid-line mesencephalic tegmentum, left and right septal region, left amygdaloid nucleus, left paraolfactory area, and over the left and right temporal cortex, left and right occipital cortex, and left and right frontal cortex. Twenty-four leads were of stainless steel .003 inch in diameter coated with Teflon; 27 were the small silver ball type electrode.[1]

ICSS studies were not initiated until a minimal period of 6 months following operation, assuring elimination of any variables introduced by operative trauma, e.g., edema, anesthetic effects.

Stimuli were delivered from a specially constructed transistorized self-contained unit[2] which was worn on the patient's belt. The unit generated a pre-set train of bi-directional stimulus pulses each time that one of the 3 control buttons was depressed. Each button directed the pulse train to a different electrode pair permitting the operator a possible selection of cerebral sites. A mechanical counter was coupled to each button to record the total number of stimuli directed toward a given area. An internal timer limited each pulse train to 0.5 second for each depression, thereby prohibiting the operator from obtaining continuous stimuli

---

[1]Stainless steel array constructed of No. 316 stainless steel wire, .003 inch in diameter, with quad Teflon-coated leads and 6 contact points 2 mm. apart. Electrode designed and fabricated by Henry A. Schryver, 110 W. Packard St., Fort Wayne, Indiana.

[2]Technical Associates of New Orleans.

merely by keeping the button depressed. An additional feature of the unit provided 3 separate level potentiometers to give wide-range control of stimuli for each electrode pair.

*Circuit details.* To minimize the effects of dc polarization, a bi-directional pulse was chosen (Figure 1). This pulse permitted restoration of the dc level to zero after each 1.0 millisecond stimulus and maintenance at zero during the entire dead time of 10 milliseconds.

A silicon unijunction timing circuit generated the basic 10 millisecond interval. The output from the unijunction transistor was gated off after 0.5 second operation by a diode gate driven from an R-G charging circuit. When the diode gate was open, the unijunction transistor generator drove two complementary one-shot multivibrators operated serially, permitting the falling edge of the first to trigger the second. The two multivibrators had equal periods of 0.5

millisecond. The multivibrator timing circuits saturated complementary output transistors which fed voltage to the load through isolating capacitors.

The stimuli were mono-polar; the indifferent pole was a plate strapped to the subject's leg.

Studies conducted on the two patients differed somewhat because of therapeutic considerations. For studies with Patient No. B-7, the narcoleptic, the 3 buttons of the unit were attached to electrodes in the septal region, hippocampus, and mesencephalic tegmentum, and he was free to stimulate any of these sites as he chose. The patient wore the stimulator for a period of 17 weeks. Before he was equipped with the unit, baseline data concerning the time he spent sleeping during an arbitrary 6-hour period each day were charted by specified ward personnel. These data were later compared with sleeping time following attachment of the unit. This study was

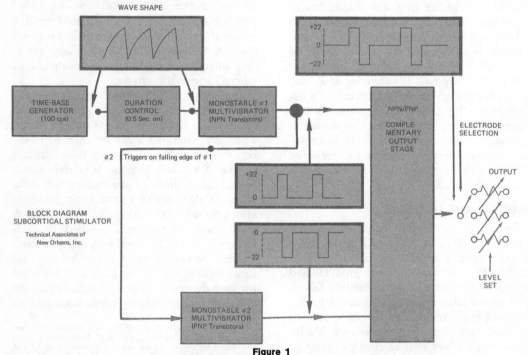

**Figure 1**
Circuit Diagram for Transistorized Intracranial Self-stimulator.

basically therapeutic (treatment results will be presented elsewhere) but from the experimental design we were able to obtain considerable subjective data regarding the effects of ICSS to several regions of the brain.

With Patient No. B-10, the psychomotor epileptic, a number of different experimental designs were employed to investigate the effects of ICSS. For illustrative purposes, the results of one study are presented herein as background for a description of the subjective responses. In the first part of the study a total of 17 different cerebral regions were stimulated. They were selected at random, the unit design permitting 3 sites to be hooked up at any one time. Each electrode was made available to the patient for stimulation for a minimal period of 2 hours. Various combinations of 3 sites were arranged. The purpose in making stimulation to different combinations of sites available was based on well-documented animal studies which indicate that rate of stimulation at a given site will vary somewhat depending upon the site stimulated beforehand. Data are presented in terms of the hourly stimulation to a given site as recorded with the automatic counter of the unit. Additionally, the same site of the brain was attached to different buttons to determine if the patient would relate a response to a given button. He reported, however, a consistent response to stimulation of a given electrode regardless of the button to which it was attached.

In the second part of the study the 3 sites of the brain which the subject had elected to stimulate most frequently during the first part of the study were compared over a 6-hour period.

## RESULTS

*Patient No. B-7.* After randomly exploring the effects of stimulation with presses of each of the 3 buttons, Patient No. B-7 almost exclusively pressed the septal button (Figure 2).

Stimulation to the mesencephalic tegmentum resulted in a prompt alerting, but was quite aversive. The patient, complaining of intense discomfort and looking fearful, requested that the stimulus not be repeated. To make certain that the region was not stimulated, he ingeniously modified a hair pin to fit under the button which directed a pulse train to the mesencephalic tegmentum so it could not be depressed.

Hippocampal stimulation was mildly rewarding.

Stimulation to the septal region was the most rewarding of the stimulations and, additionally, it alerted the patient, thereby combatting the narcolepsy. By virtue of his ability to control symptoms with the stimulator, he was employed part-time, while wearing the unit, as an entertainer in a night club.

The patient's narcolepsy was severe. He would move from an alert state into a deep sleep in the matter of a second. Recognizing that button pressing promptly awakened him, fellow patients and friends occasionally resorted to pushing the button

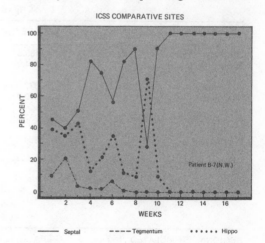

**Figure 2**
Comparative Sites, ICSS. Frequency of Stimulation to Various Intracranial Sites Expressed in Percentages in Patient with Narcolepsy and Cataplexy.
ICSS
Comparative Sites

if he fell asleep so rapidly that he was unable to stimulate himself.

The patient, in explaining why he pressed the septal button with such frequency, stated that the feeling was "good"; it was as if he were building up to a sexual orgasm. He reported that he was unable to achieve the orgastic end point, however, explaining that his frequent, sometimes frantic, pushing of the button was an attempt to reach the end point. This futile effort was frustrating at times and described by him on these occasions as a "nervous feeling."

*Patient No. B-10.* Studies conducted on the psychomotor epileptic patient were more varied and provided more information concerning subjective responses. The average number of button presses per hour for various regions of the brain is listed in Tables 1 and 2. Regions of the brain are listed in order of the frequency with which they were selectively stimulated by the subject. A summary of the principal subjective feelings is given.

The button most frequently pushed provided a stimulus to the centromedian thalamus. This stimulus did not, however, induce the most pleasurable response; in fact, it induced irritability. The subject reported that he was almost able to recall a memory during this stimulation, but he could not quite grasp it. The frequent self-stimulations were an endeavor to bring this elusive memory into clear focus.

The patient most consistently reported pleasurable feelings with stimulation to two electrodes in the septal region and one in the mesencephalic tegmentum. With the pleasurable response to septal stimuli, he frequently produced associations in the sexual area. Actual content varied considerably, but regardless of his baseline emotional state and the subject under discussion in the room, the stimulation was accompanied by the patient's introduction

### Table 1
### ICSS in Man
### Reward (?) Sites

| REGIONAL STIMULATED | AVERAGE/HOUR | SUBJECTIVE RESPONSE |
|---|---|---|
| L. Centromedian | 488.8 | Partial memory recall; anger and frustration |
| R. P. Septal | 394.9 | "Feel great"; sexual thoughts; elimination of "bad" thoughts |
| L. Caudate | 373.0 | Cool taste; "like it OK" |
| Mesenceph. Teg. | 280.0 | "Drunk feeling"; "happy button"; elimination of "bad" thoughts |
| A. Amygdala | 257.9 | Indifferent feeling; somewhat pleasant, but feeling not intense |
| P. Amygdala | 224.0 | Moderately rewarding; increase of current requested |

### Table 2
### ICSS in Man
### Aversive Sites

| REGIONAL STIMULATED | AVERAGE/HOUR | SUBJECTIVE RESPONSE |
|---|---|---|
| R. Hippocampus | 1.77 | Strongly aversive; "feel sick all over" |
| L. Paraolfactory | 0.36 | Moderately aversive |
| R. Parietal Cortex | 0.50 | |
| R. Frontal Cortex | 0.00 | No significant subjective response |
| R. Occipital Cortex | 0.00 | |
| R. Temporal Cortex | 0.00 | |

of a sexual subject, usually with a broad grin. When questioned about this, he would say, "I don't know why that came to mind—I just happened to think of it." The "happy feelings" with mesencephalic stimulation were not accompanied by sexual thoughts.

Patient No. B-10 also described as "good," but somewhat less in pleasurable-yielding quality, stimuli to two sites, the amygdaloid nucleus and the caudate nucleus. Several other septal electrodes and one other electrode in the amygdaloid nucleus were stimulated a moderate number of times. His reports concerning these stimulations suggested a lesser magnitude of pleasurable response, but definitely not an unpleasant feeling.

Minimal positive response was obtained with stimulation of several other septal electrodes. The most aversive response ("sick feeling") was obtained with stimulation to one hippocampal electrode and one lead in the paraolfactory area. With stimulation of the latter lead, he complained of light flashes, apparently due to spread to the optic nerve, and of general discomfort.

No consistent changes, either significantly aversive or rewarding, were displayed with stimulation to any of 12 cortical leads dispersed widely over the cortical surface, including the frontal, temporal, occipital, and parietal lobes.

In the second part of the study the 3 electrodes which were stimulated most during the first phase of the study were attached to the 3 buttons. The sites of these electrodes were the centromedian thalamus, the septal region, and the mesencephalic tegmentum. Data indicated that the combination of sites available influenced the number of times that a given region of the brain was stimulated (Figure 3). When coupled with the subjective reports, the data also suggested that the over-all state of the subject at a given moment was an influential determinant for selecting the region to be stimulated. For example, the

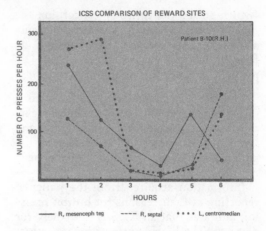

ICSS COMPARISON OF REWARD SITES

Patient B-10(R.H.)

NUMBER OF PRESSES PER HOUR

HOURS

—— R, mesenceph teg    ---- R, septal    •••• L, centromedian

**Figure 3**
Comparison of Frequency of Stimulation to Reward Sites in the Brain of Patient with Psychomotor Epilepsy.
ICSS
Comparison of Reward Sites

centromedian thalamus was stimulated up to 1,100 times per hour when in combination with relatively inactive sites of stimulation and only a maximum of 290 times per hour when in combination with two other highly rewarding areas, the septal region and the mesencephalic tegmentum.

The patient noted that the frustration and anger resulting from stimulation of the centromedian thalamus was alleviated with stimulation to the septal region and to the mesencephalic tegmentum. As Figure 3 indicates, the patient during the first two hours stimulated the centromedian thalamus most frequently. This was associated with discomfort in his attempt to recapture a fleeting memory. He reported that stimulation of the other areas relieved this discomfort. There was little activity during the next two hours. Toward the end of the study, in the 5th and 6th hours, stimulation to septal and tegmental leads increased. During the 5th hour, the mesencephalic tegmentum was stimulated most frequently; during the 6th hour, the septal lead was stimulated most frequently. The patient evolved a pattern coupling the stimulus to the centromedian thalamus (which stirred his curiosity concerning the memory) with stimuli to the more pleasurable areas to lessen the feeling of frustration[3]

## DISCUSSION

Changes in parameters of stimuli to a given region of the brain, including current intensity, wave form, pulse width, and frequency, in many instances altered the patients' responses. This has similarly been reported with animal ICSS.

Information acquired from the patients' reporting of their reasons for button pressing indicates that all ICSS is not solely for pleasure. The highest rate of button pressing occurred with Patient No. B-7 when he was somewhat frustrated in his pleasurable pursuit and as he attempted to achieve an orgastic end point. In Patient No. B-10 the highest rate of button pressing also occurred with frustration, but of a different type, evolving with attempts to bring into focus a vague memory that ICSS had evoked. The subject's emotional state in this instance built into strong anger. It was interesting that the patient would button press to stimulate the region within the centromedian thalamus for a prolonged period, but at a slower rate when buttons providing more pleasurable septal and tegmental stimulation were also available. Depression of the septal button, with resultant pleasant feelings, alleviated the painful emergency state, according to the subject's

[3]When the paper was presented, it was here that the 16 mm. sound film was shown. Clinical effects of stimulation to a variety of deep regions of the brain, as summarized herein, were demonstrated.

In the last sequence of the film, Patient No. B-10, the psychomotor epileptic, was stimulated in the septal region during a period when he was exhibiting agitated, violent psychotic behavior. The stimulus was introduced without his knowledge. Almost instantly his behavioral state changed from one of disorganization, rage, and persecution to one of happiness and mild euphoria. He described the beginning of a sexual motive state. He was unable, when questioned directly, to explain the sudden shift in his feelings and thoughts. This sequence of film was presented to demonstrate a phenomenon which appears to be consistent and which has been repeated in a large number of patients in our laboratories. This phenomenon is the ability to obliterate immediately painful emergency emotional feelings in a human subject through introduction of a pleasurable state by physical or chemical techniques.

report, and thereby provided him comfort to pursue his quest for the fleeting memory.

With septal stimulation in other patients, as well as the two subjects discussed here, a sexual motive state has frequently been induced in association with the pleasurable response. This sexual state has not developed in association with pleasurable feelings during stimulation to other regions. The consistent observation of a relation between sexual feelings and stimulation to the septal region has been described by MacLean in monkey experiments (13). These reports, in part, answer questions raised by Galambos regarding ICSS when he asked, "What motivates these animals to do such unheard-of-things? Is it some exquisite pleasure they receive, as several students of the problem staunchly contend, or the feeling of utter and complete well-being as others claim?" (4).

The ICSS techniques represent one of several methodologies that the Tulane researchers have used in man to investigate the pleasurable phenomenon associated with certain types of cerebral activity. These studies complement early subcortical electrical stimulation studies (5). The pleasurable response has also been induced in man with introduction of certain chemicals into specific deep brain regions (8-10). It is noteworthy that intense pleasurable responses induced with chemical stimulation of the brain occurred when a high amplitude spindling type of recording was set up in the septal region.

The observation that introduction of a stimulus which induces pleasure immediately eliminates painful emergency states is quite consistent. If our psychodynamic formulations are correct, this basic observation may have widespread implication for the development of therapeutic methods to alter favorably disordered behavior.

## SUMMARY

Studies are described of two human patients under treatment with ICSS. Their subjective reports in association with stimulation to reward areas of the brain are presented. The data indicate that patients will stimulate regions of the brain at a high frequency for reasons other than to obtain a pleasurable response. These data extend information obtained from ICSS in animals.

## REFERENCES

1. Becker, H. C., et al. 1954. In *Studies in schizophrenia*, p. 565. Cambridge: Harvard University Press.

2. Becker, H. C., et al. 1957. *Electroencephalography and Clinical Neurophysiology* 9:533.

3. Bishop, M. P., et al. 1963. *Science* 140:394.

4. Galambos, Robert. 1961. *Federation Proceedings* 20:603.

5. Heath, R. G., et al. 1954. *Studies in schizophrenia*, pp. 42, 46, 47, 50, 560. Cambridge: Harvard University Press.

6. Heath, R. G. 1955. *Psychosomatic Medicine* 17:383.

7. Heath, R. G. 1958. *Confinia Neurologica* 18:305.

8. Heath, R. G. In press. In *Pleasure integration and behavior*, ed. R. G. Heath. New York: Hoeber.

9. Heath, R. G., and deBalbian Verster, F. 1961. *American Journal of Psychiatry* 117:980.

10. Heath, R. G., and Founds, W. L. 1960. *Electroencephalography and Clinical Neurophysiology* 12:930.

11. Heath, R. G., et al. 1954. In *Studies in schizophrenia*, p. 555. Cambridge: Harvard University Press.

12. Heath, R. G., and Mickle, W. A. 1960. In *Electrical studies on the unanesthetized brain*, ed. R. R. Ramey and D. S. O'Doherty. New York: Hoeber.

13. MacLean, P. D., et al. 1959. *Transactions of the American Neurological Association* 84:105.

14. Olds, J. 1962. *Physiological Review* 42:554.

15. Olds, J. 1960. *American Journal of Physiology* 199:965.

16. Olds, J., and Milner, P. 1954. *Journal of Comparative and Physiological Psychology* 47:419.

17. Olds, J., and Olds, M. E. In press. In *Pleasure integration and behavior*, ed. R. G. Heath. New York: Hoeber.

# READING 11

## Critical Periods in Behavioral Development

### J. P. SCOTT

Although the concept of instinct has not been popular among psychologists for many years, ethologists have recently renewed the study of instinctive behavior under the name of "species-specific" behavior. Research has indicated that behaviors characteristic of certain species in their natural surroundings do exist. The behavior appears to be hereditary and is only displayed or "released" by specific stimuli in the environment. Scott examines the concept of the critical period, presents data in support of it, and suggests the important uses of this concept in a theory of behavioral development.

### QUESTIONS

1. What is meant by a critical period?
2. Do you believe there is such a thing as a critical period? Support your opinion. If you do not accept this conceptualization, how would you account for the data in this article?
3. If critical periods for learning and socialization exist in humans, what are the implications for child-rearing and educational processes?

A number of years ago I was given a flocklamb taken from its mother at birth. My wife and I raised it on the bottle for the first 10 days of life and then placed it out in the pasture with a small flock of domestic sheep. As might have been expected from folklore, the lamb became attached to people and followed the persons who fed it. More surprisingly, the lamb remained independent of the rest of the flock when we restored it to the pasture. Three years later it was still following an independent grazing pattern. In addition, when it was mated and had lambs of its own it became a very indifferent mother, allowing its offspring to nurse but showing no concern when the lamb moved away with the other members of the flock (1).

Since following the flock is such a universal characteristic of normal sheep, I was

The author is senior staff scientist at the Roscoe B. Jackson Memorial Laboratory, Bar Harbor, Maine.

impressed by the extensive and permanent modification of this behavior that resulted from a brief early experience. The results suggested that Freud was right concerning the importance of early experience, and pointed toward the existence of critical periods in behavioral development. As I soon discovered, there is considerable evidence that a critical period for determining early social relationships is a widespread phenomenon in vertebrates; such a critical period had long been known in ants (2).

The theory of critical periods is not a new one in either biology or psychology. It was strongly stated by Stockard in 1921, in connection with his experiments on the induction of monstrosities in fish embryos, although he gave credit to Dareste for originating the basic idea 30 years earlier (3). In experimenting with the effects of various inorganic chemicals upon the development of *Fundulus* eggs, Stockard at first thought one-eyed monsters were specifically caused by the magnesium ion. Further experiments showed him that almost any chemical would produce the same effect, provided it was applied at the proper time during development. These experiments and those of Child (4) and his students established the fact that the most rapidly growing tissues in an embryo are the most sensitive to any change in conditions, thus accounting for the specificity of effects at particular times.

Meanwhile Freud had attempted to explain the origin of neuroses in human patients as the result of early experience and had implied that certain periods in the life of an infant are times of particular sensitivity. In 1935, Lorenz (5) emphasized the importance of critical periods for the formation of primary social bonds (imprinting) in birds, remarking on their similarity to critical periods in the development of the embryo, and McGraw soon afterward (6) pointed out the existence of critical periods for optimal learning of motor skills in the human infant.

Since then, the phenomenon of critical periods has excited the imagination of a large group of experimenters interested in human and animal development. In describing this fast-moving scientific field, I shall point out some of the most significant current developments. More detailed information is available in some excellent recent reviews (7, 8).

To begin with, three major kinds of critical-period phenomena have been discovered. These involve optimal periods for learning, for infantile stimulation, and for the formation of basic social relationships. The last of these has been established as a widespread phenomenon in the animal kingdom and consequently receives major attention in this article.

## PERIODS ARE BASED ON PROCESSES

In the dog, the development of behavior may be divided into several natural periods marked off by important changes in social relationships (Table 1). Only a few other species have been studied in sufficient detail for making adequate comparisons, but enough data have been accumulated to show that similar periods can be identified in other mammals and in birds (9, 10). I originally expected to find that the course of postnatal development, like that of embryonic development, would be essentially similar in all vertebrates, and that while the periods might be extended or shortened, the same pattern of development would be evident in all (11). However, comparison of only two species, man and the dog, shows that the periods can actually occur in reverse order, and that there is an astonishing degree of flexibility in behavioral development (12).

This leads to the conclusion that the important aspect of each developmental period is not time sequence but the fact that each represents a major developmental process. Thus, the neonatal period is chiefly characterized by the process of neonatal nutrition—nursing in mammals and parental feeding in many birds. The transition period is characterized by the process of transition to adult methods of nutrition and locomotion and the appearance of adult patterns of social behavior, at least in immature form. The period of socialization is the period in which primary social bonds are formed. If we consider processes alone, it is apparent that they are not completely dependent on each other and that they can therefore be arranged in different orders. It is also apparent that certain of these processes persist beyond the periods characterized by them. For example, a mammal usually retains throughout life the ability to suck which characterizes the neonatal period, although in most cases this ability is little used.

## PROCESS OF PRIMARY SOCIALIZATION

Since one of the first acts of a young mammal is to nurse, and since food rewards are known to modify the behavior of adult animals, it once seemed logical to suppose that the process of forming a social attachment begins with food rewards and develops as an acquired drive. However, the experimental evidence does not support this extreme viewpoint. Brodbeck reared a group of puppies during the critical period of socialization, feeding half of them by hand and the other half by machine, but giving all of them the same degree of human contact (13). He found that the two sets of puppies became equally attached to people. This result was later confirmed by Stanley and his co-workers (14), who found that the only difference in response between the machine-fed and the hand-fed puppies was that the latter yelped more when they saw the experimenter. Elliot and King (15) fed all their puppies by hand but overfed one group and underfed another. The hungry puppies became more rapidly attached to the handlers. We can conclude that, in the dog, food rewards per se are not necessary for the process of socialization, but that hunger will speed it up.

Fisher (16) reared fox terrier puppies in isolation boxes through the entire socialization period. The puppies were fed mechanically (thus, food was entirely eliminated as a factor in the experiment), but they were removed from the boxes for regular contacts with the experimenter. One group of puppies was always rewarded by kind social treatment. A second group was sometimes rewarded and sometimes punished, but in a purely random way. Still a third group was always punished for any positive approach to the experimenter. The puppies that were both rewarded and punished showed most attraction and dependency behavior with respect to the experimenter, and the puppies that were always punished showed the least. After the treatment was discontinued, all the puppies began coming toward the experimenter, and the differences rapidly disappeared. This leads to the surprising conclusion that the process of socialization is not inhibited by punishment and may even be speeded up by it.

At approximately 3 weeks of age — that is, at the beginning of the period of socialization—young puppies begin to bark or whine when isolated or placed in strange places. Elliot and Scott (17) showed that the reaction to isolation in a strange place reaches a peak at 6 to 7 weeks of age, approximately the midpoint of the critical period, and begins to decline thereafter. Scott, Deshaies, and Morris (18) found that separating young puppies overnight from their mother and litter mates in a strange pen for 20 hours per day produced a strong emotional reaction and speeded up the process of socialization to human handlers. All this evidence indicates that any sort of strong emotion, whether hunger, fear, pain, or loneliness, will speed up the process of socialization. No experiments have been carried out to determine the effects of pleasant types of emotion, such as might be aroused by play and handling, but these were probably a factor in Brodbeck's experiment with machine-fed puppies.

The results of these experiments on dogs agree with evidence from other species. While they were going on, Harlow (19) was performing his famous experiments with rhesus monkeys isolated at birth and supplied with dummy "mothers." When given the choice between a comfortable cloth-covered mother without a nipple and an uncomfortable mother made of wire-screening but equipped with a functional nursing bottle, the young rhesus monkeys definitely preferred the cloth-covered models from which they had received no food rewards. Harlow concluded that the acquired-drive theory of the origin of social attachment could be discarded.

Later, Igel and Calvin (20) performed a similar but more elaborate experiment with puppies. These animals had more opportunity to choose, being provided with four kinds of mother models: comfortable and uncomfortable, each type with and without nipples. Like rhesus monkeys, the puppies preferred the comfortable "mother" but usually chose one with a nipple. Thus, it appears that food rewards do contribute something to the social relationship, although they do not form its prime basis.

Since then Harlow (21) has raised to maturity the monkeys raised on dummy mothers, has mated them, and has observed their behavior toward their own young. They become uniformly poor mothers, neglecting their offspring and often punishing them when they cry. In spite of such rejection, the young rhesus infants desperately crawl toward their mothers and give every evidence of becoming attached to them, although perhaps not as strongly as in the normal relationship. Here again punishment does not inhibit the formation of a social bond.

The hypothesis that the primary social bond originates through food rewards had already been shown to be invalid in the precocial birds, many of which form attachments prior to the time when they begin to feed. Lorenz (5) was the first to point out

the significance of this phenomenon, which he called "imprinting." He also stated that it differed from conditioning, primarily in that it was very rapid and apparently irreversible. However, rapid formation and great persistence are also characteristic of many conditioned responses and other learned behavior. Fabricius (22) pointed out that no sharp line can be drawn between imprinting and conditioning, and Collias (23) concluded that imprinting is a form of learned behavior that is self-reinforcing.

The process of imprinting in young ducklings and chicks has since been experimentally analyzed in much detail with results that invariably confirm the conclusion that it takes place without any obvious external rewards or reinforcement. Hess (24) found that if he caused young ducklings to follow a model over varying distances or over hurdles, the ducklings which had to make the greater effort became more strongly imprinted. He also found that the drug meprobamate and its congener carisoprodol, which are muscle relaxants as well as tranquilizers, greatly reduce imprinting if given during the critical period. James (25) found that chicks would become attached to an object illuminated by a flickering light, even though they were not allowed to follow, and Gray (26) later showed that they will become attached to a motionless object illuminated by a steady light and viewed from an isolation box. It is therefore apparent that chicks can become imprinted without following, although muscular tension may still be important.

Guiton (27) found that chicks allowed to follow a model in a group become less strongly imprinted than chicks exposed singly, and he attributed the results to the greater fear shown by the isolated chicks. Recently, Pitz and Ross (28) subjected young chicks following a model to a loud sound and found that this increased the speed with which they formed a social bond. Hess (29) has given a mild electric shock to chicks following a model and finds that this also increases the strength of imprinting. Instead of avoiding the model, the distressed chick runs after it more closely.

We may conclude that these young birds become attached to any object to which they are long exposed during the critical period, even when their contact is only visual. We may also conclude that the speed of formation of a social bond is dependent upon the degree of emotional arousal, irrespective of the nature of that arousal. Whether attachment is the result of the emotion itself or of the reduction of emotion as the chick or duckling approaches the model is still a matter of conjecture (30).

## TIMING MECHANISMS

The basic timing mechanisms for developmental periods are obviously the biological processes of growth and differentiation, usually called maturation. For various reasons, these are not precisely correlated with age from birth or hatching. For example, birds often retain newly formed eggs in their bodies overnight, thus incubating them for several hours before laying. By chilling duck eggs just before placing

them in an incubator (thus killing all embryos except those in the earliest stages of development) Gottlieb (31) was able to time the age of ducklings from the onset of incubation rather than from hatching and found that variation in the timing for the critical period was much reduced. No such exact timing studies have been made in mammals, but I have estimated that there is at least a week's variation in development among puppies at 3 weeks of age, and the variation among human infants must be considerably greater (32).

Another approach to the problem is to try to identify the actual mechanisms which open and close a period. Since an important part of forming a primary social relationship appears to be emotional arousal while the young animal is in contact with another, it is obvious that the critical period for socialization could be timed by the appearance of behavioral mechanisms which maintain or prevent contact, and this indeed is the case. There are demonstrable positive mechanisms, varying from species to species, which bring young animals close to other members of their kind: the clinging response of young rhesus monkeys; the

**Table 1**

Periods of development in the puppy and song sparrow. The six periods of development described by Nice (10) for the song sparrow correspond to the first four periods in the puppy, as indicated in the table. The young of the two species are born or hatched in an immature state, require intensive parental care and feeding, and go through much the same stages before becoming independent. Development is much more rapid in the bird than in the puppy, although small mammals such as mice mature at about the same rate as birds.

| | Puppy | | | Song sparrow | | |
|---|---|---|---|---|---|---|
| Name of period | Length of period (weeks) | Initial event | | Name of period | Length of period (days) | Initial event |
| I Neonatal | 0–2 | Birth, nursing | | Stage 1 (nestling) | 0–4 | Hatching, gaping |
| II Transition | 2–3 | Eyes open | | Stage 2 | 5–6 | Eyes open |
| III Socialization | 3–10 | Startle to sound | | Stage 3 | 7–9 | Cowering—first fear reactions |
| | | | | Stage 4 (fledgling) | 10–16 | Leaving nest— first flight |
| | | | | Stage 5 | 17–28 | Full flight |
| IV Juvenile | 10– | Final weaning | | Stage 6 (juvenile) | 29– | Independent feeding |

following response of chicks, ducklings, and lambs and other herd animals; the social investigation, tail wagging, and playful fighting of puppies; and the visual investigation and smiling of the human infant (33). These are, of course, accompanied by interacting responses from adult and immature members of the species: holding and clasping by primate mothers, brooding of mother hens and other birds, calling by mother sheep, investigation and play on the part of other young puppies, and the various supporting and nurturing activities of human mothers.

If contact and emotional arousal result in social attachment, there must be negative mechanisms which prevent such attachment once the critical period is past. Perhaps the most widespread of these is the development of a fear response which causes the young animal to immediately leave the vicinity of a stranger and hence avoid contact. This developing fear response is found in young chicks (7), ducklings (22, 34), dogs (35), rhesus monkeys (36), and in many other birds and mammals. Even in children there is a period between the ages of 5 and 12 months in which there is a mounting fear of strangers (37), sometimes called "8-months anxiety" (38). As already pointed out, there is a time in development when certain fear responses actually facilitate imprinting, but, as they grow stronger, the escape reaction follows so quickly that it prevents contact altogether.

Another sort of negative mechanism is the rejection of strange young by adult sheep, goats, and many other herd animals (39). In these species the mothers become strongly attached to the young within a few hours after birth and refuse to accept strangers thereafter. This indicates that the rapid formation of emotional bonds is not limited to young animals.

These timing mechanisms all depend primarily on the development of social behavior patterns, but both sensory and motor development can also influence timing. For example, a very immature animal cannot maintain contact by following, and in slowly developing altricial birds such as jackdaws and doves (5, 40), the period of imprinting comes much later than it does in the precocial species. In the human infant the process of socialization begins before the adult motor patterns develop, but contact is maintained by visual exploration and by the smiling response to human faces (33). Thus, understanding the process of socialization and its timing mechanisms in any particular species requires a systematic study of the development of the various capacities which affect the time of onset and the duration of the critical period. These include sensory, motor, and learning capacities as well as the ability to perform essential patterns of social behavior.

The fact that emotional arousal is so strongly connected with the process of primary socialization suggests that the capacity to produce emotional reactions may also govern the time of onset of a critical period. Figure 1 summarizes the results of a study of emotional development in the dog during the critical period. If puppies are kept in large fields, totally isolated from people, fear and escape responses toward human beings very nearly reach a maximum by the time the puppies are 14 weeks old—a finding that fixes the upper limit of the period of socialization (35). On the other hand, the peak of the emotional response to isolation in a strange place occurs when puppies are approximately 6 to 7 weeks old, as does the peak of the heart-rate response to handling. At this age, such emotional arousal actually contributes to the strength of the social bond. Fuller (41) was unable to condition the heart-rate response consistently until puppies were 5 weeks old. This indicates that one of the factors that brings the critical period to a close may be the developing ability of the young puppy to associate fear responses with particular stimuli.

All this suggests that if the development of the escape response to strangers could be held in check, the critical period might be extended indefinitely. Raising puppies in small isolation boxes during the critical period inhibits the development of the escape response but they still show obvious signs of fear when they are first removed from their cages. Fuller (42) reports some success in socializing these older pups by overcoming their fear responses, either by careful handling or through the use of tranquilizing drugs.

Fear responses thus have the dual effect of facilitating the formation of the social bond during the critical period (along with other emotions) and of bringing the period to a close. This is understandable because the type of fear which terminates the critical period is a developing fear of strange animals. In the early part of the critical period the escape reaction is either lacking or is momentary and weak. At the close of the period it is strong enough to prevent contact altogether.

## FORMATION OF AFFECTIONAL BONDS IN ADULT LIFE

Until recently, most investigators have concentrated their attention on the critical period for primary socialization or imprinting and few have gone on to study similar phenomena in later development. This field of investigation is just beginning to open up, though many related facts have long been known. For example, many birds form strong pair bonds which are maintained as long as both members survive. In studying the development of various types of social bonds in different species of ducks, Schutz (43) finds that, while attachments to particular individuals may be formed in the early critical period from 12 to 17 hours after hatching, the critical period for the attachment to the species may not come until sometime later, in some cases as late as 30

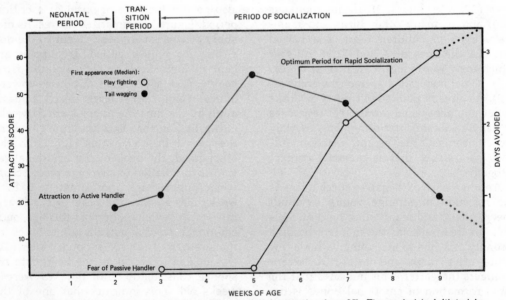

**Figure 1.** Timing mechanisms for the critical period in puppies (see 35). The period is initiated by positive behavior mechanisms, such as playful fighting, which result in attraction to a strange individual, and it is brought to a close by the development of a fear response which causes the attraction to decline. The optimum period for rapid and permanent socialization comes shortly after the appearance of prolonged avoidance reactions.

days after hatching, and the attachment to a particular member of the opposite sex, or the pair bond, does not come until the age of 5 months or so. Schutz also finds that female mallards cannot be sexually imprinted with respect to other species but always mate with other mallards no matter what their earliest experience has been. A similar phenomenon is reported by Warriner (44), who finds that male pigeons prefer to mate with birds whose color is similar to that of the parents who reared them, whether of the same or another color from themselves, but females show no preference.

Certain species of mammals, such as foxes (45), form long-lasting mating bonds. It is possible that the violence of the sexual emotions contributes to the formation of the adult bond, just as other sorts of emotional arousal are important to the primary socialization of the infant. Klopfer (46) has suggested that the rapid formation of the social bond in a mother goat toward her kid is the result of the high degree of emotional arousal which accompanies the birth of the offspring.

In short, it seems likely that the formation of a social attachment through contact and emotional arousal is a process that may take place throughout life, and that although it may take place more slowly outside of certain critical periods, the capacity for such an attachment is never completely lost.

At this point it may be remarked that, in attempting to analyze the development of affection and social bonds objectively, scientists have often tried to simplify the problem by postulating various unitary, unromantic, and sometimes unesthetic explanations. One of these was the "acquired drive" hypothesis—that children love you because you feed them. Taking a more moderate view Harlow (19) has emphasized "contact comfort" as a major variable—that the young monkey begins to love its mother because she feels warm and comfortable—

but that a number of other factors are involved. As this article indicates, evidence is accumulating that there is a much less specific, although equally unromantic, general mechanism involved — that given any kind of emotional arousal a young animal will become attached to any individual or object with which it is in contact for a sufficiently long time. The necessary arousal would, of course, include various specific kinds of emotions associated with food rewards and contact comfort.

It should not be surprising that many kinds of emotional reactions contribute to a social relationship. The surprising thing is that emotions which we normally consider aversive should produce the same effect as those which appear to be rewarding. This apparent paradox is partially resolved by evidence that the positive effect of unpleasant emotions is normally limited to early infancy by the development of escape reactions.

Nevertheless, this concept leads to the somewhat alarming conclusion that an animal (and perhaps a person) of any age, exposed to certain individuals or physical surroundings for any length of time, will inevitably become attached to them, the rapidity of the process being governed by the degree of emotional arousal associated with them. I need not dwell on the consequences for human behavior, if this conclusion should apply to our species as well as to other animals, except to point out that it provides an explanation of certain well-known clinical observations such as the development by neglected children of strong affection for cruel and abusive parents, and the various peculiar affectional relationships that develop between prisoners and jailors, slaves and masters, and so on. Perhaps the general adaptive nature of this mechanism is that since the survival of any member of a highly social species depends upon the rapid development of social relationships, a mechanism has evolved which makes it almost impossible to inhibit the formation of social bonds.

## CRITICAL PERIODS OF LEARNING

Unlike the process of socialization, the phenomenon of critical periods of learning was first noticed in children rather than in lower animals. McGraw's (47) famous experiment with the twins Johnny and Jimmy was a deliberate attempt to modify behavioral development by giving one of a pair of identical twins special early training. The result varied according to the activity involved. The onset of walking, for example, was not affected by previous practice or help. Other activities, however, could be greatly speeded up—notably roller skating, in which the favored twin became adept almost as soon as he could walk. In other activities performance was actually made worse by early practice, simply because of the formation of unskillful habits. McGraw (6) concluded that there are critical periods for learning which vary from activity to activity; for each kind of coordinated muscular activity there is an optimum period for rapid and skillful learning.

In an experiment with rats, Hebb (48) used the technique of providing young animals with many opportunities for spontaneous learning rather than formal training. Pet rats raised in the rich environment of a home performed much better on learning tasks than rats reared in barren laboratory cages. Since then, other experimenters (49) have standardized the "rich" environment as a large cage including many objects and playthings and have gotten similar effects.

Forgays (see 50) finds that the age at which the maximum effect is produced is limited to the period from approximately 20 to 30 days of age, immediately after weaning. A similar experience in adult life produces no effect. In rats, at any rate, the critical period of learning seems to coincide with the critical period of primary socializa-

tion, and it may be that the two are in some way related. Candland and Campbell (51) find that fearful behavior in response to a strange situation begins to increase in rats between 20 and 30 days after birth, and Bernstein (52) showed earlier that discrimination learning could be improved by gentle handling beginning at 20 days. It may well be that the development of fear limits the capacity for future learning as well as the formation of social relationships.

In addition to these studies on motor learning and problem solving, there are many experiments demonstrating the existence of critical periods for the learning of social behavior patterns. It has long been known that many kinds of birds do not develop the characteristic songs of their species if they are reared apart from their own kind (53). More recently, Thorpe (54) discovered a critical period for this effect in the chaffinch. If isolated at 3 or 4 days of age, a young male chaffinch produces an incomplete song, but if he hears adults singing, as a fledgling 2 or 3 weeks old or in early juvenile life before he sings himself, he will the next year produce the song characteristic of the species, even if he has been kept in isolation. In nature, the fine details of the song are added at the time of competition over territory, within a period of 2 or 3 weeks, when the bird is about a year old. At this time it learns the songs of two or three of its neighbors, and never learns any others in subsequent years. The critical period for song learning is thus a relatively long one, but it is definitely over by the time the bird is a year old. There is no obvious explanation for its ending at this particular time, but it is possible that learning a complete song pattern in some way interferes with further learning.

King and Gurney (55) found that adult mice reared in groups during youth fought more readily than animals isolated at 20 days of age. Later experiments showed that most of the effect was produced in a 10-day period just after weaning, and that similar experience as adults produced little or no effect (56). Thus, there appears to be a critical period for learning to fight through social experience, and this experience need be no more than contact through a wire. In this case the effect is probably produced by association with other mice before the fear response has been completely developed. Similarly, Fisher (16) and Fuller (57) inhibited the development of attacking behavior in fox terriers by raising them in isolation through the critical period for socialization. The animals would fight back somewhat ineffectually if attacked, but did not initiate conflicts. Tinbergen (58) found a critical period in dogs for learning territorial boundaries, coinciding with sexual maturity.

The results of corresponding experiments on sexual behavior vary from species to species. In mice, rearing in isolation produced no effects (59). Beach (60) found that male rats reared with either females or males were actually slower to respond to sexual behavior than isolated males, and he suggested that habits of playful fighting established by the group-reared animals interfered with sexual behavior later on. In guinea pigs, contact with other young animals improves sexual performance (61).

On the other hand, young chimpanzees (62) reared apart from their kind can only be mated with experienced animals. Harlow (21) discovered that his rhesus infants reared on dummy mothers did not develop normal patterns of sexual behavior, and he was able to obtain matings only by exposing females to experienced males. Normal behavior can be developed by allowing 20-minute daily play periods with other young monkeys, but if rhesus infants are reared apart from all other monkeys beyond the period when they spontaneously play with their fellows, patterns of both sexual and maternal behavior fail to develop normally. These results suggest that play has an important role in developing adult patterns of social behavior in

these primates, and that the decline of play behavior sets the upper limit of the critical period during which normal adult behavior may be developed.

Such great changes in the social environment rarely occur in humans even by accident, but Money, Hampson, and Hampson (63) have studied the development of hermaphroditic children who have been reared as one sex and then changed to the other. They find that if this occurs before 2½ years of age, very little emotional disturbance results. Thus, there is a critical period for learning the sex role, this capacity persisting unchanged up to a point in development which roughly corresponds to the age when children begin to use and understand language. Perhaps more important, this is the age when children first begin to take an interest in, and play with, members of their own age group.

It is difficult to find a common factor in these critical periods for learning. In some species, such as rats, mice, dogs, and sheep, certain critical periods for learning coincide with the period for primary socialization and seem to be similarly brought to a close by the development of fear reactions. Other critical periods, in chaffinches and dogs, coincide with the formation of adult mating bonds. However, the critical period for sexual learning in the rhesus monkey comes later than that for primary socialization (64), as do critical periods for various kinds of learning in human beings.

Part of this apparent inconsistency arises from our ignorance regarding timing mechanisms. One such mechanism must be the development of learning capacities, and we have evidence in dogs (65), rhesus monkeys (66), and human infants (12) that learning capacities change during development, sometimes in a stepwise fashion. One element in these capacities is the ability to learn things which facilitate subsequent learning.

It is equally possible, however, to "learn not to learn," and such a negative learning set may act to bring the critical period to a close. At this point, we can only state a provisional general hypothesis: that the critical period for any specific sort of learning is that time when maximum capacities —sensory, motor, and motivational, as well as psychological ones—are first present.

## CRITICAL PERIODS FOR EARLY STIMULATION

Experiments to determine the effects of early stimulation have been mainly performed on infant mice and rats, which are usually weaned at about 21 days at the earliest, and have been concerned with the effect of stimulation during this pre-weaning period. All investigators beginning with Levine (67) and Schaefer (68), agree that rats handled during the first week or 10 days of life have a lessened tendency to urinate and defecate in a strange "open field" situation, learn avoidance behavior more readily, and survive longer when deprived of food and water. In short, early stimulation produces an animal that is less timorous, learns more quickly, and is more vigorous. Levine found that the effect could be obtained by a variety of stimuli, including electric shock and mechanical shaking as well as handling. This ruled out learned behavior as an explanation of the effect, and Levine, Alpert, and Lewis (69) discovered that animals handled in the early period showed a much earlier maturation of the adrenocortical response to stress. Levine interpreted these results as indicating that the laboratory environment did not provide sufficient stimulation for the proper development of the hormonal systems of the animals. This interpretation is in agreement with Richter's finding (70) that laboratory rats are quite deficient in adrenocortical response as compared with the wild variety. Schaefer, Weingarten, and Towne (71) have duplicated Levine's results by the use of cold alone, and have suggested temperature as a possible unitary mechanism. However, their findings are not

necessarily in disagreement with those of Levine, as the hormonal stress response can be elicited by a variety of stimuli, and temperature may simply be another of the many kinds of stimuli which produce the effect.

According to Thompson and Schaefer (72) the earlier the stimulation the greater the effect. If the hormonal mechanism is the chief phenomenon involved, we can say that there is a critical period during the first week or 10 days of life, since the adrenal response in any case matures and becomes fixed by 16 days of age.

Denenberg (73) takes a somewhat different approach, pointing out that there should be optimal levels of stimulation, so that either very weak or very strong stimulation would produce poor results. He suggests that there are different critical periods for the effect of early stimulation, depending on the intensity of stimulation and the kind of later behavior measured. Working within the critical first 10 days, Denenberg found that the best avoidance learning was produced by stimulation in the second half of the period, whereas the best survival rates were produced by stimulation in the first half. Weight was approximately equally affected, except that there was little effect in the first 3 days (74).

Analyzing the effect on avoidance learning, Denenberg (75) and his associates found that both unhandled controls and rats handled for the first 20 days performed poorly, the former because they were too emotional and the latter because they were too calm to react quickly. An intermediate amount of emotional response produces the best learning, and this can be produced by handling only in the first 10 days of life; handling during the second 10 days has a lesser effect. No handling produces too much emotionality, and handling for 20 days results in too little. Irrespective of the effect on learning, the data lead to the important conclusion that emotional stimulation during a critical period early in life can lead to the reduction of emotional responses in later life.

More precisely, there appear to be two critical periods revealed by research on early stimulation of rats, one based on a physiological process (the development of the adrenal cortical stress mechanism) and extending to 16 days of age at the latest, the other based on a psychological process (the reduction of fear through familiarity) (51), beginning about 17 days when the eyes first open and extending to 30 days. The effects of handling during these two periods are additive, and many experiments based on arbitrary time rather than developmental periods undoubtedly include both.

The deleterious effects of excessive stimulation in the life of the infant may also be interpreted as a traumatic emotional experience. Bowlby (76), in studying a group of juvenile thieves, found that a large proportion of them had been separated from their mothers in early infancy, and he postulated that this traumatic emotional experience had affected their later behavior. Since this conclusion was based on retrospective information, he and his coworkers have since studied the primary symptoms of separation and have described in detail the emotional reactions of infants sent to hospitals, and thus separated from their mothers (77). Schaffer (78) found a difference in reaction to separation before 7 months and separation afterward. Both sets of infants were disturbed, but they were disturbed in different ways. Infants show increasingly severe emotional reactions to adoption from 3 through 12 months of age (33). It seems logical to place the beginning of the critical period for maximum emotional disturbance at approximately 7 months—at the end of the critical period for primary socialization, which Gray (79) places at approximately 6 weeks to 6 months. Infants whose social relationships have been thoroughly established and whose fear responses toward strangers have been fully developed are much more likely to be upset by changes than infants in which these relationships and responses have not yet been developed.

However, not all apparently "traumatic" early experiences have such a lasting effect. Experimental work shows that young animals have a considerable capacity to recover from unpleasant emotions experienced in a limited period in early life (80), and that what is traumatic in one species may not be in another. While young rats become calmer after infantile stimulation, young mice subjected to excessive auditory stimulation later become more emotional (81). At this point it is appropriate to point out that critical periods are not necessarily involved in every kind of early experience. Raising young chimpanzees in the dark produces degeneration of the retina, but this is a long and gradual process (82).

Another approach to the problem is to stimulate emotional responses in mothers and observe the effect on the offspring. Thompson (83) and other authors (84) have shown that the offspring of rats made fearful while pregnant are more likely to be overemotional in the open-field situation than the offspring of animals not so stimulated. Since any direct influence of maternal behavior was ruled out by cross-fostering experiments, it seems likely that the result is produced by modification of the adrenocortical stress mechanism—in this case, by secretion of maternal hormones acting on the embryo rather than by stimulation after birth of the young animal itself. No precise critical period for the effect has been established, but it is probably confined to the latter part of pregnancy. Similar effects have been obtained in mice (85), and if such effects can be demonstrated in other mammals, the implications for prenatal care in human beings are obvious.

It is interesting to note that, whereas shocking the mother both before and after parturition has the effect of increasing emotional responses in the young, the emotional responses of young rats are de-

*creased* when the treatment is applied directly to them. The explanation of this contradiction must await direct experiments on the endocrine system.

## GENERAL THEORY OF CRITICAL PERIODS

There are at least two ways in which experience during critical periods may act on behavioral development. The critical period for primary socialization constitutes a turning point. Experience during a short period early in life determines which shall be the close relatives of the young animal, and this, in turn, leads the animal to develop in one of two directions—the normal one, in which it becomes attached to and mates with a member of its own species, or an abnormal one, in which it becomes attached to a different species, with consequent disrupting effects upon sexual and other social relationships with members of its own kind.

The concept of a turning point applies equally well to most examples of critical periods for learning. Up to a certain point in development a chaffinch can learn several varieties of song, but once it has learned one of them it no longer has a choice. Similarly, the human infant can learn either sex role up to a certain age, but once it has learned one or the other, changing over becomes increasingly difficult. What is learned at particular points limits and interferes with subsequent learning, and Schneirla and Rosenblatt (86) have suggested that there are critical stages of learning—that what has been learned at a particular time in development may be critical for whatever follows.

A second sort of action during a critical period consists of a nonspecific stimulus producing an irrevocable result, not modifiable in subsequent development. Thus, almost any sort of stimulus has the effect of modifying the development of the endocrine stress mechanism of young rats in early infancy.

Is there any underlying common principle? Each of these effects has its counterpart in embryonic development. Up to a certain point a cell taken from an amphibian embryo and transplanted to a new location will develop in accordance with its new environment. Beyond this turning point it develops in accordance with its previous location. Some cells retain a degree of lability, but none retain the breadth of choice they had before. Similarly, specific injuries produced by nonspecific causes are also found in embryonic development: damage to an embryonic optic vesicle results in a defective eye, no matter what sort of chemical produces the injury. It is obvious that the similarity between this case and the critical period for early stimulation can be accounted for by the single common process of growth, occurring relatively late in development in the case of the endocrine stress mechanism and much earlier in the development of the eye. The effects are nonspecific because of the fact that growth can be modified in only very limited ways, by being either slowed down or speeded up.

Both growth and behavioral differentiation are based on organizing processes. This suggests a general principle of organization: that once a system becomes organized, whether it is the cells of the embryo that are multiplying and differentiating or the behavior patterns of a young animal that are becoming organized through learning, it becomes progressively more difficult to reorganize the system. That is, organization inhibits reorganization. Further, organization can be strongly modified only when active processes of organization are going on, and this accounts for critical periods of development.

## CONCLUSION

The concept of critical periods is a highly important one for human and animal welfare. Once the dangers and potential benefits for each period of life are known, it should be possible to avoid the former and take advantage of the latter.

The discovery of critical periods immediately focuses attention on the developmental processes which cause them. As these processes become understood, it is increasingly possible to deliberately modify critical periods and their results. For example, since the development of fear responses limits the period of primary socialization, we can deliberately extend the period by reducing fear reactions, either by psychological methods or by the use of tranquilizing drugs. Or, if it seems desirable, we can increase the degree of dependency of a child or pet animal by purposely increasing his emotional reactions during the critical period. Again, if infantile stimulation is desirable, parents can be taught to provide it in appropriate amounts at the proper time.

Some data suggest that for each behavioral and physiological phenomenon there is a different critical period in development. If this were literally true, the process of development, complicated by individual variability, would be so complex that the concept of critical periods would serve little useful purpose. Some sort of order can be obtained by dealing with different classes of behavioral phenomena. For example, it can be stated that the period in life in which each new social relationship is initiated is a critical one for the determination of that relationship. Furthermore, there is evidence that critical-period effects are more common early in life than they are later on, and that the critical period for primary socialization is also critical for other effects, such as the attachment to particular places (87), and may overlap with a critical period for the formation of basic food habits (88).

We may expect to find that the periods in which actual physiological damage through environmental stimulation is possible will turn out to be similarly specific and concentrated in early life.

A great deal of needed information regarding the optimum periods for acquiring motor and intellectual skills is still lacking. These skills are based not merely on age but on the relative rate of maturation of various organs. Any attempt to teach a child or animal at too early a period of development may result in his learning bad habits, or simply in his learning "not to learn," either of which results may greatly handicap him in later life. In the long run, this line of experimental work should lead to greater realization of the capacities possessed by human beings, both through avoidance of damaging experiences and through correction of damage from unavoidable accidents (89).

## REFERENCES

1. Scott, J. P. 1945. *Comparative Psychology Monographs* 18:1.

2. Fielde, A. M. 1904. *Biological Bulletin* 7:227.

3. Stockard, C. R. 1921. *American Journal of Anatomy* 28:115.

4. Child, C. M. 1941. *Patterns and problems of development.* Chicago: University of Chicago Press.

5. Lorenz, K. 1935. *Journal of Ornithology* 83:137, 289.

6. McGraw, M. B. 1946. In *Manual of child psychology*, ed. L. C. Carmichael, pp. 332–369. New York: Wiley.

7. Hess, E. H. 1959. In *Nebraska symposium on motivation*, pp. 44–77. Lincoln: University of Nebraska Press.

8. Moltz, H. 1960. *Psychological Bulletin* 57:291. Gewirtz, J. L. 1961. In *Determinants of infant behaviour*, ed. B. M. Foss, pp. 213–299. London: Methuen.

9. Scott, J. P. In press. In *Social behavior and organization in vertebrates*, ed. W. Etkin. Chicago: University of Chicago Press.

10. Nice, M. M. 1943. *Transactions of the Linnaean Society of New York* 6:1.

11. Scott, J. P., and Marston, M. V. 1950. *Journal of Genetic Psychology* 77:25.

12. Scott, J. P. In press. *Child Development Monographs.*

13. Brodbeck, A. J. 1954. *Bulletin of the Ecological Society of America* 35:73.

14. Stanley, W. C. 1962. Private communication.

15. Elliot, O., and King, J. A. 1960. *Psychological Reports* 6:391.

16. Fisher, A. E. 1955. Thesis, Pennsylvania State University.

17. Elliot, O., and Scott, J. P. 1961. *Journal of Genetic Psychology* 99:3.

18. Scott, J. P.; Deshaies, D.; and Morris, D. D. 1961. Effect of emotional arousal on primary socialization in the dog. Address to the New York State Branch of the American Psychiatric Association, November 11.

19. Harlow, H. 1958. *American Psychologist* 13:673.

20. Igel, G. J., and Calvin, A. D. 1960. *Journal of Comparative and Physiological Psychology* 53:302.

21. Harlow, H. F., and Harlow, M. K. 1962. Personal communication.

22. Fabricius, E. 1951. *Acta Zoologica Fennica* 68:1.

23. Collias, N. 1962. In *Roots of behavior*, ed. E. L. Bliss, pp. 264–273. New York: Harper.

24. Hess, E. H. 1957. *Annals of the New York Academy of Sciences* 67:724. In *Drugs and behavior*, ed. L. Uhr and J. G. Miller, pp. 268–271. New York: Wiley, 1960.

25. James, H. 1959. *Canadian Journal of Psychology* 13:59.

26. Gray, P. H. 1960. *Science* 132:1834.

27. Guiton, P. 1961. *Animal Behavior* 9:167.

28. Pitz, G. F., and Ross, R. B. 1961. *Journal of Comparative and Physiological Psychology* 54:602.

29. Hess, E. H. 1961. Influence of early experience on behavior. Paper presented before the American Psychiatric Association, New York State Divisional Meeting.

30. Moltz, H.; Rosenblum, L.; and Halikas, N. 1959. *Journal of Comparative and Physiological Psychology* 52:240.

31. Gottlieb, G. 1961. *Journal of Comparative and Physiological Psychology* 54:422.

32. Scott, J. P. 1958. *Psychosomatic Medicine* 20:42.

33. Caldwell, B. M. 1961. *American Psychologist* 16:377.

34. Hinde, R. A.; Thorpe, W. H.; and Vince, M. A. 1956. *Behaviour* 9:214.

35. Freedman, D. G.; King, J. A.; and Elliot, O. 1961. *Science* 133:1016.

36. Harlow, H. F., and Zimmermann, R. R. 1959. *Science* 130:421.

37. Freedman, D. G. 1961. *Journal of Child Psychology and Psychiatry* 242.

38. Spitz, R. A. 1950. *International Journal of Psychoanalysis* 31:138.

39. Collias, N. E. 1956. *Ecology* 37:228.

40. Craig, W. 1914. *Journal of Animal Behavior* 4:121.

41. Fuller, J. L., and Christake, A. 1959. *Federation Proceedings* 18:49.

42. Fuller, J. L. Private communication.

43. Schutz, F. Private communication.

44. Warriner, C. C. 1960. Thesis, University of Oklahoma.

45. Enders, R. K. 1945. *Sociometry* 8:53–55.

46. Klopfer, P. H. In press. *Behavioral aspects of ecology*. New York: Prentice-Hall.

47. McGraw, M. B. 1935. *Growth: A study of Johnny and Jimmy*. New York: Appleton-Century.

48. Hebb, D. O. 1947. *American Psychologist* 2:306.

49. Forgays, D. G., and Forgays, J. W. 1952. *Journal of Comparative and Physiological Psychology* 45:322.

50. Forgays, D. G. 1962. The importance of experience at specific times in the development of an organism. Address before the Eastern Psychological Association.

51. Candland, D. K., and Campbell, B. A. 1962. Private communication.

52. Bernstein, L. 1957. *Journal of Comparative and Physiological Psychology* 50:162.

53. Scott, W. E. D. 1901. *Science* 14:522.

54. Thorpe, W. H. 1961. In *Current problems in animal behaviour*, ed. W. H. Thorpe and O. L. Zangwill. Cambridge: Cambridge University Press.

55. King, J. A., and Gurney, N. L. 1954. *Journal of Comparative and Physiological Psychology* 47:326.

56. King, J. A. 1957. *Journal of Genetic Psychology* 90:151.

57. Fuller, J. L. In press. Proceedings, International Psychiatric Congress, Montreal.

58. Tinbergen, N. 1951. *The study of instinct*. Oxford: Oxford University Press.

59. King, J. A. 1956. *Journal of Genetic Psychology* 88:223.

60. Beach, F. A. 1942. *Journal of Genetic Psychology* 60:121.

61. Valenstein, E. S.; Riss, W.; and Young, W. C. 1954. *Journal of Comparative and Physiological Psychology* 47:162.

62. Nissen, H. 1954. *Symposium on sexual behavior in mammals, Amherst, Mass.*, pp. 204–227.

63. Money, J.; Hampson, J. G.; and Hampson, J. L. 1957. *Archives of Neurology and Psychiatry* 77:333.

64. Harlow, H. 1961. In *Determinants of infant behaviour*, ed. B. M. Foss, pp. 75–97. New York: Wiley.

65. Fuller, J. L.; Easler, C. A.; and Banks, E. M. 1950. *American Journal of Physiology* 160:462. Cornwell, A. C., and Fuller, J. L. 1961. *Journal of Comparative and Physiological Psychology* 54:13.

66. Harlow, H. F.; Harlow, M. K.; Rueping, R. R.; and Mason, W. A. 1960. *Journal of Comparative and Physiological Psychology* 53:113.

67. Levine, S.; Chevalier, J. A.; and Korchin, S. J. 1956. *Journal of Personality* 24:475.

68. Schaefer, T. 1957. Thesis, University of Chicago.

69. Levine, S.; Alpert, M.; and Lewis, G. W. 1957. *Science* 126:1347.

70. Richter, C. P. 1952. *American Journal of Human Genetics* 4:273.

71. Schaefer, T., Jr.; Weingarten, F. S.; and Towne, J. C. 1962. *Science* 135:41.

72. Thompson, W. R., and Schaefer, T. 1961. In *Functions of varied experience*, ed. D. W. Fiske and S. R. Maddi, pp. 81–105. Homewood, Ill.: Dorsey.

73. Denenberg, V. H. In *The behaviour of domestic animals*, ed. E. S. E. Hafez, pp. 109–138. London: Bailliere, Tindall, and Cox.

74. Denenberg, V. H. In press. *Journal of Comparative and Physiological Psychology.*

75. Denenberg, V. H., and Karas, G. G. 1960. *Psychological Reports* 7:313.

76. Bowlby, J. 1944. *International Journal of Psychoanalysis* 25:19, 107.

77. Heinicke, C. M. 1956. *Human Relations* 9:105.

78. Schaffer, H. R. 1950. *British Journal of Medical Psychology* 31:174.

79. Gray, P. H. 1958. *Journal of Psychology* 46:155.

80. Kahn, M. W. 1951. *Journal of Genetic Psychology* 79:117. Baron, A.; Brookshire, K. H.; and Littman, R. A. 1957. *Journal of Comparative and Physiological Psychology* 50:530.

81. Lindzey, G.; Lykken, D. T.; and Winston, H. D. 1960. *Journal of Abnormal and Social Psychology* 61:7.

82. Riesen, A. H. 1961. In *Functions of varied experience*, ed. D. W. Fiske and S. R. Maddi, pp. 57–80. Homewood, Ill.: Dorsey.

83. Thompson, W. R. 1957. *Science* 125:698.

84. Hockman, C. H. 1961. *Journal of Comparative and Physiological Psychology* 54:679. Ader, R., and Belfer, M. L. 1962. *Psychological Reports* 10:711.

85. Keeley, K. 1962. *Science* 135:44.

86. Schneirla, T. C., and Rosenblatt, J. S. 1960. *American Journal of Orthopsychiatry* 31:223.

87. Thorpe, W. H. 1956. *Learning and instinct in animals*. London: Methuen.

88. Hess, E. H. 1962. In *Roots of behavior*, ed. E. L. Bliss, pp. 254–263. New York: Harper.

89. Part of the research described in this article was supported by a Public Health Service research grant (No. M-4481) from the National Institute of Mental Health.

# READING 12

# "Social-Releaser Mechanisms" in Birds - A Controlled Replication of Tinbergen's Study

**MALCOLM A. McNIVEN**
**E. I. du Pont de Nemours & Company, Inc.**

One of the basic requirements of "good" research is that the results be replicable. The following article represents a situation where contradictory results occurred in the replication of a study. McNiven, on the basis of his experimental findings, refutes the work of Tinbergen's study, giving various reasons for the discrepancy, among them the possible differences in experimental procedures, equipment, etc. When a reader is faced with contradictory data, what should be his course of action? Keep this question in mind as you read this article.

**QUESTIONS**

1. Do you feel this "controlled replication" to be an adequate refutation of Tinbergen's conclusions? Support your answer.
2. How many replications of a study are necessary before we can consider the results to be valid? What are the statistical implications of many replications?
3. What is meant by a social releaser? How can this concept be used in psychology?

In the last 10 years, publications discussing human and animal learning have quoted the studies of the European ecologists (Lorenz, Tinbergen, Baerends, et al.) with increasing frequency and with increasing importance attributed to their work (Beach, 1951; Hinde, 1959; Miller, 1951; Nissen, 1951). In general, the studies have supported the thesis of the existence of in-herited neural mechanisms which control behavior.

Tinbergen's work presents an interesting hypothesis—the concept of the "social releaser." The social releaser is an innate neural releasing mechanism which, when acted upon by certain adequate stimuli in the natural environment, triggers-off certain adaptive responses. These innate releasing mechanisms are acquired by the organism through a process of species evolution and manifest themselves in such behavioral segments as mating, fright reactions, threat behavior, and other such stereotyped active patterns. Due to the fact that there is considerable generalization of response to various classes of stimuli, the resulting behavior may appear abortive and non-adjustive, as in the case of the dragonfly laying her eggs on a tar roof, or the threat behavior of the three-spined stickleback on seeing his image in the mirror. Nevertheless, the great majority of responses are appropriate and appear when the proper sign stimulus is perceived by the organism. The social releaser, which is a specialized releaser, is a materialization of the innate releasing mechanism which, through adaptive evolution, has persisted because of its appropriateness. The implications of this hypothetical mechanism are interesting when extended to the subject of nativism in human behavior, as Tinbergen does.

A study frequently referred to is that of Tinbergen's (1948) which reported the reactions of several species of birds raised in isolation to an ambiguous silhouette which resembled a predator when moving in one direction and non-predator when pulled in the other direction. Hilgard reports this study in his chapter in *Perception—an Approach to Personality* (1951); Miller reports the study in his discussion of the acquisition of fear in the *Handbook of Experimental Psychology* (1951).

In an effort to verify these rather startling findings, a series of controlled field studies was conducted to determine the frequency of occurrence of this response and its generality to other species of birds.[1]

---

[1]These studies were initiated in the Comparative Psychological Laboratory at Ohio University under the guidance of J. R. Patrick. They were continued at The Pennsylvania State University under the guidance of C. R. Carpenter and with the cooperation of the Department of Poultry Husbandry.

## PROBLEM

The general hypothesis to be tested was that birds raised in isolation will react differently to an ambiguous silhouette when it is presented to them in different directions (e.g., short neck leading vs. long neck leading). When stated in the null form:

$H_0$: There will be no differences between the number of escape responses elicited upon presentation of the silhouette in the short-neck direction and in the long-neck direction.

The sailing and swooping variable was included since Tinbergen found that swooping of a stimulus more often elicited an escape response than did the sailing response. A second null hypothesis may be stated:

$H_0{}^1$: There will be no differences in the proportion of escape responses elicited by the swooping and the sailing presentation of the silhouette.

## METHOD

The experimental treatments of all groups tested are shown in Table 1.

### Table 1
GROUP TREATMENTS

| | | IA | IB | Group IC | II | III | IV |
|---|---|---|---|---|---|---|---|
| Short-neck Leading | Sailing | X | | | X | X | X | X |
| | Swooping | | X | X | X | X | X |
| Long-neck Leading | Sailing | X | | | X | X | X | X |
| | Swooping | | X | X | X | X | X |

Subjects   The responses of domestic chickens (New Hampshires), undomesticated ducks (mallards), and undomesticated pheasants were observed in the experimental situation. These groups are described in Table 2.

**Table 2**
INFORMATION ABOUT EXPERIMENTAL GROUPS

| Group | Type Bird | N | Tested Individually or in Groups | Age | Number of Trials per Subject |
|-------|-----------|---|----------------------------------|-----|------------------------------|
| I A | Chicken | 10 | Group | 7 weeks | 12 |
| I B | Chicken | 10 | Group | 7 weeks | 12 |
| I C | Chicken | 5 | Individually | 7 weeks | 4 |
| II | Chicken | 8 | Individually | 6 weeks | 24 |
| III | Duck | 5 | Individually | 4 weeks | 24 |
| IV | Pheasant | 24 | Individually | 4 weeks | 24 |

**Apparatus**   A wire enclosure 10 feet in diameter was used as the test area. This was located close to the area where the birds were housed. A wire was strung over the enclosure at a height of 15 feet.

The silhouettes used in the experiment were similar to those described by Tinbergen. They were constructed of Masonite; one was painted black and the other was the unpainted brown color. The black silhouette used originally had a 20″ wingspan and a 10″ body. The unpainted silhouette used later was larger with a 28″ wingspan and a 14″ body. The design of these silhouettes was such that when they were pulled in the direction with the short

HAWK ←—        —→ GOOSE

**Figure 1.**   Design of silhouette used.

neck leading and the long body behind, they resembled a hawk; but when pulled in the opposite direction, the silhouettes resembled a goose. (See Figure 1.)

**Procedure**   The animals were kept in a relatively shadow-free room from the time of hatching until the experimental trials. When placed in the wire enclosure, they were allowed a ten-minute orientation period. The silhouette was then sailed over them on the wire, first in one direction then in the reverse direction. Order was rotated. In the sailing position of the design each group received six presentations of the silhouette in each direction or 12 trials in total. In the swooping portion, the same procedure was followed as above. The swooping trials always followed the sailing trials, except in the case of 10 chickens in Group IB who received only swooping trials and in Group IA which received no swooping trials. The swoop was achieved by fixing a 12-foot wire to the wire over the enclosure and then holding the silhouette up and allowing it to swoop over the enclosure and up where it was held for the next trial. Responses of the subjects were coded as follows: (1) escape response, (2) crouching response, (3) no response.

## RESULTS

Table 3 shows the proportion of escape and crouching responses combined for each group to the hawk and goose silhouette.

**Table 3**
PROPORTION OF ESCAPE RESPONSES TO DIRECTION OF STIMULUS MOVEMENT

| | | Base | Short-neck Leading | Long-neck Leading |
|---|---|------|--------------------|--------------------|
| Group | I A | 120 | .83 | .00 |
| | I B | 120 | 31.67 | 33.33 |
| | I C | 20 | 37.50 | 32.50 |
| | II | 192 | 10.42 | 10.42 |
| | III | 120 | 13.72 | 11.76 |
| | IV | 576 | 43.26 | 42.90 |
| Total | | 1148 | 32.50 | 32.26 |

**Table 4**

PROPORTION OF ESCAPE RESPONSES TO TYPE OF MOVEMENT

|       |     | Base | Sailing | Swooping |
|-------|-----|------|---------|----------|
| Group | I A | 120  | .83     | —        |
|       | I B | 120  | —       | 64.16    |
|       | I C | 20   | .00     | 65.00    |
|       | II  | 192  | 5.21    | 15.63    |
|       | III | 120  | 7.40    | 18.75    |
|       | IV  | 576  | 7.61    | 77.08    |
| Total |     | 1148 | 5.29    | 59.29    |

The results shown in Table 3 when tested by a Chi-square test indicated no differences in the number of escape responses elicited by the silhouette when pulled in the short-necked direction and when pulled in the long-necked direction. The null hypothesis $H_0$ is not rejected.

The results in Table 4 indicated that there were significant differences between the escape responses elicited by the swooping silhouette vs. the sailing silhouette. Thus $H_0^1$ is rejected (P=.001.)

## DISCUSSION

It is apparent from the results in Table 3 that the birds did not respond differentially to the shape of the silhouette when it was moved in the "long neck leading" and the "short neck leading" directions. One would conclude without question that this variable was not a factor in the birds' responses to the silhouette. It should also be noted that this finding held true for all the experimental groups.

It is equally apparent from Table 4 that the variable of type of movement was an important factor in determining the birds' responses.

The fact that none of the experimental groups was tested at various ages leaves unanswered the question of the effect of age on the evocation of a selective response to "predator" shapes. Some of Tinbergen's birds exhibited the selective response at 4 weeks. Therefore the age of our experimental animals (4-7 weeks) should have been adequate to illustrate the phenomenon.

Hirsch, Lindley and Tolman (1955) report that, when Tinbergen's hypothesis was tested under laboratory conditions with white Leghorn chickens, the form of the silhouette (changed by direction of movement) was not a significant source of variance. Tinbergen's results concerning a hypothetical "social releaser mechanism" were not supported in this study. The experimental techniques used by Hirsch, Lindley and Tolman were quite similar to those used in the present study, except for the fact that their trials were run indoors under controlled background and illumination conditions while the present study was conducted outdoors under natural conditions.

The results in Table 3 agree with those results reported by Hirsch, Lindley and Tolman.

The data presented in Tables 3 and 4 certainly bring into question the results of the Tinbergen study. However, one must ask: "How could these results differ so markedly from those obtained by Tinbergen?" Perhaps the answer lies in the different approaches to studying a problem demonstrated by American comparative psychologists and their European counterparts. Tinbergen's statement of the results merely indicated that young gallinaceous birds, ducks, and geese reacted in a frightened manner to the silhouette when moved in the "hawk" direction, but showed no escape responses when the silhouette was moved in the "goose" direction. No data were reported and no description of the details of the procedure was reported. A request to Tinbergen for specific information about the experimental procedure was not answered. The answer to the question of why the results differ may lie in the details of procedure, in the details of the subjects' environment prior to the trials, or in many other aspects of the study. But, unless these are reported by the experimenter, we will never know. Writers in

America have given wide circulation to the studies of the Lorenz-Tinbergen school without demanding corroborative evidence of the adequacy of the experimental work. Several individuals have worked closely with members of the Lorenz-Tinbergen school and have reported on their work. One such report by Lehrman (1953) criticized Lorenz's theory of instinct for the following reasons:

1. It is rigidly canalized by the merging of widely different kinds of organization under inappropriate and gratuitous categories.

2. It involves preconceived and rigid ideas of innateness and the nature of maturation.

3. It habitually depends on the transference of concepts from one level to another, solely on the basis of analogical reasoning.

4. It is limited by preconceptions of isomorphic resemblances between neural and behavioral phenomena.

5. It depends on finalistic, preformationist conceptions of the development of behavior itself.

6. As indicated by its applications to human psychology and sociology, it leads to, or depends on, (or both), a rigid, preformationist, categorical conception of development and organization.

There is no doubt that the work of the European ecologists and ornithologists will have and should have heuristic value for studies of animal and human behavior in the U.S. However, we should not accept the conclusions of the ecologist's studies until they have been replicated by more experimental techniques or until the details of the experimental procedures, equipment, and data have been fully reported.

## CONCLUSIONS

1. Chickens, ducks and pheasants fail to exhibit the escape responses to the sign-stimulus of "short-neckedness" as reported by Tinbergen.

2. Chickens, ducks, and pheasants do exhibit escape responses to a swooping movement of the silhouette, but this is true regardless of the direction in which it is moving.

3. The slow sailing of the silhouette over chickens, ducks, and pheasants does not elicit escape responses, regardless of direction.

## SUMMARY

Tinbergen reported a study which found that young gallinaceous birds, ducks, and geese reacted in a frightened manner to a silhouette when it moved in the "hawk" direction, but showed no escape responses when the silhouette was moved in the "goose" direction. In order to replicate this study, chickens, ducks, and pheasants were presented with the same type of silhouette used by Tinbergen. A total of 1178 trials were run with the three species of birds. The silhouette was presented in a sailing manner (moving horizontally over the birds), and in a swooping manner. The silhouette was presented alternately in one direction then the other. The results do not support the data reported in Tinbergen's study. There was no difference in the number of escape responses to the silhouette when it moved in the two directions.

## REFERENCES

Beach, F. A. 1951. Instinctive behavior: Reproductive activities. In *Handbook of experimental psychology*, ed. S. S. Stevens, pp. 387–434. New York: Wiley.

Hilgard, E. R. 1951. In *Perception: An approach to personality*, ed. R. R. Blake and G. V. Ramsey. New York: Ronald.

Hinde, R. A. 1959. Some recent trends in ethology. In *Psychology: A study of a science. Study 1: Conceptual and systematic*, ed. S. Koch. New York: McGraw-Hill.

Hirsch, J.; Lindley, R. H.; and Tolman, E. C. 1955. An experimental test of an alleged innate sign stimulus. *Journal of Comparative and Physiological Psychology* 48:278–280.

Lehrman, D. S. 1953. A critique of Konrad Lorenz's theory of instinctive behavior. *Quarterly Review of Biology* 27:337–359.

Miller, N. E. 1951. Learnable drives and rewards. In *Handbook of experimental psychology*, ed. S. S. Stevens, pp. 435–472. New York: Wiley.

Nissen, H. W. 1951. Phylogenetic comparison. In *Handbook of experimental psychology*, ed. S. S. Stevens, pp. 347–386. New York: Wiley.

Tinbergen, N. 1948. Social releasers and the experimental method required for their study. *Wilson Bulletin* 60:6–52.

# READING 13

# The Development of Learning in the Rhesus Monkey

**HARRY F. HARLOW**

Harry F. Harlow has done extensive work with the behavior of the rhesus monkey. In the following article, Harlow describes the maturation of this monkey's learning ability, presenting experimental data which suggest that development begins within the first few days of life and extends into the fourth or fifth year.

**QUESTIONS**

1. Harlow states: "There is a tendency to think of learning or training as intrinsically good and necessarily valuable to the organism. It is entirely possible, however, that training can either be helpful or harmful, depending upon the nature of the training and the organism's state of development." Comment on this statement in reference to child-rearing and educational techniques.

2. To what degree can information about the development of learning in monkeys apply to humans? To other animals?

3. Are the problems chosen for experimental solution good choices? Can you suggest other problems? Support your answer.

During the last five years we have conducted an integrated series of researches tracing and analyzing the learning capabilities of rhesus monkeys from birth to intellectual maturity. Control over the monkey's environment has been achieved by separating the infants from their mothers at birth and raising them independently, using techniques and methods adapted from those described by van Wagenen (12).

There are many characteristics that com-

mend the rhesus monkey as a subject for investigation of the development of learning. At birth, or a few days later, this animal attains adequate control over its head, trunk, arm, and leg movements, permitting objective recording of precise responses on tests of learning. The rhesus monkey has broad learning abilities, and even the neonatal monkey rapidly learns problems appropriate to its maturational status. As it grows older, this monkey can master a relatively unlimited range of problems suitable

A Sigma Xi-RESA National Lecture, 1958–59.

for measuring intellectual maturation. Although the rhesus monkey matures more rapidly than the human being, the time allotted for assessing its developing learning capabilities is measured in terms of years — not days, weeks, or months, as is true with most subprimate forms. During this time a high degree of control can be maintained over all experimental variables, particularly those relating to the animal's learning experiences. Thus, we can assess for all learning problems the relative importance of nativistic and experiential variables, determine the age at which problems of any level of difficulty can first be solved, and measure the effects of introducing such learning problems to animals before or after this critical period appears. Furthermore, the monkey may be used with impunity as a subject for discovering the effects of cerebral damage or insult, whether produced by mechanical intervention or by biochemical lesions.

The only other creature whose intellectual maturation has been studied with any degree of adequacy is the human child, and the data from this species attest to the fact that learning capability increases with age, particularly in the range and difficulty of learned tasks which can be mastered. Beyond this fact, the human child has provided us with astonishingly little basic information on the nature or development of learning. Obviously, there are good and sufficient reasons for any and all such deficiencies. There are limits beyond which it is impossible or unjustifiable to use the child as an experimental subject. The education of groups of children cannot be hampered or delayed for purposes of experimental control over either environment or antecedent learning history. Unusual motivational conditions involving either deprivation or overstimulation are undesirable. Neurophysiological or biochemical studies involving or threatening physical injury are unthinkable.

Even aside from these cultural limitations, the human child has certain characteristics that render him a relatively limited subject for the experimental analysis of the maturation of learning capability. At birth, his neuromuscular systems are so undeveloped that he is incapable of effecting the precise head, arm, hand, trunk, leg, and foot movements essential for objective measurement. By the time these motor functions have adequately matured, many psychological developmental-processes, including those involving learning, have appeared and been elaborated, but their history and nature have been obscured or lost in a maze of confounded variables.

By the time the normal child has matured physically, he is engaging each day in such a fantastic wealth of multiple learning activities that precise, independent control over any single learning process presents a task beyond objective realism. The multiple, interactive transfer processes going on overwhelm description, and their independent experimental evaluation cannot be achieved. Even if it were proper to cage human children willfully, which it assuredly is not, this very act would in all probability render the children abnormal and untestable and again leave us with an insuperable problem.

It might appear that all these difficulties could be overcome best by studying the development of learning abilities in infraprimate organisms rather than monkeys. Unfortunately, the few researches which have been completed indicate that this is not true. Animals below the primate order are intellectually limited compared with monkeys, so that they learn the same problems more slowly and are incapable of solving many problems that are relatively easily mastered by monkeys. Horses and rats, and even cats and dogs, can solve only a limited repertoire of learning tasks, and they learn so slowly on all but the simplest of these that they pass from infancy to maturity before their intellectual measurement can be completed. Even so, we possess scattered information within this area. We know that cats perform more adequately on the Hamilton perseverance test than do kittens and that the same relationship holds for dogs compared with puppies (2, 3). It has been demonstrated that mature and aged rats are no more proficient on a multiple-T maze than young rats (11), and that conditioned responses cannot be established in dogs before 18–21 days of age (1); but such data will never give us insight into the fundamental laws of learning or maturation of learning.

## NEONATAL AND EARLY INFANTILE LEARNING: THE FIRST SIXTY DAYS

Because learning and the development of learning are continuous, orderly processes, classifying learning into temporal intervals is an arbitrary procedure. However, a criterion that may be taken for separating early learning from later learning is the underlying motive or incentive. Solid foods are precluded as incentives for monkey learning prior to 40–60 days of age, forcing the experimenter to depend upon such rewards as liquid nutrients, shock avoidance, exploration, and home cage conditions. It is recognized that these same rewards may be used to motivate older primates on learning tasks, but for them the convenient incentive of solid food becomes available. Another arbitrary criterion that may be taken for choosing this temporal period lies in the fact that fear of strange, new situations—including test situations—only appears toward the end of this period.

## CONDITIONAL RESPONSES

The earliest unequivocal learned responses which we obtained from the rhesus monkey were conditioned responses in a situation in which an auditory stimulus was paired with electric shock. The standard procedure was to adapt the neonatal monkeys during the first two days of life by placing them for ten minutes a day in the apparatus, which consisted of a cubic Plexiglas stabilimeter with a grid floor, enclosed in a sound-deadened cabinet with a one-way-vision screen on the front. Conditioning trials were initiated on the third day, the tone and shock intervals being mechanically fixed at two seconds and one second, respecively, and administered either separately or paired. The animals were divided into three groups and were given daily trials as follows: five experimental subjects (T-S group) were given eight paired tone-shock trials and two test trials; four pseudoconditioning controls (P-C group) were given eight shock trials and two test trials in which tone only was presented; and four stimulus-sensitization controls (T-O group) received ten tone trials but never received shock from the grid floor. Conditioned and unconditioned responses were measured in terms of both the continuous, objective activity records taken from an Esterline-Angus recorder and the check-list records made by two independent human observers.

The learning data presented in Figure 1 show early and progressive learning. The differences between the frequency of conditioned responses by the five experimental subjects and the four subjects in each of the control groups were significant, even though clear-cut evidence of pseudocondi-

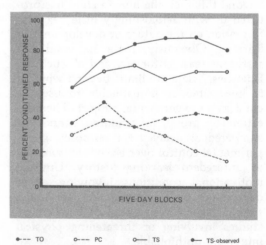

**Figure 1.** Conditioned response to tone.

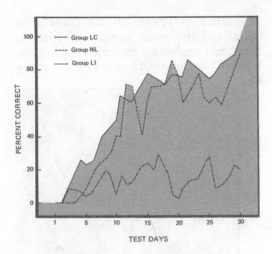

**Figure 2.** Straight-runway performance.

tioning was found in one of the P-C animals. It will be noted that the observers recorded a higher frequency of conditioned responses than could be identified from the stabilimeter record. The observational data indicate that these tone-shock conditioned responses were learned by three subjects on the second test day and that unequivocal conditioning took place in four of the five subjects. The observational data also show that the form of the conditioned response changes with training, starting as a diffuse response and gradually becoming more precise. As training progressed, most subjects responded to the conditioned stimulus by standing erect, sometimes on one foot.

Limited tests failed to demonstrate any generalization of the conditioned response to the experimenter or to auditory stimuli presented outside the test situation. Retention tests made fifteen days after the completion of the original training revealed very considerable learning loss, ranging among individual subjects from no definite indication of retention, to conditioned responses on about half the test trials.

## STRAIGHT-RUNWAY PERFORMANCE

An apparently simple learned response, which has been frequently used by psychol-

ogists in studying rat learning, is the straight runway. We produced such an apparatus by simply using the monkey's living cage as the runway and introducing a nursing booth at one end prior to each feeding period. At the time of testing, the subject was taken to the far end of the home cage, faced toward the nursing booth, released, and allowed thirty seconds to enter the booth. The number of daily trials was determined by number of feeding sessions, twelve a day during the first two weeks, and ten a day subsequently.

The subjects were divided into three groups: For the light-conditioned animals (L-C group) the nursing booth was suffused with flashing green light during each of the training trials; for the no-light monkeys (N-L group) there were no conditioning cues other than those afforded by the test situation and the act of orientation; for the light-extinguished subjects (L-I group) the nursing booth was suffused with green light, but this light was immediately extinguished when the monkey entered the booth and simultaneously there began a five-minute delay period before feeding.

The data presented in Figure 2 offer evidence of rapid and progressive improvement in performance. Many of the failures during the first ten days resulted from locomotor limitations or from the disturbing effects of reorientation and restraint by the experimenter. It is clear, however, that learning occurred early in life and that the cue of green light added little or nothing to the cues provided by the presence of the experimenter and postural orientation. The L-I group, which did not receive food upon approach to the nursing booth, was significantly inferior to the other two groups, and it is possible that the green light became a cue for absence or delay of feeding.

## SPATIAL DISCRIMINATION

Two groups of ten monkeys each were tested on a spatial discrimination problem requiring choice of right or left alley of the

Y-maze. One group of subjects began training at fifteen days of age (group 15), after four days of adaptation, and the other group started maze learning at forty-five days of age (group 45). Two trials were given each day, a correct trial being rewarded by entrance into the home cage, a highly effective incentive for the infant monkey, whereas an incorrect response, defined as entrance into the incorrect antechamber, was punished by a one-minute delay before rerunning. A rerun technique was used throughout this test, i.e., whenever the monkey made an error, it was returned to the starting position and run again until it made the correct choice and reached the home cage. Spatial discrimination learning was continued for twenty-five days; on the twenty-sixth day the position of the correct goal box was reversed and the same training schedule of two trials per day continued.

The percentage of correct initial responses made by group 15 on days 1, 2, 5, 10, and 15 are 45, 60, 75, 75, and 95, respectively. Comparable percentages for group 45 are 80, 55, 65, 85, and 100. Despite the high percentage of correct responses made by group 45 on day 1, the two learning curves, as illustrated in Figure 3, are very similar. Excluding a single member in each group that failed to adapt to the test situation and never met the criterion of 18 correct responses in 20 consecutive trials, the mean number of trials to this criterion, excluding the criterional trials, was 8.5 for group 15 and 6.2 for group 45.

The percentage of correct responses dropped below chance for both groups of monkeys during the first five reversal trials, and trial 1 was especially characterized by multiple, persistent, erroneous choices. During all these trials the animals made many violent emotional responses as indicated by balking, vocalization, and autonomic responses, including blushing, urination, and defecation. Even so, all but one subject in group 15 attained the criterion of

18 correct responses in 20 consecutive trials, and the mean number of trials to learn, not including the criterional trials, was 19.2 for group 15 and 11.9 for group 45.

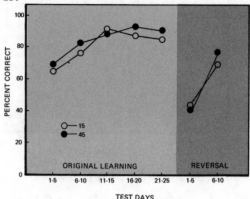

**Figure 3.**   Per cent correct response on Y-maze.

Although the performance of the older group was superior to that of the younger, particularly on the reversal problem, the differences were not statistically significant. Certainly the 15-day-old macaques solved this spatial learning task with facility, and their performance leaves little to be gained through additional maturation.

## OBJECT DISCRIMINATION

Two groups of four newborn monkeys were trained on a black-white discrimination, i.e., a nonspatial or object discrimination, by teaching them to select and climb up a black or white ramp for the reward of a full meal delivered through a nursing bottle. An incorrect choice was punished by a three-minute delay in feeding. Not only the ramp, but the entire half of the test situation was black or white, as the case might be, and the positions of these half-cages were reversed on fifty per cent of the trials. The number of test trials was stabilized at nine per day after the first few days of life.

Learning by the neonatal macaques in this test situation proved to be almost unbelievably rapid, even allowing for the fact that a maximally efficient stimulus display was provided by the totally black and totally white halves of the test chamber. As can be seen in Figure 4, the group of infants trained from birth on the object-discrimination problem attained the criterion of ninety per cent correct responses on two consecutive days beginning at nine days of age. This was a total of less than 100 trials, many of which were failed through physical inability to climb the ramp. A second group, run as a maturational control, was rewarded for climbing up either of two gray ramps for the first ten days. On day 11 the black and white ramps were substituted, and these monkeys solved the black-white discrimination problem, the first formal learning problem they had ever faced, by the second test day, averaging less than thirteen trials to achieve the criterion.

After the black-white discrimination problem was solved, the infants were tested on discrimination reversal, i.e., the color of ramp previously correct was now made incorrect, and the color of the ramp previously incorrect became correct. The results were very similar to those obtained in the spatial discrimination problem. The infants made a great many errors when the problem was first reversed and showed very severe emotional disturbances. This was particularly true when the reversal went from white correct to black, since infant monkeys strongly prefer white to black.

We have also a considerable body of data showing that the infant monkey can solve form discriminations and color discriminations as well as the black-white brightness-discrimination problem. It is not possible in these other situations, particularly in the case of form discrimination, to attain the maximally efficient stimulus display previously described. For this reason—and a control study suggests that it is for this reason alone—the number of trials required to learn increases and the age at which learning can be demonstrated also ad-

vances. Even so, it has been possible to obtain discrimination between a triangle and a circle by the 20- to 30-day-old monkey after less than 200 training trials.

## INFANT LEARNING: THE FIRST YEAR

The most surprising finding relating to neonatal learning was the very early age at which simple learning tasks could be mastered. Indeed, learning of both the simple conditioned responses and the straight runway appeared as early as the animal was capable of expressing it through the maturation of adequate skeletal motor responses. Thus, we can in no way exclude the possibility that the monkey at normal term, or even before normal term, is capable of forming simple associations.

Equally surprising is the fact that performance may reach or approach maximal facility within a brief period of time. The five-day-old monkey forms conditioned reflexes between tone and shock as rapidly as the year-old or the adult monkey. The baby macaque solves the simple straight-alley problem as soon as it can walk, and there is neither reason nor leeway for the adult to do appreciably better. Although we do not know the minimal age for solution of the Y-maze, it is obviously under fifteen days. Such data as we have on this problem indicate that the span between age of initial solution and the age of maximally efficient solution is brief. One object discrimination, the differentiation between the total-black and total-white field, shows characteristics similar to the learning already described. The developmental period for solution lies between six and ten days of age, and a near maximal learning capability evolves rapidly. However, it would be a serious mistake to assume that any sharply defined critical periods characterize the development of more complex forms of learning or problem solving.

## OBJECT DISCRIMINATION LEARNING

Although the 11-day-old monkey can solve a total-black *versus* total-white discrimination problem in less than thirteen trials, the 20- to 30-day-old monkey may require from 150 to 200 trials to solve a triangle-circle discrimination problem when the stimuli are relatively small and placed some distance apart. It is a fact that, even though the capability of solving this more conventional type of object-discrimination problem exists at twenty days, object-discrimination learning capability has by no means attained full maturity at this time.

The development of complete object-discrimination capacity was measured by testing five different age groups of naive rhesus monkeys on a single discrimination problem. Discrimination training was begun when the animals were 60, 90, 120, 150, or 366 days of age, and, in all cases, training was preceded by at least fifteen days of adaptation to the apparatus and to the eating of solid food. There were eight subjects in group 366 (as defined by age), ten in group 60, and fifteen in each of the other groups. A Wisconsin General Test Apparatus, illustrated in Figure 5, was used throughout the test sessions. A single pair of three-dimensional stimuli differing in multiple attributes such as color, form, size, and material was presented on a two-foodwell test tray of the Klüver type. The animals were given twenty-five trials a day, five days a week, for four weeks, a total of 500 trials. A noncorrection method was always used.

Figure 6 presents the number of trials taken by the five different groups of mon-

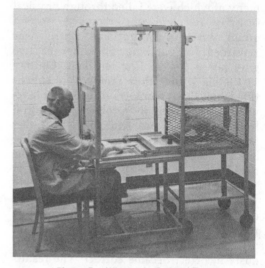

**Figure 5.**   Wisconsin General Test Apparatus.

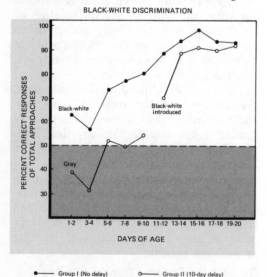

BLACK-WHITE DISCRIMINATION

**Figure 4.**   Black-white discrimination learning.

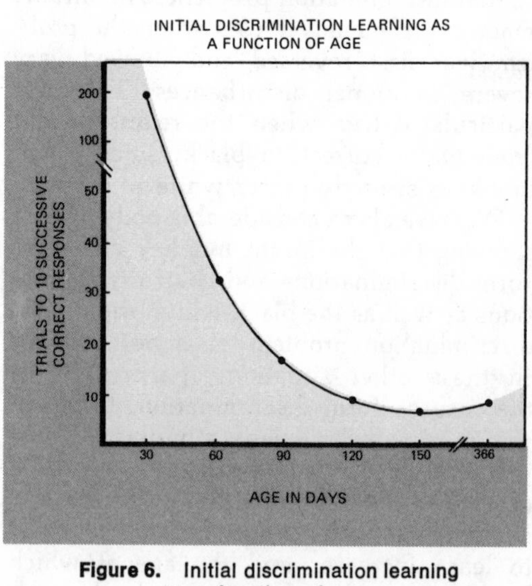

**Figure 6.**   Initial discrimination learning as a function of age.

keys, and performance by a 30-day-old group on a triangle-circle discrimination is plotted on the far left. Whether or not one includes this group, it is apparent that the ability of infant monkeys to solve the object-discrimination problem increases with age as a negatively accelerated function and approaches or attains an asymptote at 120 to 150 days.

Detailed analyses have given us considerable insight into the processes involved in the maturation of this learning function. Regardless of age, the monkeys' initial responsiveness to the problem is not random or haphazard. Instead, almost all the subjects approached the problem in some systematic manner. About twenty per cent of the monkeys chose the correct object from the beginning and stayed with their choice, making no errors! Another twenty per cent showed a strong preference for the incorrect stimulus and made many errors. Initial preference for the left side and for the right side was about equally frequent, and consistent alternation-patterns also appeared. The older, and presumably brighter, monkeys rapidly learned to abandon any incorrect response tendency. The younger, and presumably less intelligent, monkeys persisted longer with the inadequate response tendencies, and very frequently shifted from one incorrect response tendency to another before finally solving the problem. Systematic responsiveness of this type was first described by Krechevsky (8) for rats and was given the name of "hypotheses." Although this term has unfortunate connotations, it was the rule and not the exception that our monkey subjects went from one "hypothesis" to another until solution, with either no random trials or occasionally a few random trials intervening. The total number of incorrect, systematic, response tendencies before problem solution was negatively correlated with age.

These data on the maturation of discrimination learning capability clearly demonstrate that there is no single day of age nor narrow age-band at which object-discrimination learning abruptly matures. If the "critical period" hypothesis is to be entertained, one must think of two different critical periods, a period at approximately twenty days of age, when such problems can be solved if a relatively unlimited amount of training is provided, and a period at approximately 150 days of age, when a full adult level of ability has developed.

DELAYED RESPONSE

The delayed-response problem has challenged and intrigued psychologists ever since it was initially presented by Hunter (6). In this problem the animal is first shown a food reward, which is then concealed within, or under, one of two identical containers during the delay period. The problem was originally believed to measure some high-level ideational ability or "representative factor"—a capacity that presumably transcended simple trial-and-error learning. Additional interest in the problem arose from the discovery by Jacobsen (7) that the ability to solve delayed-response problems was abolished or drastically impaired by bilateral frontal lobectomy in monkeys.

Scores of researches have been conducted on delayed-response problems. Almost all known laboratory species have been tested and all conceivable parameters investigated. In so far as the delayed response is difficult, it appears to be less a function of period of delay or duration of memory than an intrinsic difficulty in responding attentively to an implicit or demonstrated reward. However, in spite of the importance of the problem and the vast literature which has accumulated, there has been no previous major attempt to trace its ontogenetic development in subhuman animals.

Ten subjects in each of four groups, a 60-, 90-, 120-, and 150-day group, were tested on so-called zero-second and five-second delayed responses (the actual delay period is approximately two seconds longer) at the same time they began their discrimination learning. A block of ten trials at each delay interval was presented five days a week for eighteen weeks, a total of ninety test days. These 900 trials at each delay interval constituted the test program for Series I, which was followed by Series II during which time delay intervals of 5, 10, 20, and 40 seconds were introduced in counterbalanced order for twelve test weeks of five days each at the rate of eight trials a day for each condition.

The results for the four infant groups on the five-second delayed responses and the performance of a group of adults with extensive previous test experience on many different problems are presented in Figure 7. The four infant groups show increasing ability to solve delayed responses both as a function of experience and as a function of age. The performance of all infant groups is inferior to the adult group, but differ-

ences in part learning experiences preclude any direct comparison.

The performance of the four infant groups of monkeys on the five-second delayed responses for trials 1-100, 201-300, 401-500, 601-700, and 801-900 is plotted in Figure 8. Because performance during trials 1-100 is poor regardless of group, it is apparent that a certain minimum experience is required to master the delayed-response task. At the same time, the increasingly steep slopes of the learning curves make it apparent that efficiency of delayed-response learning and performance is in large part a function of age. The group data suggest that, after extensive training as provided in this study, seventy per cent correct responses may be attained by 150 days of age, eighty per cent by 200 days, and ninety per cent by 250 days.

The performance at the 40-second delay interval by all monkeys tested in Series II is presented in Figure 9. The performances of the three older groups and the two younger groups are similar, and there are no significant differences between the adult group and the two older infant groups. Similar results were obtained on the 5-, 10-, and 20-second delay intervals of the Series II tests except for the fact that the differences between the younger and older groups diminished progressively with decreasing delay intervals.

Very marked individual differences were disclosed during delayed-response testing, a finding which typifies this task regardless of species or age. Some monkeys, as well as some other animals, fail to adapt to the requirements of the test. Inspection of individual records reveals that the capability of solving this problem first appears at about 125 to 135 days of age and that essentially faultless performance may appear by 200 to 250 days in perhaps half the infant monkey subjects. Thus, some monkeys at this age may possess an adult capability, and these data are in keeping with the results obtained in the Series II tests. Recently, we have completed a study on a

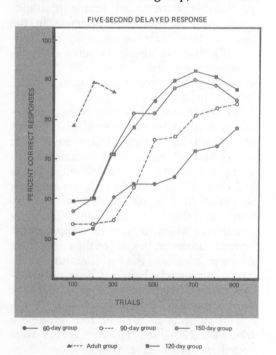

**Figure 7.** Delayed-response learning as a function of age.

30-month-old group of five monkeys on zero- and five-second delayed responses, and their learning rates and terminal performance are at adult levels. Thus, it appears that we have definitive data on the maturation and acquisition of delayed-response performance by rhesus monkeys.

It is obvious that the capability of solving the delayed-response problem matures at a later date than the capacity of solving the object-discrimination problem. This is true regardless of the criterion taken, whether it is the age at which the task can be solved after a relatively unlimited number of trials or the age at which a full adult level of mastery is attained. At the same time, it should be emphasized that this capacity does develop when the monkey is still an infant, long before many complex problems can be efficiently attacked and mastered. Thus, there is no reason to believe that the delayed response is a special measure of intelligence or of any particular or unusual intellectual function.

## OBJECT DISCRIMINATION LEARNING SET

The present writer, in 1949, demonstrated that adolescent or adult monkeys trained on a long series of six-trial discrimination problems showed progressive improvement from problem to problem. As successive blocks of problems were run, the

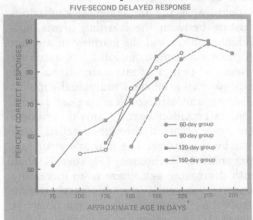

**Figure 8.** Delayed-response performance of different maturational groups with age held constant.

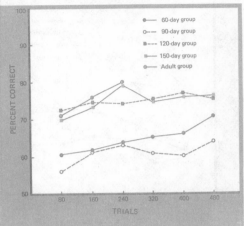

**Figure 9.** Delayed-response generalization to 40-second interval.

form of the learning curve changed from positively accelerated, to linear, to negatively accelerated; finally, there appeared to be two separate curves or functions, i.e., performance changed from chance on trial 1 to perfection or near perfection on and after trial 2. From trial 1 to 2 the curve is precipitate and from trial 2 onward it is flat. This phenomenon, called "learning set formation" or "interproblem learning," has proved to be a useful tool in comparative, physiological, and theoretical psychology. To obtain evidence concerning the maturational factors involved, the performance of various age groups of monkeys was measured on this task.

The same five infant groups previously tested on a single object-discrimination problem served as subjects for learning-set training. Upon completion of the original discrimination problem they were tested on four discrimination problems a day five days a week, each problem six trials in length. Group 366 was trained on 400 problems and the other monkeys on 600 problems. The individual test-trial procedures were identical to those employed in regular object-discrimination learning, but a new pair of stimuli was introduced for each new problem.

DISCRIMINATION LEARNING SET

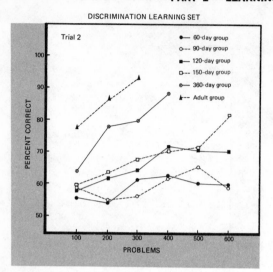

**Figure 10.** Learning set formation as a function of age.

DISCRIMINATION LEARNING SET

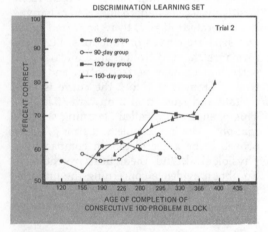

**Figure 11.** Learning set plotted for age of completion of consecutive 100 problem blocks.

The trial 2 performance of the five groups of infant monkeys is plotted in Figure 10, and data from mature monkeys tested in previous experiments are also given. The two younger groups fail to respond consistently above a sixty per cent level even though they were approximately ten and eleven months of age at the conclusion of training. The two older groups show progressive, even though extremely slow, improvement in their trial 2 performances, with groups 120 and 150 finally attaining a seventy and eighty per cent level of correct responding. These data are in general accord with those obtained from an earlier, preliminary experiment and indicate that the year-old monkey is capable of forming discrimination learning sets even though it has by no means attained an adult level of proficiency.

In Figure 11 the trial 2 learning-set performance for the various groups is plotted in terms of age of completion of consecutive 100-problem blocks, and these data suggest that the capacity of the two younger groups to form discrimination learning sets may have been impaired by their early, intensive learning-set training, initiated before they possessed any effective learning-set capability. Certainly, their performance from 260 days onward is inferior to that of the earlier groups with less experience but matched for age. The problem which these data illustrate has received little attention among experimental psychologists. There is a tendency to think of learning or training as intrinsically good and necessarily valuable to the organism. It is entirely possible, however, that training can either be helpful or harmful, depending upon the nature of the training and the organism's stage of development.

Because of the fundamental similarities existing between the learning of an individual problem and the learning of a series of problems of the same kind, it is a striking discovery that a great maturational gulf exists between efficient individual-problem learning and efficient learning-set formation. Information bearing on this problem has been obtained through detailed analyses by the author. The author's error-factor analyses technique (5) reveals that, with decreasing age, there is an increasing tendency to make stimulus-perseveration errors, i.e., if the initially chosen object is incorrect, the monkey has great difficulty in shifting to the correct object. Furthermore, with decreasing age there is an increasing tendency to make differential-cue errors, i.e., difficulty in inhibiting, on any particular trial, the ambiguous reinforcement of the position of the stimulus which is concurrent with the reinforcement of the object *per se*.

In all probability, individual-problem learning involves elimination of the same error factors or the utilization of the same hypotheses or strategies as does learning-set formation. However, as we have already seen, the young rhesus monkey's ability to suppress these error factors in individual-problem learning does not guarantee in any way whatsoever a capacity to transfer this information to the interproblem learning-set task. The learning of the infant is specific and fails to generalize from problem to problem, or, in Goldstein's terms, the infant possesses only the capacity for concrete thinking. Failure by the infant monkey to master learning-set problems is not surprising inasmuch as infraprimate animals, such as the rat and the cat, possess the most circumscribed capabilities for these interproblem learnings, and it is doubtful if the pigeon possesses any such ability at all. Indeed, discrimination learning-set formation taxes the prowess of the human imbecile and apparently exceeds the capacity of the human idiot.

Most of the findings which we have reported for the maturation of learning in the rhesus monkey had been predicted, but this was not true in the case of the string tests. We had assumed that the infant monkey would solve the parallel pattern with few or no errors, but, as can be seen in Figure 12, this assumption did not accord with fact. The infant monkeys made many errors, learned slowly, and in many cases failed to reach a level of perfect responsiveness after prolonged training. The data on the relatively simple two-crossed-strings pattern (Figure 13) show that the six-month-old rhesus monkey is just beginning to reach the age at which this problem can be mas-

tered. Unfortunately, our data on patterned-strings learning are incomplete, but it is obvious that this capacity is a function which is maturing during the second half of the first year of life and probably for a considerable period of time henceforward. In retrospect, we realized that the relatively late maturation of string-test learning was in keeping with known facts. The crossed-strings pattern has never been solved by any infraprimate animal, and this task cannot be resolved by the human infant (9, 10) until the second or third year of life.

## THE DEVELOPMENT OF TERMINAL LEARNING ABILITY

At the present time we have completed a series of experiments which clearly demonstrate that the capability of solving problems of increasing complexity develops in rhesus monkeys in a progressive and orderly manner throughout the first year of life. Furthermore, when we compare the performances of the year-old monkey and the adult monkey, it becomes obvious that maturation is far from complete at the end of the first year. Although our data on early development are more complete than our data on terminal learning capacities, we have already obtained a considerable body of information on middle and late learning growth.

### HAMILTON PERSEVERANCE TEST

Just as we were surprised by the delayed appearance of the capability of mastering the patterned-string tests, so were we surprised by the delay before performance on the Hamilton perseverance test attains maximal efficiency.

Three groups of monkeys were initially tested at 12, 30, and 50 months of age, respectively. The groups comprised six, five, and seven monkeys, and all were tested twenty trials a day for thirty days. On the perseverance problem the animal is faced with a series of four boxes having spring-loaded lids which close as soon as they are

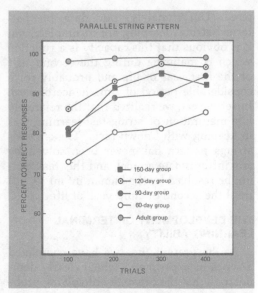

**Figure 12.** Parallel string pattern performance as a function of age.

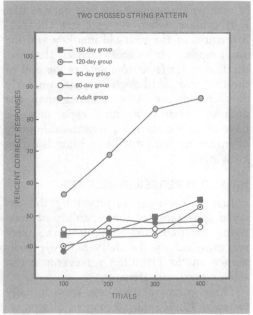

**Figure 13.** Two cross-string pattern performance as a function of age.

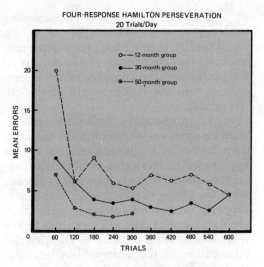

**Figure 14.** Mean number of errors per 60-trial block on Hamilton perseverance test.

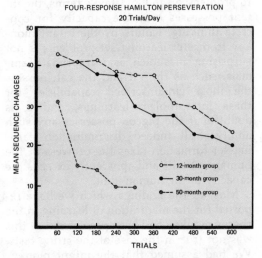

**Figure 15.** Mean number of sequence changes per 60-trial block on Hamilton perseverance test.

released. Only one box contains food, and the rewarded box is changed in a random manner from trial to trial with the provision that the same box is never rewarded twice in succession. In the present experiment the subjects were allowed only four responses per trial, whether or not the reward was obtained, and an error was defined as any additional response to an unrewarded box after the initial lifting of the lid during a trial. Infraprimate animals make many errors of this kind, but as can be seen in

Figure 14, the mature monkey makes few such errors and learns rather rapidly to eliminate these. We were surprised by the inefficient performance of the year-old monkey and unprepared to discover that maximally efficient performance was not attained by the 30-month-old monkeys.

The mature monkey finds a simple plan for attacking the perseverance problem. Typically, it chooses the extreme left or right box and works systematically toward the other end. If it adopts some more complex strategy, as responding by some such order as box 4-2-3-1, it will repeat this same order on successive trials.

Since the animal's procedural approach to the perseveration problem appeared to be an important variable, measures were taken of changes in the animal's order of responding from trial to trial, and these were defined as response-sequence changes. The data of Figure 15 show that the 50-month-old monkeys adopt the invariant type of behavior described above but that this is not true for either the 12- or 30-month-old groups. If a subject adopts an invariant response pattern, the problem is by definition simple; failure to adopt such a pattern can greatly complicate the task. In view of this fact it is not surprising that the 30-month-old subjects made so many errors; rather, it is surprising that they made so few—their error scores represent a triumph of memory over inadequate planning.

Relatively little research on the Hamilton perseverance method has been conducted by psychologists in spite of the fact that the original studies resulted in an effective ordering of Hamilton's wide range of subjects in terms of their position within the phyletic series. Furthermore, the limited ontogenetic material gave proper ordering of animal performance: kittens, puppies, and children were inferior to cats, dogs, and human adults. Above and beyond these facts, the perseverance data give support to the proposition that the rhesus monkey does not attain full intellectual status until the fourth or fifth year of life.

## ODDITY TEST

Probably the most efficient tests that have been developed for measuring the maximal intellectual capability of the subhuman primates are the multiple-sign tests, whose solution is dependent upon appropriate responses to multiple, simultaneously presented cues. One of the simplest of these tests is that of oddity. Each oddity problem utilizes two identical pairs of stimuli, the "A" and the "B" stimuli. On any trial, three of the stimuli are presented simultaneously, and the odd or different stimulus is correct and rewarded.

We have now completed a series of experiments using the two-position oddity problem, in which the correct stimulus is either in the right or left position, never in the center. In Figure 16 are presented data from a group of ten monkeys tested on 256 problems at 20 months of age and again at 36 months of age. Comparable data for a group of six adult rhesus monkeys are also graphed. These data indicate increasingly

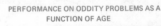

PERFORMANCE ON ODDITY PROBLEMS AS A FUNCTION OF AGE

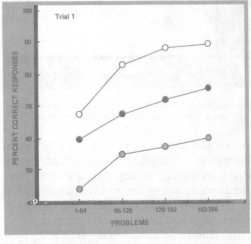

Figure 16. Performance on oddity problems as a function of age.

efficient performance as a function of age. The performance differences at each of the three age levels are statistically significant, and there is every reason to believe that intellectual maturation as measured by this test is incomplete at three years.

Additional oddity learning data obtained by the same training techniques are presented in Figure 17. Again a group of ten monkeys was trained on oddity, first at 12 months of age and subsequently at 36 months of age. At 30 months of age, however, this group was divided into two groups of five monkeys each, one group being trained on a series of 480 six-trial discrimination problems and the other, 2400 delayed response trials. The differences be-

PERFORMANCE ON ODDITY PROBLEMS AS A
FUNCTION OF AGE

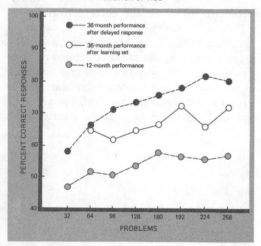

Figure 17. Performance on oddity problems as a function of age and past experience.

tween the two groups on the oddity problems are statistically significant, with every indication of negative transfer from the learning-set to the oddity training. This is consistent with the fact that a single stimulus is uniformly correct on every discrimination problem but reverses frequently during the trials of each oddity problem. The transfer from delayed response to oddity may have been positive,

since performance of the 36-month-old group with delayed-response training is superior to the comparable 36-month-old group whose performance is included in Figure 16. But, in neither case does a 36-month-old group attain an adult performance level.

For the neonatal and infant rhesus monkey each learning task is specific unto itself, and the animal's intellectual repertoire is composed of multiple, separate, and isolated learned experiences. With increasing age, problem isolation changes to problem generalization, and this fundamental reorganization of the monkey's intellectual world apparently begins in its second year of life. From here on, we can no longer specify the monkey's learning ability for any problem merely in terms of maturational age and individual differences. The variable of kind and amount of prior experience must now be given proper value. This is the characteristic of monkey learning, and, in fact, learning by all higher primates as they come of intellectual age.

Monkeys do not attain full oddity performance at three years of age, and oddity learning is by no means the most complicated learning task that the adult rhesus monkey can solve. Oddity-nonoddity learning, in which the subject is required to choose either the odd or the nonodd stimulus, depending upon the color of the test tray presented on a particular trial, can be solved relatively routinely by the adult monkey. Considerably more complex learning problems have been mastered by highly trained rhesus subjects. We are in no position to determine the monkey's age of intellectual maturity, but four or five years of age is a reasonable estimate.

## SUMMARY AND INTERPRETATION

Half a decade is entirely too brief a period to establish a definitive program on the maturation of learning ability in the rhesus monkey, particularly in the later age ranges. However, within this period of time we have developed the techniques and conducted tests which demonstrate that such a program is entirely feasible. The monkey is capable of solving simple learning problems during the first few days of life and its capability of solving ever increasingly complex problems matures progressively, probably for four to five years.

Early in life, new learning abilities appear rather suddenly within the space of a few days, but, from late infancy onward, the appearance of new learning powers is characterized by developmental stages during which particular performances progressively improve. There is a time at which increasingly difficult problems can first be solved, and a considerably delayed period before they can be solved with full adult efficiency.

The monkey possesses learning capacities far in excess of those of any other infrahuman primate, abilities probably comparable to those of low-level human imbeciles. The monkey's learning capabilities can give us little or no information concerning human language, and only incomplete information relating to thinking. These are the generalizable limits of learning research on rhesus monkeys, but they still leave us with an animal having vast research potentialities. There is a wealth of learning problems which the monkey can master, and at present the field is incompletely explored. The maturation of any learning function can be traced and the nature and mechanisms underlying interproblem and intertask transfer can be assessed. There exist great research potentialities in analyzing the fundamental similarities and differences among simple and complex learnings within a single species. The monkey is the subject ideally suited for studies involving neurological, biochemical, and pharmacological correlates of behavior. To date, such studies have been limited to adult monkeys, or monkeys of unspecified age, but such limited researches are no longer a necessity. We now know that rhesus monkeys can be raised under completely controlled conditions throughout a large part, and probably all, of their life span, and we may expect that the research of the future will correlate the neurophysiological variables, not with the behavior of the static monkey, but with the behavior of the monkey in terms of ontogenetic development.

## REFERENCES

1. Fuller, J. F.; Easler, C. A.; and Banks, E. M. 1950. Formation of conditioned avoidance responses in young puppies. *American Journal of Physiology* 160:462–466.

2. Hamilton, G. V. 1911. A study in trial and error reactions in animals. *Journal of Animal Behavior* 1:33–66.

3. Hamilton, G. V. 1916. A study of perseverance reactions in primates and rodents. *Behavior Monographs* 3, no. 2, pp. 1–63.

4. Harlow, H. F. 1949. The formation of learning sets. *Psychological Review* 56:51–65.

5. Harlow, H. F. 1950. Analysis of discrimination learning by monkeys. *Journal of Experimental Psychology* 40:26–39.

6. Hunter, W. F. 1913. The delayed reaction in animals and children. *Behavior Monographs* 2:21–30.

7. Jacobsen, C. F.; Wolfe, J. B.; and Jackson, T. A. 1935. An experimental analysis of the functions of the frontal association areas in primates. *Journal of Nervous and Mental Disease* 82:1–14.

8. Krechevsky, I. 1932. "Hypothesis" vs. "chance" in the pre-solution period in sensory discrimination learning. *University of California Publications in Psychology* 6:27–44.

9. Matheson, E. 1931. A study of problem solving behavior in pre-school children. *Child Development* 2, no. 4, 242–262.

10. Richardson, H. M. 1932. The growth of adaptive behaviour in infants. *Genetic Psychology Monographs* 12:195–357.

11. Stone, C. P. 1929. The age factor in animal learning: II. Rats on a multiple light discrimination box and a difficult image. *Genetic Psychology Monographs* 6, no. 2, 125–202.

12. van Wagenen, G. 1950. The monkey. In *The care and breeding of laboratory animals*, ed. E. J. Farris, pp. 1–42. New York: Wiley.

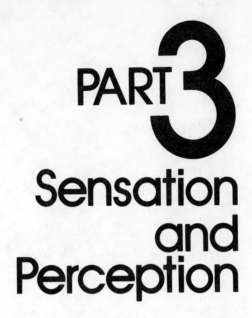

PART 3

Sensation
and
Perception

# READING 14

## The Concept of the Stimulus in Psychology

**JAMES J. GIBSON**
**Cornell University**

What is a stimulus? Although the concept of a stimulus may appear simple, Gibson presents eight areas of conflict found in this concept. He suggests that in defining a stimulus, we must know the properties of the environment. The importance of these areas of conflict cannot be overestimated if we are to have a full understanding of perception and the relationship between the effective stimulus and the subsequent alteration of behavior.

**QUESTIONS**

1. How does Gibson resolve the eight conflicts concerning stimuli?
2. In light of the body of psychological research that you are now familiar with, evaluate Gibson's analysis of "the stimulus."
3. Gibson states that learning involves "not only an alteration of behavior but also an alteration of the effective stimulus." Comment on this idea.
4. Gibson states that the concept of fixed, innate thresholds of sensation has been rejected. Do you agree with this? Why do we still study the concept of a threshold?

It seems to me that there is a weak link in the chain of reasoning by which we explain experience and behavior, namely, our concept of the stimulus. The aim of this paper is to find out what psychologists mean by the term stimulus, with the hope of deciding what they *ought* to mean by it. After a

Presidential Address to the Eastern Psychological Association, New York, New York, April 1960.

short look at the history of the term, I will try to uncover the sources of confusion in modern usage. In the end, perhaps, the concept will be clarified. If not, certain contradictions will have been brought to light.

The experimental study of the stimulus began in the eighteenth century, so far as I can tell, with an investigation of the curious things that could be done to make a frog's leg twitch. The experimenters discovered what is now called the nerve-muscle preparation. Galvani and later Volta gave their names to electricity as well as to physiology by their experiments. In the early nineteenth century Johannes Müller applied these discoveries to the philosophers' problem of the human senses, the gates of knowledge. The nerves of sense, he pointed out, can be excited by a variety of unnatural agencies such as electrical current. Since the mind is acquainted only with the qualities specific to the sensory nerves, not with the stimuli, how it gets knowledge of the material world became more puzzling than ever. Later in the century, Sherrington was to emphasize the extent to which receptors are naturally protected against such irrelevant stimuli by the structural specialization of sense organs. But meanwhile it had been discovered that the skin would yield sensations only at certain discrete points. Here was a fresh puzzle. The separate receptor cells of all the sense organs came to be seen under the microscope, and the punctate character of the sensory process seemed to be established.

During all this time, the physical scientists were discovering the laws of energy and triumphantly measuring it in its various forms, electricity, momentum, light, heat, sound, and the results of chemical reaction. It became possible to measure certain variables of energy at sense organs, at least the simple ones like frequency and amount. Thresholds of reportable sensation were established. Fechner, following Weber, conceived the grand scheme of a measurement formula for consciousness, relating its judged intensity to a simple variable of the stimulus. Psychophysics was born.

Whatever could be controlled by an experimenter and applied to an observer could be thought of as a stimulus. In the growing science of human psychology, it became evident that this was the independent variable of an experiment, to be isolated and systematically varied. Much more complex things than physical energies could be presented to the sense organs—words for instance. These were also called stimuli, although the stimulus conditions manipulated, recency, frequency, meaningfulness, were vastly different from the variables of the psychophysical experiment.

In the latter part of the nineteenth century the concept of the reflex arc was applied to the adaptive behavior of animals. It had been thought to explain the strictly mechanical actions of the body ever since Descartes. Reflexes had stimuli. The situations of animals could be systematically altered and the reactions observed. Organisms obviously responded to such stimuli, and the experimenter could apply them more freely than he could venture to do with human beings. To shorten a long story, such experiments came to be merged with human experiments and the outcome was a general stimulus-response psychology. This was a great success, especially in America. But stimuli for animal psychologists were not the same as stimuli for sensory physiologists and stimuli were still different for the students of perception and learning.

Enough has been said to show that in the twentieth century we have inherited a mixed batch of ideas about the stimulus. We constantly use the word but seldom define it. We take it for granted. We have behavior theory in full bloom, and perception theory in ripened complexity, but who ever heard of stimulus theory? As a preliminary effort in this direction, I have made a survey of what modern writers seem to mean by the term. Some writers define it, but not many. My method was to collect quotations from books. I then put them in opposition to one another. The ways of conceiving the stimulus are often in flat contradiction. Occasionally one book can be quoted against itself. The issues interlock, of course, but I have separated them into eight areas of disagreement and will treat them separately. In what follows, I will quote without comment, for the most part, keeping my own opinions to the end.

*I.* For Freud, the only use of the term stimulus that is discoverable in the *Collected Papers* (1949) is to refer to a motivating force. This, after all, is the dictionary meaning of the word—something that arouses or impels to action. In ordinary speech we refer to the stimulus of hunger or fear, which may compel extreme forms of behavior. Freud does not often use the term, but when he does, a stimulus is something to be satisfied or warded off.

Psychologists and physiologists, however, have generally used the term for the arousing of a sense organ instead of a whole individual. But they do not wholly agree about this. Some accept both meanings. Neal Miller asserts that "any stimulus has some drive value" (Miller & Dollard, 1941, p. 59). However, Skinner believes that "a drive is not a stimulus," and that although "the term has the unfortunate connotation of a goal or spur to action," we must not be misled by this popular meaning of the word (1938, p. 375). Here, then, is a first area of disagreement in our way of conceiving the stimulus: *does a stimulus motivate the individual or does it merely trigger a response?*

*II.* Pavlov said that "a stimulus appears to be connected with a given response as cause with effect" (1927, p. 10). This is a forthright assertion. Similarly Watson took as the whole aim of psychology the predicting of the response, given the stimulus, and the specifying of the stimulus, given the response (1924, p. 10). But contrast this with the caution of Hilgard and Marquis. "We refer to a stimulus as an instigator [and] no more is intended than that the stimulus is in some sense the occasion for the response" (1940, p. 73). Evidently what Pavlov and Watson meant by a stimulus is not what Hilgard and Marquis meant. Nearly all psychologists now follow the second line. It is allowed that a stimulus

may cause a reflex, but not an act. Woodworth was one of the first to emphasize that the stimulus does not in itself determine the response; factors in the organism intervene to help determine it. The discussion of intervening variables or mediating process has by now filled volumes.

The same rule is taken to hold for experience. It is allowed that a stimulus may cause a sensation, but not a perception. M. D. Vernon, for example, states that "the nature of the percept is not . . . determined by the physical qualities of the stimulus, but is largely a function of constructive tendencies in the individual" (1952, p. 47). But I have been arguing the opposite for some time, that the percept is in very good correspondence with the physical variables of the stimulus. *Can a stimulus be taken as the sufficient cause of a response, or can it not?* This is a second area of confusion in our concept of the stimulus.

*III.* Skinner has recently noted that "we frequently define the stimulus by the very doubtful property of its ability to elicit the response in question, rather than by any independent property of the stimulus itself" (1959, p. 355). He suggests no remedy, however, for this doubtful scientific behavior, and he seems to be confessing a sin without pointing the way to salvation. In truth many psychologists do give a circular definition of the stimulus. Skinner himself believed in his first book that "neither term [stimulus or response] can be defined as to its essential properties without the other" (1938, p. 9). Neal Miller has said "a response is any activity by or within the individual which can become functionally connected with an antecedent event through learning; a stimulus is any event to which a response can become so connected" (Miller & Dollard, 1941, p. 59). Miller, in fact, has argued that this circular definition of the stimulus is not only necessary but is theoretically desirable (Koch, 1959, p. 239). He seems to have abandoned completely the specifying of a stimulus by variables of physical energy. But listen to Estes. "By *stimulus*, I refer to environmental conditions, describable in physical terms without reference to the behavior of an organism" (Koch, 1959, p. 455), and Hayek says, "the distinction between different stimuli must be independent of the different effects they have on the organism" (1952, p. 9).

Here is a disagreement. The student of psychophysics will argue that we must define our stimulus by certain operations of physical science, not by the judgments of our subject. Otherwise how are we ever to discover what stimuli can be discriminated and what cannot? When the stimulus is difficult to specify in objective physical terms, however, investigators tend to avoid the difficulty and describe it as that which is responded to, or that which is perceived. A few go further and, by arguing that an experimenter cannot define the stimulus anyway except in terms of *his* perception, reach a philosophical position of subjectivism. There is an ancient puzzle to which students of philosophy are treated — whether there exists any sound when a tree crashes in the forest with no living being there to hear it. It is a question of how to conceive the auditory stimulus. It seems to remain a puzzle for a good many psychologists.

I think the central question is the following. Is a stimulus that which *does* activate a sense organ or that which *can* activate a sense organ? Some writers imply that a stimulus not currently exciting receptors is not a stimulus at all. Others imply that a stimulus need not excite receptors to be called such. They allow of *potential* stimuli. Witness Guthrie's assertion that stimuli are "potential occasions" for the initiation of sensory activity, and that "the physical stimuli, though present, may not be effective" (Koch, 1959, p. 178). The former conception allows physical energy to be called a stimulus only when some response can be observed; the latter allows of the possibility that stimulus energy may be present without necessarily being responded to. The latter seems the better concept. With the former meaning, one could never speak of a subthreshold stimulus, and this is a useful term. An effective stimulus on one occasion may be ineffective on another. And there are various response criteria by which a threshold can be measured.

The distinction between effective and potential stimuli is made by a few theorists, but its implications have not been traced, and the idea remains undeveloped. The concept of a permanent environment of *objects* is widely accepted, but not the concept of a permanent environment of *potential stimuli*.

The third area of disagreement is this: *must a stimulus be defined independently of the response it produces—in physical terms rather than terms of behavior or sensory process?*

*IV.* For Pavlov a stimulus could be anything in the terrestrial world. Any event he could think of to use in an experiment he would call a stimulus and he employed tones, bells, the sound of bubbling water, lights, rotating objects, pictures on a screen, acid in the mouth, food, a scratch on the back, or electric shock. This common sense usage of the term persists among a good many behaviorists. Spence has said that the term stimulus means to him, "the physical or world situation, with its different aspects or features" (1956, p. 39). For Neal Miller anything that is discriminable is a stimulus or, as he calls it, a cue, these terms having the same meaning. For Skinner, a stimulus is simply "a part or modification of a part, of the environment's (1938, p. 235). To be sure, he says, it must "refer to a class of events the members of which possess some property in common" (p. 34). Because stimuli have this "generic nature," the practice of calling a bell an auditory stimulus and a book a visual stimulus is, as he puts it, "frequently successful" (p. 235). All these writers persist in believing that somehow the things of the environment can *stimulate* us, and they refuse to be worried by the paradox that only receptors at the skin of an individual can actually be stimulated.

This definition of the stimulus is considered naive by perception psychologists. Stimuli are energies, not objects. In Troland's words, "the stimulus may be defined as the specific physical force, energy, or agency which brings about the stimulation of the given receptor system" (1930, p. 9). This conception has the authority of a century's research on the senses. In 1834, Johannes Müller argued that a stimulus was whatever excited one of the "nerves of sense." To the modern neurophysiologist, a stimulus is energy that depolarizes a living cell—especially, but not exclusively, a nerve cell. For Jennings in 1906, studying the ameba, a stimulus was a type of change in the immediate environment that produced a change in behavior (1906, p. 19) and there existed precisely five types: chemical, mechanical, thermal, photic, or electrical. Woodworth says that "a stimulus is any form of energy acting upon a sense organ and arousing some activity of the organism" (1929, p. 223). Koffka wishes to call stimuli "the causes of the excitations of our sense organs" (1935, p. 79), but he, more than any other theorist, faced up to the contradictory meanings of the term and proposed a formal distinction between the "proximal" stimulus and the "distal" or "distant" stimulus. He made us consider the paradox that although perception and behavior seem to be determined by the distal object, they can in fact only be aroused by the proximal stimulus.

Not all psychologists are willing to grapple with this paradox and, in truth, it is baffling. If the proximal stimulus for a given object is altered with every change of the observer's position in space, if it is different on different occasions, we are faced with an absurdity. We must suppose that a countless family of different stimuli can all arouse the same percept. Most behaviorists speak of the stimulus-object as if, by

hyphenating two words with different meanings, the absurdity were removed. As men of common sense they see the need of reducing to one the countless number of stimuli that can arouse a single percept, and in this surely they have a point. But perceptionists, being unable to take this easy way out, struggle to construct theories of how different stimuli might arouse the same percept, the theories of perceptual constancy. So far, no theory has been agreed on. Is it possible that common sense is right without knowing it, and that every family of proximal stimuli arising from one object *is*, in a sense, one stimulus?

Here is a fourth disagreement: *do stimuli exist in the environment or only at receptors?* There is a suggestion that both usages of the term are somehow correct, but it has not been explained.

V. Osgood says that "a stimulus may be defined as that form of physical energy that activates a receptor" (1953, p. 12). But he does not tell us whether he means by a receptor a single cell or a mosaic of receptor cells, that is, a sense organ. Others besides Osgood are undecided about this question, or have not thought about it. Hull knew what he thought. For him, the retinal image was a pattern of stimuli (1943, p. 37) and a single light ray was a stimulus (p. 33). "A stimulus element is a stimulus energy which activates a single receptor-organ" (p. 349). This is straightforward. Woodworth says that "of course the light entering the eye and striking many rods and cones is a collection of stimuli rather than a single stimulus," but in the next paragraph he suggests that "the sudden cessation of a light" is a stimulus (1929, p. 28). Köhler was fairly explicit on the question, saying that an organism responds to "an objective constellation of millions of stimuli" (1929, p. 179) and Koffka also assumed that stimuli on the retina or the skin were local events (1935). But Nissen, on the other hand, asserts that "a stimulus involves a pattern of stimulation, spatial or temporal" (Stevens, 1951, p.

374). Many other writers define stimuli as the occasions for activation of a sense organ, not of a receptor cell, and speak as if a pattern were a stimulus. There is a vast difference between a pattern of stimuli and a stimulus pattern, but we have not sufficiently thought about it. Is a "pattern" a single stimulus or is it a number of separate stimuli?

The notion that a stimulus is what excites a cell, and is therefore *punctate*, seems to many theorists the only rigorous definition. On this account Hull had to introduce the postulate of afferent neural interaction to explain molar behavior as distinguished from molecular responses. The gestalt psychologists had to develop the theory of sensory organization in order to explain perception. But Lashley once said that

the stimulus to any reaction above the level of a spinal reflex involves not the excitation of certain definite sensory cells but the excitation of *any* cells of a system in certain ratios, and the response may be given to the ratio even though the particular cells involved have not previously been excited in the same way (Murchison, 1934, p. 476).

This passage suggests the idea that higher levels of reaction require us to define higher orders of stimulation. Lashley seems to be saying that a ratio may be itself a stimulus, not just a relation between two stimuli. But note that the gestalt theorists, by conceiving all stimuli as local events, did not come to think in this way.

A controversy has long been going on over the question of how an individual could respond to a relation. It began with Köhler's evidence that a chick will select the brighter of two gray papers instead of the absolute brightness of a particular paper. Köhler thought it demonstrated a relational process in the brain; Spence has gone to great lengths to show that it could be explained in terms of absolute responses to each piece of paper, subject to the so-called principle of stimulus generalization. But the simplest explanation would be that the effective stimulus in the experiment was

the direction of the difference in brightness in the field of view. In line with this solution to the problem, students of vision conceive that a margin is a visual stimulus, perhaps *the* visual stimulus, and a margin in the array of light to an eye is strictly a ratio, that is, a relation between measured intensities.

Here is a fifth source of confusion: *when is a pattern or relation to be considered a single stimulus and when a number of separate stimuli?*

VI. The notion that a stimulus can only be something punctate is related to the notion that a stimulus can only be something *momentary*. The gestalt psychologists pointed out that a melody is perceived, but they never suggested that a melody was a stimulus. The notes of the melody were taken to be the stimuli. But what about the transitions between notes, or the "transients" of acoustical engineering? Are they stimuli? The investigators of speech sounds seem to think so, but the auditory literature of sensation is vague on this question. And if a short transition is a stimulus, why not a long transition or temporal pattern?

In vision, experimenters have not been able to make up their minds as to whether an optical motion was a stimulus or a series of stimuli. The retina and also the skin are very sensitive to motion. It ought to be simple, but the facts of the stroboscope and the phi-phenomenon have been interpreted to imply that it is complex. Motion is taken to be change of location, as it is in classical physics, and it is then reasoned that the impression of location must be fundamental to any perception of a change of location.

On the other hand the generalization is frequently met with that a stimulus is *always* a change. This is very confusing, in fact it is one confusion piled on another. I think that writers who make this assertion have in mind the experiments showing that an unchanging stimulus soon ceases to be effective for perception. They are thinking of sensory adaptation. What changes in that case is not the stimulus but the process of excitation. For the retina, the skin, and the olfactory organ, sensory adaptation does occur. For example, the steady application of an image to a human retina, by the method of artificially stabilizing the image, eventuates in a wholly ineffective stimulus. But note that the steady application of focusable light to a human eye does not. This stimulus never becomes wholly ineffective, even with the best voluntary fixation, because of slight movements of the eye itself. This means that retinal stimulation is by no means the same thing as optical stimulation. They are different stages in the chain of events that leads to vision. A "change in stimulation" means something quite different when it is produced by some adjustment of the sense organ itself than when it is produced by an external event.

Is optical motion, then, meaning a change in the pattern of focusable light to the eye, to be considered a stimulus? Experiments based on this assumption are beginning to appear. In the recent Cornell research with optical transformation (Gibson & Gibson, 1957) we not only think of this as a stimulus, we have come to think of nonchange of pattern as simply a special case. Stability, after all, is only definable as absence of motion. Similarly, a form is definable as a nontransformation. In this conception, sequence is a dimension of stimulation whether or not change occurs.

The great virtue of this conception of sequence is that it suggests a simple solution to the puzzle of perceptual constancy. Two types of nonchange are distinguishable, first, nonmotion of a pattern and, second, invariance of a pattern during motion. The invariant contained in a family of the perspectives arising from a single object is a single stimulus. Hence there is only one stimulus for a single object, and the common sense opinion is right after all.

The sixth conceptual issue is this: *when does a sequence constitute a single and when a number of separate stimuli; also, can a single enduring stimulus exist throughout a changing sequence?*

*VII.* Users of the Rorschach test assume that a stimulus field can be either structured or, as they put it, *unstructured.* I could find no explicit definition of unstructured stimulation in the literature but only examples of the material to which the term is applied—inkblots and other items used in the so-called projective tests. The idea of structured stimulation comes from gestalt theory but only from a vague, tentative, and undeveloped hypothesis of gestalt theory—the external forces of organization as distinguished from the internal forces of organization. Koffka, for example, was so preoccupied with the ways in which the individual *structured* his stimulus field that he scarcely considered the ways in which it might already *have* structure (1935). In fact, he wrote sometimes as if it had none, as if all structure had to be imposed on it, because the stimuli themselves were meaningless points.

This uncertainty about the existence of structure in the stimulus for perceived form still persists. But since Koffka's time, and partly inspired by him, some experimenters are beginning simply to assume it, and to apply mathematics to the structure of a stimulus. They would not agree that an inkblot is in any sense an unstructured stimulus. A picture has one structure, an inkblot has another, but it does not lack structure. That can be said only of a film-color or the cloudless blue sky. The structure of an array may have ambiguous or equivocal components, as Koffka showed, but that is not the same thing. The capacity of light to carry structure to an eye may be impoverished or reduced experimentally but it remains. The structure of light may not specify anything familiar to the subject, or to any observer, but it is a geometrical fact. The subject may be unable to register the structure because it is nonsense to him, or he overlooks it, or he was not told to look for it, or his eyes are defective, or he is too young, or for a dozen other reasons, but it is still in the light. So, at least, some experimenters would argue.

What can be meant by an unstructured stimulus field is thus a matter of disagreement. The seventh question is: *how do we specify the structure of a stimulus?*

*VIII.* The conception of stimuli as physical energies seems to imply that, in themselves, they have no significance or meaning. Especially if they are considered to be only spots of energy at brief moments of time it is clear that they specify little or nothing about the environment. Light, heat, mechanical, acoustical, chemical, and electrical energy are far from being objects, places, events, people, words, and symbols, but nevertheless they are the only stimuli that can affect receptors. This theory of the meaningless stimulus has been an accepted doctrine for a long, long time in the study of the senses. It leads to the notion of the sense datum—the bare sensation, or raw sensory impression, and thence to the persistent problem of how animals and men can be supposed to perceive objects, places, events, and one another.

Students of behavior, however, without questioning the doctrine of the empty stimulus, often act as if they did not believe it. Beach speaks for comparative psychologists when he says, in describing how birds feed their offspring, "young birds exhibit a gaping response which *stimulates* the parent to place food in the nestling's mouth" (Stevens, 1951, p. 415). He takes it for granted that light rays can specify the event called gaping and refuses to worry about it further. Students of perception do worry about this question, but they are not consistent. On the one hand, they firmly assert that nothing gets into the eye but light of variable wave length and intensity, not objects, or events, or facts of the environment. On the other hand, they often say

that light "carries" information about the environment, or that stimuli "provide" information to the perceiver. If this is so, the stimuli must specify something beyond themselves, and they cannot be empty of meaning.

A sort of compromise between the informative stimulus and the empty stimulus is provided by the use of the term *cue*. According to Woodworth, "a cue, as used in psychology, is a stimulus which serves as a sign or signal of something else, the connection having previously been learned" (1958, p. 60). Stimuli are conceived by analogy with messages, or communication in code. Brunswik thought of stimuli as *indicators* of environmental facts, by analogy with pointer readings, emphasizing, however, that they had only a probable connection with the fact in question (1956). Boring has suggested that stimuli may be taken as *clues*, and this term points to Helmholtz's theory of unconscious rational inference from the sense data (Harper & Boring, 1948).

Merely to call the stimulus a cue, **sign**, signal, message, indicator, or clue does not tell us what we need to know. The question is to what extent does the stimulus specify its source, and how does it do so? Is it possible that the use of these verbal metaphors only prevents us from facing the problem? Or consider the use by modern information theorists of a neutral term like *input*. When they compare the organism to a communication system or to a black box, the internal working of which has to be discovered, are they avoiding the obligation to consider the environment of an organism and the relation of stimuli to the environment?

The problem of the connection between stimuli and their natural sources has not been taken seriously by psychologists. Stimuli have not even been classified from this point of view, but only with respect to the sense organs and the types of energy which carry stimuli. It is a problem of ecology, as Brunswik realized when he wrote about the "ecological validity" of cues (1956). I think the problem has been obscured, and our recognition of it delayed, by our failure to separate it into parts. The connection between natural stimuli and their sources is not the same as the connection between *social* stimuli and their sources, for example, the connection between words and their referents. This latter problem, surely, is distinct. Semantics is one thing, ecology is another; and a science of environmental stimuli may not prove to be as difficult as a science of symbols, once we put our minds to it.

I have maintained that optical stimuli, for example, gradients of texture in the light to an eye, specify environmental objects by the relation of *projection*. To me this is not at all the same as the relation by which words specify objects, which I would call one of *coding*. But however this may be, we face another unanswered question, the eighth: *do stimuli carry information about their sources in the world, and how do they specify them?*

## SOME POSITIVE HYPOTHESES

Can anything useful be salvaged from these various contradictory usages and definitions? No one could be blamed for being pessimistic about it. S. S. Stevens, who has thought hard and long about stimuli, concluded that it is futile even to attempt a general definition of the stimulus in psychology. Psychology as a whole, he says, can be equated with the problem of defining the stimulus, that is, giving a complete definition of the stimulus for a given response. To be able to do so would require that we specify "all the transformations of the environment, both external and internal, that leave the response invariant." And "for no response have we yet given a complete definition of the stimulus" in this sense (Stevens, 1951, pp. 31f.). If I understand him, what Stevens chiefly had in mind is the puzzle of constancy. He was saying that we do not know how to specify, in the chaos of literal proximal-energy stimulation, the actual cause of a given response. This is a discouraging truth.

But, unlike Stevens, I have hopes, and even some positive hypotheses to suggest. Once the contradictory assumptions about stimulation are made explicit, we can try to resolve them. For one thing we might search for an invariant component in the bewildering variety of functionally equivalent stimuli. Perhaps there is an invariant stimulus for the invariant response, after all. Many sorts of higher order variables of energy may exist, only awaiting mathematical description. They will have to be described in appropriate terms, of course, not as simple functions of frequency and amount. We must not confuse a stimulus with the elements used for its analysis. We must learn to conceive an array not as a mosaic of stimuli but as a hierarchy of forms within forms, and a flux not as a chain of stimuli but as a hierarchy of sequences within longer sequences.

## MOLAR STIMULI

Ever since Tolman, behavior theorists have been agreeing that psychology is concerned with molar responses, not molecular ones. Accordingly we try to observe and measure what an organism is doing, not how all its muscles are contracting. With this kind of observation on the response side there should be a corresponding kind of observation on the stimulus side. We should try to discover what an organism is responding *to*, not what excites all the little receptors. Of course all the muscles may be contracting and all the receptors may be excited, but observation at that level is the job of the physiologists.

The same recommendation can be made for the study of perception. The gestalt theorists have demonstrated the fact of molar experience, but they did not look for molar stimuli. These may very well exist outside the laboratory and, with ingenuity, can perhaps be isolated in the laboratory. If so, we shall have a new and powerful kind of psychophysics.

This conception of molar stimuli is not wholly new. Forty-five years ago, E. B. Holt was convinced that cognition, along with behavior, was a constant function of stimulation. In this he agreed with Pavlov and Watson. But Holt emphasized that the stimulus *of which* cognitive behavior was a function was more abstract and more comprehensive than the stimulus of classical psychophysics. As one passes from reflexes to behavior, the effective stimulus "recedes," as Holt put it (1915, *passim*). By the *recession* of the stimulus he meant that it seems to be located far out in the environment rather than close by in the receptors. And he also meant that as cognition develops, the stimulus of which it is a function recedes more and more. Following this suggestion, one might conclude that a change in response implies a change in the stimulus to which the response is made. Learning would then involve not only an alteration of behavior but also an alteration in the effective stimulus. Presumably its molar character has gone up a stage in the hierarchy.

## POTENTIAL STIMULI

Evidently the hypothesis of potential stimulation, accepted casually by some theorists, has quite radical but unrecognized implications. We have long acknowledged the almost unlimited possibilities for new responses in learning theory; why not equally vast possibilities of new stimuli? The environment, so considered, would consist of a sort of reservoir of possible stimuli for both perception and action. Light, heat, sound, odor, gravity, and potential contacts with objects surround the individual. But this sea of energy has variables of pattern and sequence which can be registered by sense organs. They can be explored, either at one station-point or by moving around in the environment. The fields of radiating sound and odor, together

with the flux of light rays reflected from surfaces, make it possible to respond to things at a distance. The changes of pattern in time serve as controlling stimuli for locomotion and manipulation. The variables and covariables and invariables of this stimulus environment are inexhaustible.

Surprisingly little has been written about potential stimuli. The sensory physiologists, of course, have read their physics and chemistry. But physical science portrays a sterile world. The variables of physics make uninteresting stimuli. Why is this true? I think it is because psychologists take for stimuli only the variables of physics as they stand in the textbooks. We have simply picked the wrong variables. It is our own fault. After all, physicists are not primarily concerned with stimuli. They have enough to do to study physical energies without worrying about stimulus energies. I think that we will have to develop the needed discipline on a do-it-yourself principle. It might be called ecological physics, with branches in optics, acoustics, dynamics, and biochemistry. We cannot wait for the physical scientists to describe and classify potential stimuli. The variables would seem to them inelegant, the mathematics would have to be improvised, and the job is not to their taste. But it is necessary. And if successful, it will provide a basis for a stimulus-response psychology, which otherwise seems to be sinking in a swamp of intervening variables.

Consider, for example, the physics (that is to say the acoustics) of speech sounds. As recently as 1951, in the *Handbook of Experimental Psychology* (Stevens, p. 869), the fact that a word is perceptually the same when whispered as it is when shouted was taken to prove that the physical characteristics of sound waves, frequency, intensity, and so on, cannot tell us about speech. Speech perception would require a psychological theory, not physical measurement. But the invention of the sound spectrograph seems to have shown that certain higher order variables of acoustic energy are the critical constituents of speech and the stimuli for hearing it. These newly discovered invariant patterns of sound are completely physical, even if they had not previously been studied in physics. What was needed to understand the psychophysics of hearing words was not more psychology but more physics.

For another example consider the optics of an array of light. The physical variables applying to the point source and the image point do not explain the seeing of a surface. But my own work shows that the variables of an optical *texture* do account for the seeing of a surface, and that by manipulating textures an experimenter can produce synthetic perceptions of objects (Gibson, Purdy, & Lawrence, 1955). Gradients, patterns, and other invariants are not part of existing geometrical optics, but they are physical facts. What was needed for a psychophysics of visual perception was not more theorizing about cues but more attention to geometrical optics.

## EFFECTIVE STIMULI

An effective stimulus can now be defined. It is one which arouses receptor activity, or recorded neural impulses, or sense organ adjustments, or overt responses, or verbal judgments—whichever criterion one chooses. Note that the idea of fixed innate thresholds of sensation is rejected. It always was a myth, for every psychophysical experimenter knows that the threshold obtained depends on the method used and the response criterion chosen.

In short, whether or not a potential stimulus becomes effective depends on the individual. It depends on the species to which he belongs, on the anatomy of the sense organs, the stage of maturation, the capacities for sense organ adjustment, the habits of attention, the activity in progress, and the possibilities of educating the attention of the individual. Such facts make up

the field of perceptual development and perceptual learning. At the lower levels they are called facts of sensory physiology; at the higher levels, facts of attention or exploration, but they are all one problem. Animals seem to be driven to make potential stimuli effective. They use their receptor equipment, probably, in as great a variety of ways as they use their motor equipment. From this point of view, it seems to me, the senses begin to make sense.

## STAGES OF SPECIFICITY

Johannes Müller began the study of the way in which the modes of experience are specific to the excitations of nerve fibers. Sherrington and others showed how the excitations of fibers were generally specific to the patterns of the stimulus. Ecological physics will tell us the extent to which the proximal stimuli are specific to their sources in the world. If experience is specific to excitation, and excitation to stimulation, and stimulation to the external environment, then experience will be specific to the environment, within the limits of this chain of specificities. The first two stages have long been under investigation. The last is ripe for study. There has been a controversy over whether or not visual stimuli can specify their objects (for example, Cantril, 1950), but it can be settled, for the facts are discoverable, and arguments should await evidence.

## THE INFORMATIVE CAPACITY OF MOLAR STIMULI

If the structure and sequence of stimulus energy can be analyzed, potential stimuli can be described and arranged in a hierarchy. There will be subordinate stimuli and superordinate stimuli, of lower order and higher order. So conceived it is reasonable to assume that stimuli *carry information* about the terrestrial environment. That is, they specify things about objects, places, events, animals, people, and the actions of people. The rules by which they do so are to be determined, but there is at least enough evidence to warrant discarding the opposite assumption under which we have been operating for centuries— that stimuli are necessarily and intrinsically meaningless.

## NATURAL STIMULI, PICTORIAL STIMULI, AND CODED STIMULI

I have suggested that, instead of continuing to employ the careless analogies of our present loose terminology for stimuli—cues, clues, signals, signs, indicators, messages, inputs, and the like—we make a systematic study of the laws by which stimuli specify their sources. We need to know the laws of stimulus information. Almost certainly these will not be the laws which govern the transmission of information in human systems of communication. The natural world does not literally *communicate* with the sense organs. The potential physical stimuli arising from an event are not to be compared to the physical stimulus arising from the *word* for that event. We cannot hope to understand natural stimuli by analogy with socially coded stimuli, for that would be like putting the cart before the horse. Just this, however, is what we tend to do when we speak of the "signs" for depth perception and the "messages" of the senses. We cannot afford to speak of coded information for the sense organs when we mean stimuli, for some of these are coded and some are not.

A systematic study of the specifying power of stimuli will put the problem of meaning in perception on a new footing. It will take several forms, depending on the kinds of relations discovered. My guess is that there will be at least three, corresponding to the stimuli from things, from pictures, and from words. It is true that men, besides learning to perceive objects, also learn to apprehend things by way of perceiving pictures and words. These mediated perceptions get mixed with direct perceptions in the adult. But we shall have to dis-

entangle them before we can have a complete theory of human perception.

## CONCLUSION

The foregoing distinctions and assumptions seem promising to me. But I would agree that a stimulus theory cannot be established by merely asserting it. The scientific question is whether all these new kinds of stimuli exist. I suggest that we look for them in the environment and then try to bring them into the laboratory.

It is still true that the stimulus is the prime independent variable of a psychological experiment. I quote from Underwood (1957):

One may vary more than one stimulus condition in a given experiment . . . but to draw a conclusion about the influence of any given variable, that variable must have been systematically manipulated alone somewhere in the design. Nothing in analysis of variance, covariance, Latin squares, Greco-Latin squares, or Greco-Arabic-Latin squares has abrogated this basic principle (p. 35).

If Underwood is right, the secret of a good experiment is to discover the relevant stimulus before doing the experiment. The moral of my argument is that a systematic search for relevant stimuli, molar stimuli, potential stimuli, invariant stimuli, specifying stimuli, and information stimuli will yield experiments with positive results. Perhaps the reservoir of stimuli that I have pictured is full of elegant independent variables, their simplicity obscured by physical complexity, only waiting to be discovered.

## REFERENCES

Brunswik, E. 1956. *Perception and the representative design of experiments.* Berkeley: University of California Press.

Cantril, H. 1950. *The "why" of man's experience.* New York: Macmillan.

Freud, S. 1949. *Collected papers.* London: Hogarth Press.

Gibson, J. J., and Gibson, E. J. 1957. Continuous perspective transformations and the perception of rigid motion. *Journal of Experimental Psychology* 54:129–138.

Gibson, J. J.; Purdy, J.; and Lawrence, L. 1955. A method of controlling stimulation for the study of space perception: The optical tunnel. *Journal of Experimental Psychology* 50:1–14.

Harper, R. S., and Boring, E. G. 1948. Cues. *American Journal of Psychology* 61:343–351.

Hayek, F. A. 1952. *The sensory order.* Chicago: University of Chicago Press.

Hilgard, E. R., and Marquis, D. G. 1940. *Conditioning and learning.* New York: Appleton-Century-Crofts.

Holt, E. B. 1915. *The Freudian wish.* New York: Holt.

Hull, C. L. 1943. *Principles of behavior.* New York: Appleton-Century-Crofts.

Jennings, H. S. 1906. *Behavior of the lower organisms.* New York: Columbia University Press.

Koch, S., ed. 1959. *Psychology: A study of a science.* Vol. 2. New York: McGraw-Hill.

Koffka, K. 1935. *Principles of gestalt psychology.* New York: Harcourt, Brace.

Köhler, W. 1929. *Gestalt psychology.* New York: Liveright.

Miller, N. E., and Dollard, J. 1941. *Social learning and imitation.* New Haven: Yale University Press.

Murchison, C. 1934. *Handbook of general experimental psychology.* Worcester: Clark University Press.

Osgood, C. E. 1953. *Method and theory in experimental psychology.* New York: Oxford University Press.

Pavlov, I. P. 1927. *Conditioned reflexes.* Trans. by G. V. Anrep. London: Oxford University Press.

Skinner, B. F. 1938. *The behavior of organisms.* New York: Appleton-Century-Crofts.

Skinner, B. F. 1959. *Cumulative record.* New York: Appleton-Century-Crofts.

Spence, K. W. 1956. *Behavior theory and conditioning.* New Haven: Yale University Press.

Stevens, S. S., ed. 1951. *Handbook of experimental psychology.* New York: Wiley.

Troland, L. T. 1930. *Psychophysiology.* Vol. 2. New York: Van Nostrand.

Underwood, B. 1957. *Psychological research.* New York: Appleton-Century-Crofts.

Vernon, M. D. 1952. *A further study of visual perception.* Cambridge: Cambridge University Press.

Watson, J. B. 1924. *Psychology from the standpoint of a behaviorist.* Philadelphia: Lippincott.

Woodworth, R. S. 1929. *Psychology.* New York: Holt.

Woodworth, R. S. 1958. *Dynamics of behavior.* New York: Holt.

# READING 15

## Subliminal Stimulation: An Overview

JAMES V. McCONNELL
RICHARD L. CUTLER
ELTON B. McNEIL
University of Michigan

The following article is a review of the literature on subliminal stimulation. It is filled with experimental findings which bear on many aspects of the problem of perception without awareness. The authors raise questions about the effectiveness of subliminal stimulation, the variables that affect this kind of stimulation, and the ethical problems involved. Many of the data presented here have reference to more than one area of psychology, and you should keep this in mind as you read the article.

**QUESTIONS**

1. The authors consider the problem of thresholds. Keeping this in mind, explain how we can be stimulated subliminally.
2. Evaluate the evidence presented in this article. Pay particular attention to statements like "seem to support" or remarks to the effect that there are methodological weaknesses, or that the studies are not unequivocal.
3. Consider the ethical problems suggested by this article. What is the social and practical value of a code of ethics such as "Ethical Standards of Psychology," published by the American Psychological Association?

Seldom has anything in psychology caused such an immediate and widespread stir as the recent claim that the presentation of certain stimuli below the level of conscious awareness can influence people's behavior in a significant way. The controversy was precipitated primarily by a commercial firm which claimed that the subliminal presentation of the words "Eat Popcorn" and "Drink Coca-Cola" fantastically stimulated the respective sales of these products among the motion picture audiences who received the stimulation. Despite the fact that detailed reports of the experiment have not been made directly available in any published form, this technique was seized upon as the newest of the "new look" promises of the application of psychology to advertising. While such claims and demonstrations will be considered in greater detail below, it is important to note here that they have given rise to a series of charges and countercharges, the effects of which have reached the United States Congress and the Federal Communications Commission (7, 117).

Rarely does a day pass without a statement in the public press relating to the Utopian promise or the 1984 threat of the technique (8, 17, 29, 37, 42, 45, 118, 132). Since the process of choosing up sides promises to continue unabated, it appears wise to provide the potential combatants with a more factual basis for arriving at their positions than presently seems available. Meanwhile, the present writers have cautiously sought to avoid aligning themselves behind either of the barricades.

Obviously, the notion that one may influence the behavior of another individual without the individual's knowing about it is a fascinating one. It is of extreme interest, not only to psychologists and advertisers, but also to politicians, psychiatrists, passionate young men, and others, whose motives would be considered more or less sacred by the larger society. Equally obvious is the need for a clarification of the issues surrounding the application of subliminal perception. This clarification must involve the assessment of available scientific evidence, the answering of a series of technical questions, and the examination of what, if any, levels of behavior may indeed be influenced. Finally, a series of extremely complex ethical issues needs to be explored. It is the purpose of the present paper to undertake this task, in the hope of providing information upon which possible decisions involving its application may be based.

## RECENT HISTORY OF THE TECHNIQUE

The custom of providing a chronological review of the literature will be violated in this paper, inasmuch as three separate threads of investigation seem worth tracing: (a) the recent demonstrations by advertisers which first aroused large-scale public interest in subliminal perception, (b) systematic research by psychologists relating directly to the influencing of behavior without the individual's awareness that he is being influenced, and (c) psychological research concerned primarily with the influence of inner states of the organism upon the threshold for conscious recognition of certain stimuli.

### RECENT ADVERTISING DEMONSTRATIONS

While the advertising possibilities of subliminal stimulation were recognized by Hollingworth (59) as early as 1913, the intensive work in its application to this area has been carried out within the past two years. In 1956, BBC-TV, in conjunction with one of its regular broadcasts, transmitted the message "Pirie Breaks World Record" at a speed assumed to be subliminal (85). At the conclusion of the regular program, viewers were asked to report whether they had noticed "anything unusual" about the program. While no reliable statistical data are available, it seems possible that those few viewers responding to the message possessed sufficiently low thresholds so that for them the message was supraliminal.

A demonstration by the commercial enterprise which has been most vocal in its claims for the advertising promise of the technique consisted of projecting, during alternate periods, the words "Eat Popcorn" and "Drink Coca-Cola" during the regular presentation of a motion picture program.

As a result of this stimulation, reports contend,[1] popcorn sales rose more than 50% and Coca-Cola sales 18%, as compared to a "previous period." Despite the likelihood of serious methodological and technical defects (exposure time was reported at 1/3,000 sec., far faster than any previously reported stimulation), this demonstration has been the one which has caused the most stir in both the fields of advertising and psychology. There were no reports, however, of even the most rudimentary scientific precautions, such as adequate controls, provision for replication, etc., which leaves the skeptical scientist in a poor position to make any judgment about the validity of the study.

In a later demonstration for the press, technical difficulties permitted the viewers to become consciously aware of the fact that they were being stimulated. Although described as a purposeful and prearranged part of the demonstration, it left many of the reporters present unconvinced that the technical difficulties inherent in the technique have been surmounted.

The FCC, turning its attention to the problem, has reported that one TV station (WTWO, Bangor, Maine) has experimented with the transmission of public service announcements at subliminal levels, with "negative results" (117).

The uncontrolled and unsystematic nature of the demonstrations reported above makes very difficult the task of reaching a trustworthy conclusion about the effectiveness of subliminal stimulation in advertising. Whether the technique represents a promising means of communicating with the individual at a level of his unconsciousness or whether it reflects only the hyperenthusiasm of an entrepreneurial group remain unanswered questions.

## RESEARCH ON BEHAVIOR WITHOUT AWARENESS

In the hope of providing a more substantial foundation upon which to base judgments of the validity of advertising claims for subliminal stimulation, a systematic review of relevant scientific work was undertaken. While we believe that our review was comprehensive, we have decided not to provide an extensive critical discussion of the various studies, choosing instead to present summative statements and conclusions based upon what seems to be sufficient evidence and consensus in the literature.[2]

The work of experimental psychologists in subliminal stimulation dates from Suslowa (119) in 1863, as reported by Baker (5). Suslowa's experiments concerned the effect of electrical stimulation upon subjects' ability to make two-point threshold discriminations. He found that even when the intensity of the electrical stimulation was so low that the subjects were not aware of its presence, their ability to discriminate one- from two-point stimulation was somewhat reduced.

In 1884, Peirce and Jastrow (94) were able to show that subjects could discriminate differences between weights significantly better than chance would allow, even though the differences were so small they had no confidence whatsoever in their judgments.

Numerous experimenters have relied upon this criterion of "zero confidence" to establish that the discrimination of stimuli presented below the level of conscious awareness is possible. For example, Sidis (107) showed that subjects could reliably distinguish letters from numbers, even when the stimuli were presented at such a distance from them that the subjects thought they were relying on pure guesswork for their judgments.

---

[1]The essential facts of this study have not been reported in any journal. The discussion of this experiment and the findings reported by the commercial enterprise responsible for the study is based on reports in several general news accounts appearing in the popular press (7, 8, 16, 17, etc.).

[2]The reader who wishes a more complete technical critique of studies in the field is referred to reviews by Adams (1), Collier (27), Coover (28), Lazarus and McCleary (76), and Miller (90).

In what was essentially a replication of Sidis' research, Stroh, Shaw, and Washburn (116) found evidence to support his conclusions. They found similar results when auditory stimuli (whispers) were presented at a distance such that the subjects were not consciously aware that they were hearing anything.

Several experiments have provided further support for Peirce and Jastrow's initial conclusions (44, 127). Baker (5) found subjects able to discriminate diagonal from vertical crossed lines, and a dot-dash from a dash-dot auditory pattern. Miller (88) presented five geometric figures at four different levels of intensity below the threshold and found that, while subjects could discriminate which was being presented a significant proportion of the time, their ability to discriminate was reduced as the intensity of stimulation was further reduced. More recently, a series of studies by Blackwell (11) has shown that subjects can reliably identify during which of four time periods a subliminal spot of light is presented upon a homogeneous field. Blackwell, however, stresses that reliability of discrimination decreases as the intensity of the stimulus is further lowered. Several other supporting studies are available (28, 97, 130) which show essentially the same results, namely, that even when subjects have zero confidence in their judgments, they can discriminate reliably (though not perfectly) between stimuli.

In his review, Adams (1) points out certain general weaknesses inherent in studies of this type, but agrees with the present authors that discrimination can occur under certain circumstances. However, it is interesting to note that, in nearly all studies reporting relevant data, the reliability of the subjects' judgments increases directly with the intensity of the stimuli. If a valid extrapolation can be drawn from this finding, it would be that accuracy of perception increases as the stimulation approaches a supraliminal level.

A second series of studies has involved presenting subjects with variations of the Mueller-Lyre illusion, in which the angular lines have differed, subliminally, in hue or brightness from the background. The first of these studies, reported by Dunlap in 1909 (36), gave clear evidence that the subjects were influenced in their judgments of line length, even though they could not "see" the angular lines. Several replications of this study have been carried out, and while at least three have found partial support for Dunlap's conclusions (14, 59, 86), others have failed to find the phenomenon (123). In another experiment conducted by Sidis in 1898 (107), subjects asked to fixate on a number series in the center of a card, and then asked to pick a number from this series, systematically chose that number which was written in the periphery of the card, even though they were not consciously aware of its presence. Coover (28) in 1917 showed essentially the same results by asking subjects to pick a number at random while they were fixating on a letter in the upper right portion of a card. He found that subjects tended to pick the number printed in the lower left of the card, even though they did not *usually* know it was there. In similar experiments, Collier (27) and Perky (95) showed that subjects could be made to produce drawings, even though they were not aware that they were being influenced in their actions. While these studies are not unequivocal in their findings, nor generally rigorous in their methodology, they too seem to support the contention that behavior of a sort can be influenced by subliminal means. However, they require cautious interpretation, since the degree of the subject's attention to the stimuli seems clearly to be a factor. Further, as contrasted to those studies where the subject is actually aware in advance of at least the general nature of the stimulation, these studies reveal a somewhat less pronounced effect of subliminal stimulation upon the subject's behavior.

While the studies reported above seem to indicate that discrimination without awareness may occur, it may reasonably be asked whether stimulation below the level of conscious awareness can produce any but the most simple modifications in behavior. A series of studies (24, 26, 73, 109), beginning with Newhall and Sears in 1933 (92), have attempted to show that it is possible to condition subjects to subliminal stimuli. Newhall and Sears found it possible to establish a weak and unstable conditioned response to light presented subliminally, when the light had been previously paired with shock. Baker (6) in 1938 reported the successful conditioning of the pupillary reflex to a subliminal auditory stimulus, but later experimenters have failed to replicate his results (57, 128). In a now classic experiment, McCleary and Lazarus (79) found that nonsense syllables which had previously been associated with shock produced a greater psychogalvanic reflex when presented tachistoscopically at subliminal speeds than did nonshock syllables. Deiter (34) confirmed the McCleary and Lazarus findings and showed further that, when verbal instructions were substituted for the shock, no such differences were produced. Bach and Klein (4) have recently reported that they were able to influence subjects' judgments of whether the line drawing of a face (essentially neutral in its emotional expression) was "angry" or "happy" by projecting the appropriate words at subliminal speeds upon the drawing.

A series of related studies (58, 65, 89, 99, 105, 121, 122) have shown that, even when the subject is not aware that any cue is being given, certain responses can be learned or strengthened during the experimental process. For example, Cohen, Kalish, Thurston, and Cohen (25) showed that, when the experimenter said "right" to any sentence which the subject started with "I" or "We," the number of such sentences increased significantly. Klein (69) was able to produce both conditioning and extinction

without awareness, using the Cohen et al. technique.

Several experimenters have used subliminal or "unnoticed" reward-punishment techniques to modify subjects' responses in a variety of situations, including free or chained association tasks, performance on personality tests, and interview elicited conversation (35, 41, 50, 56, 72, 78, 93, 120, 125, 126). Typical is the work of Greenspoon (48), who reinforced the use of plural nouns by saying "mm-humm" after each plural mentioned by the subject. He found that, even though none of his subjects could verbalize the relationship between their response and his reinforcement, their use of plural nouns doubled. Sidowski (108) demonstrated essentially the same thing using a light, of which the subject was only peripherally aware, as a reinforcer for the use of plural words. Weiss (129), however, failed to find any increase in the frequency of "living things" responses, using a right-wrong reinforcement to free associations by the subjects.

This evidence suggests that subjects may either (a) "learn" certain subliminally presented stimuli or (b) make use of subliminal reinforcers either to learn or strengthen a previously learned response. Again, the critical observations of Adams (1) and the introduction of other possible explanations by Bricker and Chapanis (15) make necessary a cautious interpretation of these results.

### EFFECTS OF INNER STATES UPON THRESHOLDS

Whatever the possibility that subliminal stimulation may significantly alter behavior, there is excellent evidence that certain inner states of the organism, as well as externally induced conditions, may significantly alter the recognition threshold of the individual. This, of course, has important implications for the susceptibility of the individual to the effects of subliminal stimulation. It is well known that physiological factors, such as fatigue, visual acuity, or satiation, may change the threshold of an individual for various kinds of stimuli.

Recent evidence has accumulated to show that, in addition to these physiological factors, certain "psychological states," such as psychological need, value, conflict, and defense, may also significantly influence thresholds, as well as other aspects of the perceptual process. Early work in this area is reported by Sanford (102, 103) who showed that subjects who had been deprived of food were more prone to produce "food-relevant" responses to a series of ambiguous stimuli. McClelland and Atkinson (80) showed that levels of the hunger drive were systematically related to the ease with which food responses were made when no words were presented on the screen.

While a complete review of the experimental work on "perceptual defense" and "selective vigilance" would take us too far afield, it seems wise to indicate, by example, some of the inner state factors which allegedly produce variations in recognition threshold. Bruner and Postman (19, 20, 21) and Bruner and Goodman (18) were able to show that such factors as symbolic value, need tension and tension release, and emotional selectivity were important in the perceptual process. Ansbacher (3) had earlier demonstrated that the perception of numerosity was significantly affected by the monetary value of the stimuli. Rees and Israel (101) called attention to the fact that the mental set of the organism was an important factor in the perceptual process. Beams and Thompson (9) showed that emotional factors were important determiners of the perception of the magnitude of need-relevant objects. Other studies bearing upon the issue of inner state determiners of perception are reported by Carter and Schooler (23), Cowen and Beier (31, 32), and Levine, Chein, and Murphy (77).

More specifically related to the issue of altered recognition thresholds is a study by McGinnies (82) in which he demonstrated

that emotionally toned words had generally higher thresholds than neutral words. Blum (13) has shown that subjects tend to be less likely to choose conflict-relevant stimuli from a group presented at subliminal speeds than to choose neutral stimuli. Lazarus, Ericksen and Fonda (75) have shown that personality factors are at least in part determiners of the recognition threshold for classes of auditory stimuli. Reece (100) showed that the association of shock with certain stimuli had the effect of raising the recognition threshold for those stimuli.

While many writers have contended that the variations in threshold can be accounted for more parsimoniously than by introducing "motivational" factors such as need and value (60, 61, 111), and while the issue of the degree to which need states influence perception is still unresolved (22, 39, 40, 62, 74, 83), it is apparent that the recognition threshold is not a simple matter of intensity nor speed of presentation. Recent work by Postman and others (47, 96, 98), which has sought to illuminate the prerecognition processes operating to produce the apparent changes in threshold, does not alter the fact that individual differences in the perceptual process must be taken into account in any further work on the effects of subliminal stimulation.

## UNANSWERED METHODOLOGICAL QUESTIONS

Having now concluded that, under certain conditions, the phenomenon of subliminal perception does occur, we turn our attention next to the many unanswered questions which this conclusion raises. For example, what kinds of behavior can be influenced by subliminal stimulation? What types of stimuli operate best at subthreshold intensities? Do all subliminal stimuli operate at the same "level of unconsciousness," or do different stimuli (or modes of stimulation) affect different levels of unconsciousness? What characteristics of the perceiver help determine the effectiveness of subliminal stimulation? All of these questions, as well as many others of a technological nature, will be discussed in the ensuing paragraphs.

A few words of caution concerning the word "subliminal" seem in order, however. It must be remembered that the psychological limen is a statistical concept, a fact overlooked by far too many current textbook writers. The common definition of the limen is "that stimulus value which gives a response exactly half the time" (44, p. 111). One of the difficulties involved in analyzing the many studies on subliminal perception is the fact that many experimenters have assumed that, because the stimuli which they employed were below the statistical limen for a given subject, the stimuli were therefore never consciously perceivable by the subject. This is, of course, not true. Stimuli slightly below the statistical limen might well be consciously perceivable as much as 49% of the time. Not only this, but thresholds vary from moment to moment, as well as from day to day. All this is not to deny that stimuli which are so weak that they are never consciously reportable under any circumstances may not indeed influence behavior. We simply wish to make the point that the range of stimulus intensities which are in fact "subliminal" may be smaller than many experimenters in the past have assumed. It has been commonly assumed that the several methods of producing subliminal stimuli, i.e., reducing intensity, duration, size, or clarity, are logically and methodologically equivalent. While this may be true, it remains to be demonstrated conclusively.

## TYPES OF BEHAVIOR INFLUENCED BY SUBLIMINAL STIMULATION

One of the first questions that springs to mind concerns the types of response which can be elicited with subliminal stimulation. Let us assume for the moment that the below-threshold advertisements used in commercial demonstrations were the sole cause of increased popcorn buying among the movie audiences subjected to the ads. How did this come about? Did the stimulus "Eat Popcorn" elicit an already established response in some members of the audience? Or did the frequent repetitions of the stimulus message cause a shift in attitude towards popcorn eating which eventually resulted in the purchase of popcorn at the first opportunity the audience had? Did the ads merely raise an already existing, presumably learned, but weak need for popcorn to an above the action-threshold level, or did the ads actually create a need for popcorn where no need had existed beforehand? Did members of the audience rise like automatons during the course of the movie and thus miss part of the feature in order to satisfy a sudden craving for popcorn or in order to respond to a suddenly evoked stimulus-response connection? Or did they wait until a "rest period" to do their purchasing? How many patrons bought popcorn only after they had seen the film and were heading home? How many people purchased popcorn on their way *in* to see the next movie they attended? How many of those who purchased popcorn did so for the first time in their lives, or for the first time in recent memory? What if the message presented had been "Buy Christmas Seals," which are available only in one season? How many people failed to buy popcorn at the theater, but purchased it subsequently at the local supermarket?

Unfortunately, these pertinent questions have yet to be answered. Let us tentatively accept this demonstration that impulse buying of inexpensive items such as popcorn and Coca-Cola can be influenced by subliminal advertising, without yet knowing what the mechanism involved is. It remains to be demonstrated, however, that such ads could make a person of limited means wreck himself financially by purchasing a Cadillac merely because the ads told him to do so. Nor do we know if deep-seated, strongly emotional attitudes or long established behavior patterns can be shifted one way or another as a result of subliminal stimulation. The answers to these questions must come from further experimentation.

As we have already seen, people can make use of subthreshold stimuli in making difficult perceptual judgments in situations where they are required to call up images of various objects (*95*) and in situations where they are asked to "read the experimenter's mind" (*88*). Kennedy (*68*) believes that some extrasensory-perception (ESP) experimenters may have obtained positive results because the "senders" unconsciously transmitted slight auditory and visual cues to their "receivers," and offers many experimental findings to back up his belief. Kennedy's studies also point up the difficult dilemma faced by people who object to subliminal stimulation as being an immoral or illegal attempt to influence other people. All of us, apparently, are constantly attempting to influence the people around us by means of sounds and movements we are unconscious of making. Correspondingly, all of us make some unconscious use of the cues presented to us by the people around us.

It also seems fairly clear that learning can take place when the stimuli to which the organism must respond are presented subliminally. Hankin (*51*) learned to predict changes in the flight of birds by utilizing wing-tip adjustments which were too slight to be consciously (reportably) noticeable. As we stated previously, Baker (*6*) obtained a conditioned pupillary response to subliminal auditory stimuli, although other investigators failed to replicate his findings. Miller (*89*) had subjects look at a mirror while trying to guess geometrical forms in an ESP-type experiment. Stimuli far below the statistical limen were projected on a mirror from behind. When the subjects were rewarded by praise for correct guesses and punished by electric shock for wrong guesses, learning took place. It is interesting to note that neither punishment alone nor reward alone was sufficient to produce learning.

Whether different types of learning than those reported above can take place using subliminal stimulation, and indeed how broad a range of human behavior can be influenced in any way whatsoever by subliminal stimulation, are questions which remain unanswered.

## LEVELS OF UNCONSCIOUSNESS AFFECTED BY SUBLIMINAL STIMULATION[3]

We must now differentiate between stimuli which a subject cannot bring to awareness under any conditions (completely subliminal stimuli) and those stimuli of which he is merely not aware at the moment but could be made aware of should his set be changed. At any given moment, a vast conflux of stimuli impinges upon a subject's receptors. Few of the sensations arising from this stimulation ever enter the focus of attention. As Dolenbach was fond of reminding his freshman classes: "Until I mentioned it, you were quite unaware that your shoes are full of feet." A great many experimenters have demonstrated that subjects could make use of stimuli well above the threshold of awareness but which could not be consciously reported on. Thus in one phase of the experiment, Perky (*95*) raised the intensity of the visual stimuli she was using to such a level that other psychologists who had not participated in the study apparently refused to believe that the subjects had not been aware of the stimuli. Perky's subjects, however, operating under a set to call up "images" of the stimuli presented did not notice even relatively intense stimuli. Correspondingly, Newhall and Dodge (*91*) presented visual stimuli first at below-threshold intensities, then increased the intensities so slowly that the subjects were not aware of them even when

---

[3]For an excellent review of the many meanings of the word "unconsciousness," readers are referred to Miller, book of the same name (*90*).

the stimuli were well above threshold. When the stimuli were turned off suddenly, however, the subjects experienced after-images. Thus certain stimuli may be well above threshold and yet be "sublimined" in the sense that they cannot be reported on under certain experimental conditions.

There are other levels of "unconsciousness" which are deserving of our attention, however. Much work has been done at the animal level in which conditioning has been attempted upon animals with various parts of the brain removed (33, 43). The same is true of animals under various types of anesthesia (106, 115). Miller, in summarizing the experimental data dealing with conditioning and consciousness, concludes:

(a) That conditioning can take place in other parts of the nervous system than the cortex—even in the spinal cord;

(b) That if conditioned responses are evidences of consciousness then conscious ness is not mediated solely by the cortex;

(c) That it may be possible to develop conditioning at more than one level of the nervous system at the same time;

(d) And that . . . animals are conditionable even when anesthesized (90, p. 100).

The nervous system has many levels of anatomical integration. Should we be surprised to discover that incoming stimuli may have an effect on a lower level and not on a higher and that under certain conditions this effect can later be demonstated in terms of behavioral changes? We shall not be able to speak clearly of the effects of subliminal stimulation upon the various "levels of unconsciousness" until we have some better method of specifying exactly what these levels are and by what parts of the nervous system they are mediated. Experimentation is badly needed in this area.

## TECHNOLOGICAL PROBLEMS INVOLVED IN STIMULATING SUBJECTS SUBLIMINALLY

The paucity of data presented by those dealing with subliminal perception on a commercial basis, as well as the equivocal nature of their results, suggests that there are many technological problems yet to be solved by these and other investigators. For example, during a two-hour movie (or a one-hour television show), how many times should the stimulus be repeated to make sure that the "measure" get across to the largest possible percentage of the audience? Should the stimulus be repeated every second, every five seconds, only once a minute? Is the effect cumulative, or is one presentation really enough? Is there a satiation effect, such that the audience becomes "unconsciously tired" of the stimulation, and "unconsciously blocks" the incoming subliminal sensations? Should the stimuli be presented "between frames" of the movie (that is, when the shutter of the film projector is closed and the screen momentarily blank as it is 24 times each second), or should the message be presented only when the screen already has a picture on it? How close to the threshold (statistical or otherwise) should the stimuli be? How many words long can the message be? If the message must be short, could successive stimulations present sequential parts of a longer advertisement? How much of the screen should the stimuli fill? Should the stimuli be presented only during "happier" moments in the film, in order to gain positive affect? Does any affect transfer at all from the film to the ad? Should one use pictures, or are words best? Must the words be familiar ones? And what about subliminal auditory, cutaneous, and olfactory stimulation?

As we have stated before, there has been so much talk and so little experimentation, and much of what experimentation has been done is so inadequately reported, that we can merely hazard guesses based on related but perhaps not always applicable studies.

To begin with, we can state with some assurance that, the closer to the threshold of awareness the stimuli are, the more effect they are likely to have. Study after study has reported increased effectiveness with increased intensity of stimulation (5, 14, 88, 97, 104). The main difficulty seems to be that thresholds vary so much from subject to subject (112), and from day to day (114), that what is subliminal but effective for one person is likely to be subliminal but ineffective for a second, and supraliminal for a third. As is generally the case, anyone who wishes to use the technique of subliminal stimulation must first experiment upon the specific group of people whom he wishes to influence before he can decide what intensity levels will be most efficacious.

Somewhat the same conclusion holds for the question of how many times the stimuli should be presented. While under some conditions subliminal stimuli which did not influence behavior when presented only once seemed to "summate" when presented many times (10, 66), Bricker and Chapanis (15) found that one presentation of a stimulus slightly below the (statistical) limen was enough to increase the likelihood of its being recognized on subsequent trials. We interpret this to mean that too many presentations may well raise the "subliminal" stimuli above the limen of awareness if the stimuli themselves are not carefully chosen.

As for the physical properties of the message itself, we can but guess what the relevant issues are. Both verbal and pictorial presentations apparently are effective in the visual modality, but no one has tested the relative effectiveness of these two types of stimulation. Quite possibly subsequent experimentation will show that words are best for some situations (such as direct commands), while pictures are best for others.[4] It can be stated unequivocally, however, that advertisers should look to their basic English when writing their subliminal commercials. Several studies have shown that, the more familiar a subject is

with the stimulus he is to perceive, the more readily he perceives it (22, 54, 63, 110). We interpret these studies to mean that unfamiliar stimuli may be ineffective when presented subliminally, even though familiar messages may "get through."

The exact length the message should be, its composition, and the background in which it should be presented are variables upon which no work has been done and about which no conclusions can presently be drawn. Suffice it to say, however, that a message which would be short enough to be perceived by one person might be too long for another person to perceive under any conditions.

Which modalities are most useful for subliminal stimulation? While most of the work has been done on the visual modality, Vanderplas and Blake (124) and Kurland (71) have found subthreshold auditory stimuli to be effective, and earlier in this paper we have reported similar studies with cutaneous stimulation. Advertisers who wish to "sneak up on" their patrons by presenting subliminal stimuli in one modality while the patrons are attending to supraliminal stimuli from another modality are probably doomed to failure, however. Collier (27) presented subliminal geometric forms simultaneously to both the visual and the cutaneous modalities and found little, if any, lowering of thresholds. Correspondingly, it should be remembered that Hernandez-Peon et al. (55) found that some part of the nervous system acts as a kind of gating mechanism, and when an organism is attending strongly to one modality, the other modalities are probably "shut off" to most incoming stimuli.

Even if experimenters succeed in finding answers to many of the questions raised above concerning the physical characteristics of the stimuli to be employed, it is quite probable that they will have succeeded in discovering the source of only a small part of the variance operant in subliminal perception. For, as always, the major source of

[4]Perhaps much of the work on sensory preconditioning is applicable here. When Ellson (38) presented his subjects with both a light and a buzzer for many trials, then presented the light alone, subjects "heard" the buzzer too.

variance will come from the perceiver himself.

## CHARACTERISTICS OF THE PERCEIVER WHICH AFFECT SUBLIMINAL PERCEPTION

The following section of this paper might well be considered a plea for the recognition that individual differences exist and that they must be taken into account by anyone who wishes to deal with individuals. We know next to nothing about the relationships between such factors as age, sex, social class, etc. and subliminal perception. Perhaps only one study is relevant: Perky (95) found that children were as much influenced by subthreshold visual stimulation as were naive adults. It is quite likely that many differences in the perception of subliminal stimuli do exist between individuals of differing classes, ages, and sexes. As always only experimentation can determine what these differences are.

We do have some idea, however, of how what might be called "personality factors" influence subliminal perception. First and foremost, there seems little doubt but that a high need state affects perception. Gilchrist and Nesberg (46) found that, the greater the need state, the more their subjects tended to overestimate the brightness of objects relevant to that need. It should be noted that they were dealing with difference limens not absolute limens, but other studies to be quoted later show the same effect for absolute limens. It should be noted also that Gilchrist and Nesberg apparently overlooked evidence in their own data, that a strong need affects judgments of non-need-related objects in the same direction (but not as much) as it does need-related objects. Wispe and Drambarean, dealing with visual duration thresholds, concluded that "need-related words were recognized more rapidly as need increased" (131, p. 31). McClelland and Lieberman (81) found that subjects with high need achievement scores had lower visual thresholds for "success" words then did subjects

not scoring as high on need achievement. Do all of these findings mean that subliminal ads will work only when some fairly strong need (of any kind) is present in the viewers? Only experimentation can answer this question.

What about abnormalities of personality? What effect do they have? Kurland (71) tested auditory recognition thresholds using emotional and neutral words. He found that hospitalized neurotics perceived the emotional words at significantly lower thresholds than did a group of normal subjects. Does this mean that neurotics are more likely to respond to low-intensity subliminal commands than normals? Should advertisers take a "neurotic inventory" of their audiences?

A more pertinent problem is posed by the findings of Krech and Calvin (70). Using a Wechsler Vocabulary Score of 30.5 as their cutting point, they found that almost all college students above this score showed better visual discriminations of patterns presented at close to liminal values than did almost all students scoring below the cutting point. Does this mean that the higher the IQ, the better the subliminal perception? What is the relationship between the value of the absolute limen and intelligence? Will advertisers have to present their messages at such high intensities (in order that the "average man" might perceive the message) that the more intelligent members of the audience will be consciously aware of the advertising?

One further fascinating problem is posed by Huntley's work (64). He surreptitiously obtained photographs of the hands and profiles of his subjects, as well as handwriting samples and recordings of their voices. Six months later each subject was presented with the whole series of samples, among which were his own. Each subject was asked to make preference ratings of the samples. Huntley reports evidence of a significant tendency for subjects to prefer their own forms of expression above all others, even though in most cases they were totally unaware that the samples were their own and even though many subjects were unable to identify their own samples when told they were included in the series. If an advertiser is making a direct appeal to one specific individual, it would seem then that he should make use of the photographs and recordings of that individual's behavior as the subliminal stimuli. If an advertiser is making an appeal to a more general audience, however, it might be that he would find the use of pictures and recordings of Hollywood stars, etc., more efficacious than mere line drawings, printed messages, and unknown voices.

Nor can the advertiser afford to overlook the effects of set and attention. Miller (88), Perky (95), and Blake and Vanderplas (12), among others, discovered that giving the subject the proper set lowered the recognition threshold greatly. In fact, in many cases the stimulus intensity which was subliminal but effective for sophisticated subjects was far too subliminal to have much, if any, effect upon naive subjects. Thus advertisers might do well to tell audiences that subliminal messages were being presented to them, in order to bring all members of that audience closer to a uniform threshold. Does this not, however, vitiate some of the effect of subliminal advertising?

As for attentional effects, we have presented evidence earlier (46) that strong needs seem to have an "alerting" effect upon the organism, lowering recognition thresholds for all stimuli, not just need-related stimuli. In addition to this, two studies by Hartmann (52, 53), as well as two by Spencer (113, 114), lead us to the belief that subliminal stimuli might best be presented when either the television or movie screen was blank of other pictures. Perhaps, then, subliminal commercials in movie houses should be shown between features; while on television the commercials should consist of an appropriate period of apparent

"visual silence," during which the audience would not be aware of the subliminal stimulation presented, but might react to it later.

One fact emerges from all of the above. Anyone who wishes to utilize subliminal stimulation for commercial or other purposes can be likened to a stranger entering into a misty, confused countryside where there are but few landmarks. Before this technique is used in the market place, if it is to be used at all, a tremendous amount of research should be done, and by competent experimenters.

## THE ETHICS OF SUBLIMINAL INFLUENCE

From its beginnings as a purely academic offshoot of philosophy, psychology has, with ever increasing momentum, grown in the public perception as a practical and applied discipline. As psychologists were called upon to communicate and interpret their insights and research findings to lay persons, it was necessary to make decisions about what constituted proper professional behavior, since it was evident that the misuse of such information would reflect directly on the community of psychologists. As a growing number of our research efforts are viewed as useful to society, the problem of effective and honest communication becomes magnified, although its essential nature does not change. Recently, to our dismay, the announcement of a commercial application of long established psychological principles has assumed nightmarish qualities, and we find ourselves unwillingly cast in the role of invaders of personal privacy and enemies of society. A kind of guilt by association seems to be occurring, and, as future incidents of this kind will, it threatens to undermine the public relations we have built with years of caution and concern for the public welfare. The highly emotional public reaction to the "discovery" of subliminal perception should serve as an object lesson to our profession, for in the bright glare of publicity we can see urgent ethical issues as well as an omen of things to come. When the theoretical notion E=MC² became the applied reality of an atom bomb, the community of physicists became deeply concerned with social as well as scientific responsibility. Judging from the intensity of the public alarm when confronted with a bare minimum of fact about this subliminal social atom, there exists a clear need for psychologists to examine the ethical problems that are a part of this era of the application of their findings.

The vehemence of the reaction to the proposed use of a device to project subliminal, or from the public's point of view "hidden," messages to viewers indicates that the proposal touches a sensitive area. One of the basic contributors to this reaction seems to be the feeling that a technique which avowedly tampers with the psychological status of the individual ought to be under the regulation or control of a trusted scientific group. As a professional group, psychologists would fit this description, for in the *Ethical Standards of Psychologists* (2) there is a clear statement of their motives and relationship to society:

> Principle 1.12–1 The psychologist's ultimate allegiance is to society, and his professional behavior should demonstrate an awareness of his social responsibilities. The welfare of the profession and of the individual psychologist are clearly subordinate to the welfare of the public. . . .

Both this statement and the long record of responsible behavior of the members of the profession would certainly seem to be sufficient to reduce any anxiety the public might have over the possible unscrupulous use of this or any other device. It is precisely the fact that the public *is* aware that decisions about the use of subliminal perception devices rest not with psychologists but with commercial agencies that may be distressing to the public. The aura of open-for-business flamboyance and the sketchily presented percentages in the first public announcement tended to reinforce existing apprehensions rather than allay them.

Although subliminal perception happens now to be the focus of a great deal of reaction, it is merely the most recent in a succession of perturbing events to which the public has been exposed. It has become the focus of, and is likely to become the whipping boy for, a host of techniques which now occupy the twilight zone of infringement of personal psychological freedom. It must be remembered that to the lay person the notion of an unconscious part of the "mind" is eerie, vague, and more than a little mysterious. Unable fully to comprehend the systematic and theoretical aspects of such a concept, he must be content with overly popularized and dramatic versions of it. In every form of mass media the American public has been exposed to convincing images of the bearded hypnotist (with piercing eye) who achieves his nefarious ends by controlling the unconscious of his victim. It has been treated to the spectacle of the seeming reincarnation of Bridey Murphy out of the unconscious of an American housewife and in *Three Faces of Eve*, to complex multiple personalities hidden in the psychic recesses of a single individual. With such uncanny and disturbing images as an emotional backdrop, the appearance of *The Hidden Persuaders* on the best seller lists formed the indelible impression of the exploitation of the unconscious for purposes of profit and personal gain. In combination, this growth of emotionally charged attitudes toward the unconscious and the suspicions about commercial morality came to be a potentially explosive set of tensions which was triggered off by the first commercial use of subliminal techniques.

What is to be the psychologist's position in regard to future developments with subliminal perception? The apparent discrepancy between the claims being made for the technique and the available research evidence suggests a need for considerable scientific caution as well as extensive investigation. The responsibility of psychologists in this instance is clearly indicated in the code of ethics:

> Principle 2.12–1 The psychologist should refuse to suggest, support or condone unwarranted assumptions, invalid applications, or unjustified conclusions in the use of psychological instruments or techniques.

The flurry of claim and opinion about the effectiveness of subliminal methods seems to be based more on enthusiasm than controlled scientific experimentation, and it is here that psychology can be of service. Until acceptable scientific answers are forthcoming, we believe psychologists should guard against a premature commitment which might jeopardize public respect for them. The cause of scientific history is strewn with the dessicated remains of projects pursued with more vigor than wisdom.

Scientific caution is essential, but it falls short of meeting the ethical issue raised by the nature of subliminal perception itself. The most strident public objections have been directed toward the possibility that suggestions or attempts to influence or persuade may be administered without the knowledge or consent of the audience. Assurances that widespread adoption of this technique would provide increased enjoyment through the elimination of commercial intrusions, or that the users will establish an ethical control over the content of the messages presented, can only fail to be convincing in light of past experience. The suggestion that the public can be taught means of detecting when it is being exposed to a planned subliminal stimulation is far from reassuring since such a suggestion implies that the ability to defend oneself warrants being attacked. A captive audience is not a happy audience, and even the plan to inform the viewers in advance concerning the details of what is to be presented subliminally may not prevent the public from reacting to this technique as a demand that it surrender an additional degree of personal freedom. Fresh from similar encounters, the public may not allow this freedom to be wrested from it.

Finally, the argument that a great deal of our normal perception occurs on the fringe of conscious awareness and that subliminal events are no more effective than weak conscious stimuli rests on opinion and not fact. This seems particularly dangerous clinical ground on which to tread since the effect, on behavior, of stimuli which may possibly be inserted directly into the unconscious has yet to be explored. Assurances that this technique can only "remind" a person of something he already knows or "support" a set of urges already in existence but cannot establish a completely new set of urges or needs are reckless assertions having no evidence to support them. So it seems that the aspect of subliminal projection which is marked by the greatest potential risk to the individual's emotional equilibrium is the aspect about which the least is scientifically known.

The psychologist's ethical quandary, then, stems directly from the inescapable implication of deviousness in the use of such a technique. The appropriate guidelines for conduct are provided in this ethical statement:

> Principle 2.62–2 It is unethical to employ psychological techniques for devious purposes, for entertainment, or for other reasons not consonant with the best interests of a client or with the development of psychology as a science.

It is obvious that "devious purposes" and "the best interests . . . of psychology as a science" are not self-defining terms and must be interpreted by the individual psychologist in light of the circumstances of each situation. It is a trying and complex decision to make. If in his mature judgment the intended uses of the principles of subliminal perception do not meet acceptable ethical standards, the psychologist is obligated to disassociate himself from the endeavor and to labor in behalf of the public welfare to which he owes his first allegiance. In this respect, the responsibility of the social scientist must always be that of watchdog over his own actions as well as the actions of those to whom he lends his professional support.

The furor which promises to accompany the further application of a variety of devices involving subliminal perception is certain to embroil psychology in a dispute not of its own choosing. The indiscriminate and uncontrolled application of psychological principles is increasing at a fearsome rate in the form of motivation research, propaganda, public relations, and a host of other "useful" practices based on the work of psychologists. In a very real sense this era of applied psychology will be a test of the workability of the psychologist's code of ethics and promises to stimulate the profession to give further consideration to its responsibility for assisting society to use its findings wisely.

## REFERENCES

1. Adams, J. K. 1957. Laboratory studies of behavior without awareness. *Psychological Bulletin* 54:383–405.

2. American Psychological Association, Committee on Ethical Standards for Psychology. 1953. *Ethical standards of psychologists*. Washington: APA.

3. Ansbacher, H. 1937. Perception of number as affected by the monetary value of the objects. *Archives of Psychology* 30, no. 215.

4. Bach, S., and Klein, G. S. 1957. Conscious effects of prolonged subliminal exposures of words. *American Psychologist* 12:397 (abstract).

5. Baker, L. E. 1937. The influence of subliminal stimuli upon verbal behavior. *Journal of Experimental Psychology* 20:84–100.

6. Baker, L. E. 1938. The pupillary response conditioned to subliminal auditory stimuli. *Psychological Monographs* 50, no. 3 (whole no. 223).

7. Ban on subliminal ads, pending FCC probe, is urged. 1957. *Advanced Age* 28, no. 45.

8. Battelle, Phyllis. 1957. The lady objects to id tampering. *Publishers Auxiliary* 92, no. 40.

9. Beams, H. L., and Thompson, G. G. 1952. Affectivity as a factor in the perception of the magnitude of food objects. *American Psychologist* 7:323 (abstract).

10. Beitel, R. J., Jr. 1934. Spatial summation of subliminal stimuli in the retina of the human eye. *Journal of General Psychology* 10:311–327.

11. Blackwell, H. R. 1958. Personal communication.

12. Blake, R. R., and Vanderplas, J. M. 1950–1951. The effects of prerecognition hypotheses on veridical recognition thresholds in auditory perception. *Journal of Personality* 19:95–115.

13. Blum, G. S. 1955. Perceptual defense revisited. *Journal of Abnormal and Social Psychology* 56:24–29.

14. Bressler, J. 1931. Illusion in the case of subliminal visual stimulation. *Journal of General Psychology* 5:244–250.

15. Bricker, P. D., and Chapanis, A. 1953. Do incorrectly perceived tachistoscopic stimuli convey some information? *Psychological Review* 60:181–188.

16. Britt, S. H. 1957. Subliminal advertising—fact or fantasy? *Advanced Age* 28:103.

17. Brooks, J. 1957. The little ad that isn't there. *Consumer Reports* 23, no. 1.

18. Bruner, J. S., and Goodman, C. C. 1947. Value and need as organizing factors in perception. *Journal of Abnormal and Social Psychology* 42:33–44.

19. Bruner, J. S., and Postman, L. 1947. Emotional selectivity in perception and action. *Journal of Personality* 16:69–77.

20. Bruner, J. S., and Postman, L. 1947. Tension and tension-release as organizing factors in perception. *Journal of Personality* 16:300–308.

21. Bruner, J. S., and Postman, L. 1948. Symbolic value as an organizing factor in perception. *Journal of Social Psychology* 27:203–208.

22. Bruner, J. S., and Postman, L. 1949. Perception, cognition, and behavior. *Journal of Personality* 18:14–31.

23. Carter, L. F., and Schooler, K. 1949. Value, need, and other factors in perception. *Psychological Review* 56:200–207.

24. Cason, H., and Katcher, Naomi. 1934. An attempt to condition breathing and eyelid responses to a subliminal electric stimulus. *Journal of Experimental Psychology* 16:831–842.

25. Cohen, B. D.; Kalish, H. I.; Thurston, J. R.; and Cohen, E. 1954. Experimental manipulation of verbal behavior. *Journal of Experimental Psychology* 47:106–110.

26. Cohen, L. H.; Hilgard, E. R.; and Wendt, G. R. 1933. Sensitivity to light in a case of hysterical blindness studied by reinforcement-inhibition and conditioning methods. *Yale Journal of Biology and Medicine* 6:61–67.

27. Collier, R. M. 1940. An experimental study of the effects of subliminal stimuli. *Psychological Monographs* 52, no. 5 (whole no. 236).

28. Coover, J. E. 1917. Experiments in psychical research. *Psychical Research Monographs*, no. 1.

29. Cousins, N. 1957. Smudging the subconscious. *Saturday Review* 40, no. 40.

30. Cowen, E. L., and Beier, E. G. 1950–1951. The influence of "threat-expectancy" on perception. *Journal of Personality* 19:85–94.

31. Cowen, E. L., and Beier, E. G. 1952. A further study of the "threat-expectancy" variable in perception. *American Psychologist* 7:320–321 (abstract).

32. Cowen, E. L., and Beier, E. G. 1954. Threat-expectancy, word frequencies, and perceptual prerecognition hypotheses. *Journal of Abnormal and Social Psychology* 49:178–182.

33. Culler, E., and Mettler, F. A. 1934. Conditioned behavior in a decorticate dog. *Journal of Comparative Psychology* 18:291–303.

34. Deiter, J. 1953. The nature of subception. Unpublished doctoral dissertation, University of Kansas.

35. Diven, K. 1937. Certain determinants in the conditioning of anxiety reactions. *Journal of Psychology* 3:291–308.

36. Dunlap, K. 1900. Effect of imperceptible shadows on the judgments of distance. *Psychological Review* 7:435–453.

37. DuShane, G. 1957. The invisible word, or no thresholds barred. *Science* 126:681.

38. Ellson, D. G. 1941. Hallucinations produced by sensory conditioning. *Journal of Experimental Psychology* 28:1–20.

39. Eriksen, C. W. 1954. The case for perceptual defense. *Psychological Review* 61:175–182.

40. Eriksen, C. W. 1956. Subception: Fact or artifact? *Psychological Review* 63:74–80.

41. Eriksen, C. W., and Kuethe, J. L. 1956. Avoidance conditioning of verbal behavior without awareness: A paradigm of repression. *Journal of Abnormal and Social Psychology* 53:203–209.

42. Fink, A. A. 1957. Questions about subliminal advertising. New York: Author.

43. Foley, J. P., Jr. 1933. The cortical interpretation of conditioning. *Journal of General Psychology* 9:228–234.

44. Fullerton, G. S., and Cattell, J. McK. 1892. On the perception of small differences. *University of Pennsylvania Publications, Philos. Ser.*, no. 2.

45. "Ghost" ads overrated. 1957. *Science Newsletter* 72, no. 17.

46. Gilchrist, J. C., and Nesberg, L. S. 1952. Need and perceptual change in need-related objects. *Journal of Experimental Psychology* 44:369–376.

47. Goodnow, Jacqueline J., and Postman, L. 1955. Probability learning in a problem-solving situation. *Journal of Experimental Psychology* 49:16–22.

48. Greenspoon, J. 1955. The reinforcing effect of two spoken sounds on the frequency of two responses. *American Journal of Psychology* 68:409–416.

49. Guilford, J. P. 1936. *Psychometric methods.* New York: McGraw-Hill.

50. Haggard, E. A. 1943. Experimental studies in affective processes: I. Some effects of cognitive structure and active participation on certain autonomic reactions during and following experimentally induced stress. *Journal of Experimental Psychology* 33:257–284.

51. Hankin, H. 1926. *Common sense.* New York: Dutton.

52. Hartmann, G. W. 1933. I. The increase of visual acuity in one eye through the illumination of the other. *Journal of Experimental Psychology* 16:383–392.

53. Hartmann, G. W. 1933. II. Changes in visual acuity through simultaneous stimulation in other sense organs. *Journal of Experimental Psychology* 16:393–407.

54. Henle, Mary. 1942. An experimental investigation of past experience as a determinant of visual form perception. *Journal of Experimental Psychology* 30:1–21.

55. Hernandez-Peon, R.; Scherrer, H.; and Michel, J. 1955. Modification of electrical activity of cochlear nucleus during "attention" in unanesthetized cats. *Science* 123:331–332.

56. **Hildum, D. C., and Brown, R. W. 1956.** Verbal reinforcement and interviewer bias. *Journal of Abnormal and Social Psychology* 53:108–111.

57. Hilgard, E. R.; Miller, J.; and Ohlson, J. A. 1941. Three attempts to secure pupillary conditioning to auditory stimuli near the absolute threshold. *Journal of Experimental Psychology* 29:89–103.

58. Hilgard, E. R., and Wendt, G. R. 1933. The problem of reflex sensitivity to light studied in a case of hemianopsia. *Yale Journal of Biology and Medicine* 5:373–385.

59. Hollingworth, H. L. 1913. *Advertising and selling.* New York: Appleton.

60. Howes, D. 1954. A statistical theory of the phenomenon of subception. *Psychological Review* 61:98–110.

61. Howes, D. 1954. On the interpretation of word frequency as a variable affecting speed of recognition. *Journal of Experimental Psychology* 48:106–112.

62. Howes, D., and Solomon, R. L. 1950. A note on McGinnies' "Emotionality and perceptual defense." *Psychological Review* 57:235–240.

63. Howes, D., and Solomon, R. L. 1951. Visual duration threshold as a function of word probability. *Journal of Experimental Psychology* 41:401–410.

64. Huntley, C. W. 1953. Judgments of self based upon records of expressive behavior. *Journal of Abnormal and Social Psychology* 48:398–427.

65. Irwin, F. W.; Kaufman, K.; Prior, G.; and Weaver, H. B. 1934. On "Learning without awareness of what is being learned." *Journal of Experimental Psychology* 17:823–827.

66. Karn, H. W. 1935. The function of intensity in the spatial summation of subliminal stimuli in the retina. *Journal of General Psychology* 12:95–107.

67. Kennedy, J. L. 1938. Experiments on "unconscious whispering." *Psychological Bulletin* 35:526 (abstract).

68. Kennedy, J. L. 1939. A methodological review of extrasensory perception. *Psychological Bulletin* 36:59–103.

69. Klein, G. S.; Meister, D.; and Schlesinger, H. J. 1949. The effect of personal values on perception: An experimental critique. *American Psychologist* 4:252–253 (abstract).

70. Krech, D., and Calvin, A. 1953. Levels of perceptual organization and cognition. *Journal of Abnormal and Social Psychology* 48:394–400.

71. Kurland, S. H. 1954. The lack of generality in defense mechanisms as indicated in auditory perception. *Journal of Abnormal and Social Psychology* 49:173–177.

72. Lacey, J. I., and Smith, R. L. 1954. Conditioning and generalization of unconscious anxiety. *Science* 120:1045–1052.

73. Lacey, J. I.; Smith, R. L.; and Green, A. 1955. Use of conditioned autonomic responses in the study of anxiety. *Psychosomatic Medicine* 17:208–217.

74. Lazarus, R. S. 1956. Subception: Fact or artifact? A reply to Eriksen. *Psychological Review* 63:343–347.

75. Lazarus, R. S.; Eriksen, C. W.; and Fonda, C. P. 1950–1951. Personality dynamics and auditory perceptual recognition. *Journal of Personality* 19:471–482.

76. Lazarus, R. S., and McCleary, R. A. 1951. Autonomic discrimination without awareness: A study of subception. *Psychological Review* 58:113–122.

77. Levine, R.; Chein, I.; and Murphy, G. 1942. The relation of the intensity of a need to the amount of perceptual distortion. *Journal of Psychology* 13:283–293.

78. Lysak, W. 1954. The effects of punishment upon syllable recognition thresholds. *Journal of Experimental Psychology* 47:343–350.

79. McCleary, R. A., and Lazarus, R. S. 1949. Autonomic discrimination without awareness: An interim report. *Journal of Personality* 18:171–179.

80. McClelland, D. C., and Atkinson, J. W. 1948. The projective expression of needs: I. The effect of different intensities of the hunger drive on perception. *Journal of Psychology* 25:205–222.

81. McClelland, D. C., and Lieberman, A. M. 1949. The effect of need for achievement on recognition of need-related words. *Journal of Personality* 18:236–251.

82. McGinnies, E. 1949. Emotionality and perceptual defense. *Psychological Review* 56:244–251.

83. McGinnies, E. 1950. Discussion of Howes' and Solomon's note on "Emotionality and perceptual defense." *Psychological Review* 57:229–234.

84. Mandler, G., and Kaplan, W. K. 1956. Subjective evaluation and reinforcing effect of a verbal stimulus. *Science* 124:582–583.

85. Mannes, Marya. 1957. Ain't nobody here but us commercials. *Reporter* 17, no. 6.

86. Manro, H. M., and Washburn, M. F. 1908. Effect of imperceptible lines on judgment of distance. *American Journal of Psychology* 19:242–243.

87. Michigan State prof. tells weaknesses of invisible commercials. 1957. *Publishers Auxiliary* 92, no. 40.

88. Miller, J. G. 1939. Discrimination without awareness. *American Journal of Psychology* 52:562–578.

89. Miller, J. G. 1940. The role of motivation in learning without awareness. *American Journal of Psychology* 53:229–239.

90. Miller, J. G. 1942. *Unconsciousness.* New York: Wiley.

91. Newhall, S. M., and Dodge, R. 1927. Colored after images from unperceived weak chromatic stimulation. *Journal of Experimental Psychology* 10:1–17.

92. Newhall, S. M., and Sears, R. R. 1933. Conditioning finger retraction to visual stimuli near the absolute threshold. *Comparative Psychology Monographs* 9, no. 43.

93. Nuthmann, Anne M. 1957. Conditioning of a response class on a personality test. *Journal of Abnormal and Social Psychology* 54:19–23.

94. Peirce, C. S., and Jastrow, J. 1884. On small differences of sensation. *Memoirs of the National Academy of Sciences* 3:73–83.

95. Perky, C. W. 1910. An experimental study of imagination. *American Journal of Psychology* 21:422–452.

96. Philbrick, E. B., and Postman, L. 1955. A further analysis of "learning without awareness." *American Journal of Psychology* 68:417–424.

97. Pillai, R. P. B. K. 1939. A study of the threshold in relation to the investigations on subliminal impressions and allied phenomena. *British Journal of Educational Psychology* 9:97–98.

98. Postman, L., and Jarrett, R. F. 1952. An experimental analysis of "learning without awareness." *American Journal of Psychology* 65:244–255.

99. Razran, G. 1949. Stimulus generalization of conditioned responses. *Psychological Bulletin* 46:337–365.

100. Reece, M. M. 1954. The effect of shock on recognition thresholds. *Journal of Abnormal and Social Psychology* 49:165–172.

101. Rees, H. J., and Israel, H. E. 1935. An investigation of the establishment and operation of mental sets. *Psychological Monographs* 46, no. 6 (whole no. 210).

102. Sanford, R. N. 1936. The effects of abstinence from food upon imaginal processes: A preliminary experiment. *Journal of Psychology* 2:129–136.

103. Sanford, R. N. 1937. The effects of abstinence from food upon imaginal processes: A further experiment. *Journal of Psychology* 3:145–159.

104. Schafer, T. H. 1950. Influence of the preceding item on units of the noise masked threshold by a modified constant method. *Journal of Experimental Psychology* 40:365–371.

105. Sears, R. R., and Cohen, L. H. 1933. Hysterical anesthesia, analgesia, and astereognosis. *Archives of Neurology and Psychiatry* 29:260–271.

106. Settlage, T. 1936. The effect of sodium amytal on the formation and elicitation of conditioned reflexes. *Journal of Comparative Psychology* 22:339–343.

107. Sidis, B. 1898. *The psychology of suggestion.* New York: Appleton.

108. Sidowski, J. B. 1954. Influence of awareness of reinforcement on verbal conditioning. *Journal of Experimental Psychology* 48:355–360.

109. Silverman, A., and Baker, L. E. 1935. An attempt to condition various responses to subliminal electrical stimulation. *Journal of Experimental Psychology* 18:246–254.

110. Smoke, K. L. 1932. An objective study of concept formation. *Psychological Monographs* 42, no. 4 (whole no. 191).

111. Solomon, R. L., and Howes, D. H. 1951. Word frequency, personal values, and visual duration thresholds. *Psychological Review* 58:256–270.

112. Solomon, R. L., and Postman, L. 1952. Frequency of usage as a determinant of recognition thresholds for words. *Journal of Experimental Psychology* 43:195–201.

113. Spencer, L. T. 1928. The concept of the threshold and Heymans' law of inhibition: I. Correlation between the visual threshold and Heymans' coefficient of inhibition of binocular vision. *Journal of Experimental Psychology* 11:88–97.

114. Spencer, L. T., and Cohen, L. H. 1928. The concept of the threshold and Heymans' law of inhibition. II. *Journal of Experimental Psychology* 11:194–201.

115. Sterling, K., and Miller, J. G. 1941. Conditioning under anesthesia. *American Journal of Psychology* 54:92–101.

116. Stroh, M.; Shaw, A. M.; and Washburn, M. F. 1908. A study in guessing. *American Journal of Psychology* 19:243–245.

117. Subliminal ad okay if it sells: Lessler; FCC peers into subliminal picture on TV. 1957. *Advanced Age* 28, no. 48.

118. Subliminal ads wash no brains, declare Moore, Becker, developers of precon device. 1957. *Advanced Age* 28, no. 48.

119. Suslowa, M. 1863. Veranderungen der Hautgefule unter dem Einflusse electrischer Reizung. *Zeitschrift für Rationelle Medicin* 18:155–160.

120. Taffel, C. 1955. *Anxiety* and the conditioning of verbal behavior. *Journal of Abnormal and Social Psychology* 51:496–501.

121. Thorndike, E. L. 1932. *The fundamentals of learning.* New York: Teachers College, Columbia University.

122. Thorndike, E. L., and Rock, R. T. 1934. Learning without awareness of what is being learned or intent to learn it. *Journal of Experimental Psychology* 17:1–19.

123. Titchner, E. B., and Pyle, W. H. 1907. Effect of imperceptible shadows on the judgment of distance. *Proceedings of the American Philosophical Society* 46:94–109.

124. Vanderplas, J. M., and Blake, R. R. 1949. Selective sensitization in auditory perception. *Journal of Personality* 18:252–266.

125. Verplanck, W. S. 1955. The control of the content of conversation: Reinforcement of statements of opinion. *Journal of Abnormal and Social Psychology* 51:668–676.

126. Verplanck, W. S. 1956. The operant conditioning of human motor behavior. *Psychological Bulletin* 53:70–83.

127. Vinacke, W. E. 1942. The discrimination of color and form at levels of illumination below conscious awareness. *Archives of Psychology* 38, no. 267.

128. Wedell, C. H.; Taylor, F. V.; and Skolnick, A. 1940. An attempt to condition the pupillary response. *Journal of Experimental Psychology* 27:517–531.

129. Weiss, R. L. 1955. The influence of "set for speed" on "learning without awareness." *American Journal of Psychology* 68:425–431.

130. Williams, A. C. 1938. Perception of subliminal visual stimuli. *Journal of Psychology* 6:187–199.

131. Wispe, L. G., and Drambarean, N. C. 1953. Physiological need, word frequency, and visual duration thresholds. *Journal of Experimental Psychology* 46:25–31.

132. Woolf, J. D. 1957. Subliminal perception is nothing new. *Advanced Age* 28, no. 43.

# READING 16

## A Classroom Demonstration of "Extra Sensory Perception"

**N. H. PRONKO**
**University of Wichita**

Extrasensory perception is a very controversial area in psychology today. Many psychologists dismiss the entire area as nonsense; others recognize that some type of phenomenon may exist, but see no means to explore it experimentally; and a very few support ESP and the work in this area. The root of the matter lies in the fact that it is very difficult to do "scientific experimentation" on this subject, and, as a result, few scientific psychologists will risk their reputations in support of these concepts.

The following article is a short description of an ESP demonstration done in the classroom. Pronko demonstrates how pure sensory perception can appear to be perception beyond the known limits of our sensory systems.

### QUESTIONS

1. One of the underlying issues in this area is the assumption by many people that we have delineated the limits of our perceptual systems. The idea of *extra*sensory perception implies that our sensory systems cannot function in this type of perception. Comment on this idea.

2. Did Pronko choose a situation which influenced his students in the direction of his own thinking? Did he set out to trick his students, or to perform an actual open-minded experiment?

3. Could the findings of demonstrations such as this be used in argument against ESP? Support your answer.

The demonstration to be described in the present paper is one that the author has

Appreciation to Mr. Gerald Brazil for help with his photographic skill is hereby gratefully acknowledged.

The author wishes to express his gratitude to Dr. Margaret Habein, Dean of Liberal Arts, University of Wichita, for her financial support of the present study.

used successfully in his classes for a number of years. It is always presented as a problem-solving situation which the students are urged to come to grips with and to solve with analytical tools of scientific psychology (such as stimulus-response, setting factors, etc. ). As an introduction to the demonstration, students are told that just as engineering or chemistry has questions that must be answered and as algebra or geometry has its problems that demand solution, so what they are about to witness must be studied so that they understand *what* has happened and *how* it happened.

The instructor then takes a deck of ESP cards, preferably of the earlier edition and hands them to a student at random in the first row of the class. He requests the student to shuffle the cards thoroughly and to ask one or more other students to cut the deck. He then asks the student who shuffled the cards to place the deck face down on the table that is usually found at the front of a lecture room. He further instructs this same student to sit close by the cards and to keep his hands off the deck until the experimenter calls each card in turn, at which point the card handler must hold up the card so that the class may clearly note each hit (or miss) of the instructor's call.

After the instructor surrenders the deck of cards to his assistant, at no time must he come into contact with the cards until after the demonstration is over. In fact, to be most effective, from the time he hands the cards over to the assistant, the instructor walks back away from the table about six feet and stays in this position. He then calls the cards properly, practically as fast as his assistant can turn them, to the complete amazement of his audience.

## HOW THE TRICK IS DONE

A number of years ago, the writer stumbled across the fact of his "ESP powers" as he looked at a deck of ESP cards, face down, several feet away, on his desk. To his surprise, he found that under the existing conditions of illumination he could make out the symbol on the back of the card. Analysis of the situation showed that the light reflected from the back of the card reflected differentially from the area in which the symbol had been imprinted on the under side (i.e., the face of the card). Continuing with the rest of the deck, he had equal success, predicting the symbol of each card *before* turning it face up. Fired with such quick success, he continued practice under varied conditions permitting him to build up quick and subtle (non-extra) sensory perceptions. The only precaution necessary prior to demonstration (i.e., before the class or group assembles) is to make a quick check of the illumination for best placement of the cards and the demonstrator. With these conditions fulfilled, no amount of card shuffling or cutting the deck can confound the experimenter's "powers." Perfect runs are the rule and even a single miss out of 25 calls is aggravating! The problem has been consistently difficult for the class to solve.

It should be stressed that the earlier printing of the ESP cards is preferable to the more recent issue. However, the writer is making progress in developing reaction sensitization to cards of the later printing.

## SUMMARY

A classroom demonstration of what appears to be extrasensory perception achieved through inapparent, plain "sensory perception" is described.

# READING 17

# ESP and Credibility in Science

**R. A. McCONNELL**
**University of Pittsburgh**

The following article on ESP is a discussion of why most psychologists are not interested in the topic. McConnell presents some of the available data on ESP experimentation and questions psychologists' motivation in rejection not only of the data, but of the concepts themselves.

## QUESTIONS

1. "Why are psychologists not interested in ESP?"
2. What are some of the methodological problems involved in laboratory investigations of ESP?
3. Is the evidence for ESP any less substantial than that for subliminal perception? Compare the ESP evidence with other areas of psychological experimentation. What conclusions can you draw from these comparisons?

In discussing extrasensory perception (ESP) before psychology students, it is not uncommon to stress the credulity of the public. Perhaps, instead, we ought to examine the credibility of scientists—including those on both sides of the controversy.

In ESP research whom shall we trust? One can rather easily imagine experimental precautions to keep participating subjects from cheating. But how do we know whether the experimenter is deliberately deceiving us? And in a world where people

An invited lecture to the introductory psychology classes at Carnegie-Mellon University, December 18 and 19, 1967.

believe all kinds of nonsense, how can we be sure that the experimenter is not deceiving himself?

Let us suppose that 10 experimenters independently get the same result. Can we accept it? Ten is not a large number. There are about 150,000 names in *American Men of Science*. We may reasonably assume that at least 10,000 of these hold beliefs about the nature of reality that the majority of scientists would regard as wholly without foundation. Thus, on a subject like ESP, where there are no recognized authorities, why should we accept the word of 10 experimenters — or, for that matter, a thousand? Are we not, all of us, creatures of our culture? Is there any way we can be sure that a scientist in any field is as rational as he pretends to be?

Questions concerning the credibility of scientists are rarely asked in our classrooms. I have wondered why. Perhaps it makes us uncomfortable to consider the possibility of incompetence, dishonesty, or mental illness among professional people. Whatever the reason, this is forbidden territory for study.

Once in a long while, these embarrassing ideas do come to the surface. Someone, a little bolder or a little more eccentric than the rest of us, may write an article that slips by the editorial censor. When that happens, we have a chance to learn what people really think.

When I accepted this invitation to talk to you, I was told I could give you an advance reading assignment. I asked that you read an eight-page article on ESP by G. R. Price (1955) that appeared in *Science* together with several letters to the editor (Soal; Rhine; Meehl & Scriven; Bridgman; Price; Rhine, 1956) written in reply to Price. These papers are currently available as part of the Bobbs-Merrill reprint series that is widely used for teaching psychology, and they have thus acquired a quasi-official status as source documents to which the very young may be exposed.

I also suggested that you read an analysis of Price's article (McConnell, 1955) that appeared in the *Journal of Parapsychology* and that was not included in the Bobbs-Merrill series. I hope that most of you have had a chance to study these references, which I shall now discuss briefly.

Price, a chemist by profession, presented a well-supported argument showing that existing experimental evidence constitutes conclusive proof of ESP if one accepts the good faith and sanity of the experimenters. But he went on to say that all of the otherwise convincing evidence for ESP can be easily explained away if one assumes that experimenters, working in collaboration with their witnesses, have intentionally faked their results.

Perhaps the most interesting thing about this unsubstantiated suggestion of fraud is that it was published on the first page of the most influential scientific journal in the United States. I will not say whether Price intended what he wrote as a joke. That is a riddle that I leave to you to answer. The important question is not whether Price took himself seriously, but whether you and I ought to do so.

I believe, as apparently does Price, that all kinds of fraud, even by highly placed scientists, are possible and that it is conceivable that there might be collaboration between two scientists in perpetuating a scientific hoax. Nevertheless, I think that those who accept Price's argument fail to understand two important things about science as a social enterprise.

First, they fail to realize that the way to tell whether a number of scientists are collaborating in a hoax is to consider the intricate web of public and private motivation, belief, and retribution that determines the behavior of professional people in our culture. Price suggested that scientists, university teachers, medical doctors, and intellectually prominent persons who have assisted in the investigation of ESP may have engaged in conscious collusive fraud. Price answered the question of how one might get such people to become willing accomplices by saying: "In recruiting, I would appeal not to desire for fame or material gain but to the noblest motives, arguing that much good to humanity could result from a small deception designed to strengthen religious belief." An experienced lawyer or even a politician would laugh at this explanation of a supposed conspiracy among well-educated and fully engaged members of our society, but evidently quite a few scientists find it plausible.

Second, those who take Price

seriously do not understand scientific method. Price suggested that the way to establish the scientific truth of ESP is to carry out a fraudproof experiment. In his words: "What is needed is one completely convincing experiment." He described in specific detail how this might be done by using prominent scientists and stage magicians as witnesses, backed up by motion pictures of the entire proceedings, plus photomicrographs of welded seals, and so on. This is nonsense because it assumes that scientific proof is of the same nature as legal proof. On the contrary, the acceptance of a scientific principle does not, and never can, depend upon the honesty of individual scientists.

I wish I had time to pursue with you the subtle psychological question of the nature of scientific proof and of how the method of science deals with individual experimenter error as well as mass irrationality. Those of you who are especially interested may wish to read a book by T. S. Kuhn (1962) titled *The Structure of Scientific Revolutions*.[1] Here today, I can only say that in my opinion, wittingly or unwittingly, Price's article is a hoax about hoaxes and about the nature of science.

If you were to ask: "What does it signify that Price successfully placed his article in our most important journal of science?" I would answer as follows: There is a facade of respectability and belief that covers all of the activities of society and makes it possible for men to work together and for society to exist. Most people—including those who are well educated—are unaware of this false front and lose their equilibrium when they are forced by circumstances to penetrate behind it. On the other hand, those of you who are intellectually alienated from our culture understand quite well that this pretense exists. I hope that some day you will also understand why it is necessary and it is not the contrivance of a group of evil men but reflects what exis-

_____
[1]For a condensation of this book see McConnell (1968b).

tential philosophers refer to as "the human condition."

This curtain of propriety and convention exists in science also, where it allows us to believe that all is well with our knowledge system. ESP or any other revolutionary discovery may seem to threaten science. From time to time, when such a challenge is offered, the stagehands nervously fumble, the curtain slips, and we see a little of the normally concealed machinery. We get a glimpse of underlying reality, a glimpse of the ignorance and fear that govern the inner affairs of the mind of men. Such was the case when *Science* published Price's critique of ESP. That is why his article is important.

## EVIDENCE AND BELIEF

Then, what about ESP? If laboratory scientists lack sophistication about human nature and even about the methodology of science, how do we decide for ourselves whether ESP is real or imaginary, true or false?

Before we try to answer so difficult a question, let us go back to the beginning. I shall give you an operational definition of ESP that you may find a bit confusing. Then I shall describe a test for ESP that I hope will make the matter clear to you.

The definition goes this way: "Extrasensory perception is a response to an unknown event not presented to any known sense." I shall not try to explain it. Instead, let me describe the test.

I have brought with me a deck of ESP cards. These cards have five different kinds of symbols printed on them: a circle, a square, a plus, a star, and wavy lines. Altogether, there are 25 cards, 5 of each kind.

Suppose I shuffle these cards, hide them, and ask you to guess them. By the theory of chance probability, the number you would most often get right is five. Sometimes you would get four or six or seven. Only once in a long while would you get 15 right out of 25. In fact if you got more than

10 right very often, you would begin to suspect that it was not just good luck. It might even be ESP.

Of course, you could not be sure. It might be luck—or it might be something else. If you look closely at the backs of these cards, sometimes you can see the symbol showing through. Perhaps in this way you recognized some of the cards when I shuffled them. Or again, every time I asked whether you were ready for your next guess, perhaps I gave you a hint without knowing it. Perhaps, unconsciously, I raised the tone of my voice just a little when I came to each star—because I think of stars as being "higher" than the other symbols, or for some other trivial reason.

You can see that there are many subtle ways for information to leak through by sight or by sound. No serious scientist would try to conduct an ESP experiment in this fashion. My only purpose in showing you these cards is to let you know how some of the early tests for ESP were done at Duke University 35 years ago. I regard these cards as a museum piece, although they are a lot of fun and can be used in preliminary testing.

The experiments that are carried out today are often so complex that one cannot evaluate them without advanced training in statistics, physics, and psychology. For this reason, and because the field is too large to describe in one lecture, I have prepared a list of reading materials. Some of these are intended to show the scope of the subject (Heywood, 1964; Langdon-Davies, 1961; McConnell, 1966; Murphy & Dale, 1961); others are experimental reports (Anderson & McConnell, 1961; McConnell & Forwald, 1967a, 1967b, 1968; McConnell, Snowdon, & Powell, 1955; Sinclair, 1962; Soal & Bateman, 1954).

You will notice that I have listed only my own journal articles. For this I offer my apology along with the following explanation. In any frontier field of science there are experimental hazards. If someone questions the soundness of what I recommend to you as evidence, I can probably do a better job of explaining if I have chosen research with which I am most familiar. I also want to convey the idea that there has been a large amount of work done in this field. If you study my papers and cannot find anything wrong with them, you ought to remember that there have been perhaps a hundred investigators who have found substantial evidence for ESP under controlled experimental conditions.

ESP is a controversial idea in psychology. Nevertheless, the psychologists whom I know personally agree with me on many things. I am sure we agree on what constitutes good quality experimental laboratory research. We also agree that there is a sizable body of high-grade evidence for ESP in the literature.

In 1947 I visited Duke University in North Carolina where a man by the name of Rhine was doing experiments on ESP. I wanted to get acquainted with Rhine and with the people who were working under him. Even more important, I wanted to talk to those faculty members who rejected Rhine's work. I rented a dormitory room, and during four weeks I interviewed everyone I could, beginning with the President of the University and working down to assistant professors in various departments. I shall not have time to describe that adventure, but I will tell you what I was told by one professor of psychology in a private interview.

He said that he was familiar with the experimental literature of ESP and that, in his opinion, if it were anything else *but* ESP, one-tenth of the published evidence would already have established the phenomenon. He also explained that he would not accept ESP himself because, as he put it, he found "a world without ESP a more comfortable place in which to live."

That trip to Duke University was part of a larger investigation that made me decide to leave engineering electronics, in which

I had acquired some experience, and to devote my life to the investigation of ESP and related effects.

That was 20 years ago. What has happened in this field since then? Among other things, there has been time to publish 20 more volumes of the *Journal of Parapsychology.* That comes to about 4,000 pages of research. There have been several thousand additional pages in the *Journal of the American Society for Psychical Research* and in the English and Continental journals. You might think that the argument would be settled by now.

Only recently, a brilliant young psychologist, who is here on your campus, gave a lecture on ESP in which he said "I tend to believe the evidence is as good as it is for many of our other psychological phenomena." He also said that "Psychologists will not be interested in ESP until there is a repeatable experiment."

Where my psychologist friends and I disagree, is that I believe that the available evidence for ESP is sufficient to establish its reality beyond all reasonable doubt. My psychologist friends think that the evidence is not yet conclusive. I do not regard this difference of opinion as very important. I am happy to allow anyone the privilege of doubt.

How else does the position of professional psychologists whom I know differ from my own? Perhaps the main difference —the really important difference—lies in our interpretation of the history and methodology of science—in what today we call the philosophy of science.

For one thing, my friends seem to believe that the only good evidence for ESP must come from controlled experimentation in a laboratory. My own belief is that all available evidence must be weighed, taking into account its source and the conditions under which it was gathered.

Perhaps it will clarify the problem if I say that there are only two important kinds of scientific evidence in this world: our own evidence and someone else's. Since most of us are not in a position to gather evidence of ESP, my remarks apply especially to other people's evidence.

The first thing to remember is that, no matter how reputable the scientific journal, someone else's evidence is always suspect. And if the matter is important, we ought to be *aggressively* skeptical about it.

Whether we are listening to a tale of a ghost in a haunted house or reading the tightly edited *Journal of Experimental Psychology,* we have to concern ourselves with two questions: what is the content of the report and what are the competence and motivation of the observer?

What I am suggesting is that our attitude toward *all* supposedly scientific reports must be that of the psychologist in receiving an introspective account from a human subject in a laboratory experiment—for it must be remembered that, as far as the reader is concerned, a journal article by a distant scientist is in some ways even less dependable than what psychologists, often condescendingly, refer to as a "verbal report."

From a study of the history of science, I have come to two conclusions in this connection: (*a*) the evidence presented in scientific journals by professional scientists for all kinds of ordinary phenomena is not as good as commonly supposed, and (*b*) on a controversial subject where the professionals do not agree, the evidence of the layman may have considerable scientific value. As corollaries, I suggest that the textbooks of science are often wrong and that contrary popular opinion is sometimes right. Let us examine these ideas.

## STOREHOUSES OF KNOWLEDGE?

Textbooks are the storehouses of man's knowledge. They are presumed to contain all of the things we know to be true. If you are becoming a scientist, you will spend at least 18 years studying from books. It would be not entirely unfair to call most of this training a "brainwashing" process. Nearly everything you learn as factual reality must be accepted upon the word of some recognized authority and not upon your own firsthand experience. It should be a matter of concern to you whether you have been told the truth for those 18 years. Just how bad are the textbooks we use? Let me take an example from the field of geology.

Did you know that until the year 1800 the highest scientific authorities thought that there was no such thing as a meteorite? After all, there are no stones in the sky; so stones cannot fall out of the sky. Only a superstitious person would believe in meteorites.

Many of you are familiar with the work of Lavoisier. He was the founder of modern chemistry. He discovered that burning is the combining of oxygen with other things, and he helped to show that the formula for water is $H_2O$. He was one of the great scientists of all time.

In 1772 Lavoisier signed a report to the French Academy of Science in which he said he had examined a stone that was believed to have fallen from the sky in a great blaze of light. Lavoisier said in his report that this was just an ordinary stone that had been struck by lightning and had melted partly into glass while lying on the ground.

Eventually, of course, the leaders of science decided that meteorites do come from outer space, and they revised the textbooks accordingly. But in doing so, they forgot to mention that there had ever been any argument about the matter. So here we are, living in the space age, without realizing how hard it is to discover the truth about even a simple thing like meteorites, which can be seen as meteors in the sky on any clear night, and which have been found upon the surface of the earth since the dawn of history.

Even worse, as students, we have no way of estimating how many arguments are still going on in science and how many mistakes—truly serious mistakes—there are in the textbooks from which we study. It is my guess that we can safely believe nearly all of what is said in the physics and chemistry books. But we ought to believe only half of the ideas in the biological sciences—although I am not sure which half. And we should accept as final very little in the social sciences, which try to explain why groups of people behave as they do.

Our subject today is extrasensory perception, which belongs in psychology, one of the biological sciences. ESP is something about which the "authorities" are in error. Most psychology textbooks omit the subject entirely as unworthy of serious attention. But these books are mistaken, because ESP is a real psychological phenomenon.

Of course, I am only giving you my individual opinion about ESP. I do not want you to base your belief upon what I tell you. When you have studied advanced psychology and statistics, and when you come to realize that your professors cannot be expected to teach you everything you wish to know, then I hope you will go to the scientific journals and study the experiments that have been done and decide for yourself.

## MENTAL RADIO

I have already discussed the credibility of experts and the errors we find in science textbooks. I would like to turn to the other half of my thesis, namely, that evidence from a layman may sometimes have scientific value.

Most of you are familiar with the name Upton Sinclair, who was a socialist reformer and a writer active in the first half of the twentieth century. He died in 1968 at the age of 90. In his time he wrote nearly 90 books. One of the best known of these, published in 1906, was called *The Jungle*. It told about the cruel and unsanitary conditions in the processing of beef in the Chicago stock yards. As a result of that book, laws were passed, and today the situation is much improved. In a very real sense, all of us are indebted to this man.

Sinclair discovered that his wife had an unusual amount of what was then known as "psychic ability." (That was before the beginning of the ESP controversy.) After three years of serious experimentation, he wrote a book about it: *Mental Radio* (1962, orig. publ. 1930).

In his experiments, Sinclair, or someone else, would draw a secret picture and ask Mrs. Sinclair to draw another picture to to match it. Some of the pairs of pictures are presented in the following examples.[2] The one on the left is always the original picture, and the one on the right is what Mrs. Sinclair got by ESP.

Sometimes the pictures were made as far apart as 40 miles. At other times the target picture was held by Mrs. Sinclair in her hand—without looking, of course—while she concentrated before drawing her matching picture. The degree of success did not seem to depend upon distance.

Let us examine some of the pictures. In Example 1 we see an almost perfect ESP

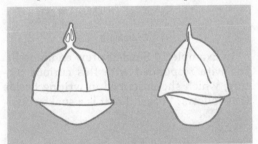

Example 1

response. It is a knight's helmet. Notice that for every important line in the left-hand picture there is a corresponding line on the right.

Compare that with Example 2. Here, the response on the right is not quite the same as the target on the left, but the idea is the same.

Example 2

The next slide is Example 3. Sinclair drew a football as a target. Mrs. Sinclair made the drawing on the right, but she thought

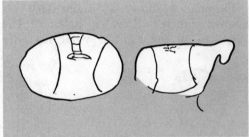

Example 3

it was "a baby calf with a belly band." Why did her ESP make this mistake? We cannot be sure, but we think it had something to do with the fact that in her childhood she had known a queer old man who raised calves as parlor pets and dressed them in embroidered belly bands.

Example 4 is another instance of the right shape with a wrong interpretation. Upton Sinclair drew a volcano, and Mrs. Sinclair

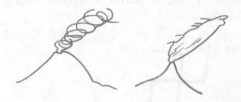

Example 4

drew what she called a black beetle. The beetle is upside down. If you turn the example over, you can more easily recognize its antennae and legs.

[2]Illustrations from *Mental Radio* by Upton Sinclair are reproduced by permission of the publisher, Charles C. Thomas, Springfield, Illinois.

In Example 5 Sinclair drew a fish hook, which turned into two flowers.

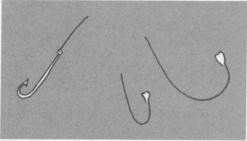

Example 5

Example 6 shows a fragmentary response. Sinclair drew a balloon. The response on the right is what his wife

Example 6

received by "mental radio." She was not sure what it was, so she wrote beside the picture: "Shines in sunlight, must be metal, a scythe hanging among vines or strings."

Example 7 on the left is a swastika. Mrs. Sinclair drew the response on the right. She did not know what it meant, but she wrote beside it, "These things somehow belong

Example 7

together, but won't get together." You can see some of her words which were ac-

cidentally included when the printer made the book. Here is the beginning of "These" and "belong" and "but won't" and "together."

Example 8 is a pair of drawings in which a stick man became a skull and crossbones.

Example 8

Notice that in Example 9, Mrs. Sinclair left out some of the stars and added a moon instead.

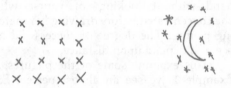

Example 9

In Example 10 Sinclair drew an umbrella. His wife responded with this curious picture, which she described in writing beside it as follows: "I feel that it is a snake crawl-

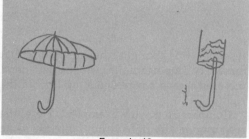

Example 10

ing out of something—vivid feeling of snake, but it looks like a cat's tail." I might mention that she had a special fear of snakes, having grown up on a plantation in a Mississippi swamp.

The last example is the American flag and a response to it that could hardly be called a chance coincidence (Example 11).

Example 11

You have seen a selection of 11 pictures out of a total of 290 trials made by Mrs. Sinclair. Perhaps 4 of the 11 would be called direct target hits. The rest are partial hits. Out of the 290 tries, 23% were rated by Upton Sinclair as hits, 53% were partial hits, and 24% were failures.

Of course, before you can be sure that these pictures were made by ESP, many questions must be answered. Because Upton Sinclair and his wife were laymen, you will have to pay particular attention to their competence and motivation. On the other hand, one imporant feature of Sinclair's book is that you do not have to be a scientist to understand it. Even though you may not have studied statistics and psychology, you can read the book yourself and make up your mind as to its value on the basis of common sense. When you do, I think you will arrive at the same conclusion that many scientists have reached by entirely different kinds of experiments. I think you will decide that extrasensory perception is a reality regardless of the skepticism of the psychological profession.

## A MATTER OF INTEREST

I have been told by my friends that psychologists will not be interested in ESP until someone discovers a repeatable experiment. Upton Sinclair repeated his experiments over a period of three years. In London, a mathematician by the name of Soal (Soal & Bateman, 1954) repeated certain card-guessing experiments again and again over a period of six years using two subjects and many different witnesses. What do psychologists mean by a repeatable experiment?

Evidently, they mean an experiment that is "repeatable by prescription." They want a standard experimental procedure that can be described on paper by which any qualified person—or at least some qualified persons—can guarantee to produce ESP upon demand. I must confess that we have not yet reached that stage in ESP research. And, until we do, I can sympathize with my skeptical friends. I can see why they, as busy individuals with other interests, are unwilling to reach a firm position about the reality of ESP.

What I cannot understand is why they say: "Psychologists will not be *interested* in ESP until there is a repeatable experiment."

It is a statement of fact that psychologists are *not* interested in ESP. Recently, I had occasion to examine a number of psychology textbooks. Only one of them mentioned ESP—that book, by Hilgard and Atkinson (1967). After reading the four pages which these authors devote to ESP, I have only two minor critical observations to offer.

The first is that the authors have given too much space to finding fault with unimportant papers. They go back 25 years to a journal article in which they accuse an ESP experimenter of overanalyzing his data. I am sure that comparable examples of weak statistical method could be found in any one of the quantitative journals of the APA —and we would not need to go back a generation in time to do it.

My second comment is that Hilgard and Atkinson may have tended to damage their own scholarly reputations by recommending as a "scholarly review" a book by

C. E. M. Hansel (1966) titled *ESP: A Scientific Evaluation*. This book has been reviewed by S. S. Stevens of Harvard, who regards ESP as a Rabelaisian joke and who gave Hansel his unqualified approval. If you like amusing book reviews, I suggest that you read Stevens (1967). I regret that I do not have time here today to document for you the basis of my unfavorable opinion of Hansel's book.[3]

I have wandered over many facets of ESP. I shall now summarize what I think are the most important ideas. Since the scientific study of ESP was begun by the London Society for Psychical Research in 1882, there have been hundreds and perhaps thousands of experiments done with a care typical of the journals of the APA. Many psychologists of high repute admit that the evidence is as good as that for other phenomena that are accepted by their profession.

Surprising though it may seem, most of this research on ESP has been done by people who were not psychologists. From this fact and from the usual psychology textbook treatment of the subject as well as from private discussion, we know that psychologists are *not* interested in ESP. This raises a question—a very mysterious question that I invite you to try to answer: Why are psychologists not interested in ESP?[4]

## REFERENCES

Anderson, M. L., and McConnell, R. A. 1961. Fantasy testing for ESP in a fourth and fifth grade class. *Journal of Psychology* 52:491–503.

Clark, K. E., et al. 1967. The scientific and professional aims of psychology. *American Psychologist* 22:49–76.

Hansel, C. E. M. 1966. *ESP: A scientific evaluation.* New York: Scribner's.

Heywood, R. 1964. *ESP: A personal memoir.* New York: Dutton.

Hilgard, E. R., and Atkinson, R. C. 1967. *Introduction to psychology.* New York: Harcourt, Brace & World.

Kuhn, T. S. 1962. *The structure of scientific revolutions* (vol. II, no. 2, of the *International encyclopedia of unified science*). Chicago: University of Chicago Press.

Langdon-Davies, J. 1961. *On the nature of man.* New York: New American Library Corporation.

Linder, R. 1967. Light one candle. *American Psychologist* 22:804–805.

McConnell, R. A. 1955. Price in *Science. Journal of Parapsychology* 19:258–261.

McConnell, R. A. 1966. ESP research at three levels of method. *Journal of Parapsychology* 30:195–207.

McConnell, R. A. 1968a. The ESP scholar. *Contemporary Psychology* 13:41.

McConnell, R. A. 1968b. The structure of scientific revolutions: An epitome. *Journal of the American Society for Psychical Research* 62:321–327.

McConnell, R. A., and Forwald, H. 1967a. Psychokinetic placement: I. A re-examination of the Forwald-Durham experiment. *Journal of Parapsychology* 31:51–69.

McConnell, R. A., and Forwald, H. 1967b. Psychokinetic placement: II. A factorial study of successful and unsuccessful series. *Journal of Parapsychology* 31:198–213.

McConnell, R. A., and Forwald, H. 1968. Psychokinetic placement: III. Cube-releasing devices. *Journal of Parapsychology* 32:9–38.

McConnell, R. A.; Snowdon, R. J.; and Powell, K. F. 1955. Wishing with dice. *Journal of Experimental Psychology* 50:269–275.

Murphy, G., and Dale, L. A. 1961. *Challenge of psychical research.* New York: Harper.

Price, G. R. 1955. Science and the supernatural. *Science* 122:359–367.

Sinclair, U. 1962. *Mental radio.* Springfield, Ill.: Charles C. Thomas.

Soal, S. G., and Bateman, F. 1954. *Modern experiments in telepathy.* London: Faber & Faber.

Soal, S. G.; Rhine, J. B.; Meehl, P. E., and Scriven, M.; Bridgman, P. W.; Price, G. R.; and Rhine, J. B. 1956. Letters to the editor in rejoinder to G. R. Price. *Science* 123:9–19.

Stevens, S. S. 1967. The market for miracles. *Contemporary Psychology* 12:1–3.

---

[3]This has since been done. See McConnell (1968a).

[4]Those who wish to answer this question might start their odyssey by visiting Clark et al. (1967) and Linder (1967).

# READING 18 Readaptation and Decay after Exposure to Optical Tilt

**SHELDON M. EBENHOLTZ**
**University of Wisconsin**

Sensory adaptation has long been subject to experimentation by psychologists. Sheldon Ebenholtz provides us with a compact report on two experiments in this area. Ebenholtz is concerned with the question of readaptation to a normal environment after the subjects have adapted to wearing prism lenses. Is this readaptation or simple forgetting of the previous adaptation?

## QUESTIONS

1. "The assumption that adaptation and perceptual development share many common processes (Held & Bossom, 1961) carries the implication that the 'normal' preadaptation state is itself a state of adaptation." Discuss this implication.

2. Ebenholtz states: "The results indicate that forgetting and re-adaptation proceed at different rates with the latter significantly more rapid than the former." Explain how the results indicate this. Could the results suggest something else?

3. Give data to support this statement: "Continued visual support is necessary for sustained adaptation."

The assumption that adaptation and perceptual development share many common processes (Held & Bossom, 1961) carries the implication that the "normal" pre-adaptation state is itself a state of adaptation (Ebenholtz, 1967). In the context of adaptation to optical tilt, the normal state

This research was supported by Grant MH-13006-02 from the National Institute of Mental Health, United States Public Health Service.

therefore may be regarded as one in which S is exposed to a tilt of 0°. It follows that exposure to the normal environment, after a period of adaptation, should yield a growth curve similar to that obtained during the initial adaptation period, but in the opposite direction. Thus S may be expected to adapt and then to readapt to the normal environment, both at the same rate. There is, however, the possibility that transfer to a tilt of 0° produces not readaptation but rather a decay or simply forgetting of the previous adaptation. In the present study the rates of readaptation and decay were compared.

## METHOD

In Exp. I two groups of eight female Ss each were exposed monocularly to an optical tilt of 15° for a period of 30 min. Throughout this interval Ss walked back and forth along a corridor. Only the right eye was used and the clockwise (CW) or counterclockwise (CCW) direction of tilt was counterbalanced over Ss within each group. The level of adaptation (LA) was determined by having S set a 12-in. luminous line to the apparent vertical in an otherwise light-free room. The Ss viewed the line monocularly at a distance of 5 ft. without prisms and with the head stabilized in a chin and forehead rest. Four measures of the upright were taken, with the rod starting position counterbalanced over CW and CCW positions, immediately prior to the adaptation period and at 15-min. periods thereafter for a total of 1 hr. The LA was defined in terms of the difference between the means of the pre- and postadaptation settings.

After the initial ½-hr. period there was an additional ½-hr. interval in which Ss of Group O continued to move through the corridor but with prisms removed and both eyes open. The Ss of Group C were guided over the same path as that of Group O with their eyes covered by blindfolds.

In Exp. II Ss were exposed to a 30° prism tilt and two rather than four measures of the upright were taken at each test interval. In addition, during the transfer period, Ss of Group O viewed the scene monocularly through prisms with an optical tilt of 0°. There were two males and six females in each group. All other procedures and conditions were identical with those of Exp. I, the major purpose of Exp. II being to maintain the conditions of monocular observation both during initial adaptation and subsequent readaptation.

## RESULTS

The LA during acquisition and transfer periods of Exp. I for both groups is represented in Figure 1. After 15 min. of exposure to an optical tilt of 15° Groups O and C yielded LAs of 3.4° and 3.8°, respectively, $t(14) = .97$ $p > .05$. The corresponding values after 30 min. were 4.6° and 4.7°, $t(14) = .15$, $p > .05$. After 15 min. of transfer the LA for Group C dropped to 2.6° whereas Group O yielded an LA of 1.7°. The difference was not significant, $t(14) = 1.29$, $p > .05$. As Figure 1 indicates, the differences between the two transfer conditions increased with time so that at the final test the LAs were .6° and 2.2° for Groups O and C, respectively, $t(14) = 2.25$, $p < .05$. Although both Groups O and C showed a significant decrement in LA at the end of the transfer period, $t(7) = 6.22$

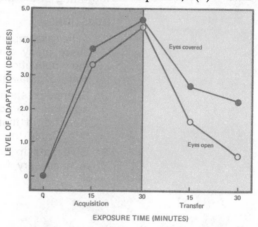

**Figure 1.** Level of adaptation as a function of exposure time during acquisition and transfer phases (Exp. I).

and 4.06, $p < .01$, respectively, the final LA for Group O only, of .6°, was not significantly different from zero, $t(7) = 1.02$, $p > .05$.

The analysis of Exp. II data revealed a

pattern of significant (and nonsignificant) differences identical with that reported above, with the one exception that Group C yielded a significantly higher LA than Group O after 15 min. of transfer ($p < .01$). Thus after 30 min. of adaptation the LAs for Groups O and C were 6.6° and 6.8°, respectively, $t(14) = .183$, $p > .05$. The comparable values after the 30-min. transfer period were .22° and 2.1°, $t(14) = 2.81$, $p < .05$. As in the case of Exp. I only the former value failed to differ significantly from zero, $t(7) = .601$, $p > .05$.

## DISCUSSION

The results indicate that forgetting and readaptation proceed at different rates with the latter significantly more rapid than the former. This, taken together with the fact that readaptation was completed in the same amount of time as that required for initial adaptation suggests that (a) exposure to the normal environment is not unique relative to the effects of exposure to other optical tilts, and (b) continued visual sup-

port is necessary for sustained adaptation.

The present results are not consistent with those of Hamilton and Bossom (1964). These authors failed to find a significant difference between the effects of decay and readaptation after exposure to a laterally displaced visual field. Direct comparisons of the effects of exposure to the two types of optical transformations are needed in order to determine whether or not the disparate results reflect fundamental differences or merely procedural ones.

## REFERENCES

Ebenholtz, S. M. 1967. Transfer of adaptation as a function of interpolated optical tilt to the ipsilateral and contralateral eye. *Journal of Experimental Psychology* 73:263–267.

Hamilton, C., and Bossom, J. 1964. Decay of prism aftereffects. *Journal of Experimental Psychology* 67:148–150.

Held, R., and Bossom, J. 1961. Neonatal deprivation and adult rearrangement: Complementary techniques for analyzing plastic sensory-motor coordinations. *Journal of Comparative and Physiological Psychology* 54:33–57.

# READING 19

# To Perceive Is to Know

**W. R. GARNER**
**Johns Hopkins University**

Garner sets forth three aspects of perception: to perceive is to know; the factors known in perception are properties of sets of stimuli; and, to perceive is an active process. He then discusses experimental data in support of these ideas. His emphasis on the activity of the perceiver and the relationship of sets of stimuli provides the reader with many interesting insights into the study of perception.

## QUESTIONS

1. What does Garner mean by, "to perceive is to know"?
2. Do Garner and Gibson have similar theories of perception as reflected by their respective articles? Discuss.
3. Evaluate the logic used by Garner. Do the data he presents support his conclusions? Could the data mean something else?

This paper is a progress report of research on perception in the broad sense. The experiments reported are chosen with the expectation that they will illustrate three aspects of perception. These three aspects are:

First, and most general, *to perceive is to know*. Perceiving is a cognitive process involving knowing, understanding, comprehending, organizing, even cognizing. Most

The research reported here has been supported by the Veterans Administration, the Office of Naval Research, and the National Institutes of Health. The preparation of this paper was supported by Grant No. MH11062 from the National Institute of Mental Health.

of our current research on the topic would suggest that perceiving is responding, naming, discriminating, and analyzing. These psychological processes all exist, and it does not matter that they are *also* called perception. What does matter is that we study perception as a cognitive process. As such, perception is much more closely related to classification, conceptualization, and free-recall learning than to sensory or discriminatory processes.

Second, *the factors known in perception are properties of sets of stimuli*, not properties of individual stimuli (to say nothing of the elements which make up these individual stimuli). Gestalt psychologists have emphasized that perception is concerned with organized wholes, not analyzed parts, but they were talking about the single stimulus. Yet a single stimulus can have no real meaning without reference to a set of stimuli, because the attributes which define it cannot be specified without knowing what the alternatives are.

It is convenient to think of three levels of stimulus set. There is the *single stimulus* itself, and often we do want to talk about it. But that stimulus has attributes whose combinations define a total set, and the real or assumed properties of this total are also the properties of the single stimulus. In addition, there is usually a *subset* of the total set, a subset which does not include all stimuli from the total set, but which does include the particular stimulus we are concerned about. This subset is redundant in some fashion, since it is smaller than the total set; and it has properties of its own which are not identical to those of the total set.

Now the important point is simply this: How the single stimulus is perceived is a function not so much of what it is, but is rather a function of what the total set and the particular subset are. The properties of the total set and the subset are also the perceived properties of the single stimulus, so we cannot understand the knowing of the single stimulus without understanding the properties of the sets within which it is contained.

Third, *to perceive is an active process*, one in which the perceiver participates fully. The perceiver does not passively *receive* information about his environment; he actively *perceives* his environment. Nor does he simply impose his organization on an otherwise unstructured world—the world is structured. But he does select the structure to which he will attend and react, and he even provides the missing structure on occasion. In particular, as we shall see, the perceiver provides his own total set and subset when these do not physically exist.

## FREE VERSUS CONSTRAINED CLASSIFICATION

The first experiment I want to discuss was done in collaboration with Shiro Imai (Imai & Garner, 1965), and it is concerned with perceptual classification of sets of stimuli defined by different numbers and kinds of attributes. More specifically, we compared two types of classification task: a constrained classification, in which the experimenter specifies the attribute by which the subject is to classify; and a free classification, in which the subject chooses his own mode of classification.

The stimuli we used in this experiment are shown in Figure 1. Each stimulus consisted of a small card on which were placed two dots. The locations of these dots could be varied so as to produce three perceived attributes: *Position*, in that the pair of dots

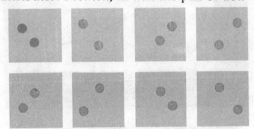

**Figure 1.** Types of stimuli used in free and constrained classification (after Imai & Garner, 1965).

could be to the left or right of center; *Distance* between the dots, large or small; and *Orientation*, with rotation to the right or left of vertical. The two levels of each of the three attributes provide the eight possible stimuli in a set. In some cases the sets involved the various combinations of just pairs of these attributes, and such sets contain four different stimuli. And in one situation the stimuli varied on just a single attribute.

Each attribute varied also in discriminability, which we changed by using larger or smaller differences in the two levels of the attribute. We used four degrees of discriminability for each attribute, as equally matched between attributes as we could make them, and we used the degrees of discriminability in all possible combinations to determine the effect of discriminability of attribute on classification.

## CONSTRAINED CLASSIFICATION

In the constrained-classification task the subject was required to sort a deck of 32 cards into two piles as fast as he could, and the attribute by which he was required to sort was specified by the experimenter.

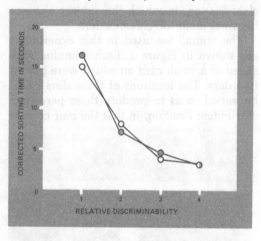

●—— With competing attributes      ○—— With no competing attributes

**Figure 2.** Sorting times for decks of 32 cards as a function of relative discriminability of the criterion attribute, with and without the existence of competing attributes (from Imai & Garner, 1965).

With this task the experimental result is the time required to sort the deck of cards.

The major result of this part of the experiment is shown in Figure 2. In this figure, a corrected sorting time is shown as a function of the relative discriminability (on the abscissa) of the attribute by which the subject was sorting. The drop in this function makes it quite clear that sorting is much faster with higher discriminability. So we do know that discriminability of attribute

affects how well subjects can do in this constrained task.

The results for all three attributes have been combined in this figure because there were no differences between the attributes. So we also know that the discriminabilities of different attributes can at least be adjusted so that they are quite equivalent with regard to sorting speed.

**Table 1**
PERCENTAGE CHOICE OF ATTRIBUTE BY THREE TYPES OF SUBJECTS IN FREE CLASSIFICATION

| Subject type | Attribute chosen | | | |
| --- | --- | --- | --- | --- |
| | Distance | Orienta-tion | Position | Other |
| D preferring (12) | 69.0 | 22.3 | 5.3 | 3.4 |
| O preferring (8) | 22.8 | 61.9 | 12.2 | 3.1 |
| DO preferring (4) | 39.5 | 40.0 | 19.0 | 1.5 |
| All subjects (24) | 48.7 | 38.4 | 9.9 | 3.0 |

Note.—From Imai and Garner (1965).

But there are two functions shown here. One is the function obtained when the stimuli differed on just one attribute. The other function is for all conditions in which there were one or two competing attributes with different degrees of discriminability. All these other conditions have been combined because once again there were no differential effects: Neither the number nor the discriminability of the competing attributes had any effect on sorting speed.

Thus our conclusion is that only the discriminability of the differentiating or classifying attribute affects the nature of the perceived organization.

In free classification, the task was somewhat different. A set of either four or eight stimuli (depending on whether two or three attributes were used) was placed in front of the subject, and he was simply required to arrange the stimuli into two groups. With this task we do not measure how well the subject can do what he is told to do, but rather we measure what in fact he does—that is, what attribute he classifies by.

Some of the results with free classification are shown in Table 1. On the bottom row is shown the percentage of times that subjects used each of the attributes in making the classification. Distance between dots was used nearly 50% of the time, Orientation was used nearly 40% of the time, and Position was used less than 10% of the time. Since all combinations of discriminabilities had been used in producing the stimulus sets, these results are due entirely to an overall preference of subjects to classify by some attributes rather than by others.

These preferences for attributes are not the same for all subjects, as is shown on the other three rows of data. On the top row, 12 of the subjects preferred Distance, using it 69% of the time. On the second row, 8 of the subjects preferred Orientation, using it nearly 62% of the time. And on the third row, 4 subjects preferred both Distance and Orientation equally, using each of them about 40% of the time. No subject preferred Position as the classifying attribute.

So not only are there overall preferences for attributes, but there are also strong individual differences in these preferences. And I hasten to add that these individual differences are not correlated with equivalent differences in speed of sorting with the various attributes.

Still further results are shown in Figure 3. This graph shows data for all the cases where there were just four stimuli in the set; that is, there were just two attributes the subject could use to classify. For each set of stimuli we knew which attribute was preferred over the other on the average, and the discriminability of this attribute is shown on the abscissa. The discriminability of the nonpreferred attribute is shown separately for each of the curves; and the ordinate shows the percentage of times that the preferred attribute was actually chosen. Notice, on the right, that when the preferred attribute has high discriminability, it is chosen regardless of the discriminability of the nonpreferred attribute. However, on the left, where the preferred attribute has low discriminability, the discriminability of the nonpreferred attribute affects the choice, even to the extent that it will be chosen more often than the preferred attribute.

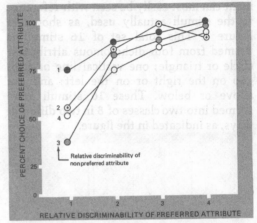

**Figure 3.** Percentage choice of a preferred attribute in free classification as a function of its discriminability and the discriminability of a competing nonpreferred attribute (from Imai & Garner, 1965).

So this experiment has shown us that what the subject can do is one thing, but that what he does do is quite another. What he can do is to ignore all attributes of the stimulus which define a larger set except the differentiating one, and he shows no performance advantage of one attribute over another. What he does do is to have definite and personal preferences for attributes, and his perceptual organization is affected by all attributes defining the set of stimuli. To perceive is to know—all properties of the stimulus set, not just those immediately relevant to discrimination.

## CLASSIFICATION LEARNING

The next experiment I shall discuss was done in collaboration with James Whitman (Whitman & Garner, 1963), and it concerns the learning of classifications. This type of task is, in a sense, another form of constrained classification since the experimenter sets the rules (that is, he defines the subsets or classes of stimuli to be learned) and the subject is required to perform according to these rules, even having to discover them.

The particular purpose of this experiment can most easily be seen with reference to the stimuli actually used, as shown in Figure 4. This total set of 16 stimuli is formed from four dichotomous attributes: circle or triangle; one vertical line or two; gap on the right or on the left; and dot above or below. These 16 stimuli were formed into two classes of 8 in two different ways, as indicated in the figure.

**Figure 4.** Stimuli used in classification learning (after Whitman & Garner, 1963).

First, notice the two classes formed by a vertical separation. Each of these classes has an equal number of each level of each attribute. For example, the class of stimuli labeled "A" has four triangles and four circles, and so does the remaining set of stimuli, those labeled "B". The same is true for location of gap, number of lines, and location of dot. In addition, within each of these two classes one pair of attributes is

perfectly correlated. Specifically, in the eight Class A stimuli, the gap is always on the left of the triangle and on the right of the circle. This same pair of attributes is also correlated in the Class B stimuli, except now the gap is on the right of the triangle and on the left of the circle. The structure of these two classes is called simple because we know from a previous experiment (Whitman & Garner, 1962) that subsets with these simple contingencies or correlations are easy to learn.

Now notice the classes formed with a horizontal separation. Once again, each of the classes has an equal number of each level of each attribute. So there is no difference between the two methods of classification in this regard. However, these classes with complex structure have no pair correlations. To illustrate, in the J class, half the time the gap is on the right of the circle and half the time on the left, and the same is true for the triangles. Nor is any other pair of attributes correlated.

Now our specific experimental question was whether the nature of the classification system affected the ease of classification learning. But more importantly, we wanted to know whether the difference in difficulty of learning (which we really knew to exist in some cases at least) depended on how the stimuli were presented to the subject. In particular, we wanted to know whether presenting classes with simple structure as intact groups, rather than as single stimuli, facilitated learning.

## BOTH CLASSES PRESENTED MIXED

In the more-or-less traditional method used in concept or classification learning, stimuli from both classes are presented singly and in a mixed order, and this is one of the methods we used. On each trial all 16 stimuli were presented, with the stimuli randomly arranged in order, and with each stimulus labeled. The subject read out the label—the A or B, the J or K—on each stimulus card. At the end of each trial, a shuffled deck of all 16 cards was handed to the subject, who was then required to sort them into the two separate classes.

The learning curves obtained with this method are shown in Figure 5. The percentage of correct responses is shown on the ordinate as a function of trials. These two curves cross and recross, and there is no significant difference between them. The conclusion with this method is that the nature of the structure in the subset does not affect the ease of learning.

## ONE CLASS PRESENTED ALONE

With the other method, we presented just one class of stimuli to the subject—either the A stimuli or the J stimuli, depending on which classification was being learned.

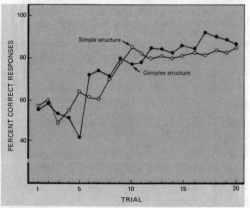

**Figure 5.** Learning curves for simple and complex classifications when both classes are presented mixed (after Whitman & Garner, 1963).

Once again the subject read aloud the label on each stimulus, but the label that he read was always the same. The other stimuli were never shown to the subject on the presentation trials. After each trial, the subject was again given the full set of stimuli and required to sort them into the two classes.

The results with this method are shown in Figure 6. Here there is a very clear separation between the two curves, showing that the classification with simple structure is much easier to learn than the classification

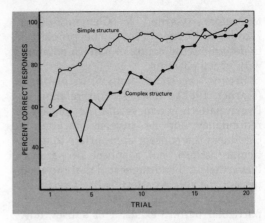

**Figure 6.** Learning curves for simple and complex classifications when one class is presented alone (after Whitman & Garner, 1963).

with complex structure. Incidentally, the bottom curve here is not significantly different from the two curves obtained with mixed stimulus presentation, so this method facilitates learning of the classification with simple structure, rather than making it more difficult with complex structure.

This last point is of some importance, because if we just look at learning of sets with simple structure and compare learning with the two methods of stimulus presentation, we see that learning improves when we show the subject only half the stimuli. This result does not seem reasonable unless we realize that the subjects are in fact learning sets of stimuli, not individual stimuli.

The conclusion is clear: People do perceive properties of sets of stimuli, and these properties affect ease of learning. But the stimuli must be presented so that it is clear to the subject what constitutes a single class or group or subset. If the stimuli are presented so that the subject must learn them as individual stimuli, he can do so, but then he cannot take advantage of some facilitating properties of sets.

## VISUAL PATTERN PERCEPTION

The next problem area I want to discuss involves two experiments, in which David Clement and Stephen Handel were my collaborators (Garner & Clement, 1963; Handel & Garner, 1966). The problem is to determine the nature of pattern goodness with visual patterns.

In my *Uncertainty and Structure* book (Garner, 1962) I discussed the relation between pattern goodness and the concept of redundancy, or its inverse uncertainty. Goodness is a concept appropriate to a particular pattern, not a subset of patterns. Nevertheless, I had suggested that the goodness of the single pattern is itself related to the size of a subset of patterns in which the particular pattern exists. This subset, however, is not defined objectively, or even by the experimenter, but rather is inferred by the subject. I had stated the specific hypothesis that good patterns come from small inferred subsets, and poor patterns come from large ones. These experiments are concerned with this hypothesis.

The kinds of stimuli used in these two experiments are shown in Figure 7. These stimulus patterns are produced by placing five dots in the cells of a 3 × 3 imaginary matrix. Although there are 126 patterns which can be formed in this manner, in our first experiment we used just 90 of them, eliminating those patterns in which a row or a column had no dot in it. These 90 patterns form several subsets of patterns by the objective rule that all patterns which can produce each other by rotation or reflection are to be considered as a single subset. In this figure, 1 pattern from each of the 17 such subsets is shown, and our data will be given for these 17 prototypical patterns.

In this first experiment, subjects did two things with these 90 patterns. One group of subjects rated each of the 90 patterns for goodness on a 7-point scale, and we obtained a mean rating for each of the patterns. Another group of subjects was required to sort the 90 patterns into approximately eight groups, keeping similar patterns in the same group. These subjects were not, however, required to have all groups be of the same size, and in fact the

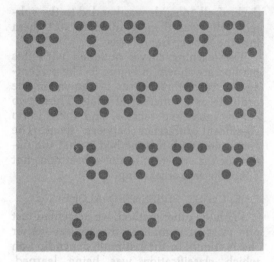

**Figure 7.** Prototypical dot patterns used in experiments on pattern goodness. (Each of these patterns is 1 from a subset of 1, 4, or 8 patterns which are equivalent when rotated or reflected.)

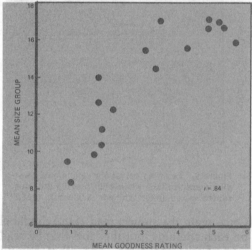

**Figure 8.** Mean goodness rating versus mean size group for 17 dot patterns (after Garner & Clement, 1963).

measure we used for each pattern was the size of the group in which it had been placed. We used a mean size of group as the summary statistic for this second task.

Now we have for each of the 90 patterns a mean goodness rating and a mean size group, and the hypothesis states that these two measures should be correlated. The re-

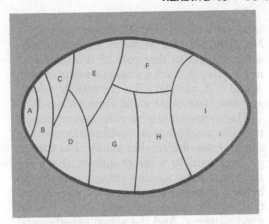

**Figure 9.** A conception of subsets of unequal size produced by partitioning. (All subsets are mutually exclusive.)

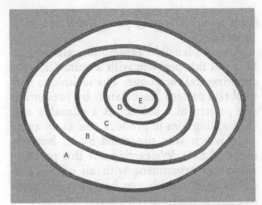

**Figure 10.** A conception of subsets of unequal size produced by nesting. (Each subset includes all smaller ones.)

lation between these measures for the 17 prototypical patterns is shown in Figure 8. Here the mean goodness rating (with a small numerical rating meaning a good pattern) is shown on the abscissa, and the mean size group is on the ordinate. The correlation between these two measures is .84, which is quite high enough for us to conclude that the basic hypothesis is essentially correct: Good patterns come from small inferred subsets, and poor patterns come from large inferred subsets.

## NESTED OR PARTITIONED SETS?

Our basic conception of the different sizes of inferred subsets was as shown in Figure 9. Here the outer bound represents the total set of stimulus patterns, and the smaller regions inside represent the inferred subsets, whose sizes we obtained experimentally. Notice that these subsets differ in size, and are also mutually exclusive; that is, the subsets do not overlap each other. Subset A is, to illustrate, a small subset of good patterns, and Subset I is a large subset of different, poor patterns. This method of obtaining subsets from a total set is called partitioning, and it corresponds exactly to what we required our subjects to do, since they had to form different groups using all

of the stimuli, and no stimulus was allowed to be in more than one group.

After this experiment had been completed, it occurred to us that there is at least one other highly possible way in which subjects can infer subsets of different sizes, and that is with the use of nested sets. A diagram of such a system of subsets is shown in Figure 10. In this conception, Set A includes Subset B and Subset C, and in fact all of the stimuli. Subset B includes Subset C and Subset D, and in fact all of the stimuli except those in Set A which do not overlap with Subset B; and likewise for Set C. In other words, these sets form a kind of inclusive ordering with respect to size of set, since the most inclusive set will contain all stimuli, the next most will contain all but a few of those in the largest set, until finally the smallest set may well contain only a single stimulus.

This conception would have satisfied the requirements of the original hypothesis perfectly well, since all the hypothesis required is that inferred subsets have different sizes. In fact, if the nesting conception of the perceptual process is correct, our obtaining of such a high correlation between goodness and inferred subset size might have been a little fortunate, since in our experimental procedure we forced the subjects to partition, and the partitions formed from nonoverlapping parts need not vary in size.

A very plausible assumption allowed us to get at this problem with a quite different experimental technique. The technique was to obtain pattern "associates" by presenting one pattern to a subject as a stimulus and then asking him to produce one as an associate which was suggested by it, but not identical to it. We carried out this pattern-associates experiment with all of the 126 dot patterns which can be generated with five dots in the nine-cell matrix.

The assumption which makes this experimental procedure interpretable to the nesting conception is simply this: A pattern will be used as an associate to another stimulus pattern only if it lies in the smallest subset in which the stimulus pattern exists. To illustrate, suppose Stimulus x exists in Set A but not in B or any smaller set—that is, it exists in the outer ring. Its smallest subset is the total set, so any pattern in the

total set can be used as an associate to it. Now suppose that Stimulus y exists in Subset B but not in that part of A which does not overlap B. Such a stimulus exists in both A and in B, but since B is the smaller subset, any associate must come from Subset B.

The consequence of this assumption is that the associates are unidirectional—they can go toward a smaller subset, but cannot go backward to a larger subset. If we are right that these smaller subsets contain the better patterns, then this assumption means that pattern associates will move toward good patterns. And the actual experimental result will be that some patterns (the poor ones) will have many other patterns as associates, while other patterns (the good ones) will have very few different associates.

The results we obtained with this association experiment are illustrated in Figure 11. In this figure each column stands for a pattern used as a stimulus and each equiv-

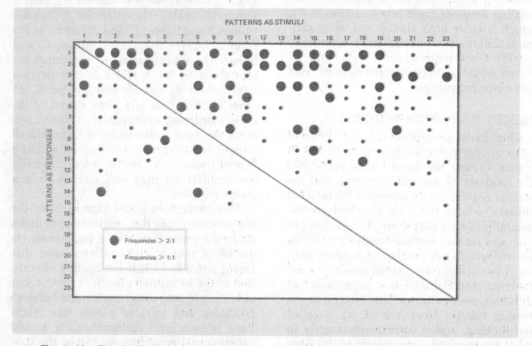

PATTERNS AS STIMULI

PATTERNS AS RESPONSES

Frequencies > 2:1

Frequencies > 1:1

**Figure 11.** The distribution of patterns used as associates to different patterns used as stimuli. (The filled circles indicate a greater than expected ratio of occurrences—after Handel & Garner, 1966).

alent row for the same pattern used as a response. If our nesting idea is correct, it should be possible to arrange the order of the patterns so that practically all of the associates are above the diagonal line, that is, go toward better patterns, and the ordering shown here is the best that can be obtained with this criterion. (Again, incidentally, we are showing data for prototypical patterns rather than for each individual pattern.)

These actual results strongly confirm our hypothesis (with its working assumption). The small circles represent cells whose frequencies are greater than the expected value (assuming all associates equally likely) and the large circles represent cells where the expected frequency has been exceeded by a factor of 2. The vast majority of the associates are clearly unidirectional. Only with the lower numbered patterns—those presumably nested well within the total set—do we get apparent bidirectionality of associates. We must remember, however, that our technique is limited since subjects were required to produce an associate different from the stimulus. So these bidirectional associates may be an artifact of our method.

The ordering of these stimulus patterns in this figure is based entirely on the association data. We also did obtain goodness ratings of the patterns, and the correlation between the orderings based on associations and those based on goodness ratings is .85. Thus, not only can we feel that the nesting conception is fundamentally correct, but we also know that it is related to pattern goodness.

Furthermore, both of these experiments show that sets and subsets of stimuli do exist for subjects even though we, as experimenters, present a single stimulus and want to act as though the single stimulus exists in isolation. The subject actively participates in the perceptual process by forming sets and subsets of stimuli and his perception of the individual stimulus is really perception of the properties of these sets.

## AUDITORY PATTERN PERCEPTION

The last experiment I shall describe concerns auditory pattern perception, and was done in collaboration with Fred Royer (Royer & Garner, 1966). In changing from visual pattern perception to auditory pattern perception, it is inevitable that we change from thinking of patterns as existing in space (which is the primary way in which visual patterns are perceived) to thinking of patterns as existing in time (which is the primary way in which auditory patterns are perceived).

The questions we undertook to investigate were: first, whether the concept of pattern complexity or goodness is appropriate to auditory temporal pattern perception; second, whether such pattern goodness is related to the size of an inferred subset of stimuli; and third, whether the difficulty of

| Pattern | Uncertainty of Point of Response (Bits) | Average Response Delay | Average No. Errors |
|---------|------------------------------------------|------------------------|--------------------|
| G 11111000 | 1.45 | 20.5 | 0.34 |
| K 11110010 | 2.02 | 33.4 | 1.59 |
| T 11011010 | 2.73 | 48.8 | 3.34 |

**Figure 12.** Response uncertainty, delay, and errors for three auditory temporal patterns (after Royer & Garner, 1966).

perceiving a perceptual organization or pattern is related to the complexity and the size of the inferred subset.

The stimuli we used consisted of dichotomous, qualitatively different elements (two different door buzzers worked quite well for us), presented in a rigidly fixed time schedule of two per second, and at the same intensity and duration. We worked with a basic sequence of eight elements, and actually used all of the 256 sequences which can be generated with dichotomous elements in sequences of eight. However, once a particular sequence was started, it continued indefinitely with no break at the end of the eight elements.

Three of the sequences used, and some results obtained with them, are shown in Figure 12. The three actual patterns are shown on the left, with the 0's and 1's standing for the two dichotomous elements or buzzers. These 256 different sequences, when repeated, reduce to a much smaller number, because on repetition many of the patterns become the same. To illustrate, Pattern G is shown here as 11111000. Another actual sequence is 11100011, but this sequence, when repeated, becomes exactly the same as Pattern G, and can be considered the same as Pattern G except that it is started at the third position of the pattern. Most of the 256 patterns are one of a subset of eight, all of which are the same with continued repetition, and the three patterns illustrated here are all of this type.

Our experimental procedure was moderately straightforward. We started a particular pattern and the subject was required simply to listen to it. As soon as he thought he could, he was to produce the pattern by pushing two telegraph keys in synchrony with the auditory pattern, which continued until the subject had been correct for two complete cycles.

We measured three things: Two of them are measures which reflect the difficulty of a pattern to a subject—first, the delay after the stimulus sequence had begun and before the subject attempted to respond, shown as the average response delay in the middle column; and second, the number of errors made after responding began, shown on the far right as an average per subject per sequence.

The third measure requires a slight explanation. Each pattern was started at each of its eight possible starting points, but there was no requirement that the subject begin responding at that particular point— he was free to begin responding at any point

in the sequence. We noted the exact point in the sequence at which the subject started to respond. Not all subjects started at the same point, nor did the same subject start at the same point each time he heard a particular pattern but with a different stimulus starting point. So we have a distribution of beginning response points for each pattern, and the variability of this distribution was measured in bits of uncertainty. It is the measure shown in the first column of numbers.

This number tells us one of the things we want to know. There are not in fact 256 perceived temporal patterns, but considerably fewer, because all alternative modes of organization are not acceptable to subjects. But more important, it makes clear that the number of alternative modes of organization does vary from pattern to pattern, and by a substantial amount. These three patterns have uncertainties which are the equivalent of less than three alternative organizations for Pattern G, to about four for Pattern K, to almost seven for Pattern T.

So there is a difference in size of an inferred, or subjective, subset of patterns which is quite analogous to what we find with visual patterns. Furthermore, this size is obviously related to pattern complexity or goodness—so much so that we did not think it necessary to obtain direct goodness ratings of the various patterns. Good or simple auditory patterns have few alternative modes of organization; poor patterns have many alternative modes.

Now to return to our measures of perceptual difficulty. The average response delay does vary with complexity and uncertainty, being just over 20 elements for Pattern G and almost 49 elements for Pattern T. In like manner, the number of errors made after starting to respond varies from about one error for every three sequences with Pattern G to over three per sequence with Pattern T. So both delay and errors are highly correlated with each other, and either or both of them are highly correlated with the uncertainty of the point at which responding begins.

To summarize, there are simple and complex auditory temporal patterns. Simple patterns (good, in the Gestalt sense) are stable, have few alternative modes of perceptual organization, and are quickly organized with little error. Complex patterns are unstable, have many alternative modes of perceptual organization, are organized only after considerable time, and even after that are organized imperfectly. And again it is clear that the perceiver actively participates in the organizing process.

## CONCLUSION

In conclusion, I hope that these experiments have illustrated for you that to perceive is to know. It is to know and comprehend the nature of a stimulus; it is to know the nature of the alternatives to a stimulus; and it is to know the structure and organization of sets of stimuli. Furthermore, the perception of stimuli as existing in sets and subsets is an active process for the perceiver, one in which he will define and organize sets of stimuli which he may never have experienced, if the nature of a stimulus clearly requires such an inference in order for it to be known.

## REFERENCES

Garner, W. R. 1962. *Uncertainty and structure as psychological concepts.* New York: Wiley.

Garner, W. R., and Clement, D. E. 1963. Goodness of pattern and pattern uncertainty. *Journal of Verbal Learning and Verbal Behavior* 2:446–452.

Handel, S., and Garner, W. R. 1966. The structure of visual pattern associates and pattern goodness. *Journal of Perception and Psychophysics.*

Imai, S., and Garner, W. R. 1965. Discriminability and preference for attributes in free and constrained classification. *Journal of Experimental Psychology* 69:596–608.

Royer, F. L., and Garner, W. R. 1966. Response uncertainty and perceptual difficulty of auditory temporal patterns. *Journal of Perception and Psychophysics.*

Whitman, J. R., and Garner, W. R. 1962. Free recall learning of visual figures as a function of form of internal structure. *Journal of Experimental Psychology* 64:558–564.

Whitman, J. R., and Garner, W. R. 1963. Concept learning as a function of form of internal structure. *Journal of Verbal Learning and Verbal Behavior* 2:195–202.

# PART 4

# Complex Learning and Thinking

# PART 4

# Complex Learning and Thinking

# READING 20

## The Interpretive Cortex

### WILDER PENFIELD

Some of the best-known electrophysiological studies on the human brain have been done by Wilder Penfield. His surgery on epileptic patients has done much to clarify our understanding of the structure and functions of the human brain. His work has had application in the areas of physiological psychology and the influence of the brain in perception and memory. In this article, Penfield tells how "the stream of consciousness" in the brain is reactivated through electrical stimulation.

### QUESTIONS

1. What type of memory model does Penfield's research suggest? Do you agree with this model?
2. What type of research has Penfield's work stimulated?
3. It has been suggested that the patient's recall may not be valid, that the reports are too vague, and that the patient is producing what he feels is expected of him. Do you think these are valid criticisms of Penfield's research?

There is an area of the surface of the human brain where local electrical stimulation can call back a sequence of past experience. An epileptic irritation in this area may do the same. It is as though a wire recorder, or a strip of cinematographic film with sound track, had been set in motion within the brain. The sights and sounds, and the thoughts, of a former day pass through the man's mind again.

The author is director of the Montreal Neurological Institute, McGill University, Montreal, Quebec.

The purpose of this article is to describe, for readers from various disciplines of science, the area of the cerebral cortex from which this neuron record of the past can be activated and to suggest what normal contribution it may make to cerebral function.

The human brain is the master organ of the human race. It differs from the brains of other mammals particularly in the greater extent of its cerebral cortex. The gray matter, or cortex, that covers the two cerebral hemispheres of the brain of man is so vast in nerve cell population that it could never have been contained within the human skull if it were not folded upon itself, and refolded, so as to form a very large number of fissures and convolutions (Figure 1). The fissures are so deep and so devious that by far the greater portion of this ganglionic carpet (about 65 percent) is hidden in them, below the surface (Figure 2).

The portion that is labeled "interpretive" in Figures 1 and 3 covers a part of both temporal lobes. It is from these two homologous areas, and from nowhere else, that electrical stimulation has occasionally produced physical responses which may be divided into (i) experiential responses and (ii) interpretive responses.

## EXPERIENTIAL RESPONSES

Occasionally during the course of a neurosurgical operation under local anesthesia, gentle electrical stimulation in this temporal area, right or left, has caused the conscious patient to be aware of some previous experience (1). The experience seems to be picked out at random from his own past. But it comes back to him in great detail. He is suddenly aware again of those things to which he paid attention in that distant interval of time. This recollection of an experiential sequence stops suddenly when the electrical current is switched off or when the electrode is removed from contact with the cortex. This phenomenon we have chosen to call an experiential response to stimulation.

## CASE EXAMPLES (2)

The patient S.Be. observed, when the electrode touched the temporal lobe (right superior temporal convolution), "There was a piano over there and someone playing. I could hear the song you know." When the cortex was stimulated again without warning, at approximately the same point, the patient had a different experience. He said: "Someone speaking to another, and he mentioned a name but I could not understand it

. . . It was like a dream." Again the point was restimulated without his knowledge. He said quietly: "Yes, 'Oh Marie, Oh Marie'! Someone is singing it." When the point was stimulated a fourth time he heard the same song again and said it was the "theme song of a radio program."

The electrode was then applied to a point 4 centimeters farther forward on the first temporal convolution. While the electrode was still in place, S.Be. said: "Something brings back a memory. I can see Seven-Up Bottling Company—Harrison Bakery." He was evidently seeing two of Montreal's large illuminated advertisements.

The surgeon then warned him that he was about to apply the electrode again. Then, after a pause, the surgeon said "Now," but he did not stimulate. (The patient has no means of knowing when the electrode is applied, unless he is told, since the cortex itself is without sensation.) The patient replied promptly, "Nothing."

A woman (D.F.) (3) heard an orchestra playing an air while the electrode was held in place. The music stopped when the electrode was removed. It came again when the electrode was reapplied. On request, she hummed the tune, while the electrode was held in place, accompanying the orchestra. It was a popular song. Over and over again, restimulation at the same spot produced the same song. The music seemed always to begin at the same place and to progress at the normally expected tempo. All efforts to mislead her failed. She believed that a gramaphone was being turned on in the operating room on each occasion, and she asserted her belief stoutly in a conversation some days after the operation.

A boy (R.W.) heard his mother talking to someone on the telephone when an electrode was applied to his right temporal cortex. When the stimulus was repeated without warning, he heard his mother again in the same conversation. When the stimulus was repeated after a lapse of time, he said, "My mother is telling my brother he has

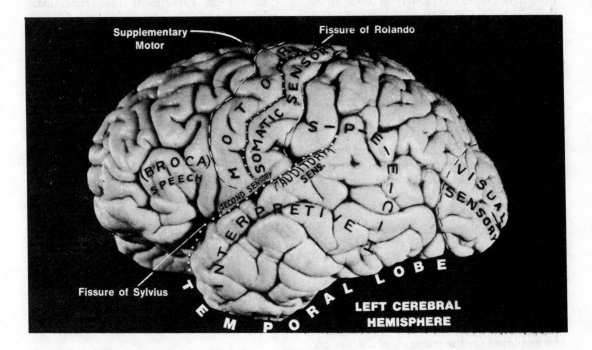

**Figure 1.**  Photograph of the left hemisphere of a human brain. The frontal lobe is on the left, the occipital lobe on the right. The major motor and sensory areas are indicated, as well as the speech areas and the interpretive area. [Penfield and Roberts (18)]

got his coat on backwards. I can just hear them."

The surgeon then asked the boy whether he remembered this happening. "Oh yes," he said, "just before I came here." Asked again whether this seemed like a dream, he replied: "No, it is like I go into a daze."

J. T. cried out in astonishment when the electrode was applied to the temporal cortex; "Yes doctor, yes doctor. Now I hear people laughing—my friends in South Africa!"

When asked about this, he explained the reason for his surprise. He seemed to be laughing with his cousins, Bessie and Ann Wheliow, whom he had left behind him on a farm in South Africa, although he knew he was now on the operating table in Montreal.

## INTERPRETIVE RESPONSES

On the other hand, similar stimulation in this same general area may produce quite a different response. The patient discovers, on stimulation, that he has somehow changed his own interpretation of what he is seeing at the moment, or hearing or thinking. For example, he may exclaim that his present experience seems familiar, as though he had seen it or heard it or thought it before. He realizes that this must be a false interpretation. Or, on the contrary, these things may seem suddenly strange, absurd. Sights or sounds may seem distant and small, or they may come unexpectedly close and seem loud or large. He may feel suddenly afraid, as though his environment were threatening him, and he is possessed by a nameless dread or panic. Another patient may say he feels lonely or aloof, or as though he were observing himself at a distance.

Under normal circumstances anyone may make such interpretations of the present, and these interpretations serve him as guides to action or reaction. If the interpretations are accurate guides, they must be based upon previous comparable experience. It is conceivable, therefore, that the recall mechanism which is activated by the electrode during an experiential response and the mechanism activated in an interpretive response may be parts of a common inclusive mechanism of reflex recognition or interpretation.

No special function had been previously assigned by neurologists to the area in each temporal lobe that is marked "interpretive" in Figures 1 and 3, though some clinicians have suggested it might have to do with the recall of music. The term *interpretive cortex*, therefore, is no more than slang to be employed for the purposes of discussion. The terms *motor cortex, sensory cortex,* and *speech cortex* began as slang phrases and have served such a purpose. But such phrases must not be understood to signify independence of action of separated units in the case of any of these areas. Localization of function in the cerebral cortex means no more than specialization of function as compared with other cortical regions, not separation from the integrated action of the brain.

Before considering the interpretive cortex further, we may turn briefly to the motor and sensory areas and the speech areas of the cortex. After considering the effects of electrical stimulation there, we should be better able to understand the results of stimulation in the temporal lobes.

## SPECIALIZATION OF FUNCTION IN THE CORTEX

Evidence for some degree of localization within the brain was recognized early in the 19th century by Flourens. He con-

cluded from experiment that functional subdivision of "the organ of the mind" was possible. The forebrain (4), he said [cerebral hemispheres and higher brain stem (Figure 4)] had to do with thought and will power, while the cerebellum was involved in the coordination of movement.

In 1861, Paul Broca showed that a man with a relatively small area of destruction in a certain part of the left hemisphere alone might lose only the power of speech. It was soon realized that this was the speech area of man's dominant (left) hemisphere. In 1870 Fritsch and Hitzig applied an electric current to the exposed cortex of one hemisphere of a lightly anesthetized dog and caused the legs of the opposite side to move. Thus, an area of cortex called motor was discovered.

After that, localization of function became a research target for many clinicians and experimentalists. It was soon evident that in the case of man, the precentral gyrus

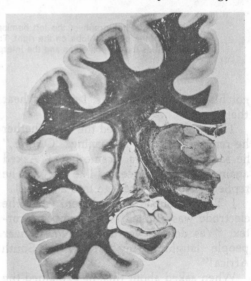

**Figure 2a.** Photograph of a cross section of the left cerebral hemisphere [Jelgersma (19)]. The white matter is stained black and the gray matter is unstained. The major convolutions of the cerebral cortex and the subcortical masses of gray matter can be identified by reference to Figure 2b.

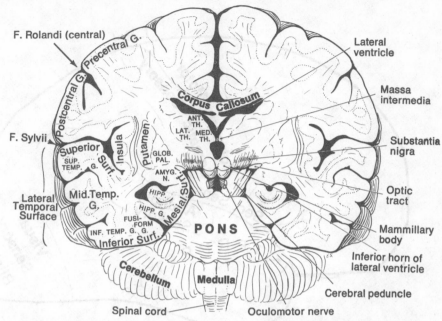

F. Rolandi (central)
Precentral G.
Postcentral G.
F. Sylvii
Superior Surf.
SUP. TEMP. G.
Insula
Putamen
GLOB. PAL.
AMYG. N.
Lateral Temporal Surface
Mid.Temp. G.
HIPP.
HIPP. G.
Mesial Surf.
FUSI-FORM
INF. TEMP. G. G.
Inferior Surf.
Cerebellum
Medulla
Spinal cord
Corpus Callosum
ANT. TH.
LAT. TH.
MED. TH.
**PONS**
Oculomotor nerve
Lateral ventricle
Massa intermedia
Substantia nigra
Optic tract
Mammillary body
Inferior horn of lateral ventricle
Cerebral peduncle

**Figure 2b.** Drawing of the cross section shown in Figure 2a, with additions. The surfaces and convolutions of the temporal lobe are identified, and the relationship of one hemisphere to the other and the relationship of the hemispheres to the brain stem and cerebellum are shown.

(Figure 5) in each hemisphere was related to voluntary control of the contralateral limbs and that there was an analogous area of motor cortex in the frontal lobes of animals. It appeared also that other separate areas of cortex (Figures 1 and 5) in each hemisphere were dedicated to sensation (one for visual sensation, others for auditory, olfactory, and discriminative somatic sensation, respectively).

It was demonstrated, too, that from the "motor cortex" there was an efferent bundle of nerve fibers (the pyramidal tract) that ran down through the lower brain stem and the spinal cord to be relayed on out to the muscles. Through this efferent pathway, voluntary control of these muscles was actually carried out. It was evident, too, that there were separate sensory tracts carrying nerve impulses in the other direction, from the principal organs of special sense

(eye, ear, nose, and skin and muscle) into separate sensory areas of the cortex.

These areas, motor and sensory, have been called "projection areas." They play a role in the projection of nerve currents to the cortex from the periphery of the body, and from the cortex to the periphery. This makes possible (sensory) awareness of environment and provides the individual with a means of outward (motor) expression. The motor cortex has a specialized use during voluntary action, and each of the several sensory areas has a specialized use, when the individual is seeing, hearing, smelling, or feeling.

## TRAVELING POTENTIALS

The action of the living brain depends upon the movement, within it, of "transient electrical potentials traveling the fibers of the nervous system." This was Sherring-

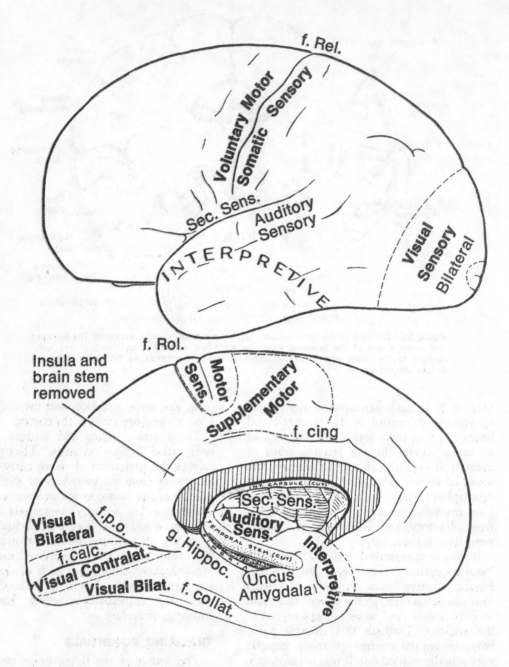

**Figure 3.** The left cerebral hemisphere; the lateral surface is shown above and the mesial surface below. In the lower drawing the brain stem with the Island of Reil has been removed to show the inner banks of the fissure of Sylvius and the superior surface of the temporal lobe. The interpretive cortex extends from the lateral to the superior surface of the temporal lobe. [Penfield and Roberts (18)]

ton's phrase. Within the vast circuits of this master organ, potentials travel, here and there and yonder, like meteors that streak across the sky at night and line the firmament with trails of light. When the meteors pass, the paths of luminescence still glow a little while, then fade and are gone. The changing patterns of these paths of passing energy make possible the changing content of the mind. The patterns are never quite the same, and so it is with the content of the mind.

Specialized areas in the cortex are at times active and again relatively quiet. But, when a man is awake, there is always some central integration and coordination of the traveling potentials. There must be activity within the brain stem and some areas of the cortex. This is centrencephalic integration (5).

## SENSORY, MOTOR, AND PSYCHICAL RESPONSES TO CORTICAL STIMULATION

My purpose in writing this article is to discuss in simple words (free of technical terms) the meaning of the "psychical" responses which appear only on stimulation of the so-called interpretive cortex. But before considering these responses let us consider the motor and sensory activity of the cortex for a moment.

When the streams of electrical potentials that pass normally through the various areas of sensory cortex are examined electrically, they do not seem to differ from each other except in pattern and timing. The essential difference is to be found in the fact that the visual stream passes to the visual cortex and then to one subcortical target and the auditory stream passes through the auditory cortex and then on to another subcortical target.

When the surgeon stimulates the intact sensory cortex he must be sending a current along the next "piece of road" to a subcortical destination. This electrode (delivering, for example, 60 "waves" per second of 2-millisecond duration and 1-volt intensity)

produces no more than elementary sight when applied to visual cortex. The patient reports colors, lights, and shadows that move and take on crude outlines. The same electrode, applied to auditory cortex, causes him to hear a ringing or hissing or thumping sound. When applied to postcentral gyrus it produces tingling or a false sense of movement.

Thus, sensation is produced by the passage inward of electrical potentials. And when the electrode is applied to the motor cortex, movement is produced by passage of potentials outward to the muscles. In each case positive response is produced by conduction in the direction of normal physiological flow—that is, by dromic conduction (6).

Responses to electrical stimulation that may be called "psychical," as distinguished from sensory or motor, have been elicited from certain areas of the human cortex (Figure 6). But they have never been produced by stimulation in other areas. There are, of course, other large areas of cortex which are neither sensory nor motor in function. They seem to be employed in other neuron mechanisms that are also associated with psychical processes. But the function of these other areas cannot, it seems, be activated by so simple a stimulus as an electric current applied to the cortex.

### DREAMY STATES OF EPILEPSY

"Epilepsy" may be defined, in Jackson's words, as "the name for occasional, sudden, excessive, rapid and local discharges of grey matter." Our aim in the operations under discussion was to remove the gray matter responsible for epileptic attacks if that gray matter could be spared. When the stimulating electrode reproduced the psychical phenomenon that initiated the fit, it provided the guidance sought (7).

During the 19th century clinicians had recognized these phenomena as epileptic. They applied the term *intellectual aura* to such attacks. Jackson substituted the expression *dreamy states* (see *8*). These were, he said, "psychical states during the onset of certain epileptic seizures, states which are much more elaborate than crude sensations." And again, he wrote, "These are all voluminous mental states and yet of different kinds; no doubt they ought to be classified, but for my present purpose they may be considered together."

"The state," he said, "is often like that occasionally experienced by healthy people as a feeling of 'reminiscence.'" Or the patient has "dreamy feelings," "dreams mixing up with present thoughts," "double consciousness," a "feeling of being somewhere else," a feeling "as if I went back to all that occurred in my childhood," "silly thoughts."

Jackson never did classify these states, but he did something more important. He localized the area of cortex from which epileptic discharge would produce dreamy states. His localization was in the anterior and deep portions of the temporal lobes, the

same area that is labeled "interpretive" cortex in Figure 3.

### CASE EXAMPLE

Brief reference may be made to a specific case. The patient had seizures, and stimulation produced responses which were first recognized as psychical.

In 1936, a girl of 16 (J.V.) was admitted to the Montreal Neurological Institute complaining of epileptic attacks, each of which was ushered in by the same hallucination. It was a little dream, she said, in which an experience from early childhood was reenacted, always the same train of events. She would then cry out with fear and run to her mother. Occasionally this was followed immediately by a major convulsive seizure.

At operation, under local anesthesia, we tried to set off the dream by a gentle electrical stimulus in the right temporal lobe. The attempt was successful. The dream was produced by the electrode. Stimulation at other points on the temporal cortex pro-

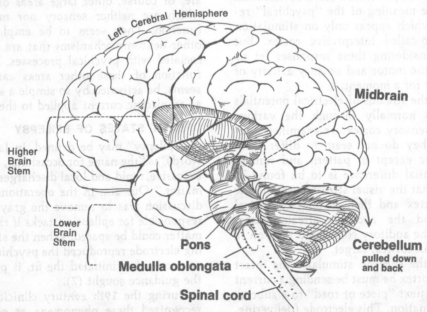

**Figure 4.** Drawing of the left cerebral hemisphere, showing the higher brain stem, including the thalamus, within and the lower brain stem and spinal cord emerging below. The cerebellum is shown, attached to the lower brain stem. [Penfield and Roberts (*18*)]

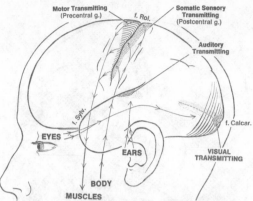

**Figure 5.** Sensory and motor projection areas. The sensory areas are stippled, and the afferent pathways to them from eyes, ears, and body are indicated by entering arrows. The motor cortex is indicated by parallel lines, and the efferent corticospinal tract is indicated by emerging arrows. [Penfield and Roberts (18)]

duced sudden fear without the dream. At still other points, stimulation caused her to say that she saw "someone coming toward me." At another point, stimulation caused her to say she heard the voices of her mother and her brothers (9).

This suggested a new order of cortical response to electrical stimulation. When the neighboring visual sensory area of the cortex is stimulated, any patient may report seeing stars of light or moving colors or black outlines but never "someone coming toward me." Stimulation of the auditory sensory cortex may cause any patient to report that he hears ringing, buzzing, blowing, or thumping sounds, perhaps, but never voices that speak. Stimulation in the areas of sensory cortex can call forth nothing more than the elements of visual or auditory or tactile sensation, never happenings that might have been previously experienced.

During the 23 years that have followed, although practically all areas of the cerebral cortex have been stimulated and studied in more than 1000 craniotomies, performed under local anesthesia, psychical responses of the experiential or interpretive variety have been produced only from

the temporal cortex in the general areas that are marked "psychical responses" in Figure 3 (10, 11).

## CLASSIFICATION

It seems reasonable to subdivide psychical responses and psychical seizures (epileptic dreamy states) in the same way, classifying them as "interpretive" or "experiential." Interpretive psychical responses are those involving interpretations of the present experience, or emotions related to it; experiential psychical responses are re-enactments of past experiences. Interpretive seizures are those accompanied by auras and illusions; experiential seizures are those accompanied by auras and hallucinations.

The interpretive responses and seizures may be divided into groups (11) of which the commonest are as follows: (i) recognition, the illusion that things seen and heard and thought are familiar (déjà vu phenomenon); (ii) visual illusion, the illusion that things seen are changing—for example, coming nearer, growing larger (macropsia); (iii) auditory illusion, the illusion that things heard are changing—for example, coming near, going away, changing tempo; (iv) illusional emotion, the emotion of fear or, less often, loneliness, sorrow, or disgust.

Experiential phenomena (hallucinations) are an awareness of experiences from the past that come into the mind without complete loss of awareness of the present.

## DISCUSSION

What, then, is the function of the interpretive cortex? This is a physiological question that follows the foregoing observations naturally.

An electrode, delivering, for example, 60 electrical pulses per second to the surface of the motor cortex, causes a man to make crude movements. When applied to the various sensory areas of the cortex, it causes him to have crude sensations of sight or sound or body feeling. This indicates only that these areas have something to do with the complicated mechanism of voluntary action or conscious sensation. It does not reveal what contribution the cortex may make, or in what way it may contribute to skill in making voluntary movement or qualify the incoming sensory streams.

In the case of the interpretive cortex, the observations are similar. We may say that the interpretive cortex has something to do with a mechanism that can reactivate the vivid record of the past. It has also something to do with a mechanism that can present to consciousness a reflex interpretation of the present. To conclude that here is the mechanism of memory would be an unjustified assumption. It would be too simple.

What a man remembers when he makes a voluntary effort is apt to be a generalization. If this were not so, he might be hopelessly lost in detail. On the other hand, the experiential responses described above are detailed reenactments of a single experience. Such experiences soon slip beyond the range of voluntary recall. A man may summon to mind a song at will. He hears it then in his mind, not all at once but advancing phrase by phrase. He may sing it or play it too, and one would call this memory.

But if a patient hears music in response to the electrode, he hears it in one particular strip of time. That time runs forward again at the original tempo, and he hears the orchestration, or he sees the player at a piano "over there." These are details he would have thought forgotten.

A vast amount of work remains to be done before the mechanism of memory, and how and where the recording takes place, are understood. This record is not laid down in the interpretive cortex, but it is kept in a part of the brain that is intimately connected with it.

Removal of large areas of interpretive cortex, even when carried out on both sides, may result in mild complaints of memory defect, but it does not abolish the capacity to remember recent events. On the other

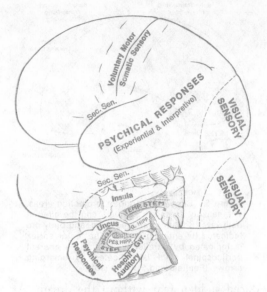

**Figure 6.** The left cerebral hemisphere is shown with the temporal lobe cut across and turned down. The areas of cortex from which psychical responses have been elicited are indicated. [Penfield (1)]

hand, surgical removals that result in bilateral interference with the underlying hippocampal zone do make the recording of recent events impossible, while distant memory is still preserved (12, 13).

The importance of the hippocampal area for memory was pointed out long ago in a forgotten publication by the Russian neurologist Bechterew (14). The year before publication Bechterew had demonstrated the case before the St. Petersburg Clinic for Nervous and Mental Diseases. The man on whom Bechterew reported had "extraordinary weakness of memory, falsifications of memory and great apathy." These defects were shown at autopsy to be secondary to lesions of the mesial surface of the cortex of both temporal lobes. The English neurologists Glees and Griffith (15) reported similar defects, a half century later, in a patient who had symmetrical lesions of the hippocampus and of hippocampal and fusiform gyri on both sides.

The way in which the interpretive cortex

seems to be used may be suggested by an example: After years of absence you meet, by chance, a man whose very existence you had forgotten. On seeing him, you may be struck by a sudden sense of familiarity, even before you have time to "think." A signal seems to flash up in consciousness to tell you that you've seen that man before. You watch him as he smiles and moves and speaks. The sense of familiarity grows stronger. Then you remember him. You may even recall that his name was Jones. The sight and the sound of the man has given you an instant access, through some reflex, to the records of the past in which this man has played some part. The opening of this forgotten file was subconscious. It was not a voluntary act. You would have known him even against your will. Although Jones was a forgotten man a moment before, now you can summon the record in such detail that you remark at once the slowness of his gait or a new line about the mouth.

If Jones had been a source of danger to you, you might have felt fear as well as familiarity before you had time to consider the man. Thus, the signal of fear as well as the signal of familiarity may come to one as the result of subconscious comparison of present with similar past experience.

One more example may be given from common experience. A sudden increase in the size of objects seen and in sounds heard may mean the rapid approach of something that calls for instant avoidance action. These are signals that, because of previous experience, we sometimes act upon with little consideration.

## SUMMARY

The interpretive cortex has in it a mechanism for instant reactivation of the detailed record of the past. It has a mechanism also for the production of interpretive signals. Such signals could only be significant if past records are scanned and relevant experiences are selected for comparison with present experience. This is a subconscious process. But it may well be that this scanning of past experience and selection from it also renders the relevant past available for conscious consideration as well. Thus, the individual may refer to the record as he employs other circuits of the brain.

Access to the record of the past seems to be as readily available from the temporal cortex of one side as from that of the other. Auditory illusions (or interpretations of the distance, loudness, or tempo of sounds) have been produced by stimulation of the temporal cortex of either side. The same is true of illusional emotions, such as fear and disgust.

But, on the contrary, visual illusions (interpretations of the distance, dimension, erectness, and tempo of things seen) are only produced by stimulation of the temporal cortex on the nondominant (normally, right) side of the brain. Illusions of recognition, such as familiarity or strangeness, were also elicited only from the nondominant side, except in one case.

## CONCLUSION

"Consciousness," to quote William James (16), "is never quite the same in successive moments of time. It is a stream forever flowing, forever changing." The stream of changing states of mind that James described so well does flow through each man's waking hours until the time when he falls asleep to wake no more. But the stream, unlike a river, leaves a record in the living brain.

Transient electrical potentials move with it through the circuits of the nervous system, leaving a path that can be followed again. The pattern of this pathway, from neuron to neuron along each nerve-cell body and fiber and junction, is the recorded pattern of each man's past. That complicated record is held there in temporal sequence through the principle of durable facilitation of conduction and connection.

A steady stream of electrical pulses applied through an electrode to some point in the interpretive cortex causes a stream of excitation to flow from the cortex to the place where past experience is recorded. This stream of excitation acts as a key to the past. It can enter the pathway of recorded consciousness at any random point, from childhood on through adult life. But having entered, the experience moves forward without interference from other experiences. And when the electrode is withdrawn there is a likelihood, which lasts for seconds or minutes, that the stream of excitation will enter the pathway again at the same moment of past time, even if the electrode is reapplied at neighboring points (17).

Finally, an electric current applied to the surface of what may be called the interpretive cortex of a conscious man (i) may cause the stream of former consciousness to flow again or (ii) may give him an interpretation of the present that is unexpected and involuntary. Therefore, it is concluded that, under normal circumstances, this area of cortex must make some functional contribution to reflex comparison of the present with related past experience. It contributes to reflex interpretation or perception of the present.

The combination and comparison of present experience with similar past experience must call for remarkable scanning of the past and classification of similarities. What contribution this area of the temporal cortex may make to the whole process is not clear. The term *interpretive cortex* will serve for identification until students of human physiology can shed more light on these fascinating findings.

## REFERENCES AND NOTES

1. W. Penfield, *Journal of Mental Science* 101 (1955): 451.

2. These patients, designated by the same initials, have been described in previous publications in much greater detail. An index of patients (designated by initials) may be found in any of my books.

3. This case is reported in detail in W. Penfield and H. Jasper, *Epilepsy and the Functional Anatomy of the Human Brain* (Boston: Little, Brown, 1954) (published in abridged form in Russian [translation by N. P. Graschenkov and G. Smirnov] by the Soviet Academy of Sciences, 1958).

4. The forebrain, or prosencephalon, properly includes the diencephalon and the telencephalon, or higher brain stem, and hemispheres. Flourens probably had cerebral hemispheres in mind as distinguished from cerebellum.

5. "Within the brain, a central transactional core has been identified between the strictly sensory or motor systems of classical neurology. This central reticular mechanism has been found capable of grading the activity of most other parts of the brain"—H. Magoun, *The Waking Brain* (Springfield, Ill.: Thomas, 1958).

6. W. Penfield, *The Excitable Cortex in Conscious Man* (Springfield, Ill.: Thomas, 1958).

7. It did more than this; it produced illusions or hallucinations that had never been experienced by the patient during a seizure.

8. J. Taylor, ed., *Selected Writings of John Hughlings Jackson* (London: Hodder and Stoughton, 1931), vol. 1, *On Epilepsy and Epileptiform Convulsions*.

9. Twenty-one years later this young woman, who is the daughter of a physician, was present at a meeting of the National Academy of Sciences in New York while her case was discussed. She could still recall the operation and the nature of the "dreams" that had preceded her seizures (W. Penfield, *Proceedings of the National Academy of Sciences of the United States* 44 (1958): 51).

10. In a recent review of the series my associate, Dr. Phanor Perot, has found and summarized 35 out of 384 temporal lobe cases in which stimulation produced experiential responses. All such responses were elicited in the temporal cortex. In a study of 214 consecutive operations for temporal lobe epilepsy, my associate Sean Mullan found 70 cases in which interpretive illusion occurred in the minor seizures before operation, or in which an interpretive response was produced by stimulation during operation. In most cases it occurred both before and during operation.

11. S. Mullan and W. Penfield, *American Medical Association Archives of Neurology and Psychiatry* 81 (1959): 269.

12. This area is marked "Hipp" and "Hipp. G" in Figure 2 (bottom) and "g. Hippoc." and "amygdala" in Figure 3.

13. W. Penfield and B. Milner, *American Medical Association Archives of Neurology and Psychiatry* 79 (1958): 475.

14. W. V. Bechterew, "Demonstration eines Gehirns mit Zerstörung der vorderen und inneren Theile der Hirnrinde beider Schläfenlappen," *Neurol. Zentralbl. Leipzig* 19 (1900): 990. My attention was called to this case recently by Dr. Peter Gloor of Montreal.

15. P. Glees and H. B. Griffith, *Monatsschr. Psychiat. Neurol.* 123 (1952): 193.

16. W. James, *The Principles of Psychology* (New York: Holt, 1910).

17. Thus, it is apparent that the beam of excitation that emanates from the interpretive cortex and seems to scan the record of the past is subject to the principles of transient facilitation already demonstrated for the anthropoid motor cortex (A. S. F. Grünbaum and C. Sherrington, *Proceedings of the Royal Society [London]* 72B [1901]: 152; T. Graham Brown and C. S. Sherrington, *ibid.* 85B [1912]: 250). Similarly subject to the principles of facilitation are the motor and the sensory cortex of man (W. Penfield and K. Welch, *J. Physiol. [London]* 109 [1949]: 358). The patient D. F. heard the same orchestra playing the same music in the operating room more than 20 times when the electrode was reapplied to the superior surface of the temporal lobe. Each time the music began in the verse of a popular song. It proceeded to the chorus, if the electrode was kept in place.

18. W. Penfield and L. Roberts, *Speech and Brain Mechanisms* (Princeton, N.J.: Princeton University Press, 1959).

19. G. Jelgersma, *Atlas anatomicum cerebri humani* (Amsterdam: Scheltema and Holkema).

# READING 21

# Magical Number Seven, Plus or Minus Two: Some Limits on Our Capacity for Processing Information

**GEORGE A. MILLER**
**Harvard University**

How much information can a person process at one time? How many items can be retained in immediate memory at one time? Miller discusses both of these questions and in each case comes up with the number seven. The data presented suggest that our information processing capacity has definite limits and that these limits depend on the number of dimensions existing in the information input. The data also suggest definite limits to the temporary storage of our memory system. Miller suggests that by recoding information or by adding dimensions to the stimulus input, the limit of seven items can be changed.

### QUESTIONS

1. Would "chunking" be an effective study tool? Why?
2. Is the limit of information processing constant? Does it vary from dimension to dimension or from single to multidimensions?
3. Is Miller's method of recoding information useful? What are the implications of this method for learning and memory capacities?

My problem is that I have been persecuted by an integer. For seven years this number has followed me around, has intruded in my most private data, and has assaulted me from the pages of our most public journals. This number assumes a variety of disguises, being sometimes a little larger and sometimes a little smaller than usual, but never changing so much as to be unrecognizable. The persistence with which this number

This paper was first read as an Invited Address before the Eastern Psychological Association in Philadelphia on April 15, 1955. Preparation of the paper was supported by the Harvard Psycho-Acoustic Laboratory under Contract N5ori-76 between Harvard University and the Office of Naval Research, U. S. Navy (Project NR142-201, Report PNR-174). Reproduction for any purpose of the U. S. Government is permitted.

plagues me is far more than a random accident. There is, to quote a famous senator, a design behind it, some pattern governing its appearances. Either there really is something unusual about the number or else I am suffering from delusions of persecution.

I shall begin my case history by telling you about some experiments that tested how accurately people can assign numbers to the magnitudes of various aspects of a stimulus. In the traditional language of psychology these would be called experiments in absolute judgment. Historical accident, however, has decreed that they should have another name. We now call them experiments on the capacity of people to transmit information. Since these experiments would not have been done without the appearance of information theory on the psychological scene, and since the results are analyzed in terms of the concepts of information theory, I shall have to preface my discussion with a few remarks about this theory.

## INFORMATION MEASUREMENT

The "amount of information" is exactly the same concept that we have talked about for years under the name of "variance." The equations are different, but if we hold tight to the idea that anything that increases the variance also increases the amount of information we cannot go far astray.

The advantages of this new way of talking about variance are simple enough. Variance is always stated in terms of the unit of measurement—inches, pounds, volts, etc.—whereas the amount of information is a dimensionless quantity. Since the information in a discrete statistical distribution does not depend upon the unit of measurement, we can extend the concept to situations where we have no metric and we would not ordinarily think of using the variance. And it also enables us to compare results obtained in quite different experimental situations where it would be meaningless to compare variances based on different metrics. So there are some good reasons for adopting the newer concept.

The similarity of variance and amount of information might be explained this way: When we have a large variance, we are very ignorant about what is going to happen. If we are very ignorant, then when we make the observation it gives us a lot of information. On the other hand, if the variance is very small, we know in advance how our observation must come out, so we get little information from making the observation.

If you will now imagine a communication system, you will realize that there is a great deal of variability about what goes into the system and also a great deal of variability about what comes out. The input and the output can therefore be described in terms of their variance (or their information). If it is a good communication system, however, there must be some systematic relation between what goes in and what comes out. That is to say, the output will depend upon the input, or will be correlated with the input. If we measure this correlation, then we can say how much of the output variance is attributable to the input and how much is due to random fluctuations or "noise" introduced by the system during transmission. So we see that the measure of transmitted information is simply a measure of the input-output correlation.

There are two simple rules to follow. Whenever I refer to "amount of information," you will understand "variance." And whenever I refer to "amount of transmitted information," you will understand "covariance" or "correlation."

The situation can be described graphically by two partially overlapping circles. Then the left circle can be taken to represent the variance of the input, the right circle the variance of the output, and the overlap the covariance of input and output. I shall speak of the left circle as the amount of input information, the right circle as the amount of output information, and the overlap as the amount of transmitted information.

In the experiments on absolute judgment, the observer is considered to be a communication channel. Then the left circle would represent the amount of information in the stimuli, the right circle the amount of information in his responses, and the overlap the stimulus-response correlation as measured by the amount of transmitted information. The experimental problem is to increase the amount of input information and to measure the amount of transmitted information. If the observer's absolute judgments are quite accurate, then nearly all of the input information will be transmitted and will be recoverable from his responses. If he makes errors, then the transmitted information may be considerably less than the input. We expect that, as we increase the amount of input information, the observer will begin to make more and more errors; we can test the limits of accuracy of his absolute judgments. If the human observer is a reasonable kind of communication system, then when we increase the amount of input information the transmitted information will increase at first and will eventually level off at some asymptotic value. This asymptotic value we take to be the *channel capacity* of the observer: it represents the greatest amount of information that he can give us about the stimulus on the basis of an absolute judgment. The channel capacity is the upper limit on the extent to which the observer can match his responses to the stimuli we give him.

Now just a brief word about the *bit* and we can begin to look at some data. One bit of information is the amount of information that we need to make a decision between two equally likely alternatives. If we must decide whether a man is less than six feet tall or more than six feet tall and if we know that the chances are 50–50, then we need one bit of information. Notice that this unit of information does not refer in any way to the unit of length that we use—feet, inches, centimeters, etc. However you measure the man's height, we still need just one bit of information.

Two bits of information enable us to decide among four equally likely alternatives. Three bits of information enable us to decide among eight equally likely alternatives. Four bits of information decide among 16 alternatives, five among 32, and so on. That is to say, if there are 32 equally likely alternatives, we must make five successive binary decisions, worth one bit each, before we know which alternative is correct. So the general rule is simple: every time the number of alternatives is increased by a factor of two, one bit of information is added.

There are two ways we might increase the amount of input information. We could increase the rate at which we give information to the observer, so that the amount of information per unit time would increase. Or we could ignore the time variable completely and increase the amount of input information by increasing the number of alternative stimuli. In the absolute judgment experiment we are interested in the second alternative. We give the observer as much time as he wants to make his response; we simply increase the number of alternative stimuli among which he must discriminate and look to see where confusions begin to occur. Confusions will appear near the point that we are calling his "channel capacity."

## ABSOLUTE JUDGMENTS OF UNIDIMENSIONAL STIMULI

Now let us consider what happens when we make absolute judgments of tones. Pollack (17) asked listeners to identify tones by assigning numerals to them. The tones were different with respect to frequency, and covered the range from 100 to 8000 cps in equal logarithmic steps. A tone was sounded and the listener responded by giving a numeral. After the listener had made his response he was told the correct identification of the tone.

When only two or three tones were used the listeners never confused them. With four different tones confusions were quite rare, but with five or more tones confusions were frequent. With fourteen different tones the listeners made many mistakes.

These data are plotted in Figure 1. Along the bottom is the amount of input information in bits per stimulus. As the number of alternative tones was increased from 2 to 14, the input information increased from 1 to 3.8 bits. On the ordinate is plotted the

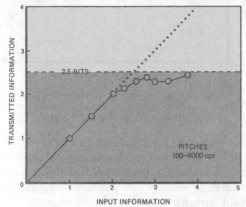

**Figure 1.** Data from Pollack (*17, 18*) on the amount of information that is transmitted by listeners who make absolute judgments of auditory pitch. As the amount of input information is increased by increasing from 2 to 14 the number of different pitches to be judged, the amount of transmitted information approaches as its upper limit a channel capacity of about 2.5 bits per judgment.

amount of transmitted information. The amount of transmitted information behaves in much the way we would expect a communication channel to behave; the transmitted information increases linearly up to about 2 bits and then bends off toward an asymptote at about 2.5 bits. This value, 2.5 bits, therefore, is what we are calling the channel capacity of the listener for absolute judgments of pitch.

So now we have the number 2.5 bits. What does it mean? First, note that 2.5 bits corresponds to about six equally likely alternatives. The result means that we cannot pick more than six different pitches that the listener will never confuse. Or, stated slightly differently, no matter how many alternative tones we ask him to judge, the

best we can expect him to do is to assign them to about six different classes without error. Or, again, if we know that there were $N$ alternative stimuli, then his judgment enables us to narrow down the particular stimulus to one out of $N/6$.

Most people are surprised that the number is as small as six. Of course, there is evidence that a musically sophisticated person with absolute pitch can identify accurately any one of 50 or 60 different pitches. Fortunately, I do not have time to discuss these remarkable exceptions. I say it is fortunate because I do not know how to explain their superior performance. So I shall stick to the more pedestrian fact that most of us can identify about one out of only five or six pitches before we begin to get confused.

It is interesting to consider that psychologists have been using seven-point rating scales for a long time, on the intuitive basis that trying to rate into finer categories does not really add much to the usefulness of the ratings. Pollack's results indicate that, at least for pitches, this intuition is fairly sound.

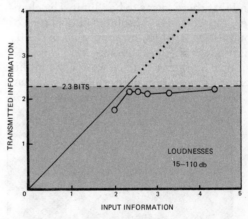

**Figure 2.** Data from Garner (7) on the channel capacity for absolute judgments of auditory loudness.

Next you can ask how reproducible this result is. Does it depend on the spacing of the tones or the various conditions of judgment? Pollack varied these conditions in a number of ways. The range of frequencies can be changed by a factor of about 20 without changing the amount of information transmitted more than a small percentage. Different groupings of the pitches decreased the transmission, but the loss was small. For example, if you can discriminate five high-pitched tones in one series and five low-pitched tones in another series, it is reasonable to expect that you could combine all ten into a single series and still tell them all apart without error. When you try it, however, it does not work. The channel capacity for pitch seems to be about six and that is the best you can do.

While we are on tones, let us look next at Garner's (7) work on loudness. Garner's data for loudness are summarized in Figure 2. Garner went to some trouble to get the best possible spacing of his tones over the intensity range from 15 to 110 db. He used 4, 5, 6, 7, 10, and 20 different stimulus intensities. The results shown in Figure 2 take into account the differences among subjects and the sequential influence of the immediately preceding judgment. Again we find that there seems to be a limit. The channel capacity for absolute judgments of loudness is 2.3 bits, or about five perfectly discriminable alternatives.

Since these two studies were done in different laboratories with slightly different

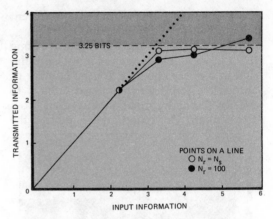

**Figure 4.** Data from Hake and Garner (8) on the channel capacity for absolute judgments of the position of a pointer in a linear interval.

techniques and methods of analysis, we are not in a good position to argue whether five loudnesses is significantly different from six pitches. Probably the difference is in the right direction, and absolute judgments of pitch are slightly more accurate than absolute judgments of loudness. The important point, however, is that the two answers are of the same order of magnitude.

The experiment has also been done for taste intensities. In Figure 3 are the results obtained by Beebe-Center, Rogers, and O'Connell (1) for absolute judgments of the concentration of salt solutions. The concentrations ranged from 0.3 to 34.7 gm. NaCl per 100 cc. tap water in equal subjective steps. They used 3, 5, 9, and 17 different concentrations. The channel capacity is 1.9 bits, which is about four distinct concentrations. Thus taste intensities seem a little less distinctive than auditory stimuli, but again the order of magnitude is not far off.

On the other hand, the channel capacity for judgments of visual position seems to be significantly larger. Hake and Garner (8) asked observers to interpolate visually between two scale markers. Their results are shown in Figure 4. They did the experiment in two ways. In one version they let the observer use any number between zero and 100 to describe the position, although they

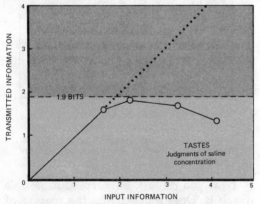

**Figure 3.** Data from Beebe-Center, Rogers, and O'Connell (1) on the channel capacity for absolute judgments of saltiness.

presented stimuli at only 5, 10, 20, or 50 different positions. The results with this un-limited response technique are shown by the filled circles on the graph. In the other version the observers were limited in their responses to reporting just those stimulus values that were possible. That is to say, in the second version the number of different responses that the observer could make was exactly the same as the number of different stimuli that the experimenter might present. The results with this limited response tech-nique are shown by the open circles on the graph. The two functions are so similar that it seems fair to conclude that the number of responses available to the observer had nothing to do with the channel capacity of 3.25 bits.

The Hake-Garner experiment has been repeated by Coonan and Klemmer. Al-though they have not yet published their results, they have given me permission to say that they obtained channel capacities ranging from 3.2 bits for very short ex-posures of the pointer position to 3.9 bits for longer exposures. These values are slightly higher than Hake and Garner's, so we must conclude that there are between 10 and 15 distinct positions along a linear interval. This is the largest channel capacity that has been measured for any unidimensional variable.

At the present time these four experi-ments on absolute judgments of simple, undimensional stimuli are all that have appeared in the psychological journals. However, a great deal of work on other stimulus variables has not yet appeared in the journals. For example, Eriksen and Hake (6) have found that the channel capacity for judging the sizes of squares is 2.2 bits, or about five categories, under a wide range of experimental conditions. In a separate experiment Eriksen (5) found 2.8 bits for size, 3.1 bits for hue, and 2.3 bits for brightness. Geldard has measured the channel capacity for the skin by placing vi-brators on the chest region. A good observer can identify about four intensities, about five durations, and about seven locations.

One of the most active groups in this area has been the Air Force Operational Applica-tions Laboratory. Pollack has been kind enough to furnish me with the results of their measurements for several aspects of visual displays. They made measurements for area and for the curvature, length, and direction of lines. In one set of experiments they used a very short exposure of the stim-ulus—1/40 second—and then they repeated the measurements with a 5-second expo-sure. For area they got 2.6 bits with the short exposure and 2.7 bits with the long exposure. For the length of a line they got about 2.6 bits with the short exposure and about 3.0 bits with the long exposure. Direc-tion, or angle of inclination, gave 2.8 bits for the short exposure and 3.3 bits for the long exposure. Curvature was apparently harder to judge. When the length of the arc was constant, the result at the short exposure duration was 2.2 bits, but when the length of the chord was constant, the result was only 1.6 bits. This last value is the lowest that anyone has measured to date. I should add, however, that these values are apt to be slightly too low because the data from all subjects were pooled before the transmitted information was computed.

Now let us see where we are. First, the channel capacity does seem to be a valid notion for describing human observers. Sec-ond, the channel capacities measured for these unidimensional variables range from 1.6 bits for curvature to 3.9 bits ror posi-tions in an interval. Although there is no question that the differences among the var-iables are real and meaningful, the more im-pressive fact to me is their considerable similarity. If I take the best estimates I can get of the channel capacities for all the stim-ulus variables I have mentioned, the mean is 2.6 bits and the standard deviation is only 0.6 bit. In terms of distinguishable alter-natives, this mean corresponds to about 6.5 categories, one standard deviation includes from 4 to 10 categories, and the total range is from 3 to 15 categories. Considering the wide variety of different variables that have been studied, I find this to be a remarkably narrow range.

There seems to be some limitation built into us either by learning or by the design of our nervous systems, a limit that keeps our channel capacities in this general range. On the basis of the present evidence it seems safe to say that we possess a finite and rather small capacity for making such unidimensional judgments and that this capacity does not vary a great deal from one simple sensory attribute to another.

## ABSOLUTE JUDGMENTS OF MULTIDIMENSIONAL STIMULI

You may have noticed that I have been careful to say that this magical number seven applies to one-dimensional judgments. Everyday experience teaches us that we can identify accurately any one of several hundred faces, any one of several thousand words, any one of several thousand objects, etc. The story certainly would not be complete if we stopped at this point. We must have some understanding of why the one-dimensional variables we judge in the laboratory give results so far out of line with what we do constantly in our behavior outside the laboratory. A possible explanation lies in the number of independently variable attributes of the stimuli that are being judged. Objects, faces, words, and the like differ from one another in many ways, whereas the simple stimuli we have considered thus far differ from one another in only one respect.

Fortunately, there are a few data on what happens when we make absolute judgments of stimuli that differ from one another in several ways. Let us look first at the results Klemmer and Frick (13) have reported for the absolute judgment of the position of a dot in a square. In Figure 5 we see their results. Now the channel capacity seems to have increased to 4.6 bits, which

means that people can identify accurately any one of 24 positions in the square.

The position of a dot in a square is clearly a two-dimensional proposition. Both its horizontal and its vertical position must be identified. Thus it seems natural to compare the 4.6-bit capacity for a square with the 3.25-bit capacity for the position of a point in an interval. The point in the square requires two judgments of the interval type. If we have a capacity of 3.25 bits for estimating intervals and we do this twice, we should get 6.5 bits as our capacity for locating points in a square. Adding the second independent dimension gives us an increase from 3.25 to 4.6, but it falls short of the perfect addition that would give 6.5 bits.

Another example is provided by Beebe-Center, Rogers, and O'Connell. When they asked people to identify both the saltiness and the sweetness of solutions containing various concentrations of salt and sucrose, they found that the channel capacity was 2.3 bits. Since the capacity for salt alone was 1.9, we might expect about 3.8 bits if the two aspects of the compound stimuli were judged independently. As with spatial locations, the second dimension adds a little to the capacity but not as much as it conceivably might.

A third example is provided by Pollack (18), who asked listeners to judge both the loudness and the pitch of pure tones. Since pitch gives 2.5 bits and loudness gives 2.3 bits, we might hope to get as much as 4.8 bits for pitch and loudness together. Pollack obtained 3.1 bits, which again indicates that the second dimension augments the channel capacity but not so much as it might.

A fourth example can be drawn from the work of Halsey and Chapanis (9) on confusions among colors of equal luminance. Although they did not analyze their results in informational terms, they estimate that there are about 11 to 15 identifiable colors, or, in our terms, about 3.6 bits. Since these colors varied in both hue and saturation, it is probably correct to regard this as a two-dimensional judgment. If we compare this with Eriksen's 3.1 bits for hue (which is a questionable comparison to draw), we again have something less than perfect addition when a second dimension is added.

It is still a long way, however, from these two-dimensional examples to the multidimensional stimuli provided by faces, words, etc. To fill this gap we have only one experiment, an auditory study done by Pollack and Ficks (*19*). They managed to get six different acoustic variables that they could change: frequency, intensity, rate of interruption, on-time fraction, total duration, and spatial location. Each one of these six variables could assume any one of five different values, so altogether there were $5^6$, or 15,625 different tones that they could present. The listeners made a separate rating for each one of these six dimensions. Under these conditions the transmitted information was 7.2 bits, which corresponds to about 150 different categories that could be absolutely identified without error. Now we are beginning to get up into the range that ordinary experience would lead us to expect.

Suppose that we plot these data, fragmentary as they are, and make a guess about how the channel capacity changes with the dimensionality of the stimuli. The result is given in Figure 6. In a moment of

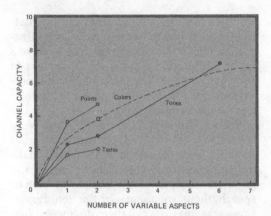

**Figure 6.** The general form of the relation between channel capacity and the number of independently variable attributes of the stimuli.

considerable daring I sketched the dotted line to indicate roughly the trend that the data seemed to be taking.

Clearly, the addition of independently variable attributes to the stimulus increases the channel capacity, but at a decreasing rate. It is interesting to note that the channel capacity is increased even when the several variables are not independent. Eriksen (*5*) reports that, when size, brightness, and hue all vary together in perfect correlation, the transmitted information is 4.1 bits as compared with an average of about 2.7 bits when these attributes are varied one at a time. By confounding three attributes, Eriksen increased the dimensionality of the input without increasing the amount of input information; the result was an increase in channel capacity of about the amount that the dotted function in Figure 6 would lead us to expect.

The point seems to be that, as we add more variables to the display, we increase the total capacity, but we decrease the accuracy for any particular variable. In other words, we can make relatively crude judgments of several things simultaneously.

We might argue that in the course of evolution those organisms were most successful that were responsive to the widest range of stimulus energies in their environment.

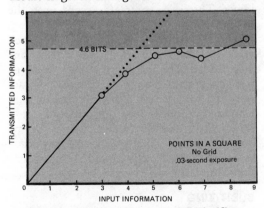

**Figure 5.** Data from Klemmer and Frick (*13*) on the channel capacity for absolute judgments of the position of a dot in a square.

In order to survive in a constantly fluctuating world, it was better to have a little information about a lot of things than to have a lot of information about a small segment of the environment. If a compromise was necessary, the one we seem to have made is clearly the more adaptive.

Pollack and Ficks's results are very strongly suggestive of an argument that linguists and phoneticians have been making for some time (11). [According to the linguistic analysis of the sounds of human speech, there are about eight or ten dimensions—the linguists call them *distinctive features*—that distinguish one phoneme from another.] These distinctive features are usually binary, or at most ternary, in nature. For example, a binary distinction is made between vowels and consonants, a binary decision is made between oral and nasal consonants, a ternary decision is made among front, middle, and back phonemes, etc. This approach gives us quite a different picture of speech perception than we might otherwise obtain from our studies of the speech spectrum and of the ear's ability to discriminate relative differences among pure tones. I am personally much interested in this new approach (15), and I regret that there is not time to discuss it here.

It was probably with this linguistic theory in mind that Pollack and Ficks conducted a test on a set of tonal stimuli that varied in eight dimensions, but required only a binary decision on each dimension. With these tones they measured the transmitted information at 6.9 bits, or about 120 recognizable kinds of sounds. It is an intriguing question, as yet unexplored, whether one can go on adding dimensions indefinitely in this way.

In human speech there is clearly a limit to the number of dimensions that we use. In this instance, however, it is not known whether the limit is imposed by the nature of the perceptual machinery that must recognize the sounds or by the nature of the speech machinery that must produce them. Somebody will have to do the experiment to find out. There is a limit, however, at about eight or nine distinctive features in every language that has been studied, and so when we talk we must resort to still another trick for increasing our channel capacity. Language uses sequences of phonemes, so we make several judgments successively when we listen to words and sentences. That is to say, we use both simultaneous and successive discriminations in order to expand the rather rigid limits imposed by the inaccuracy of our absolute judgments of simple magnitudes.

These multidimensional judgments are strongly reminiscent of the abstraction experiment of Külpe (14). As you may remember, Külpe showed that observers report more accurately on an attribute for which they are set than on attributes for which they are not set. For example, Chapman (4) used three different attributes and compared the results obtained when the observers were instructed before the tachistoscopic presentation with the results obtained when they were not told until after the presentation which one of the three attributes was to be reported. When the instruction was given in advance, the judgments were more accurate. When the instruction was given afterwards, the subjects presumably had to judge all three attributes in order to report on any one of them and the accuracy was correspondingly lower. This is in complete accord with the results we have just been considering, where the accuracy of judgment on each attribute decreased as more dimensions were added. The point is probably obvious, but I shall make it anyhow, that the abstraction experiments did *not* demonstrate that people can judge only one attribute at a time. They merely showed what seems quite reasonable, that people are less accurate if they must judge more than one attribute simultaneously.

## SUBITIZING

I cannot leave this general area without mentioning, however briefly, the experiments conducted at Mount Holyoke College on the discrimination of number (12). In experiments by Kaufman, Lord, Reese, and Volkmann random patterns of dots were flashed on a screen for ⅕ of a second. Anywhere from 1 to more than 200 dots could appear in the pattern. The subject's task was to report how many dots there were.

The first point to note is that on patterns containing up to five or six dots the subjects simply did not make errors. The performance on these small numbers of dots was so different from the performance with more dots that it was given a special name. Below seven the subjects were said to *subitize;* above seven they were said to *estimate.* This is, as you will recognize, what we once optimistically called "the span of attention."

This discontinuity at seven is, of course, suggestive. Is this the same basic process that limits our unidimensional judgments to about seven categories? The generalization is tempting, but not sound in my opinion. The data on number estimates have not been analyzed in informational terms; but on the basis of the published data I would guess that the subjects transmitted something more than four bits of information about the number of dots. Using the same arguments as before, we would conclude that there are about 20 or 30 distinguishable categories of numerousness. This is considerably more information than we would expect to get from a unidimensional display. It is, as a matter of fact, very much like a two-dimensional display. Although the dimensionality of the random dot patterns is not entirely clear, these results are in the same range as Klemmer and Frick's for their two-dimensional display of dots in a square. Perhaps the two dimensions of numerousness are area and density. When the subject can subitize, area and density may not be the significant variables, but when the subject must estimate perhaps they are significant. In any event, the comparison is not so simple as it might seem at first thought.

This is one of the ways in which the magical number seven has persecuted me. Here we have two closely related kinds of experiments, both of which point to the significance of the number seven as a limit on our capacities. And yet when we examine the matter more closely, there seems to be a reasonable suspicion that it is nothing more than a coincidence.

## THE SPAN OF IMMEDIATE MEMORY

Let me summarize the situation in this way. There is a clear and definite limit to the accuracy with which we can identify absolutely the magnitude of a unidimensional stimulus variable. I would propose to call this limit the *span of absolute judgment,* and I maintain that for unidimensional judgments this span is usually somewhere in the neighborhood of seven. We are not completely at the mercy of this limited span, however, because we have a variety of techniques for getting around it and increasing the accuracy of our judgments. The three most important of these devices are (*a*) to make relative rather than absolute judgments; or, if that is not possible, (*b*) to increase the number of dimensions along which the stimuli can differ; or (*c*) to arrange the task in such a way that we make a sequence of several absolute judgments in a row.

The study of relative judgments is one of the oldest topics in experimental psychology, and I will not pause to review it now. The second device, increasing the dimensionality, we have just considered. It seems that by adding more dimensions and requiring crude, binary, yes-no judgments on each attribute we can extend the span of absolute judgment from seven to at least 150. Judging from our everyday behavior, the limit is probably in the thousands, if indeed there is a limit. In my opinion, we cannot go on compounding dimensions indefinitely. I suspect that there is also a *span of perceptual dimensionality* and that this span is somewhere in the neighborhood of ten, but I must add at once that there is no objective evidence to support this suspicion. This is a question sadly needing experimental exploration.

Concerning the third device, the use of successive judgments, I have quite a bit to say because this device introduces memory as the handmaiden of discrimination. And, since mnemonic processes are at least as complex as are perceptual processes, we can anticipate that their interactions will not be easily disentangled.

Suppose that we start by simply extending slightly the experimental procedure that we have been using. Up to this point we have presented a single stimulus and asked the observer to name it immediately thereafter. We can extend this procedure by requiring the observer to withhold his response until we have given him several stimuli in succession. At the end of the sequence of stimuli he then makes his response. We still have the same sort of input-output situation that is required for the measurement of transmitted information. But now we have passed from an experiment on absolute judgment to what is traditionally called an experiment on immediate memory.

Before we look at any data on this topic I feel I must give you a word of warning to help you avoid some obvious associations that can be confusing. Everybody knows that there is a finite span of immediate memory and that for a lot of different kinds of test materials this span is about seven items in length. I have just shown you that there is a span of absolute judgment that can distinguish about seven categories and that there is a span of attention that will encompass about six objects at a glance. What is more natural than to think that all three of these spans are different aspects of a single underlying process? And that is a fundamental mistake, as I shall be at some pains to demonstrate. This mistake is one of the malicious persecutions that the magical number seven has subjected me to.

My mistake went something like this. We have seen that the invariant feature in the span of absolute judgment is the amount of information that the observer can transmit.

There is a real operational similarity between the absolute judgment experiment and the immediate memory experiment. If immediate memory is like absolute judgment, then it should follow that the invariant feature in the span of immediate memory is also the amount of information that an observer can retain. If the amount of information in the span of immediate memory is a constant, then the span should be short when the individual items contain a lot of information and the span should be long when the items contain little information. For example, decimal digits are worth 3.3 bits apiece. We can recall about seven of them, for a total of 23 bits of information. Isolated English words are worth about 10 bits apiece. If the total amount of information is to remain constant at 23 bits, then we should be able to remember only two or three words chosen at random. In this way I generated a theory about how the span of immediate memory should vary as a function of the amount of information per item in the test materials.

The measurements of memory span in the literature are suggestive on this question, but not definitive. And so it was necessary to do the experiment to see. Hayes (10) tried it out with five different kinds of test ma-

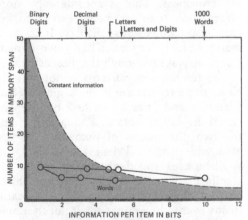

**Figure 7.** Data from Hayes (10) on the span of immediate memory plotted as a function of the amount of information per item in the test materials.

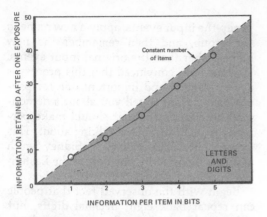

**Figure 8.** Data from Pollack (*16*) on the amount of information retained after one presentation plotted as a function of the amount of information per item in the test materials.

terials: binary digits, decimal digits, letters of the alphabet, letters plus decimal digits, and with 1,000 monosyllabic words. The lists were read aloud at the rate of one item per second and the subjects had as much time as they needed to give their responses. A procedure described by Woodworth (*20*) was used to score the responses.

The results are shown by the filled circles in Figure 7. Here the dotted line indicates what the span should have been if the amount of information in the span were constant. The solid curves represent the data. Hayes repeated the experiment using test vocabularies of different sizes but all containing only English monosyllables (open circles in Figure 7). This more homogeneous test material did not change the picture significantly. With binary items the span is about nine and, although it drops to about five with monosyllabic English words, the difference is far less than the hypothesis of constant information would require.

There is nothing wrong with Hayes's experiment, because Pollack (*16*) repeated it much more elaborately and got essentially the same result. Pollack took pains to measure the amount of information transmitted and did not rely on the traditional procedure for scoring the responses. His results

are plotted in Figure 8. Here it is clear that the amount of information transmitted is not a constant, but increases almost linearly as the amount of information per item in the input is increased.

And so the outcome is perfectly clear. In spite of the coincidence that the magical number seven appears in both places, the span of absolute judgment and the span of immediate memory are quite different kinds of limitations that are imposed on our ability to process information. Absolute judgment is limited by the amount of information. Immediate memory is limited by the number of items. In order to capture this distinction in somewhat picturesque terms, I have fallen into the custom of distinguishing between *bits* of information and *chunks* of information. Then I can say that the number of bits of information is constant for absolute judgment and the number of chunks of information is constant for immediate memory. The span of immediate memory seems to be almost independent of the number of bits per chunk, at least over the range that has been examined to date.

The contrast of the terms *bit* and *chunk* also serves to highlight the fact that we are not very definite about what constitutes a chunk of information. For example, the memory span of five words that Hayes obtained when each word was drawn at random from a set of 1000 English monosyllables might just as appropriately have been called a memory span of 15 phonemes, since each word had about three phonemes in it. Intuitively, it is clear that the subjects were recalling five words, not 15 phonemes, but the logical distinction is not immediately apparent. We are dealing here with a process of organizing or grouping the input into familiar units or chunks, and a great deal of learning has gone into the formation of these familiar units.

## RECODING

In order to speak more precisely, therefore, we must recognize the importance of grouping or organizing the input sequence into units or chunks. Since the memory span is a fixed number of chunks, we can increase the number of bits of information that it contains simply by building larger and larger chunks, each chunk containing more information than before.

A man just beginning to learn radiotelegraphic code hears each *dit* and *dah* as a separate chunk. Soon he is able to organize these sounds into letters and then he can deal with the letters as chunks. Then the letters organize themselves as words, which are still larger chunks, and he begins to hear whole phrases. I do not mean that each step is a discrete process, or that plateaus must appear in his learning curve, for surely the levels of organization are achieved at different rates and overlap each other during the learning process. I am simply pointing to the obvious fact that the dits and dahs are organized by learning into patterns and that as these larger chunks emerge the amount of message that the operator can remember increases correspondingly. In the terms I am proposing to use, the operator learns to increase the bits per chunk.

In the jargon of communication theory, this process would be called *recoding*. The input is given in a code that contains many chunks with few bits per chunk. The operator recodes the input into another code that contains fewer chunks with more bits per chunk. There are many ways to do this recoding, but probably the simplest is to group the input events, apply a new name to the group, and then remember the new name rather than the original input events.

Since I am convinced that this process is a very general and important one for psychology, I want to tell you about a demonstration experiment that should make perfectly explicit what I am talking about. This experiment was conducted by Sidney Smith and was reported by him before the Eastern Psychological Association in 1954.

Begin with the observed fact that people can repeat back eight decimal digits, but only nine binary digits. Since there is a large discrepancy in the amount of information recalled in these two cases, we suspect at once that a recoding procedure could be used to increase the span of immediate memory for binary digits. In Table 1 a method for grouping and renaming is illustrated. Along the top is a sequence of 18 binary digits, far more than any subject was able to recall after a single presentation. In the next line these same binary digits are grouped by pairs. Four possible pairs can occur: 00 is renamed 0, 01 is renamed 1, 10 is renamed 2, and 11 is renamed 3. That is to say, we recode from a base-two arithmetic to a base-four arithmetic. In the recorded sequence there are now just nine digits to remember, and this is almost within the span of immediate memory. In the next line the same sequence of binary digits is regrouped into chunks of three. There are eight possible sequences of three, so we give each sequence

**Table 1**

WAYS OF RECODING SEQUENCES OF BINARY DIGITS

| Binary Digits (Bits) | 1 0 | 1 0 | 0 0 | 1 0 | 0 1 | 1 1 | 0 0 | 1 1 | 1 0 |
|---|---|---|---|---|---|---|---|---|---|
| 2:1  Chunks | 10 | 10 | 00 | 10 | 01 | 11 | 00 | 11 | 10 |
|       Recoding | 2 | 2 | 0 | 2 | 1 | 3 | 0 | 3 | 2 |
| 3:1  Chunks | 101 | 000 | | 100 | | 111 | | 001 | 110 |
|       Recoding | 5 | 0 | | 4 | | 7 | | 1 | 6 |
| 4:1  Chunks | 1010 | | 0010 | | 0111 | | 0011 | | 10 |
|       Recoding | 10 | | 2 | | 7 | | 3 | | |
| 5:1  Chunks | 10100 | | 01001 | | 11001 | | 110 | | |
|       Recoding | 20 | | 9 | | 25 | | | | |

a new name between 0 and 7. Now we have recoded from a sequence of 18 binary digits into a sequence of 6 octal digits, and this is well within the span of immediate memory. In the last two lines the binary digits are grouped by fours and by fives and are given decimal-digit names from 0 to 15 and from 0 to 31.

It is reasonably obvious that this kind of recoding increases the bits per chunk, and packages the binary sequence into a form that can be retained within the span of immediate memory. So Smith assembled 20 subjects and measured their spans for binary and octal digits. The spans were 9 for binaries and 7 for octals. Then he gave each recoding scheme to five of the subjects. They studied the recoding until they said they understood it—for about 5 or 10 minutes. Then he tested their span for binary digits again while they tried to use the recoding schemes they had studied.

The recoding schemes increased their span for binary digits in every case. But the increase was not as large as we had expected on the basis of their span for octal digits. Since the discrepancy increased as the recoding ratio increased, we reasoned that the few minutes the subjects had spent learning the recoding schemes had not been sufficient. Apparently the translation from one code to the other must be almost automatic or the subject will lose part of the next group while he is trying to remember the translation of the last group.

Since the 4:1 and 5:1 ratios require considerable study, Smith decided to imitate Ebbinghaus and do the experiment on himself. With Germanic patience he drilled himself on each recoding successively, and obtained the results shown in Figure 9. Here the data follow along rather nicely with the results you would predict on the basis of his span for octal digits. He could remember 12 octal digits. With the 2:1 recoding, these 12 chunks were worth 24 binary digits. With the 3:1 recoding they were worth 36 binary digits. With the 4:1 and 5:1 recod-

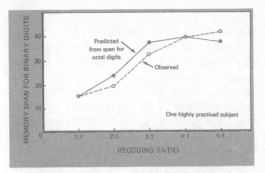

**Figure 9.** The span of immediate memory for binary digits is plotted as a function of the recoding procedure used. The predicted function is obtained by multiplying the span for octals by 2, 3 and 3.3 for recoding into base 4, base 8, and base 10, respectively.

ings, they were worth about 40 binary digits.

It is a little dramatic to watch a person get 40 binary digits in a row and then repeat them back without error. However, if you think of this merely as a mnemonic trick for extending the memory span, you will miss the more important point that is implicit in nearly all such mnemonic devices. The point is that recoding is an extremely powerful weapon for increasing the amount of information that we can deal with. In one form or another we use recoding constantly in our daily behavior.

In my opinion the most customary kind of recoding that we do all the time is to translate into a verbal code. When there is a story or an argument or an idea that we want to remember, we usually try to rephrase it "in our own words." When we witness some event we want to remember, we make a verbal description of the event and then remember our verbalization. Upon recall we recreate by secondary elaboration the details that seem consistent with the particular verbal recoding we happen to have made. The well-known experiment by Carmichael, Hogan, and Walter (3) on the influence that names have on the recall of visual figures is one demonstration of the process.

The inaccuracy of the testimony of eye-witnesses is well known in legal psychology, but the distortions of testimony are not random—they follow naturally from the particular recoding that the witness used, and the particular recoding he used depends upon his whole life history. Our language is tremendously useful for repackaging material into a few chunks rich in information. I suspect that imagery is a form of recoding, too, but images seem much harder to get at operationally and to study experimentally than the more symbolic kinds of recoding.

It seems probable that even memorization can be studied in these terms. The process of memorizing may be simply the formation of chunks, or groups of items that go together, until there are few enough chunks so that we can recall all the items. The work by Bousfield and Cohen (2) on the occurrence of clustering in the recall of words is especially interesting in this respect.

## SUMMARY

I have come to the end of the data that I wanted to present, so I would like now to make some summarizing remarks.

First, the span of absolute judgment and the span of immediate memory impose severe limitations on the amount of information that we are able to receive, process, and remember. By organizing the stimulus input simultaneously into several dimensions and successively into a sequence of chunks, we manage to break (or at least stretch) this informational bottleneck.

Second, the process of recoding is a very important one in human psychology and deserves much more explicit attention than it has received. In particular, the kind of linguistic recoding that people do seems to me to be the very lifeblood of the thought processes. Recoding procedures are a constant concern to clinicians, social psychologists, linguists, and anthropologists and yet, probably because recoding is less accessible to experimental manipulation than nonsense syllables or T mazes, the traditional experimental psychologist has contributed little or nothing to their analysis. Nevertheless, experimental techniques can be used, methods of recoding can be specified, behavioral indicants can be found. And I anticipate that we will find a very orderly set of relations describing what now seems an uncharted wilderness of individual differences.

Third, the concepts and measures provided by the theory of information provide a quantitative way of getting at some of these questions. The theory provides us with a yardstick for calibrating our stimulus materials and for measuring the performance of our subjects. In the interests of communciation I have suppressed the technical details of information measurement and have tried to express the ideas in more familiar terms; I hope this paraphrase will not lead you to think they are not useful in research. Informational concepts have already proved valuable in the study of discrimination and of language; they promise a great deal in the study of learning and memory; and it has even been proposed that they can be useful in the study of concept formation. A lot of questions that seemed fruitless twenty or thirty years ago may now be worth another look. In fact, I feel that my story here must stop just as it begins to get really interesting.

And finally, what about the magical number seven? What about the seven wonders of the world, the seven seas, the seven deadly sins, the seven daughters of Atlas in the Pleiades, the seven ages of man, the seven levels of hell, the seven primary colors, the seven notes of the musical scale, and the seven days of the week? What about the seven-point rating scale, the seven categories for absolute judgment, the seven objects in the span of attention, and the seven digits in the span of immediate memory? For the present I propose to withhold judgment. Perhaps there is something deep and profound behind all these sevens, something just calling out for us to discover it. But I suspect that it is only a pernicious, Pythagorean coincidence.

## REFERENCES

1. Beebe-Center, J. G.; Rogers, M. S.; and O'Connell, D. N. 1955. Transmission of information about sucrose and saline solutions through the sense of taste. *Journal of Psychology* 39:157–160.

2. Bousfield, W. A., and Cohen, B. H. 1955. The occurrence of clustering in the recall of randomly arranged words of different frequencies-of-usage. *Journal of General Psychology* 52:83–95.

3. Carmichael, L.; Hogan, H. P.; and Walter, A. A. 1932. An experimental study of the effect of language on the reproduction of visually perceived form. *Journal of Experimental Psychology* 15:73–86.

4. Chapman, D. W. 1932. Relative effects of determinate and indeterminate *Aufgaben*. *American Journal of Psychology* 44:163–174.

5. Eriksen, C. W. 1954. Multidimensional stimulus differences and accuracy of discrimination. *USAF, WADC Technical Report*, no. 54–165.

6. Eriksen, C. W., and Hake, H. W. 1955. Absolute judgments as a function of the stimulus range and the number of stimulus and response categories. *Journal of Experimental Psychology* 49:323–332.

7. Garner, W. R. 1953. An informational analysis of absolute judgments of loudness. *Journal of Experimental Psychology* 46:373–380.

8. Hake, H. W., and Garner, W. R. 1951. The effect of presenting various numbers of discrete steps on scale reading accuracy. *Journal of Experimental Psychology* 42:358–366.

9. Halsey, R. M., and Chapanis, A. 1954. Chromaticity-confusion contours in a complex viewing situation. *Journal of the Optical Society of America* 44:442–454.

10. Hayes, J. R. M. 1952. Memory span for several vocabularies as a function of vocabulary size. In *Quarterly Progress Report*, Acoustics Laboratory, Massachusetts Institute of Technology, Jan.–June.

11. Jakobson, R.; Fant, C. G. M.; and Halle, M. 1952. *Preliminaries to speech analysis*. Cambridge, Mass.: Acoustics Laboratory, Massachusetts Institute of Technology. Technical Report no. 13.

12. Kaufman, E. L.; Lord, M. W.; Reese, T. W.; and Volkmann, J. 1949. The discrimination of visual number. *American Journal of Psychology* 62:498–525.

13. Klemmer, E. T., and Frick, F. C. 1953. Assimilation of information from dot and matrix patterns. *Journal of Experimental Psychology* 45:15–19.

14. Külpe, O. 1904. Versuche über Abstraktion. *Bericht über das Internationale Kongress für Experimentalle Psychologie* 56–68.

15. Miller, G. A., and Nicely, P. E. 1955. An analysis of perceptual confusions among some English consonants. *Journal of the Acoustical Society of America* 27:338–352.

16. Pollack, I. 1953. The assimilation of sequentially encoded information. *American Journal of Psychology* 66:421–435.

17. Pollack, I. 1952. The information of elementary auditory displays. *Journal of the Acoustical Society of America* 24:745–749.

18. Pollack, I. 1953. The information of elementary auditory displays. II. *Journal of the Acoustical Society of America* 25:765–769.

19. Pollack, I., and Ficks, L. 1954. Information of elementary multi-dimensional auditory displays. *Journal of the Acoustical Society of America* 26:155–158.

20. Woodworth, R. S. 1938. *Experimental psychology*. New York: Holt.

# READING 22

# Interference and Forgetting

**BENTON J. UNDERWOOD**
**Northwestern University**

Psychologists have been trying to solve the problem of forgetting for many years. Some have suggested that a person forgets a name or item because a (hypothetical) memory trace decays over time. Others have suggested that forgetting occurs because of interference either from items already learned or from items which will be learned at a later time. Another group of psychologists suggests that a combination of both of these concepts occurs at the same time.

Underwood discusses the relative merits of the concepts of proactive interference and retroactive interference. After concluding that proactive interference is a major cause of forgetting, Underwood analyzes some of the variables that affect forgetting.

## QUESTIONS

1. Underwood states: "Science does not deal at will with all natural events. Science deals with natural events only when ingenuity in developing methods and techniques of measurement allows these events to be brought within the scope of science." Discuss this statement.

2. If proactive interference accounts for most forgetting, is it reasonable to assume that more and more forgetting must occur as a person continues his education? What is the implication for techniques like rote learning?

3. Underwood lists several variables that influence forgetting. Which variables do you think are most important? Why?

I know of no one who seriously maintains that interference among tasks is of no con-

Address of the president, Midwestern Psychological Association, St. Louis, Missouri, May, 1956.

Most of the data from my own research referred to in this paper were obtained from work done under Contract N7 onr-45008, Project NR 154-057, between Northwestern University and The Office of Naval Research.

sequence in the production of forgetting. Whether forgetting is conceptualized at a strict psychological level or at a neural level (e.g., neural memory trace), some provision is made for interference to account for at least some of the measured forgetting. The many studies on retroactive inhibition are probably responsible for this general agreement that interference among tasks must produce a sizable proportion of forgetting. By introducing an interpolated interfering task very marked decrements in recall can be produced in a few minutes in the laboratory. But there is a second generalization which has resulted from these studies, namely, that most forgetting must be a function of the learning of tasks which interfere with that which has already been learned (19). Thus, if a single task is learned in the laboratory and retention measured after a week, the loss has been attributed to the interference from activities learned outside the laboratory during the week. It is this generalization with which I am concerned in the initial portions of this paper.

Now, I cannot deny the data which show large amounts of forgetting produced by an interpolated list in a few minutes in the laboratory. Nor do I deny that this loss may be attributed to interference. But I will try to show that use of retroactive inhibition as a paradigm of forgetting (via interference) may be seriously questioned. To be more specific: if a subject learns a single task, such as a list of words, and retention of this task is measured after a day, a week, or a month, I will try to show that very little of the forgetting can be attributed to an interfering task learned outside the laboratory during the retention interval. Before pursuing this further, I must make some general comments by way of preparation.

Whether we like it or not, the experimental study of forgetting has been largely dominated by the Ebbinghaus tradition, both in terms of methods and materials used. I do not think this is due to sheer perversity on the part of several generations of scientists interested in forgetting. It may be noted that much of our elementary knowledge can be obtained only by rote learning. To work with rote learning does not mean that we are thereby not concerning ourselves with phenomena that have no counterparts outside the laboratory. Furthermore, the investigation of these phenomena can be handled by methods which are acceptable to a science. As is well known, there are periodic verbal revolts against the Ebbinghaus tradition (e.g., 2, 15, 22). But for some reason nothing much even happens in the laboratory as a consequence of these revolts. I mention these matters neither by way of apology nor of justification for having done some research in rote learning, but for two other reasons. First, it may very well be true, as some have suggested (e.g., 22), that studies of memory in the Ebbinghaus tradition are not getting at all of the important phenomena of memory. I think the same statement—that research has not got at all of the important processes—could be made about all areas in psychology; so that the criticism (even if just) should not be indigenous to the study of memory. Science does not deal at will with all natural events. Science deals with natural events only when ingenuity in developing methods and techniques of measurement allow these events to be brought within the scope of science. If, therefore, the studies of memory which meet scientific acceptability do not tap all-important memorial processes, all I can say is that this is the state of the science in the area at the moment. Secondly, because the bulk of the systematic data on forgetting has been obtained on rote-learned tasks, I must of necessity use such data in discussing interference and forgetting.

Returning to the experimental situation, let me again put in concrete form the problem with which I first wish to deal. A subject learns a single task, such as a list of syllables, nouns, or adjectives. After an interval of time, say, 24 hours, his retention of this list is measured. The explanatory problem is what is responsible for the forgetting which commonly occurs over the 24 hours. As indicated earlier, the studies of retroactive inhibition led to the theoretical generalization that this forgetting was due largely to interference from other tasks learned during the 24-hour retention interval. McGeoch (20) came to this conclusion, his last such statement being made in 1942. I would, therefore, like to look at the data which were available to McGeoch and others interested in this matter. I must repeat that the kind of data with which I am concerned is the retention of a list without formal interpolated learning introduced. The interval of retention with which I am going to deal in this, and several subsequent analyses, is 24 hours.

First, of course, Ebbinghaus' data were available and in a sense served as the reference point for many subsequent investigations. In terms of percentage saved in relearning, Ebbinghaus showed about 65 per cent loss over 24 hours (7). In terms of recall after 24 hours, the following studies are representative of the amount forgotten: Youtz, 88 per cent loss (37); Luh, 82 per cent (18); Krueger, 74 per cent (16); Hovland, 78 per cent (11); Cheng, 65 per cent and 84 per cent (6); Lester, 65 per cent (17). Let us assume as a rough average of these studies that 75 per cent forgetting was measured over 24 hours. In all of these studies the list was learned to one perfect trial. The percentage values were derived by dividing the total number of items in the list into the number lost and changing to a percentage. Thus, on the average in these studies, if the subject learned a 12-item list and recalled three of these items after 24 hours, nine items (75 per cent) were forgotten.

The theory of interference as advanced by McGeoch, and so far as I know never seriously challenged, was that during the 24-hour interval subjects learned something outside the laboratory which interfered with the list learned in the laboratory. Most of the materials involved in the investigations cited above were nonsense syllables, and the subjects were college students. While realizing that I am viewing these results in the light of data which McGeoch and others did not have available, it seems to me to be an incredible stretch of an interference hypothesis to hold that this 75 per cent forgetting was caused by something which the subjects learned outside the laboratory during the 24-hour interval. Even if we agree with some educators that much of what we teach our students in college is nonsense, it does not suffice to be the kind of learning that would interfere with nonsense syllables.

If, however, this forgetting was not due to interference from tasks learned outside the laboratory during the retention interval, to what was it due? I shall try to show that most of this forgetting was indeed produced by interference—not from tasks learned outside the laboratory, but from tasks learned previously in the laboratory. Following this I will show that when interference from laboratory tasks is removed, the amount of forgetting which occurs is relatively quite small. It then becomes more plausible that this amount could be produced by interference from tasks learned outside the laboratory, although, as I shall also point out, the interference very likely comes from prior, not interpolated, learning.

In 1950 a study was published by Mrs. Greenberg and myself (10) on retention as a function of stage of practice. The orientation for this study was crassly empirical; we simply wanted to know if subjects learn how to recall in the same sense that they learn how to learn. In the conditions with which I am concerned, naive subjects learned a list of ten paired adjectives to a criterion of eight out of ten correct on a single trial. Forty-eight hours later this list was recalled. On the following day, these same subjects learned a new list to the same criterion and recalled it after 48 hours. This continued for two additional lists, so that the subjects had learned and recalled four lists, but the learning and recall of each list was complete before another list was learned. There was low similarity among these lists as far as conventional symptoms of similarity are concerned. No

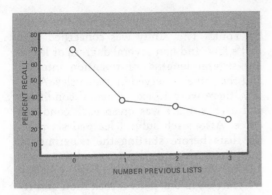

**Figure 1.** Recall of paired adjectives as a function of number of previous lists learned (10).

words were repeated and no obvious similarities existed, except for the fact that they were all adjectives and a certain amount of similarity among prefixes, suffixes, and so on must inevitably occur. The recall of these four successive lists is shown in Figure 1.

As can be seen, the more lists that are learned, the poorer the recall, from **69 per** cent recall of the first list to 25 per cent recall of the fourth list. In examining errors at recall, we found a sufficient number of intrusion responses from previous lists to lead us to suggest that the increasing decrements in recall were a function of proactive interference from previous lists. And, while we pointed out that these results had implications for the design of experiments on retention, the relevance to an interference theory of forgetting was not mentioned.

Dr. E. J. Archer has made available to me certain data from an experiment which still is in progress and which deals with this issue. Subjects learned lists of 12 serial adjectives to one perfect trial and recalled them after 24 hours. The recall of a list always took place prior to learning the next list. The results for nine successive lists are shown in Figure 2. Let me say again that there is no laboratory activity during the 24-hour interval; the subject learns a list, is dismissed from the laboratory, and returns after 24 hours to recall the list. The percent-

age of recall falls from 71 per cent for the first list to 27 per cent for the ninth.

In summarizing the more classical data on retention above, I indicated that a rough estimate showed that after 24 hours 75 per cent forgetting took place, or recall was about 25 per cent correct. In viewing these values in the light of Greenberg's and Archer's findings, the conclusion seemed inescapable that the classical studies must have been dealing with subjects who had learned many lists. That is to say, the subjects must have served in many conditions by use of counterbalancing and repeated cycles. To check on this I have made a search of the literature on the studies of retention to see if systematic data could be compiled on this matter. Preliminary work led me to establish certain criteria for inclusion in the summary to be presented. First, because degree of learning is such an important variable, I have included only those studies in which degree of learning was one perfect recitation of the list. Second, I have included only studies in which retention was measured after 24 hours. Third, I have included only studies in which recall measures were given. (Relearning measures add complexities with which I do not wish to deal in this paper.) Fourth, the summary includes only material learned by relatively massed practice. Finally, if an

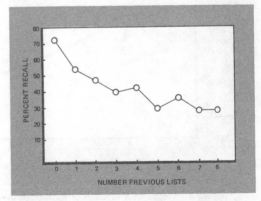

**Figure 2.** Recall of serial adjective lists as a function of number of previous lists learned. Unpublished data, courtesy of Dr. E. J. Archer.

investigator had two or more conditions which met these criteria, I averaged the values presentation in this paper. Except for these restrictions, I have used all studies I found (with an exception to be noted later), although I do not pretend to have made an exhaustive search. From each of these studies I got two facts: first, the percentage recalled after 24 hours, and second, the average number of previous lists the subjects had learned before learning the list on which recall after 24 hours was taken. Thus, if a subject had served in five experimental conditions via counterbalancing, and had been given two practice lists, the average number of lists learned before learning the list for which I tabulated the recall was four. This does not take into account any previous experiments in rote learning in which the subject might have served.

For each of these studies the two facts, average number of previous lists learned and percentage of recall, are related as in Figure 3. For example, consider the study by Youtz. This study was concerned with Jost's law, and had several degrees of learning, several lengths of retention interval, and the subjects served in two cycles. Actually, there were 15 experimental conditions and each subject was given each condition twice. Also, each subject learned six practice lists before starting the experimental conditions. Among the 15 conditions was one in which the learning of the syllables was carried to one perfect recitation and recall was taken after 24 hours. It is this particular condition in which I am interested. On the average, this condition would have been given at the time when the subject had learned six practice lists and 15 experimental lists, for a total of 21 previous lists.

The studies included in Figure 3 have several different kinds of materials, from geometric forms to nonsense syllables to nouns; they include both paired-associate and serial presentation, with different

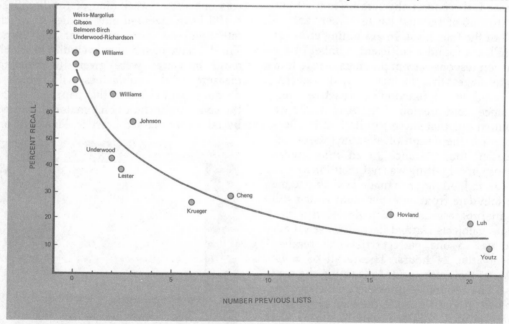

**Figure 3.** Recall as a function of number of previous lists learned as determined from a number of studies. From left to right: Weiss and Margolius (*35*), Gibson (*9*), Belmont and Birch (*3*), Underwood and Richardson (*33*), Williams (*36*), Underwood (*27, 28, 29, 30*), Lester (*17*), Johnson (*14*), Krueger (*16*), Cheng (*6*), Hovland (*11*), Luh (*18*), Youtz (*37*).

speeds of presentation and different lengths of lists. But I think the general relationship is clear. The greater the number of previous lists learned the greater the forgetting. I interpret this to mean that the greater the number of previous lists the greater the *proactive* interference. We know this to be true (*26*) for a formal proactive-inhibition paradigm; it seems a reasonable interpretation for the data of Figure 3. That there are minor sources of variance still involved I do not deny. Some of the variation can be rationalized, but that is not the purpose of this report. The point I wish to make is the obvious one of the relationship between number of previous lists learned—lists which presumably had no intentionally built-in similarity—and amount of forgetting. If you like to think in correlational terms, the rank-order correlation between the two variables is —91 for the 14 points of Figure 3.

It may be of interest to the historian that, of the studies published before 1942 which met the criteria I imposed, I did not find a single one in which subjects had not been given at least one practice task before starting experimental conditions, and in most cases the subjects had several practice lists and several experimental conditions. Gibson's study (1942) was the first I found in which subjects served in only one condition and were not given practice tasks. I think it is apparent that the design proclivities of the 1920s and 1930s have been largely responsible for the exaggerated picture we have had of the rate of forgetting of rote-learned materials. On the basis of studies performed during the 1920s and 1930s, I have given a rough estimate of forgetting as being 75 per cent over 24 hours, recall being 25 per cent. On the basis of modern studies in which the subject has learned no previous lists—where there is no proactive inhibition from previous laboratory tasks—a rough estimate would be that forgetting is 25 per cent; recall is 75 per cent. The values are reversed. (If in the above and subsequent discussion my use of percentage values as

if I were dealing with a cardinal or extensive scale is disturbing, I will say that it makes the picture easier to grasp, and in my opinion no critical distortion results.)

Before taking the next major step, I would like to point out a few other observations which serve to support my general point that proactive inhibition from laboratory tasks has been the major cause of forgetting in the more classical studies. The first illustration I shall give exemplifies the point that when subjects have served in several conditions, forgetting after relatively short periods of time is greater than after 24 hours if the subject has served in only one condition. In the Youtz study to which I have already referred, other conditions were employed in which recall was taken after short intervals. After 20 minutes recall was 74 per cent, about what it is after 24 hours if the subject has not served in a series of conditions. After two hours recall was 32 per cent. In Ward's (*34*) well-known reminiscence experiment, subjects who on the average had learned ten previous lists showed a recall of only 64 per cent after 20 minutes.

In the famous Jenkins-Dallenbach (*13*) study on retention following sleep and following waking, two subjects were used. One subject learned a total of 61 lists and the other 62 in addition to several practice lists. Roughly, then, if the order of the conditions was randomized, approximately 30 lists had been learned prior to the learning of a list for a given experimental condition. Recall after eight waking hours for one subject was 4 per cent and for the other 14 per cent. Even after sleeping for eight hours the recall was only 55 per cent and 58 per cent.

I have said that an interpolated list can produce severe forgetting. However, in one study (*1*), using the A-B, A-C paradigm for original and interpolated learning, but using subjects who had never served in any previous conditions, recall of the original list was 46 per cent after 48 hours, and in another comparable study (*24*), 42 per cent. Thus, the loss is not nearly as great as in the classical studies I have cited where there was no interpolated learning in the laboratory.

My conclusion at this point is that, in terms of the gross analysis I have made, the amount of forgetting which might be attributed to interference from tasks learned outside the laboratory has been "reduced" from 75 per cent to about 25 per cent. I shall proceed in the next section to see if we have grounds for reducing this estimate still more. In passing on to this section, however, let me say that the study of factors which influence proactive inhibition in these counterbalanced studies is a perfectly legitimate and important area of study. I mention this because in the subsequent discussion I am going to deal only with the case where a subject has learned a single list in the laboratory, and I do not want to leave the impression that we should now and forevermore drop the study of interference produced by previous laboratory tasks. Indeed, as will be seen shortly, it is my opinion that we should increase these studies for the simple reason that the proactive paradigm provides a more realistic one than does the retroactive paradigm.

When the subject learns and recalls a single list in the laboratory, I have given an estimate of 25 per cent as being the amount forgotten over 24 hours. When, as shown above, we calculate percentage forgotten of lists learned to one perfect trial, the assumption is that had the subjects been given an immediate recall trial, the list would have been perfectly recalled. This, of course, is simply not true. The major factor determining how much error is introduced by this criterion-percentage method is probably the difficulty of the task. In general, the overestimation of forgetting by the percentage method will be directly related to the difficulty of the task. Thus, the more slowly the learning approaches a given criterion, the greater the drop on the trial immediately after the criterion trial. Data from a study by Runquist (24), using eight paired adjectives

(a comparatively easy task), shows that amount of forgetting is overestimated by about 10 per cent. In a study (32) using very difficult consonant syllables, the overestimation was approximately 20 per cent. To be conservative, assume that on the average the percentage method of reporting recall overestimates the amount forgotten by 10 per cent. If we subtract this from the 25 per cent assumed above, the forgetting is now re-estimated as being 15 per cent over 24 hours. That is to say, an interference theory, or any other form of theory, has to account for a very small amount of forgetting as compared with the amount traditionally cited.

What are the implications of so greatly "reducing" the amount of forgetting? There are at least three implications which I feel are worth pointing out. First, if one wishes to hold to an interference theory of forgetting (as I do), it seems plausible to assert that this amount of forgetting could be produced from learning which has taken place outside of the laboratory. Furthermore, it seems likely that such interference must result primarily from proactive interference. This seems likely on a simple probability basis. A 20-year-old college student will more likely have learned something during his 20 years prior to coming to the laboratory that will interfere with his retention than he will during the 24 hours between the learning and retention test. However, the longer the retention interval the more important will retroactive interference become relative to proactive interferences.

The second implication is that these data may suggest greater homogeneity or continuity in memorial processes than hitherto supposed. Although no one has adequately solved the measurement problem of how to make comparisons of retention among conditioned responses, prose material, motor tasks, concept learning, and rote-learned tasks, the gross comparisons have indicated that rote-learned tasks were forgotten much more rapidly than these other tasks. But the rote-learning data used for comparison have been those derived with the classical design in which the forgetting over 24 hours is approximately 75 per cent. If we take the revised estimate of 15 per cent, the discrepancies among tasks become considerably less.

The third implication of the revised estimate of rate of forgetting is that the number of variables which appreciably influence rate of forgetting must be sharply limited. While this statement does not inevitably follow from the analyses I have made, the current evidence strongly supports the statement. I want to turn to the final section of this paper which will consist of a review of the influence of some of the variables which are or have been thought to be related to rate of forgetting. In considering these variables, it is well to keep in mind that a variable which produces only a small difference in forgetting is important if one is interested in accounting for the 15 per cent assumed now as the loss over 24 hours. If appropriate for a given variable, I will indicate where it fits into an interference theory, although in no case will I endeavor to handle the details of such a theory.

*Time.* Passage of time between learning and recall is the critical defining variable for forgetting. Manipulation of this variable provides the basic data for which a theory must account. Previously, our conception of rate of forgetting as a function of time has been tied to the Ebbinghaus curve. If the analysis made earlier is correct, this curve does not give us the basic data we need. In short, we must start all over and derive a retention curve over time when the subjects have learned no previous materials in the laboratory. It is apparent that I expect the fall in this curve over time to be relatively small.

In conjunction with time as an independent variable, we must, in explanations of forgetting, consider why sleep retards the processes responsible for forgetting. (My conception, which does not really explain anything, is that since forgetting is largely produced by proactive interference, the amount of time which a subject spends in sleep is simply to be subtracted from the total retention interval when predicting the amount to be forgotten.) It is known that proactive interference increases with passage of time (5); sleep, I believe, brings to a standstill whatever these processes are which produce this increase.

*Degree of learning.* We usually say that the better or stronger the learning the more or better the retention. Yet, we do not know whether or not the *rate* of forgetting differs for items of different strength. The experimental problem is a difficult one. What we need is to have a subject learn a single association and measure its decline in strength over time. But this is difficult to carry out with verbal material, since almost of necessity we must have the subject learn a series of associations, to make it a reasonable task. And, when a series of associations are learned, complications arise from interaction effects among associations of different strength. Nevertheless, we may expect, on the basis of evidence from a wide variety of studies, that given a constant degree of similarity, the effective interference varies as some function of the strength of associations.

*Distribution of practice.* It is a fact that distribution of practice during acquisition influences retention of verbal materials. The facts of the case seem to be as follows. If the subject has not learned previous lists in the laboratory, massed practice gives equal or better retention than does distributed practice. If, on the other hand, the subject has learned a number of previous lists, distributed practice will facilitate retention (32). We do not have the theoretical solution to these facts. The point I wish to make here is that whether or not distribution of learning inhibits or facilitates retention depends upon the amount of interference from previous learning. It is reasonable to expect, therefore, that the solution to the problem will come via principles handling interference in general. I might also say that a theoretical solution to this problem will also provide a solution for Jost's laws.

*Similarity.* Amount of interference from other tasks is closely tied to similarity. This similarity must be conceived of as similarity among materials as such and also situational similarity (4). When we turn to similarity within a task, the situation is not quite so clear. Empirically and theoretically (8) one would expect that intratask similarity would be a very relevant variable in forgetting. As discussed elsewhere (31), however, variation in intratask similarity almost inevitably leads to variations in intertask similarity. We do know from a recent study (33) that with material of low meaningfulness forgetting is significantly greater with high intralist similarity than with low. While the difference in magnitude is only about 8 per cent, when we are trying to account for a total loss of 15 per cent, this amount becomes a major matter.

*Meaningfulness.* The belief has long been held that the more meaningful the material the better the retention—the less the forgetting. Osgood (21) has pointed out that if this is true it is difficult for an interference theory to handle. So far as I know, the only direct test of the influence of this variable is a recent study in which retention of syllables of 100 per cent association value was compared with that of zero association value (33). There was no difference in the recall of these syllables. Other less precise evidence would support this finding when comparisons are made among syllables, adjectives, and nouns, as plotted in Figure 3. However, there is some evidence that materials of very low meaningfulness are forgotten more rapidly than nonsense syllables of zero association value. Consonant syllables, both serial (32) and paired associates (unpublished), show about 50 per cent loss over 24 hours. The study using serial lists was the one mentioned earlier as knowingly

omitted from Figure 3. These syllables, being extremely difficult to learn, allow a correction of about 20 per cent due to criterion overestimation, but even with this much correction the forgetting (30 per cent) is still appreciably more than the estimate we have made for other materials. To invoke the interference theory to account for this discrepancy means that we must demonstrate how interference from other activities could be greater for these consonant syllables than for nonsense syllables, nouns, adjectives, and other materials. Our best guess at the present time is that the sequences of letters in consonant syllables are contrary to other well-established language habits. That is to say, letter sequences which commonly occur in our language are largely different from those in consonant syllables. As a consequence, not only are these consonant syllables very difficult to learn, but forgetting is accelerated by proactive interference from previously well-learned letter sequences. If subsequent research cannot demonstrate such a source of interference, or if some other source is not specified, an interference theory for this case will be in some trouble.

*Affectivity.* Another task dimension which has received extensive attention is the affective tone of the material. I would also include here the studies attaching unpleasant experiences to some items experimentally and not to others, and measuring retention of these two sets of items. Freud is to a large extent responsible for these studies, but he cannot be held responsible for the malformed methodology which characterizes so many of them. What can one say by way of summarizing these studies? The only conclusion that I can reach is a statistical one, namely, that the occasional positive result found among the scores of studies is about as frequent as one would expect by sampling error, using the 5 per cent level of confidence. Until a reliable body of facts is established for this variable and associated variables, no theoretical evaluation is possible.

*Other variables.* As I indicated earlier, I will not make an exhaustive survey of the variables which may influence rate of forgetting. I have limited myself to variables which have been rather extensively investigated, which have immediate relevance to the interference theory, or for which reliable relationships are available. Nevertheless, I would like to mention briefly some of these other variables. There is the matter of *warm-up* before recall; some investigators find that this reduces forgetting (12); others, under as nearly replicated conditions as is possible to obtain, do not (23). Some resolution must be found for these flat contradictions. It seems perfectly reasonable, however, that inadequate set or context differences could reduce recall. Indeed, an interference theory would predict this forgetting if the set or context stimuli are appreciably different from those prevailing at the time of learning. In our laboratory we try to reinstate the learning set by careful instructions, and we simply do not find decrements that might be attributed to inadequate set. For example, in a recent study (33) subjects were given a 24-hour recall of a serial list after learning to one perfect trial. I think we would expect that the first item in the list would suffer the greatest decrement due to inadequate set, yet this item showed only .7 per cent loss. But let it be clear that when we are attempting to account for the 15 per cent loss over 24 hours, we should not overlook any possible source for this loss.

Thus far I have not said anything about forgetting as a function of characteristics of the subject, that is, the personality or intellectual characteristics. As far as I have been able to determine, there is not a single valid study which shows that such variables have an appreciable influence on forgetting. Many studies have shown differences in learning as a function of these variables, but not differences in rate of forgetting. Surely there must be some such variables. We do know that if subjects are severely insulted, made to feel stupid, or generally led to believe that they have no justification for continued existence on the earth just before they are asked to recall, they will show losses (e.g., 25, 38), but even the influence of this kind of psychological beating is short lived. Somehow I have never felt that such findings need explanation by a theory used to explain the other facts of forgetting.

Concerning the causes of forgetting, let me sum up in a somewhat more dogmatic fashion than is probably justified. One of the assumptions of science is finite causality. Everything cannot influence everything else. To me, the most important implication of the work on forgetting during the last ten years is that this work has markedly *reduced* the number of variables related to forgetting. Correspondingly, I think the theoretical problem has become simpler. It is my belief that we can narrow down the cause of forgetting to interference from previously learned habits, from habits being currently learned, and from habits we have yet to learn. The amount of this interference is primarily a function of similarity and associative strength, the latter being important because it interacts with similarity.

## SUMMARY

This paper deals with issues in the forgetting of rote-learned materials. An analysis of the current evidence suggests that the classical Ebbinghaus curve of forgetting is primarily a function of interference from materials learned previously in the laboratory. When this source of interference is removed, forgetting decreases from about 75 per cent over 24 hours to about 25 per cent. This latter figure can be reduced by at least 10 per cent by other methodological considerations, leaving 15 per cent as an estimate of the forgetting over 24 hours. This estimate will vary somewhat as a function of intratask similarity, distributed practice, and with very low meaningful material. But the overall evidence suggests that *similarity with other material and situational similarity are by far the most critical factors in forgetting.* Such evidence is consonant with a general interference theory, although the details of such a theory were not presented here.

## REFERENCES

1. Archer, E. J., and Underwood, B. J. 1951. Retroactive inhibition of verbal associations as a multiple function of temporal point of interpolation and degree of interpolated learning. *Journal of Experimental Psychology* 42:283–290.

2. Bartlett, F. C. 1932. *Remembering: A study in experimental and social psychology.* London: Cambridge University Press.

3. Belmont, L., and Birch, H. G. 1951. Re-individualizing the repression hypothesis. *Journal of Abnormal and Social Psychology* 46:226–235.

4. Bilodeau, I. McD., and Schlosberg, H. 1951. Similarity in stimulating conditions as a variable in retroactive inhibition. *Journal of Experimental Psychology* 41:199–204.

5. Briggs, G. E. 1954. Acquisition, extinction, and recovery functions in retroactive inhibition. *Journal of Experimental Psychology* 47:285–293.

6. Cheng, N. Y. 1929. Retroactive effect and degree of similarity. *Journal of Experimental Psychology* 12:444–458.

7. Ebbinghaus, H. 1913. *Memory: A contribution to experimental psychology.* Trans. by H. A. Ruger and C. E. Bussenius. New York: Bureau of Publications, Teachers College, Columbia University.

8. Gibson, Eleanor J. 1940. A systematic application of the concepts of generalization and differentiation to verbal learning. *Psychological Review* 47:196–229.

9. Gibson, Eleanor J. 1942. Intra-list generalization as a factor in verbal learning. *Journal of Experimental Psychology* 30:185–200.

10. Greenberg, R., and Underwood, B. J. 1950. Retention as a function of stage of practice. *Journal of Experimental Psychology* 40:452–457.

11. Hovland, C. I. 1940. Experimental studies in rote-learning theory. VI. Comparison of retention following learning to same criterion by massed and distributed practice. *Journal of Experimental Psychology* 26:568–587.

12. Irion, A. L. 1948. The relation of "set" to retention. *Psychological Review* 55:336–341.

13. Jenkins, J. G., and Dallenbach, K. M. 1924. Oblivescence during sleep and waking. *American Journal of Psychology* 35:605–612.

14. Johnson, L. M. 1939. The relative effect of a time interval upon learning and retention. *Journal of Experimental Psychology* 24:169–179.

15. Katona, G. 1940. *Organizing and memorizing: Studies in the psychology of learning and teaching.* New York: Columbia University Press.

16. Krueger, W. C. F. 1929. The effect of overlearning on retention. *Journal of Experimental Psychology* 12:71–78.

17. Lester, O. P. 1932. Mental set in relation to retroactive inhibition. *Journal of Experimental Psychology* 15:681–699.

18. Luh, C. W. 1922. The conditions of retention. *Psychological Monographs* 31, no. 3 (whole no. 142).

19. McGeoch, J. A. 1932. Forgetting and the law of disuse. *Psychological Review* 39:352–370.

20. McGeoch, J. A. 1942. *The psychology of human learning.* New York: Longmans, Green.

21. Osgood, C. E. 1953. *Method and theory in experimental psychology.* New York: Oxford University Press.

22. Rapaport, D. 1943. Emotions and memory. *Psychological Review* 50:234–243.

23. Rockway, M. R., and Duncan, C. P. 1952. Pre-recall warming-up in verbal retention. *Journal of Experimental Psychology* 43:305–312.

24. Runquist, W. 1956. Retention of verbal associations as a function of interference and strength. Unpublished doctor's dissertation, Northwestern University.

25. Russell, W. A. 1952. Retention of verbal material as a function of motivating instructions and experimentally-induced failure. *Journal of Experimental Psychology* 43:207–216.

26. Underwood, B. J. 1945. The effect of successive interpolations on retroactive and proactive inhibition. *Psychological Monographs* 59, no. 3 (whole no. 273).

27. Underwood, B. J. 1952. Studies of distributed practice: VII. Learning and retention of serial nonsense lists as a function of intralist similarity. *Journal of Experimental Psychology* 44:80–87.

28. Underwood, B. J. 1953. Studies of distributed practice: VIII. Learning and retention of paired nonsense syllables as a function of intralist similarity. *Journal of Experimental Psychology* 45:133–142.

29. Underwood, B. J. 1953. Studies of distributed practice: IX. Learning and retention of paired adjectives as a function of intralist similarity. *Journal of Experimental Psychology* 45:143–149.

30. Underwood, B. J. 1953. Studies of distributed practice: X. The influence of intralist similarity on learning and retention of serial adjective lists. *Journal of Experimental Psychology* 45:253–259.

31. Underwood, R. J. 1954. Intralist similarity in verbal learning and retention. *Psychological Review* 3:160–166.

32. Underwood, B. J., and Richardson, J. 1955. Studies of distributed practice: XIII. Interlist interference and the retention of serial nonsense lists. *Journal of Experimental Psychology* 50:39–46.

33. Underwood, B. J., and Richardson, J. 1956. The influence of meaningfulness, intralist similarity, and serial position on retention. *Journal of Experimental Psychology* 52:119–126.

34. Ward, L. B. 1937. Reminiscence and rote learning. *Psychological Monographs* 49, no. 4 (whole no. 220).

35. Weiss, W., and Margolius, G. 1954. The effect of context stimuli on learning and retention. *Journal of Experimental Psychology* 48:318–322.

36. Williams, M. 1950. The effects of experimentally induced needs upon retention. *Journal of Experimental Psychology* 40:139–151.

37. Youtz, Adella C. 1941. An experimental evaluation of Jost's laws. *Psychological Monographs* 53, no. 1 (whole no. 238).

38. Zeller, A. F. 1951. An experimental analogue of repression: III. The effect of induced failure and success on memory measured by recall. *Journal of Experimental Psychology* 42:32–38.

# READING 23

# Primary Memory

**NANCY C. WAUGH**
**Harvard Medical School**

**DONALD A. NORMAN**
**Center for Cognitive Studies,**
**Harvard University**

The following article develops and tests a theoretical model specific to short-term memory. Waugh and Norman utilize a "probe-digit" technique which has many interesting implications for experimental methodology. In analyzing their data and data from other experiments, the authors conclude that (1) interference, rather than decay, is responsible for short-term forgetting, and (2) there is a dual storage mechanism in memory which allows an item to be retained in both states simultaneously.

**QUESTIONS**

1. Do you agree with this model of memory? Are there two memory mechanisms?
2. If this model is correct, how can these principles be applied to teaching methods and study habits?
3. What is the relationship between the concepts in this article and those found in the G. A. Miller article? Is Miller talking about primary memory, as defined by the Waugh and Norman model?

It is a well-established fact that the longest series of unrelated digits, letters, or words that a person can recall verbatim

This research was supported in part by Research Grants No. MH 05120-02 and MH 08119-01 from the National Institutes of Health, United States Public Health Service, to Harvard University, Center for Cognitive Studies and to Harvard Medical School, respectively. The second author was supported by a National Science Foundation Postdoctoral Fellowship at the Center for Cognitive Studies.

after one presentation seldom exceeds 10 items. It is also true, however, that one can nearly always recall the most recent item in a series, no matter how long the series—but only if this item may be recalled immediately, or if it may be rehearsed during the interval between its presentation and recall. Otherwise it is very likely to be lost.

If we may assume that attending to a current item precludes reviewing a prior one, we can say that the span of immediate memory must be limited in large part by our inability to rehearse, and hence retain, the early items in a sequence while attempting to store the later ones. Our limited memory span would then be but one manifestation of our general inability to think about two things at the same time.

Why should an unrehearsed item in a list be forgotten so swiftly? Is its physiological trace in some sense written over by the traces of the items that follow it? Or does this trace simply decay within a brief interval, regardless of how that interval is filled? Tradition, in the guise of interference theory, favors the first explanation (McGeoch, 1932; Postman, 1961), although some psychologists now think that new memory traces must fade autonomously in time (Brown, 1958; Conrad, 1957; Hebb, 1949). Until now, no one has reported any data which clearly contradict either of these ideas. In fact, when we first considered the problem of the instability of recent memory traces, we thought it entirely possible that both decay and interference operate over brief retention intervals to produce forgetting, and we therefore designed an experiment to weigh their respective effects. The results of this experiment were unexpectedly straightforward — and seemingly inconsistent with certain other existing data on immediate retention. We have been able, however, to formulate a simple quantitative model which relates our results to those reported by other investigators. What began as an attempt to evaluate two very general hypotheses about the forgetting of recent events has therefore resulted in a specific theory of short-term memory.

We shall describe our experiment in Section I below. A major portion of this paper, Section II, will be concerned with the description and application of our model. In Section III we shall discuss this model in relation to the general question of whether short- and long-term retention represent distinguishably different psychological processes.

## I. PROBE-DIGIT EXPERIMENT

Our experiment was designed to measure the recall of a minimally rehearsed verbal item as a joint function of the number of seconds and the number of other items following its presentation. The general procedure was as follows. Lists of 16 single digits were prepared with the aid of a standard table of random numbers, under the constraint that no digit should appear more than twice in a row. The last digit in every list was one that had occurred exactly once before, in Position 3, 5, 7, 9, 10, 11, 12, 13, or 14. On its second appearance, this "probe-digit" was a cue for the recall of the digit that had followed it initially.

The lists were recorded on two magnetic tapes; they were read in a montone voice by a male speaker at a constant rate of either one or four digits per second. Each of the nine possible probe-digit positions was tested 10 times. The two tapes accordingly contained 90 test lists (plus 8 practice lists apiece, all read at the same rate. The last digit in every list, the probe-digit, was accompanied by a high-frequency tone to aid the subject in detecting the end of the list. The position of the initial presentation of the probe varied randomly from list to list on each of the two tapes.

The subject's task was to write down the digit that had followed the probe digit in the list, guessing if he did not know. Since the probe-digit was unique in Positions 1 through 15, there was only one possible correct answer on any trial. Every subject listened to the list through earphones for a total of 12 experimental sessions, 6 with each tape, alternating between fast and slow lists. The first session under each condition and the first eight lists listened to in each session were considered to be practice and, unknown to the subject, were not scored.

The subjects received explicit instructions

to control rehearsal by "thinking only of the last digit you have heard and never of any of the earlier ones." These instructions were repeated before the second session, and occasional reminders were given throughout the course of the experiment. Thus, the subjects were to rehearse every item during the interitem interval immediately following it. Our instructions were not designed to eliminate the rehearsal of single items as such, but rather to eliminate the rehearsal of *groups* of digits. The experiment actually tested the retention of a digit pair, the probe-digit and its successor. The retention of this pair should be independent of the interitem interval, if the instructions to avoid grouping were followed faithfully. We hoped, in effect, to test the retention of unrehearsed pairs of digits under two rates of presentation.

The subjects were four Harvard undergraduates, three males and one female.

The responses were scored and analyzed to yield a serial position curve for each rate of presentation, relating the relative frequency of an item's correct recall to its distance from the end of the list. A comparison of the two functions allows us to assess the relative effects of decay and interference on short-term forgetting, according to the following line of reasoning. Consider the recall of Item $i$ from the end of the line. If the list was read at the rate of one item per second, then $i$ items would have intervened, and $i$ seconds would have elapsed between the time the subject heard the item and the time he attempted to recall it. (We count the second appearance of the probe-digit as an intervening event.) If the items were read at the rate of four per second, on the other hand, then only $i/4$, rather than $i$, seconds would have elapsed between the occurrence of Item $i$ and the subject's attempt to recall it. A total of $i$ other items would, of course, still have intervened between these two events. Therefore, if the probability of recalling Item $i$ from the end of a slow list were identical

with the probability of recalling Item $4i$ from a fast list, we could conclude that recent memory traces decay in time, independently of one another. Conversely, if the probability of recalling Item $i$ were invariant with rate of presentation, we could conclude that rapid forgetting is caused primarily by retroactive interference.

The results of the experiment are shown in Figure 1. The scores for the individual subjects are presented in Figures 1A and 1B. The pooled data, corrected for guessing, are shown in Figure 1C.[1] Each point in Figures 1A and 1B is based on 50 observations; each point in Figure 1C, on 200. It is evident that there are consistent differences among subjects, but little interaction between subjects and serial positions. Furthermore, although there appears to be a slight interaction between relative frequency of recall, or $R(i)$, and rate of presentation, it is clear that the effect of rate is relatively small compared to the effect of serial position. The main source of forgetting in our experiment was interference.

The differences between the two sets of points shown in Figure 1C are not statistically reliable, according to an analysis of variance performed on the number of items recalled by each subject at each value of $i$ under the two rates of presentation ($F < 1$ for the mean square between rates tested against the interaction between subjects and rates). This conclusion is borne out by the results of nine Kolmogorov-Smirnov two-sample tests, one for each value of $i$, performed on the distributions of number of items recalled per subject per session under the two rates of presentation. We have therefore fitted the points shown in Figure 1C with a funtion that represents the probability of recalling Item $i$ from the end of a series, estimated across rates of presenta-

---

[1]The response set—the 10 digits—was known to the subjects, and they knew that the probe would not be the same as the test digit. Thus the probability of correctly guessing the answer, $g$, was 1/9. A standard normalizing technique was used to eliminate the effects of guessing from the data, namely, $p(\text{recall}) = [p(\text{correct}) - g]/(1 - g)$.

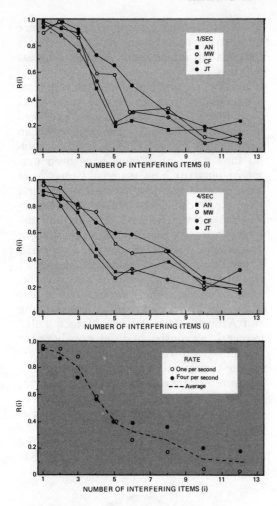

**Figure 1.** Results of the probe-digit experiment. (Figures 1A and 1B represent retention functions for individual subjects under two rates of presentation; in Figure 1C these data have been pooled.)

tion. This function decreases monotonically with $i$, attaining a value of about .07 at $i = 12$.

## II. MODEL FOR PRIMARY MEMORY

When we compared the foregoing results with the typical outcome of the first trial in a standard list-learning experiment, we found ourselves facing two dilemmas. In the first place, it often happens that an item

in a long list is recalled after 10 or 20, or even more, items have followed it. But in our experiment, probability of recall was effectively zero for the eleventh item in from the end of a list. In the second place, various investigators have shown that probability of recall increases with presentation time (see Posner, 1963), yet in our experiment this probability, for all practical purposes, was independent of the rate at which the digits were read.

In seeking for a way to account for these discrepancies, it occurred to us that one difference between our experiment and previous ones in this area is that we instructed our subjects not to think about any item in a list once the next had been presented. This instruction to avoid rehearsal is, to be sure, rather unorthodox, although not completely without precedent (Underwood & Keppel, 1962). In order to minimize rehearsal, many experimenters try to keep the subject so busy that he does not have time to rehearse; but we think it highly likely that a well-motivated subject who is trying to learn a list will rehearse unless specifically enjoined from doing so. The typical subject's account of how he learns a list (Bugelski, 1962; Clark, Lansford, & Dallenbach, 1960) bears us out on this point. In fact, it is probably very difficult *not* to rehearse material that one is trying to memorize.

We shall assume here that rehearsal simply denotes the recall of a verbal item—either immediate or delayed, silent or overt, deliberate or involuntary. The initial perception of a stimulus probably must also qualify as a rehearsal. Obviously a very conspicuous item or one that relates easily to what we have already learned can be retained with a minimum of conscious effort. We assume that relatively homogeneous or unfamiliar material must, on the other hand, be deliberately rehearsed if it is to be retained. Actually, we shall not be concerned here with the exact role of rehearsal in the memorization process. We are simply noting that, in the usual verbal-learning experiment, the likelihood that an item in a homogeneous list will be recalled tends to increase with the amount of time available for its rehearsal. The probe-digit experiment has shown, conversely, that material which is not rehearsed is rapidly lost, regardless of the rate at which it is presented. It is as though rehearsal transferred a recently perceived verbal item from one memory store of very limited capacity to another more commodious store from which it can be retrieved at a much later time.

We shall follow James (1890) in using the terms *primary* and *secondary memory* (PM and SM) to denote the two stores. James defined these terms introspectively: an event in PM has never left consciousness and is part of the psychological present, while an event recalled from SM has been absent from consciousness and belongs to the psychological past. PM is a faithful record of events just perceived; SM is full of gaps and distortions. James believed that PM extends over a fixed period of time. We propose instead that it encompasses a certain number of events regardless of the time they take to occur. Our goal is to distinguish operationally between PM and SM on the basis of the model that we shall now describe.

Consider the general scheme illustrated in Figure 2. Every verbal item that is attended to enters PM. As we have seen, the capacity of this system is sharply limited. New items displace old ones; displaced items are permanently lost. When an item is rehearsed, however, it remains in PM, and it may enter into SM. We should like to assume, for the sake of simplicity, that the probability of its entering SM is independent of its position in a series and of the time at which it is rehearsed. Thus, it would not matter whether the item was rehearsed immediately on entering PM or several seconds later: as long as it was in PM, it would make the transition into SM with fixed probability. (Our PM is similar to

Broadbent's, 1958, *P* system. One difference between our two systems is that ours relates rehearsal to longer term storage, whereas his does not.)

Finally, we shall assume that response-produced interference has the same effect on an item in PM as does stimulus-produced interference. That is, the probability that an item in PM will be recalled depends upon (*a*) how many new items have been perceived plus (*b*) how many old ones have been recalled between its presentation and attempted recall. Thus, if an item appears in Position $n$ from the end of a list and the subject attempts to recall it after recalling $m$ other items, it is as if the item had appeared in position $i = n + m$ in the list, and recall was attempted at the end of the list. This assumption is rather strong, but recent studies by Murdock (1963) and by Tulving and Arbuckle (1963) have, in fact, failed to reveal any consistent differences between stimulus- and response-induced interference in the retention of paired associates. It may not be unreasonable to suppose, therefore, that the two sources of interference exert equivalent effects on free and serial recall.

According to our hypothesis, then, the probability of recalling an item which has been followed by $i$ subsequent items is given

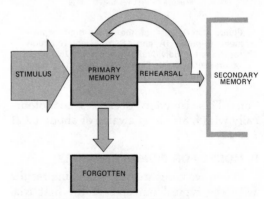

**Figure 2.** The primary and secondary memory system. (All verbal items enter PM, where they are either rehearsed or forgotten. Rehearsed items may enter SM.)

by the probability that it is in PM, in SM, or in both. Assuming that these probabilities combine independently,

$$R(i) = P(i) + S(i) - P(i)S(i) \qquad [1]$$

where $R(i)$ is the probability that Item $i$ will be recalled, $P(i)$ is the probability that it is in PM, and $S(i)$ the probability that it is in SM. The probability that this item is in PM is then given by

$$P(i) = [R(i) - S(i)]/[1 - S(i)]. \qquad [2]$$

We assume that $P(i)$ is a monotonic decreasing function of $i$ and that

$$\lim_{i \to \infty} P(i) = 0.$$

We should like specifically to test the hypothesis that $P(i)$ is independent of the value of $S(i)$ and, in fact, varies with $i$ in the manner of the probe-digit data. (This hypothesis is stated more formally in the Appendix.) In order to do so, we need data on verbal retention that meet the following requirements.

1. They should come from an experimental situation where at least some of the items are retrieved from PM.

2. The subject should have been allowed to rehearse, so that $S(i) > 0$.

3. The value of $S(i)$ should preferably be constant and independent of $i$.

4. The experimental lists should be long enough to let us estimate $S(i)$ for $i > 12$.

5. We should know the location of a given item in the stimulus list ($n$) and in the recall list ($m$), so as to be able to estimate the total number of interfering items ($i = n + m$).

## FREE RECALL

The free-recall experiment is well suited to our purposes. Subjects can (and usually do) recall the last few items in a list right away, and the middle portion of the serial position curve (after the first three and before the last seven items) is effectively flat, thereby providing a convenient estimate of $S(i)$ (Deese & Kaufman, 1957; Murdock, 1962; Waugh, 1962).

Testing our hypothesis against data collected in a free-recall experiment therefore involves the following steps:

1. First, we estimate $S(i)$ from the average proportion of items recalled from the middle of a long list.

2. We then estimate $P(i)$ for each of the last seven items in the list by Equation 2.

3. We plot this estimate against $n + m = i$ and compare the resulting function with that shown in Figure 1.

Fortunately, we did not have to perform a free-recall experiment especially for this purpose: several such studies have been carried out and reported in sufficient detail to enable us to test our hypothesis against their results. We have chosen to analyze four sets of data collected by three different investigators: Deese and Kaufman (1957), Murdock (1962), and two as yet unpublished experiments conducted by Waugh. The two principal variables that affect $S(i)$ in free recall appear to be length of list (the amount of material that is to be retained) and presentation time (the amount of time available for the rehearsal of a given item). Manipulating these variables results in orderly changes in the value of $S(i)$, so that our estimates range from .08 to .45 across the four experiments.

1. In Deese and Kaufman's study, the subjects listened to lists of 32 unrelated English words read at a rate of one per second, and began recalling them immediately after the last had been spoken. Deese and Kaufman have presented a serial position curve based on these data and have also reported the relation between an item's serial position in recall and its position in the original list. We can thereby estimate $i$ for each item in their lists, letting an item's average position in recall be our estimator of the amount of response interference ($m$).[2] We estimated

---

[2] It is not really correct to use the average of the serial positions in recall as an estimate of $m + 1$: the total effect of response interference should depend on the variance of this distribution as well as on its mean or median. It is the only alternative open to us, however, since our correction for asymptote must be applied to the average proportion of items retained, estimated across serial position in recall.

**Table 1**

PROPORTION OF ITEMS FREELY RECALLED AS A FUNCTION
OF SERIAL POSITION AND TOTAL TIME PER LIST

| Number of intervening items | List length × seconds per item | | | | | | |
|---|---|---|---|---|---|---|---|
| | 32 × 1 | 40 × 1 | 20 × 2 | 30 × 1 | 15 × 2 | 20 × 1 | 10 × 2 |
| 0 | .72 | .96 | .95 | .97 | .97 | .96 | .95 |
| 1 | .67 | .85 | .88 | .89 | .88 | .84 | .83 |
| 2 | .60 | .71 | .75 | .74 | .80 | .76 | .71 |
| 3 | .42 | .51 | .57 | .52 | .62 | .62 | .67 |
| 4 | .32 | .40 | .43 | .39 | .58 | .39 | .58 |
| 5 | .27 | .27 | .38 | .33 | .49 | .30 | .45 |
| 6 | .22 | .22 | .38 | .24 | .42 | .26 | .45 |
| 6+[a] | .17 | .12 | .27 | .19 | .38 | .15 | .45 |

Note.—Deese and Kaufman (1957), Column 1; Murdock (1961), Columns 2–6.
[a]Entries in this row represent the asymptotic value of $R(n)$.

$S(i)$ by the proportion of items recalled after the first three and before the last seven serial positions in the original list.[3] (This same general procedure will be followed in our subsequent analyses.)

The last seven points of Deese and Kaufman's serial position curve, taken from their Figure 1 and corrected for asymptote according to Equation 2, are plotted as a function of $i$ in Figure 3. The dashed lines in Figure 3 represent the 99% confidence limits for the probe-digit function: a standard error for each point was estimated across subjects and experimental sessions. The uncorrected data are shown in Table 1.

2. Waugh's experiments were concerned with determining the number of items freely recalled from long lists as a function of presentation time. In her first experiment, 24, 30, 40, 60, or 120 different monosyllabic English words were read to the subjects at a rate of one per second. The proportion of items recalled varied inversely with list length, so that for each length of list there is a different serial position function. The asymptotes of these functions range from approximately .08 to .20. Median serial position in recall $(m + 1)$ was calculated for

---

[3]In estimating $S(i)$, we ignored the recall of the first three items on a list because they invariably show a primacy effect, perhaps the result of selective attention and rehearsal.

each of the last six items in a list; Figure 4 shows $S(i)$ as a function of $i$ for each of these items. The uncorrected data appear in Table 2.

In Waugh's second experiment, the subjects listened to 30 different words presented at a rate of 1, 2, 3, 4, or 6 seconds per word. In each case the presentations were either massed—that is, each word was read one, two, or three times in a row, at a rate of one word per second or of one word every two seconds—or they were distributed —each word was read once at one, two, three, four, or six different places in a list, at a rate of one word per second. The results of this experiment indicate that whether the repetitions are massed or distributed is of no importance; the probability that a word will be recalled is determined simply by the total number of seconds for which it is presented. Since this probability increases as a negatively accelerated function of presentation time, the asymptotic values of the serial position function obtained in this experiment ranged from approximately .14 (for 30 words each read once) to .45 (for 30 words each read six times). Average serial position in recall was again calculated for each of the last six items in a list. The retention functions for massed and distributed repetitions, corrected for asymptote and response interference, are shown in Figures 5 and 6, respectively, along with the PM function obtained in our probe-digit experiment. The uncorrected data are shown in Table 2.

3. In Murdock's experiment, the subjects listened to lists of 20, 30, or 40 words read at a rate of 1 word per second and to lists of 10, 15, and 20 words read at a rate of 1 word every 2 seconds. Murdock found, as has Waugh (1963), that the probability of recalling a word that has been listened to for 2 seconds is almost exactly twice the probability of recalling a word that has been listened to for 1 second. Murdock's data can therefore be grouped into three pairs of

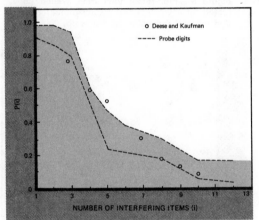

**Figure 3.** Free-recall data from Deese and Kaufman (1957), corrected for asymptote and response interference.

**TABLE 2**

PROPORTION OF ITEMS FREELY RECALLED AS A FUNCTION OF STIMULUS INTERFERENCE AND NUMBER OF ITEMS PER LIST

| Number of intervening items | List Length | | | | |
|---|---|---|---|---|---|
| | 24 | 30 | 40 | 60 | 120 |
| 0 | .95 | .97 | 1.00 | .95 | 1.00 |
| 1 | .85 | .85 | .90 | .93 | .95 |
| 2 | .92 | .69 | .81 | .86 | .92 |
| 3 | .42 | .46 | .51 | .53 | .57 |
| 4 | .47 | .35 | .31 | .32 | .57 |
| 5 | .21 | .17 | .22 | .14 | .14 |
| 5+ [a] | .15 | .17 | .16 | .12 | .08 |

[a]Entries in this row represent the symptotic value of $R(n)$.

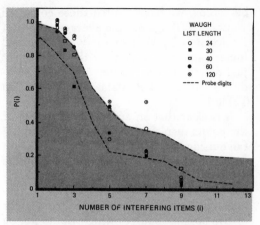

**Figure 4.** Free-recall data from Waugh corrected for asymptote and response interference.

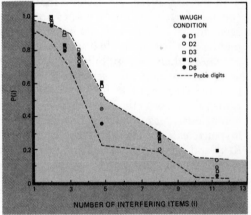

**Figure 5.** Free-recall data from Waugh corrected for asymptote and response interference (1-6 distributed presentations per word).

serial position curves: 10 words read at a rate of 1 every 2 seconds versus 20 words read at a rate of 1 per second; 15 words read at a rate of 1 every 2 seconds versus 30 read at a rate of 1 per second; and 20 words read at a rate of 1 every 2 seconds versus 40 read at a rate of 1 per second. Within each pair, there are two asymptotes, one of which is approximately twice the value of the other.

We have corrected Murdock's curves for asymptote—that is, for $S(i)$—and since he did not calculate serial position in recall for his words, we have plotted these corrected values of $P(i)$ against the average values of $i$ calculated by Waugh for words recalled under similar conditions in the experiment just described (see Figures 5 and 6).[4] Murdock's uncorrected data are shown in Table 1.

It is clear that an appreciable number of the points displayed in Figures 3 through 7 fall outside the confidence limits we have set for the probe-digit function. In general, the discrepancies between theoretical and observed values of $P(i)$ appear to be unsystematic. They may have resulted from either of two possible sources which would not be reflected in the variance of the probe-digit function.

In the first place, we assume that $S(i)$ is constant for all $i$. While $S(i)$ does not in fact seem to vary systematically with $i$ in the middle of a list, individual words do differ greatly in their susceptibility of storage in secondary memory: the serial position function for free recall is haphazardly jagged rather than perfectly flat. Thus, even one anomalously easy word in Location $n$, for instance, can greatly inflate our estimate of $R(n)$ and hence $P(n)$. The probe-digit data would presumably not be subject to this kind of variability.

A second source of errors may lie in our estimation of $i$, or $m + n$. We have used average position in recall—call it $m + 1$—as our estimate of $m + 1$. Even a small error in this estimate can lead to a sizable discrepancy between a theoretical and an observed value of $P(i)$, especially around the steep early portion of the function. Errors of this sort would be reflected in Figures 4–7, where $i$ and $P(i)$ are derived from either partially or completely independent sets of data (in Figures 4–6 and Figure 7, respectively). Furthermore, we should in any case expect some discrepancy on purely mathematical grounds between $P(i)$, where $(i)$ is the mean

<hr>

[4]The asymptotes for Murdock's curves were obtained by complementing his tabulated values for $v$ (shown in his Table 2).

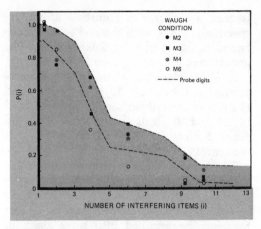

**Figure 6.** Free-recall data from Waugh corrected for asymptote and response interference (2-6 massed presentations per word).

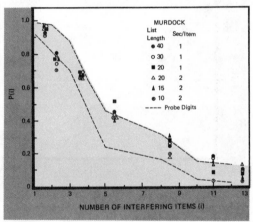

**Figure 7.** Free-recall data from Murdock (1961), corrected for asymptote and response interference.

of a point distribution, as in the probe-digit experiment, and $P(m + n)$, where $m$ can assume any of a number of values, as in the free-recall data we have analyzed. Unfortunately, we are unable to specify the magnitude of this expected discrepancy.

In view, therefore, of the likelihood of the errors we have just described, we believe that the fit between the probe-digit function and the free-recall data is fairly good and is, in fact, probably too close to attribute to chance. Actually, in one respect it is surprising that the probe-digit function should describe the free-recall data as well as it does. The probe-digit experiment tested the retention of digit pairs, whereas the free-recall experiments tested the retention of individual items. How are we justified in equating the two? One possibility is to assume that in the probe-digit experiment the subjects perceived and stored the digits as a series of overlapping pairs, rather than as single digits. In this case, the measure of interference would be given by the number of digit-pairs that follow any given pair, which is, of course, equal to the number of single digits that follow it. In the free-recall experiment, on the other hand, the subjects may have perceived the words as independent units, and the effective interference would then consist of single words, as we have in fact been assuming. The problem, then, can be restated as follows: why do pairs of digits and single words exert equal amounts of retroactive interference on like items in primary memory? There is little in the existing literature that sheds much light on this point.

## PAIRED ASSOCIATES

Our model should, of course, be able to describe ordered as well as free recall. We face serious problems, however, in attempting to apply it to serial learning: if a list is long enough to furnish a stable estimate of $S(i)$, the probability that a given item will be in PM at the time of testing is negligible, since serial items are customarily tested in the order in which they were presented. We must therefore turn to paired associates. In a recent study, Tulving and Arbuckle (1963) systematically varied the positions of the items on the recall list, and we have therefore applied our hypothesis to their data in the manner described above.

Tulving and Arbuckle presented number-word pairs to their subjects and then tested for the recall of each word by presenting only the number with which it had been paired. They were interested in measuring probability of recall after one trial as a func-

tion of an item's serial position in both the original list and the test list. We have estimated $S(i)$ by averaging the recall probabilities for $i > 13$, excluding Items 1 and 2. The value of their serial position curve is fortunately constant in this region, as it was for free recall. Note that in this task, each pair presented after a given number and before the cue for its recall actually consists of *two* interfering items: a word plus a number. We have counted all items occurring between the test item and its recall—including the test number—as interfering items. We have analyzed the proportion of items presented in Positions 1 through 6 from the end of the stimulus list and tested in Positions 1 through 6 of the response list. These proportions are shown in Tulving and Arbuckle's Tables 2 and 4; we have pooled those that correspond to a given value of $i$. Thus $i$, or $n + m$ (where $n = j$ and $m = i - j$), ranges from 1 to 11. These data are presented in Figure 8, along with our own estimate of $P(i)$. Again, considering the variability of $S(i)$ that is not taken into account by our model, the fit between data and theory appears to be reasonably good.

In sum, then, we believe we can say that the similarity between our probe-digit function and the various other, initially disparate, serial position curves shown in Figures 3–8 is consistent with the hypothesis that there is a primary memory store that is independent of any longer term store. The capacity of the primary store appears to be invariant under a wide variety of experimental conditions which do, however, affect the properties of the longer term store.

## SINGLE-ITEM RETENTION

Much of the experimental work on memory in the past 5 years has focused on measuring the retention of a single verbal item —or of a brief list of items—over short intervals. A widely used procedure which was introduced by Peterson and Peterson (1959) is to expose an item (for example, a meaningless three-letter sequence) to a subject;

have him perform some task that presumably monopolizes his attention (such as counting backwards by three's) for a specified number of seconds; and, finally, at the end of this interval, have him attempt to recall the critical item. The universal finding has been that retention decreases monotonically with the length of the retention interval. It has generally been assumed that the subject does not rehearse during the retention interval, that a number spoken by him does not interfere with a trigram previously spoken by the experimenter, and that therefore the observed decline over time in the retention of such an item reflects the pure decay of its memory trace. This general conclusion is clearly inconsistent with our results, since we have found that the length of the retention interval as such—within the limits we tested, naturally—is of relatively little importance in determining retention loss.

In seeking for a way to account for this discrepancy, it occurred to us to question the assumption that, in an experiment of the sort described above, the numbers spoken by the subject during the retention interval do not interfere with the memory trace of the item he is supposed to retain. Some experimenters have, after all, reported that dissimilar items seem to interfere with one another just as much as do similar ones in the immediate recall of very short lists (Brown, 1958; Pillsbury & Sylvester, 1940). What would happen, therefore, if we were to define a three-digit number uttered by a subject in the course of a simple arithmetic calculation — counting backwards — as one unit of mnemonic interference? Could our model then describe the forgetting of single items over brief intervals? We have attempted to fit the data of two experimenters, Loess (in press) and Murdock (1961), by converting the retention interval into a corresponding number of interfering items. Murdock's subjects were trained to count at a steady rate of one number per second, so the number of interfering items in his experiment is equal to the retention interval

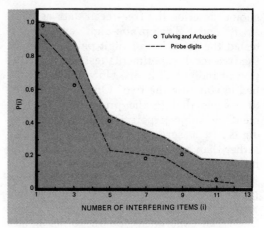

**Figure 8.** Paired-associate data from Tulving and Arbuckle (1963) corrected for asymptote and response interference.

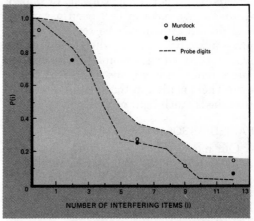

**Figure 9.** The retention of three-item lists compared with the probe-digit function, (Loess' data denote the proportion of consonant trigrams recalled after various retention intervals; Murdock's data represent the average proportion of trigrams and word triads retained after a given interval.)

in seconds. Loess' subjects counted at a rate of one number every 1.5 seconds; we have therefore multiplied the length of his retention intervals by $\frac{2}{3}$ in order to obtain the equivalent number of interfering items. We estimate $S(i)$ in both cases by the relative frequency of recall at $i = 18$.[5]

---

[5]We have also tried to analyze the results of Peterson and Peterson (1959) but without success. Part of the difficulty may result from the fact that their subjects may not have adhered strictly to a prescribed rate of counting during the retention interval (L. Peterson, personal communication, 1964).

The two sets of data, corrected for asymptote, are shown in Figure 9, along with the probe-digit function. The correspondence between them is reasonably close. It is possible, of course, that this agreement between theory and fact is simply a matter of luck, depending, as it does, on the arbitary assumption that a three-digit number generated by the subject himself is psychologically equivalent to a one-digit number presented by the experimenter during the retention interval (as in the probe-digit study). Obviously we cannot draw any firm conclusions about the effect of interference on the retention of single items until this assumption is justified empirically. We can only point out that the results of Murdock and Loess do not necessarily contradict our model.

## DISCUSSION

We should at this point like to consider the general question of whether all verbal information is stored in the same system or whether, as we have assumed here, there are two independent mnemonic processes that contribute to retention even over very short intervals. The proponents of a unitary theory of memory, eloquently led by Melton (1963), have argued that recall after a few seconds is affected in very similar ways by the variables that govern recall over much longer intervals; and that therefore the distinction between a short-term memory mechanism, on the one hand, and a longer term mechanism, on the other, is purely arbitrary. The following facts have been cited in support of this argument:

1. Short-term retention improves, just as does long-term retention, when the material to be recalled is repeated before a test of retention, or when it is repeated between successive tests (Hebb, 1961; Hellyer, 1962).

2. Retention after a brief delay is subject to proactive interference, as is retention after a long delay (Keppel & Underwood, 1962; Loess, in press). Why, asks the unitary theorist, should we distinguish between

short- and long-term retention if we cannot find any quantitative and experimentally manipulatable differences between them? This question might well be disturbing if one took the position that the two processes have sharply defined nonoverlapping temporal boundaries such that items recalled within some critical interval after their initial occurrence must have been retrieved from one system, whereas items recalled beyond this interval must have been retrieved from another. (Such a view would imply, interestingly enough, that an item would have to remain in a short-term storage for some specified number of seconds before passing into longer term storage, if it did so at all.)

But what if we do not require that the two systems be mutually exclusive? Then the probability that an item will be recalled will depend on both the probability that it is still in PM and the probability that it has entered into SM in the interval between its presentation and the start of the interfering sequence (or even during this sequence, if the subject is able to rehearse). All those variables that determine $S(i)$ for a given item—such as its position in a closely spaced series of tests, or the number of times it has been repeated—will then determine the observed proportion recalled after a brief interval. We believe we have shown, however, that $P(i)$ depends only on $i$ and remains invariant with changes in $S(i)$; and we submit that most of the published data on short-term retention actually reflect the properties of both memory systems.

We would like to make one final point: the existence of some rather compelling introspective evidence in favor of two distinct mnemonic systems. PM, as we have defined it here, is best illustrated by a person's ability to recall verbatim the most recent few words in a sentence that he is hearing or speaking, even when he is barely paying attention to what is being said, or to what he is saying. Given that the flow of speech is intelligible, failures in the immediate recall of words we have just heard—errors of either omission, transposition, or substitution—are probably so rare as to be abnormal. Indeed, we believe that it would be impossible to understand or to generate a grammatical utterance if we lacked this rather remarkable mnemonic capacity. In order to recall a sentence verbatim at a later time, however, we usually have to rehearse it while it is still available in PM.

The same effect holds for meaningless arrangements of verbal items. If we present a subject with a random string of words, letters, or digits, and ask him to reproduce them in any order he chooses, he can maximize the number he recalls by "unloading" the last few items immediately. Most subjects in free-recall experiments report that these very late items tend to be lost if they are not recalled immediately, whereas items that came earlier in the list can be retrieved at leisure, if they can be recalled at all. In the colorful terminology of one such subject (Waugh, 1961), the most recent items in a verbal series reside temporarily in a kind of "echo box," from which they can be effortlessly parroted back. When an experienced subject is trying to memorize a list of serial items, moreover, he "fills up" successive echo boxes as the list is read to him and attempts to rehearse the contents of each. He will invariably lose some items if rehearsal is delayed too long or if he attempts to load his echo box with more items than it can hold. We think it very likely that the PM function describes the (variable) capacity of this mechanism. We would remind you in this connection that, within very broad limits, the rate at which someone is speaking does not affect your ability to follow his words—just as differences in the rate at which meaningless lists of digits are presented do not exert any profound effect on the PM function.

## CONCLUSIONS

We have tried to demonstrate the existence of a short-term or PM system that is independent of any longer term or secondary store by showing that one function relating probability of recall to number of intervening items can describe a number of seemingly disparate sets of experimental results. In doing so, we have deliberately avoided discussing a number of problems raised in our analyses. Foremost in our list of problems is the definition of an item. Certainly the idea of a discrete verbal unit is crucial to our theory. The interference effect that we have studied seems to be invariant over a broad class of units and combinations of units—single digits, nonsense trigrams, and meaningful words. How long a string of such primitive units can we combine and still have one item? Is an item determined

**TABLE 3**

PROPORTION OF ITEMS FREELY RECALLED AS A FUNCTION OF
STIMULUS INTERFERENCE AND PRESENTATION TIME

| Number of intervening items | Seconds per item | | | | | | | | |
|---|---|---|---|---|---|---|---|---|---|
| | Distributed | | | | | Massed | | | |
| | 1 | 2 | 3 | 4 | 6 | 2 | 3 | 4 | 6 |
| 0 | .96 | .99 | .97 | 1.00 | .97 | .98 | .97 | 1.00 | 1.00 |
| 1 | .82 | .90 | .91 | .86 | .89 | .82 | .96 | .87 | .91 |
| 2 | .76 | .81 | .86 | .82 | .87 | .75 | .63 | .76 | .63 |
| 3 | .54 | .64 | .73 | .76 | .65 | .51 | .58 | .58 | .50 |
| 4 | .38 | .40 | .50 | .57 | .60 | .40 | .31 | .51 | .44 |
| 5 | .21 | .36 | .36 | .49 | .48 | .27 | .36 | .45 | .44 |
| 5+[a] | .14 | .26 | .32 | .38 | .45 | .25 | .31 | .38 | .42 |

[a]Entries in this row represent the asymptotic value of $R(n)$.

by our grammatical habits? Is it determined by the duration of the verbal stimulus? Is it determined by both? We do not know.

We have also avoided discussing the possible rules whereby items now in PM are displaced by later items. Are items lost independently of one another, or do they hang and fall together? It may perhaps prove difficult to answer this question experimentally, but it should not be impossible.

Finally, at what stage in the processing of incoming information does our PM reside? Is it in the peripheral sensory mechanism? Probably not. The work of Sperling (1960) indicates that "sensory memory"—to use Peterson's (1963) phrase—decays within a matter of milliseconds, whereas we have dealt in our analysis with retention intervals on the order of seconds. Does storage in PM precede the attachment of meaning to discrete verbal stimuli? Must a verbal stimulus be transformed into an auditory image in order to be stored in PM, even if it was presented visually? We refer the reader to a recent paper by Sperling (1963) for some thoughts on the latter question.

## REFERENCES

Atkinson, R. C., and Crothers, E. J. 1964. A comparison of paired-associate learning models having different acquisition and retention axioms. *Journal of Mathematical Psychology* 1:285–315.

Broadbent, D. E. 1958. *Perception and communication.* New York: Pergamon Press.

Brown, J. 1958. Some tests of the decay theory of immediate memory. *Quarterly Journal of Experimental Psychology* 10:12–21.

Bugelski, B. R. 1962. Presentation time, total time, and mediation in paired-associate learning. *Journal of Experimental Psychology* 63:409–412.

Clark, L. L.; Lansford, T. E.; and Dallenbach, K. M. 1960. Repetition and associative learning. *American Journal of Psychology* 73:22–40.

Conrad, R. 1957. Decay theory of immediate memory. *Nature* 179:831–832.

Deese, J., and Kaufman, R. A. 1957. Sequential effects in recall of unorganized and sequentially organized material. *Journal of Experimental Psychology* 54:180–187.

Hebb, D. O. 1949. *The organization of behavior.* New York: Wiley.

Hebb, D. O. 1961. Distinctive features of learning in the higher animal. In *Brain mechanisms and learning,* ed. J. F. Delafresnaye, pp. 37–46. London: Oxford University Press.

Hellyer, S. 1962. Supplementary report: Frequency of stimulus presentation and short-term decrement in recall. *Journal of Experimental Psychology* 64:650.

James, W. 1890. *The principles of psychology.* Vol. 1, chap. 16. New York: Holt.

Keppel, G., and Underwood, B. J. 1962. Proactive inhibition in short-term retention of single items. *Journal of Verbal Learning and Verbal Behavior* 1:153–161.

Loess, H. In press. Proactive inhibition in short-term memory. *Journal of Verbal Learning and Verbal Behavior.*

McGeoch, J. A. 1932. Forgetting and the law of disuse. *Psychological Review* 39:352–370.

Melton, A. W. 1963. Implications of short-term memory for a general theory of memory. *Journal of Verbal Learning and Verbal Behavior* 2:1–21.

Murdock, B. B., Jr. 1961. The retention of individual items. *Journal of Experimental Psychology* 62:618–625.

Murdock, B. B., Jr. 1962. The serial position effect in free recall. *Journal of Experimental Psychology* 64:482–488.

Murdock, B. B., Jr. 1963. Interpolated recall in short-term memory. *Journal of Experimental Psychology* 66:525–532.

Peterson, L. R. 1963. Immediate memory: Data and theory. In *Verbal behavior and learning: Problems and processes,* ed. C. N. Cofer and Barbara Musgrave, pp. 336–353. New York: McGraw-Hill.

Peterson, L. R., and Peterson, M. J. 1959. Short-term retention of individual verbal items. *Journal of Experimental Psychology* 58:193–198.

Pillsbury, W. B., and Sylvester, A. 1940. Retroactive and proactive inhibition in immediate memory. *Journal of Experimental Psychology* 27:532–545.

Posner, M. I. 1963. Immediate memory in sequential tasks. *Psychological Bulletin* 60:333–349.

Postman, L. 1961. The present status of interference theory. In *Verbal learning and verbal behavior,* ed. C. N. Cofer, pp. 152–179. New York: McGraw-Hill.

Sperling, G. 1960. The information available in brief visual presentations. *Psychological Monographs* 74, no. 11 (whole no. 498).

Sperling, G. 1963. A model for visual memory tasks. *Human Factors* 5:19–36.

Tulving, E., and Arbuckle, T. Y. 1963. Sources of intratrial interference in immediate recall of paired associates. *Journal of Verbal Learning and Verbal Behavior* 1:321–334.

Underwood, B. J., and Keppel, G. 1962. An evaluation of two problems of method in the study of retention. *American Journal of Psychology* 75:1–17.

Waugh, N. C. 1961. Free versus serial recall. *Journal of Experimental Psychology* 62:496–502.

Waugh, N. C. 1962. The effect of intralist repetition on free recall. *Journal of Verbal Learning and Verbal Behavior* 1:95–99.

Waugh, N. C. 1963. Immediate memory as a function of repetition. *Journal of Verbal Learning and Verbal Behavior* 2:107–112.

# READING 24

## The "Tip of the Tongue" Phenomenon

**ROGER BROWN**
**Harvard University**
**DAVID McNEILL**
**University of Chicago**

The TOT experience is familiar to us all. The variables surrounding this state have been studied experimentally by Brown and McNeill. Because of the nature of the TOT state, one of the problems that faced the authors was the statistical analysis of the data. As you read this article, keep in mind the problems—both methodological and analytical—and note how the authors solved these problems.

**QUESTIONS**

1. As the authors stated, statistical analysis of the data was difficult. Do you find their analyses meaningful? Should experimental design be limited by statistical methods? Support your answer.
2. Do you think Brown and McNeill's model of long-term memory for words is valid? Comment.
3. What is the value of studying something like the TOT phenomenon? Is it a waste of valuable research time, or can this type of research add constructive information to the pool of psychological knowledge?

William James wrote, in 1893: "Suppose we try to recall a forgotten name. The state of our consciousness is peculiar. There is a gap therein; but no mere gap. It is a gap that is intensely active. A sort of wraith of the name is in it, beckoning us in a given direction, making us at moments tingle with the sense of our closeness and then letting us sink back without the longed-for term. If wrong names are proposed to us, this singu-larly definite gap acts immediately so as to negate them. They do not fit into its mould. And the gap of one word does not feel like the gap of another, all empty of content as both might seem necessarily to be when described as gaps" (p. 251).

The "tip of the tongue" (TOT) state involves a failure to recall a word of which one has knowledge. The evidence of knowledge is either an eventually successful recall or else an act of recognition that occurs, without additional training, when recall has failed. The class of cases defined by the conjunction of knowledge and a failure of recall is a large one. The TOT state, which James described, seems to be a small subclass in which recall is felt to be imminent.

For several months we watched for TOT states in ourselves. Unable to recall the name of the street on which a relative lives, one of us thought of *Congress* and *Corinth* and *Concord* and then looked up the address and learned that it was *Cornish*. The words that had come to mind have certain properties in common with the word that had been sought (the "target word"): all four begin with *Co*; all are two-syllable words; all put the primary stress on the first syllable. After this experience we began putting direct questions to ourselves when we fell into the TOT state, questions as to the number of syllables in the target word, its initial letter, etc.

Woodworth (1934), before us, made a record of data for naturally occurring TOT states and Wenzl (1932, 1936) did the same for German words. Their results are similar to those we obtained and consistent with the following preliminary characterization. When complete recall of a word is not presently possible but is felt to be imminent, one can often correctly recall the general type of the word; *generic* recall may succeed when particular recall fails. There seem to be two common varieties of generic recall. (a) Sometimes a part of the target word is recalled, a letter or two, a syllable, or affix. Partial recall is necessarily also *generic* since the class of words defined by the possession of any *part* of the target word will include words other than the target. (b) Sometimes the abstract form of the target is recalled, perhaps the fact that it was a two-syllable sequence with the primary stress on the first syllable. The whole word is represented in *abstract form recall* but not on the letter-by-letter level that constitutes its identity. The recall of an abstract form is also necessarily *generic*, since any such form

defines a class of words extending beyond the target.

Wenzl and Woodworth had worked with small collections of data for naturally occurring TOT states. These data were, for the most part, provided by the investigators; were collected in an unsystematic fashion; and were analyzed in an impressionistic nonquantitative way. It seemed to us that such data left the facts of generic recall in doubt. An occasional correspondence between a retrieved word and a target word with respect to number of syllables, stress pattern or initial letter is, after all, to be expected by chance. Several months of "self-observation and asking-our-friends" yielded fewer than a dozen good cases and we realized that an improved method of data collection was essential.

We thought it might pay to "prospect" for TOT states by reading to *S* definitions of uncommon English words and asking him to supply the words. The procedure was given a preliminary test with nine *S*s who were individually interviewed for 2 hrs. each.[1] In 57 instances an *S* was, in fact, "seized" by a TOT state. The signs of it were unmistakable; he would appear to be in mild torment, something like the brink of a sneeze, and if he found the word his relief was considerable. While searching for the target *S* told us all the words that came to his mind. He volunteered the information that some of them resembled the target in sound but not in meaning; others he was sure were similar in meaning but not in sound. The *E* intruded on *S*'s agony with two questions: (a) How many syllables has the target word? (b) What is its first letter? Answers to the first question were correct in 47% of all cases and answers to the second question were correct in 51% of the cases. These outcomes encouraged us to believe that generic recall was real and to devise a group procedure that would further speed up the rate of data collection.

---

[1] We wish to thank Mr. Charles Hollen for doing the pretest interviews.

## METHOD
### SUBJECTS

Fifty-six Harvard and Radcliffe undergraduates participated in one of three evening sessions; each session was 2 hrs. long. The *S*s were volunteers from a large General Education Course and were paid for their time.

### Word List.

The list consisted of 49 words which according to the Thorndike-Lorge *Word Book* (1952) occur at least once per four million words but not so often as once per one million words. The level is suggested by these examples: *apse, nepotism, cloaca, ambergris,* and *sampan.* We thought the words used were likely to be in the passive or recognition vocabularies of our *S*s but not in their active recall vocabularies. There were 6 words of 1 syllable; 19 of 2 syllables; 20 of 3 syllables; 4 of 4 syllables. For each word we used a definition from *The American College Dictionary* (Barnhart, 1948) edited so as to contain no words that closely resembled the one being defined.

### Response Sheet.

The response sheet was laid off in vertical columns headed as follows:

*Intended word (+ One I was thinking of).*
*(— Not).*

*Number of syllables (1–5).*
*Initial letter.*
*Words of similar sound.*

> (1. *Closest in sound* )
> (2. *Middle*　　　　　 )
> (3. *Farthest in Sound*)

*Words of similar meaning.*
*Word you had in mind if not intended word.*

## PROCEDURE

We instructed *S*s to the following effect.

In this experiment we are concerned with that state of mind in which a person is unable to think of a word that he is certain he knows, the state of mind in which a word seems to be on the tip of one's tongue. Our technique for precipitating such states is, in general, to read definitions of uncommon words and ask the subject to recall the word.

(1) We will first read the definition of a low-frequency word.

(2) If you should happen to know the word at once, or think you do, or, if you should simply not know it, then there is nothing further for you to do at the moment. Just wait.

(3) If you are unable to think of the word but feel sure that you know it and that it is on the verge of coming back to you then you are in a TOT state and should begin at once to fill in the columns of the response sheet.

(4) After reading each definition we will ask whether anyone is in the TOT state. Anyone who is in that state should raise his hand. The rest of us will then wait until those in the TOT state have written on the answer sheet all the information they are able to provide.

(5) When everyone who has been in the TOT state has signalled us to proceed, we will read the target word. At this time, everyone is to write the word in the leftmost column of the response sheet. Those of you who have known the word since first its definition was read are asked not to write it until this point. Those of you who simply did not know the word or who had thought of a different word will write now the word we read. For those of you who have been in the TOT state two eventualities are possible. The word read may strike you as definitely the word you have been seeking. In that case please write '+' after the word, as the instructions at the head of the column direct. The other possibility is that you will not be sure whether the word read is the one you have been seeking or, indeed, you may be sure that it is not. In this case you are asked to write the sign '—' after the word. Sometimes when the word read out is not the one you have been seeking your actual target may come to mind. In this case, in addition to the minus sign in the leftmost column, please write the actual target word in the rightmost column.

(6) Now we come to the column entries

themselves. The first two entries, the guess as to the number of syllables and the initial letter, are required. The remaining entries should be filled out if possible. When you are in a TOT state, words that are related to the target word do almost always come to mind. List them as they come, but separate words which you think resemble the target in sound from words which you think resemble the target in meaning.

(7) When you have finished all your entries, but before you signal us to read the intended target word, look again at the words you have listed as 'Words of similar sound.' If possible, rank these, as the instructions at the head of the column direct, in terms of the degree of their seeming resemblance to the target. This must be done without knowledge of what the target actually is.

(8) The search procedure of a person in the TOT state will sometimes serve to retrieve the missing word before he has finished filling in the columns and before we read out the word. When this happens please mark the place where it happens with the words "Got it" and *do not provide any more data.*

## RESULTS

### CLASSES OF DATA

There were 360 instances, across all words and all Ss, in which a TOT state was signalled. Of this total, 233 were positive TOTs. A positive TOT is one for which the target word is known and, consequently, one for which the data obtained can be scored as accurate or inaccurate. In those cases where the target was not the word intended but some other word which S finally recalled and wrote in the rightmost column his data were checked against that word, his effective target. A negative TOT is one for which the S judged the word read out not to have been his target and, in addition, one in which S proved unable to recall his own functional target.

The data provided by S while he searched for the target word are of two kinds: explicit guesses as to the number of syllables in the target and the initial letter of the target; words that came to mind while he searched for the target. The words that came to mind were classified by S into 224 words similar in sound to the target (hereafter called "SS" words) and 95 words similar in meaning to the target (hereafter called "SM" words). The S's information about the number of syllables in, and the initial letter of the target may be inferred from correspondences between the target and his SS words as well as directly discovered from his explicit guesses. For his knowledge of the stress pattern of the target and of letters in the target, other than the initial letter, we must rely on the SS words alone since explicit guesses were not required.

To convey a sense of the SS and SM words we offer the following examples. When the target was *sampan* the SS words (not all of them real words) included: *Saipan, Siam, Cheyenne, sarong, sanching,* and *sympoon.* The SM words were: *barge, houseboat,* and *junk.* When the target was *caduceus* the SS words included *Casadesus, Aeschelus, cephalus,* and *leucosis.* The SM words were: *fasces, Hippocrates, lictor,* and *snake.* The spelling in all cases is S's own.

We will, in this report, use the SM words to provide baseline data against which to evaluate the accuracy of the explicit guesses and of the SS words. The SM words are words produced under the spell of the positive TOT state but judged by S to resemble the target in meaning rather than sound. We are quite sure that the SM words are somewhat more like the target than would be a collection of words produced by Ss with no knowledge of the target. However, the SM words make a better comparative baseline than any other data we collected.

### GENERAL PROBLEMS OF ANALYSIS

The data present problems of analysis that are not common in psychology. To begin with, the words of the list did not reliably precipitate TOT states. Of the original 49 words, all but *zither* succeeded at least once; the range was from one success to nine. The *S*s made actual targets of 51 words not on the original list and all but five of these were pursued by one *S* only. Clearly none of the 100 words came even close to precipitating a TOT state in all 56 *S*s. Furthermore, the *S*s varied in their susceptibility to TOT states. There were nine who experienced none at all in a 2-hr. period; the largest number experienced in such a period by one *S* was eight. In our data, then, the entries for one word will not usually involve the same *S*s or even the same number of *S*s as the entries for another word. The entries for one *S* need not involve the same words or even the same number of words as the entries for another *S*. Consequently for the tests we shall want to make there are no significance tests that we can be sure are appropriate.

In statistical theory our problem is called the "fragmentary data problem."[2] The best thing to do with fragmentary data is to report them very fully and analyze them in several different ways. Our detailed knowledge of these data suggests that the problems are not serious for, while there is some variation in the pull of words and the susceptibility of *S*s there is not much variation in the quality of the data. The character of the material recalled is much the same from word to word and *S* to *S*.

## NUMBER OF SYLLABLES

As the main item of evidence that *S* in a TOT state can recall with significant success the number of syllables in a target word he has not yet found we offer Table 1. The entries on the diagonal are instances in which guesses were correct. The order of the means of the explicit guesses is the same as the order of the actual numbers of syllables in the target words. The rank order correlation between the two is 1.0 and such a correlation

---

[2] We wish to thank Professor Frederick Mosteller for discussing the fragmentary data problem with us.

**TABLE 1**

ACTUAL NUMBERS OF SYLLABLES AND
GUESSED NUMBERS FOR ALL TOTs
IN THE MAIN EXPERIMENT

|  |  | Guessed numbers | | | | | No | | |
|---|---|---|---|---|---|---|---|---|---|
|  |  | 1 | 2 | 3 | 4 | 5 | guess | Mode | Mean |
| Actual numbers | 1 | 9 | 7 | 1 | 0 | 0 | 0 | 1 | 1.53 |
|  | 2 | 2 | 55 | 22 | 2 | 1 | 5 | 2 | 2.33 |
|  | 3 | 3 | 19 | 61 | 10 | 1 | 5 | 3 | 2.86 |
|  | 4 | 0 | 2 | 12 | 6 | 2 | 3 | 3 | 3.36 |
|  | 5 | 0 | 0 | 3 | 0 | 1 | 1 | 3 | 3.50 |

relation is significant with a $p < .001$ (one-tailed) even when only five items are correlated. The modes of the guesses correspond exactly with the actual numbers of syllables, for the values one through three; for words of four and five syllables the modes continue to be three.

When all TOTs are combined, the contributions to the total effects of individual *S*s and of individual words are unequal. We have made an analysis in which each word counts but once. This was accomplished by calculating the mean of the guesses made by all *S*s for whom a particular word precipitated a TOT state and taking that mean as the score for that word. The new means calculated with all words equally weighted were, in order: 1.62; 2.30; 2.80; 3.33; and 3.50. These values are close to those of Table 1 and *rho* with the actual numbers of syllables continues to be 1.0.

We also made an analysis in which each *S* counts but once. This was done by calculating the mean of an *S*'s guesses for all words of one syllable, the mean for all words of two syllables, etc. In comparing the means of guesses for words of different length one can only use those *S*s who made at least one guess for each actual length to be compared. In the present data only words of two syllables and three syllables precipitated enough TOTs to yield a substantial number of such matched scores. There were 21 *S*s who made guesses for both two-syllable and three-syllable words.

The simplest way to evaluate the significance of the differences in these guesses is with the Sign Test. In only 6 of 21 matched scores was the mean guess for words of two syllables larger than the mean for words of three syllables. The difference is significant with a $p = .039$ (one-tailed). For actual words that were only one syllable apart in length, $S$s were able to make a significant distinction in the correct direction when the words themselves could not be called to mind.

The 224 SS words and the 95 SM words provide supporting evidence. Words of similar sound (SS) had the same number of syllables as the target in 48% of all cases. This value is close to the 57% that were correct for explicit guesses in the main experiment and still closer to the 47% correct already reported for the pretest. The SM words provide a clear contrast; only 20% matched the number of syllables in the target. We conclude that $S$ in a positive TOT state has a significant ability to recall correctly the number of syllables in the word he is trying to retrieve.

In Table 1 it can be seen that the modes of guesses exactly correspond with the actual numbers of syllables in target words for the values one through three. For still longer target words (four and five syllables) the means of guesses continue to rise but the modes stay at the value three. Words of more than three syllables are rare in English and the generic entry for such words may be the same as for words of three syllables; something like "three or more" may be used for all long words.

### INITIAL LETTER

Over all positive TOTs, the initial letter of the word $S$ was seeking was correctly guessed 57% of the time. The pretest result was 51% correct. The results from the main experiment were analyzed with each word counting just once by entering a word's score as "correct" whenever the most common guess or the only guess was in fact correct; 62% of words were, by this reckoning, correctly guessed. The SS words had initial letters matching the initial letters of the target words in 49% of all cases. We do not know the chance level of success for this performance but with 26 letters and many words that began with uncommon letters the level must be low. Probably the results for the SM words are better than chance and yet the outcome for these words was only 8% matches.

We did an analysis of the SS and SM words, with each $S$ counting just once. There were 26 $S$s who had at least one such word. For each $S$ we calculated the proportion of SS words matching the target in initial letter and the same proportion for SM words. For 21 $S$s the proportions were not tied and in all but 3 cases the larger value was that of the SS words. The difference is significant by Sign Test with $p = .001$ (one-tailed).

The evidence for significantly accurate generic recall of initial letters is even stronger than for syllables. The absolute levels of success are similar but the chance baseline must be much lower for letters than for syllables because the possibilities are more numerous.

### SYLLABIC STRESS

We did not ask $S$ to guess the stress pattern of the target word but the SS words provide relevant data. The test was limited to the syllabic location of the primary or heaviest stress for which *The American College Dictionary* was our authority. The number of SS words that could be used was limited by three considerations. (a) Words of one syllable had to be excluded because there was no possibility of variation. (b) Stress locations could only be matched if the SS word had the same number of syllables as the target, and so only such matching words could be used. (c) Invented words and foreign words could not be used because they do not appear in the dictionary. Only 49 SS words remained.

As it happened all of the target words involved (whatever their length) placed the primary stress on either the first or the second syllable. It was possible, therefore, to make a 2 × 2 table for the 49 pairs of target and SS words which would reveal the correspondences and noncorrespondences. As can be seen in Table 2 the SS words tended to stress the same syllable as the target words. The $X^2$ for this table is 10.96 and that value is significant with $p < .001$. However, the data do not meet the independence requirement, so we cannot be sure that the matching tendency is significant. There were not enough data to permit any other analyses, and so we are left suspect-

**TABLE 2**

SYLLABLES RECEIVING PRIMARY STRESS
IN TARGET WORDS AND SS WORDS

|  |  | Target words | |
|---|---|---|---|
|  |  | 1st syllable | 2nd syllable |
| SS Words | 1st syllable | 25 | 6 |
| | 2nd syllable | 6 | 12 |

ing that $S$ in a TOT state has knowledge of the stress pattern of the target, but we are not sure of it.

## LETTERS IN VARIOUS POSITIONS

We did not require explicit guesses for letters in positions other than the first, but the SS words provide relevant data. The test was limited to the following positions: first, second, third, third-last, second-last, and last. A target word must have at least six letters in order to provide data on the six positions; it might have any number of letters larger than six and still provide data for the six (relatively defined) positions. Accordingly we included the data for all target words having six or more letters.

Figure 1 displays the percentages of letters in each of six positions of SS words which matched the letters in the same positions of the corresponding targets. For comparison purposes these data are also provided for SM words. The SS curve is at all points above the SM curve; the two are

closest together at the third-last position. The values for the last three positions of the SS curve quite closely match the values for the first three positions. The values for the last three positions of the SM curve, on the other hand, are well above the values for

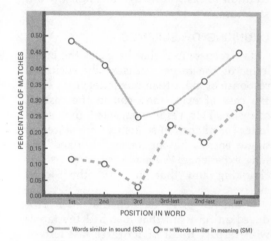

**Figure 1.** Percentages of letter matches between target words and SS words for six serial positions.

the first three positions. Consequently the *relative* superiority of the SS curve is greater in the first three positions.

The letter-position data were also analyzed in such a way as to count each target word just once, assigning each position in the target a single score representing the proportion of matches across all $Ss$ for that position in that word. The order of the SS and SM points is preserved in this finer analysis. We did Sign Tests comparing the SS and SM values for each of the six positions. As Figure 1 would suggest the SS values for the first three positions all exceeded the SM values with $p$'s less than .01 (one-tailed). The SS values for the final two positions exceeded the SM values with $p$'s less than .05 (one-tailed). The SS values for the third-last position were greater than the SM values but not significantly so.

The cause of the upswing in the final three positions of the SM curve may be some difference in the distribution of information in early and late positions of English words. Probably there is less variety in the later positions. In any case the fact that the SS curve lies above the SM curve for the last three positions indicates that $S$ in a TOT state has knowledge of the target in addition to his knowledge of English word structure.

## CHUNKING OF SUFFIXES

The request to $S$ that he guess the initial letter of the target occasionally elicited a response of more than one letter; e.g., *ex* in the case of *extort* and *con* in the case of *convene*. This result suggested that some letter (or phoneme) sequences are stored as single entries having been "chunked" by long experience. We made only one test for chunking and that involved three-letter suffixes.

It did not often happen that an $S$ produced an SS word that matched the target with respect to all of its three last letters. The question asked of the data was whether such three-letter matches occurred more often when the letters constituted an English suffix than when they did not. In order to determine which of the target words terminated in such a suffix, we entered *The American College Dictionary* with final trigrams. If there was an entry describing a suffix appropriate to the grammatical and semantic properties of the target we considered the trigram to be a suffix. There were 20 words that terminated in a suffix, including *fawning, unctuous,* and *philatelist*.

Of 93 SS words produced in response to a target terminating in a suffix, 30 matched the target in their final three letters. Of 130 SS words supplied in response to a target that did not terminate in a suffix only 5 matched the target in their final three letters. The data were also analyzed in a way that counts each $S$ just once and uses only $S$s who produced SS words in response to both kinds of target. A Sign Test was made of the difference between matches of suffixes and matches of endings that were not

suffixes; the former were more common with $p = .059$ (one-tailed). A comparable Sign Test for SM words was very far from significance. We conclude that suffix-chunking probably plays a role in generic recall.

## PROXIMITY TO THE TARGET AND QUALITY OF INFORMATION

There were three varieties of positive TOT states: (1) Cases in which $S$ *recognized* the word read by $E$ as the word he had been seeking; (2) Cases in which $S$ *recalled* the intended word before it was read out; (3) Cases in which $S$ *recalled* the word he had been seeking before $E$ read the intended word and the recalled word was not the same as the word read. Since $S$ in a TOT state of either type 2 or type 3 reached the target before the intended word was read and $S$ in a TOT state of type 1 did not, the TOTs of the second and third types may be considered "nearer" the target than TOTs of the first type. We have no basis for ordering types 2 and 3 relative to one another. We predicted that $S$s in the two kinds of TOT state that ended in recall (types 2 and 3) would produce more accurate information about the target than $S$s in the TOT state that ended in recognition (type 1).

The prediction was tested on the explicit guesses of initial letters since these were the most complete and sensitive data. There were 138 guesses from $S$s in a type 1 state and 58 of these, or 42%, were correct. There were 36 guesses from $S$s in a type 2 state and, of these, 20, or 56%, were correct. There were 59 guesses from $S$s in a type 3 state and of these 39, or 66%, were correct. We also analyzed the results in such a way as to count each word only once. The percentages correct were: for type 1, 50%; type 2, 62%; type 3, 63%. Finally, we performed an analysis counting each $S$ just once but averaging together type 2 and type 3 results in order to bring a maximum number of $S$s into the comparison. The combining action is justified since both type 2 and type 3 were states ending in recall. A Sign

Test of the differences showed that guesses were more accurate in the states that ended in recall than in the states that ended in recognition; one-tailed $p < .01$. Supplementary analyses with SS and SM words confirmed these results. We conclude that when S is nearer his target his generic recall is more accurate than when he is farther from the target.

Special interest attaches to the results from type 2 TOTs. In the method of our experiment there is nothing to guarantee that when S said he recognized a word he had really done so. Perhaps when E read out a word, S could not help thinking that that was the word he had in mind. We ourselves do not believe anything of the sort happened. The single fact that most Ss claimed fewer than five positive TOTs in a 2-hr. period argues against any such effect. Still it is reassuring to have the 36 type 2 cases in which S recalled the intended word *before* it was read. The fact that 56% of the guesses of initial letters made in type 2 states were correct is hard-core evidence of generic recall. It may be worth adding that 65% of the guesses of the number of syllables for type 2 cases were correct.

## JUDGMENTS OF THE PROXIMITY OF SS WORDS

The several comparisons we have made of SS and SM words demonstrate that when recall is imminent S can distinguish among the words that come to mind those that resemble the target in form from those that do not resemble the target in form. There is a second kind of evidence which shows that S can tell when he is getting close (or "warm").

In 15 instances Ss rated two or more SS words for comparative similarity to the target. Our analysis contrasts those rated "most similar" (1) with those rated next most similar (2). Since there were very few words rated (3) we attempted no analysis of them. Similarity points were given for all the features of a word that have now been demonstrated to play a part in generic recall —with the single exception of stress. Stress had to be disregarded because some of the words were invented and their stress patterns were unknown.

The problem was to compare pairs of SS words, rated 1 and 2, for overall similarity to the target. We determined whether each member matched the target in number of syllables. If one did and the other did not, then a single similarity point was assigned the word that matched. For each word, we counted, beginning with the initial letter, the number of consecutive letters in common with the target. The word having the longer sequence that matched the target earned one similarity point. An exactly comparable procedure was followed for sequences starting from the final letter. In sum, each word in a pair could receive from zero to three similarity points.

We made Sign Tests comparing the total scores for words rated most like the target (1) and words rated next most like the target (2). This test was only slightly inappropriate since only two target words occurred twice in the set of 15 and only one S repeated in the set. Ten of 12 differences were in the predicted direction and the one-tailed $p = .019$. It is of some interest that similarity points awarded on the basis of letters in the middle of the words did not even go in the right direction. Figure 1 has already indicated that they also do not figure in Ss' judgments of the comparative similarity to the target of pairs of SS words. Our conclusion is that S at a given distance from the target can accurately judge which of two words that come to mind is more like the target and that he does so in terms of the features of words that appear in generic recall.

## CONCLUSIONS

When complete recall of a word has not occurred but is felt to be imminent there is likely to be accurate generic recall. Generic recall of the *abstract form* variety is evidenced by *S's* knowledge of the number of syllables in the target and of the location of the primary stress. Generic recall of the *partial* variety is evidenced by *S's* knowledge of letters in the target word. This knowledge shows a bowed serial-position effect since it is better for the ends of a word than for the middle and somewhat better for beginning positions than for final positions. The accuracy of generic recall is greater when *S* is near the target (complete recall is imminent) than when *S* is far from the target. A person experiencing generic recall is able to judge the relative similarity to the target of words that occur to him and these judgments are based on the features of words that figure in partial and abstract form recall.

## DISCUSSION

The facts of generic recall are relevant to theories of speech perception, reading the understanding of sentences, and the organization of memory. We have not worked out all the implications. In this section we first attempt a model of the TOT process and then try to account for the existence of generic memory.

### A MODEL OF THE PROCESS

Let us suppose (with Katz and Fodor, 1963, and many others) that our long-term memory for words and definitions is organized into the functional equivalent of a dictionary. In real dictionaries, those that are books, entries are ordered alphabetically and bound in place. Such an arrangement is too simple and too inflexible to serve as a model for a mental dictionary. We will suppose that words are entered on keysort cards instead of pages and that the cards are punched for various features of the words entered. With real cards, paper ones, it is possible to retrieve from the total deck any subset punched for a common feature by putting a metal rod through the proper hole. We will suppose that there is in the mind some speedier equivalent of this retrieval technique.

The model will be described in terms of a single example. When the target word was *sextant*, *Ss* heard the definition: "A navigational instrument used in measuring angular distances, especially the altitude of sun, moon, and stars at sea." This definition precipitated a TOT state in 9 *Ss* of the total 56. The SM words included: *astrolabe, compass, dividers,* and *protractor*. The SS words included: *secant, sextet,* and *sexton*.

The problem begins with a definition rather than a word and so *S* must enter his dictionary backwards, or in a way that would be backwards and quite impossible for the dictionary that is a book. It is not impossible with keysort cards, providing we suppose that the cards are punched for some set of semantic features. Perhaps these are the semantic "markers" that Katz and Fodor (1963) postulate in their account of the comprehension of sentences. We will imagine that it is somehow possible to extract from the definition a set of markers and that these are, in the present case: "navigation, instrument, having to do with geometry." Metal rods thrust into the holes for each of these features might fish up such a collection of entries as: *astrolabe, compass, dividers,* and *protractor*. This first retrieval, which is in response to the definition, must be semantically based and it will not, therefore, account for the appearance of such SS words as *sextet* and *sexton*.

There are four major kinds of outcome of the first retrieval and these outcomes correspond with the four main things that happen to *Ss* in the TOT experiment. We will assume that a definition of each word retrieved is entered on its card and that it is possible to check the input definition against those on the cards. The first possible outcome is that *sextant* is retrieved along with *compass* and *astrolabe* and the others and that the definitions are specific enough so that the one entered for *sextant* registers as matching the input and all the others as not-matching. This is the case of correct recall; *S* has found a word that matches the definition and it is the intended word. The second possibility is that *sextant* is not among the words retrieved and, in addition, the definitions entered for those retrieved are so imprecise that one of them (the definition for *compass*, for example) registers as matching the input. In this case *S* thinks he has found the target though he really has not. The third possibility is that *sextant* is not among the words retrieved, but the definitions entered for those retrieved are specific enough so that none of them will register a match with the input. In this case, *S* does not know the word and realizes the fact. The above three outcomes are the common ones and none of them represents a TOT state.

In the TOT case the first retrieval must include a card with the definition of *sextant* entered on it but with the word itself incompletely entered. The card might, for instance, have the following information about the word: two-syllables, initial s, final t. The entry would be a punchcard equivalent of S_ _ _ _T. Perhaps an incomplete entry of this sort is James's "singularly definite gap" and the basis for generic recall.

The *S* with a correct definition, matching the input, and an incomplete word entry will know that he knows the word, will feel that he almost has it, that it is on the tip of his tongue. If he is asked to guess the number of syllables and the initial letter he should, in the case we have imagined, be able to do so. He should also be able to produce SS words. The features that appear in the incomplete entry (two-syllables, initial s, and final t) can be used as the basis for a second retrieval. The subset of cards defined by the intersection of all three features would include cards for *secant* and *sextet*. If one feature were not used then *sexton* would be added to the set.

Which of the facts about the TOT state can now be accounted for? We know that *S*s were able, when they had not recalled a target, to distinguish between words resembling the target in sound (SS words) and words resembling the target in meaning only (SM words). The basis for this distinc-

tion in the model would seem to be the distinction between the first and second retrievals. Membership in the first subset retrieved defines SM words and membership in the second subset defines SS words.

We know that when *S* had produced several SS words but had not recalled the target he could sometimes accurately rank-order the SS words for similarity to the target. The model offers an account of this ranking performance. If the incomplete entry for *sextant* includes three features of the word then SS words having only one or two of these features (e.g., *sexton*) should be judged less similar to the target than SS words having all three of them (e.g., *secant*).

When an SS word has all of the features of the incomplete entry (as do *secant* and *sextet* in our example) what prevents its being mistaken for the target? Why did not the *S* who produced *sextet* think that the word was "right?" Because of the definitions. The forms meet all the requirements of the incomplete entry but the definitions do not match.

The TOT state often ended in recognition; i.e., *S* failed to recall the word but when *E* read out *sextant S* recognized it as the word he had been seeking. The model accounts for this outcome as follows. Suppose that there is only the incomplete entry S_ _ _T in memory, plus the definition. The *E* now says (in effect) that there exists a word *sextant* which has the definition in question. The word *sextant* then satisfies all the data points available to *S*; it has the right number of syllables, the right initial letter, the right final letter, and it is said to have the right definition. The result is recognition.

The proposed account has some testable implications. Suppose that *E* were to read out, when recall failed, not the correct word *sextant* but an invented word like *sekrant* or *saktint* which satisfies the incomplete entry as well as does *sextant* itself. If *S* had nothing but the incomplete entry and *E*'s testimony to guide him then he should "recognize" the invented words just as he recognizes *sextant*.

The account we have given does not accord with intuition. Our intuitive notion of recognition is that the features which could not be called were actually in storage but less accessible than the features that were recalled. To stay with our example, intuition suggests that the features of *sextant* that could not be recalled, the letters between the first and the last, were entered on the card but were less "legible" than the recalled features. We might imagine them printed in small letters and faintly. When, however, the *E* reads out the word *sextant*, then *S* can make out the less legible parts of his entry and, since the total entry matches *E*'s word, *S* recognizes it. This sort of recognition should be "tighter" than the one described previously. *Sekrant* and *saktint* would be rejected.

We did not try the effect of invented words and we do not know how they would have been received but among the outcomes of the actual experiment there is one that strongly favors the faint-entry theory. Subjects in a TOT state, after all, sometimes recalled the target word without any prompting. The incomplete entry theory does not admit of such a possibility. If we suppose that the entry is not S__ __T but something more like S*ex tan*T (with the italicized lower-case letters representing the faint-entry section) we must still explain how it happens that the faintly entered, and at first inaccessible, middle letters are made accessible in the case of recall.

Perhaps it works something like this. The features that are first recalled operate as we have suggested, to retrieve a set of SS words. Whenever an SS word (such as *secant*) includes middle letters that are matched in the faintly entered section of the target then those faintly entered letters become accessible. The match brings out the missing parts the way heat brings out anything written in lemon juice. In other words, when *secant* is retrieved the target entry grows from S*ex tan*T to SE*x t*ANT. The retrieval of *sextet* brings out the remaining

letters and *S* recalls the complete word— *sextant*.

It is now possible to explain the one as yet unexplained outcome of the TOT experiment. Subjects whose state ended in recall had, before they found the target, more correct information about it than did *S*s whose state ended in recognition. More correct information means fewer features to be brought out by duplication in SS words and so should mean a greater likelihood that all essential features will be brought out in a short period of time.

All of the above assumes that each word is entered in memory just once, on a single card. There is another possibility. Suppose that there are entries for *sextant* on several different cards. They might all be incomplete, but at different points, or, some might be incomplete and one or more of them complete. The several cards would be punched for different semantic markers and perhaps for different associations so that the entry recovered would vary with the rule of retrieval. With this conception we do not require the notion of faint entry. The difference between features commonly recalled, such as the first and last letters, and features that are recalled with difficulty or perhaps only recognized, can be rendered in another way. The more accessible features are entered on more cards or else the cards on which they appear are punched for more markers; in effect, they are wired into a more extended associative net.

## THE REASON FOR GENERIC RECALL

In adult minds words are stored in both visual and auditory terms and between the two there are complicated rules of translation. Generic recall involves letters (or phonemes), affixes, syllables, and stress location. In this section we will discuss only letters (legible forms) and will attempt to explain a single effect—the serial position effect in the recall of letters. It is not clear how far the explanation can be extended.

In brief overview this is the argument.

The design of the English language is such that one word is usually distinguished from all others in a more-than-minimal way, i.e., by more than a single letter in a single position. It is consequently *possible* to recognize words when one has not stored the complete letter sequence. The evidence is that we do not store the complete sequence if we do not have to. We begin by attending chiefly to initial and final letters and storing these. The order of attention and of storage favors the ends of words because the ends carry more information than the middles. An incomplete entry will serve for recognition, but if words are to be produced (or recalled) they must be stored in full. For most words, then, it is eventually necessary to attend to the middle letters. Since end letters have been attended to from the first they should always be more clearly entered or more elaborately connected than middle letters. When recall is required, of words that are not very familiar to S, as it was in our experiment, the end letters should often be accessible when the middle are not.

In building pronounceable sequences the English language, like all other languages, utilizes only a small fraction of its combinatorial possibilities (Hockett, 1958). If a language used all possible sequences of phonemes (or letters) its words could be shorter, but they would be much more vulnerable to misconstruction. A change of any single letter would result in reception of a different word. As matters are actually arranged, most changes result in no word at all; for example: *textant, sixtant, sektant.* Our words are highly redundant and fairly indestructible.

Underwood (1963) has made a distinction for the learning of nonsense syllables between the "nominal" stimulus which is the syllable presented and the "functional" stimulus which is the set of characteristics of the syllable actually used to cue the response. Underwood reviews evidence showing that college students learning paired-associates do not learn any more of a stimulus

trigram than they have to. If, for instance, each of a set of stimulus trigrams has a different initial letter, then Ss are not likely to learn letters other than the first, since they do not need them.

Feigenbaum (1963) has written a computer program (EPAM) which simulates the selective-attention aspect of verbal learning as well as many other aspects. " . . . EPAM has a *noticing order for letters of syllables,* which prescribes at any moment a letter-scanning sequence for the matching process. Because it is observed that subjects generally consider end letters before middle letters, the noticing order is initialized as follows: first letter, third letter, second letter" (p. 304). We believe that the differential recall of letters in various positions, revealed in Figure 1 of this paper, is to be explained by the operation in the perception of real words of a rule very much like Feigenbaum's.

Feigenbaum's EPAM is so written as to make it possible for the noticing rule to be changed by experience. If the middle position were consistently the position that differentiated syllables, the computer would learn to look there first. We suggest that the human tendency to look first at the beginning of a word, then at the end and finally the middle has "grown" in response to the distribution of information in words. Miller and Friedman (1957) asked English speakers to guess letters for various open positions in segments of English text that were 5, 7, or 11 characters long. The percentages of correct first guesses show a very clear serial position effect for segments of all three lengths. Success was lowest in the early positions, next lowest in the final positions, and at a maximum in the middle positions. Therefore, information was greatest at the start of a word, next greatest at the end, and least in the middle. Attention needs to be turned where information is, to the parts of the word that cannot be guessed. The Miller and Friedman segments did not necessarily break at word boundaries but their discovery that the middle positions of continuous text are more easily guessed than the ends applies to words.

Is there any evidence that speakers of English do attend first to the ends of English words? There is no evidence that the eye fixations of adult readers consistently favor particular parts of words (Woodworth and Schlosberg, 1954). However, it is not eye fixation that we have in mind. A considerable stretch of text can be taken in from a single fixation point. We are suggesting that there is selection within this stretch, selection accomplished centrally; perhaps by a mechanism like Broadbent's (1958) "biased filter."

Bruner and O'Dowd (1958) studied word perception with tachistoscopic exposures too brief to permit more than one fixation. In each word presented there was a single reversal of two letters and the S knew this. His task was to identify the *actual* English word responding as quickly as possible. When the *actual* word was AVIATION, Ss were presented with one of the following: VAIATION, AVITAION, AVIATINO. Identification of the actual word as AVIATION was best when S saw AVITAION, next best when he saw AVIATINO, and most difficult when he saw VAIATION. In general, a reversal of the two initial letters made identification most difficult, reversal of the last two letters made it somewhat less difficult, reversal in the middle made least difficulty. This is what should happen if words are first scanned initially, then finally, then medially. But the scanning cannot be a matter of eye movements; it must be more central.

Selective attention to the ends of words should lead to the entry of these parts into the mental dictionary, in advance of the middle parts. However, we ordinarily need to know more than the ends of words. Underwood has pointed out (1963), in connection with paired-associate learning, that while partial knowledge may be enough for

a stimulus syllable which need only be recognized it will not suffice for a response item which must be produced. The case is similar for natural language. In order to speak one must know all of a word. However, the words of the present study were low-frequency words, words likely to be in the passive or recognition vocabularies of the college-student Ss but not in their active vocabularies; stimulus items, in effect, rather than response items. If knowledge of the parts of new words begins at the ends and moves toward the middle we might expect a word like *numismatics*, which was on our list, to be still registered as NUM__- __ICS. Reduced entries of this sort would in many contexts serve to retrieve the definition.

The argument is reinforced by a well-known effect in spelling. Jensen (1962) has analyzed thousands of spelling errors for words of 7, 9, or 11 letters made by children in the eighth and tenth grades and by junior college freshmen. A striking serial position effect appears in all his sets of data such that errors are most common in the middle of the word, next most common at the end, and least common at the start. These results are as they should be if the order of attention and entry of information is first, last, and then, middle. Jensen's results show us what happens when children are forced to produce words that are still on the recognition level. His results remind us of those bluebooks in which students who are uncertain of the spelling of a word write the first and last letters with great clarity and fill in the middle with indecipherable squiggles. That is what should happen when a word that can be only partially recalled must be produced in its entirety. End letters and a stretch of squiggles may, however, be made quite adequate for recognition purposes. In the TOT experiment we have perhaps placed adult Ss in a situation comparable to that created for children by Jensen's spelling tests.

There are two points to clarify and the argument is finished. The Ss in our experiment were college students, and so in order to obtain words on the margin of knowledge we had to use words that are very infrequent in English as a whole. It is not our thought, however, that the TOT phenomenon occurs only with rare words. The absolute location of the margin of word knowledge is a function of S's age and education, and so with other Ss we would expect to obtain TOT states for words more frequent in English. Finally the need to produce (or recall) a word is not the only factor that is likely to encourage registration of its middle letters. The amount of detail needed to specify a word uniquely must increase with the total number of words known, the number from which any one is to be distinguished. Consequently the growth of vocabulary, as well as the need to recall, should have some power to force attention into the middle of a word.

## REFERENCES

Barnhart, C. L., ed. 1948. *The American college dictionary*. New York: Harper.

Broadbent, D. E. 1958. *Perception and communication*. New York: Macmillan.

Bruner, J. S., and O'Dowd, D. 1958. A note on the informativeness of words. *Language and Speech* 1:98–101.

Feigenbaum, E. A. 1963. The simulation of verbal learning behavior. In *Computers and thought*, ed. E. A. Feigenbaum and J. Feldman, pp. 297–309. New York: McGraw-Hill.

Hockett, C. F. 1958. *A course in modern linguistics*. New York: Macmillan.

James, W. 1893. *The principles of psychology*. Vol. I. New York: Holt.

Jensen, A. R. 1962. Spelling errors and the serial-position effect. *Journal of Educational Psychology* 53:105–109.

Katz, J. J., and Fodor, J. A. 1963. The structure of a semantic theory. *Language* 39:170–210.

Miller, G. A., and Friedman, Elizabeth A. 1957. The reconstruction of mutilated English texts. *Information Control* 1:38–55.

Thorndike, E. L., and Lorge, I. 1952. *The teacher's word book of 30,000 words*. New York: Columbia University.

Underwood, B. J. 1963. Stimulus selection in verbal learning. In *Verbal behavior and learning: Problems and processes*, ed. C. N. Cofer and B. S. Musgrave, pp. 33–48. New York: McGraw-Hill.

Wenzl, A. 1932. Empirische und theoretische Beiträge zur Erinnerungsarbeit bei erschwerter Wortfindung. *Archiv für die Gesamte Psychologie* 85: 181–218.

Wenzl, A. 1936. Empirische und theoretische Beiträge zur Erinnerungsarbeit bei erschwerter Wortfindung. *Archiv für die Gesamte Psychologie* 97:294–318.

Woodworth, R. S. 1934. *Psychology*. 3d ed. New York: Holt.

Woodworth, R. S., and Schlosberg, H. 1954. *Experimental psychology*. Rev. ed. New York: Holt.

# READING 25

# Cognitive Effects of Perceptual Isolation

**T. H. SCOTT**
**W. H. BEXTON**
**W. HERON**
**B. K. DOANE**

What happens to a person who is isolated from all perceptual stimulation? The authors of this article have experimentally tested the cognitive abilities of their subjects in an effort to determine if perceptual isolation impairs cognitive functioning. The results indicate impaired performance by the experimental group, and suggest that some level of stimulation is necessary for normal cognitive functioning. The relative effect of propaganda was also examined in experimental and control subjects.

**QUESTIONS**

1. Do you think adequate control procedures were used in this experiment? Support your answer.
2. What is the relationship between perceptual isolation and the effectiveness of propaganda? What does this imply?
3. A current trend in movies, television, music, etc., has been to increase the stimulation of the senses. What is the relationship between this trend and the findings of this article?

In earlier preliminary reports (1, 3, 4) we have described some of the effects of exposing human subjects to a relatively unchanging sensory environment. The present paper reports a more systematic investigation of the effects of perceptual isolation on certain tests of cognitive function given during the

D.R.B. Project no. D77–94–85–01.

experimental period and shortly after the subject had returned to a normal environment.

**METHOD**

The subject was paid to lie 24 hrs. a day on a comfortable bed in a lighted, semi-soundproof cubicle, 8 ft. × 4 ft. × 6 ft., which had an observation window. Throughout the experiment he wore translucent goggles which admitted diffuse light but prevented pattern vision. Except when eating or at the toilet, he also wore cotton gloves and cardboard cuffs which extended from below the elbows to beyond the fingertips, so as to limit tactual perception. A U-shaped foam-rubber pillow, the walls of the cubicle, the masking noise of the thermostatically regulated air-conditioner, and other equipment severely limited auditory perception. A two-way speaker system allowed communication between S and E.

The subjects were asked to stay as long as they could (usually 3 to 4 days), and during this period were prevented as far as possible from finding out what time it was. An experimenter was always in attendance, and Ss were told that if they needed anything they had only to call for it. They were fed and went to the toilet on request. These breaks occupied, on the average, 2 to 3 hrs. a day.

## TESTS

We used two batteries of tests, one given during the isolation period, and one afterwards. We also tried to measure S's susceptibility to propaganda, as another means of assessing the cognitive effects of isolation.

The first set of tests ("cubicle battery") had two parts: A, five types of problems taken from various intelligence tests; and B, associative learning and digit span from the Wechsler memory battery, as well as an analogies test. The tests in Part A were given before, during, and after the isolation period, those in Part B were given shortly before the subject left isolation. The tests in the cubicle battery were given orally, and the subject did them in his head.

The types of problem in Part A of the battery were (1) multiplication of two and three digit numbers; (2) arithmetic "catch" problems, such as "how many times greater is twice 2½ than half of 2½?"; (3) number series completion; (4) word-making, in which S had to make as many words as he could using the letters of a given word, and following certain rules (he could not make the same word twice, use proper nouns, and so on); and (5) anagrams, in which he had to make a word from a group of jumbled letters.

We took great care to make sure that S was awake some time before he was tested. All problems were read to him twice, and, except in the arithmetic "catch" problems and number series completion, he had to repeat the problem aloud to prove that he had heard it correctly. He was told that if he forgot the problem it would be repeated on request.

In the first three types of problem in Part A, S worked until he had the correct answer, or until 8 min. were up. In word-making he worked for 5 min. In the anagrams, if the correct word was not formed in 4 min., its first letter was supplied, subsequent letters being given at 3-min. intervals when necessary. Three scores were obtained from each test: time spent on the problem, number of wrong answers, and the number of requests for the problem to be repeated.

The second ("post-cubicle") battery contained the following tests: Kobs' blocks, Wechsler digit-symbol, Thurstone-Gottschaldt figures, transcribing a passage of unfamiliar technical material, the McGill Picture Anomaly test, and an unpublished block-design test (Delta Blocks) described by Hebb (2).

## PROPAGANDA

The propaganda material dealt with psychical phenomena. It consisted of a 90-min. talk read in a deliberately boring monotone, and was recorded on discs. Although there were general arguments in favour of believing in all types of psychical phenomena, four main topics were concentrated upon: telepathy, clairvoyance, ghosts, and poltergeists. In addition, the general importance of psychical research was discussed.

To measure attitudes towards psychical phenomena, we used a questionnaire consisting of a series of Bogardus-type scales. The questionnaire was divided into five sections, dealing with attitudes towards telepathy, clairvoyance, ghosts, poltergeists, and psychical research. There was a total of fourteen scales in the questionnaire, three in each of the first four sections and two in the fifth. Each scale consisted of five statements indicating different degrees of belief in the relevant phenomenon.

For scoring purposes, a three-point interval was set between successive statements on the scale. S had to indicate the statement with which he agreed most. If he was unable to decide between two statements, the average weight of the statements concerned was ascertained. A score of zero indicated that S did not believe in the particular psychical phenomenon at all, while a score of twelve indicated that he believed in it firmly. Since each of the first four sections of the questionnaire consisted of three scales, complete belief in some subject (telepathy, for example) would be indicated by a score of 36, complete disbelief by a score of zero. A score of 18 would, of course, indicate uncertainty.

Each section of the questionnaire also had a secondary series of scales. These were concerned with the amount of interest which S felt in the topic, and how important he felt the topic was.

## SUBJECTS

The subjects were English-speaking male college students. The mean age of the experimental group was 22 years, 1 month (range 19–30), of the control group 22 years, 2 months (range 19–32). Each group had the same proportion of Arts and Science students. Of the 29 experimental Ss only 18 stayed in isolation long enough to complete the testing schedule for Part A of the cubicle battery. Twenty-seven control Ss were tested on both parts of this battery.

There was some variation in the number

**TABLE 1**

SEQUENCE OF TESTS GIVEN BEFORE, DURING, AND AFTER ISOLATION

| | Pre-isolation | | Immediately pre-isolation |
|---|---|---|---|
| 1-2 weeks | 48 hours | 24 hours | |
| Interview | First form of post-cubicle battery | Practice on cubicle battery A | Cubicle battery A |
| First attitude questionnaire | | Test on cubicle battery B | Second attitude questionnaire |

| | Isolation | | 1 hour pre-emergence |
|---|---|---|---|
| 12 hours | 24 hours | 48 hours | |
| Cubicle battery A | Cubicle battery A | Cubicle battery A | Cubicle battery B |
| | Records | Records | |

| | Post-isolation | | 4 days |
|---|---|---|---|
| Immediately | 3 hours | 3 days | |
| Post-cubicle battery | Third attitude questionnaire | Cubicle battery A | Cubicle battery A |
| | Interview | Interview | |

of $S$s on each test in the post-cubicle battery, as shown in Table 2, since some tests were added to this battery later.

Of the 29 experimental $S$s 24 were in isolation long enough to be given the propaganda. Data from 8 additional control $S$s are available on the propaganda questionnaire. Though these data did not alter the statistical probabilities of the results, they are included, so that the control group for this test totals 35.

## PROCEDURE

The testing schedule of the experimental $S$s is shown in Table 1. The control $S$s were given the same tests at the same intervals; they were not, of course, placed in isolation, but came to the laboratory at the appropriate times and were tested in a quiet room.

The subjects were given the questionnaire twice before they were placed in isolation. This was done because preliminary experiments showed that the reliability of the questionnaire was much greater between the second and third administrations than between the first and second.

The propaganda was given as follows: after $S$ had been in isolation for approximately 18 hrs. he was told that there was a series of records that he could listen to if he wished. If he asked for a record, only one would be played at that time, but he could ask for another whenever he wished. He was not told anything about the content of the records. The nine records were played through in series as $S$ requested them. When they were finished he was told, "Those are all the records. You may have any of them you want played through again." On further requests, if no specific record was mentioned, the series was given in the original order, one record for each request.

The control subject was treated in a similar way. He was told about the records at approximately the same time in the testing schedule as the experimental $S$s, and was made to hear the records at least once. He did not have to do this all at one sitting, but could hear any of the records as often as he liked during his subsequent visits. He was put in a room with the records and a machine for playing them, and listened to them through ear-phones. The attitude questionnaire was not given for the third and final time until the subject had definitely stated that he did not want to hear any of the records again.

## RESULTS

Table 2 shows the results of the post-cubicle battery of tests. The $p$-values are for the difference between the mean scores of the experimental and control subjects immediately after isolation, relative to their scores before isolation. The experimental subjects were inferior to the controls on six of the seven tests. Only in the case of mirror drawing was there no difference between the groups.

The five graphs in Figure 1 show the mean time scores (except in the word-making test, where number of correct words is given) for the experimental and control groups on the five types of problem in cubicle battery Part A for each of the six test periods. A statistical analysis based on a comparison of the mean difference scores (between the pre-isolation and subsequent test periods) of the two groups reveals the following differences: on the word-making test the experimental group was significantly poorer on all three test periods during isolation ($p < .02$), and on the number series test poorer on the first cubicle test period ($p < .05$). The experimental group was also poorer on all the other problems, but the difference approached significance only in the case of anagrams ($p < .10$). No significant difference between the groups was obtained on tests given outside the cubicle.

When we compare the two groups on error scores, and on the number of requests for repetition of the problem, we find that during the isolation period the experimental group was again inferior to the control

## TABLE 2

MEAN SCORES OF THE EXPERIMENTAL AND CONTROL GROUPS ON THE
POST-CUBICLE BATTERY: p-VALUES BASED ON DIFFERENT SCORES

| Test | Score basis | Experiment group | | | Control group | | | p |
| | | N | Before | After | N | 1st test | 2nd test | |
|---|---|---|---|---|---|---|---|---|
| Kohs' Blocks | Total time (sec.)* | 20 | 1088 | 931 | 25 | 1095 | 762 | .01 |
| Digit symbol | Number correct | 19 | 52.9 | 68.2 | 24 | 52.0 | 74.5 | .01 |
| Thurstone-Gottschaldt | Number correct | 12 | 5.5 | 5.4 | 18 | 5.2 | 8.1 | .01 |
| Copy passage | Time (sec.) | 18 | 594 | 640 | 25 | 634 | 639 | .05 |
| Delta Blocks | Number correct | 12 | 9.4 | 13.2 | 19 | 11.4 | 19.9 | .01 |
| Picture anomaly | Number errors | 15 | 3.0 | 5.9 | 23 | 4.0 | 4.9 | .01 |
| Mirror drawing | Time | 12 | 219 | 108 | 19 | 223 | 103 | .10 |

*The number of Kohs' items on which the time score increased, in the second test, was also significantly greater for the experimental group ($p < .001$).

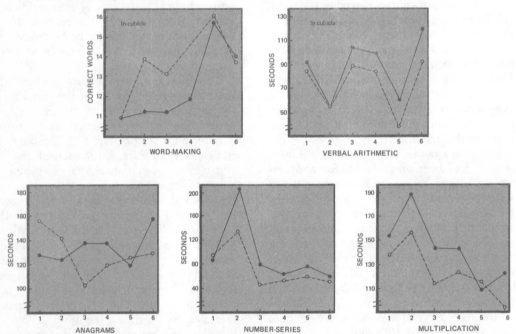

**Figure 1.** Scores for the experimental and control subjects on the five types of problem in cubicle battery A. Numbers along the abscissae indicate the test period. During test periods 2–4 the experimental subjects were in isolation.

group. This is true for all tests and test periods during isolation, though the differences were significant only in the following cases: on the anagrams test the difference between the error scores of the two groups at the 24-hour period is significant at the 5 per cent level of confidence; on the word-making test the experimental subjects made significantly more errors at the first test period in the cubicle ($p < .05$) and at the last ($p < .02$). It is worth noting that they also made fewer words altogether (correct plus incorrect words) than did the control subjects (significantly fewer at the second test period in the cubicle, $p < .01$). On this same test, requests for repetition were significantly different at the first test period during isolation ($p < .05$).

There was virtually no difference in performance between the two groups on the digit span and analogies tests (cubicle battery, Part B). In associative learning the experimental subject did somewhat more poorly than the controls, but the difference did not approach significance ($p > .10$).

We must now consider the effects of propaganda. The $t$-test was used to find out whether the subjects had been affected by propaganda, and whether one group was more affected than the other. The results are summarized in Table 3.

Both groups showed a significant change in attitude after listening to the propaganda, but the change was much greater for the ex-

**TABLE 3**

MEAN TOTALS ON 5 ATTITUDE SCALES FOR 24 EXPERIMENTAL AND 35 CONTROL Ss, SHOWING INCREASED BELIEF IN PHYSICAL PHENOMENA AFTER EXPOSURE TO POSITIVE PROPAGANDA*

| Scale | Possible score | Experimental Pre | Post | Control Pre | Post | p |
|---|---|---|---|---|---|---|
| Attitude | 168 | 68.7 | 106.5 | 73.4 | 91.5 | .02 |
| Interest | 45 | 23.5 | 31.0 | 26.9 | 29.6 | .01 |
| Importance | 20 | 9.0 | 13.0 | 9.4 | 11.3 | .01 |

*Scores showing increased interest and estimate of importance are also shown. p-values are based on a comparison of the mean difference scores (between the pre- and post-propaganda tests) for the two groups.

perimental subjects than it was for the controls. On the total questionnaire (all scales) the difference between the groups was significant ($p < .02$). If we consider the various sections, we find that the differences are most marked on the sections dealing with ghosts, poltergeists, and clairvoyance, where the levels of confidence are beyond the 3, 5, and 7 per cent respectively. In the sections dealing with telepathy and psychical research, the differences, while in the same direction, do not approach signifi-

cance. Table 3 also shows the results from two other subsidiary scales which measured the degree of interest which the subjects felt about the various topics, their previous familiarity with the topic, and the degree of importance which they felt that each topic had. Scores for the entire questionnaire are considered. It can be seen that although both groups are more interested in the subject after they have listened to the propaganda than they were before, and feel that it is of greater importance, the experimental subjects are affected to a greater degree than are the controls.

## DURING ISOLATION

Of the 29 experimental subjects, nearly all reported inability to concentrate on any topic for long, lack of clarity in their thinking, or difficulty in organizing their thoughts. Most had originally planned to review their studies, solve problems, or "think about things" generally. But, after a few hours in isolation, they found that such efforts tended to be abortive. They reported that the disorganization in their thinking became more pronounced as the experimental period advanced, and described their thinking in the later stages with such words as sterile, garbled, disjointed, confused, ineffectual, shallow. They frequently experienced "blank periods" during which, though fully awake, they did not seem to be thinking of anything, and attributed this to the fact that they had "run out of topics" and "couldn't think of anything to think about." This, they felt, was one reason why the experimental situation became unpleasantly boring. The content of their thinking also changed as time went on: they reported that at first they did make some attempt to review studies, and to solve personal problems, but later resorted to reminiscence and idle day dreaming, making no attempt to control the direction of their thoughts.

There seemed to be some evidence of impaired judgment and loss of sense of proportion while the subjects were in isolation.

Thus, one left the experimental situation highly pleased with his solution to a musical problem only to find that the phrase he had invented was, note for note, one that he already had in his manuscript. Another, towards the end of his stay, adopted the irrational procedure of "lying back and letting the problem sink in" in the hope that the answer would come to him "intuitively." Subjects frequently developed a childish sense of humour, and had exaggerated emotional reactions, becoming excessively irritated by small things and sometimes very annoyed with the experimenters. A few reported that they brooded about things unduly, dwelling on imaginary injustices. Some committed small deceptions (readily admitted later), and others became obsessive about trying to stay in the cubicle. Later, the subjects were frequently surprised by the way they felt during the isolation period, and said they had "magnified things," or had been "irritated out of all proportion."

## AFTER ISOLATION

The subjects' condition did not return to normal immediately after they emerged from isolation. That their behaviour was still impaired is evident from their test performance during the first 2½ hours after isolation (already described); it is confirmed by observation and their own reports. They appeared dazed and somewhat unresponsive. Sometimes, during the tests, their attention would wander off the problem in hand, and they would sit staring into space. They commonly reported feeling remote and confused, and that they had difficulty in concentrating. Thus, one subject complained that he "had to relearn concentration"; some said they had to make a deliberate effort to concentrate on, and grasp, anything to which their attention was directed. Comments such as "I felt 'wooden' during testing," "impulses had difficulty getting to the brain," "my brain was fuzzy and couldn't grasp—it wouldn't take things

in," "the patterns [of the Kohs' blocks] didn't sink into my mind—I had to *get* my mind to work," were common.

We gave no formal tests later than 2½ hours after emergence, other than final tests of the post-cubicle battery on the third and fourth days. Some subjects, however, indicated that they noticed some effects for two days after the experimental session ended, and reported a generalized lack of interest and loss of motivation to study. In addition, some reported behaviour of an "absent-minded" type. Two had difficulty driving their cars, one double-exposed his camera, another took a shower while partially clothed, and another forgot to bring his books to college. Several of our early subjects reported that they tended to plunge across the street without noticing or looking for traffic, and we had subsequently to warn subjects to be careful about this. In addition, almost all subjects reported an increased irritability during this period which made it difficult for them to get on with their associates.

The cubicle experience may have made the subjects unusually analytical of their own behaviour, and suggestion probably played a role, but it was clear that they regarded the incidents reported as unusual; moreover, most subjects reported the same symptoms, and were able to say when they disappeared.

## DISCUSSION

The results, then, indicate that perceptual isolation produces a decline in intellectual ability. However, several puzzling results are evident. The difference between the groups did not increase as time went on, so that it seems as if there was no progressive deterioration. There are a number of possibilities why this result was obtained. One is that the cognitive abilities measured by the tests were affected early during isolation, but that there is no marked decline in performance between 12 and 48 hours of isolation, when the last test of the cubicle battery was given. Had we given another set of tests at 72 hours, say, the difference between the groups might have been greater than it was at 48 hours.

Another possible reason is that each test session of the cubicle battery took up to two hours, and it became apparent that the control subjects regarded the tests as an unpleasant chore. Their motivation began to flag after about the second session. It is therefore possible that the control subjects' performance may also have been declining, so that the difference between the groups remained approximately constant.

When we consider the section of the experiment dealing with propaganda, we find that only 4 of the 35 control subjects wanted to hear the records more than once, in spite of the fact that they were paid by the hour to listen. On the other hand, 16 of the 24 experimental subjects asked for repetitions. This might lead the reader to believe that the results obtained were due solely to the fact that the experimental subjects spent a longer time listening to the propaganda than did the controls. Even if this were so, the results could still be attributed to isolation since one of the effects of isolating the individual is that he will listen to material which he would normally avoid, and listen to it often. Presumably, he becomes so bored that any form of stimulation is better than nothing at all. It happens, however, that there does not seem to be any relationship between the number of times that the subject listened to the records and the degree to which his attitudes were changed. No significant correlation can be detected.

To sum up, the results indicate that the experimental conditions produced some deterioration in performance on some tests of cognitive ability while the subjects were in isolation and after they had emerged. Subjects reported that their minds wandered, and that they were no longer able to find anything to think about. It seems too, that they became abnormally preoccupied with whatever patterned stimulation they did receive. These results may be attributed to some general disorganization of brain function which is also involved in the hallucinatory activity, disturbances of visual function and abnormal EEGs which occur under conditions of perceptual isolation (4).

## SUMMARY

Twenty-nine male subjects were placed in isolation for as long as they would stay (usually 3 to 4 days). Two batteries of tests were given to them, before, during, and after isolation. In addition, they were subjected to propaganda during the isolation period. Twenty-seven control subjects, who were not isolated, were given the same tests and propaganda material.

The results indicate that the experimental subjects performed worse than the controls both during and after the isolation period on some tests, and that they were more susceptible to propaganda, though both groups showed a significant change in attitude.

## REFERENCES

1. Bexton, W. H.; Heron, W.; and Scott, T. H. 1954. Effects of decreased variation in the sensory environment. *Canadian Journal of Psychology* 8:70–76.

2. Hebb, D. O. 1945. Man's frontal lobes. *Archives of Neurology and Psychiatry* 54:10–24.

3. Heron, W. 1957. The pathology of boredom. *Scientific American*, vol. 196, no. 1, pp. 52–56.

4. Heron, W.; Doane, B. K.; and Scott, T. H. 1956. Visual disturbances after prolonged perceptual isolation. *Canadian Journal of Psychology* 10:13–18.

# READING 26

# Computer Simulation of Thinking

**CARL I. HOVLAND**
**Yale University**

Computer simulation of psychological processes is a relatively new and exciting area of research. Hovland indicates many advantages of computer simulation of problem-solving tasks. He notes that in order to simulate a program for problem-solving, we must first understand the processes involved, and that the simulation provides the psychologist with a good test of these processes. Other advantages of computer simulation lie in its predictive capacity and the fact that we can manipulate many complex variables at one time.

**QUESTIONS**
1. In research utilizing computer simulation, what is the relationship between the computer data and human behavior? How much can we generalize from computer performance to human performance?
2. Is it valid to use a computer to study an isolated process such as problem-solving without taking into consideration all of the other factors which influence this process in the human?
3. What is the role of the computer and computer simulation in psychological research? What are some of the problems involved?

---

It is commonplace in the history of science for developments in one field of knowledge to have profound effects on other related areas. The dramatic influence of advances in atomic physics on biology, genetics, and

Adapted from a talk given over the *Voice of America* in September 1959. Unrestricted use of this material is available to the United States Government without cost.

The author is a member of the Social Science Research Council Committee on Simulation of Cognitive Processes. This committee supports relevant work in this field and welcomes suggestions for fellowships or research projects from interested investigators.

medicine is a good case in point. We are currently witnessing a similar phenomenon in the repercussions of high speed computer technology on research in the behavioral sciences. The initial impact came from the computational efficiency of these devices which permitted calculations formerly prohibitive in terms of time and effort. A more recent and less direct effect has been in stimulating machine-like methods of analysis of human thought and behavior through simulation on high speed computers. It is these newer techniques and their applicability to psychological problems that is the topic of the present paper.

The analogy between the high speed computer and human thinking has long been noted. We frequently see the Univacs, Johniacs, Illiacs referred to in the popular press as "giant brains" or "thinking machines." In most uses of high speed computers, however, there is an attempt to attain objectives beyond the scope of human capabilities, either because of their speed or their extensive storage capacity (called, interestingly enough, their "memory"). But in the investigations I shall be describing, the utilization is quite different. Here we are primarily concerned with the use of computing machines to simulate in exact fashion the way a human solves a problem. Both human weaknesses, such as limited and fallible memory, and strengths, such as the ability to choose an efficient solution out of innumerable alternatives, must be represented. We say that we can simulate human problem solving when we are able to specify both the prior information a human possesses and the sequence of steps by which he utilizes this information in the solution of the problem. We are then able to set up a computing machine to carry out this same sequence of operation.

Those familiar with the operation of high speed computers will readily understand the way in which simulation proceeds. Just as in ordinary operations of a computer, one gives the machine a set of "instructions" to execute. These constitute a "program." In arithmetical operations these are sentences like the following: "square the product of the first and second number," "store the product in memory," "compare the first and second number," "select the larger of the two numbers compared." Or such instructions as: "find the number of dollars paid to the individual last month," "add to this amount the number of dollars earned this month," and so forth. The machine then executes each of these instructions through an intricate electronic system, printing out its answers on an electric typewriter. Sequences of instructions can then solve the most complicated numerical problems, such as making out a payroll with each individual working different numbers of hours, at different wage rates, with advance payments to some workers, with different deductions for subscriptions to health and accident insurance, different income tax credits, and so forth. The nub of the simulation problem involves the use of similar types of "programs" of "instructions" to the machine in order to reproduce the steps an individual goes through in thinking out the solution to a difficult problem. One specifies the steps the individual uses by stating them in an unambiguous way so that a computing machine is able to carry them out. These may be instructions like: "store the answer to the last problem," "determine whether you have stored in memory any similar problems," "if so, what are the differences between the past problem and the present problem," "see if applying Rule a will convert the old problem into the new one," and "apply Rule b" to convert the answer to the former problem into the solution to the present one. Thus the computer can be given information which is exactly equivalent to that of the human problem solver, as well as a specification of the way the human goes about processing that information to reach a solution.

The obvious point is that if we can be precise enough about a process to describe it in terms which can be programmed and executed by a machine, we indeed know quite a bit about that process. And if we can specify singly each of the subprocesses involved, we can determine the effects of combinations of them and of variations in order of execution of the steps. The outcomes are almost impossible to foresee without actually carrying out the combinations and variations.

Let me begin by giving a concrete

example of the new techniques, namely, simulation of the solving of geometry problems. We certainly think of the solving of theorems in Euclidian geometry by a high school sophomore as constituting a clear-cut example of intelligent human behavior. But Gelernter and Rochester (1958) of the International Business Machines Company have now successfully developed a program whereby a high speed computer is able to solve many of the theorems in Euclid's geometry, for example, that the diagonals of a parallelogram bisect one another. A human learner who tries to solve such a problem has usually been taught a series of fundamental principles, or axioms, together with a set of rules for inferring relationships by which the basic symbols in the system may be manipulated. He is then asked to prove a new theorem. He tries to find a way of transforming and combining previous axioms through the set of rules until he achieves the proof of the new theorem. Typically he starts out in rather routine fashion, then has a flash of insight as to a possible means of solution, and then methodically tests the adequacy of the solution. The geometry computing machine is set up to operate in an analogous fashion. It is given a set of basic formulas and axioms, together with rules as to possible ways of manipulating them in order to form new theorems. The new theorem is then presented to the machine to prove. The machine is equipped with a number of rules of thumb for possible ways of solving problems. For example, it is instructed that if the proposition to be proved involves parallel lines and equality of angles, there is a good chance that it may be useful to try the theorem: "If two parallel lines are intersected by a third line, the opposite interior angles are equal." This instruction constitutes a short-cut which often works well but is by no means sure to be of value. Successful solution typically involves setting up a series of sub goals which are then worked in succession. For example, in the problem cited earlier the machine ascertains that it can solve the theorem if it can establish the fact that the distance from one corner of the base of the parallelogram to the point of intersection must equal the distance from the intersection to the opposite corner of the parallelogram. This is then a subgoal, which in turn can be proved if the triangle formed by the bisecting lines and one of the sides of the parallelogram is equal to the triangle formed by the opposite side and the corresponding bisects. A device is incorporated into the computer which makes constructions and measures lines and angles. This operates by means of coordinate geometry. Once the sequence of subgoals leads from the initial axioms to the theorem to be proved, the machine routinely tests the accuracy of the proof. This it can do in an exhaustive manner, since once one has a possible proof, checking it is largely clerical. The chief problem is to find a possible method of proceeding, out of the almost infinite number of alternatives. It is here that the short-cut methods operate. They permit the use of likely and plausible methods of solution, just the way a clever high school student would proceed. Once the proof has been verified, the machine prints QED. Throughout the entire operation the machine prints out on paper a complete tracing of the steps it tries—this is analogous to an individual's account of the way he solves a problem in geometry. Some of the machine's failures in finding proofs closely resemble those made by beginning geometry students.

It will be noted that the methods of solution built into the computer closely resemble those used by humans' solving similar problems. Let me again call attention to the fact that in this way they differ from the usual uses of high speed computers which methodically go through every possible solution in a deliberate way. The complete methods guarantee that if there is a solution it will be found, although an extraordinary number of trials may be required.

Solutions of this type are referred to as "algorithms." These are used here to check proofs. In contrast, finding a possible solution is facilitated by short-cuts and rules of thumb programed into the machine. In this way it simulates a human subject in making leaps in the solution and trying out schemes which have been successful in the past, rather than exhaustively trying out each possible alternative. Mathematicians call these short-cut solutions "heuristics."

One may wonder whether we have gained anything by the simulation since we initially derive processes from study of how students work and then program into the computer their ways of proceeding. In fact, at the outset, we may operate in a somewhat circular fashion—that is, we may only get out of the machine what we put into it. But as one proceeds, new combinations are tested which could not have been predicted from the individual steps. Some results, although strictly determined by the processes programed, are impossible to foresee because so many complex operations interact in the final solution. One can find out the effect of increased complexity of problems, and then determine with human subjects whether the order of difficulty is the same that would be predicted from the computer's information processing routines. In this way one is constantly working back and forth from experiments with human subjects to simulation on the computing machine. Furthermore one frequently finds that one must make assumptions about certain steps in the process to get the computer to execute its program correctly. Here the simulation comes first and suggests later experiments with human subjects.

The geometry machine just described involves solving problems rather than learning how to solve them, in the sense that the computer would solve the same problem in the same way on a second trial. Humans, of course, do learn and improve through practice. So the interesting task is to build into the computer this capability as well. Simula-

tion of learning is one of the most interesting potential applications of computer simulation techniques, since the ability to learn is one of the clear-cut differences between human and machine performance. A number of different types of learning are currently being simulated. The first involves stimulus-response learning. It is rather simple to simulate this type of learning with rewards ("reinforcements") given when certain types of behavior occur and not given when other types of responses are made. The probability that the response followed by reward will occur on later trials can then be made to increase. Failure of reward, or punishment, can be made to lead to a decreased probability of response ("extinction"). The studies of Herman, a computing machine, carried out by Friedberg (1958), and of the Perceptron, investigated by Rosenblatt (1958), are interesting examples of artificial learning machines. Other related possibilities are discussed in Miller, Galanter, and Pribram (1960).

At a somewhat more complex level is the type of learning involved in the recognizing patterns imbedded in complex stimuli. It seems a simple thing for a human to respond to a triangle as a triangle whether it is large or small, short or tall, tilted or upright, and to distinguish it clearly from a square. But to specify rigorously the criteria in such a way that a machine can learn to recognize it invariably is quite a job. And the difficulty clearly hints that there is a lot we do not understand about the phenomenon even at the human level where we take the process for granted. Selfridge (1955) and Dinneen (1955) have worked most extensively on this problem and have been able to develop methods for getting the salient features of patterns to stand out so that some uniform response is given to a particular pattern. With two techniques, one of "averaging," to get rid of random elements, and a second, of "edging," to maximize the most distinctive features, they are able to insure that a variety of different ways of writing the letter A, for example, are registered as the same letter in the computer as a basis for further processing.

The third type of learning is made possible by keeping records of success and failure attained when different methods are pursued and using these records to improve performance. Thus, in the case of the geometry computer it is possible to store theorems which have already been proved. Similar mechanisms have been incorporated into the General Problem Solver developed by Newell, Shaw, and Simon (1958). It is also possible for these machines to be selective in their choice of theorems for permanent storage, rejecting those which do not seem sufficiently general to be useful later on. The most highly developed simulation of this type of learning is that incorporated in a checker-playing machine developed by Samuel (1959). His machine utilizes a type of rote learning which stores all of the checkerboard positions it encounters in play, together with the outcomes following each move. In addition this machine has some capacity to generalize on the basis of past experience and to store the generalizations themselves. With these learning mechanisms it appears possible for the computer to learn in a short period of time to play a better game of checkers than can be played by the person who wrote the program.

Many of the formulations of learning are made without any special assumptions that learning processes are consistent with known neurophysiological mechanisms. A number of students are attempting to close this gap by simulation studies of the way in which nerve networks become organized into systems and are then modified through use. There is quite extensive investigation along these lines, some of it instigated by the speculations of Hebb about the nature of nervous organization. Suffice it to say that a number of researchers have been able to program computers to simulate the changing of neural organization patterns as a result of repeated stimulation of nerve fibers and further work of a similar type is in progress (cf. Clark & Farley, 1955, and Rochester, Holland, Haibt, & Duda, 1956).

In the work in our laboratory the emphasis is on understanding and simulating the processes involved in acquiring complex concepts through experience (Hovland & Hunt, 1960). The learner acquires a particular concept when he is told which of a series of specific instances presented to him belong in the concept class and which do not. This is similar to the way in which a child learns the concept of "animate" through some experiences in which parents and teachers label a given stimulus as "animate" and others in which they label it as "inanimate" (Hovland, 1952).

Our type of problem is illustrated by a situation in which there are a large number of slides of cancer cells, some of which are known to be malignant and other nonmalignant. The task of the individual (or the machine) is one of inducing the base of difference between the two types and subsequently labeling correctly new slides previously unidentified. Medical pathologists have just such a task and have achieved considerable success, although not 100% accuracy, in making such distinctions. It is of interest in passing that there is a machine available which can make such a distinction on the basis of slides presented to it, but here the combination of characteristics (the "concept") was formulated by the scientist who developed the instrument (Tolles & Bostrom, 1956). The machine's task is to see whether the new specimen conforms to certain specifications, that is, whether on the basis of density and structure the cell belongs in the "malignant" or "normal" category. Thus it has the "concept" built into it, obviating the need to start from the beginning in order to induce it.

The input to the type of concept learning in which we are interested is a series of pictures, say flower designs (Hovland, 1953), some of which are labeled "positive" instances (examples of the concept) and some "negative" instances (examples of what the concept *is not*). The characteristics of the instances are represented as symbols for processing by the machine. It is hoped later to have this transformation automatic through the use of techniques developed at the Bell Telephone Laboratories which employ a television camera to convert the visual representation into electrical impulses as input to the computer. Thus the picture would become converted into one set of symbols representing the characteristics which constitute the instances of the concept (like A1B2C1D1E2F1G1H2), while another string of symbols will represent instances of what the concept *is not* (like A2B1C1D2E1F1G1H2).

Potentially, a machine can then consider combinations of all of these characteristics as possible ways of categorizing and distinguishing between the class of "A" and of "not A." Typically, human learners only attend to part of the potential set of characteristics because of perceptual limitations. We have devoted considerable research effort toward determining just how attention and perception vary during the course of learning. We have incorporated in the machine simulation a selective scanning of possible aspects of the complex stimuli with provision for the fact that some individuals see only some of the characteristics while other individuals pay attention to different aspects.

Human subjects, at least at the adult level, operate on material of this type by developing strategies involving some generalization as to what concepts are like. Some details of these strategies have been investigated by Bruner, Goodnow, and Austin (1956). The strategies may be different for different types of concepts. Logicians describe some concepts as being of the *conjunctive* type, where all the members of the class share certain common characteristics. For example, rubies share the characteristics of hardness, translucence, and redness. A second type of concept is called *disjunctive*, in which possession of either one characteristic or possession of a different characteristic makes the instance subsumable under the general class. This is illustrated by the concept of "strike" in American baseball which is either a pitched ball across the plate and between the batter's knees and shoulders *or*, alternatively, any pitch at which the batter strikes but fails to send into the field. A third type of concept is *relational*, where the instances of the concept share no common fixed characteristics but do have certain relationship in common. A sample would be the concept of "isosceles triangles." All instances of this concept involve triangles with two equal sides. But any fixed characteristics, such as lengths of the equal sides, lengths of the third side, or sizes of angles, are not an adequate basis for inclusion or exclusion in the concept class.

In preparation for later simulation, we have carried out extensive experimentation to determine the order in which these various types of concepts are considered by human learners. We find that for our type of stimulus materials, conjunctive and relational concepts are considered much more commonly than disjunctive ones (Hunt and Hovland, 1960). So our present machine will have built into it a hierarchy of responses in which the first attempts to organize the material will be in terms of shared characteristics—conjunctive type concepts. Alternatively the machine will consider concepts which are based on relationships between the stimuli. Only when these have been extensively and unsuccessfully explored will the machine try disjunctive concept patterns.

At present, then, we have the program for a machine which is able to receive drawings having a number of different dimensions. It is then able to try a number of possible ways of organizing into a concept the prior information it has received regarding confirming and nonconfirming instances. First it considers possibilities of concepts which have various combinations of features. When none of these suffice, it considers relational concepts. When these are not successful, it considers various disjunctive concepts where one set of features or another alternative set define the concept. When a solution is reached the description of what constitutes a concept is printed out on tape and subsequent unlabeled instances are classified A's or non-A's. A scanning device is built into the machine to take into account only certain of the characteristics available for consideration. The present machine remembers all that has been presented to it. We are currently considering various devices to simulate the gradual loss of information, or forgetting, which is all too human a characteristic. Our experimental studies have indicated the overall mathematical form which the loss should take, but there are alternative means of producing such a loss (Cahill & Hovland, 1960). Each alternative represents a different theory of the way in which forgetting occurs and investigation of the different theories is of fundamental importance. Simulation again provides a powerful tool for specifying the operation of the process of forgetting.

A high proportion of our research effort goes into new experimentation with human learners to determine their methods of handling various aspects of the problem, as compared to other efforts which stress programming the actual simulation. It is expected that this type of imbalance in effort will continue, but we are perennially hopeful that as more and more information becomes available an increasing amount of our effort will go into the simulation itself.

Work has now progressed to the point where I think we can see more clearly both the opportunities provided by these methods and some of the difficulties involved. I hope that the foregoing discussion has suggested some of the advantages of these new techniques. Let me briefly summarize the potentialities. First, simula-

tion methods have a tremendous role in sharpening our formulations concerning mental processes and phenomena. It is one thing to say, as earlier students have said, that problem solving involves a number of different stages, for example, those of preparation, incubation, illumination, and verification, and quite another thing for one to specify exactly what is involved in each stage. The pioneering studies by Newell, Shaw, and Simon (1958) on the General Problem Solver indicate the great forward strides which result from specifying the nature of these processes in such complete detail that a computer is able to solve problems by following the sequence of steps programed into the machine.

Closely related is the second advantage of the computer, the emphasis which it places on developing theories that have both descriptive and predictive power. Many of the theories which exist in psychology and sociology are so general and vague that they have little real predictive power. The program written for the computer to describe a particular process constitutes a theory which, if successful in carrying out the process in the same way as the human, is highly efficient in predicting the effects of changes in conditions and in specifying what other individuals will do under particular conditions.

Lastly, the simulation of human responses has the same overwhelming advantages for our understanding of behavioral phenomena as similar methods in other sciences. For example, the use of the wind tunnel represents a complex set of interacting conditions in actuality which could not be duplicated and whose effects could not be predicted from theory alone. Analogously in the present case, for single factors one can analyze effects without simulation, but when one seeks to understand the combined action of a number of factors interacting in complex ways, no satisfactory way of predicting the exact outcome may be possible. Those working on the geometry simulator, the General Problem Solver, and the chess and checker-playing machines, all testify to the fact that many of the moves made by the computer greatly surprised their inventors.

I hope that my remarks on the importance of simulation methods do not give rise to the feeling that these methods automatically lead to quick success in areas which have been investigated for decades using other techniques. Two examples of the difficulties confronting us may be mentioned. The first is the complexity of the process to be simulated. At present we consider ourselves fortunate if we can simulate on a machine the typical performance of a single individual in solving a particular problem. This is indeed a great step forward. But for simulation to be maximally effective we would like to be able to predict machine solutions which simulate not only a single individual under some specified condition, but also the effects for different individuals under different environmental conditions, and after various amounts of experience. To date, most simulation has been of the performance of one individual, either real or an imaginary average individual. It may prove to be extremely difficult to carry out the next step, that of specifying which characteristics must be known about each individual to be able to simulate the way he varies from the typical pattern. In addition, the effects of environmental variables, such as the effects of drugs on performance, or of pressure to complete a task, should then be simulated. Finally, the effects of experience should be specified, so that the way in which a problem is attacked is appropriately changed as a result of the machine's ability to learn. This leaves for the future such a complex problem as analysis of the interactions between type of individual and amount of learning under different environmental conditions. It is apparent that a long and difficult road lies ahead before we can accomplish successful simulation of a single type of task which has all of these variables

programed. But when they can be successfully specified we will know a great deal about the problem. Most research generalizations in the social sciences are only true for a group of people, not for each individual. Computer methodology may make possible a broadening of our understanding of behavior by emphasizing the simulation of single individuals and then studying variations between them. The integration of these complementary approaches in new computer work will help us to reduce the gap between group averages and individual processes.

A second example of the difficulties of machine simulation is attributable to the nature of the process with which we are concerned. Simulation methods have most successfully been employed where it is possible to define the final performance of a task as an outcome of a succession of single steps. Thus where the mental process involves steps in a sequence one can synthesize the process by having the computing machine work first on stage one, then stage two, etc. Much more difficult are those processes where a number of stages are going on simultaneously, in parallel fashion. It certainly appears that much of our perceptual and thought process operates in this way. Under these conditions it is much more difficult to untangle the processes at work prior to simulation. In addition, present machines are not as suitable for these purposes as they are for sequential operation. New and radically different machines may ultimately be required to cope with this problem. Most of our present work is being carried out with computers which were built for quite other purposes, namely, high speed arithmetical computation. It would be possible to design machines more closely simulating thought processes and more flexible in their operation, but they would be expensive to construct and would not have the large number of potential purchasers who ordinarily help defray the costs of development.

Despite the difficulties mentioned, work on simulation of complex psychological processes is yielding results of increasing importance. Processes which were thought to be understood turn out to require much more explicit statement. But along with the increased explicitness comes new understanding and precision. At present most computer programs grapple with only one phase of complex processes, but we are beginning to see common features in a number of different programs, permitting the construction of comprehensive programs from simpler subprograms. Work on simulation has also had a stimulating effect on research on the higher thought processes themselves. Attempts to program computers have repeatedly revealed that we lacked much information as to how humans carry out seemingly simple thought operations. This has led to the return of workers to the laboratory which in turn has further enriched our knowledge of the human thought process.

Let not this enthusiastic report on the scientific potentialities of simulation research arouse anxieties of the sort raised by Norbert Wiener (1960) and other writers that machines will take over our civilization and supplant man in the near future. Rather, I think, there is great hope that detailed knowledge of how humans learn, think, and organize will redound to human welfare in removing much of the mystery which surrounds these processes and in leading to better understanding of the limitations of current ways of solving problems. It may, of course, become possible for us to then build machines which will work out solutions to many problems which we now consider distinctively human and to do so in a manner surpassing present human performance. But that this will lead to the machine becoming master and the designer, slave, seems to me most unlikely. Rather it will free man for novel creative tasks which are progressively beyond the capability of machines designed by man.

## REFERENCES

Bruner, J. S.; Goodnow, Jacqueline J.; and Austin, G. A. 1956. *A study of thinking.* New York: Wiley.

Cahill, H., and Hovland, C. I. 1960. The role of memory in the acquisition of concepts. *Journal of Experimental Psychology* 59:137–144.

Clark, W. A., and Farley, B. G. 1955. Generalization of pattern recognition in a self-organizing system. In *Proceedings of the Western Joint Computer Conference,* pp. 86–91. Institute of Radio Engineers.

Dinneen, G. P. 1955. Programming pattern recognition. In *Proceedings of the Joint Western Computer Conference,* pp. 94–100. Institute of Radio Engineers.

Friedberg, R. M. 1958. A learning machine. Part I. *IBM Journal of Research and Development* 2:2–13. (Cf. also 1959, 3:282–287.)

Gelernter, H. L., and Rochester, N. 1958. Intelligent behavior in problem-solving machines. *IBM Journal of Research and Development* 2:336–345.

Hovland, C. I. 1952. A "communication analysis" of concept learning. *Psychological Review* 59:461–472.

Hovland, C. I. 1953. A set of flower designs for concept learning experiments. *American Journal of Psychology* 66:140–142.

Hovland, C. I., and Hunt, E. B. 1960. Computer simulation of concept attainment. *Behavioral Science* 5:265–267.

Hunt, E. B., and Hovland, C. I. 1960. Order of consideration of different types of concepts. *Journal of Experimental Psychology* 59:220–225.

Miller, G. A.; Galanter, E.; and Pribram, K. H. 1960. *Plans and the structure of behavior.* New York: Holt.

Newell, A.; Shaw, J. C.; and Simon, H. A. 1958. Elements of a theory of human problem solving. *Psychological Review* 65:151–166.

Rochester, N.; Holland, J. H.; Haibt, L. H.; and Duda, W. L. 1956. Tests on a cell assembly theory of the action of the brain, using a large digital computer. *Transactions on Information Theory,* IT-2(3), 80–93.

Rosenblatt, F. 1958. The perceptron: A probabilistic model for information storage and organization in the brain. *Psychological Review* 65:386–408.

Samuel, A. L. 1959. Some studies in machine learning using the game of checkers. *IBM Journal of Research and Development* 3:211–229.

Selfridge, O. G. 1955. Pattern recognition and modern computers. In *Proceedings of the Western Computer Conference*, pp. 91–93. Institute of Radio Engineers.

Tolles, W. E., and Bostrom, R. C. 1956. Automatic screening of cytological smears for cancer: The instrumentation. *Annals of the New York Academy of Sciences* 63:1211–1218.

Wiener, N. 1960. Some moral and technical consequences of automation. *Science* 131:1355–1358.

# PART 5 The Individual

# READING 27

# Rating Diversity and Measures of Convergent and Divergent Intelligence

**CHARLES NEURINGER**
**GAYLE R. WHEELER**
**JAMES V. BEARDSLEY**
**University of Kansas and University of
North Dakota**

What is intelligence? We all use the word; most of us have taken IQ tests; and we often discuss factors which might influence it. Researchers have worked in many areas developing theories of intelligence, attempting to define what intelligence is, and selecting tasks whose successful completion reflects intelligence.

The two following articles are examples of this kind of research. They are concerned with what factors could influence intelligence (as it is measured by IQ tests) and discovering relationships between measured intelligence and performance on other tasks.

In an attempt to dissect intelligence into meaningful components, Neuringer and his associates discuss the distinction between two different kinds of intelligence—convergent and divergent. Their main interest lies in discovering whether a relationship exists between either of these two kinds of intelligence and the rating patterns made by subjects on Osgood's Semantic Differential.

## QUESTIONS

1. Discuss the differences between convergent and divergent intelligence. Are these differences real? What do you think they mean?
2. Consider the following statement by the authors: "Negative results do not infirm an hypothesis, although they may weaken it considerably. A great deal of negative evidence needs to be brought forward before an hypothesis is abandoned. On the other hand only one instance of positive evidence is needed to substantiate an hypothesis." Do you agree with this statement? Is it logical?
3. What is Osgood's Semantic Differential? What are its uses in psychology?

## A. INTRODUCTION

The hypothesis that a person's capacity to perceive concepts in a varied manner (as measured by the diversity of semantic differential ratings) is related to intelligence was evaluated by Ware (11). Using high school students of differing intelligence levels, he was unable to find a significant relationship between IQ and diversity of semantic differential ratings. Osgood (7), however, still felt that the diversity of semantic differential scoring ought to be related to intelligence.

Neuringer (5) working with adult subjects reported a nonsignificant correlation between the Information Subtest of the Wechsler-Bellevue Intelligence Scale and a diversity of rating intensity measure based on semantic differential protocols. At that time Neuringer felt that the failure to substantiate the existence of a relationship between intelligence and rating diversity could be traced to the error of considering intelligence as a unified entity and therefore accepting single global intelligence scores as the measure of that entity.

The present study attempted to relate rating diversity to particular intellectual styles and factors. Guilford (4) has distinguished two broad classes of intellectual strategies known as convergent and divergent thinking. Convergent intelligence involves a person's ability to channel or control his thinking in a particular direction toward one correct solution. This is the kind of thinking demanded by standard intelligence tests. Divergent intelligence is reflected by an individual's ability to create freely and consider a multitude of adequate responses to a problem. Divergent thinking ranges outwards (as in finding as many meanings as possible for a word) in distinction to convergent thinking where a person zeros in on the one possible solution to a problem. It was felt that divergent intelligence should be more related to diversity of ratings than convergent intelligence. In addition this study also allowed for an inspection of the relationship between rating diversity and several common intellectual factors (numerical ability, verbal comprehension, etc.).

## B. METHOD

The subjects in this study consisted of 198 male undergraduates chosen at random from introductory psychology courses at the University of Kansas and University of North Dakota. All selectees participated in the study. The 99 students at the University of North Dakota were administered the Wechsler Adult Intelligence Scale (WAIS) and a semantic differential. The WAIS was the measure of convergent intelligence. The other 99 students at the University of Kansas received a battery of divergent intelligence test measures and the same semantic differential as given to the North Dakota students. A perusal of the School and College Ability Test scores for entering freshmen at the two universities, for the academic years 1964-1965 and 1965-1966, indicated that there was no significant difference between their scholastic abilities.

### 1. CONVERGENT INTELLIGENCE

The WAIS, a standard intelligence test, was used as the measure of convergent thinking. The test demands a correct answer to a series of subtest problems. It is also constructed so as to yield scores on 11 different subtests presumably measuring different intellectual abilities. However factor analyses (1, 2, 9, 10) have indicated that there exist intellectual ability factors that do not correspond to Wechsler's subtest categories. In this study both the subtest scores and the factor scores, constructed from the 12 factors described by Cohen and Saunders, were related to rating diversity.

### 2. DIVERGENT INTELLIGENCE

The scores from a battery of divergent intelligence measures designed by Guilford (4) and Getzels and Jackson (3) were related to rating diversity. They were the (a) Word Association Test, (b) Uses Test, (c) Fables

Test, and (d) Make Up Problems Test. On the Word Association Test, a subject is asked to give as many associations as he can to particular stimulus words. On the Uses Test, the examinees are requested to list as many uses as they can think of for a brick and a pencil. This test is scored for originality and the number of response classes. Subjects on the Fables Test are asked to give a moralistic, humorous, and sad ending to a series of fables. The test is scored in terms of appropriateness (whether the endings are moralistic, humorous, or sad) and relatedness (the logicality of the ending). On the Make Up Problems Tests, subjects are asked to make up as many problems as they can based on information read to them.

## 3. RATING DIVERSITY

A semantic differential, consisting of 18 concepts (democracy, death, God, honor, communism, mother, success, love, life, murder, devil, father, myself, shame, failure, other people, hate, and suicide) and nine scales (good-bad, dirty-clean, nice-awful, unpleasant- pleasant, fair-unfair, worthless-valuable, happy-sad, dishonest-honest, and beautiful-ugly) high on the evaluation factor, was used. The format and administration procedures follow those suggested by Osgood, Suci, and Tannenbaum (8). Each subject made 162 scale judgments.

The method of evaluating the amount of rating diversity made by the subjects was done in the following manner: the usual seven rating spaces per scale were collapsed into four rating spaces by ignoring the direction of the judgment and by only utilizing the magnitude of the ratings. The derived four rating spaces are (a) very, (b) moderately, (c) mildly, and (d) neutral. The dispersion of ratings on the nine four-rating-space scales for each concept were used as the basis of evaluating the amount of variability in a subject's rating of that concept. If a subject rated a concept in the extreme category on all nine scales, he was considered to be showing no amount of variability.

However, if a subject placed three out of the nine ratings in one of the four rating spaces and the other six judgments were equally dispersed among the other three rating spaces, this reflected a high degree of diversification of ratings.

All of the possible ways of rating a concept on nine scales for four rating spaces were ordered and ranked in terms of the amount of diversification reflected in the orderings. The magnitude was then ignored, since a person making nine judgments in the extreme category is considered as undiversified as another person making nine judgments in the neutral category. Only the pattern of distribution of ratings indicates the amount of dispersion. There are 18 possible ways of assigning nine judgments to nine four-rating-space scales for any single concept. The pattern reflecting the least amount of dispersion—9,0,0,0—received a rank of 1. The next least diversified pattern —8,1,0,0—received a rank score of 2, etc., until the pattern of greatest diversification —3,2,2,2—received a rank score of 18. The possible groupings of nine ratings for the four scoring spaces are presented in Table 1 with their accompanying assigned rank diversity scores. The greater the mean Dispersion Index Score (ID), the greater is the use of varied rating spaces on the semantic differential.

The mean Dispersion Index score was computed for each subject by summing the

### TABLE 1

INDEX OF DISPERSION RANK SCORES
FOR NINE RATING-SPACE-SCALES

| Diversity pattern | ID | Diversity pattern | ID |
|---|---|---|---|
| 9,0,0,0 | 1 | 5,2,2,0 | 10 |
| 8,1,0,0 | 2 | 5,2,1,1 | 11 |
| 7,2,0,0 | 3 | 4,4,1,0 | 12 |
| 7,1,1,0 | 4 | 4,3,2,0 | 13 |
| 6,3,0,0 | 5 | 4,3,1,1 | 14 |
| 6,2,1,0 | 6 | 4,2,2,1 | 15 |
| 6,1,1,1 | 7 | 3,3,3,0 | 16 |
| 5,4,0,0 | 8 | 3,3,2,1 | 17 |
| 5,3,1,0 | 9 | 3,2,2,2, | 18 |

ID rankings across the 18 concepts. The greater the score, the greater the amount of rating diversity.

## C. RESULTS

The Pearson Product Moment Correlation Coefficients between the Index of Dispersion scores from the semantic differential and measures of convergent and divergent intelligence can be found in Table 2. Five of the 23 convergent intelligence measures were found to correlate significantly with the Index of Dispersion. They were the Arithmetic and Comprehension Subtests, Saunders' factor IV (Scientific Information), and Cohen's factors A (Verbal Comprehension) and C (Memory). These correlations may be somewhat redundant, since the two

subtests contribute to the three factor scores.

Three of the six divergent intelligence measures were found to be significantly correlated to rating diversity. They were the Word Association Test, Uses Test (originality Measure), and the Make Up Problems Test. While 50 per cent of the divergent intelligence tests, as compared to 21 per cent of the convergent intelligence measures, correlated significantly with the Index of Dispersion, the magnitude of these correlations, which ranged from .20 to .31, was rather low.

## D. DISCUSSION

If one expected that the results of this study would confirm the existence of a ro-

## TABLE 2

PEARSON PRODUCT MOMENT CORRELATION COEFFICIENTS BETWEEN THE INDEX OF DISPERSION SCORES FROM THE SEMANTIC DIFFERENTIAL AND MEASURES OF CONVERGENT AND DIVERGENT INTELLIGENCE

| Convergent intelligence measures | r | Divergent intelligence measures | r |
|---|---|---|---|
| *WAIS subtests* | | | |
| Information | .15 | Word Association Test | .29** |
| Comprehension | .09 | Uses Test (classes) | .15 |
| Arithmetic | .20* | Uses Test (originality) | .24* |
| Similarities | .21* | Fables Test (appropriateness) | .06 |
| Digit span | .10 | Fables Test (relatedness) | .01 |
| Vocabulary | .15 | Make Up Problems Test | .22* |
| Digit symbol | .16 | | |
| Picture completion | .09 | | |
| Block design | .04 | | |
| Picture arrangement | .04 | | |
| Object assembly | .10 | | |
| *Saunders' factors* | | | |
| I. General information | .14 | | |
| II. Contemporary affairs | .12 | | |
| III. Cultural information | .13 | | |
| IV. Scientific information | .31** | | |
| V. Numerical information | .19 | | |
| VI. Numerical operations | .19 | | |
| VII. Maintenance of contact | .06 | | |
| VIII. Maintenance of perspective | .11 | | |
| IX. Effect of uncertainty | .05 | | |
| *Cohen's factors* | | | |
| A. Verbal comprehension | .20* | | |
| B. Perceptual organization | .08 | | |
| C. Memory | .24* | | |

*Significant at .05 level.
**Significant at .01 level.

bust relationship between rating diversity with either convergent and divergent intelligence, or various intellectual abilities, one would be disappointed. The significant correlations were too few and too small. Saunders' factor IV (Scientific Information) correlated highest of all the measures with the Index of Dispersion. However only nine per cent of the correlation variance can be attributed to the relationship between the two measures.

It was hypothesized that divergent intelligence would be more related to rating diversity than convergent intelligence. This prediction was substantiated. Half of the divergent intelligence measures correlated significantly with rating diversity. Less than one fourth of the convergent intelligence measures were significantly correlated with the diversification of rating space index. However, in all cases the magnitude of the correlations would indicate that they have very low predictive value. It is, of course, possible that there exists an intellectual or cognitive factor or ability which determines or influences rating diversity. It was not uncovered in this or previous research. Negative evidence is peculiar due to the fact that it is not as informative as positive evidence. Negative results do not infirm an hypothesis, although they may weaken it considerably. A great deal of negative evidence needs to be brought forward before an hypothesis is abandoned. On the other hand only one instance of positive evidence is needed to substantiate an hypothesis.

It seems feasible to conclude that intelligence has only a minor relationship to rating diversity and that other factors play a more powerful role in determining how many rating spaces a person will utilize. Neuringer (5) has shown that pathology is a crucial factor determining diversity ratings. O'Donovan (6) has tried to relate rating extremity to "meaningfulness." These factors, and others like them, may provide the key to understanding the determinants of the rating judgments.

## E. SUMMARY

In order to clarify further the relationship between rating diversity and intelligence, rating patterns made by subjects on the Semantic Differential were related to scores made on measures of divergent and convergent intelligence. Half the subjects were administered the WAIS (a convergent intelligence measure) and a semantic differential. The other half received the same semantic differential paired with several divergent intelligence tests. An Index of Dispersion score was constructed from the patterns of responses on the Semantic Differential and correlated with the WAIS subtest scores, WAIS factor scores, and the divergent intelligence measures. It was found that rating diversity correlated significantly more often with the divergent intelligence measures than with the convergent intelligence measures. However, the low magnitude of the correlations indicated that the intelligence measures had very low rating diversity predictive value. It was concluded that intelligence has only a minor influence on rating diversity.

## REFERENCES

1. Cohen, J. 1957. The factorial structure of the WAIS between early adulthood and old age. *Journal of Consulting Psychology* 21:283–290.

2. Cohen, J. 1957. A factor-analytically based rationale for the WAIS. *Journal of Consulting Psychology* 21:451–457.

3. Getzels, J. W., and Jackson, P. W. 1962. *Creativity and intelligence.* New York: Wiley.

4. Guilford, J. P. 1959. *Personality.* New York: McGraw-Hill.

5. Neuringer, C. 1963. Effect of intellectual level and neuropsychiatric status on the diversity of semantic differential ratings. *Journal of Consulting Psychology* 27:280.

6. O'Donovan, D. 1965. Rating extremity: Pathology or meaningfulness. *Psychological Review* 72:358–372.

7. Osgood, C. E. 1962. Studies on the generality of effective meaning systems. *American Psychologist* 17:10–28.

8. Osgood, C. E.; Suci, G. J.; and Tannenbaum, F. H. 1957. *The measurement of meaning.* Urbana, Ill.: University of Illinois Press.

9. Saunders, D. R. 1960. A factor analysis of the information and arithmetic items of the WAIS. *Psychological Reports* 6:367–383.

10. Saunders, D. R. 1960. A factor analysis of the picture completion items of the WAIS. *Journal of Clinical Psychology* 16:146–149.

11. Ware, E. E. 1958. Relationships of intelligence and sex to diversity of individual semantic meaning spaces. Unpublished doctoral dissertation, University of Illinois, Urbana, Illinois.

# READING 28

## Infant Development, Preschool IQ, and Social Class

LEE WILLERMAN
SARAH H. BROMAN
National Institute of Neurological Diseases and Stroke
MIRIAM FIEDLER
Children's Hospital Medical Center of Boston

The Willerman, Broman, and Fiedler article takes a developmental viewpoint of intelligence. Through a program of longitudinal research they evaluate the relationships between infant development, IQ as measured at a preschool level, and social class.

### QUESTIONS

1. What is the relationship between infant development, preschool IQ, and socioeconomic status? Support your answer.
2. Discuss the methodology of this study. Is this type of longitudinal research program valuable? What are some problems inherent in this type of research?
3. Discuss some of the developmental aspects of intelligence.

Studies relating infant developmental status to later IQ have generally yielded two distinct classes of findings. Those on the negative side have shown essentially no correlation between infant scores and later IQ. (Bayley 1955). Those on the positive side

This paper was presented at the Biennial Meeting of the Society for Research in Child Development, Santa Monica, California, March 25–29, 1969. Author Willerman's address: Perinatal Research Branch, National Institute of Neurological Diseases and Stroke, National Institutes of Health, Bethesda, Maryland 20014.

such as Knobloch and Pasamanick (1967), and Erickson (1968) have found moderately high correlations between the earlier and later assessments. Explanations of the negative results have focused upon the lack of overlapping content between infant scales and IQ tests (Anderson 1939), or suggested that poor predictability is evidence for the prepotency of environmental influences in determining IQ (Hunt 1961).

It has been pointed out that the difficulty

with some studies yielding negative results is that they were designed in such a way as to minimize the inclusion of abnormal infants or infants from the lower classes. This interpretation has received some support since studies with positive findings have sampled infants likely to have had a much higher incidence of abnormality and have included children from lower socioeconomic strata. Knobloch, Rider, Harper and Pasamanick (1956), in obtaining positive findings, utilized a sample of infants, approximately half of which were premature. Erickson's (1968) positive results included infants subsequently found to be mentally defective (mean Cattell IQ=52). Their findings support the generally held view that infant tests are more useful in predicting low IQs than in predicting average or above average IQs (Illingworth and Birch 1959).

There is some evidence suggesting that the long-term effects of a particular adverse experience during infancy are strongly dependent on socioeconomic status (SES). Werner, Simonian, Bierman, & French (1967) assessed the severity of complications around delivery for a large number of neonates. When these children were given the Cattell Infant Intelligence Scale at 20 months, it was found that social class produced only small differences in IQ if the delivery had been an uncomplicated one, but that social class was strongly related to IQ among deliveries with severe complications. Drillien (1964) found that among full-term infants, social class differences in developmental quotient between the higher and lower classes were approximately of the same magnitude at 4 years of age as they had been at 6 months of age. However, among premature infants, less than 3 pounds 9 ounces, differences in developmental quotient between the higher- and lower-class children were far greater at 4 years than they had been at 6 months. Though based on small numbers of subjects, a reanalysis of Knobloch and Pasamanick's (1967) results also suggests that the risk to

the abnormal infant is disproportionately greater when the child comes from a less stimulating cultural milieu. Using the Gesell examination and the Chapin Living-Room Scale (1930) to estimate the degree of cultural stimulation provided in the home, they found that abnormal infants from homes given the highest cultural ratings averaged 5 points increase from the DQ (Developmental Quotient) in infancy to the IQ obtained during the school years. Those abnormal infants from the middle group dropped 28 points from their DQ to IQ, and those from the group given the lowest stimulation rating dropped 16.7 points between DQ and IQ. Among the "normal" cases the respective changes between DQ and IQ were +5, −4, and −11 points. In view of this suggestive differential effect of infant developmental status on IQ as a function of SES, it becomes particularly important to treat SES in a systematic fashion in predicting IQ from infant status. The present report includes a large sample of children widely varying in SES and infant development and relates infant scores to IQs at 4 years of age.

## PROCEDURE
### SUBJECTS

Subjects were 3037 white children born at Boston Lying-in Hospital (BLI). This hospital is a member of the Collaborative Perinatal Research Project sponsored by the National Institute of Neurological Diseases and Stroke. The project, still in progress, has included gravidae who delivered approximately 50,000 infants at 12 collaborating institutions throughout the country. The children are now being followed until 8 years of age with batteries of neurological, speech, language, hearing, and psychological tests. Only 12 percent of the subjects served by the Medical Center are Negro, and they are not included in the present report. Also excluded were the few children identified as having Down's syndrome. The subjects included in the present analysis are those who received the 8-month as well as the 4-year psychological examinations.

## METHOD

At 8 months of age, the infants were routinely brought to either BLI or to the Children's Hospital Medical Center (CHMC) and administered the Collaborative Research Form of the Bayley Scales of Mental and Motor Development. At 4 years of age these children returned to CHMC and were given the abbreviated version of the Stanford-Binet Intelligence Scale, Form L–M.

The point scores on the infant Mental and Motor Scales were divided as nearly as possible into quartiles and the results are presented as a function of these quartiles. The point scores based on the number of items for which the infant received credit for each of the quartiles are as follows:

Mental Scale, $Q_4 = \leq 78$, $Q_3 = 79–81$, $Q_2 = 82–84$, $Q_1 = 85–106$;

Motor Scale, $Q_4 = \leq 29$, $Q_3 = 30–33$, $Q_2 = 34–36$, $Q_1 = 37–43$.

A socioeconomic index (SEI) devised especially for the project by Myrianthopoulos and French (1968) was employed to assess the SES of the subjects. This multidimensional index is based on the average of a set of rankings of paternal (or other head of household) education and occupation, and family income. The SEI, because it is multidimensional, does not permit a concrete description of the population at various SEI intervals. A graduate student, for example, would rank high on education and occupation, but rank low on income. Another parent with only a high school education, but high income, may have the same SEI, yet there may be substantial differences in their methods of child rearing. Be that as it may, the subjects were arbitrarily divided into three levels of SEI; high, middle, and low. As an oversimplified description of the modal low SEI parent (SEI 0–39), he might be characterized as an unskilled worker having completed no more

than 2 years of high school, with a family income of less than $3,500 per year. The middle SEI (40–69) member would be a skilled worker with a high school education and a family income of less than $5,000 per year. The high SEI (70–93) member would have completed at least 1 year of college, be employed as a clerical worker, proprietor or manager, and have a family income of at least $6,000 a year.

## RESULTS

Table 1 gives the mean scores by sex for the major psychological variables. As can be seen from this table, females obtain significantly higher scores on the Bayley Motor Test at 8 months as well as on the Binet IQ test at 4 years. In the standardization of the Revised Form of the Bayley Motor Scales, Bayley (1965) found a significant ($< .05$) sex difference at 8 months of age in favor of males. Though the population in that report differed considerably from the present one, no ready explanation can be offered for the difference. Despite this difference between her results and ours, since the point biserial correlations between sex and these variables are so low ($r_{pb} = .052$ for sex and Motor Test and $r_{pb} = .117$ for sex and IQ) as to account for only a very small proportion of the variance, and because preliminary analysis revealed essentially similar patterns of results for the sexes, only combined scores will be presented in the figures that follow.

Mean Bayley Mental Test scores do not differ significantly between the SEI levels. The mean low SEI Mental Test score = 80.80, middle = 81.23, and high = 81.00.

Shown in figure 1 are the mean Binet IQs by Bayley Mental quartiles for each SEI level. Within each of the SEI levels it can be seen that infants from the lowest quartile ($Q_4$) are significantly and consistently lower in IQ at 4 years of age.

As might be expected, the largest main effect is related to SEI, and it is interesting to note that in the low SEI level not even

**TABLE 1**
PRIMARY DATA BY SEX

| Variable | Males | Females | Total | SD | t |
|---|---|---|---|---|---|
| Number ........................ | 1624 | 1413 | 3037 | ... | ... |
| Mean Bayley Mental Test .......... | 80.93 | 81.30 | 81.11 | 6.11 | 1.67* |
| Mean Bayley Motor Test .......... | 32.73 | 33.24 | 32.97 | 4.92 | 2.85** |
| Mean Binet IQ ................... | 106.04 | 109.44 | 107.62 | 14.55 | 6.43*** |

\* $p < .10$.
\*\* $p < .01$.
\*\*\* $p < .001$.

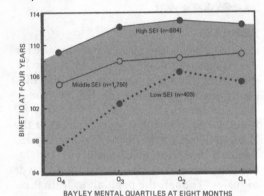

**Figure 1.** Mean 4-year IQ as Bayley Mental quartile at 8 months and SC.

the 4-year olds who were most advanced as infants ($Q_1$) obtain mean IQs as high as 4-year olds from the high SEI level who were retarded ($Q_4$) as infants.

Mean Bayley Motor scores show a slight, but statistically significant relationship to SEI. The mean Motor score of the low SEI = 32.46, middle SEI = 32.90, and high SEI = 33.30. The low SEIs differ significantly from both the middle and high SEIs, and the mean difference between the middle and high SEIs is of borderline statistical significance ($t$ low vs. middle = 2.41, $p < .05$, $df = 2151$; $t$ low vs. high = 3.51, $p < .001$, $df = 704$; $t$ middle vs. high = 1.84, $p < .10$, $df = 2632$).

Figure 2 gives mean Binet IQ by Bayley Motor quartiles and SEI. Within each SEI level, infants from the lowest Motor quartile obtain the lowest mean IQs. This figure also shows that the greatest differences in mean IQ between the quartiles are found among those with the lowest SEI. The maximum

difference in IQ within the low SEIs is between those from $Q_4$ and $Q_2$, where a mean difference of 10 IQ points exists. Among the middle SEIs the maximum difference is less, only 4.5 IQ points between $Q_4$ and $Q_1$. The maximum IQ difference among the high SEIs is about 6 IQ points, between $Q_4$ and $Q_1$. This finding suggests greater vulnerability of poorly developed infants to the adverse effects of environment.

A clearer picture emerges of the increased susceptibility of poorly developed infants to their environment when Mental and Motor scores are combined and only those infants who performed in the lowest quartiles on both Mental and Motor tests are examined. This small group, only 11.6 percent of the total number of subjects, contains 58 percent of those children with IQ $\leq 79$ at 4 years. These infants might be said to display no islands of strength. As a contrast group, those infants who are in the

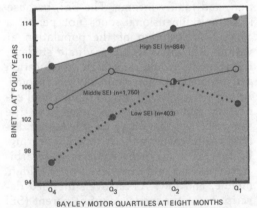

**Figure 2.** Mean 4-year IQ as a function of Bayley Motor quartile at 8 months and SC.

highest quartiles on both Mental and Motor tests are presented. These advanced infants might be said to display no weaknesses.

Figure 3 presents the percentage of these retarded and advanced infants who obtained IQs $\leqq$ 79 at 4 years as a function of SEI level. Among advanced infants the frequency of occurrence of IQ $\leqq$ 79 is unrelated to SEI. However, among infants retarded at 8 months, SEI level is related to subsequent low IQ. Retarded infants were seven times more likely to obtain IQs $\leqq$ 79 if they came from the lowest SEI than if they came from the highest SEI $X^2$, $df =$ 6.34, $p <$ .02 (corrected for continuity).

## DISCUSSION

The major finding of the present study is that infant developmental status interacts with SES in the incidence of low 4-year IQ. Retarded infant development augurs disproportionately poorer intellectual performance in the context of low SES than in the context of higher SES, and it appears that retarded low SES infants are more vulnerable to the adverse effects of their environment. Conversely, it seems that advanced infant development can minimize the occurrence of low IQ among low SES individuals. Just how this occurs is a subject for further investigation.

There is no question that the SEI has many weaknesses and that it is not accounting for what influences accelerated infant development. Our data, as well as Bayley and Schaefer's (1964) indicate a very poor relation between social class and test performance in infancy. During the interval between 1 and 2 years, Caldwell and Richmond (1967) have reported moderate correlations between mother's affective and achievement behavior and the child's Cattell IQ. The genic or environmental influences which lead to accelerated early infant maturational status remain a mystery.

Among high SES groups the present results suggest that the infant test is a poorer predictor of later intellectual status. Infant

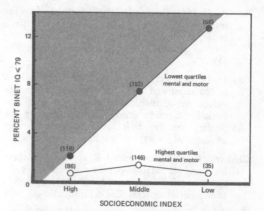

**Figure 3.** Percentage of children IQ $\leq$ 79 at 4 years as a function of quartile category on Mental and Motor tests at 8 months and SC (*N* in parentheses).

developmental status bore little relation to 4-year IQ. The process by which poorly developed infants from high SES environments overcome their deficits is unclear. However, Drillion (1964) has suggested that even these high SES children will display deficits if they are compared to their siblings. The fact that high SES can mask presumptive constitutional deficits points to the necessity of taking SES into account in gauging the effects of infant experience such as perinatal stress.

These results also suggest that poverty, which produces a higher incidence of perinatal morbidity as well as mortality (Yudkin & Yudkin, 1968) will amplify the IQ deficit in poorly developed infants. The next step in the present research program is to study the fate of neurologically impaired infants as a function of social class.

## REFERENCES

Anderson, J. E. 1939. The limitations of infant and preschool tests in the measurement of intelligence. *Journal of Psychology* 8:351–379.

Bayley, N. 1955. On the growth of intelligence. *American Psychologist* 10:805–818.

Bayley, N. 1958. COLR research form of the Bayley scales of mental and motor development. Perinatal Research Branch, National Institute of Neurological Diseases and Stroke.

Bayley, N. 1965. Comparisons of mental and motor test scores for ages 1–15 months, by sex, birth order, race, geographical location, and education of parents. *Child Development* 36:379–411.

Bayley, N., and Schaefer, E. S. 1964. Correlations of maternal and child behaviors with the development of mental abilities. Data from the Berkeley Growth Study. *Monographs of the Society for Research in Child Development* 29 (6, serial no. 97).

Caldwell, B., and Richmond, J. B. 1967. Social class level and stimulation potential of the home. In *Exceptional infant*, ed. J. Hellmuth, pp. 453–466. Seattle: Special Child Publications.

Chapin, F. S. 1930. *Scale for rating living room equipment*. Minneapolis: Institute of Child Welfare.

Drillien, C. M. 1964. *The growth and development of the prematurely born infant*. Baltimore: Williams & Wilkins.

Erickson, M. T. 1968. The predictive validity of the Cattell Infant Intelligence Scale for young mentally retarded children. *American Journal of Mental Deficiency* 72:728–733.

Hunt, J. McV. 1961. *Intelligence and experience*. New York: Ronald.

Illingworth, R. S., and Birch, L. B. 1959. The diagnosis of mental retardation in infancy: A follow-up study. *Archives of Diseases in Childhood* 34:269–273.

Knobloch, H., and Pasamanick, B. 1967. Prediction from the assessment of neuromotor and intellectual status in infancy. In *Psychopathology of mental development*, ed. J. Zubin and G. A. Jervis, pp. 387–400. New York: Grune & Stratton.

Knobloch, H.; Rider, R.; Harper, P.; and Pasamanick, B. 1956. Neuropsychiatric sequelae of prematurity. *Journal of the American Medical Association* 161:581–585.

Myrianthopoulos, N. C., and French, K. S. 1968. An application of the U.S. Bureau of the Census socioeconomic index to a large diversified population. *Social Science and Medicine* 2:283–299.

Werner, E.; Simonian, K.; Bierman, J. M.; and French, F. E. 1967. Cumulative effect of perinatal complications and deprived environment on physical, intellectual, and social development of preschool children. *Pediatrics* 39:480–505.

Yudkin, S., and Yudkin, G. 1968. Poverty and child development. *Developmental Medicine and Child Neurology* 10:569–579.

# READING 29

# Task Complexity and IQ as Variables in Piaget's Problem of Conservation

## KENNETH D. FEIGENBAUM
### Wayne State University

Jean Piaget has devoted many years to the study of mental development in children. His experimentation has included the areas of perception, language, intelligence, thinking, and the emergence of children's concepts of morality and causality. During one state of development, a child begins to master the principle of invariances or conservation. Working within this theoretical framework, Kenneth Feigenbaum concerns himself with the variables of task complexity and IQ. Using conservation problems, he demonstrates that a child's grasp of the conservation concept varies with his tested intelligence and the nature of the experimental operations.

### QUESTIONS
1. What is the value of a principle of "conservation"? What is the use of such a principle in psychology?
2. Write a critical review of this study. Can you find any confounding of variables? Are the statistical tests adequate and meaningful?
3. Piaget states that the attainment of conservation follows a sequence which has been verified experimentally. He suggests that there are definite age ranges associated with this sequence. Do you think it is possible to teach a child to conserve before the age of seven? How definitive are these age barriers?

In Piaget's genetic epistemological theory one dimension of cognitive development is reflected in how the child utilizes the principle of conservation of discontinuous quantities (8).

As used by Piaget, understanding of the principle of "conservation" involves understanding that the number or quantitative aspect of an aggregate is considered to be

This study was part of a doctoral dissertation submitted to the Committee on Human Development, University of Chicago. The author wishes to express his gratitude to Helen L. Koch for her generous advice.

independent of the spatial arrangements of the items or the material in the aggregate, e.g., if beads are moved from one container to another of smaller dimensions, the number of beads remains constant even though there "looks to be" a larger amount in the smaller container.

In order to study mastery of the "conservation" principle, Piaget presented children 4 to 7 years of age with two glasses of equal size and a number of beads. He put one bead into one glass while the child put one into the other, or he allowed the child to put one bead into one glass with one hand while putting another bead into the other glass with the other hand. Piaget then asked questions such as "Which glass has more beads?" to ascertain if the child "understood" one-to-one correspondence. He then poured the contents from a given container into another of smaller dimensions and asked the child whether there were more, fewer, or the same number of beads in the smaller one. If the child understood that there were still the same number of beads in the smaller glass, Piaget concluded that the child understood the principle of conservation of discontinuous quantities.

Piaget contends that "mastery" of the conservation concept occurs in three definite stages. In stage I, "Absence of Conservation," the quantity of an aggregate tends to be estimated on the basis of aspects of the perceptual situation that are irrelevant to the number of items. The number of items is judged to change as their spatial distribution changes. According to Piaget, the child in the first stage of reasoning is egocentric and judges on the basis of global properties or centers upon one aspect of a problem at a time. In stage II, "Beginning of Construction of Permanent Set," there is a vacillating belief that alteration of the spatial arrangement of items does not alter their number or quantity. The child begins to show awareness of the principles of reversibility, identity, and compensated relations, principles which are necessary for the

understanding of conservation. In stage III, "Conservation and Quantifying Coordination," the child understands the concept of conservation. His cognitive field has become a coherent organized whole from which he can abstract.

Piaget indicates that each of the stages constitutes a new way of thinking about the problem. The stages are derived from the logical operations available to the child, which in turn determine the method he employs in the solving of the problem. A dominant mode of operation prevails during any particular age span. Furthermore, without reference to a general measure of abstract ability such as mental age, Piaget suggests that analysis of the operations employed by a child can account for his success or failure with a given set of problems involving the conservation principle.

Unfortunately Piaget limits his study and discussion of conservation to one type or level of complexity of problem. He states that, for the greater part of childhood, logical operations are not independent of their concrete content. However, nowhere in his discussion of the development of the conservation principle does he consider the following relationships: (a) the difficulty of the problem and the child's propensity for solution; (b) the effect of practice with one set of problems on changing performance in others; or (c) the relation between ability to generalize a solution to a new problem involving the conservation principle and the similarity between the two problems. Let us assume that the subject has only partially assimilated[1] conservation; that is, he cannot generalize the principle in all contexts. It is reasonable that such variables as familiarity of stimuli, past training, and "reinforcement" would play some role in determining the child's ability to cope with the principle involved in the problems presented.

The conceptual difficulties of Piaget's ap-

---

[1]Assimilation as defined by Piaget (9) is the action of the organism on surrounding objects, insofar as this action depends on previous behavior involving the same or similar objects.

proach are partially based upon his reportorial techniques. As in many of his studies, Piaget fails to give an accurate report of his procedures (5). Nowhere does he tell his reader exactly what he said to all his subjects, how many children he employed in the sample, how many succeeded or failed to comprehend the conservation principle at each level, or what the IQs of the subjects were. Nor does he give any idea as to the standard of the materials used (i.e., how many beads were employed, their sizes, the dimensions of the glasses used). These variables are relevant if they influence the empirical data upon which Piaget's theory is based. It has been shown by at least one experimenter (3) that intelligence is a factor in number concept attainment. Furthermore, if success varies with the complexity of the task, Piaget's logical stages would be dependent upon the particular conditions and materials involved in the experiment. To be able to generalize, he would have to incorporate his learning principles of assimilation and accommodation into his discussion of conservation.

The purpose of this experiment was to test whether Piaget's explanation emphasizing logical operations occurring in an invariable age-stage system is sufficient to account for success or failure in understanding the principle of conservation.

Hypotheses

1. The levels of thinking involved in the development of conservation of discontinuous quantities are not solely the product of age.

2. The level of success that subjects achieve on tests of correspondence and conservation is related to IQ, as measured by the Stanford-Binet Test. This hypothesis is based on the assumptions that the acquisition of the concepts of correspondence and conservation involves the ability to abstract and that there is a correlation between this ability and IQ.

3. (a) The greater the number of beads used, the more difficult the attainment of conservation and correspondence tends to become.[2] (b) There is a relation between differential size of the containers employed and the solution of the conservation problem. The greater the container size differential, the more difficult the attainment of the solution.[3]

## METHOD
### PROCEDURE
#### Preliminary Testing

Since the E was interested in the relation between the child's IQ and his understanding of the principle of conservation, each of the Ss participating in the study was given a Stanford-Binet Test (Short Form L).

Correspondence Test I.  In order to ascertain the child's understanding of the principle of one-to-one correspondence, the following procedure was employed. Each S was presented with 28 white beads all of the same dimensions and was instructed to drop one bead into a glass, G-1 (1⅜ in. circumference) and one bead into a second glass of different dimensions (1 in. circumference). After S put all of the 14 bead pairs into the two glasses, he was asked: "Which glass has more beads in it, or do the two glasses both have the same number of beads?" "Can you tell me why?"

After the above procedures, the Ss were placed into three experimental subgroups. The treatments applied to each subgroup consisted exactly of the same sequence of tests, the materials employed being different for each treatment (relative size of containers, number of beads). The description of the tests is given under treatment I.

#### Treatment I

Correspondence Test II  The Ss in treatment group I were presented with 28 beads all of same dimensions. They were instructed to drop simultaneously one bead into one glass and another bead into a second glass of the same dimensions. After

---

[2]This relation need not be considered linear.
[3]This relation need not be considered linear.

putting all of the beads into the two glasses, S was asked the following questions: "What glass has more beads in it, or do the two glasses both have the same number of beads?" "Can you tell me why?"

Correspondence Test with prompting. If the Ss failed Correspondence Test II by indicating that they thought that one glass contained more beads than the other, they were asked to count the number of beads in the glasses. If after counting they still could not state that there were the same number of beads in the two glasses, the beads were removed from the glasses. They were then placed into the glasses by the E. After each pair of beads was placed into the glasses, the question of Correspondence Test II was asked, "Now are there still the same number of beads in both glasses?" This procedure was continued until all of the beads were placed into the glasses.

Conservation Test I. E took the beads that the S had put into one of the glasses of equal size and poured them into a glass of smaller dimensions, causing the level of the beads in the smaller glass to appear higher than the level in the other glass. The Ss were then asked the following questions: "Which glass has more beads in it or do the two glasses both have the same number of beads?" "Can you tell me why?" The Ss were considered to have solved the problem referred to as Conservation Test I if their answers were not "guesswork" or based upon perceptual equivalence ("They're the same because they look the same"), but rather by reference to the operation of provoked correspondence ("Because I put them in one by one") or conservation of set ("Because we poured them all out").

Tests for understanding of "more and "bigger." Following the tests for Correspondence II and Conservation I, the Ss were presented a form board consisting of one large triangle and one smaller triangle, one large circle and a smaller circle, one large square and a smaller square, one large triangle and two smaller triangles, one large

circle and two smaller circles, and one large square and two smaller squares. Each set of these geometric figures was arranged horizontally on a single line, and the area of the larger figure was always greater than the sum of the areas of the smaller ones. The Ss were also questioned to see if they could differentiate the concept "more" (number) from "bigger" (size), in order to test the notion that the development of the understanding of mathematical concepts may proceed concurrently with the development of the understanding of the conservation principle.

Conservation Test II and Correspondence Test III. In order to determine if the experience on the form board had any positive transfer, the Ss were retested on correspondence (this is referred to as Correspondence Test III) and conservation (this is referred to as Conservation Test II), using the original materials.

## Treatment II

In order to assess if any relation exists between the number of beads employed and solution of the tests of correspondence and conservation, a second group of 21 Ss matched approximately as to IQ, age, and social class with the Ss in treatment group I were given the same set of tests as those employed in treatment group I with one exception. In the tasks labeled Conservation Tests I and II and Correspondence Tests II and III the number of beads employed was one half the number of beads employed in treatment I.

## Treatment III

In order to test the hypothesis that the greater the size differential of the containers the more difficult would the tests of correspondence and conservation become, 15 Ss approximating in IQ, age, and social class the Ss in treatment groups I and II were given the same set of tests as those in the treatment group I with the following exceptions: (a) the number of beads employed in

TABLE 1

DEMOGRAPHIC CHARACTERISTICS OF THE SUBJECTS IN VARIOUS
TREATMENT GROUPS

| | Number of Subjects | | | Age in Months | | IQ | |
| | Total | Male | Female | Mean | SD | Mean | SD |
|---|---|---|---|---|---|---|---|
| Treatment Group I ................ | 54 | 34 | 20 | 65.4 | 11.4 | 119.3 | 14.7 |
| Treatment Group II .............. | 21 | 10 | 11 | 67.7 | 10.2 | 121.1 | 14.2 |
| Treatment Group III .............. | 15 | 8 | 7 | 65.3 | 9.3 | 117.0 | 16.0 |
| Total ..................... | 90 | 52 | 38 | | | | |

Correspondence Test II and III and Conservation Tests I and II was one half of those used in treatment group I. (b) In the test labeled Conservation I and II the size differential of the glasses was smaller so as to produce less perceptual distortion that in the case of either treatments I or II.

## Mode Analysis

An area of inquiry relating age to understanding of the conservation principle involved an analysis of the modes employed by the children in their attempt at solution of the correspondence and conservation problems. Modes refer to categories of responses deduced from the $Ss'$ responses to the question "Why?" posed after the Test of Correspondence and Conservation. The reasons offered by the $Ss$ were classified as follows: (a) perceptual (looks bigger); (b) conservation of set ("We poured them all out"); (c) reference to provoked correspondence ("We put them in two-by-two").[4]

Due to the fact that the investigator did not have complete protocols for all his subjects, a subpopulation of 66 $Ss$ (those for whom remarks were complete) furnished the data for this analysis. The mean age of the sample was 65.5 months and the mean IQ was 119.8.

The $E$ and an assistant listened to the transcripts and attempted to characterize the reasons the children gave in accounting for their answers in Conservation Tests I and II.

[4]The latter two modes imply some understanding of what Piaget calls the operations of reversibility, identity, and compensated relation.

## POPULATION

The sample for this study consisted of 90 $Ss$ drawn from nursery and elementary schools. As in Piaget's study, their ages ranged between 4 and 7 years.

The sample consisted of bright normals (*see* Table I), and there were no significant differences between the sexes with respect to age and IQ.

## RESULTS AND DISCUSSION
### AGE AND THE MASTERY OF THE PRINCIPLES OF CORRESPONDENCE AND CONSERVATION

It was anticipated that the age variable would account for only part of the variance of the ability or method used to solve the problems of correspondence and conservation. This investigation supports this view.

As Piaget suggests, however, there was a strong positive relation between age and success in understanding the conservation principle (Table 2). An age-numerical ability relation was computed employing chi squares or Fisher exact tests of the difference between $Ss$ below the median age of the group (designated as younger [45 to 64 months]) and those above the median (65 to 87 months). There was a significant difference between the performance of the two age groups for all groups tested ($p < .01$). In contrast with Piaget's report, which describes stages defined by definite age barriers, inspection of the results indicated that the frequency of success in solving the problems gradually increased with age. Furthermore, in the youngest age group (45 to 54

## TABLE 2

PERCENTAGE OF SUBJECTS AT DIFFERENT AGE LEVELS WHO SUCCEEDED
WITH THE TESTS OF CORRESPONDENCE AND CONSERVATION

|  | Age in Months | | | |
|---|---|---|---|---|
|  | 45–54 | 55–64 | 65–74 | 75–87 |
| Correspondence Test I ........................... | 7 | 21 | 32 | 71 |
| Correspondence Test II ........................... | 14 | 31 | 67 | 100 |
| Correspondence Test III ........................... | 45 | 61 | 80 | 100 |
| Conservation Test I ............................. | 0 | 47 | 56 | 91 |
| Conservation Test II ............................. | 16 | 49 | 73 | 91 |

## TABLE 3

PERCENTAGE OF SUBJECTS AT DIFFERENT AGE LEVELS EMPLOYING THE
VARIOUS MODES OF SOLUTION

| Mode | AGE IN MONTHS | | | |
|---|---|---|---|---|
|  | 45–54 | 55–64 | 65–74 | 75–87 |
| Conservation of Set ............................. | 0 | 10 | 50 | 77 |
| Provoked Correspondence ........................ | 14 | 13 | 14 | 9 |
| Perceptual ....................................... | 72 | 63 | 27 | 7 |
| Counts .......................................... | 14 | 14 | 9 | 7 |

months) (Table 2) there were some subjects who could solve most of the problems. These findings are not congruent with Piaget's thesis that the child cannot comprehend the conservation principle until the age of approximately 65 months.

### Mode Analysis (Table 3)

Eight different modes were discriminated in the analysis: two major ones, into which a majority of the responses fell, and six minor ones. The rater agreement on the individual protocols was 86.2 per cent.

I. Perceptual. A group of 22 $Ss$ employed this category. The mean age of this subgroup was 59 months and the mean IQ was 118. An analysis of variance indicated that $Ss$ who used the perceptual mode differed significantly ($F = 14.73$; $p < .01$) in age from the children who employed the other modes. The $Ss$ who employed the perceptual mode were the youngest subjects in the sample. This suggests that the perceptual "stage," as Piaget indicates, tends to be first in the developmental sequence of "modes of operation."

2. Conservation of set. There were 22 $Ss$ who employed this mode of reasoning. The mean age of this subgroup was 77 months and the mean IQ was 125. An analysis of variance comparing the age of this subgroup with the rest of the sample produced a significant difference ($F = 44.1$; $p < .01$). The mean age of this subgroup was higher than that of the subgroups employing other modes. The result indicated that conservation of set was the most employed by the older children in the sample and constituted the most advanced of the developmental states explored.

3. Provoked correspondence. There were four $Ss$ who employed this mode. Their mean age was 61 months and the mean IQ was 120. The $N$ was too small for any meaningful statistical analysis.

4. Marginal group. There were 13 $Ss$ who used combinations of the above three modes, employing one mode on Conservation Test I and another one on Conservation Test II. This group of $Ss$ constituted a marginal group advancing from one mode of thought to another.

**TABLE 4**

RESULTS OF $X^2$ TESTS OF DIFFERENCES IN TESTS OF CORRESPONDENCE
AND CONSERVATION BETWEEN BRIGHTER AND DULLER
SUBJECTS (OVER AND UNDER AN IQ OF 119)

| Test | $X^2$ | $p$ |
|---|---|---|
| Correspondence I | 7.05 | .01 |
| Correspondence II | 3.76 | .05–.10 |
| Conservation I | 4.49 | .05 |
| Conservation II | 5.02 | .05 |
| Correspondence III | 2.75 | .10 |

5. Counts.   When Piaget analyzed the children's approaches to the problem he presented, he did not mention that any of his Ss attempted to use the counting method. Among the Ss of the present study, however, when asked, "Are there the same number of beads in the two glasses?" etc., some proceeded to count the beads in the glass. The mean age was 67.7 months. This group is older than the group of Ss who used the perceptual mode ($p < .01$).

In summary, Piaget is generally correct in stating that perception tends to overrule one-to-one correspondence in the earliest stages of development of the conservation principle. But this mode of response is not confined to children of a particular age period. As can be seen from Table 3, a mode may be dominant during a particular age period, but it may also be employed by children over the entire age continuum encompassed by this sample. In addition, there were a number of cases in which the Ss employed more than one method in their attempt to fathom the conservation principle. It appears that any claim for rigid stages of development needs qualification.

[5]The use of 14 beads rather than two or three or four beads, etc., was dictated by two factors. First, in a pretest it was found that some of the Ss who failed the problems with 14 pairs of beads could solve it with seven pairs. Second, under Piaget's definition of the conservation problem, an ability to resist the suggestion created by the perceptual distortion of the aggregates in the containers, the employment of two, three, or four beads, etc., could not produce the perceptual distortion required. It is quite probable, however, as McLaughlin (6) has indicated, that the crucial difference in the Ss' performance might be in their ability to discriminate between one and more than one, two and more than two, and three and more than three, rather than between 14 and 28. By using Piaget's definition of conservation, one therefore in effect limits the possibility of a more adequate test of the hypothesis, suggesting that reducing the number of beads would increase success with the conservation test.

## IQ AND FREQUENCY OF SUCCESS

The second hypothesis states that a positive relation exists between IQ, as measured by the Stanford-Binet, and ability to solve the problems concerning correspondence and conservation. From Table 4, one can discern a positive relation between IQ and success in the tasks labeled Correspondence Tests I and II and Conservation Tests I and II. In the case of Correspondence Test III, the incidence of success among children above the median in IQ was not significantly greater than the incidence among children with IQ below 119. In a number of cases the performance of younger subjects with higher IQs was also superior to that of older children with the lower IQs. These findings are in agreement with Dodwell (3). It is apparent that age does not account completely for differences in levels of success with the "conservation problems." One might suggest that there is an interplay between general intelligence and possession or propensity for assimilation of the logical operations involved in the comprehension of the conservation principle.

## PROBLEM DIFFICULTY AND THE COMPLEXITY VARIABLES
### Relation between Number of Beads Employed and Success on the Tasks

The performance differences for groups equated as to IQ, age, and ability in the performance of the task of Correspondence Test I were assessed with regard to the number of beads employed in the problem (treatment I, 28 beads; treatment II, 14 beads).[5] In the case of Conservation Test I, no significant difference was noted ($X^2 = 1$).

However, in the case of Correspondence Test II, the difference was significant at the 5 per cent level ($X^2 = 4.4$). Inspection of the data indicated that success by the younger children accounted for the difference. In addition, evidence from the protocols suggested that some Ss solved the relevant problems with 2, 3, or 4 pairs of beads, but failed when the number was increased. The evidence gives tentative support to a view that the complexity of the stimuli presented affected Ss' frequency of success in case of incomplete assimilation of the principle of one-to-one correspondence and to a view that the crucial discrimination for young children regarding enumeration or logical derivatives of a number sort occurs in the first few numbers of the system (6).

## Effect of Perceptual Distortion on Facility with the Tasks

In order to determine the effect of degree of similarity of the containers on the child's ability to resist the influence of irrelevant characteristics of the perceptual field in his thinking about conservation, the results of treatment III were compared with those of treatment II. These two treatments were the same except for the size of containers. Chi square tests revealed no significant differences between treatments II and III in the cases of Conservation Tests I and II or Correspondence Test III. In the case of Correspondence Test II there was a significant difference between the performance of the two treatment groups. Since Correspondence Test II, however, did not involve different size containers, the data cannot be looked upon as proof for hypothesis 3b.

## DISCUSSION

The study has been fruitful in indicating overlapping stages of development in the acquisition of the conservation principle and a positive relation between IQ and knowledge of the concept of conservation. However, the inconclusive results of the study regarding the role of complexity lead to the suggestion that further testing is necessary in order to unravel the relation among the irrelevant perceptual stimuli, the number of beads employed, and the logical processes used by children and the relation between understanding one-to-one correspondence and conservation. Another type of approach to the study of the development of the concept of conservation is indicated. A test of understanding of conservation which is independent of that of correspondence is needed. It would be reasonable to take as evidence for some understanding of conservation the ability to see number constancy when aggregates are simply moved from one area to another. The investigator could then test for understanding of one-to-one correspondence by varying the degree of the irrelevant perceptual stimuli, while under independent conditions varying the number and kinds of aggregates employed to test the subject's possession of a conception of the simplest form of conservation.

## SUMMARY

The present investigation was part of an evaluation of Piaget's study of the child's development of the concept of conservation of discontinuous quantities. The sample consisted of 90 children, 4 to 7 years of age, drawn from nursery and elementary schools in Chicago and Greater Detroit. The evidence indicated that "stages of development" in the acquisition of the conservation concept were not defined by definite age barriers, but rather descriptive general trends. The data also indicated that the children's grasp of the conservation concept tended to vary with their IQ and with the nature of the concrete experimental operations.

## REFERENCES

1. Dennis, W. 1953. Animistic thinking among college and university students. *Scientific Monthly* 76:247–249.

2. Deutsche, J. M. 1937. *The development of children's concepts of causal relations.* Minneapolis: University of Minnesota Press.

3. Dodwell, P. C. 1960. Children's understanding of number and related concepts. *Canadian Journal of Psychology* 14:191–205.

4. Estes, B. W. 1956. Some mathematical and logical concepts in children. *Journal of Genetic Psychology* 88:219–222.

5. Huang, I. 1943. Children's conceptions of physical causality: A critical summary. *Journal of Genetic Psychology* 63:71–121.

6. McLaughlin, K. 1932. A study of number ability in children of ages three to six. Unpublished doctoral dissertation, University of Chicago.

7. Nass, M. L. 1956. The effect of three variables on children's concepts of physical causality. *Journal of Abnormal and Social Psychology* 53: 191–196.

8. Piaget, J. 1950. *Child's conception of number.* London: Routledge, Kegan Paul.

9. Piaget, J. 1950. *The psychology of intelligence.* New York: Harcourt, Brace.

# READING 30

# Self-Understanding and Social Feeling

**JAMES F. BRENNAN**
**Western State School and Hospital**
**Cannonsburg, Pennsylvania**

Since the dawn of man, self-understanding has been sought, and perhaps psychology has come into existence because of this prime motivation. Although all areas of psychology are related directly or indirectly to this problem, it has been the specific concern of personality theorists and clinicians. The following three articles discuss some of the methods and directions in this area.

James Brennan discusses how a person can become more aware of himself and understand his behavior through the use of the Adlerian concept of social feeling. He maintains that self-understanding is attainable only through understanding others and suggests that the practice of social feeling in day-to-day existence will help an individual to understand himself.

## QUESTIONS

1. Discuss the concept that "self-understanding is only attained through understanding others." Is this valid? Is it possible to understand others without understanding yourself first?
2. What is Adler's meaning of social feeling?
3. Why are there so many different personality theories? What is their practical value?

I discover that I am everybody, and that I discover myself in discovering my fellow man, and vice versa.     —Erich Fromm (6, p. 186)

For the psychologist the rule is never to worry about his own success; if he does so, he forfeits it. The psychotherapist must lose all thought of himself.     —Alfred Adler (2, p. 341)

Adler's concept of social feeling offers the psychologist a means by which he is better able to comprehend the process of self-understanding, and most important, articulate his comprehension of the process to others. This statement implies that at present many psychologists are unclear as to the nature of self-understanding and consequently refrain from discussing it, specially as an issue in itself. It is the author's contention that the nature of self-understanding as process is a problem for therapeutic psychology. It is simple enough to say that mental health is to know thyself, but precisely how one goes about knowing thyself remains an enigma.

The purpose of this paper is to examine self-understanding as a problem, study this problem in terms of the Adlerian notion of social feeling, formulate a definition of self-understanding, illuminate this definition with examples, and present its therapeutic implication through a case study.

## SELF-UNDERSTANDING AS A PROBLEM

"Know thyself." This utterance has been handed down through the ages as the criterion of wisdom and peace of mind until our present day where it is transformed through psychological sophistication from a religious-philosophical notion into a slogan of mental health or the central theme of an academic course in mental hygiene. Today it is assumed that one gets to know himself by learning about man in the abstract, i.e., man as a social, psychological, biological, economic, and religious being. Consequently, the "knowledgeable person" ends up knowing about a fictive man constructed from a web of ideas, not the man who lives and breathes, nor the one to whom the personal pronouns "I" and "me" apply.

Then how does one "know thyself"? This slogan or academic theme implies that one does not ordinarily come to know himself; that is why it is conceived as a goal to be attained or a lesson to be learned. Then knowledge of one's self is not the exclusive goal of amnesiacs; rather, insight into self is understanding why we behave as we do. For instance a person may still not understand the reason why he yells at his wife in certain situations, although he knows his socio-economic status, genealogical descent, IQ score, level of academic achievement, physiological make-up, and religious heritage. Clearly, such information is not wisdom, nor does it bring about peace of mind, nor does mental hygiene commence and mental health prevail because of it. Instead, self-understanding appears to be particularized knowledge involving one's unique individuality which is constantly situated with and implicating others. How then does one come to understand himself as a unique individual always situated and involved with others?

## DEFINITION OF SOCIAL FEELING

Adler's concept of social feeling offers us a powerful conceptual tool which we may bring to bear upon the thorny question of self-understanding.

What does social feeling mean? Basically, it is a notion which refers to a person's ability to empathize with another: to see, hear, and feel with him (2, p. 135). Buchheimer's analysis of the original German term *Gemeinschaftsgefühl* is helpful here: *Gemeinschaft* means specifically community with general aspects implicating also the universe; *Gefühl* signifies a person's attitude and action tendency (5, p. 242). The English translation of *Gemeinschaftsgefühl* as social feeling or interest loses merely the implication of one's relation to the universe. What is interesting and rather paradoxical is that Adler combined the idea of social, an objective referent of commonality, with feeling or interest, a subjective referent of personality. The former implicates common meaning; the latter indicates private experience and desire. The synthesis of the objective "social" with the subjective "feeling" or "interest" seems to indicate a triumph over the dichotomous relationship of common meaning and private meaning, a bridge between "you" and "me." Now let us be more specific.

Ansbacher states that Adler considered social feeling to be "an innate cognitive aptitude" (3, p. 50), an aptitude, the author believes, which allows one to transcend his private meanings and feelings by focusing his interest on the other's words and behaviors in terms of what they mean to the other, a feeling with the other. This point can be seen in the way Adler sums up the notion of social interest: "The capacity for identification, which alone makes us capable of friendship, love of mankind, sympathy, occupation, and love, is the basis of social interest and can be practiced and exercised only in conjunction with others" (2, p. 136).

Such identification is a self-transcendence, a going beyond the limited horizons of one's private motives and thoughts to an understanding or sharing of another's aims and desires. In the context of this paper, the nature of social feeling is seen as an aptitude to understand one's self through the understanding of others. At this point it is possible to make more definitive statements concerning the nature of self-understanding conceived as social feeling.

## DEFINITION OF SELF-UNDERSTANDING

Self-understanding is, paradoxically, self-transcendence, i.e., focusing one's interest and feeling upon the other in order to discover what his words, gestures, and postures mean to him. It is becoming less involved with one's own hopes, fears, shame, and doubt in order to become more concerned about how the other sees and experiences the world and others. Self-understanding conceived as social feeling means to see one's self (insight) by participating with another, sharing mutual concern, or more succinctly, being an "I" for a "thou" as Buber (4) would say. It is precisely in such an "I-thou" relation that one is able to establish the necessary distance between himself as figure and his self-seeking pragmatic involvement as ground, for self-understanding to come about. Schultz, the late social philosopher of common sense life, comes to a similar conclusion through a phenomenology of face-to-face relations: "I

experience myself through you, and you experience yourself through me" (7, p. 30).

## THE PRACTICE OF SOCIAL FEELING: SELF-UNDERSTANDING

How can one practice social feeling and thereby understand himself? This question is not easily answered, for we lack adequate descriptive-explanatory concepts with which to exemplify social feeling in action. Here I ask you to imagine along with me. Suppose, for the purpose of exemplification, that you finish eating supper and sit down in the easy-chair and begin to read the newspaper. Your wife enters and begins to nag you about never doing anything around the house and calls you "lazy."

You can respond in different ways. You can mimic her actions as she scolds you, thereby causing her to break into tears. Or, you can not listen to her words, and slip into your own thoughts of self-pity, or think of some ideal love who is always affectionate to you. Or, you can try to understand her point of view, i.e., what her words mean in terms of herself. You actively direct your interest toward how she must feel in making such remarks. All of your knowledge, past experience, and emotional sensitivity is summoned in order to understand why she behaves in such a manner. At this point you are not self-conscious (ashamed, embarrassed, enraged, threatened, etc.), but totally directed toward understanding her point of view. This self-transcending movement achieves distance from self and affords you the possibility of understanding her and hence yourself. For instance, you may realize that she acts as though she is inadequate to the task of being a home-maker, leading you to see that she needs some encouragement and help in doing household chores. It then impresses you that the reason for not helping her in the past springs from an inflated idea of manliness which you unknowingly harbored. On the other hand, you may suddenly see that she is afraid to be affectionate and feels that only harsh words bring results. This understanding also brings with it insight, for you realize that you have been treating her abruptly due to your own mistrust of affection. Let us now pursue what psychotherapeutic implication the reciprocal aspect of self-understanding has in terms of a case study.

## THERAPEUTIC IMPLICATION OF A CASE STUDY

In the analysis of an apparently paranoid woman with a persecution complex, Adler (1, pp. 183–185) revealed how lack of social feeling can make wrong spring from right. It so happened that Adler's patient was actually being disparaged by her supposed friend who in truth depreciated others behind their backs. At first not even the patient's husband and friends believed the patient's accusation: that the apparently kind lady was prone to assassinate a person's good name, and had already done so in the patient's case. In the end the hostile side of the accused woman was revealed for all to see. However, in the interim, the patient suffered alienation from her husband and friends, became hostile and anxiety ridden even though she was right. The point Adler makes is that his patient failed to understand her two-faced friend; instead, she became so hurt and insulted that she risked her own sanity to prove herself right and the other wrong.

Adler's patient responded to the other's depreciating remarks in terms of her injured self-esteem; she depreciated her deceptive friend in the name of truth instead of understanding what the depreciatory tendency meant to this two-faced woman. If the patient had practiced social feeling she would have become aware of this same tendency within herself and everyone else and thereby been able to see that everybody has faults. Despite the fact that this patient was right in what she said, her behavior was not adaptive; she failed to understand the other and to understand herself. Reciprocal understanding of self and others transcends the argumentative mode of being with others, i.e., being interested in being right and proving the other wrong.

## SUMMARY

Self-understanding is only attained through understanding others. Understanding others is a function of social feeling. Social feeling implies self-transcendence. The self-transcending movement of social feeling overcomes self-centeredness and leads to greater reciprocity between self and others. Fostering social feeling in psychotherapy allows the patient to transcend the struggle between right and wrong through a reciprocal understanding of self and others.

## REFERENCES

1. Adler, A. 1964 (originally published 1933). *Social interest: A challenge to mankind.* New York: Capricorn Books.

2. Adler, A. 1956. *The individual psychology of Alfred Adler.* New York: Basic Books.

3. Ansbacher, H. L. 1965. Sensus privatus versus sensus communis. *Journal of Individual Psychology* 21:48–50.

4. Buber, M. 1958. *I and thou.* New York: Scribner.

5. Buchheimer, A. 1959. From group to "Gemeinschaft." In *Essays in individual psychology,* ed. K. A. Adler and Danica Deutsch, pp. 242–247. New York: Grove Press.

6. Fromm, E. 1962. *Beyond the chains of illusion.* New York: Pocket Books.

7. Schutz, A. 1964. *Collected papers.* Vol. 2. The Hague: Martinus Nyhoff.

# READING 31

# Video Tape and Other Therapeutic Procedures with Nude Marathon Groups

**STEPHEN B. LAWRENCE**
**San Bernardino County Hospital**
**San Bernardino, California**

S. B. Lawrence is concerned with the therapeutic relationships involved in group associations. At a time when sensitivity groups, T-groups, etc., are so popular, Lawrence gives us some insight into the techniques that are being tried and their success.

**QUESTIONS**

1. What are our cultural attitudes toward nudity? Why do they exist? Are these attitudes healthy?
2. Why was the use of video tape feedback effective? Were the participants developing "social feeling" toward themselves?
3. Is the tone of this article defensive? Discuss.

Nude group therapy has come into being at this time partially because many of the old taboos are dying or dead. A more permissive society is already upon us. This is seen in the increasing nudity and frankness in today's films, in the blunt, often obscene, dialogue in American plays and novels, in the candid lyrics of popular songs, in the open discussion programs on television, in the political consciousness of the young, and in

freer fashions and the often discussed "sexual revolution." Behind this expanding permissiveness stands a society that has lost its consensus on such crucial issues as premarital sex, the purpose of education, race relations, drug usage, and the meaningful good life, a society that no longer agrees on the basic issues of what constitutes normal standards of conduct.

While some perceive this new candor as a release from an American era of Victorian hypocrisy and repression, many are bewildered, concerned, and often angered at

An earlier version of this article was presented at the meeting of the California State Psychological Association, Santa Barbara, California, 1968.

344

the swiftness with which all the old restraints are crumbling. These mores are changing so rapidly that many alarmed social thinkers fear a dangerous swing toward irresponsible hedonism and, ultimately, social decay. The analogy of the decline and fall of the Roman Empire has been applied to what is now perceived as developing in Western Society.

Although most agree that this new freedom of expression is unlikely to reverse itself because the forces that have produced it are a permanent and irresistible part of modern life, many responsible individuals reject the notion that the new permissiveness is a sign of impending moral collapse. It is clear, however, that until recently agencies of moral order like the church, the government, the community, and the family have dictated what type of behavior will be allowed. Now these institutions have simply been overrun by individuals who are deciding for themselves which experiences they feel are rewarding and growth producing.

With the typical cultural lag now receding behind us, many social scientists are beginning to see the tumbling of the old codes not as the beginning of moral decline but rather as the beginning of a search for new values. The breakdown of traditional values has broadened the options available to each individual as to how he will conduct his life and how he will deal with the new freedoms. Areas that were so heavily guarded or suppressed, such as nudism, are now open to this new moral atmosphere.

We are just beginning to discover what morality is all about. It is concerned with how we treat one another, not how much of our body we display. Nudity is just a part of a new way of being able to express feelings and this area must be faced and accepted as a part of a general confrontation with life. And like the youth of today who demand the truth, psychology and social science must also "tell it straight; tell it the way it really is."

## CHANGES IN PSYCHOLOGY

In the field of clinical psychology and especially psychotherapy, change is developing with a bewildering rapidity. The traditional 1 to 1 therapy situation with its sharply defined roles and the therapist firmly secured behind his desk with the door closed and secrets flowing in one direction only has almost become passé. From personal experience, I know both the exhilaration and the fear that has accompanied coming out from behind that desk: coming out to participate in psychotherapy on live television watched by hundreds of observers; to experience the aliveness of sensory-awareness procedures and nonverbal techniques, often utilizing physical contact; to attempt to defend oneself in the Synanon games' "attack therapy"; to intimately share the tears and joy of 24–48 hour continuous marathon groups; to accept the jolting experience of watching your own behavior on video tape playback; and now nude marathon groups. Frankly, the intellectual and emotional nakedness in the above experiences was felt to be considerably more revealing than the experience of simple physical nudity.

For this author, the introspection, speculation, and preliminary planning for a nude marathon, now in retrospect, seem as valuable and enlightening as the actual group experience itself. The whole procedure, it was found, was steeped in caution and a strong concern of how my professional colleagues would judge such a venture. From previous personal experience, I have found that innovations in therapeutic approaches often lead to spirited opposition that at times has openly developed into hostile, defensive rejection by other social scientists and therapists of other schools. It has appeared to me that change, innovation, and pioneering in clinical psychology meets with the same forces of opposition and suppression that the establishment everywhere instantly seems to be able to muster. This reactionary element in a science dedicated to change is a problem in psychology that warrants deep concern. So before a nude marathon was planned, this author carefully considered the contingencies of professional criticism and possible censure, being labeled as unethical, cultist, unscientific, and other similar tags usually given to those whose ideas and values differ from the majority. The fact that papers such as this one are now being presented at psychological conventions indicates there definitely are strong elements of openness and permissiveness in psychology, and this is considerably reassuring.

## PRELIMINARY EVENTS

In preparing for the nude marathon it was felt, for a variety of reasons, that an appropriate and natural setting for the group would be on the grounds of a nudist camp. Since social nudism is legal in only some counties in California, an appropriate and convenient camp was selected and arrangements for a marathon completed with the camp's director. The 24-hour session was held in one of the homes of the camp so that the problems of food and other necessities were easily solved.

The participants, who were all over 21 years old, were volunteers solicited informally by word of mouth. Each gave his written agreement to follow the simple camp rules and also permission for video recordings to be taken with the knowledge that an abstract discussion of the group's experiences might be given for professional and educational purposes at a later date. The participants included two married couples and several single male and female individuals, most of whom had considerable background in psychotherapeutic experiences both as therapists and clients. None were social nudists, although all had some very minor experiences with nudity.

The video tape nude marathon lasted 24 continuous hours during which the group remained intact with no subgrouping. Brief periods were spent in jointly exploring the

camp grounds, in group sensory-awareness exercises, and using the camp swimming pool. Video tape recordings and playback occurred during most of the session. Conveniently, the camp director sat in on parts of the marathon and was available for questions and feedback concerning his extensive experience with social nudism.

The group began fully clothed in the early evening with a discussion of anxious feelings the members might have about social nudism. There was also a brief discussion of each individual's previous experiences with nudity, most of which were solitary or in childhood. It was then jointly decided the group would walk to the swimming pool, disrobe, and swim briefly before continuing on with the session. At the time and later, all agreed this was a comfortable and smooth transition to group nudity.

As the group confronted its own nudity, there initially was much good-natured joking and laughter, with several members noting how pleasant and enjoyable the immediate experience had become. A number of topics related to the nudity were then discussed by the group, including present voyeuristic needs, the surprisingly easy control of sexual impulses, degrees of inhibition, physical imperfections, and the emotional adjustment to the new situation. In less than one hour, however, the group felt the topic of nudity and its peripheral areas had essentially been exhausted, and it was agreed to move on to other verbal encounters. At that point, the group felt that the nudity itself did essentially contribute to a feeling of group solidarity. This was to gradually develop as the marathon continued.

## VIDEO TAPE FEEDBACK

During the session each participant was given several opportunities to view his behavior and physical appearance through video tape playbacks. The first tape consisted of five-minute segments of each group member walking, standing, turning, sitting, and talking and included facial closeups, shots from the waist up, and finally video tapes of full body profiles. The participants viewed this five-minute taped segment twice; once in the group setting immediately after it was recorded, and again the next day alone, one at a time while the rest of the group ate lunch. The second tape was one-hour long and consisted of candid views of the free group interaction including group discussions and the participants moving about, changing seats, listening, and talking. This second-hour tape was played back to the group approximately 12 hours later at the evening meal. During the playbacks the group members could comment and discuss what they perceived while watching their behavior and appearance on the video tape. Following the marathon, the author studied both tapes several times before they were erased. It might be noted that as in regular video tape marathon groups, the taping equipment and activities did not interfere or inhibit the free-flowing group interaction.

The group's reaction to the video tape feedback appeared to be consistently and often dramatically effective. Without a doubt it is a useful and meaningful tool in communicating another form or type of information in these group encounters. For example, most of the members had highly specific concepts and self-perceptions of their own physical appearance. These perceptions were not always shared by the rest of the group. Following the video tape feedback, however, these self-perceptions appeared to alter more in the direction of objective reality. Most of the group members' original self-body perception tended to focus on what they felt were negative characteristics, such as over- or under-weight, poor body proportioning, unattractive changes due to aging, and other similar deviations from what is generally considered the ideal human physique. Despite repeated assurances that others did not perceive them in this manner, members continued to maintain these beliefs. Following the video tape playback of themselves, however, body self-

perceptions were judged more congruent with group perception.

One rather startling alteration in self-body image occurred in a male individual who felt all his life he had been physically unattractive, especially to women, and that now he had gradually become a "fat, little old man." Contrary opinions by the female participants were simply not accepted by him. Laughing and smiling while watching his video replay he excitedly informed the group that, "I'm not fat at all; I'm really rather husky and stocky and there is a nice masculine powerfulness about me. I like what I see!"

In general, the women tended to be much more critical of their physical appearance and video feedbacks often confirmed their original body perceptions, especially the usual shift in weight and proportion that occurs with aging. There did not, however, appear to be any critical evaluation of physiques by one member of another, but rather as one participant aptly put it, "each body seems to fit nicely with each face."

The group voiced a consensus that none of us had previously taken a very careful look at ourselves in the nude. One couple noted that although they had been married many years, neither had a very accurate perception of how his mate appeared nude. All agreed the video tape had given them a dramatically more accurate image of their own body and judged this element of the nude marathon experience as very valuable.

## OTHER ACTIVITIES

During a brief period in the marathon session, the group strolled around the camp grounds and jointly observed the other nudists. The most consistent impression was that now that we had been initiated, the nudists, and especially the nude families, seemed very natural and rather appropriate. Also noted was a feeling that other than the nudism, the camp activities seemed rather dull and lacking in the ability to sustain our interest for very long. Although our initial experience with nudism was uniformly judged as valuable, none of the group indicated any strong interest in the nudist style of life and, in fact, were rather critical of the typical nudist's rationale and the seeming overcautiousness and often incongruent rules and regulations of the camp.

Initially the participants exhibited some hesitancy and inhibition concerning physical contact, especially between men and women. These receded rather slowly until appropriate physical contact became comfortable and spontaneously natural. There were no observable sexual overtones to these contacts and the group agreed that sexual arousal in this setting would not only be socially inappropriate, but a serious breach of our personal and group mores.

Throughout the marathon, physical contact was frequently initiated as a nonverbal therapeutic technique and spontaneously arose during shared episodes of intimate and warm personal feelings. Physical contact was also experienced during a series of sensory-awareness exercises conducted outside on the camp grounds. The members unanimously agreed these experiences were significantly enhanced by being conducted nude. Several felt the procedures were joyfully enriching with an accompaniment of deep personal feelings of warmth and oneness with the group.

## CONCLUSIONS

In conclusion it is observed that a therapeutic encounter facilitated by nudity is not as radically new a concept as it may first appear. The approach has previously been used intermittently at some residential training centers, and mixed communal bathing and massage have been a standard adjunct for several years now at one of the leading California centers for exploration in the social sciences. Also, Abraham Maslow, president of the APA in 1967, has been quoted as directly encouraging and sanctioning the concept of nude psychotherapy.

Like the new morality, this technique is already upon us whether we agreed with it or not. Possibly it might be discarded tomorrow as other approaches are found to be more effective, but for now this author would appeal for a period of objective testing and evaluation of this new approach. Certainly much more objective data are needed, but even more vital would be the need for a fair and adequate hearing for nude therapy.

This is not to say that nude therapy might be appropriate for all therapists with all clients in all situations; it obviously is not! But our very preliminary evidence suggests that nudity as a facilitator in the group process can be significantly effective with some therapists and some clients in some settings. In any case, video tape nude marathon groups with emphasis on sensory awareness and nonverbal physical techniques is "where it's at" today. The general thrust of all these new approaches developing so rapidly may leave most of us hesitant to deal with them, but, in conclusion, let me quote Bob Dylan, the popular singer and one of the spokesmen for the new generation. He proclaims, "Something is happening Mr. Jones and you don't know what it is, do you?" I suggest we find out what is happening in this area.

# READING 32

## The Necessary and Sufficient Conditions of Therapeutic Personality Change

**CARL R. ROGERS**
**University of Chicago**

The article by Carl Rogers devotes itself to a therapeutic situation. He lists six conditions that he feels are necessary before personality change and self-understanding can occur. These conditions are a reflection of the system of treatment and theory of personality which Rogers has developed.

**QUESTIONS**

1. Why is Rogers concerned with defining the six conditions operationally? Do you think this definition is necessary?

2. Rogers suggests that the six conditions apply to any situation in which the goal is personality change. How many (if any) of these conditions are met in work with delinquents? Conditions four and five appear to be contradictory to the role of a parole officer. What are your ideas concerning this?

3. Do you agree with Rogers concerning the conditions he terms nonessential? Why?

For many years I have been engaged in psychotherapy with individuals in distress. In recent years I have found myself increasingly concerned with the process of abstracting from that experience the general principles which appear to be involved in it. I have endeavored to discover any orderliness, any unity which seems to inhere in the subtle, complex tissue of interpersonal relationship in which I have so constantly been immersed in therapeutic work. One of the current products of this concern is an attempt to state, in formal terms, a theory of psychotherapy, of personality, and of interpersonal relationships which will encompass and contain the phenomena of my experience.[1] What I wish to do in this paper is to take one very small segment of that theory,

[1] This formal statement is entitled "A theory of therapy, personality and interpersonal relationships, as developed in the client-centered framework," by Carl R. Rogers. The manuscript was prepared at the request of the Committee of the American Psychological Association for the Study of the Status and Development of Psychology in the United States. It will be published by McGraw-Hill in one of several volumes being prepared by this committee. Copies of the unpublished manuscript are available from the author to those with special interest in this field.

spell it out more completely, and explore its meaning and usefulness.

## THE PROBLEM

The question to which I wish to address myself is this: Is it possible to state, in terms which are clearly definable and measurable, the psychological conditions which are both necessary and sufficient to bring about constructive personality change? Do we, in other words, know with any precision those elements which are essential if psychotherapeutic change is to ensue?

Before proceeding to the major task let me dispose very briefly of the second portion of the question. What is meant by such phrases as "psychotherapeutic change," "constructive personality change"? This problem also deserves deep and serious consideration, but for the moment let me suggest a common-sense type of meaning upon which we can perhaps agree for purposes of this paper. By these phrases is meant: change in the personality structure of the individual, at both surface and deeper levels, in a direction which clinicians would agree means greater integration, less internal conflict, more energy utilizable for effective living; change in behavior away from behaviors generally regarded as immature and toward behaviors regarded as mature. This brief description may suffice to indicate the kind of change for which we are considering the preconditions. It may also suggest the ways in which this criterion of change may be determined.[2]

## THE CONDITIONS

As I have considered my own clinical experience and that of my colleagues together with the pertinent research which is available, I have drawn out several conditions which seem to me to be necessary to initiate constructive personality change, and when taken together, appear to be sufficient to inaugurate that process. As I have worked on this problem I have found myself surprised at the simplicity of what has emerged. The

statement which follows is not offered with any assurance as to its correctness, but with the expectation that it will have the value of any theory, namely that it states or implies a series of hypotheses which are open to proof or disproof, thereby clarifying and extending our knowledge of the field.

Since I am not, in this paper, trying to achieve suspense, I will state at once, in severely rigorous and summarized terms, the six conditions which I have come to feel are basic to the process of personality change. The meaning of a number of the terms is not immediately evident, but will be clarified in the explanatory sections which follow. It is hoped that this brief statement will have much more significance to the reader when he has completed the paper. Without further introduction let me state the basic theoretical position.

For constructive personality change to occur, it is necessary that these conditions exist and continue over a period of time:

1. Two persons are in psychological contact.

2. The first, whom we shall term the client, is in a state of incongruence, being vulnerable or anxious.

3. The second person, whom we shall term the therapist, is congruent or integrated in the relationship.

4. The therapist experiences unconditional positive regard for the client.

5. The therapist experiences an empathic understanding of the client's internal frame of reference and endeavors to communicate this experience to the client.

6. The communication to the client of the therapist's empathic understanding and unconditional positive regard is to a minimal degree achieved.

No other conditions are necessary. If these six conditions exist, and continue over a period of time, this is sufficient. The process of constructive personality change will follow.

## A RELATIONSHIP

The first condition specifies that a minimal relationship, a psychological contact, must

---

[2]That this is a measurable and determinable criterion has been shown in research already completed. See (7), especially chapters 8, 13, and 17.

exist. I am hypothesizing that significant positive personality change does not occur except in a relationship. This is of course an hypothesis, and it may be disproved.

Conditions 2 through 6 define the characteristics of the relationship which are regarded as essential by defining the necessary characteristics of each person in the relationship. All that is intended by this first condition is to specify that the two people are to some degree in contact, that each makes some perceived difference in the experiential field of the other. Probably it is sufficient if each makes some "subceived" difference, even though the individual may not be consciously aware of this impact. Thus it might be difficult to know whether a catatonic patient perceives a therapist's presence as making a difference to him—a difference of any kind—but it is almost certain that at some organic level he does sense this difference.

Except in such a difficult borderline situation as that just mentioned, it would be relatively easy to define this condition in operational terms and thus determine, from a hard-boiled research point of view, whether the condition does, or does not, exist. The simplest method of determination involves simply the awareness of both client and therapist. If each is aware of being in personal or psychological contact with the other, then this condition is met.

This first condition of therapeutic change is such a simple one that perhaps it should be labeled an assumption or a precondition in order to set it apart from those that follow. Without it, however, the remaining items would have no meaning, and that is the reason for including it.

## THE STATE OF THE CLIENT

It was specified that it is necessary that the client be "in a state of incongruence, being vulnerable or anxious." What is the meaning of these terms?

Incongruence is a basic construct in the theory we have been developing. It refers to a discrepancy between the actual experience of the organism and the self picture of the individual insofar as it represents that experience. Thus a student may experience, at a total or organismic level, a fear of the university and of examinations which are given on the third floor of a certain building, since these may demonstrate fundamental inadequacy in him. Since such a fear of his inadequacy is decidedly at odds with his concept of himself, this experience is represented (distortedly) in his awareness as an unreasonable fear of climbing stairs in this building, or any building, and soon an unreasonable fear of crossing the open campus. Thus there is a fundamental discrepancy between the experienced meaning of the situation as it registers in his organism and the symbolic representation of that experience in awareness in such a way that it does not conflict with the picture he has of himself. In this case to admit a fear of inadequacy would contradict the picture he holds of himself; to admit incomprehensible fears does not contradict his self concept.

Another instance would be the mother who develops vague illnesses whenever her only son makes plans to leave home. The actual desire is to hold on to her only source of satisfaction. To perceive this in awareness would be inconsistent with the picture she holds of herself as a good mother. Illness, however, is consistent with her self concept, and the experience is symbolized in this distorted fashion. Thus again there is a basic incongruence between the self as perceived (in this case as an ill mother needing attention) and the actual experience (in this case the desire to hold on to her son).

When the individual has no awareness of such incongruence in himself, then he is merely vulnerable to the possibility of anxiety and disorganization. Some experience might occur so suddenly or so obviously that the incongruence could not be denied. Therefore, the person is vulnerable to such a possibility.

If the individual dimly perceives such an incongruence in himself, then a tension state occurs which is known as anxiety. The incongruence need not be sharply perceived. It is enough that it is subceived—that is, discriminated as threatening to the self without any awareness of the content of that threat. Such anxiety is often seen in therapy as the individual approaches awareness of some element of his experience which is in sharp contradiction to his self concept.

It is not easy to give precise operational definition to this second of the six conditions, yet to some degree this has been achieved. Several research workers have defined the self concept by means of a Q sort by the individual of a list of self-referent items. This gives us an operational picture of the self. The total experiencing of the individual is more difficult to capture. Chodorkoff (2) has defined it as a Q sort made by a clinician who sorts the same self-referent items independently, basing his sorting on the picture he has obtained of the individual from projective tests. His sort thus includes unconscious as well as conscious elements of the individual's experience, thus representing (in an admittedly imperfect way) the totality of the client's experience. The correlation between these two sortings gives a crude operational measure of incongruence between self and experience, low or negative correlation representing of course a high degree of incongruence.

## THE THERAPIST'S GENUINENESS IN THE RELATIONSHIP

The third condition is that the therapist should be, within the confines of this relationship, a congruent, genuine, integrated person. It means that within the relationship he is freely and deeply himself, with his actual experience accurately represented by his awareness of himself. It is the opposite of presenting a facade, either knowingly or unknowingly.

It is not necessary (nor is it possible) that the therapist be a paragon who exhibits this degree of integration, of wholeness, in every aspect of his life. It is sufficient that he is accurately himself in this hour of this rela-

tionship, that in this basic sense he is what he actually is, in this moment of time.

It should be clear that this includes being himself even in ways which are not regarded as ideal for psychotherapy. His experience may be "I am afraid of this client" or "My attention is so focused on my own problems that I can scarcely listen to him." If the therapist is not denying these feelings to awareness, but is able freely to be them (as well as being his other feelings), then the condition we have stated is met.

It would take us too far afield to consider the puzzling matter as to the degree to which the therapist overtly communicates this reality in himself to the client. Certainly, the aim is not for the therapist to express or talk out his own feelings, but primarily that he should not be deceiving the client as to himself. At times he may need to talk out some of his own feelings (either to the client, or to a colleague or supervisor) if they are standing in the way of the two following conditions.

It is not too difficult to suggest an operational definition for this third condition. We resort again to Q technique. If the therapist sorts a series of items relevant to the relationship (using a list similar to the ones developed by Fiedler [3, 4] and Bown [1]), this will give his perception of his experience in the relationship. If several judges who have observed the interview or listened to a recording of it (or observed a sound movie of it) now sort the same items to represent *their* perception of the relationship, this second sorting should catch those elements of the therapist's behavior and inferred attitudes of which he is unaware, as well as those of which he is aware. Thus a high correlation between the therapist's sort and the observer's sort would represent in crude form an operational definition of the therapist's congruence or integration in the relationship; and a low correlation, the opposite.

## UNCONDITIONAL POSITIVE REGARD

To the extent that the therapist finds himself experiencing a warm acceptance of each aspect of the client's experience as being a part of that client, he is experiencing unconditional positive regard. This concept has been developed by Standal (8). It means that there are no *conditions* of acceptance, no feeling of "I like you only *if* you are thus and so." It means a "prizing" of the person, as Dewey has used that term. It is at the opposite pole from a selective evaluating attitude—"You are bad in these ways, good in those." It involves as much feeling of acceptance for the client's expression of negative, "bad," painful, fearful, defensive, abnormal feelings as for his expression of "good," positive, mature, confident, social feelings, as much acceptance of ways in which he is inconsistent as of ways in which he is consistent. It means a caring for the client, but not in a possessive way or in such a way as simply to satisfy the therapist's own needs. It means a caring for the client as a *separate* person, with permission to have his own feelings, his own experiences. One client describes the therapist as "fostering my possession of my own experience . . . that [this] is *my* experience and that I am actually having it: thinking what I think, feeling what I feel, wanting what I want, fearing what I fear: no 'ifs,' 'buts,' or 'not reallys.'" This is the type of acceptance which is hypothesized as being necessary if personality change is to occur.

Like the two previous conditions, this fourth condition is a matter of degree,[3] as immediately becomes apparent if we attempt to define it in terms of specific research operations. One such method of giving it definition would be to consider the

---

[3]The phrase "unconditional positive regard" may be an unfortunate one, since it sounds like an absolute, an all or nothing dispositional concept. It is probably evident from the description that completely unconditional positive regard would never exist except in theory. From a clinical and experiential point of view I believe the most accurate statement is that the effective therapist experiences unconditional positive regard for the client during many moments of his contact with him, yet from time to time he experiences only a conditional positive regard—and perhaps at times a negative regard, though this is not likely in effective therapy. It is in this sense that unconditional positive regard exists as a matter of degree in any relationship.

Q sort for the relationship as described under Condition 3. To the extent that items expressive of unconditional positive regard are sorted as characteristic of the relationship by both the therapist and the observers, unconditional positive regard might be said to exist. Such items might include statements of this order: "I feel no revulsion at anything the client says"; "I feel neither approval nor disapproval of the client and his statements—simply acceptance"; "I feel warmly toward the client—toward his weaknesses and problems as well as his potentialities"; "I am not inclined to pass judgment on what the client tells me"; "I like the client." To the extent that both therapist and observers perceive these items as characteristic, or their opposites as uncharacteristic, Condition 4 might be said to be met.

## EMPATHY

The fifth condition is that the therapist is experiencing an accurate, empathic understanding of the client's awareness of his own experience. To sense the client's private world as if it were your own, but without ever losing the "as if" quality—this is empathy, and this seems essential to therapy. To sense the client's anger, fear, or confusion as if it were your own, yet without your own anger, fear, or confusion getting bound up in it, is the condition we are endeavoring to describe. When the client's world is this clear to the therapist, and he moves about in it freely, then he can both communicate his understanding of what is clearly known to the client and can also voice meanings in the client's experience of which the client is scarcely aware. As one client described this second aspect: "Every now and again, with me in a tangle of thought and feeling, screwed up in a web of mutually divergent lines of movement, with impulses from different parts of me, and me feeling the feeling of its being all too much and suchlike—then whomp, just like a sunbeam thrusting its way through cloudbanks and tangles of foliage to spread a circle of light on a tangle of forest paths, came some comment from you. [It was] clarity, even disentanglement, an additional twist to the picture, a putting in place. Then the consequence—the sense of moving on, the relaxation. These were sunbeams." That such penetrating empathy is important for therapy is indicated by Fiedler's research (3) in which items such as the following placed high in the description of relationships created by experienced therapists:

The therapist is well able to understand the patient's feelings.

The therapist is never in any doubt about what the patient means.

The therapist's remarks fit in just right with the patient's mood and content.

The therapist's tone of voice conveys the complete ability to share the patient's feelings.

An operational definition of the therapist's empathy could be provided in different ways. Use might be made of the Q sort described under Condition 3. To the degree that items descriptive of accurate empathy were sorted as characteristic by both the therapist and the observers, this condition would be regarded as existing.

Another way of defining this condition would be for both client and therapist to sort a list of items descriptive of client feelings. Each would sort independently, the task being to represent the feelings which the client had experienced during a just completed interview. If the correlation between client and therapist sortings were high, accurate empathy would be said to exist, a low correlation indicating the opposite conclusion.

Still another way of measuring empathy would be for trained judges to rate the depth and accuracy of the therapist's empathy on the basis of listening to recorded interviews.

## THE CLIENT'S PERCEPTION OF THE THERAPIST

The final condition as stated is that the client perceives, to a minimal degree, the acceptance and empathy which the therapist experiences for him. Unless some communication of these attitudes has been achieved, then such attitudes do not exist in the relationship as far as the client is concerned, and the therapeutic process could not, by our hypothesis, be initiated.

Since attitudes cannot be directly perceived, it might be somewhat more accurate to state that therapist behaviors and words are perceived by the client as meaning that to some degree the therapist accepts and understands him.

An operational definition of this condition would not be difficult. The client might, after an interview, sort a Q-sort list of items referring to qualities representing the relationship between himself and the therapist. (The same list could be used as for Condition 3.) If several items descriptive of acceptance and empathy are sorted by the client as characteristic of the relationship, then this condition could be regarded as met. In the present state of our knowledge the meaning of "to a minimal degree" would have to be arbitrary.

## SOME COMMENTS

Up to this point the effort has been made to present, briefly and factually, the conditions which I have come to regard as essential for psychotherapeutic change. I have not tried to give the theoretical context of these conditions nor to explain what seem to me to be the dynamics of their effectiveness. Such explanatory material will be available, to the reader who is interested, in the document already mentioned (see footnote 1).

I have, however, given at least one means of defining, in operational terms, each of the conditions mentioned. I have done this in order to stress the fact that I am not speaking of vague qualities which ideally should be present if some other vague result is to occur. I am presenting conditions which are crudely measurable even in the present state of our technology, and have suggested specific operations in each instance even though I am sure that more adequate methods of measurement could be devised by a serious investigator.

My purpose has been to stress the notion that in my opinion we are dealing with an if-then phenomenon in which knowledge of the dynamics is not essential to testing the hypotheses. Thus, to illustrate from another field: if one substance, shown by a series of operations to be the substance known as hydrochloric acid, is mixed with another substance, shown by another series of operations to be sodium hydroxide, then salt and water will be products of this mixture. This is true whether one regards the results as due to magic, or whether one explains it in the most adequate terms of modern chemical theory. In the same way it is being postuated here that certain definable conditions precede certain definable changes and that this fact exists independently of our efforts to account for it.

## THE RESULTING HYPOTHESES

The major value of stating any theory in unequivocal terms is that specific hypotheses may be drawn from it which are capable of proof or disproof. Thus, even if the conditions which have been postulated as necessary and sufficient conditions are more incorrect than correct (which I hope they are not), they could still advance science in this field by providing a base of operations from which fact could be winnowed out from error.

The hypotheses which would follow from the theory given would be of this order:

If these six conditions (as operationally defined) exist, then constructive personality change (as defined) will occur in the client.

If one or more of these conditions is not present, constructive personality change will not occur.

These hypotheses hold in any situation whether it is or is not labeled "psychotherapy."

Only Condition 1 is dichotomous (it either is present or is not), and the remaining five occur in varying degree, each on its continuum. Since this is true, another hypothesis follows, and it is likely that this would be the simplest to test:

If all six conditions are present, then the greater the degree to which Conditions 2 to 6 exist, the more marked will be the constructive personality change in the client.

At the present time the above hypothesis can only be stated in this general form—which implies that all of the conditions have equal weight. Empirical studies will no doubt make possible much more refinement of this hypothesis. It may be, for example, that if anxiety is high in the client, then the other conditions are less important. Or if unconditional positive regard is high (as in a mother's love for her child), then perhaps a modest degree of empathy is sufficient. But at the moment we can only speculate on such possibilities.

## SOME IMPLICATIONS
### SIGNIFICANT OMISSIONS

If there is any startling feature in the formulation which has been given as to the necessary conditions for therapy, it probably lies in the elements which are omitted. In present-day clinical practice, therapists operate as though there were many other conditions in addition to those described, which are essential for psychotherapy. To point this up it may be well to mention a few of the conditions which, after thoughtful consideration of our research and our experience, are not included.

For example, it is *not* stated that these conditions apply to one type of client, and that other conditions are necessary to bring about psychotherapeutic change with other types of client. Probably no idea is so prevalent in clinical work today as that one works with neurotics in one way, with psychotics in another; that certain therapeutic conditions must be provided for compulsives, others for homosexuals, etc. Because of this heavy weight of clinical opinion to the contrary, it is with some "fear and trembling" that I advance the concept that the essential conditions of psychotherapy exist in a single configuration, even though the client or patient may use them very differently.[4]

It is *not* stated that these six conditions are the essential conditions for client-centered therapy, and that other conditions are essential for other types of psychotherapy. I certainly am heavily influenced by my own experience, and that experience has led me to a viewpoint which is termed "client centered." Nevertheless my aim in stating this theory is to state the conditions which apply to *any* situation in which constructive personality change occurs, whether we are thinking of classical psychoanalysis, or any of its modern offshoots, or Adlerian psychotherapy, or any other. It will be obvious then that in my judgment much of what is considered to be essential would not be found, empirically, to be essential. Testing of some of the stated hypotheses would throw light on this perplexing issue. We may of course find that various therapies produce various types of personality change, and that for each psychotherapy a separate set of conditions is necessary. Until and unless this is demonstrated, I am hypothesizing that effective psychotherapy of any sort produces similar changes in personality and behavior, and that a single set of preconditions is necessary.

It is *not* stated that psychotherapy is a special kind of relationship, different in kind

from all others which occur in everyday life. It will be evident instead that for brief moments, at least, many good friendships fulfill the six conditions. Usually this is only momentarily, however, and then empathy falters, the positive regard becomes conditional, or the congruence of the "therapist" friend becomes overlaid by some degree of facade or defensiveness. Thus the therapeutic relationship is seen as a heightening of the constructive qualities which often exist in part in other relationships, and an extension through time of qualities which in other relationships tend at best to be momentary.

It is *not* stated that special intellectual professional knowledge — psychological, psychiatric, medical, or religious—is required of the therapist. Conditions 3, 4, and 5, which apply especially to the therapist, are qualities of experience, not intellectual information. If they are to be acquired, they must, in my opinion, be acquired through an experiential training—which may be, but usually is not, a part of professional training. It troubles me to hold such a radical point of view, but I can draw no other conclusion from my experience. Intellectual training and the acquiring of information has, I believe, many valuable results—but becoming a therapist is not one of those results.

It is *not* stated that it is necessary for psychotherapy that the therapist have an accurate psychological diagnosis of the client. Here too it troubles me to hold a viewpoint so at variance with my clinical colleagues. When one thinks of the vast proportion of time spent in any psychological, psychiatric, or mental hygiene center on the exhaustive psychological evaluation of the client or patient, it seems as though this *must* serve a useful purpose insofar as psychotherapy is concerned. Yet the more I have observed therapists, and the more closely I have studied research such as that done by Fiedler and others (4), the more I am forced to the conclusion that such diagnostic knowledge

---

[4] I cling to this statement of my hypothesis even though it is challenged by a just completed study by Kirtner (5). Kirtner has found, in a group of 26 cases from the Counseling Center at the University of Chicago, that there are sharp differences in the client's mode of approach to the resolution of life difficulties, and that these differences are related to success in psychotherapy. Briefly, the client who sees his problem as involving his relationships, and who feels that he contributes to this problem and wants to change it, is likely to be successful. The client who externalizes his problem, feeling little self-responsibility, is much more likely to be a failure. Thus the implication is that some other conditions need to be provided for psychotherapy with this group. For the present, however, I will stand by my hypothesis as given, until Kirtner's study is confirmed, and until we know an alternative hypothesis to take its place.

is not essential to psychotherapy.[5] It may even be that its defense as a necessary prelude to psychotherapy is simply a protective alternative to the admission that it is, for the most part, a colossal waste of time. There is only one useful purpose I have been able to observe which relates to psychotherapy. Some therapists cannot feel secure in the relationship with the client unless they possess such diagnostic knowledge. Without it they feel fearful of him, unable to be empathic, unable to experience unconditional regard, finding it necessary to put up a pretense in the relationship. If they know in *advance* of suicidal impulses they can somehow be more acceptant of them. Thus, for some therapists, the security they perceive in diagnostic information may be a basis for permitting themselves to be integrated in the relationship, and to experience empathy and full acceptance. In these instances a psychological diagnosis would certainly be justified as adding to the comfort and hence the effectiveness of the therapist. But even here it does not appear to be a basic precondition for psychotherapy.[6]

Perhaps I have given enough illustrations to indicate that the conditions I have hypothesized as necessary and sufficient for psychotherapy are striking and unusual primarily by virtue of what they omit. If we were to determine, by a survey of the behaviors of therapists, those hypotheses which they appear to regard as necessary to psychotherapy, the list would be a great deal longer and more complex.

## IS THIS THEORETICAL FORMULATION USEFUL?

Aside from the personal satisfaction it

gives as a venture in abstraction and generalization, what is the value of a theoretical statement such as has been offered in this paper? I should like to spell out more fully the usefulness which I believe it may have.

In the field of research it may give both direction and impetus to investigation. Since it sees the conditions of constructive personality change as general, it greatly broadens the opportunities for study. Psychotherapy is not the only situation aimed at constructive personality change. Programs of training for leadership in industry and programs of training for military leadership often aim at such change. Educational institutions or programs frequently aim at development of character and personality as well as at intellectual skills. Community agencies aim at personality and behavioral change in delinquents and criminals. Such programs would provide an opportunity for the broad testing of the hypotheses offered. If it is found that constructive personality change occurs in such programs when the hypothesized conditions are not fulfilled, then the theory would have to be revised. If however the hypotheses are upheld, then the results, both for the planning of such programs and for our knowledge of human dynamics, would be significant. In the field of psychotherapy itself, the application of consistent hypotheses to the work of various schools of therapists may prove highly profitable. Again the disproof of the hypotheses offered would be as important as their confirmation, either result adding significantly to our knowledge.

For the practice of psychotherapy the theory also offers significant problems for consideration. One of its implications is that the techniques of the various therapies are relatively unimportant except to the extent that they serve as channels for fulfilling one of the conditions. In client-centered therapy, for example, the technique of "reflecting feelings" has been described and commented on (6, pp. 26–36). In terms of the theory here being presented, this tech-

[5]There is no intent here to maintain that diagnostic evaluation is useless. We have ourselves made heavy use of such methods in our research studies of change in personality. It is its usefulness as a precondition to psychotherapy which is questioned.

[6]In a facetious moment I have suggested that such therapists might be made equally comfortable by being given the diagnosis of some other individual, not of this patient or client. The fact that the diagnosis proved inaccurate as psychotherapy continued would not be particularly disturbing, because one always expects to find inaccuracies in the diagnosis as one works with the individual.

nique is by no means an essential condition of therapy. To the extent, however, that it provides a channel by which the therapist communicates a sensitive empathy and an unconditional positive regard, then it may serve as a technical channel by which the essential conditions of therapy are fulfilled. In the same way, the theory I have presented would see no essential value to therapy of such techniques as interpretation of personality dynamics, free association, analysis of dreams, analysis of the transference, hypnosis, interpretation of life style, suggestion, and the like. Each of these techniques may, however, become a channel for communicating the essential conditions which have been formulated. An interpretation may be given in a way which communicates the unconditional positive regard of the therapist. A stream of free association may be listened to in a way which communicates an empathy which the therapist is experiencing. In the handling of the transference an effective therapist often communicates his own wholeness and congruence in the relationship. Similarly for the other techniques. But just as these techniques *may* communicate the elements which are essential for therapy, so any one of them may communicate attitudes and experiences sharply contradictory to the hypothesized conditions of therapy. Feeling may be "reflected" in a way which communicates the therapist's lack of empathy. Interpretations may be rendered in a way which indicates the highly conditional regard of the therapist. Any of the techniques may communicate the fact that the therapist is expressing one attitude at a surface level, and another contradictory attitude which is denied to his own awareness. Thus one value of such a theoretical formulation as we have offered is that it may assist therapists to think more critically about those elements of their experience, attitudes, and behaviors which are essential to psychotherapy, and those which are nonessential or even deleterious to psychotherapy.

Finally, in those programs—educational, correctional, military, or industrial—which aim toward constructive changes in the personality structure and behavior of the individual, this formulation may serve as a very tentative criterion against which to measure the program. Until it is much further tested by research, it cannot be thought of as a valid criterion, but, as in the field of psychotherapy, it may help to stimulate critical analysis and the formulation of alternative conditions and alternative hypotheses.

## SUMMARY

Drawing from a larger theoretical context, six conditions are postulated as necessary and sufficient conditions for the initiation of a process of constructive personality change. A brief explanation is given of each condition, and suggestions are made as to how each may be operationally defined for research purposes. The implications of this theory for research, for psychotherapy, and for educational and training programs aimed at constructive personality change, are indicated. It is pointed out that many of the conditions which are commonly regarded as necessary to psychotherapy are, in terms of this theory, nonessential.

## REFERENCES

1. Bown, O. H. 1954. An investigation of therapeutic relationship in client-centered therapy. Unpublished doctoral dissertation, University of Chicago.
2. Chodorkoff, B. 1954. Self-perception, perceptual defense, and adjustment. *Journal of Abnormal and Social Psychology* 49:508–512.
3. Fiedler, F. E. 1950. A comparison of therapeutic relationships in psychoanalytic, non-directive and Adlerian therapy. *Journal of Consulting Psychology* 14:436–445.
4. Fiedler, F. E. 1953. Quantitative studies on the role of therapists' feelings toward their patients. In *Psychotherapy: Theory and research*, ed. O. H. Mowrer. New York: Ronald.
5. Kirtner, W. L. 1955. Success and failure in client-centered therapy as a function of personality variables. Unpublished master's thesis, University of Chicago.

6. Rogers, C. R. 1951. *Client-centered therapy.* Boston: Houghton Mifflin.

7. Rogers, C. R., and Dymond, Rosalind F., eds. 1954. *Psychotherapy and personality change.* Chicago: University of Chicago Press.

8. Standal, S. 1954. The need for positive regard: A contribution to client-centered theory. Unpublished doctoral dissertation, University of Chicago.

# READING 33

## The Uses of Naming and the Origin of the Myth of Mental Illness

**THOMAS S. SZASZ**
**State University of New York,**
**Upstate Medical Center, Syracuse**

What is mental illness? Does the use of the term *mental illness* give us any understanding of the causes and conditions of the behavior classified under this name? Thomas Szasz argues that this term is misleading, transmits little information, and is used more often than not to induce mood or promote action instead of giving understanding. The naming of an existing condition can often lead to problems, which, in turn, require more labeling, and so forth. Szasz points out how the term *mental illness* has been used and the problems involved with this term. He suggests as an answer to this problem the use of a different frame of reference.

### QUESTIONS

1. Szasz states: "like 'malingering,' then, 'mental illness' now denotes behavior considered unpleasant and socially deviant by the user of the label." Do you agree with this statement? Why?

2. Today there is a trend to call alcoholism and drug addiction illnesses rather than criminal behavior. How do you think Szasz would comment on this trend?

3. What are the cultural and social attitudes toward mental illness today? Are "voiced" attitudes the same as "inner" feelings? Defend your position.

"What's the use of their having names," the Gnat said, "if they won't answer them?"

"No use to *them*," said Alice; "but it's useful to the people that name them, I suppose. If not, why do things have names at all?"

Lewis Carroll ([1865] 1946, p. 182)

When we say that someone has or suffers from a mental illness, we assert a logically highly dubious proposition. It is virtually impossible to ascertain whether this proposition is true or false, because of the wide range of meaning that may be assigned to the term "mental illness." In the face of such logical opacity, what is required, of course, is clarification. The clarifiation of poorly defined terms or obscure concepts is mainly a problem for logical analysis. Such an analysis of the concept of mental illness was presented previously (Szasz, 1960a). While this usually suffices for concepts used in the physical sciences, in the social sciences further analyses in terms of sociohistorical and ethical considerations may prove useful or even indispensable. The aim of this essay, accordingly, is to undertake a clarification of the concept of mental illness by examining its hidden or inexplicit historical antecedents and ethical implications.

## USES OF LANGUAGE

According to linguists and logicians, language has three main functions: to transmit information, to induce mood, and to promote action (Reichenbach, 1947). While the details of the functions of language (or communication) need not concern us here, it should be noted that conceptual clarity is required only for the cognitive or information transmitting use of language. Lack of clarity may be no handicap in using language to influence people. Indeed, it might even be helpful. Since the social sciences, psychiatry among them, are concerned precisely with this phenomenon—namely, with how people influence each other—the so-called promotive use of language is a significant part of the observational data that they endeavor to describe and explain. A major source of difficulty in such undertakings in that the social sciences themselves use everyday language which is often logically obscure or ambiguous and which lends itself readily to promotive rather than cognitive usage. Thus, psychiatric or sociologic descriptions and explanations may themselves present a barrier to recognizing and comprehending the very phenomena which they allegedly seek to elucidate, because in their formulations they frequently

offer promotive statements in the guise of cognitive assertions. Or, to put it more simply, psychiatrists often *prescribe* conduct, while claiming merely to *describe* it. The phenomenon of calling someone "sick" —bodily, physically, mentally, emotionally, or in any other way—constitutes an excellent example of the promotive use of language. This claim will be buttressed by evidence. If successful, this analysis should provide further epistemological clarification of the concept of mental illness.

The rules of the game of society determine whether it is good or bad for a person to be called "sick." A remarkable bit of psychological insight into the fact that the word "sickness" is merely a *name* for some permissible moves in a game, rather than for the state of being disabled, is to be found in Samuel Butler's inspired little book, *Erewhon* ([1872] 1954). There, Butler described an imaginary society in which "sickness" was punished like "crime" is in our culture, whereas "criminality" was treated like "illness."

Without reviewing the details of the social history of illness, the sick role, and related variables, let us merely note that during the latter half of the nineteenth century—that is, when so-called modern neurology and psychiatry originated—the rules of the game of living were such that if a person was disabled, there was an advantage to his being called "sick." It might be said, therefore, that physicians had two basic choices. One was to classify (or rename) all who were disabled (in whatever way) as "sick," to "cash in" on the instrumental use of this symbol and thus improve the lot of these people. The other was, or would have been, to make the rules themselves clear and then extend the humane treatment accorded to the "sick" to other members of society. This would have involved expanding, so to speak, man's humanity to man. As is well known, the first alternative was invariably adopted by physicians. Moreover, this choice is still constantly made whenever this problem, which appears in many guises, arises. Preferring to use the word "sick" (or some other word) promotively, rather than making the rules of the game explicit and perhaps altering them, seems to be generally regarded as the easier of the two choices. This fact seems to be attributable to its consonance with the Christian ethic, which places much greater emphasis on charitableness than on truthfulness or scientific clarity. I shall try to demonstrate the social consequence of each of these choices and indicate the basis for my preference of the latter.

More specifically, the decision which faced the pioneer neuropsychiatrists—Charcot, Janet, Bernheim, Kraepelin, Freud, and others—was what to label persons exhibiting disability by means of certain so-called neuromuscular and sensory symptoms? Should they be called physically ill, malingerers, hysterics, mentally ill, or perhaps something else? On the whole, the pre-Charcotian predilection was to label all those not demonstrably physically ill "malingerers." One of Charcot's alleged discoveries was not a "discovery" at all, however, but consisted rather in promoting the relabeling of these persons as "hysterics" (Freud [1893] 1948; Guillain, 1959). It is this process of relabeling that will occupy our attention in this study.

## TWO CONVERSIONS: MALINGERERS TO HYSTERICS—JEWS TO CHRISTIANS

The maneuver of renaming is insidious because it has certain, at least consciously, undesired consequences. There are many similarities between it and religious conversion. This thesis will be illustrated by taking the social game of anti-Semitism as an example. In Europe in Freud's day, anti-Semitism amounted to the following rule: To be a Jew was a disability in that it made life more difficult in various ways. For a Christian (particularly a Roman Catholic in Austria-Hungary), life was easier, all other things being equal. Hence, there is a com-

pelling analogy between being sick, with say a congenital hip injury, or chronic peptic ulcer, or a chronic low grade infection, on the one hand, and being Jewish on the other. Conversely, there was a similarity between being Catholic and being healthy. If Jews desired to improve their status, they had two choices. These were the same choices that Charcot and Freud had when they faced the problem of malingering and hysteria. First, there was the option of being renamed and reclassified. This, of course, must be taken quite literally. Jews could adopt German names instead of their Jewish ones, and they could also be reclassified as Christians. That is, they could be converted. This process involved being placed in a group (Christian) in which, in a sense, they did not belong. Conversion of this kind constitutes a sort of socially accepted form of lying. People *agree* to call something by a name which, in one sense, is a false denoter. This is done in full awareness of the cognitive falsity of the new semantics for the instrumental purpose of insuring a better life for the renamed. I submit that when "malingerers" were renamed "hysterics"—to secure for them the rights and privileges of the "sick"—what was accomplished was essentially similar to the restoring of the full range of human rights to the disenfranchised Jews by promoting their conversion to Catholicism (Szasz, 1956).

It is important to note that only the instrumental use of language was involved here. The cognitive proposition underlying the rules—namely, that Jews are inferior to Christians, or that "malingerers" are inferior to "patients"—remained unaltered! This is very different from explicitly adopting a Jeffersonian kind of humanism—however idealistic—according to which all men have the same rights and dignities, irrespective of their religions or disabilities. If we were to classify human beings—instead of their disembodied disabilities—into classes, according to which some would have more rights and opportunities than others (I am speaking here of legal rules, not of physical abilities to perform), then I think most physicians would hesitate to make any distinctions whatever. As matters still stand, however, certain disabilities are much more honorable—and hence more socially useful —than others. In other words, although society no longer recognizes aristocracies of birth, at least not in the forms in which these were honored in medieval monarchies, there are today aristocracies of illness. A residual paralysis from poliomyelitis, for example, ranks with the nobility; chronic peptic ulcer is on the level of the bourgoisie; schizophrenia is slavery.

The rules of anti-Semitism having been what they were in, say, Austria-Hungary, Jews had the option of converting to Christianity. I have commented on how this worked. Presently, I shall trace its consequences beyond this initial stage. The second basic choice whereby the game of life could be altered was by immigrating, especially to America. This meant, in essence, to leave the field of current action, hoping that the new life— the new game—would not be played by the same rules, but by rules more favorable to the subject. The process of immigration has its exact analog in the psychiatric situation. It is for the physician (psychiatrist) to decide that the sufferer should be better treated, *not because he is sick, but because he is human!* But this means that the physician leaves his social role as doctor and adopts another role. Now this, in fact, happened to Freud and psychoanalysis, but it came about in a very complicated and confused manner. For, it has become clear that psychoanalysis—not only in theory but even more in actual practice—has little in common with medicine (Szasz, 1959a, 1959b). Hence, a new social role was created. Freud and the psychoanalysts who followed him immigrated, as it were, by leaving medicine behind, and by engaging in a new life, that is psychotherapy. But the new life, as it usually happens, was built partly after the image of the old. Instead of building a "New England," Freud built a "New Medicine." The similarities between the old and the new, however, were slight except in *name*.

As a result of the ways in which psychoanalysis, and modern dynamic psychiatries in general, originated and developed, it came to pass that the psychiatric study of problems in human living became incorporated into medicine, much as converted Jews were incorporated into the social body of Austria-Hungary. This maneuver may be paraphrased as follows: "Psychoanalysis *is* a part of medicine because it deals with mental health and illness." The covert corollary of this statement is: "Psychoanalysis *should* be a part of medicine because this will be good for psychoanalysts." (By analogy: "Jews *are* citizens of Austria-Hungary because they speak German, which is the official language of the country." And its corollary: "Jews *should* be considered citizens of the country because it will be good for them.")

This method of solving the problem of the disenfranchisement of psychoanalytic psychology (among the sciences)—or of the Jews—makes it impossible to take advantage of a solution which is scientifically more accurate and socially more promising. It may be paraphrased as follows: "Psychoanalysis, which clearly differs in many ways from other branches of medicine, *may be regarded* as a part of it because its subject matter is relevant to the broad idea of human abilities and disabilities." The covert implication of this statement is that psychoanalysts *do not* plead for the special privileges bestowed on the physician by Western European and American socities. Rather, it is as though they had said: "Psychoanalysis is a form of scientific activity, composed of an abstract or theoretical part and an applied or therapeutic part. As such, its primary aspiration is not the improvement of the social role of its practitioners. Its aims are, rather, first, increasing and improving the sum total of scientific knowledge concerning man as a social being, and second, helping certain persons by means of a special method (for influencing people), known as 'psychoanalytic treatment'." The Jewish-Gentile analogy to this would run as follows: "Jews, while different from Gentiles—e.g., in language, religion, physical appearance, etc.—nevertheless may be regarded as citizens of Austria-Hungary because they do in fact constitute a part of its social body." The corollary of this would be to state that: "We, as Jews, do not claim the special privileges which are usually bestowed on citizens in contrast to foreigners. On the contrary, we are also opposed to discriminations against, say, Czechs and Rumanians." The latter position, while equalizing the differences between Jews and Gentiles at one stroke, creates new differences between them with the next. This, I submit, is the reason why it has been avoided in all situations in which the participants' purpose does not lie chiefly in enlarging cognitive horizons but lies rather in the (immediate) improvement of human conditions.

## PROBLEM OF RECONVERSION

Adopting the first alternative, that is, naming all disabilities "illness," left the underlying rules of the game unaltered and thus invited the participants to continue playing by the old rules, whenever possible. Specifically, the renaming of "malingering" as "hysteria" left untouched the basic rule that some disabilities could be treated with kindness, and others with hostility (by psysicians and others). This maneuver was simply a trick to provide an advantage for certain participants in the game who had been previously handicapped. Similarly, the conversion of Jews recodified the correctness, as it were, of the premise and rule that it was a "good" thing for members of an in-group to discriminate against, and debase, members of certain out-groups. The conversion, once again, is merely a trick or maneuver whereby members of the out-

group became converted into members of the in-group.

Such a maneuver, it seems to me, invites its converse. In other words, two can play at this game of "conversion" as well as one. For each step of "conversion," there is a corresponding step of "reconversion." This has occurred in both the Jew-Gentile relationship in Europe and in the relationship of psychiatry to medicine. Each of these processes has been facilitated, or so I submit, by earlier social changes which have not only left the basic rules of discrimination unaltered, but covertly strengthened them—and the beliefs they embodied—by the very attempts to evade them. In so describing the "return of the old rules" I am speaking, of course, of the same sort of occurrence which Freud subsumed under the expression "return of the repressed." The former emphasizes the rule-following aspects of behavior (Peters, 1958), and the fate of inexplicit rules; the latter focuses on the tendency of old patterns of human relationships to reappear in new forms, especially when the most significant past relationships drop out of awareness.

One of the things that happened in medicine and psychiatry in regard to the so-called problem of mental illness during the past half-century could be briefly summarized as follows. Human disabilities previously called "malingering" (or "sin," or by still other names) were renamed "mental illnesses." This was done in part to give the bearers of these names a new citizenship, so to speak, in the land of the "sick." And for a while, perhaps, this maneuver worked. But soon, people bearing the names of mental illnesses—much like Jews with certain distinguishing German names or physical characteristics—began to reacquire their former ill repute. And so it has come to pass that the new label "mental illness"—and all its variants—has in everyday language come to mean much the same thing as had been denoted by the previously abandoned words of denigration. This is not to say that in the context of some psychoanalytic writings certain terms, such as "hysteria" or "schizophrenia," do not have a more precise, technical meaning. They do, and to that extent have a limited scientific (cognitive) usefulness. More often than not, however, these terms are used, even by psychiatrists and psychoanalysts, only for their instrumental-promotive effect. When used in this way, as for instance when it is asserted that "Mr. A. is mentally ill," what is meant is some thing such as this: "Do not pay any attention to what Mr. A. says," or "Do not take Mr. A. seriously," or "I suggest that you deprive Mr. A. of his civil liberties," and so forth (Szasz, 1958a, 1958c). If the person so labeled is a fellow psychiatrist, psychologist, or psychoanalyst, then the assertion means: "Dr. A. is all wrong," or "Dr. A. is a poor psychotherapist, do not send him any patients," and so forth. The expression "mental illness," as a convenient term of derogation, denigration, or thinly veiled attack, has thus been woven into the very fabric of everyday life. Indeed, even psychoanalysts have been unable to resist adopting this usage.

This thesis may be illustrated by considering Ernest Jones' (1953-57), otherwise surely most praiseworthy, biography of Freud, and some of the reactions to it. In a recent essay, Fromm (1958) decried what he considered to be Jones' unjust attack on Ferenczi and Rank as "mentally ill." The gist of Fromm's thesis was that they were healthy mentally (whatever he meant by that), but that Jones called them "sick" only to impugn their stature. Fromm went even further by implying that it was not Ferenczi and Rank who were "sick," but rather Freud and Jones. It is curious that although Fromm must have been well aware of this derogatory use of the expression "mental illness," he did not consider the possibility that this notion is devoid of a clear cognitive meaning, and that its main function might be precisely such an instrumental one. This game of psychiatric name calling tends to go

on and on, with new players aspiring to the status of power of being able to denigrate and injure others by such linguistic exhortation.

It is consistent with this view that not only did Freud, Jones, and others use the expression "mental illness" to depreciate and injure others (particularly fellow professionals), but they also used its converse, "mental health," to promote the good fortune of those whom they liked and respected. For example, Freud failed to find any signs of "mental illness" in the American psychiatrist, Frink, whom he analyzed, although the latter had apparently behaved in a socially disordered manner before his analysis and "passed through a psychotic phase" during it.[1] The same was true for Freud's earlier relationship with Ferenczi, when, for example, the latter showed disap-

[1] In this connection, see Jones' (1957) following comments concerning the Frink affair:

"This year brought Freud a keen personal disappointment, second only to that concerning Rank. Frink of New York had resumed his analysis in Vienna in April, 1922, continuing until February, 1923, and Freud had formed the very highest opinion of him. He was, so Freud maintained, by far *the ablest American he had come across, the only one from whose gifts he expected something* [italics added]. Frink had passed through a psychotic phase during his analysis—he had indeed to have a male nurse with him for a time—but Freud considered he had quite overcome it, and *he counted on his being the leading analyst in America* [italics added]. Unfortunately, on returning to New York Frink behaved very arrogantly to the older analysts, particularly Brill, telling everyone how out of date they were. Frink's second marriage, which had caused so much scandal and on which high hopes of happiness had been set, had proved a failure, and his wife was suing for a divorce. That, together with the quarrels just mentioned, must have precipitated another attack. Frink wrote to me in November, 1923, that for reasons of ill health he had to give up his work for the Journal and also his private practice. In the following summer he was a patient in the Phipps Psychiatric Institute, and he never recovered his sanity. He died in the Chapel Hill Mental Hospital in North Carolina some ten years later" (pp. 105–106).

The Frink affair, I think, might be paradigmatic of many later—and now current—problems of *psychoanalytic training*. I refer to the disposition training analysts seem to have to see mental health in those of their candidates of whom they approve. This is especially true for those training analysts who have proselytizing tendencies; they will be disposed to think well of those candidates whom they consider worthy disciples. Contrariwise, training candidates whom their analysts dislike—or with whom they find themselves in serious disagreement—are in danger of being found mentally unhealthy, requiring prolonged or repeated analyses. Needless to say, I am not implying that this is the *only* criterion used for assessing "psychopathology" in training analyses. I only wish to point out a significant bias inherent in the present organization of the psychoanalytic training system. I have examined this problem in greater detail in my two papers on this subject (Szasz, 1958b, 1960b).

pointment over Freud's reluctance to confide in him *all* of his (i.e., Freud's) dreams, while the two spent their vacations together (Jones, 1955, pp. 82–84). The point I wish to make is that Freud (and others after him) tended to view those whom he considered talented and promising spokesmen for his new science as "mentally healthy," irrespective of other indications which might conflict with this appraisal. In this usage, the old rules of the game according to which "mental illness" is but a form of imitating illness or malingering are evident. In brief, then, "mental illness" is considered to be a bit of nasty behavior, the purpose of which is to antagonize those toward whom it is directed.

In this connection, Eisendorfer's (1959) recent review of the policies governing admission for training to the New York Psychoanalytic Institute is pertinent. He stated that candidates diagnosed as having "perversions" or "overt psychopathology" are *automatically* excluded from acceptance. He did not specify the definition of perversion or psychopathology that was used. This makes for a convenient arrangement for the admissions committee, but provides no help for those wishing to ascertain the actual practices described. It is worth noting, too, that inasmuch as analytic training organizations have adopted this openly anti-psychopathology attitude, it may not be a coincidence that their applicants present them with a facade of normality! At the same time, this allegedly pseudonormal attitude of present-day candidates seems to be resented by many analysts.[2] The possible connections between the currently prevalent psychoanalytic position toward the candidate's so-called psychopathology and

his facade of normality are, curiously, never drawn in discussions of this subject.

For a final illustration of the contemporary usage of "mental illness," we may consider a portion of *Time* magazine's recent (June 23, 1958) commentary on Taft's (1958) biography of Rank. It read, in part, as follows:

> In Rank's later years his behavior was more appropriate to the role of patient than of therapist. He went through one emotional crisis after another (diagnosed by famed Freud Biographer Ernest Jones as a mild manic-depressive psychosis), even suffered artist's and writer's block—a symptom that analysts claim to relieve most effectively. One thing certain from Biographer Taft's candid pages: in the post-Freud patter of the cocktail hour, Otto Rank was "sick, sick, sick" (p. 68).

Surely, in this context the word "sick" is used very differently than it is when the patient develops in his later life, say, generalized arteriosclerosis or coronary heart disease. Thus, the expression "mental illness," and the phenomena to which it refers, has, since the early days of psychoanalysis, traversed a full cycle. Like "malingering," then, "mental illness" now denotes behavior considered unpleasant and socially deviant by the user of the label. There is a parallel between this turn of events and the recrudescence of anti-Semitism in Central Europe that began after the first World War. The period during which the life of the Jews by means of religious and social conversion was greatly improved was soon followed by another during which the semantic and social changes were reconverted, as it were, into their original form. Thus, certain people who bore German names and professed to believe in the Christian religion were—under the Nazi

[2]According to Eisendorfer (1959): "Such factors as overt psychopathology, perversions, homosexuality, and antisocial psychopathic acting out automatically eliminate the candidate" (p. 376). Barely one paragraph later he noted that "A not uncommon characteristic of a considerable number of candidates (about ten per cent) is a facade of normality" (p. 377); adding that "A dogged determination to present himself as being normal, more often than not, serves as veneer to conceal chronic pathology" (p. 377). Apparently

Eisendorfer did not regard these two requirements—namely, presenting *no* overt psychopathology on the one hand, and presenting *no* facade of normality on the other—as mutually contradictory. But what else is left for the candidate to present, except, of course, having precisely the "right kind of psychopathology" (my formulation). Eisendorfer's statements offer rather clear evidence that psychoanalytic training organizations use the notion of psychopathology, and the process of *naming*, to promote their particular ends, rather than to communicate verifiable observations.

laws (rules)—once again treated as though they were Jews, and further, as though persecuting Jews was the "right" thing to do. The rule which stated that hostility to members of out-groups (Jewish or otherwise) was a social "good"—in other words, that it was the sign by which (German) patriotism was to be recognized—could be readapted to the new conditions with a minimum of effort. All this was inherent, as I suggested, in the fact that these rules—which in a way constitute the rules of a primitive sort of patriotism everywhere—were never challenged by those who sought to improve their lot in life by semantic and religious conversion. Indeed, it is well known that many converted European Jews became identified with their aggressors, which is to say that they continued to play by their rules. Thus, not only was this type of conversion not a successful revolt against anti-Semitism, but it was a covert way of pouring oil on the fires of this sort of social orientation. Accordingly, anti-Semitism was not given up by the in-group, and all that had happened was that some Jews removed themselves from the group of the "hated" and enlisted themselves in the group of "haters." I do not cite these facts to dwell on the recent history of European Jews, and can only hope that the events depicted will not distract the reader from the primary purpose of this analysis, which is the clarification of the vicissitudes of the notion of mental illness.

The events sketched above are paralleled by the following developments in the history of medical psychology. The psychiatrists of the late nineteenth and early twentieth century—that is, the former "alienists"—were distinctly depreciated by their medical colleagues. They were medical outcasts. Contrast this with the public image and social role of the mid-twentieth century psychiatrist (in the United States of America) whose prestige often outranks that of other physicians. He has become a kind of supertherapist. But this is not all.

He has joined with his medical colleagues in enthusiastic "togetherness" and has become a leader in proclaiming his "loyalty" to medicine. And how is this loyalty demonstrated? By an aggressively depreciating posture vis-à-vis psychologists and other nonmedical psychotherapists. But it is evident that such a trend is bound to be corrupting to the scientific-technical integrity of psychiatry. Movement in this direction, moreover, is inimical to another trend, namely to that which would further professional integrity by ever-increasing professional competence (Szasz, 1959a).

## CONVERSION, RELABELING, AND THE PROBLEM OF PROFESSIONAL INTEGRITY

Summing up this analysis, it is possible to identify a parallel development in the Nazi reclassification of formerly Jewish Christians to the status of (persecutable) Jews on the one hand, and in the contemporary trend to interpret the notion of "mental illness" (which was created in an effort to improve the lot of those designated as "malingerers") as meaning nothing but a derogation of the subject who is so named, on the other hand. Similarly, when "hysteria" was taken out of the large group called "malingering," what happened was only that some members of the latter group were promoted to a higher status. The notion of malingering, and all it implied, was retained—just as, during periods when conversion from Judaism to Christianity was encouraged, the social operations of anti-Semitism continued unabated.

Even today there are those who expect human betterment for all types of suffering to come via the path of labeling everything "illness." This position would correspond to the conversion of *all* Jews to Christianity, or, in a larger sense, to the abolition of all out-groups by their open adherence to the values and behavior of the dominant in-group. But what could this accomplish—even if it were feasible—so long as those basic rules of conduct which include the positive valuation of human destructiveness toward certain out-groups (e.g., minorities, "criminals," etc.) are retained unaltered? It would seem to me that under such conditions the rules would tend to be implemented essentially as before, although changes in semantic usage may make it *appear* as though great progress had been made. I think it behooves all physicians, psychologists, social scientists—and, for that matter, the intelligent layman as well—to examine carefully the precise nature of the present status of our scientific (as well as everyday) attitudes toward problems of so-called mental illness. This is not to gainsay the progress that has been made in our science since the days of Charcot, much of it through the efforts of Freud and psychoanalysis. Yet, in this very progress—based as it has been in large part on an adventitious acquisition of positive values through a partly misleading professional association with the practice of medicine—may lie the seeds of its destruction! In order to secure the scientific advances that have been made in our field, I believe we could do no better than to recast our knowledge in a psychosocial, linguistic, and ethical framework. This would entail a re-emphasis of the differences, rather than the similarities, between man the social being and man the mammal. It would also result in abandoning the persistent attempts to convert psychologists and sociologists to biologists (physicians) or physicists, and they themselves would no longer need to aspire to these roles. The integrity of the science of man as social being thus requires—just as does the integrity of the individual—a forthright recognition of its historical origins together with an accurate assessment of its individual unique characteristics and potentialities. It is in this way, and not by imitating the greatness of the older, more securely established sciences, that the psychosocial disciplines must establish their rightful place among the sciences.

## REFERENCES

Butler, S. 1954 (originally published 1872). *Erewhon*. Harmondsworth, Middlesex: Penguin Books.

Carroll, L. 1946 (originally published 1865, 1872). *Alice in wonderland and through the looking glass*. New York: Grosset & Dunlap.

Eisendorfer, A. 1959. The selection of candidates applying for psychoanalytic training. *Psychoanalytic Quarterly* 28:374–378.

Freud, S. 1948 (originally published 1893). Charcot. In *Collected papers*, vol. 1, pp. 9–23. London: Hogarth.

Fromm, E. 1958. Freud, friends, and feuds: I. Scientism or fanaticism? *Saturday Review*, June 14, p. 11.

Guillain, G. 1959. *J. M. Charcot, 1825–1893: His life—his work*. Trans. by Pearce Bailey. New York: Hoeber.

Jones, E. 1953, 1955, 1957. *The life and work of Sigmund Freud*. Vols. I–III. New York: Basic Books.

Peters, R. S. 1958. *The concept of motivation*. London: Routledge & Kegan Paul.

Reichenbach, H. 1947. *Elements of symbolic logic*. New York: Macmillan.

Szasz, T. S. 1956. Malingering: "Diagnosis" or social condemnation? *AMA Archives of Neurology and Psychiatry* 76:432–443.

Szasz, T. S. 1958a. Psychiatry, ethics, and the criminal law. *Columbia Law Review* 58:183–198.

Szasz, T. S. 1958b. Psychoanalytic training: A socio-psychological analysis of its history and present status. *International Journal of Psychoanalysis* 39:598–613.

Szasz, T. S. 1958c. Politics and mental health: Some remarks apropos of the case of Mr. Ezra Pound. *American Journal of Psychiatry* 115:508–511.

Szasz, T. S. 1959a. Psychiatry, psychotherapy, and psychology. *AMA Archives of General Psychiatry* 1:455–463.

Szasz, T. S. 1959b. Psychoanalysis and medicine. In *Readings in psychoanalytic psychology*, ed. M. Levitt, pp. 355–374. New York: Appleton-Century-Crofts.

Szasz, T. S. 1960a. The myth of mental illness. *American Psychologist* 15:113–118.

Szasz, T. S. 1960b. Three problems in contemporary psychoanalytic training. *AMA Archives of General Psychiatry* 3:82–94.

Taft, J. 1958. *Otto Rank*. New York: Julian.

# READING 34

# On Keeping Mental Patients Chronic

**HORACE STEWART**
**West Georgia College**
**Carrollton, Georgia**

The days of the "snake pit" are supposedly long gone, and in many respects this is the case. However, the situation in mental hospitals today is often deplorable, and Horace Stewart has pointed out some of the problems for us. His rather satiric account makes very serious accusations concerning conditions, methodology, and practices in mental hospitals today. We would do well to listen to him.

**QUESTIONS**
1. Is this article an overstatement of the problems of mental hospitals or an accurate picture? (Have you ever visited a mental hospital?)
2. Are mental hospitals necessary? Do they serve a valid purpose?
3. Try to design a method of helping mental patients. Would you include hospitals, treatment centers, drugs, therapy, testing, et cetera? What sorts of problems would you expect to encounter?

The methods employed in keeping a mental patient chronic are becoming clearer as scientific investigation continues. A long step forward was made by Heckel and Salzberg (1964) in elaborating the more commonly observed techniques. J. L. Bernard (personal communication, 1965) reported that chronicity can be established within a week of admission to a state hospital. The report by Kissinger (1963) on "The un-therapeutic community: a team approach that failed" gives invaluable insight into the powerful role of interdisciplinary disharmony in re-enforcement of chronicity. The following rules are a resume of current research reported by observers located in treatment centers for the mentally disordered throughout the world.

**RULES**

## 1. THE INSTITUTION'S GENERAL APPEARANCE

The importance of over-crowding, under-staffing, and poorly maintained buildings and grounds cannot be overestimated. They immediately impress upon the patient the utter hopelessness of his situation. The fight is taken out of him, preparing the way for treatment. Also, the importance of a good name cannot be set aside lightly. The old names were the best, e.g., The Institution for Lunatics, Insane Asylum, The Asylum for the Relief of Persons Deprived of the Use of Their Reason.

## 2. IN ALL DECISIONS, PLAY IT SAFE

Never allow the patient freedom that may, in any way, give him an opportunity to kill himself, fall in love, interact with normal, honest, God-fearing folk, or simply be alone. Never believe the patient's account of any event. Decisions are best put off for several weeks, and longer if possible. The effects of a positive experience can be completely reversed by careful timing.

## 3. SUPPLY ONLY THE BARE NECESSITIES OF LIFE

The mental patient requires very little of the luxuries of life. The Spartan life was best. Some observers (notably state legislators) have made this observation and have attempted to make luxuries impossible through parsimonious budgeting commitments. Actually, the money is better spent on public highways, an impressive governor's mansion, and foreign aid.

## 4. KEEP ALL RECORDS STRICTLY CONFIDENTIAL

Under no circumstances discuss a diagnosis with the patient. The records of commitment and conversations with relatives should be completely inaccessible to the patient. Knowledge of results has been known to lead to a complete remission.

## 5. INSIST ON PHYSICAL DISEASE

The patient should have his attention continually drawn to any physical defects or illnesses. Not only can many of these disorders be successfully treated, but this keeps the patient's mind on the fact that his mental problems are basically physical. The whole idea of pills and medical treatment precludes any thought of the possibility of underlying psychological processes.

## 6. NEVER MENTION ANY INTERPERSONAL DYNAMICS

This only confuses the patient. Also, it tends to undermine the good work of the physician, often making an alert patient doubt the ability of the professionally trained person to cure mental illness. Any allusion to social factors, emotional conflicts or sibling rivalry is detrimental, as would be such foolish projects as ward government.

## 7. LIBERALLY MIX THE PATIENT POPULATION WITH CRIMINALS, ADDICTS, AND PROSTITUTES

This helps the patient identify himself with the proper element of society. It also adds to his confusion concerning the real status of his illness. The introduction of a psychopathic criminal has been known to frighten schizophrenics into complete withdrawal for a period of weeks. A pretty prostitute enlivens a drab ward considerably and furnishes young trainees with candidates for dynamic psychotherapy. However, the sexes must be strictly segregated.

## 8. SPECIAL CARE FOR CHILDREN AND ADOLESCENTS

The institution is in a unique position to teach these young impressionable minds lessons which will never be forgotten. Children placed on a back ward with several hundred regressed patients are furnished with remarkable lessons in futility. If several children or adolescents are allowed to band together, they are able to learn to steal, lie, cheat and practice sexual perversions that otherwise may take a life-time to learn.

## 9. MAINTAIN THE PATIENT'S IDENTITY

The old custom of photographing mental

patients considerably helped to remind the patient that he was potentially dangerous. It is well to continually remind the new attendants of the early reporting of possible escapes and bring to their attention the classic cases of various crimes that have been committed by escaped mental patients. Above all, do not allow patients to become friendly with staff personnel. I need not point out the problems which arise with male staff members and certain female patients.

## 10. ENCOURAGE THE RELATIVES TO LIE TO THE PATIENT

This is especially important during commitment procedures. Never tell the patient where he is going to be taken. They often just become resistive and fight. A small lie enables you to have them safely transported to the institution where they can be properly managed by hospital personnel. The doctor-relative relationship should not include the patient.

## CONCLUSIONS

The results of careful observation indicate that these are time-honored methods of establishing and maintaining chronicity in the mental patient. That these principles may be generalized to other situations is not denied. It should be pointed out that there are certainly other methods available. However, with some refinement and further research other procedures may well become acceptable.

## REFERENCES

Heckel, R. V., and Salzberg, H. C. 1964. How to make your patients chronic. *Mental Hospitals* 15:37–38.

Kissinger, R. D. 1963. The un-therapeutic community: A team approach that failed. Paper read at the Eastern Psychological Association meeting in Philadelphia.

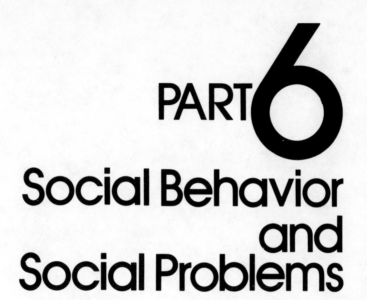

# PART 6

# Social Behavior and Social Problems

# READING 35

# The Marihuana Problem: An Overview

**WILLIAM H. McGLOTHLIN, Ph.D.**
**LOUIS JOLYON WEST, M.D.**

Drug usage and experimentation have received considerable notice in the last few years, and today the news media are filled with programs discussing drugs and the problems associated with them. McGlothlin and West provide us with an interesting overview of marihuana use. They discuss the relationship between this drug and crime, dependence or addiction, other drug use, and social policy. The authors also present data from a group of adults relating frequency of usage, motivation to use the drug, and the characteristics of this group.

## QUESTIONS

1. The authors suggest that much drug legislation is an attempt to enforce a specific moral code on the members of our society. Discuss this question.

2. Gather some of the new experimental data on marihuana. How do the effects of this drug compare with the effects of alcohol? Other drugs?

3. What type of education should young children be given concerning drugs? What points do you think are important?

The combination of a very rapid increase in marihuana use and the severe penalties prescribed for violation of the marihuana

Read at the 124th annual meeting of the American Psychiatric Association, Boston, Mass., May 13–17, 1968.

Dr. McGlothlin is research psychologist, U.C.L.A. Institute of Government and Public Affairs, Los Angeles, Calif. 90024. Dr. West is chairman, department of psychiatry, University of Oklahoma School of Medicine, Oklahoma City, Okla.

Some of the work reported in this paper was supported by Public Health Service grant MH-13484 from the National Institute of Mental Health.

laws has brought about a social crisis. These two phenomena are not necessarily independent. The extreme legal penalties and the gross exaggerations of the consequences of marihuana use as fostered by the Federal Bureau of Narcotics make it an ideal target for rebellious youth to point to as an example of adult hypocrisy.

The situation is especially crucial in California. In 1967 there were 37,500 marihuana arrests in California, compared to 7,000 in 1964. Three-fourths of the cases are dismissed without trial, yet marihuana cases still accounted for 17 percent of all felony complaints issued by the Los Angeles district attorney's office during the period June through September 1967. The present rate of increase in marihuana arrests would indicate that such cases would comprise over 50 percent of the felony complaints within two years. On the other hand, in one highly publicized recent case of arrest for violation of marihuana laws, the defense collected 2,000 affidavits, the majority from persons who stated that they used marihuana and found it harmless.

A reappraisal of the social policies controlling marihuana is clearly needed, but unfortunately there is very little recent research to provide a basis for rational decisions. Virtually all the studies done in this country were conducted some 25 to 30 years ago. The dearth of recent research and absence of long-term studies is a situation largely brought about by giving the same governmental agency control of both enforcement and research.

In assessing the current state of knowledge pertaining to the use of marihuana, probably the most important fact to keep in mind is that the range in amount used is extremely wide. Since marihuana use has been traditionally defined in legal rather than in health terms, there is a tendency to consider all users as a single group. In fact, there are no physiologically addictive qualities, and the occasional users have always far outnumbered those using it in a habitual manner.

The older studies in this country found that regular users consumed around 6 to 10 cigarettes per day (4, 8); however, a much larger number used it on an irregular basis (3). Studies done in Eastern countries, especially India and North Africa, have concentrated on users of the highly potent hashish. Heavy users consume 2 to 6 grams of hashish per day which is equiva-lent to smoking at least 20 to 60 marihuana cigarettes (5, 9). Moderate use of the less potent cannabis preparations in the East is not considered to be a health problem; and, in fact, bhang (the Indian equivalent of marihuana) is not even considered to fall within the definition of cannabis by Indian authorities and so is excluded from U.N. treaty control (6).

The recent increase in marihuana use in the U. S. is primarily among middle- and upper-class youth, the large majority of whom do not average more than two or three cigarettes a week. Some members of the hippie subculture and certain other individuals use marihuana in amounts comparable to that found in the older studies (6 to 10 cigarettes per day).

With this as preface, we propose to provide a brief overview of what is known about the effects of marihuana use, followed by some preliminary data from a current study.

## CLASSIFICATION

In small amounts marihuana acts as a mild euphoriant and sedative somewhat like alcohol, although in comparable doses it is probably more disruptive of thought processes. In larger doses marihuana effects more closely resemble those of the hallucinogens than any other group of drugs. Most of the phenomena experienced with LSD, such as depersonalization, marked visual and temporal distortion, and hallucinations have been observed with sufficiently large amounts of marihuana and especially with hashish. The effects, however, are generally much milder and easier to control than those of LSD. Isbell and associates recently demonstrated a similar dose effect with tetrahydrocannabinol (THC), an active constituent of marihuana (7).

On the other hand, there are considerable differences in users' descriptions of marihuana and LSD effects; also, marihuana acts as a sedative and tends to produce sleep, whereas the strong hallucinogens cause long periods of wakefulness. In addition, marihuana produces virtually no tolerance, whereas very rapid tolerance accompanies use of LSD-like drugs. Isbell found no cross tolerance to THC in subjects tolerant to LSD, indicating that the two drugs probably act by different mechanisms.

## DEPENDENCE

Mild irritability frequently follows withdrawal from heavy use of marihuana, but there are virtually no other symptoms of physical dependence. Psychological dependence may develop in the sense that the individual prefers the mood state resulting from marihuana use to the undrugged state. The fact that 65 percent of the hashish users in a recent Egyptian survey indicated they would like to get rid of the habit indicates appreciable psychological dependence (9).

Of course, many forms of socially acceptable behavior (e.g., smoking tobacco, watching TV) may produce a form of psychic dependence. The harmfulness of such behavior should be based on the consequences of the activity rather than its existence.

## PHYSICAL AND MENTAL EFFECTS

No long-term physical effects of marihuana use have been demonstrated in this country, although more current studies are needed before this issue can be resolved with any degree of certainty. Eastern studies of chronic users, who consume several times the amounts generally used in this country, report a variety of cannabis-induced physical ailments. Conjunctivitis is the most frequent, followed by chronic bronchitis and various digestive ailments (5). Sleep difficulties frequently occur, as is the case with opiate users in this country (5, 9). It is interesting to note that from 25 to 70 percent of regular hashish users in two Eastern surveys reported some impairment in physical health due to the use of the drug (5, 9).

There have been several cases of marihuana-induced temporary psychosis reported in this country (3, 8). Panic reactions are not uncommon among inexperienced users, and such reactions occasionally develop into a psychotic episode. These very rarely last more than a day or so, and they do not usually require hospitalization. The danger of a prolonged psychosis from marihuana is very small compared to that for LSD.

On the other hand, in India and other Eastern countries, cannabis has long been regarded as an important cause of psychosis. One study reported that 25 percent of some 2,300 men admitted to psychiatric hospitals were diagnosed as having cannabis psychoses; of the total male admissions 70 percent of the patients admitted to smoking cannabis and one-third were regular users (1). Other investigators have argued that the 3 to 1 ratio of male to female hospitalized psychotics is a result of cannabis use being almost entirely restricted to males.

These studies are definitely not in agreement with the findings in this country, and many Western authorities question the adequacy of both the diagnoses made and the methodology of the studies themselves. Although part of the difference may be due to the fact that much larger amounts of the drug are used in the East, it is doubtful that this could reasonably account for the wide discrepancy in the findings.

While there is little concern about marihuana-induced psychosis in this country, there is considerable interest in the possibility of personality changes resulting from marihuana use, particularly in the development of what has been called an "amotivational" syndrome. The older studies of regular users in this country typically described them as tending to be passive and nonproductive. Eastern studies characterize heavy users in a similar manner. However, there has generally been no attempt to distinguish between pre-existing personality traits and the effect of the drug use.

While systematic studies of the recent wave of young marihuana users are not yet available, clinical observations indicate that regular marihuana use may contribute to the development of more passive, inward-turning, amotivational personality characteristics. For numerous middle-class students, the subtly progressive change from conforming, achievement-oriented behavior to a state of relaxed and careless drifting has followed their use of significant amounts of marihuana.

It is difficult to parcel out social factors, as well as the occasional use of LSD, but it appears that regular use of marihuana may very well contribute to some characteristic personality changes, especially among highly impressionable young persons. Such changes include apathy, loss of effectiveness, and diminished capacity or willingness to carry out complex long-term plans, endure frustration, concentrate for long periods, follow routines, or successfully master new material. Verbal facility is often impaired, both in speaking and writing.

Such individuals exhibit greater introversion, become totally involved with the present at the expense of future goals, and demonstrate a strong tendency toward regressive, child-like magical thinking. They report a greater subjective creativity but less objective productivity; and, while seeming to suffer less from vicissitudes and frustrations of life, at the same time they seem to be subtly withdrawing from the challenge of it.

## MARIHUANA AND CRIME

Enforcement agencies have long attempted to justify existing punitive marihuana laws by contending that marihuana use is criminogenic. No acceptable evidence has ever been offered to support these claims, and virtually every serious investigator who has attempted to examine the question has found no relationship between marihuana and major crime. Indeed, many feel that the characteristic passive reaction to marihuana use tends to inhibit rather than cause crime whereas alcohol consumption is more likely to release aggressive behavior.

The recent study of drug use among juveniles reported that those who were most delinquent preferred alcohol, whereas the "pot-heads" tended to be nonaggressive and stayed away from trouble(2). Moreover, a shift from alcohol to marihuana use tended to be correlated with a change toward less delinquent behavior in other respects. There apparently is some validity to the claim that professional criminals sometimes use marihuana as a means of fortifying themselves in their criminal operations; however, other drugs such as alcohol, amphetamines, and barbiturates are equally popular for this purpose.

## RELATION OF MARIHUANA TO OTHER DRUG USE

A possible indirect hazard of marihuana smoking has been much debated. According to the stepping-stone theory, the use of marihuana will lead to the use of heroin in the search for greater thrills. Proponents cite the fact that most heroin users have previously used marihuana. Opponents deny that this indicates causality and cite the fact that while heroin use has remained at virtually the same level during the last few years marihuana use has experienced a rapid rise.

Although present-day marihuana use has not been shown to predispose to heroin use, it does play a role in initiation to other potent drugs, particularly LSD. To the extent that marihuana contributes to a general disregard for the realistic consequences of behavior in young persons, its use increases the probability of the abuse of other more dangerous drugs. Thus, members of the hippie subculture frequently use methamphetamine and a host of other drugs. There is also some experimentation with heroin.

Finally, to the extent that hashish is available, its use is causally related to marihuana use. Many if not most marihuana users would welcome the opportunity to try hashish, and, if it were available, many would probably continue to use it in preference to the low-potency marihuana. Of course, the use of hashish does not necessarily lead to excess any more than does a preference for distilled liquor over beer or wine. However, the history of mind-altering drugs invariably shows that excessive indulgence increases sharply as more potent preparations of a given drug become available.

## MARIHUANA USE AMONG A SELECTED GROUP OF ADULTS

Table 1 presents some characteristics of users and nonusers of marihuana among a sample of 189 persons randomly drawn from a population of 750 who received LSD from a physician in either an experimental or psychotherapy setting during the period 1955-61. The marihuana data are incidental to an ongoing follow-up interview study of

LSD effects; however, these results are of interest in two respects. First, they provide information on the use of marihuana among an older group of largely professional persons. Second, the observations of this group concerning the effects of marihuana are based on more experience and are considered to be more objective than assessments made by the less reality-oriented younger groups of marihuana users.

Forty-two percent of this group of 189 have had some experience with marihuana, although only 17 percent have used it ten or more times. One-half of the latter group were introduced to marihuana prior to 1954. About one-third of those who had not tried marihuana indicated that they might do so in the future, and a slightly higher proportion stated that they might try it if it were legal. The large majority of those who had used marihuana favored its legalization, and about one-half of those who had not tried it indicated a similar preference.

The remainder of the data apply to the 32 respondents who used marihuana ten or

**TABLE 1**

CHARACTERISTICS OF USERS AND NONUSERS OF MARIHUANA AMONG A SAMPLE OF PERSONS
RECEIVING LSD UNDER MEDICAL CONDITIONS, 1955-61

| Characteristic | Marihuana Use | | |
| --- | --- | --- | --- |
| | None (N = 110) | Less Than Ten Times (N = 47) | Ten or More Times (N = 32) |
| Percent of total group | 58 | 25 | 17 |
| Mean age (years) | 46 | 40 | 39 |
| Percent male | 63 | 72 | 66 |
| Education: B.A. degree or higher (percent) | 56 | 64 | 44 |
| Income: $10,000 or more (percent) | 68 | 66 | 58 |
| Used LSD under nonmedical conditions (percent) | 7 | 19 | 64 |
| Median year of initial marihuana use | — | 1962 | 1954 |
| Used marihuana prior to LSD (percent) | — | 30 | 69 |
| Use of marihuana in future: | | | |
| No (percent) | 65 | 40 | 12 |
| Yes (percent) | 7 | 30 | 72 |
| Possibly (percent) | 28 | 30 | 16 |
| Use of marihuana in future if legalized: | | | |
| No (percent) | 54 | 32 | 9 |
| Yes (percent) | 15 | 36 | 84 |
| Possibly (percent) | 30 | 32 | 6 |
| Favor removal of legal penalties against: | | | |
| Possession (percent) | 54 | 81 | 97 |
| Both possession and sale to persons over 21 (percent) | 40 | 74 | 84 |

## TABLE 2

PROFESSION AND FREQUENCY OF USE OF
MARIHUANA AMONG 32 RESPONDENTS WHO HAVE
USED IT TEN OR MORE TIMES

| Variable | Number |
| --- | --- |
| Profession | |
| Arts (artist, writer, actor, TV-radio, designer, etc.) | 14 |
| Physician, dentist, psychologist | 7 |
| Housewife | 4 |
| Engineer | 2 |
| Other | 5 |
| Frequency of use | |
| Daily | 5 |
| Two or three times per week | 6 |
| Once a week | 4 |
| Less than once a week | 8 |
| Do not use currently | 9 |

## TABLE 3

MOTIVATION FOR USE OF MARIHUANA AMONG 32
RESPONDENTS WHO HAVE USED IT TEN OR
MORE TIMES

| Motivation | Percent | |
| --- | --- | --- |
| | Frequently | Occasionally |
| Produce "high" or euphoria | 66 | 25 |
| Relax | 50 | 32 |
| Relieve tensions or stress | 38 | 44 |
| Increase sociability | 25 | 50 |
| Increase sexual satisfaction | 35 | 38 |
| Increase enjoyment of plays, movies, etc. | 22 | 44 |
| Increase enjoyment of food | 32 | 32 |
| To go along with group | 16 | 41 |
| To cope with uncomfortable social situations | 13 | 28 |
| Relieve depression | 16 | 25 |

more times. Table 2 provides profession and frequency of use. Table 3 presents data on various motivations for marihuana use.

Inquiry was made concerning the effect of marihuana on driving competence. Of the 32 respondents, eight stated that they never drove under the influence of marihuana. Twenty of the remaining 24 felt that their driving competence was impaired. The

reasons given were: perceptual distortion, speed distortion, slower reaction time, less alert, disoriented, poor judgment, and less careful.

Fourteen of the 32 indicated that they sometimes worked under the influence of marihuana; five stated that the effect on work was positive, four, that it was negative, and five, neutral or mixed. Fifteen of the 32 indicated that they sometimes used marihuana to enhance creative endeavors such as art, writing, music, singing, and design. Those who felt it aided in writing generally indicated that the ideas occurred to them while under the influence of marihuana. But the actual writing was done in an undrugged state.

A frequently reported advantage of marihuana over alcohol is the absence of hangover effects. Twelve of the 32 respondents reported that they sometimes experienced undesirable aftereffects the day following the use of marihuana; however, nine of the 12 indicated that such effects occurred only when large amounts were used or when it was smoked just prior to retiring. The most frequently reported symptom was lethargy, followed by inability to concentrate, irritability, and headaches.

Twenty-five of the 32 felt marihuana had resulted in no long-term effects; six reported positive long-term effects (increased insight, tolerance, spontaneity, and sexual freedom); one respondent regarded the long-term effects as mixed. It is interesting to compare these results with those of heavy hashish users in India and Egypt, where up to 70 percent report some harmful effects.

Nine of the 32 respondents were not currently using marihuana. Three said they stopped because they did not particularly like the effect, two stopped due to legal concerns, and four, due to other reasons. Of the 23 currently using marihuana, 18 indicated that they planned to continue at the same level of use and five stated they planned to decrease the frequency of use.

Four of the 32 had been arrested in connection with their marihuana use—two cases were dismissed and two received probation. Twenty of the 32 had used LSD under non-medical conditions and 17 had used other strong hallucinogens such as peyote, mescaline, and psilocybin. Six had some experience with heroin—one had been addicted.

## SOCIAL POLICY

Social policy with respect to marihuana and other psychoactive drugs has many important dimensions other than those already mentioned. The most basic issue is whether or not the prohibition of behavior whose direct effects are limited to the individual is within the function of the state. Those who feel it is not argue that the state has no more right to intervene with respect to the use of harmful drugs than it does with regard to harmful overeating.

Those who take the contrary position argue that the harms are not limited to the individual but burden society in a variety of ways; hence the state is entitled to prohibit its use in the public interest. It is certainly clear that the very existence of government entails individual restraints. Whether or not individual freedoms should be curbed with respect to drug use depends on the extent of the threat to society and whether or not the sanctions against it are effective.

An objective assessment of the threat or benefit to society resulting from the non-medical use of a drug should consider: physiological effects resulting from occasional or chronic use; tendency to produce physiological or psychological dependence as a function of period of use; release of antisocial behavior; effect on motor activity, especially driving safety; and tendency to produce long-lasting personality changes. Other relevant considerations are: cost; ability to control and measure potency; convenience of mode of intake, oral vs. intravenous, for example; capacity for self-titration to control effect; protection against overdose; availability of an antidote; specific effects attainable without unpredictable

side effects; predictable length of action; hangover or other short-term properties which may spill over to affect work or other activities; ability to return to normalcy on demand; and ability to detect the drug, as for monitoring drivers, etc.

One of the most neglected questions in evaluating drug effects concerns the individual benefits which motivate the user. Drug use in many instances may well be an attempt to alleviate symptoms of psychiatric illness through self-medication. In some cases, marihuana use might postpone or prevent more serious manifestations of an illness. Especially for recreational drugs, such as alcohol and marihuana, an objective assessment of user motivation should consider: effectiveness in producing pleasure, relaxation, and aesthetic appreciation; enhancement of appetite and other senses; enhancement of interpersonal rapport, warmth, and emotionality; utility of variety or newness of perception and thinking; and enhancement of enjoyment of vacations, weekends, or other periods devoted to recreation, rest, and pleasure.

Other effects of nonmedical drug use may have more far-reaching ramifications for society in general. Does the drug use provide an emotional escape-valve similar to institutionalized festivities employed by other cultures? What is its effect on personality, life style, aggressiveness, competitiveness, etc.? Does it affect military effectiveness through increased passivity? Would its adoption by large numbers affect the direction of society? For example, the use of peyote changed the direction of the American Indian culture by creating a pan-Indian movement—the hippies would advocate a similar cure for the ills of the present society.

In considering the effectivness of legal sanctions against the use of a drug, three related questions must be considered at the outset: 1) How many persons would abuse the drug if legal controls were removed or not adopted? 2) Do the laws deter use, or perhaps encourage it, as has been suggested with relation to rebellious youth? 3) Is the drug abuser a sick person who, if one drug is prohibited, will find another drug or some equally destructive behavior as a substitute? More specifically, each of these questions must be examined in the context of criminal sanctions against both the user and the distributor as opposed to sanctions against sale only.

Clearly, if the law protects against a non-existing harm, society is better off without the law. The recent elimination of all laws pertaining to written pornography in Denmark, for example, apparently resulted in no ill effects. The incidence of marihuana use as opposed to LSD use supports the position that legal penalties are by no means the overriding determiner of drug usage. The number of persons who have used marihuana is several times that for LSD and is increasing in spite of severe penalties. LSD usage is apparently declining because of concern over the hazards rather than because of any deterrent effect of the relatively moderate laws.

The argument that the drug abuser would simply find another means of escape or self-destructive behavior if the drug were not available is probably only partially correct. It is clear that persons are more vulnerable to the abuse of drugs at certain times in their lives, such as during adolescence or other highly stressful periods. If a potential drug-of-abuse is unavailable at these times an undesirable chain of events may well be avoided. Also, it is known that alcoholism results from sociogenic as well as psychogenic causes, and marihuana abuse can undoubtedly follow a similar pattern.

Concerning the kind of drug-control laws which should be enacted and enforced, there is general agreement that the government has not only the right but also the obligation to enforce certain practices with regard to the distribution of drugs. Disagreement exists as to the point at which the advantages of restricting availability are outweighed by the harm resulting from the illicit supplying of the demand for the drug, such as occurred during the prohibition of alcohol.

Regulation, as opposed to prohibition, permits the orderly control of potency and the conditions of sale, such as age of purchaser, hours of sale, and licensing. It also permits taxation and eliminates the support of organized crime as well as the criminogenic aspects of forcing the user to deal with illegal sources. On the other hand, prohibition of sale clearly indicates social disapproval, whereas open sale does not.

Arguments for criminal sanctions against the drug user primarily stress: 1) their deterrent effect and 2) the aid such laws give to enforcement agencies in apprehending sources of supply. Major arguments against such laws stress that enforcement inevitably encourages the violation of constitutional guarantees of privacy, as well as various other practices, such as informers posing as students, hippies, or other potential drug users, which are ethically questionable though technically legal.

The social control of drug use is most difficult to handle via legal means when the drug in question permits both use and abuse e.g., alcohol and marihuana. The problem of penalizing the majority because of the abuse by the minority was specifically dealt with by the Supreme Court at the time of the Volstead Act. The Court ruled that the state had the right to deny access to alcohol to those who would not abuse it in order to remove the temptation from those who would abuse it.

On a few occasions, exceptions have actually been carved out of the law to permit use of a drug otherwise prohibited: e.g., sacramental use of wine and religious use of peyote by the Indians. More frequently, society has informally disregarded the enforcement of the law for various groups, conditions, or in certain districts of the city. For example, during the '40s, police frequently overlooked the use of marihuana by all musicians because they were otherwise productive and did not cause trouble.

Another means of allowing use but controlling abuse is through compulsory treatment.

## CONCLUSION

What is especially needed is a concerted effort to produce congruence among the various drug policies and laws. What we have at present is an assortment of approaches which are not only lacking in consistency but often operate in clearly opposite directions. Much of the incongruity is based on unrecognized attitudes and fears which must be made conscious and explicit before a congruent policy can emerge. One means of forcing some of the most glaring inconsistencies into perspective is to treat alcohol abuse and drug abuse as a single problem, an approach suggested by the World Health Organization(10).

A national approach to reducing the harm caused to society by excessive drug use must include examination of the contributions of the massive advertising programs for alcohol and tobacco and weigh this against the economic and other costs of intervening in our free enterprise system. If public drunkenness is the manifestation of an illness to be treated rather than punished, is dependency on other drugs not also an illness?

We should critically examine the legal reasoning which concludes that being an addict is not a crime, but possessing the substance necessary to be an addict is a felony deserving a five- or ten-year sentence. The methods of controlling narcotics supply should be weighed against the expense to the victim burglarized, the increased number of prostitutes, and the large profits to organized crime, all of which accompany illegal drug traffic. The deterring effect of the current marihuana laws should be evaluated against the resulting alienation, disrespect for the law, and secondary deviance involving a sizeable portion of an entire generation.

Finally, in a somewhat speculative vein, part of the lack of congruence among drug policies in this country may be due to the fact that economic and technological factors are changing at a faster rate than are cultural attitudes and values. The drug laws in this country have always been an attempt to legislate morality, although they have been justified in terms of preventing antisocial acts. These laws and attitudes evolved at a time when the Protestant ethic and the competitive, achievement-oriented value system were very much in dominance. The freely chosen, passive withdrawal to a life of drug-induced fantasy was an extremely threatening concept.

Now we are told we are verging on an economy of abundance rather than scarcity; an age of automation will eliminate half or more of the labor force necessary for the production of goods. The concept of work will have to be redefined to include nonproductive pursuits which are now considered hobbies; a guaranteed annual income program will likely be in effect within five or ten years. The children of today's middle class have never experienced a depression or any appreciable difficulty in satisfying their material needs. They do not share the materialistic value system to the same extent as their parents because they have little fear of material deprivation.

There also appears to be an increasing acceptance of pleasure in its own right rather than as something that needs to be earned as a reward for hard work. The traditional American attitude toward pleasure was quite evident in the opinion recently given by Judge Tauro in upholding the constitutionality of the Massachusetts marihuana laws. In denying that the fundamental right to the pursuit of happiness is violated by the marihuana laws, he argues that such rights must be "essential" to continued liberty and are particularly those "closely related to some commonly acknowledged moral or legal duty and not merely to a hedonistic seeking of pleasure." In affirming that the state was justified in permitting alcohol and prohibiting marihuana, Judge Tauro argued that alcohol was used most frequently as a relaxant and "as an incident of other social activities," whereas marihuana was "used solely as a means of intoxication," i.e., pleasure.

If the age of economic abundance, automation, and greatly increased leisure time becomes a reality, it is doubtful that these viewpoints toward pleasure (hedonistic and otherwise) can survive. Excessive drug use would be seen as a threat to the individual —not as "a threat to the very moral fabric of society." The over-all welfare of society would be much less dependent on the productivity of the individual, and a value system which demands that pleasure be earned through work would be obsolete.

In conclusion, whether or not the age of abundance arrives, social policy, with some minor reversals, will probably move in the direction of permitting greater individual freedom with respect to drug use. Society will promote the concept of allowing adults the privilege of informed decision. The crucial problem which will remain is that of protecting those who are too young to make an informed decision.

## REFERENCES

1. Benabud, A. 1957. Psycho-pathological aspects of the Cannabis situation in Morocco: Statistical data for 1956. *Bulletin on Narcotics* 9:1–16.

2. Blumer, H.; Sutter, A.; Ahmed, S.; and Smith, R. 1967. *The world of youthful drug use, ADD center project—final report.* Berkeley: University of California Press.

3. Bromberg, W. 1934. Marihuana intoxication. *American Journal of Psychiatry* 91:303–330.

4. Charen, S., and Perelman, L. 1946. Personality studies of marihuana addicts. *American Journal of Psychiatry* 102:674–682.

5. Chopra, R. N., and Chopra, G. S. 1939. The present position of hemp-drug addiction in India. *Indian Journal of Medical Research Memoirs* 31:1–119.

6. Commission on Narcotic Drugs. 1965. Report of the twentieth session, November 29–December 21, E/4140, E/CN.7/488, United Nations.

7. Isbell, H.; Gorodetzsky, C. W.; Jasinski, D.; Claussen, U.; Spulak, F.; and Korte, F. 1967. Effects of (−)$\Delta^9$-Trans-Tetrahydrocannabinol in man. *Psychopharmacologia* 11:184–188.

8. Mayor's Committee on Marihuana. 1944. *The marihuana problem in the city of New York.* Lancaster, Pa.: Jacques Cattell Press.

9. Soueif, M. I. 1967. Hashish consumption in Egypt with special reference to psychosocial aspects. *Bulletin on Narcotics* 19:1–12.

10. World Health Organization. 1967. Services for the prevention and treatment of dependence on alcohol and other drugs. WHO Technical Report, ser. no. 363.

# READING 36

# Psychosocial Aspects of Drug Addiction

**SHERWIN S. RADIN, M.D.**
**Upstate Medical Center, Syracuse, New York**

One important aspect of drugs is their addictive effect. Radin begins his paper with a number of valid questions about drug addiction. What is drug addiction, and why does it occur? Is a person who takes aspirin daily a drug addict? Radin reviews the effects of several different drugs, discusses some of the literature on the subject, and addresses himself to the problems involved in helping the drug-addicted person. In conclusion, he suggests that one of the most effective tools in the prevention of drug addiction could be our educational system, but in order for this to be possible, our educational system will have to undergo some changes.

**QUESTIONS**

1. What is the rationale behind government restriction of drug usage? Is it valid? Should the government be able to restrict doctors from prescribing certain drugs to their patients?
2. Do you agree with Radin's suggested solution to the psychosocial problem of addiction? Do you agree it is a psychosocial problem?
3. Is there such a thing as the "narcotic character" or an addictive personality type? Support your answer.

Drug addiction is a complex issue involving physiological, sociological, psychological, medical and legal parameters. There are many questions raised by this problem:

What is drug addiction?

Why does it occur?

Where and under what circumstances does one become addicted?

Who is most likely to become addicted?

What is the relationship to genetics and to developmental phenomena?

Are there specific personality characteristics of drug addicts?

Is narcotic addiction a crime or a disease or neither or both?

Presented to Nurses, Health Educators, Public Health Workers, Administrators, May 10, 1966, at a session in Syracuse, sponsored by the New York State Departments of Mental Hygiene and Education.

What is the natural course?

How do the cultural and personality aspects relate to one another?

What are the problems of treatment?

Is there anything to be done to prevent drug addiction?

Many papers have been written by persons from a variety of disciplines attempting to answer these questions. Unfortunately far too few answers have emerged. The complexity of the problem itself makes it difficult to arrive at valid conclusions. I will stress some of the psychosocial phenomena related to drug usage.

From time immemorial man has sought to ease his tensions of living and to make life more bearable. His adaptive maneuvers may be sanctioned or not. People utilize realistic endeavors or resort to magic and to phantasy.

The adaptive challenge may be met by the alteration of the environment. If one is unable to accomplish this or elects not to, he may alter his perception of the environment, or alter himself or his perception of himself.

There are available a variety of drugs that enables one to alter his perceptual stage. How tempting for someone with a depreciated depicted self image to resort to a magical potion! The effortless miracle is accomplished simply by introducing a foreign object into the body. The ability to change one's private world by altering one's view of it is reminiscent of the state of infantile omnipotence. The cry of the helpless infant signals the feeding mother whose ministrations rapidly alter his state of tension and hunger to one of calmness, satiation and perhaps blissful drowsiness or sleep. It is postulated that this is the paradigm for drug addiction. Just as the infant is dependent upon his mother for need gratification the addict is dependent upon his drug. Not everyone is tempted to try drugs and of those who do or are required to for medical reasons, only a relatively small percentage become addicted. It

is thus postulated that there must be some physical and/or psychological predisposition necessary for addiction to take place. Drug addiction includes a compulsive need for the drug; an increase in tolerance and in intake; a withdrawal syndrome. The addict believes he cannot function without the drug and strives to obtain it regardless of the price. The period of elation during which the sense of self is grossly expanded and the individual's problems minimized lasts for a period of time and is then generally followed by depression as the drug wears off and the harsh realities of life are magnified. The addict vigorously seeks drugs to alter the depression and regain elation as rapidly as possible. Painful reality plus the memory of the state of bliss motivates him strongly to seek the drug. There has been a shift in the population using narcotics and in the cultural reasons for addiction in this country during the past 150 years. During the early part of the 19th century the addictive powers of opium and other drugs were not recognized. People of all ages and from all social strata were exposed to a variety of patient medicines as well as to doctor's prescriptions containing opium. These remedies were sold without restraint and were publicized as being a "cure-all" for practically "anything that ails you." Opium, morphine, codeine and cocaine were the main drugs. By the middle of the 19th century some 3–4% of the population were addicted. During the 1890's the dangers of addiction were recognized and institutions were opened to treat the patients. Toward the turn of the century heroin was discovered and promoted as a cure for morphine addiction. Heroin did relieve the withdrawal symptoms of morphine but was even more of a pernicious addictive agent in its own right.

Thus the first group of addicts in this country were predisposed persons who were medically or quasi-medically exposed via perfectly legal channels. During the past 50 years a series of events, both legal and social, have resulted in a shift in the nature of the problem.

The early addicts were considered patients and were primarily under medical care. Dr. Charles Towns of New York was one of the early doctors who realized how dangerous addiction was and used his influence to help control it. He helped draft the Boylan Law in 1904 designed to enable physicians to assist in the control of the narcotic problem. Although this law was passed, the section drafted by Towns concerning treatment was dropped. The Harrison Narcotic Act passed by Congress in 1914 was primarily for the purpose of control of production, manufacture and distribution of narcotic drugs. It too mimimized the physician's role in treatment. The enforcement of the revenue act was placed under the Bureau of Internal Revenue within its Bureau of Narcotics.

The essence of this change was that not only enforcement of production and distribution but also medical treatment came under the sway of the Bureau. The enforcement of the law was quite severe so that doctors were even imprisoned for administering to their patients, now considered criminals. The net effect of all this was that many persons who previously, while using the drug under medical supervision, lived a fairly regular life, now had to go underground in order to obtain illegally that which had become necessary for their psychosocial and even physiological survival. The criminal associations and traffic in narcotics is familiar to everyone. Since the drugs have become more valuable and more difficult to obtain, forbidden fruit connotations in defiance of authority have provided additional motivation to obtain drugs. Thus there is a shift from patients to criminals and from all social strata to a preponderance of addicts in high incidence lower socio-economic areas: where in order to gain acceptance amongst one's peers it is necessary to join in. The few cigarettes of marijuana in the 9-10 year old frequently gives way to heroin in the teen-ager. Recently another shift is under way: to the college campus where morphine, marijuana, L.S.D. and other drugs are currently in vogue as youth seeks psychedelic experiences.

The incidence of narcotic addiction in the United States today is difficult to determine because of its illegal aspects. Estimates vary from 60,000 to 1 million. The majority are found in the larger cities, particularly New York, Los Angeles, Detroit and Chicago. The number of addicts has increased some 5 to 10 fold over the past 15 years. Males outnumber females by 5 to 1. These figures are based upon the number of arrests. The majority are young adults from 21 to 30, but there is a significant increase in addiction in children.

Even though many people from deprived areas become addicted, others exposed to the same socio-economic milieu do not. Apparently these sociological conditions help to produce addiction only in those with physical or psychological vulnerabilities. Since addiction is flourishing in a variety of colleges, it is inaccurate to accent the lower socio-economic area as the breeding place for addiction. Some authors have stated that boredom, hopelessness and the need for immediate gratification frequently seen in slum areas lead to addiction. These traits might be prevalent upon a college campus despite the intellectually stimulating atmosphere with its abundant opportunities for creative endeavors and discourse. A number of college students disregard this atmosphere and seek answers in a world of altered self perceptions, created by their ingestation of drugs. Proponents of a mystique, such as Timothy Leary and Allen Ginzberg, reinforce and promote drug cults. Young sensitive people are particularly susceptible since their natural developmental dilemma is to search for a true sense of identity. When authority purports to be able to delve into the depths of the mind and to uncover the essence of mental revelations a ray of hope is afforded to many which may become their religion or philosophy of life. It thus appears that the social milieu per se is not a crucial determinant of addiction; although it may provide the individual with the opportunity to obtain the drug, it doesn't guarantee that he will.

Is there an addict personality type? Are there qualities that all or most addicts possess? Does addiction itself lead to the development of characteristics such as impulsive, aggressive, assaultive behavior or passive dependent behavior? There are studies in the literature where traits of character as diverse as those indicated are thought to be related in some way to drug addiction. The overall consensus, however, is that there isn't any succinct pattern that is readily identifiable as the "Narcotic Character."

Most studies indicate that the addict may be in one of several psychiatric diagnostic categories: psychotic, neurotic, character disorder. There are common personality qualities which are described in many studies. However they are not exclusively found in addicts or are not in any way pathognomonic of narcotic addiction.

During the addiction phase most addicts reveal emotional blunting, immaturity, and a narcissistic orientation primarily related to the drug rather than to his family. His mind is usually clear, rational, logical and coherent. These qualities may be drastically altered during periods of overdose or withdrawal.

Many studies of hospitalized male addicts describe non-aggressivity, sociability, closeness to mother, interests in the arts and in creativity, passivity, omnipotent ideals and narcissism, orality with regressive tendencies as the significant qualities of addicts. These traits refer primarily to opium and its derivatives.

Drugs such as marijuana and alcohol act by releasing inhibitions and therefore aggresive and sexual behavior is much more common than in the case of opium where

relaxation of tensions usually results in a state of pleasure, euphoria and relaxation. Dexedrine is an exhilarating stimulant. Cocaine stimulates the central nervous system and may produce wild excitement with hallucinations and paranoid ideas. The latter may lead to retaliatory aggression and even to homicide. Peyote or mescaline produces colored geometric hallucinations. Barbiturates may lead to poor motor control and speech that may be inarticulate. Emotional lability is common. He may suddenly change from a warm and friendly demeanor to an outburst of violence. His judgment is poor, resorting to inner fantasies is common.

Lysergic acid diethylamide (LSD-25) is a drug which recently has been the subject of much concern. Like mescaline or psilocybin it is a hallucinogenic drug. Some persons, such as Timothy Leary, advocate it as a mind stimulant enabling one to experience fantastic sensory impressions. Their influence has been primarily upon the college campus. The potential of this drug to induce an underlying psychosis has been frequently reported. Some claim that no permanent damage to the brain results from LSD, while others state the contrary. At any rate it is a dangerous drug which is still in its experimental stage and should be primarily reserved for the laboratory. It may have its prime function in action upon the integration mechanisms of the mind.

Lauretta Bender has found that addicts under 16 years of age are more disturbed in the psychosocial areas than are those from 16-21. In some hospitalized adolescents there is the possibility that addiction to opiates protects against the development of underlying psychosis.

In her informative book, "The Drug Addict as a Patient," Dr. Marie Nyswander reviews several formulations which are related to drug addiction. She notes that addiction usually begins during adolescence and spends itself by the middle forties. These 30 years or so are the most active and productive ones for most people. It is postulated that morphine serves to quell the anxiety associated with normal sexual and aggressive drives. This enables the addict to avoid sexuality and aggression. His history generally reveals disappointment and failure in ordinary sexual experiences. Morphine provides in many a substitute orgastic experience. It obviates the need for sexual relations. When addicts indulge in opiates sexual activity is not sought. In some addicts sexual feelings are enhanced but at the expense of sexual performance. This not only refers to opiates but other drugs such as LSD, alcohol and marijuana. "Whether this avoidance of sexuality is a cause or a result of addiction is open to question. But regardless of this aspect, the addict's life does not include what could by any stretch of the imagination be called normal sexuality." (1)

According to the Avoidance of Aggression theory, the drug prevents the addict from assuming his normal role in life associated with mature assertive strivings toward responsible behavior. The diminished interest in aggression and in sexuality in the addict predates adolescence and reflects distorted family life and developmental phenomena.

Many of the addict's qualities are reminiscent of early childhood, such as immaturity, omnipotent strivings, narcissism, inability to give, etc. The closeness and the identification of the addict with the opposite sex parent forges a personality that is poorly equipped to deal with life's problems. Through the vehicle of the drug and the providers of the same he fashions for himself an illusory world where his infantile strivings are gratified. He triumphs in his magical drug dependency as his self expands in omnipotent grandeur.

It is no mystery that the relapse rate is well over 90% in most studies regardless of the treatment, ambulatory or hospitalized and with or without vigorous case work and psychiatric treatment. It is extremely difficult to substitute reality which is painful for pleasurable fantasy.

There is apparently greater success in dealing with the management of this problem in England than in the United States. The legal problems are minimized and the treatment is primarily in medical hands. This enables a greater number of people to function effectively while under medical supervision. The person is not considered a criminal and motivations such as defiance of authority are eliminated. Those suggestible persons who are influenced by "dope peddlers" are no longer fair bait. Thus in all the total number of addicts is less and those who are still addicted function in the main stream of life to a greater extent than those in this country who are forced to wear the criminal label. Since many of the drugs, when properly supervised, do not constitute a health hazard to the user or a menace to society, the English approach is a warranted one. These comments, of course, do not exclude a psychosocial and educational program to aid those addicted.

Freedman and Wilson outline an educational approach to the prevention of addiction. (2, 3) They stress a program for the 16 year olds who leave schools in slum areas where they are frequently exposed to narcotics. According to these authors group and recreation workers should provide an opportunity for the children to identify with an attitude counter to the narcotic one. This is particularly important when the child's family provides little direction or education. An informative approach to the use of drugs in the schools is readily implemented. Small discussion groups rather than formal lectures are more effective. "Two kinds of attack through environmental change are indicated: first, a general strengthening of population resistance to the addictive disorders, and, second, amelioration or elimination of the contributary environmental factors." (3) Since the addiction problem seems to flourish under conditions of frustration and failure, and since the schools might inadvertently provide such experience for some disadvantaged children, special programming is indicated for them, in which a positive and non-frustrating environment is created.

Many of these children have emotional problems of great severity. It isn't theoretical that such children can be helped. My experiences with the Syracuse Scholastic Rehabilitation Program for children with emotional problems has dramatically demonstrated how educators and clinicians working together can effect the rehabilitation of many children with emotional and learning problems. (4, 5) The overall approach is both clinical and educational. The two reinforce each other. The teacher learns to utilize the clinical knowledge of the child, his development and his family to aid him in overcoming his learning problems. The child may simultaneously be receiving psychotherapy. His family may be involved if they appear to be playing a significant role. Usually they do and it is necessary to treat a child-family unit, rather than the child alone. Both clinician and educator working together are able to accomplish what either alone might not. The child's sense of self worth expands as he succeeds in school. He now enjoys learning. The clinician helps free those parts of his mind which were directed at containing the emotional problems. The teacher learns from the clinician the best way of approaching the child and presenting the academic program. The end result of this is that many children who were chronic failures in school are now able to learn. A number of these children come from the same areas where drug addiction is a problem. Many of these children enter the program at a very early age, 6-9 or ten. This perhaps is early enough to prevent their later developing such psychosocial problems as addiction and delinquency.

This approach is not adequate enough to prevent these problems. We are dealing with only a small number of children. It is necessary to enrich the normal child's academic program by utilizing proper mental health principles and personnel. The child must be viewed as a total person in order to accomplish this task. He has social and psychological needs as well as educational ones. How can we enable children to utilize their native equipment optimally? This is the area where new approaches are warranted. How much of the pressure on young people brought to bear today for the purpose of enabling them to learn and enter colleges is exacting an unnecessary and deleterious effect? The argument that we are living in a competitive world and they might as well start now may be valid for some but not for all. In addition this extra stress might lead to a variety of emotional disorders and breakdowns and possibly to drug addiction. If the sense of self worth is diminished significantly and drugs serve to elevate the sense of self then the latter possibility must be considered.

Let us use the potential inherent in the school structure for all children not just for those with emotional problems. The days of teaching just the 3R's are long past. This means more than just a quantitative change to the 20, 50 or 100 R's. The effectiveness of our educational systems must be broadened by the utilization of psychological knowledge in collaboration with educators. A more effective model for children to learn, develop and flourish under will emerge. Only then will psycho-social problems such as addiction be remedied.

## REFERENCES

1. Nyswander, M. 1956. *The drug addict as a patient*, p. 65. New York: Grune & Stratton.
2. Freedman, A. M., and Wilson, E. A. 1964. Childhood and adolescent addictive disorders. *Pediatrics*, August, pp. 273–290.
3. Freedman, A. M., and Wilson, E. A. 1964. Childhood and adolescent addictive disorders. *Pediatrics*, September, pp. 425–430.
4. Radin, S. S. 1962. Mental health problems of school children. *Journal of School Health* 32 (no. 10): 250–257.
5. Radin, S. S. 1965. The teacher and the rehabilitation of the emotionally disturbed child. *Journal of School Health*, vol. 35, no. 3.

# READING 37

## Effects of Manipulated Self-Esteem on Persuasibility Depending on Threat and Complexity of Communication

**HARRY F. GOLLOB**
University of Michigan

**JAMES E. DITTES**
Yale University

The variables affecting a change in social attitudes are many, and their interrelationships are often complex. Gollob and Dittes have provided us with a good example of an experimental study of attitude change. They are mainly concerned with persuasibility and how the variables of self-esteem, threat, and complexity of communication affect a person's susceptibility to influence by communication. They present three hypotheses in hopes of explaining the complex relationship among the variables involved. After experimentation, they conclude that self-esteem has variable effects depending upon its interaction with the characteristics of the communication and the communicator and how self-esteem is conceived by the subject.

### QUESTIONS

1. Should research be published when no significant differences between conditions are found? Why?
2. How were the main variables represented experimentally? Was their representation accurate?
3. What is the relationship of studies in social attitudes to the mass media, advertising, and propaganda techniques?

The purpose of this experiment was to investigate some possible relationships between self-esteem and persuasibility. It was expected that these relationships would vary with different characteristics of a communication.

The hypothesis is widespread that self-esteem is inversely related to various forms of conformity behavior, including persuasibility. Evidence for the inverse relation between self-esteem and persuasibility has been reported by Janis (1953b, 1954, 1955), Janis and Field (1959), Janis and Rife (1959), and, for children, Lesser and Abelson (1959). However, it seems probable that different types of communication would interact with self-esteem and produce different effects on persuasibility. We reasoned that the findings of increased persuasibility with lower self-esteem probably depended on quite specific characteristics of the communication. By varying crucial aspects of the communication, we predicted varying relationships between self-esteem and persuasibility.

## SIMPLE HYPOTHESIS

When the advocated opinion is nonthreatening and clearly and unambiguously stated, there is an inverse relationship between self-esteem and persuasibility. This hypothesis, without any limiting conditions being imposed on the content and form of the communications, is the one which has been tested in the research cited above. It may be derived from the following considerations: Subjects feeling low in self-esteem think more unfavorably of themselves and their opinions, and therefore, in attempting to enhance their self-esteem are more likely to accept the opinions of others. In addition, it is assumed that being in

This experiment was supported by Grant M-3857 to James E. Dittes from the National Institute of Mental Health, United States Public Health Service. Part of the results were presented to the 1963 American Psychological Association convention.

The authors wish to thank Howard Leventhal, George Wolf, Philip K. Oltman, and Alan Feirstein for their helpful comments on this paper, and Sally Kasparek and Karen White for assistance in conducting the experimental sessions.

agreement with others has, for most people in our culture, an acquired reward value, and that reassurance resulting from agreeing with others enhances self-esteem.

## FEAR HYPOTHESIS

In cases where acceptance of a clearly and simply stated opinion would cause a substantial threat to the self, there is a direct positive relationship between self-esteem and persuasibility. It is assumed, except perhaps in some cases of pathological depression, that people with threatend self-esteem do what they can to compensate for or minimize their feelings of inferiority, that is, they try to raise their level of self-esteem. They are likely to defend against accepting any opinion that would make them feel still more insecure and threatened.

## COMPLEXITY HYPOTHESIS

There is a direct positive relation between self-esteem and persuasibility when the communication is complex, and especially when it contains the kind of complexity which results from the presence of misleading, closure-inducing phrases. The simple and fear hypotheses concern the effect of self-esteem on the *acceptance* of the communicator's opinion, and assume negligible effects on learning the content of the communicator's position. These hypotheses assume that people understand the communication but do or do not accept its opinion, according to the conditions specified in the hypotheses. The complexity hypothesis, however, concerns the effect of threatened self-esteem on the *learning* of the communicator's position. If people do not learn the position, they cannot be "persuaded" by it. The distinction between acceptance and learning, as distinct components of persuasibility, has also been made by Janis (1953a).

Several studies have shown that anxiety facilitates performance on simple tasks and interferes with performance on complex tasks (*Child, 1954*). The complexity hypothesis applies these findings regarding task complexity and anxiety to the relation of self-esteem and persuasibility. For present purposes it is assumed that threatened self-esteem functions as anxiety.

Taylor and Spence (1952) present the theory that when complex tasks evoke many competing response tendencies, high anxiety may lead to poorer performance by increasing the probability that conflicting or erroneous responses will occur. Child (1954) has pointed out that high anxiety may result in more task-irrelevant responses, which interfere especially with performance on complex tasks.

In studying the effects of threatened self-esteem on closure, Dittes (1959, 1961) has specified circumstances under which conditions of threat lead to increased probability that competing erroneous responses will occur. He has proposed that the act of closure commonly acquires a reward value as a means of enhancing self-esteem and that damage to self-esteem increases the strength of the tendency to achieve closure as one means of restoring or enhancing self-esteem.

Applied to persuasibility, Dittes' theory states that the reading of a communication without obtaining closure (i.e., a feeling of having understood the communication) is threatening to self-esteem, and that subjects with already lowered or threatened self-esteem are particularly motivated to this further threat and therefore impose closure readily. When a communication is simple, such a tendency to form rapid closure should facilitate performance; but when a communication is complex, and particularly when it contains misleading, closure-inducing phrases, such an effort toward rapid closure is likely to result in misunderstanding the communication.

The theoretical positions of Taylor and Spence, Child, and Dittes all lead to the hypothesis that if a communication is complex, and especially if it also contains misleading closure-inducing cues, subjects with threat-ened self-esteem will not learn the content of the communication as well as subjects with enhanced self-esteem.

## INTERACTIONS BETWEEN HYPOTHESES

The effects postulated by all the hypotheses of this study are presumably operating with all communications. It is assumed that they can interact with each other and, depending on the relative strength of the various processes which are activated, result in a net relationship between self-esteem and persuasibility which, theoretically, can range anywhere between a correlation of $-1.00$ and $+1.00$. Thus, in testing the fear hypothesis, we selected a threatening opinion which we felt would activate processes which would *override* the effects postulated by the simple hypothesis. In a similar manner, again in order to override the effects hypothesized by the simple hypothesis, we emphasized the complexity and misleading, closure-inducing features of the portion of the communication used to test the complexity hypothesis.

## RELATION BETWEEN MANIPULATED AND PREDISPOSITIONAL SELF-ESTEEM

Previous studies of the relation between self-esteem and persuasibility have been concerned with predispositional self-esteem, as measured by subjects' self-report on questionnaires. In this study we have experimentally manipulated self-esteem by varying failure or success on an ego-involving task. It was, however, a secondary purpose of the study to compare the effects on persuasibility of predispositional and manipulated self-esteem. Although we recognize that there are probably several important differences in manipulated and predispositional self-esteem, we expected that the hypotheses advanced above would hold for both manipulated, situationally affected levels of self-esteem, and predispositional levels of self-esteem. In presenting our hypotheses we have cited studies which supported analogous hypotheses using self-report measures of predispositional self-esteem or predispositional anxiety.

Cohen (1959), though, has proposed that people high in predispositional self-esteem tend to use avoidance defenses which lead them to reject threatening communications and accept optimistic ones; while people low in self-esteem tend to use sensitizing defenses which lead them to reject optimistic communications and accept threatening ones. Thus, Cohen's hypotheses concerning predispositional self-esteem are contrary to the predictions of our simple and fear hypotheses. Cohen's hypotheses have been partially supported by Goldstein (1959) and Leventhal and Perloe (1962). Dabbs (1962), though, found that the optimism-pessimism of communications produced no effect. He did find that the effect of predispositional self-esteem on persuasibility depended on whether the communicator was portrayed as a "coper" or "noncoper."

## METHOD

Subjects were made to experience either success or failure on an ego-involving task. They then gave their opinion on three questions (pretest), read the communication, and then again, in the light of what they had just read, stated their opinion on the same three questions (posttest). Then, in order to measure possible differences in learning factors, the subjects were given an information test which asked for the communicator's opinion on these same three questions. At the end of the experimental session subjects completed a questionnaire which included questions intended to check on the effectiveness of the experimental manipulations.

Two self-report measures of predispositional self-esteem were administered to subjects at the beginning of the experimental session. The questionnaires were presented to subjects as unrelated to the later procedures and were completed in a room separate from the one in which the experimental procedures were conducted. The questionnaires

were the 23-item measure of "feelings of inadequacy" which Janis and Field (1959) found was positively related to persuasibility in male high-school students, and the 12-item scale previously found by Dittes (1959, 1961) to interact with the effects of manipulated self-esteem on closure.

## SUBJECTS

The experimental materials were completed by 165 Yale freshmen who were recruited from their dormitories and paid for participating in the experiment. To minimize any effects of interpersonal interaction and anticipated opinion of others, all work was anonymous. After a brief general introduction, subjects began work on the tasks, which were all self-administered. The various experimental materials were presented as a series of unrelated tasks. Each subject took a folder of experimental materials as he entered the room. The folders containing the experimental manipulations had been shuffled in advance.

## SUCCESS-FAILURE MANIPULATION

Subjects took Items 1-10 and Items 31-40 of the Space Relations Test published by the Psychological Corporation. This test is difficult enough to prevent subjects from having much subjective certainty about the quality of their performance and it is therefore open to manipulation of reported performance results, and thus of success or failure. The test is also abstract enough to allow it to be represented as measuring almost anything; this provided opportunity for making it an ego-involving task. A special answer sheet was devised, so that answers were recorded, by carbon, onto a keyed sheet so as to permit self-scoring after the seal was broken. Anonymity was emphasized by repeated written instructions during the procedures that subjects should not write their names on the materials and that the experimenter's interest was only in group averages and not individual results.

In order to make it an ego-involving task,

the written instructions described the Space Relations Test as one measuring

> skills of abstraction . . . of central importance in almost all occupations . . . highly related to personal effectiveness and professional success.

Fictitious keys and norms were used to affect the subjects' feelings of having performed well or poorly on the Space Relations Test. For subjects assigned to the success condition ($N=79$), a special answer key was devised, to maximize the number of apparently correct responses. A fictitious set of norms was provided so that all success subjects would find their scores ranging among the high percentiles of Yale freshmen. For subjects in the failure condition ($N=86$) a false key was provided indicating that many of the common responses were incorrect. A set of norms was also devised in such a way as to make the scores of all failure subjects range in the lower percentiles as compared with other Yale freshmen. To guarantee that subjects would inspect the norms carefully, a form was provided on which they were required to record their own score and percentile.

A final questionnaire was intended to check on the effectiveness of the experimental manipulations. On four items on this questionnaire, success subjects reported that their results were above average, higher than they had expected, pleasing, and esteem enhancing, while subjects in the failure condition reported that their results were below average, lower than they expected, disturbing, and not esteem enhancing. The differences between the success and failure subjects on these four items were all significant at well beyond the .001 level of probability.

## COMMUNICATION AND MEASURES OF OPINION CHANGE

The communication was about 1,200 words long and was entitled, "How Much Should We Spend on Cancer Research?" The stated source of the article was either a low prestige, poorly qualified author (Mr. Lewis — sophomore student at Andover High School) or a high prestige, well-qualified author: (Dr. Lewis — Executive Director of the American Association for Medical Research).[1] Different segments of the communication were constructed to test the different hypotheses. The threatening portion occupied the first segment, and the complex, closure-inducing portion occupied the final segment. The point which was neither threatening nor complex was introduced in the middle of the communication. For reasons to be given later, two counterbalanced forms of the final segment were used.

**Simple Hypothesis.** Both forms of the communication clearly expressed the belief that a diffuse research program is now the best strategy for using research facilities in doing research on career. Opinion was measured, on a 6-point scale, by asking subjects:

> Consider the following two strategies for using research facilities in doing research on cancer: (1) a massive, concentrated crash program, focusing on a few clear problems, vs. (2) a widespread, diffuse program of many people working in many different places and in many different ways. Which do you think is *now* the best strategy?

This item was intended to provide a measure of opinion change in which impulsive closure would play a negligible role and in which affective reactions to the content of the question would be relatively slight.

**Fear Hypothesis.** The first two paragraphs clearly stated and elaborated the opinion, "At present the whole cancer problem seems almost hopeless." The communication included statements such as:

> When your chances of getting a disease are as high as one in four, you might as well admit that it COULD happen to you! . . . your chances of escaping cancer are not better than just that—

---

[1]The manipulation of qualifications and prestige of communicator did not show any statistically significant effects on any of the measures of opinion change used in this report. The main effects and first- and second-order interactions with the failure-success conditions and with Forms A and B of the communication were all nonsignificant.

four to one. . . . What is more, cancer is becoming a bigger problem every year. . . . You can't be vaccinated against cancer. . . . You can't even rely on the latest wonder drug in your doctor's black bag to pull you through once you have it.

In order to measure opinion change on this issue, subjects gave one of six responses ranging from "Agree very much" to "Disagree very much" to the following statement: "At present the whole cancer problem seems almost hopeless."

This item was intended to provide a measure of opinion change where any effects of impulsive closure would be negligble and where it would be probable that subjects would feel threatened by the content of the item, and the relevant portion of the communication.

Complexity Hypothesis.    The complexity hypothesis states that subjects with lowered self-esteem, when given a complex communication, will be more likely to misread the communication and not learn the communicator's intended opinion, and hence not be influenced by it.

To test the complexity hypothesis, we constructed a portion of the communication as follows: The communication presented a complex argument in favor of one opinion—on the relative costliness of a crash program versus a diffuse program of cancer research. It also provided — by means of underlining, quotation marks, and otherwise making selected phrases prominent — certain closure-inducing cues which could lead the subject to a conclusion the opposite of that actually expressed in the total communication.

In this way we ensured that at least one competing erroneous response would be very high on the response hierarchy, and also made it easy for a subject, particularly if he felt threatened and was seeking closure, to jump to a quick, but incorrect, conclusion as to the communicator's opinion. Through this technique we were able to study an extreme case of the common situation in which a rapid, impulsive closure-producing reading of a complex communication leads to a misunderstanding of the communicator's actual opinion.

Two counterbalanced forms of the communication were used to test the complexity hypothesis. One form actually argued that a diffuse research program is more expensive than a concentrated program; but the complex closure-inducing portions of the communication made it easy for subjects, if they were so inclined, to come to the conclusion that the author was arguing in favor of the opposite position, that is, that a crash research program is more expensive than a diffuse research program. The second form argued in the opposite direction.

Counterbalanced forms were used in order to control for the possibility of an effect of the success-failure manipulation on subjects' preferences for spending more or less money on cancer research. Opinion change results showed no significant interaction between the two forms of communication and the success-failure manipulation ($t = -.51$).

The item used in testing the complexity hypothesis was: "Which type of strategy in cancer research do you think is more expensive, a massive concentrated crash program, or a widespread diffuse program?" Subjects gave one of four responses ranging from "The crash program is much more expensive" to "The diffuse program is much more expensive." To aid comparison with other scales, these four responses are expanded to a 6-point scale.

The information test for this item provides a measure of whether or not subjects correctly learned the communicator's position on the issue. Subjects were asked to indicate on a similar 4-point scale whether the author regarded the diffuse or crash program as more expensive. Subjects whose responses were consistent with the misleading closure-inducing phrases, rather than with the communicator's actual opinion, were regarded as having misunderstood or misread the communication.

## RESULTS AND DISCUSSION

The proportion of subjects changing in the direction advocated by the communication was used as a measure of opinion change. The mean change on each item showed the same pattern of results as the proportion of subjects changing positively.[2]

### SIMPLE HYPOTHESIS

An inverse relationship between manipulated self-esteem and persuasibility was observed when the advocated opinion was not threatening and the communicator's position was clearly stated. As shown in Row 1 of Table 1, failure subjects showed significantly more opinion change than success subjects ($p < .02$).

The fact that the difference between the mean information scores of the two groups was so small (Row 1 of Table 2) permits us to conclude that the experimental manipulation probably had its effect on *acceptance* of the communicator's position rather than on *learning* his position on the issue.

There were no differences in initial opinion between the failure and success groups that could account for the observed differences in opinion changes. Similarly, with the opinions used to test the fear and complexity hypotheses, initial positions were virtually identical; all $t$'s were $< .60$.

### FEAR HYPOTHESIS

A direct positive relationship between manipulated self-esteem and persuasibility was observed when acceptance of the advocated opinion would generally result in substantially increased threat to subjects. Row 2 of Table 1 shows that, as compared with success subjects, the subjects in the failure condition showed significantly less acceptance of the threatening opinion, "At present the whole cancer problem seems almost hopeless" ($p < .02$). Since there is no significant difference between the groups on the information test for this item (Row 2 of Table 2), it is again concluded that the experimental manipulation probably affected the *acceptance* component of opinion change, rather than *learning* components.

### TABLE 1

PROPORTION OF SUBJECTS CHANGING IN DIRECTION ADVOCATED BY COMMUNICATION

| Hypothesis | Opinion question | Experimental conditions | | t |
|---|---|---|---|---|
| | | Failure | Success | |
| 1. Simple | Diffuse versus crash program as best strategy | .50 | .34 | —2.08* |
| 2. Fear | Cancer problem seems hopeless | .31 | .48 | —2.22* |
| 3. Complexity | Diffuse versus crash program as most expensive | .26 | .43 | —2.34* |

* $p < .02$, one-tailed test.

[2] The investigators wish to thank Robert P. Abelson for suggesting use of the arc-sine transformation (Walker & Lev, 1953, p. 424) in analyzing the data.

Straightforward applications of the arc-sine transformation were used to test for interactions of the failure and success conditions with other variables. This test, unlike most other tests for analyzing interactions among proportions, does not require the assumption that no main effects exist in order to test for the significance of interaction terms.

For the benefit of those readers who distrust statistical transformations of this type, chi-square tests of the main effects for all the hypotheses of this study gave $p$ values of approximately the same magnitude as those obtained using the arc-sine transformation.

### TABLE 2

MEAN INFORMATION SCORE: LEARNING OF COMMUNICATOR'S POSITION

| Hypotheses | Opinion question | Experimental conditions | | t |
|---|---|---|---|---|
| | | Failure | Success | |
| 1. Simple | Diffuse versus crash program as best strategy | 5.0 | 4.8 | .79 |
| 2. Fear | Cancer problem seems hopeless | | | |
| 3. Complexity | Diffuse versus crash program as most expensive | 4.9 | 4.8 | .55 |
| | | 4.1 | 5.2 | —3.12* |

* $p < .001$, one-tailed test.

## COMPLEXITY HYPOTHESIS

A direct positive relationship between manipulated self-esteem and persuasibility was observed in the case where the communication presented a complex argument in favor of an opinion and contained misleading, closure-inducing phrases. As shown in Row 3 of Table 1, success subjects showed significantly more opinion change than failure subjects ($p < .01$).

**Difference in learning, not acceptance.** On this item, it was predicted that the experimental manipulation of self-esteem would affect opinion change via *learning* components of persuasibility. Row 3 of Table 2 shows that the information score on this item, unlike that of the other items, was significantly higher for success subjects than for failure subjects ($p < .001$). Thus, on the complexity item, the finding of more opinion change by success subjects (Row 3 of Table 1) can be adequately explained by the fact that significantly more of the success subjects had correctly learned the communicator's actual opinion.

## RESULTS WITH PREDISPOSITIONAL SELF-ESTEEM

Our results provided little illumination concerning comparisons between the effects on persuasibility of manipulated and predispositional self-esteem. Neither of the two measures of self-esteem was significantly related to any of the opinion measures, nor was an interaction between predispositional self-esteem and the success-failure conditions significant. We are not clear about the reasons for failure to replicate previous findings obtained using these measures of self-esteem; perhaps the intrusion of the experimental manipulation swamped any overall effects of predispositional self-esteem.

## A FINAL "COMPLEXITY" HYPOTHESIS

The results of this experiment, and other recent work, emphasize that the relation between self-esteem and persuasibility is quite complex. Our results or others' indicate that increased self-esteem may enhance or decrease persuasibility, or have no effect, depending on how it interacts with such variables as the following: the characteristics of the communication, the characteristics of the communicator, and whether self-esteem is conceived as predispositional or situationally manipulated. Finally, our results emphasize that self-esteem may affect persuasibility through differential *learning* of the communication as well as through the more commonly considered process of the *acceptance* of the communication.

## REFERENCES

Child, I. L. 1954. Personality. *Annual Review of Psychology* 5:149–170.

Cohen, A. R. 1959. Some implications of selfesteem for social influence. In *Personality and persuasibility*, ed. C. I. Hovland and I. L. Janis, pp. 102–120. New Haven: Yale University Press.

Dabbs, J. M., Jr. 1962. Self-esteem, coping, and influence. Unpublished doctoral dissertation, Yale University.

Dittes, J. E. 1959. Effect of changes in self-esteem upon impulsiveness and deliberation in making judgments. *Journal of Abnormal and Social Psychology* 58:348–356.

Dittes, J. E. 1961. Impulsive closure as reaction to failure-induced threat. *Journal of Abnormal and Social Psychology* 63:562–569.

Goldstein, M. J. 1959. The relationship between coping and avoiding behavior and response to fear-arousing propaganda. *Journal of Abnormal and Social Psychology* 58:247–252.

Janis, I. L. 1953a. Fear-arousing appeals. In C. I. Hovland, I. L. Janis, and H. H. Kelley, *Communication and persuasion*, pp. 56–98. New Haven: Yale University Press.

Janis, I. L. 1953b. Personality and susceptibility to persuasion. In C. I. Hovland, I. L. Janis, and H. H. Kelley, *Communication and persuasion*, pp. 174–214. New Haven: Yale University Press.

Janis, I. L. 1954. Personality correlates of susceptibility to persuasion. *Journal of Personality* 22:505–518.

Janis, I. L. 1955. Anxiety indices related to susceptibility to persuasion. *Journal of Abnormal and Social Psychology* 51:663–667.

Janis, I. L., and Field, P. B. 1959. Sex differences and personality factors related to persuasibility. In *Personality and persuasibility*, ed. C. I. Hovland and I. L. Janis, pp. 55–68. New Haven: Yale University Press.

Janis, I. L., and Rife, E. 1959. Persuasibility and emotional disorder. In *Personality and persuasibility*, ed. C. I. Hovland and I. L. Janis, pp. 121–137. New Haven: Yale University Press.

Lesser, G. S., and Abelson, R. P. 1959. Personality correlates of persuasibility in children. In *Personality and persuasibility*, ed. C. I. Hovland and I. L. Janis, pp. 187–206. New Haven: Yale University Press.

Leventhal, H., and Perloe, S. I. 1962. A relationship between self-esteem and persuasibility. *Journal of Abnormal and Social Psychology* 64: 385–388.

Taylor, J. A., and Spence, K. W. 1952. The relationship of anxiety level to performance in serial learning. *Journal of Experimental Psychology* 44:61–64.

Walker, Helen M., and Lev, J. 1953. *Statistical inference*. New York: Holt.

# READING 38

# Behavioral Study of Obedience

**STANLEY MILGRAM**
**Yale University**

A child is taught to obey almost from birth—to obey his parents, his teachers, and virtually all authority figures. In the following article, Milgram presents us with an amazing study into the nature of obedience. Subjects were ordered to administer increasingly severe punishment to another person, and the degree to which they obey these orders provides us with much food for thought. In the beginning of the article, Milgram discusses some of the implications of obedience, and it is good to keep these thoughts clearly in mind as you read the article.

## QUESTIONS

1. Why was the tendency to obey so strong? What do you honestly think you would have done if you were a subject in this experiment? Why?
2. As suggested by Milgram, the implications of this study to events in history are revealing. What are the implications for our future?
3. List the factors that govern the tendency to obey, and discuss their relative influences.

Obedience is as basic an element in the structure of social life as one can point to. Some system of authority is a requirement of all communal living, and it is only the man dwelling in isolation who is not forced to respond, through defiance or submission, to the commands of others. Obedience, as a determinant of behavior, is of particular relevance to our time. It has been reliably established that from 1933–45 millions of innocent persons were systematically slaughtered on command. Gas chambers were built, death camps were guarded, daily quotas of corpses were produced with the same efficiency as the manufacture of appliances. These inhumane policies may have originated in the mind of a single person,

This research was supported by a grant (NSF G-17916) from the National Science Foundation. Exploratory studies conducted in 1960 were supported by a grant from the Higgins Fund at Yale University. The research assistance of Alan C. Elms and Jon Wayland is gratefully acknowledged.

Stanley Milgram is now at Harvard University.

but they could only be carried out on a massive scale if a very large number of persons obeyed orders.

Obedience is the psychological mechanism that links individual action to political purpose. It is the dispositional cement that binds them to systems of authority. Facts of recent history and observation in daily life suggest that for many persons obedience may be a deeply ingrained behavior tendency, indeed, a prepotent impulse overriding training in ethics, sympathy, and moral conduct. C. P. Snow (1961) points to its importance when he writes:

> When you think of the long and gloomy history of man, you will find more hideous crimes have been committed in the name of obedience than have ever been committed in the name of rebellion. If you doubt that, read William Shirer's "Rise and Fall of the Third Reich." The German Officer Corps were brought up in the most rigorous code of obedience . . . in the name of obedience they were party to, and assisted in, the most wicked large scale actions in the history of the world [p. 24].

While the particular form of obedience dealt with in the present study has its antecedents in these episodes, it must not be thought all obedience entails acts of aggression against others. Obedience serves numerous productive functions. Indeed, the very life of society is predicated on its existence. Obedience may be ennobling and educative and refer to acts of charity and kindness, as well as to destruction.

## GENERAL PROCEDURE

A procedure was devised which seems useful as a tool for studying obedience (Milgram, 1961). It consists of ordering a naive subject to administer electric shock to a victim. A simulated shock generator is used, with 30 clearly marked voltage levels that range from 15 to 450 volts. The instrument bears verbal designations that range from Slight Shock to Danger: Severe Shock. The responses of the victim, who is a trained confederate of the experimenter, are standardized. The orders to administer shocks are given to the naive subject in the context of

a "learning experiment" ostensibly set up to study the effects of punishment on memory. As the experiment proceeds the naive subject is commanded to administer increasingly more intense shocks to the victim, even to the point of reaching the level marked Danger: Severe Shock. Internal resistances become stronger, and at a certain point the subject refuses to go on with the experiment. Behavior prior to this rupture is considered "obedience," in that the subject complies with the commands of the experimenter. The point of rupture is the act of disobedience. A quantitative value is assigned to the subject's performance based on the maximum intensity shock he is willing to administer before he refuses to participate further. Thus for any particular subject and for any particular experimental condition the degree of obedience may be specified with a numerical value. The crux of the study is to systematically vary the factors believed to alter the degree of obedience to the experimental commands.

The technique allows important variables to be manipulated at several points in the experiment. One may vary aspects of the source of command, content and form of command, instrumentalities for its execution, target object, general social setting, etc. The problem, therefore, is not one of designing increasingly more numerous experimental conditions, but of selecting those that best illuminate the *process* of obedience from the sociopsychological standpoint.

## RELATED STUDIES

The inquiry bears an important relation to philosophic analyses of obedience and authority (Arendt, 1958; Friedrich, 1958; Weber, 1947), an early experimental study of obedience by Frank (1944), studies in "authoritarianism" (Adorno, Frenkel-Brunswik, Levinson, & Sanford, 1950; Rokeach, 1961), and a recent series of analytic and empirical studies in social power (Cartwright, 1959). It owes much to the long concern with *suggestion* in social psychology, both in its normal forms (e.g., Binet, 1900) and in its clinical manifestations (Charcot, 1881). But it derives, in the first instance, from direct observation of a social fact; the individual who is commanded by a legitimate authority ordinarily obeys. Obedience comes easily and often. It is a ubiquitous and indispensable feature of social life.

## METHOD
### SUBJECTS

The subjects were 40 males between the ages of 20 and 50, drawn from New Haven and the surrounding communities. Subjects were obtained by a newspaper advertisement and direct mail solicitation. Those who responded to the appeal believed they were to participate in a study of memory and learning at Yale University. A wide range of occupations is represented in the sample. Typical subjects were postal clerks, high school teachers, salesmen, engineers, and laborers. Subjects ranged in educational level from one who had not finished elementary school, to those who had doctorate and other professional degrees. They were paid $4.50 for their participation in the experiment. However, subjects were told that payment was simply for coming to the laboratory, and that the money was theirs no matter what happened after they arrived. Table 1 shows the proportion of age and occupational types assigned to the experimental condition.

**TABLE 1**

DISTRIBUTION OF AGE AND OCCUPATIONAL TYPES IN THE EXPERIMENT

| Occupations | 20–29 years $n$ | 30–39 years $n$ | 40–50 years $n$ | Percentage of total (Occupations) |
|---|---|---|---|---|
| Workers, skilled and unskilled | 4 | 5 | 6 | 37.5 |
| Sales, business, and white-collar | 3 | 6 | 7 | 40.0 |
| Professional | 1 | 5 | 3 | 22.5 |
| Percentage of total (Age) | 20 | 40 | 40 | |

Note.—Total $N = 40$.

## PERSONNEL AND LOCALE

The experiment was conducted on the grounds of Yale University in the elegant interaction laboratory. (This detail is relevant to the perceived legitimacy of the experiment. In further variations, the experiment was dissociated from the university, with consequences for performance.) The role of experimenter was played by a 31-year-old high school teacher of biology. His manner was impassive, and his appearance somewhat stern throughout the experiment. He was dressed in a gray technician's coat. The victim was played by a 47-year-old accountant, trained for the role; he was of Irish-American stock, whom most observers found mild-mannered and likable.

## PROCEDURE

One naive subject and one victim (an accomplice) performed in each experiment. A pretext had to be devised that would justify the administration of electric shock by the naive subject. This was effectively accomplished by the cover story. After a general introduction on the presumed relation between punishment and learning, subjects were told.

> But actually, we know *very little* about the effect of punishment on learning, because almost no truly scientific studies have been made of it in human beings.
>
> For instance, we don't know how *much* punishment is best for learning—and we don't know how much difference it makes as to who is giving the punishment, whether an adult learns best from a younger or an older person than himself—or many things of that sort.
>
> So in this study we are bringing together a number of adults of different occupations and ages. And we're asking some of them to be teachers and some of them to be learners.
>
> We want to find out just what effect different people have on each other as teachers and learners, and also what effect *punishment* will have on learning in this situation.
>
> Therefore, I'm going to ask one of you to be the teacher here tonight and the other one to be the learner.
>
> Does either of you have a preference?

Subjects then drew slips of paper from a hat to determine who would be the teacher and who would be the learner in the experiment. The drawing was rigged so that the naive subject was always the teacher and the accomplice always the learner. (Both slips contained the word "Teacher.") Immediately after the drawing, the teacher and learner were taken to an adjacent room and the learner was strapped into an "electric chair" apparatus.

The experimenter explained that the straps were to prevent excessive movement while the learner was being shocked. The effect was to make it impossible for him to escape from the situation. An electrode was attached to the learner's wrist, and electrode paste was applied "to avoid blisters and burns." Subjects were told that the electrode was attached to the shock generator in the adjoining room.

In order to improve credibility the experimenter declared, in response to a question by the learner: "Although the shocks can be extremely painful, they cause no permanent tissue damage."

Learning task. The lesson administered by the subject was a paired-associate learning task. The subject read a series of word pairs to the learner, and then read the first word of the pair along with four terms. The learner was to indicate which of the four terms had originally been paired with the first word. He communicated his answer by pressing one of four switches in front of him, which in turn lit up one of four numbered quadrants in an answer-box located atop the shock generator.

Shock generator. The instrument panel consists of 30 lever switches set in a horizontal line. Each switch is clearly labeled with a voltage designation that ranges from 15 to 450 volts. There is a 15-volt increment from one switch to the next going from left to right. In addition, the following verbal designations are clearly indicated for groups of four switches going from left to right: Slight Shock, Moderate Shock, Strong Shock, Very Strong Shock, Intense Shock, Extreme Intensity Shock, Danger: Severe

Shock. (Two switches after this last designation are simply marked XXX.)

Upon depressing a switch: a pilot light corresponding to each switch is illuminated in bright red; an electric buzzing is heard; an electric blue light, labeled "voltage energizer," flashes; the dial on the voltage meter swings to the right; various relay clicks are sounded.

The upper left-hand corner of the generator is labeled Shock Generator, Type ZLB, Dyson Instrument Company, Waltham, Mass. Output 15 Volts–450 Volts.

Details of the instrument were carefully handled to insure an appearance of authenticity. The panel was engraved by precision industrial engravers, and all components were of high quality. No subject in the experiment suspected that the instrument was merely a simulated shock generator.[1]

Sample shock. Each naive subject is given a sample shock on the shock generator, prior to beginning his run as teacher. This shock is always 45 volts, and is applied by pressing the third switch of the generator. The shock is applied to the wrist of the naive subject, and has its source in a 45-volt battery wired into the generator. This further convinces the subject of the authenticity of the generator.

Shock instructions. The subject is told to administer a shock to the learner each time he gives a wrong response. Moreover—and this is the key command—the subject is instructed to "move one level higher on the shock generator each time the learner flashes a wrong answer." He is also instructed to announce the voltage level before administering a shock. This serves to

---

[1] A related technique, making use of a shock generator, was reported by Buss (1961) for the study of aggression in the laboratory. Despite the considerable similarity of technical detail in the experimental procedures, both investigators proceeded in ignorance of the other's work. Milgram provided plans and photographs of his shock generator, experimental procedure, and first results in a report to the National Science Foundation in January 1961. This report received only limited circulation. Buss reported his procedure 6 months later, but to a wider audience. Subsequently, technical information and reports were exchanged. The present article was first received in the Editor's office on December 27, 1961; it was resubmitted with deletions on July 27, 1962.

continually remind subjects of the increasing intensity of shocks administered to the learner.

Preliminary and regular run. Pretests revealed that the procedure of reading words and administering shocks requires some practice before it can be handled smoothly. Therefore, immediately preceding the regular run, the teacher is given a preliminary series of 10 words to read to the learner. There are 3 neutral words in the practice series (i.e., words that the learner answers correctly), so that shocks are administered for 7 of the words, with the maximum shock at 105 volts (moderate shock). Almost all subjects master the procedure by the time the preliminary run is over.

Subjects are then presented with a second list, and are told that the procedure is the same as for the first list; the experimenter adds, however:

When you get to the bottom of the list, repeat it over again, and continue giving shocks, until the learner has learned all the pairs correctly.

The experimenter instructs the subject to,

start from 15 volts and increase the shock level one step each time the learner gives a wrong answer.

Feedback from the victim. In all conditions the learner gives a predetermined set of responses to the word pair test, based on a schedule of approximately three wrong answers to one correct answer. In the present experimental condition no vocal response or other sign of protest is heard from the learner until Shock Level 300 is reached. When the 300-volt shock is administered, the learner pounds on the wall of the room in which he is bound to the electric chair. The pounding can be heard by the subject. From this point on, the learner's answers no longer appear on the four-way panel.

At this juncture, subjects ordinarily turn to the experimenter for guidance. The experimenter instructs the subject to treat the absence of a response as a wrong answer, and to shock the subject according to the usual schedule. He advises the subjects to allow 5–10 seconds before considering no response as a wrong answer, and to increase the shock level one step each time the learner fails to respond correctly. The learner's pounding is repeated after the 315-volt shock is administered; afterwards he is not heard from, nor do his answers reappear on the four-way signal box.

Experimenter feedback. At various points in the experiment the subject may turn to the experimenter for advice on whether he should continue to administer shocks. Or he may indicate that he does not wish to go on. It was important to standardize the experimenter's responses to these inquiries and reactions.

If the subject indicated his unwillingness to go on, the experimenter responded with a sequence of "prods," using as many as necessary to bring the subject into line.

Prod 1: Please continue, *or* Please go on.
Prod 2: The experiment requires that you continue.
Prod 3: It is absolutely essential that you continue.
Prod 4: You have no other choice, you must go on.

The prods were always made in sequence: Only if Prod 1 had been unsuccessful, could Prod 2 be used. If the subject refused to obey the experimenter after Prod 4, the experiment was terminated. The experimenter's tone of voice was at all times firm, but not impolite. The sequence was begun anew on each occasion that the subject balked or showed reluctance to follow orders.

Special prods. If the subject asked if the learner was liable to suffer permanent physical injury, the experimenter said:

Although the shocks may be painful, there is no permanent tissue damage, so please go on. [Followed by Prods 2, 3, and 4 if necessary.]

If the subject said that the learner did not want to go on, the experimenter replied:

Whether the learner likes it or not, you must go on until he has learned all the word pairs correctly. So please go on. [Followed by Prods 2, 3, and 4 if necessary.]

## DEPENDENT MEASURES

The primary dependent measure for any subject is the maximum shock he administers before he refuses to go any further. In principle this may vary from 0 (for a subject who refuses to administer even the first shock) to 30 (for a subject who administers the highest shock on the generator). A subject who breaks off the experiment at any point prior to administering the thirtieth shock level is termed a *defiant* subject. One who complies with experimental commands fully, and proceeds to administer all shock levels commanded, is termed an *obedient* subject.

Further records. With few exceptions experimental sessions were recorded on magnetic tape. Occasional photographs were taken through one-way mirrors. Notes were kept on any unusual behavior occurring during the course of the experiments. On occasion, additional observers were directed to write objective descriptions of the subjects' behavior. The latency and duration of shocks were measured by accurate timing devices.

Interview and dehoax. Following the experiment, subjects were interviewed; open-ended questions, projective measures, and attitude scales were employed. After the interview, procedures were undertaken to assure that the subject would leave the laboratory in a state of well being. A friendly reconciliation was arranged between the subject and the victim, and an effort was made to reduce any tensions that arose as a result of the experiment.

## RESULTS

### PRELIMINARY NOTIONS

Before giving an account of the experimental results, it is instructive to consider how persons predict others will perform when commanded to administer powerful shocks to another person. Fourteen Yale seniors, all psychology majors, were provided with a detailed description of the experimental situation. They were asked to reflect carefully on it, and to predict the behavior of 100 hypothetical subjects. More specifically, they were instructed to plot the distribution of obedience of "100 Americans of diverse occupations, and ranging in age from 20 to 50 years," who were placed in the experimental situation.

There was considerable agreement among the respondents on the expected behavior of hypothetical subjects. All respondents predicted that only an insignificant minority would go through to the end of the shock series. (The estimates ranged from 0 to 3%; i.e., the most "pessimistic" member of the class predicted that of 100 persons, 3 would continue through to the most potent shock available on the shock generator—450 volts.) The class mean was 1.2%. The question was also posed informally to colleagues of the author, and the most general feeling was that few if any subjects would go beyond the designation Very Strong Shock.

## RESULT OF EXPERIMENT I

Subjects Accept Situation. With few exceptions subjects were convinced of the reality of the experimental situation, that they were administering shocks to another person, and the most potent shocks were extremely painful. In the post-experimental interview subjects were asked: "How painful to the learner were the last few shocks that you administered to him?" Subjects were instructed to indicate their answers on a printed 14-point scale ranging from "Not at all painful" to "Extremely painful." The modal response was 14 (Extremely painful) with the mean at 13.42.

Signs of Extreme Tension. Many subjects showed signs of nervousness in the experimental situation, and especially upon administering the more powerful shocks. In a large number of cases the degree of tension reached extremes that are rarely seen in sociopsychological laboratory studies. Subjects were observed to sweat, tremble, stutter, bite their lips, groan, and dig their fingernails into their flesh. These were characteristic rather than exceptional responses to the experiment.

One sign of tension was the regular occurrence of nervous laughing fits. Fourteen of the 40 subjects showed definite signs of nervous laughter and smiling. The laughter seemed entirely out of place, even bizarre. Full-blown, uncontrollable seizures were observed for 3 subjects. On one occasion we observed a seizure so violently convulsive that it was necessary to call a halt to the experiment. The subject, a 46-year-old encyclopedia salesman, was seriously embarrassed by his untoward and uncontrollable behavior. In the post-experimental interviews subjects took pains to point out that they were not sadistic types, and that the laughter did not mean they enjoyed shocking the victim.

Distribution of Scores. It had been conjectured that persons would not, in general, agree to administer shocks beyond the level designated as Very Strong Shock. The distribution of maximum shocks for this experiment is shown in Table 2. The obtained distribution of scores deviates radically from the prediction.

Upon command of the experimenter, each of the 40 subjects went beyond the expected breakoff point. No subject stopped prior to administering Shock Level 20. (At this level—300 volts—the victim kicks on the wall and no longer provides answers to the teacher's multiple-choice questions.)

Of the 40 subjects, 5 refused to obey the experimental commands beyond the 300-volt level. Four more subjects administered one further shock, and then refused to go on. Two broke off at the 330-volt level, and 1 each at 345, 360, and 375 volts. Thus a total of 14 subjects defied the experimenter. It is instructive to reprint their remarks at the point of defiance, as transcribed from the tape recordings:

> [0124] I think he's trying to communicate, he's knocking. ... Well it's not fair to shock the guy ... these are terrific volts. I don't think this is very humane. ... Oh, I can't go on with this;

no, this isn't right. It's a hell of an experiment. The guy is suffering in there. No, I don't want to go on. This is crazy. [Subject refused to administer more shocks.]

> [0123] He's banging in there. I'm gonna chicken out. I'd like to continue, but I can't do that to a man. ... I'm sorry I can't do that to a man. I'll hurt his heart. You take your check. ... No really, I couldn't do it.

## TABLE 2

### DISTRIBUTION OF BREAKOFF POINTS

| Verbal designation and voltage indication | Number of subjects for whom this was maximum shock |
|---|---|
| **Slight Shock** | |
| 15 | 0 |
| 30 | 0 |
| 45 | 0 |
| 60 | 0 |
| **Moderate Shock** | |
| 75 | 0 |
| 90 | 0 |
| 105 | 0 |
| 120 | 0 |
| **Strong Shock** | |
| 135 | 0 |
| 150 | 0 |
| 165 | 0 |
| 180 | 0 |
| **Very Strong Shock** | |
| 195 | 0 |
| 210 | 0 |
| 225 | 0 |
| 240 | 0 |
| **Intense Shock** | |
| 255 | 0 |
| 270 | 0 |
| 285 | 0 |
| 300 | 5 |
| **Extreme Intensity Shock** | |
| 315 | 4 |
| 330 | 2 |
| 345 | 1 |
| 360 | 1 |
| **Danger: Severe Shock** | |
| 375 | 1 |
| 390 | 0 |
| 405 | 0 |
| 420 | 0 |
| **XXX** | |
| 435 | 0 |
| 450 | 26 |

These subjects were frequently in a highly agitated and even angered state. Sometimes, verbal protest was at a minimum, and the subject simply got up from his chair in front of the shock generator, and indicated that he wished to leave the laboratory.

Of the 40 subjects, 26 obeyed the orders of the experimenter to the end, proceeding to punish the victim until they reached the most potent shock available on the shock generator. At that point, the experimenter called a halt to the session. (The maximum shock is labeled 450 volts, and is two steps beyond the designation: Danger: Severe Shock.) Although obedient subjects continued to administer shocks, they often did so under extreme stress. Some expressed reluctance to administer shocks beyond the 300-volt level and displayed fears similar to those who defied the experimenter; yet they obeyed.

After the maximum shocks had been delivered, and the experimenter called a halt to the proceedings, many obedient subjects heaved sighs of relief, mopped their brows, rubbed their fingers over their eyes, or nervously fumbled cigarettes. Some shook their heads, apparently in regret. Some subjects had remained calm throughout the experiment, and displayed only minimal signs of tension from beginning to end.

## DISCUSSION

The experiment yielded two findings that were surprising. The first finding concerns the sheer strength of obedient tendencies manifested in this situation. Subjects have learned from childhood that it is a fundamental breach of moral conduct to hurt another person against his will. Yet 26 subjects abandon this tenet in following the instructions of an authority who has no special powers to enforce his commands. To disobey would bring no material loss to the subjects, no punishment would ensue. It is clear from the remarks and outward behavior of many participants that in punishing the victim they are often acting against their own values. Subjects often expressed deep disapproval of shocking a man in the face of his objections and others denounced it as stupid and senseless. Yet the majority

complied with the experimental commands. This outcome was surprising from two perspectives: first, from the standpoint of predictions made in the questionnaire described earlier. (Here, however, it is possible that the remoteness of the respondents from the actual situation, and the difficulty of conveying to them the concrete details of the experiment, could account for the serious underestimation of obedience.)

But the results were also unexpected to persons who observed the experiment in progress, through one-way mirrors. Observers often uttered expressions of disbelief upon seeing a subject administer more powerful shocks to the victim. These persons had a full acquaintance with the details of the situation, and yet systematically underestimated the amount of obedience that subjects would display.

The second unanticipated effect was the extraordinary tension generated by the procedures. One might suppose that a subject would simply break off or continue as his conscience dictated. Yet, this is very far from what happened. There were striking reactions of tension and emotional strain. One observer related:

> I observed a mature and initially poised businessman enter the laboratory smiling and confident. Within 20 minutes he was reduced to a twitching, stuttering wreck, who was rapidly approaching a point of nervous collapse. He constantly pulled on his earlobe, and twisted his hands. At one point he pushed his fist into his forehead and muttered: "Oh God, let's stop it." And yet he continued to respond to every word of the experimenter, and obeyed to the end.

Any understanding of the phenomenon of obedience must rest on an analysis of the particular conditions in which it occurs. The following features of the experiment go some distance in explaining the high amount of obedience observed in the situation.

1. The experiment is sponsored by and takes place on the grounds of an institution of unimpeachable reputation, Yale University. It may be reasonably presumed that the personnel are competent and reputable.

The importance of this background authority is now being studied by conducting a series of experiments outside of New Haven, and without any visible ties to the university.

2. The experiment is, on the face of it, designed to attain a worthy purpose—advancement of knowledge about learning and memory. Obedience occurs not as an end in itself, but as an instrumental element in a situation that the subject construes as significant, and meaningful. He may not be able to see its full significance, but he may properly assume that the experimenter does.

3. The subject perceives that the victim has voluntarily submitted to the authority system of the experimenter. He is not (at first) an unwilling captive impressed for involuntary service. He has taken the trouble to come to the laboratory presumably to aid the experimental research. That he later becomes an involuntary subject does not alter the fact that, initially, he consented to participate without qualification. Thus he has in some degree incurred an obligation toward the experimenter.

4. The subject, too, has entered the experiment voluntarily, and perceives himself under obligation to aid the experimenter. He has made a commitment, and to disrupt the experiment is a repudiation of this initial promise of aid.

5. Certain features of the procedure strengthen the subject's sense of obligation to the experimenter. For one, he has been paid for coming to the laboratory. In part this is canceled out by the experimenter's statement that:

> Of course, as in all experiments, the money is yours simply for coming to the laboratory. From this point on, no matter what happens, the money is yours.[2]

6. From the subject's standpoint, the fact that he is the teacher and the other man the learner is purely a chance consequence (it is determined by drawing lots) and he, the subject, ran the same risk as the other man in being assigned the role of learner. Since the assignment of positions in the experiment was achieved by fair means, the learner is deprived of any basis of complaint on this count. (A similar situation obtains in Army units, in which—in the absence of volunteers—a particularly dangerous mission may be assigned by drawing lots, and the unlucky soldier is expected to bear his misfortune with sportsmanship.)

7. There is, at best, ambiguity with regard to the prerogatives of a psychologist and the corresponding rights of his subject. There is a vagueness of expectation concerning what a psychologist may require of his subject, and when he is overstepping acceptable limits. Moreover, the experiment occurs in a closed setting, and thus provides no opportunity for the subject to remove these ambiguities by discussion with others. There are few standards that seem directly applicable to the situation, which is a novel one for most subjects.

8. The subjects are assured that the shocks administered to the subject are "painful but not dangerous." Thus they assume that the discomfort caused the victim is momentary, while the scientific gains resulting from the experiment are enduring.

9. Through Shock Level 20 the victim continues to provide answers on the signal box. The subject may construe this as a sign that the victim is still willing to "play the game." It is only after Shock Level 20 that the victim repudiates the rules completely, refusing to answer further.

These features help to explain the high amount of obedience obtained in this experiment. Many of the arguments raised need not remain matters of speculation, but can be reduced to testable propositions to be confirmed or disproved by further experiments.[3]

The following features of the experiment concern the nature of the conflict which the subject faces.

10. The subject is placed in a position in

---

[2] Forty-three subjects, undergraduates at Yale University, were run in the experiment without payment. The results are very similar to those obtained with paid subjects.

[3] A series of recently completed experiments employing the obedience paradigm is reported in Milgram (1964).

which he must respond to the competing demands of two persons: the experimenter and the victim. The conflict must be resolved by meeting the demands of one or the other; satisfaction of the victim and the experimenter are mutually exclusive. Moreover, the resolution must take the form of a highly visible action, that of continuing to shock the victim or breaking off the experiment. Thus the subject is forced into a public conflict that does not permit any completely satisfactory solution.

11. While the demands of the experimenter carry the weight of scientific authority, the demands of the victim spring from his personal experience of pain and suffering. The two claims need not be regarded as equally pressing and legitimate. The experimenter seeks an abstract scientific datum; the victim cries out for relief from physical suffering caused by the subject's actions.

12. The experiment gives the subject little time for reflection. The conflict comes on rapidly. It is only minutes after the subject has been seated before the shock generator that the victim begins his protests. Moreover, the subject perceives that he has gone through but two-thirds of the shock levels at the time the subject's first protests are heard. Thus he understands that the conflict will have a persistent aspect to it, and may well become more intense as increasingly more powerful shocks are required. The rapidity with which the conflict descends on the subject, and his realization that it is predictably recurrent may well be sources of tension to him.

13. At a more general level, the conflict stems from the opposition of two deeply ingrained behavior dispositions: first, the disposition not to harm other people, and second, the tendency to obey those whom we perceive to be legitimate authorities.

## REFERENCES

Adorno, T.; Frenkel-Brunswik, Else; Levinson, D. J.; and Sanford, R. N. 1950. *The authoritarian personality.* New York: Harper.

Arendt, H. 1958. What was authority? In *Authority,* ed. C. J. Friedrich, pp. 81–112. Cambridge: Harvard University Press.

Binet, A. 1900. *La suggestibilité.* Paris: Schleicher.

Buss, A. H. 1961. *The psychology of aggression.* New York: Wiley.

Cartwright, S., ed. 1959. *Studies in social power.* Ann Arbor: University of Michigan Institute for Social Research.

Charcot, J. M. 1881. *Oeuvres complètes.* Paris: Bureaux du Progrès Médical.

Frank, J. D. 1944. Experimental studies of personal pressure and resistance. *Journal of General Psychology* 30:23–64.

Friedrich, C. J., ed. 1958. *Authority.* Cambridge: Harvard University Press.

Milgram, S. 1961. Dynamics of obedience. Mimeo. Washington: National Science Foundation.

Milgram, S. 1964. Some conditions of obedience and disobedience to authority. *Human Relations.*

Rokeach, M. 1961. Authority, authoritarianism, and conformity. In *Conformity and deviation,* ed. I. A. Berg and B. M. Bass, pp. 230–257. New York: Harper.

Snow, C. P. 1961. Either-or. *Progressive,* February, p. 24.

Weber, M. 1947. *The theory of social and economic organization.* Oxford: Oxford University Press.

# READING 39

# Film Violence and the Cue Properties of Available Targets

**LEONARD BERKOWITZ**
**RUSSELL G. GEEN**
**University of Wisconsin**

The next two articles provide us with different insights into the problems of aggression and the nature of the variables that influence aggressive behavior. Berkowitz and Geen created an experimental stress situation by means of special anger-induction methods. In reading this study, the student should devote himself to discovering how the authors derived their hypotheses from theoretical considerations, the techniques used to obtain objective measures of the variables, the procedures used to check the success of experimental manipulations, and how a realistic situation was constructed.

## QUESTIONS

1. Discuss the experimental methodology of this study. What are the variables manipulated; how are these variables measured, etc.
2. Children's stories are often filled with violence. Cowboy stories, pirates, adventurers, etc., usually involve killing and physical harm. What is the influence of these books on children, as suggested by the results of this article?
3. Discuss the problems involved with violence on television. What measures should be taken? Is there more violence on the news broadcasts than in the entertainment programs?

According to a number of experiments, the display of aggression on the movie or television screen is more likely to increase than reduce the probability of aggressive behavior by members of the audience (Bandura & Walters, 1963; Berkowitz, 1962, 1964, 1965; Berkowitz & Rawlings, 1963; Walters, Thomas, & Acker, 1962). This heightened likelihood of aggression is not

This study was carried out by RGG under LB's supervision as part of a project sponsored by Grant C-23988 from the National Science Foundation and the senior author.

always apparent, however. If the audience regards the depicted aggression as being unwarranted or morally wrong, inhibitions will be aroused. Such restraints against hostility can weaken the intensity of the aggressive actions shown by the audience members, or may even cause them to avoid displaying any overt hostility at all (Berkowitz & Rawlings, 1963).

There is some question as to what the specific role of the witnessed hostility is. Bandura and Walters (1963) generally prefer to emphasize two processes in accounting for film-engendered aggression: imitative learning and inhibitory and disinhibitory effects (cf. p. 60). By watching the actions of another person, they state, "the observer may acquire new responses that did not previously exist in his repertory." In addition, the observed model's behavior may also either arouse or weaken the audience's inhibitions against particular actions. Thus, according to this analysis, witnessed hostility presumably gives rise to a persistent action tendency, a readiness to display aggression toward *anyone*. If certain persons are attacked rather than other people, the former supposedly have produced a disinhibition against aggression, for example, by somehow reminding the observer that hostility toward these people is permissible. (As the reader will recognize, the Bandura-Walters analysis is reminiscent of the classic scapegoat theory of prejudice. This latter doctrine also contends that the frustrated or prejudiced person is ready to attack just anyone and aggresses against those groups who are visible and safe to attack.)

But while modeling and inhibition effects are undoubtedly important, filmed violence may also serve to elicit aggressive responses from the observer (Berkowitz, 1962, 1964). The depicted aggression may increase the probability of attacks upon *particular targets*, depending upon the aggression-evoking cue properties of these objects. Observed aggression presumably is likely to have aggressive consequences as a function of: the strength of the observer's previously acquired aggressiveness habits; the association between the witnessed event and both the situations in which the observer had learned to act aggressively, and the post-observation setting; and the intensity of the guilt and/or aggression-anxiety also aroused by the observed violence( Berkowitz, 1962, p. 238). Putting it simply, this reasoning implies that the aggressiveness habits activated by witnessed hostility are often only in "low gear," so to speak. Other appropriate, aggression-evoking cues must be present before the observed violence can lead to strong aggressive responses by the observer. These cues are stimuli in the postobservation situation which have some association with the depicted event, or which may be connected with previous aggression-instigating situations. Thus, a person who sees a brutal fight may not himself display any detectable aggression immediately afterwards, even if his inhibitions are relatively weak, unless he encounters stimuli having some association with the fight. (Returning to the problem of scapegoating, this analysis maintains that the victimized groups evoke hostile responses from people who are ready to act aggressively; these groups have appropriate cue properties as well as being safe and visible targets—cf. Berkowitz, 1962; Berkowitz & Green, 1962).

Although there is considerable evidence that is consistent with this formulation (cf. Berkowitz, 1964), attempts to apply it to the consequences of movie aggression have led to somewhat ambiguous results (Berkowitz, 1965). Male college students were either angered or treated in a neutral fashion by a person who had been labeled either as a college boxer or a speech major. After this, the subjects witnessed either a prize fight or neutral film scene. It was found that the anger instigator received the greatest volume of aggression when the subjects had seen the prize fight and the anger instigator was said to be a college boxer; his label-induced association with the aggressive scene could have caused him to elicit aggressive responses from the men who were ready to act aggressively. However, there was also an indication that the label "boxer" could have strengthened the person's cue value for aggression regardless of the nature of the film witnessed by the subjects. This latter finding confirms the importance of the available target's cue value for aggression. But in the context of this study it raises a question as to whether the target's association with the observed violence had contributed to his aggression-eliciting properties. The present experiment is another test of the eliciting-cue hypothesis. This time, however, the association with the aggressive scene is varied by means of the available target's name rather than his supposed role.

## METHOD
### SUBJECTS

The subjects were 88 male undergraduates at the University of Wisconsin. Seventy-two of these people had volunteered from sections of the introductory psychology course in order to earn points counting toward their final grade. The remaining 16 subjects were recruited from an introductory sociology course several weeks later without offering any grade-increasing inducements and were distributed evenly among the eight treatment groups.

### PROCEDURE

Three independent variables were arranged in a 2 × 2 × 2 factorial design so that some subjects would be (a) angered, (b) by a person having a name-mediated association, (c) with an aggressive scene. When each subject arrived at the laboratory he was met by a peer (actually the experimenter's accomplice) and the experimenter. The first experimental treatment was carried out by asking the two men what their names were. For half of the cases the accomplice identified himself as *Kirk* Anderson while for the remaining men he said his name was *Bob* Anderson.

Following this, the experimenter said the experiment involved the administration of a mild electric shock and gave the subject an opportunity to withdraw from the study if he so desired. He then showed the men two rooms, one containing various sorts of apparatus which, he said, were instruments for giving and receiving electric shocks, and the second containing a motion picture projector and screen. In this latter room the experimenter described the experiment as dealing with problem-solving ability under stress. One person, and the experimenter indicated that the subject was to take this role, would have to work on a problem knowing the other person (the accomplice) would judge the quality of his solution. The accomplice would evaluate the subject's performance by giving the subject from 1 to 10 electric shocks; the poorer the solution the greater the number of shocks that the subject was to receive.

The accomplice then left to go into the room containing the electrical apparatus, and the subject was given his problem: to suggest how an automotive service station could attract new customers. Five minutes later the experimenter returned, picked up the subject's written solution, and strapped the shock electrode onto the subject's arm. He then left the room again, ostensibly to bring the subject's work to the other person for judging. One minute later the accomplice in the adjoining room administered either one shock (*nonangered* condition) or seven shocks (*angered* condition) to the subject. After waiting 30 seconds, the experimenter returned to the subject, asked him how many shocks he had received, and then administered a brief questionnaire on which the subject rated his mood on four separate scales.[1]

---

[1] The one shock given to the men in the nonangered conditions could have introduced a ceiling effect limiting the number of shocks administered in these conditions by defining what was the appropriate number. Contrary to this possibility, however, questionnaire findings indicate that the subjects receiving one shock were much less hostile toward the confederate than subjects getting seven shocks.

While the subject was responding to this form, the experimenter recalled the accomplice. Then as soon as the subject had finished, the experimenter said he would show the two men a brief film in order to study the effects of a diversion upon problem-solving effectiveness. Half of the subjects (*aggressive movie* condition) saw the fight scene from the movie *Champion*. The experimenter introduced this 7-minute film clip by giving them the "justified aggression" synopsis. According to earlier findings (Berkowitz & Rawlings, 1963), this context seems to lower inhibitions against aggression. Further, in the *aggressive movie-Kirk* condition the experimenter casually but pointedly remarked that the first name of the movie protagonist was the same as that of the other person, that is, the accomplice. This was done to make sure that there was a name-mediated connection between the experimenter's confederate and the witnessed violence when the accomplice was said to be "Kirk Anderson." The other half of the subjects were shown an equally long and exciting movie of a track race between the first two men to run the mile in less than 4 minutes.

Upon conclusion of the 7-minute film clip, the experimenter again sent the accomplice from the room with instructions to write his solution to the sale-promotion problem. The subject was informed that he would be given the other person's solution and then was to evaluate it by shocking the other person from 1 to 10 times. Five minutes later the experimenter brought the subject a written problem solution saying this was the other person's work but which was actually previously constructed to be standard for all conditions. He told the subject to shock the other person as many tmes as he thought appropriate. The experimenter then went to the control room to record the number and duration of the shocks supposedly being given to the accomplice.[2] After waiting 30 seconds, the experimenter returned to the experimental room and gave the sub-

ject the final questionnaire on which the subject indicated how much he liked the accomplice. When this form was completed the experimenter explained the deceptions that had been practiced upon the subject and asked him not to discuss the experiment with anyone else for the remainder of the semester.

## RESULTS
### EFFECTIVENESS OF THE EXPERIMENTAL MANIPULATIONS

Since the experiment depended upon the proper registering of the accomplice's name, the final questionnaire asked each subject to write down "the other person's" name. All 88 men were correct.

There also were several checks of the success of the anger induction. First, each subject was asked how many shocks he had received and, again, each person correctly recalled the number of shocks given to him. More directly relevant to the arousal of emotion, after receiving the shocks each subject also rated his mood on a brief four-item questionnaire. The only item yielding a significant effect by analysis of variance was the measure of how "angry" or "placid" the subject felt; the men given seven shocks reported themselves as being reliably angrier than the men shocked only once. There were no other significant differences. Table 1 presents the mean anger rating in each of the eight experimental conditions.

We might also note at this time the significant main effects for anger-nonanger on the final questionnaire. In comparison to the men getting only one shock, those people receiving seven shocks expressed a significantly lower preference for the accomplice as a partner in any subsequent experiment,

---

[2]Earlier studies in our program employed total shock duration as one of the aggression measures. Since this score obviously has a high positive correlation with number of shocks, we here experimented with another measure, mean shock duration. Our results with this score proved quite disappointing. There were negative correlations between shock number and the mean duration of each shock in six of the eight conditions, suggesting that a "law of least effort" may have been operating to some extent, and that this could have restricted the utility of the duration measure.

indicated a reliably weaker desire to know the accomplice better, and were significantly more opposed to him as a possible roommate. All in all, there can be little doubt that the seven shocks had made the subjects angry with the experimenter's accomplice. The findings obtained with these ratings and the earlier mood reports, also suggest that the confederate's name had not influenced either the subjects' level of felt anger or their attitudes toward this person.

## TEST OF THE AGGRESSION-EVOKING-CUE HYPOTHESIS

The primary measure of aggression in this experiment was the number of shocks administered by each subject. As we had expected, the men displaying the greatest number of aggressive responses were those who had seen the prize-fight film after they were provoked and who then had an opportunity to attack their frustrater named "Kirk Anderson." The accomplice's name had apparently caused him to be associated with the violent scene so that he could then elicit strong overt hostility from the people who, being angered, were primed to act aggressively. These subjects gave a significantly greater number of shocks than the men in any of the other conditions. The mean number of shocks in each condition is given in Table 2.

## OTHER QUESTIONNAIRE FINDINGS

We have already summarized the major findings obtained with the final questionnaire, administered after the subjects had given the accomplice the electric shocks; in

### TABLE 1
MEAN RATING OF FELT ANGER

| Accomplice's name | Aggressive film | | Track film | |
|---|---|---|---|---|
| | Angered | Nonangered | Angered | Nonangered |
| Kirk | 7.36$_a$ | 11.27$_b$ | 7.27$_a$ | 10.55$_b$ |
| Bob | 6.00$_a$ | 12.09$_b$ | 7.27$_a$ | 11.27$_b$ |

Note.—The lower the score the greater the felt anger. Cells having a subscript in common are not significantly different (at the .05 level) by Duncan multiple range test.

### TABLE 2
MEAN NUMBER OF SHOCKS GIVEN TO ACCOMPLICE

| Accomplice's name | Aggressive film | | Track film | |
|---|---|---|---|---|
| | Angered | Nonangered | Angered | Nonangered |
| Kirk | 6.09$_a$ | 1.73$_c$ | 4.18$_b$ | 1.54$_c$ |
| Bob | 4.55$_b$ | 1.45$_c$ | 4.00$_b$ | 1.64$_c$ |

Note.—Cells having a subscript in common are not significantly different (at the .05 level) by Duncan multiple range test.

general, at the end of the experiment the subjects still disliked the accomplice more after having received seven shocks from him than after getting only one shock. Aside from this, however, the pattern of condition differences obtained with the questionnaire data did not resemble the findings obtained with the shock measure. Many of the men could have become somewhat anxious or guilty after administering the electrical punishment. This reaction might have then affected the questionnaire responses—either decreasing or *intensifying* the verbal expressions of hostility (cf. Berkowitz, 1962, Ch. 8).

But we can make an assumption here that seems warranted in the light of other findings. Those people experiencing a strong instigation to aggression may display persistently strong aggressive responses over time, responses that are not quickly altered by anxiety-guilt reactions (cf. Berkowitz & Holmes, 1960, cited in Berkowitz, 1962, p. 96). Thus, if the final questionnaire ratings are, at least in part, expressions of hostility, the condition in which the strongest aggressive response tendencies had been activated should exhibit the highest positive correlation between shock number and questionnaire ratings. In order to test this reasoning four product-moment correlations were computed in each of the eight conditions: between the number of shocks given by each subject and his verbal expression of hostility on each of the four hostility items in the final questionnaire. A mean correlation was then obtained for each condition after first employing the $r$ to $s$ transformation. The results are shown in Table 3.

While none of the condition differences are statistically reliable, the general pattern is consistent with the shock data and our theoretical expectations. First, combining the four angered and the four nonangered groups, we find that 62.5% of the 16 correlations in the strongly provoked groups were positive but only 25% of the relationships in the nonangered conditions were in this direction ($r^2 = 4.58$, $p = .05$, if we treat the correlations within a group as independent events). Thus, strong anger arousal tended to produce relatively persistent hostile tendencies; the people exhibiting comparatively strong open aggression on the first occasion generally expressed a high level of aggression the next time measurements were obtained shortly afterwards.

Turning now to the specific theoretical expectations, Table 3 also shows that the condition having the highest mean positive correlation was the one predicted to have the strongest aggressive responses: the angered-aggressive film-Kirk group. The strong activation of aggression in this condition resulting from the combination of provocation and aggression-eliciting cues led to longer lasting aggressive response tendencies as well as the high volume of electrical attacks upon the accomplice.

These effects of the name attributed to the accomplice raised a further question. Did the name "Kirk" serve as an aggression-evoking cue after the subjects had seen Kirk Douglas being beaten in part because of prior attitudes? Disliked objects may have the cue properties enabling them to elicit aggressive responses from people who are ready to act aggressively (Berkowitz, 1962; Berkowitz & Green, 1962). It is conceivable, then, that the present college students had some negative attitudes toward the name "Kirk" and/or the actor Kirk Douglas which generalized to the accomplice, "Kirk Anderson." These attitudes could have facilitated the expression of open hostility toward Kirk Anderson. An additional investigation was conducted as an examination of this possibility. A sample of 44 male university students comparable to those who participated in the experiment was given a list of 14 masculine and feminine first names and was asked to indicate how much they liked or disliked each name on a 7-point scale. The results demonstrated that there were no particularly strong feelings connected with the name Kirk. Although the subjects tended to rate the name on the negative side of the scale (mean rating = 4.50), this mean rating was not significantly different from the neutral point ($p = .22$, one-tailed test).

These subjects, however, did tend to associate the name Kirk with Kirk Douglas. When asked on a subsequent form to write down what family names came to mind in response to each of the 17 first names, 40 of the 44 respondents listed the patronym "Douglas" after the first name Kirk. But while Kirk may be connected with a particular person, this individual is not necessarily disliked. This is indicated by the findings of a third questionnaire on which the respondents rated their attitudes toward each of 14 public figures. Kirk Douglas obtained a mean rating of 3.75 on the 7-point scales used in this instrument, a mean score which

**TABLE 3**

MEAN PRODUCT-MOMENT CORRELATION BETWEEN SHOCK NUMBER AND SUBSEQUENT QUESTIONNAIRE HOSTILITY

| Accomplice's name | Aggressive film | | Track film | |
|---|---|---|---|---|
| | Angered | Nonangered | Angered | Nonangered |
| Kirk | .37(4)[a] | —.09(1) | —.18(2) | —.15(1) |
| Bob | —.16(1) | —.27(1) | .10(3) | —.01(1) |

[a]The numbers in parentheses refer to the number of positive correlations of the four computed in each condition. One of the four positive correlations in the aggressive film-angered-Kirk condition attained statistical significance while none of the four remaining significant $r$'s were positive.

again is not significantly different from the neutral point.

## DISCUSSION

All in all, the above findings lend comparatively clear support to the theoretical analysis upon which the present study was based. Observed aggression, we have shown, does not necessarily lead to open aggression against anyone. Particular targets are most likely to be attacked, and these are objects having appropriate, aggression-eliciting cue properties. In the present case the target's cue value is derived from a label-mediated association with the witnessed aggressive scene—or more specifically, with the victim of the observed hostility. Having this association, the target evokes aggressive responses from the audience members who are primed to act aggressively and whose restraints against aggression are fairly weak.

But assuming the essential validity of this analysis, we can also raise a number of important unanswered questions. For one thing, did the accomplice draw the greatest number of aggressive responses from the people in the angered-aggressive film-Kirk group because of his connection with aggression *generally*, or because he was most closely associated with the *victim* of the observed violence? It is conceivable that an object's aggressive cue properties are derived fundamentally from the object's connection with aggressive behavior, whether these acts are given or received. Thus, if college boxers tend to draw stronger hostility than do speech majors, as seems to be the case (Berkowitz, 1965), this may be due to the former role's closer association with fighting in general. The same point can perhaps be made with regard to the presumed aggression-eliciting properties of disliked people. Here again the disliked object may somehow be associated with aggression.

A second question has to do with the frequently exciting nature of observed aggression. In addition to their specific content, violent scenes typically are fairly exciting. This excitement means, of course, that there is a relatively strong arousal state within the observer, and this high arousal level might well contribute to the strength of the aggressive responses elicited in the situation. There is a suggestion to this effect in the data summarized in Table 2. Looking at the mean number of shocks delivered to the accomplice "Bob," we can see that the angered subjects seeing the prize fight did not express reliably stronger hostility than the men witnessing the exciting track race. Other experiments have obtained a much more substantial difference when the same aggressive scene was compared with a less arousing neutral film (e.g., Berkowitz & Rawlings, 1963). The exciting nature of the prize fight might have contributed to the condition differences obtained in the earlier research. Whether this is true or not, however, film-engendered differences in degree of arousal cannot account for the present findings. The aggressive scene was probably not more exciting when the accomplice's name was Kirk than when he was called Bob. For that matter, as is shown in Table 1, the subjects did not feel greater anger toward Kirk than toward Bob.[3]

## REFERENCES

Bandura, A., and Walters, R. H. 1963. *Social learning and personality development.* New York: Holt, Rinehart & Winston.

Berkowitz, L. 1962. *Aggression: A social psychological analysis.* New York: McGraw-Hill.

Berkowitz, L. 1964. Aggressive cues in aggressive behavior and hostility catharsis. *Psychological Review* 71:104–122.

[3]An experiment by the present writers, conducted after this article went to press, indicates that associations with nonaggressive, exciting scenes do not increase the available target's aggresive cue properties. Subjects were made to be angry with a confederate, whose name in some cases was said to be either "Landy" or "Bannister," and then either saw the track race film or sat still for an equivalent time. For the people shown the track film the confederates never connected him either with the winner or loser in the observed race. The confederate did *not* receive more shocks after the track film than after the no-film treatment and regardless of whether or not his name connected him with the track film did not do so. The important association evidently is with an aggressive scene.

READING 39 — FILM VIOLENCE AND THE CUE PROPERTIES OF AVAILABLE TARGETS

Berkowitz, L. 1965. Some aspects of observed aggression. *Journal of Personality and Social Psychology* 2:359–369.

Berkowitz, L., and Green, J. A. 1962. The stimulus qualities of the scapegoat. *Journal of Abnormal and Social Psychology* 64:293–301.

Berkowitz, L., and Rawlings, E. 1963. Effects of film violence on inhibitions against subsequent aggression. *Journal of Abnormal and Social Psychology* 66:405–412.

Walters, R. H.; Thomas, E. L.; and Acker, C. W. 1962. Enhancement of punitive behavior by audio-visual displays. *Science* 136:872–873.

# READING 40

# Aggression Themes in a Binocular Rivalry Situation

**MARV MOORE**
**Colorado State University**

How do aggressive tendencies grow in children? Moore illustrates a cross-sectional approach to the study of aggression. The use of binocular rivalry is an ingenious method for examining the perception of aggression in children. His results indicate sexual differences and an age trend in the children's perception of aggression.

**QUESTIONS**

1. Does the phenomenon of binocular rivalry suggest that we see what we want to see or have been taught to see?

2. Moore suggests that the process of socialization changes aggressive expression, and that competition is one of the culturally reinforced expressions of aggression. Do you agree with this statement? Support your answer.

3. Moore states that there are "learned variant sensitivities of males and females to aggressive situations." What evidence supports this statement? Are there methodological criticisms to be considered here?

Several recent experimenters have studied the effects of presenting differentially meaningful figures simultaneously to both eyes by means of a stereoscope. Engel (1956) showed that a more familiar figure

This research was done as a master's thesis and supported by Grant F1-MH-20,820 from the National Institute of Mental Health, United States Public Health Service.

I would like to thank Charles Hanley for so helpfully serving as my thesis supervisor and Hans Toch for the use of his stereoscope while he was on sabbatical leave. I especially wish to thank them for their aid in editing and preparing this manuscript for publication.

(an upright face) will predominate in binocular rivalry over a less familiar figure (an inverted face). Using postage stamps with busts of persons such as John Adams as stimuli, Hastorf and Myro (1959) confirmed Engel's results. Bagby (1959) paired photographs of "Mexican" scenes and presented them to Mexican and American subjects. Cultural familiarity tended to determine which picture any given subject saw; whereas Mexicans tended to see the Mexican scenes, Americans more often reported the American scenes.

Toch and Schulte (1961) paired violent and neutral scenes in the stereoscope; subjects with 3 years of "Police Administration" training saw significantly more violent pictograms than a matched group of liberal arts students and a group entering the police training program. Shelley and Toch (1962) studied a group of institutionalized offenders using the same slides; they concluded that the tendency to perceive violence in the stereoscope was diagnostic of a tendency to behave in a troublesome manner. Berg and Toch (1964) showed prison inmates pictures including drives other than aggression (oral and sexual); each pair of stereoscope slides contained a "blatant" and a "socialized" form of drive expression. They confirmed Shelley and Toch's use of the stereoscope as a diagnostic indicator of impulsive behavior and were also able to discriminate between inmates classified by means of other psycho-diagnostic measures as either "impulsive" or "neurotic."

The studies described above tested implications of the general hypothesis that specific past experiences acquired under particular conditions or training sensitize a person to related content in the binocular rivalry situation. Elevated perception of violence, in particular, results from training which exposes one to violent material and in certain populations is positively correlated with the tendency towards aggressive acting out.

The present study investigates: the effects of differential socialization of the sexes on the perception of violence, and the relation of age to the perception of violence.

Clearly, males and females in Western cultures learn specific sex roles. One aspect of this socialization process where there is a noticeable difference between the sexes is the expression of aggressive behavior. Males learn to be more active, overtly aggressive, and socially assertive than females. Various investigations have both

**Figure 1.** Stereogram pair Number 1 used in this experiment.

documented these sex differences (e.g., MacFarlane, Allen, & Honsik, 1954) and demonstrated how these differences are acquired (e.g., Bandura & Walters, 1964).

Furthermore, the socialization of sex roles is a gradual and continual process from childhood through adulthood; the American youngster does not master the social expression of his drives in a day. It follows that sex-role training in the expression and control of aggression should differentially sensitize males and females to related content in the binocular rivalry situation, and the amount of sensitization should vary in some way with age.

Hypothesis 1. When presented with a paired series of violent/nonviolent stereograms in the binocular rivalry situation, males see more of the violent slides than females of the same age.

Hypothesis 2. When presented with a paired series of violent/nonviolent stereograms in the binocular rivalry situation, different age groups perceive different amounts of violence, regardless of sex.

## METHOD
### SUBJECTS

The subjects came from two sources. Some were drawn from three schools in the Waverly School District, a middle-class suburb near Lansing, Michigan: 15 boys and 15 girls were drawn from each of five grades (3, 5, 7, 9, and 11—ages 8, 10, 12, 14, and 16, respectively). Fifteen male and 15 female 18-year-old freshmen were obtained from introductory psychology classes at Michigan State University.

## APPARATUS

The apparatus was a modified stereoscope designed by Engel (1956). In the present experiment, light intensity was .2 candles/ft² for both fields. An interval timer attached to the stereoscope set exposure time of stimulus figures at .5 second throughout the study.

## STIMULUS FIGURES

Toch and Schulte's (1961) pairs of slides were used. Each "violent" slide was matched with a "nonviolent" slide of similar size and outline, covering roughly the same part of the visual field. See Figure 1 for an example. Content of the stereogram pairs was as follows:

1. Mailman-knifed man.
2. Man with suitcase-hanged man.
3. Farmer pushing plow-man with gun standing over dead person.
4. Man standing at microphone-man shooting self in head.
5. Man at drill press-man knifing another man.
6. Man showing another man a picture-man shooting another man.

## EXPERIMENTAL PROCEDURE

Subjects of both sexes in all six groups saw the six pairs of violent/nonviolent slides twice. On the second viewing the slide presented first on the right side was changed to the left, and vice versa. Thus each eye was exposed to all the possible figures. Order of presentation was randomized for *each* subject to control for any series effects.

To check whether the subjects reported what they actually saw, a pair of "lie slides" (two identical pictures of blatant violence) was presented after the 12 violent/nonvio-

lent exposures. Subjects who do not honestly report their perceptions should give a nonviolent description of the thirteenth pair. A few subjects in all age groups failed to give an accurate description of these lie slides; their scores were not used in the analysis, and enough other subjects were sampled in the needed groups to make the total usable ($N = 180$).

Subjects who needed glasses wore them. The experimenter dismissed a few subjects who had forgotten their glasses, as well as subjects who planned to obtain glasses because of a known visual problem.

After adjusting the stereoscope for optimal fusion, the experimenter gave subjects the following instructions:

> When I put the top down look into the eyepiece with both eyes open. You will see a picture flash on for a very short time. After you see the picture look away from the eyepiece, then tell me all you can about the picture; describe whatever you see. There are no wrong answers.

If at any point an inattentive subject stated that a pair of slides "just didn't make sense," he was told to "look carefully" and allowed a second trial; this seldom happened.

Verbatim responses were scored according to the standards below; Slide Pair 1 (see Figure 1) is used for the example in every scoring category.

| Points | Description |
| --- | --- |
| 2 | Clearly the violent stereogram is described by the subject, for example, "A man with a knife in his back." |

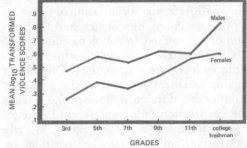

**Figure 2.** The perception of violence as a function of sex and age.

1   Fusion is described with a sensible percept including violent content (a compromise response), for example, "A mailman with a knife in his back."

1   Clearly the violent stereogram is described, but not in violent terms (a compromise response), for example, "A man with arms out in front and a stick out in the back."

0   Clearly the nonviolent stereogram is described by the subject, for example, "A mailman with pouch and letter in his hand."

0   Fusion is described with a sensible or incomprehensible percept, but *not* including violent content, for example, "A man running with his arms going in all directions."

Thus a subject could obtain a score from 0 (violence never reported) to 24 (violent slide reported on all 12 trials). Actual scores ranged from 0–11. Two persons independently scored all responses according to the above standards. The Pearson $r$ between the two sets of total violence scores of subjects was .98.

## RESULTS

The raw violence scores were transformed logarithmically (Base 10) to eliminate the correlation between grade means and variances. Figure 2 shows the mean transformed violence scores[1] for each grade tested. First, there was a difference between sexes at every grade level, and across grades the sex difference was significant at the .01 level ($F = 15.97$, $df = 1/168$). Second, the amount of violence perceived increased in a linear fashion for both sexes as age increased; both linear trends were significant at the .01 level (males, $F = 14.78$, $df = 1/84$; females, $F = 14.09$, $df = 1/84$).

## DISCUSSION

Both experimental hypotheses were confirmed. In the binocular rivalry situation males perceived significantly more violence

[1]Use of raw scores gives the same results.

than females over the grades sampled (*3, 5, 7, 9, 11,* and freshmen), and the increased sensitization to violence with age was demonstrated by statistically significant linear trends for both sexes.

One way to explain the sex differences in perceptual orientation to the world lies in learning theory. As Bandura and Walters (1964) have illustrated, such personality responses as the expression of dependency and aggression may be learned. For example, in gaining aggression control the child learns to discriminate object, form, and intensity appropriateness for expression of his anger. Such discriminations are learned and predictable under various schedules of positive and negative reinforcement and under conditions fostering imitation and modeling of significant others. Some of the most important discriminations that the child learns are the socially reinforced differences between the sexes in the expression of aggressive behavior. We are especially interested in the fact that males are taught, directly and indirectly, to be more overtly aggressive and assertive than females. Such sex-role training, as discussed by Bandura and Walters, could account for the differences in the perception of violence between sexes found at all ages in this study.

Why under the circumstances of this experiment does perception of violence increase regularly with age for both sexes? One interpretation is that subjects can, as a function of age, discriminate more clearly the vague features of the stimulus and/or verbalize better what they see. An analysis of subjects' responses to Slide Pair 13 (lie slides) in which identical stereograms were presented to each eye simultaneously provides negative evidence for the accuracy hypothesis. Table 1 shows the number of subjects accurately describing the lie slides for each grade tested. A cursory glance will convince the reader that there were no systematic or significant differences in accuracy between age (grade) levels.

**TABLE 1**

COMPARISON OF SUBJECTS ON DESCRIPTION
ACCURACY FOR SLIDE PAIR 13 (LIE SLIDE)

| Grade | Number of subjects out of 15 (group $N$) who described accurately Slide Pair 13 | |
|---|---|---|
| | Males | Females |
| 3 | 14 | 13 |
| 5 | 13 | 14 |
| 7 | 15 | 12 |
| 9 | 13 | 14 |
| 11 | 15 | 12 |
| Freshmen | 14 | 13 |

Assuming the accuracy hypothesis to be unverified, how is the linear age effect to be explained? Previous research suggests that the binocular rivalry technique is a direct measure of aggressiveness (Berg & Toch, 1964; Shelley & Toch, 1962). Assuming this knowledge to be true, we may conclude in the present study that as persons age they display more aggression or perceive the world as a more hostile place. As mentioned in relation to the sex differences in violence perception, socialization involves learning when and how to aggress. For example, children gain with age better control of anger, while at the same time they are taught to be competitive, and the older they are the greater the repertoire of responses approved as means of competition, In other words, aggression expression gets socialized with age from overt anger to more culturally reinforced avenues, particularly means of competition, which are instrumental to social adaptation. It seems, therefore, plausible that the developmental trends in this study are a reflection of culturally sanctioned "instrumental aggressiveness" increasing with age.

From the point of view presented in this paper socialization is similar to the process underlying the fact that advanced police-administration students reported seeing more violent stereograms than novices in the same training program (Toch & Schulte, 1961)—a process of education into the policeman's reality. As children mature they are educated into a reality that is a slow motion facsimile of the police training situation—a reality where they become increasingly familiar with the abundance of aggression loose in the world. Finally then, the sex and developmental differences found in this study represent learned variant sensitivities of males and females to aggressive situations and feelings which they must know about to operate effectively within a social and cultural context.

## REFERENCES

Bagby, J. A. 1959. A cross-cultural study of perceptual predominance in binocular rivalry. *Journal of Abnormal and Social Psychology* 54:33–34.

Bandura, A. B., and Walters, R. H. 1964. *Social learning and personality development.* New York: Holt, Rinehart & Winston.

Berg, S. D., and Toch, H. H. 1964. "Impulsive" and "neurotic" inmates: A study in personality and perception. *Journal of Criminal Law, Criminology, and Police Science* 55:230–234.

Engel, E. 1956. The role of content in binocular resolution. *American Journal of Psychology* 69:87–91.

Hastorf, A. H., and Myro, G. 1959. The effect of meaning on binocular rivalry. *American Journal of Psychology* 72:393–400.

MacFarlane, J.; Allen, L.; and Honsik, M. 1954. *A developmental study of the behavior problems of normal children between twenty-one months and fourteen years.* Berkeley: University of California Press.

Shelley, E. L. V., and Toch, H. H. 1962. The perception of violence as an indicator of adjustment in institutionalized offenders. *Journal of Criminal Law, Criminology, and Police Science* 53:463–469.

Toch, H. H., and Schulte, W. H. 1961. Readiness to perceive violence as a result of police training. *British Journal of Psychology* 52:389–393.

# READING 41

# Paradoxes of Student Protests

**ELI A. RUBINSTEIN**
**National Institute of Mental Health**

American students have involved themselves in social demonstrations and protests in the last few years. The following article by Rubinstein discusses some of the paradoxes involved in the students' actions. His viewpoint is, necessarily, one of a nonstudent, and his perceptions of the problems involved, and the means to solve them, can give the student insight into the feelings of the group attitudes that he represents.

## QUESTIONS

1. Do you think the paradoxes presented are valid?
2. What is the role(s) of the mass communication media in social protest? Have these media been precipitating causes of demonstrations in the grade schools and junior high schools?
3. Is it possible to study group behaviors (such as student protests) in a meaningful way? What are some of the problems involved? How can principles derived from one situation generalize to other situations?

Early in the spring of 1968 when I was approached about making this presentation on student protests, I hesitated, primarily because my credentials in this field were neither very solid nor of any long duration. Had I anticipated the increased number and

Invited address, Division of Clinical Psychology, at the meeting of the American Psychological Association, San Francisco, August 1968.

Eli A. Rubinstein is assistant director for Extramural Programs and Behavioral Sciences at the National Institute of Mental Health, Chevy Chase, Maryland.

intensity of national and international incidents in this area the past year, I would have been even more reluctant to add still one more set of interpretations to the many statements which are now being published on student protests.

Since the recent turmoil at Columbia University and the riots in Paris, almost every periodical, professional as well as popular, which might have any relevance to the topic of student unrest, has published one or more articles on the subject. From the *American Scholar* to *Barron's Financial Weekly*, there have been specific descriptions and general interpretations of student protests. It is perhaps a measure of the complexity of this phenomenon that with everything that has been written subsequent to Berkeley in 1964, and the more recent incidents at Columbia and other universities here and abroad, we have only the most superficial and obvious understanding of the dynamics of the process of confrontation which is involved in these student protests.

Social flux is so intense these days that it reveals new depths of our ignorance of social systems more rapidly than we are able to add new knowledge. It reminds me of the classic *New Yorker* cartoon in which the gas station attendant, trying to fill the gas tank of an unbelievably high-powered and luxurious automobile, says to the driver, "Would you please turn off the motor, you're gaining on me."

As I read about the succession of incidents on campuses throughout the country, and think about the insights and understanding that we as behavioral scientists can offer to assist in solving the problems, I have the same uneasy feeling that they are gaining on us. It was partly because of that uneasiness and the belief that behavioral scientists can improve understanding of this phenomenon, that a group of scholars in July 1968 at the Center for Advanced Study in the Behavioral Sciences published a recommendation for a national study to examine the individual and group patterns of response to student protests (Abrams et al., 1968).

I would like to take just a moment to describe the background to that recommendation. In 1967, at the Center for Advanced Study in the Behavioral Sciences, a small group initiated a seminar which was entitled "The College Environment as a Place to Learn." Original discussions were devoted to various aspects of the relationship

between the student and the institution which influence the learning experience. However, toward the end of the fall when student demonstrations began to occur on a number of college campuses around the country, we began to concentrate on that aspect of the college environment.

In keeping with the seminar format, and trying to take a somewhat different approach to an examination of student activism, we invited five college presidents—all from various California campuses—to come individually to meet with the seminar participants and give us their viewpoints on student activism. The five presidents included Robert Clark of San Jose State College, John Summerskill of San Francisco State College, Roger Heyns of the University of California at Berkeley, Dean McHenry of the University of California at Santa Cruz, and Louis Benezet of Claremont University Center. I will reveal my own biases when I characterize these five administrators as thoughtful, sensitive, and perceptive individuals who were aware of the stresses which now exist on the college campus and who were sincerely trying to respond to some of the demands being made by the student activists. It was the repercussions of those demands, incidentally, which forced John Summerskill to resign in the spring of 1968.

In preparation for meeting with these college presidents, a colleague and I visited six campuses around the country in February and March of 1968, on all of which some form of student demonstration had occurred. We interviewed representatives from the faculty, the administration, and the student body about student demonstrations on their respective campuses. At this point I must again mention the timing of my presentation here. My original intention in spring 1968 had been to use the meetings with the college presidents and my visits to the various campuses as a basis for commenting on some of the characteristics of student protests. Two things have happened since then which made me modify what I have to say. One, the events on campuses such as Columbia and in Paris have changed and intensified the situation somewhat and, two, a number of recent articles have discussed some of the points I had intended to make.

I would like, therefore, to touch on some of the more recent interpretations of student unrest, relate these to some of the things I have been involved in this past year, and then try to raise some additional questions about this most intriguing development among the youth of today.

In July 1967 a series of papers on student activism in the *Journal of Social Issues* presented a perspective on some of the research done since the Berkeley days. It is interesting to note that in a summary article Sampson (1967) equivocates on the "future of student activism," but he suggests that activism will not be maintained. The year of 1968 at least suggests otherwise.

And it is within this past year that the statements and articles on student activism have become too numerous to follow. It would be an interesting statistic to know how many college—and high school—commencement addresses in June of 1968 were on student protest or student power. My uninformed guess is that the vast majority were on some variant of that theme. And I would suspect that those addresses reflect an increasing degree of polarization on the subject. People are either for or against student protest per se. The issues on which the protests were initiated tend to be lost sight of in the intensity of the process of confrontation itself. It is not insignificant that the State Education Department in New York was recently reported as seeking an expert on college uprisings, who would be sent around to troubled campuses to interview persons involved in the riots.

The unanswered question in all this is what have been the factors which produced student protest? A number of themes run through much of the present literature.

Sampson (1967), in the summary paper I mentioned earlier, discussed a number of "activism inducing contexts." It is obvious that the factors are multiple and interrelated: The affluent family, the unresponsive university environment, the political and social climate, the ever-present mass media, Vietnam and the draft, and the usual problems of adolescence are all invoked as the basis for protests.

More recently, Halleck (1968) has written a paper which summarizes the various hypotheses identified as the basis for, or influence on, student activism. Interestingly enough, Halleck's paper reflects the kind of polarization in attitude I just mentioned. He divided his hypotheses into groups, one of which he calls the "critical hypotheses." These are the hypotheses which find student activism a function of something which is wrong with the student protesters themselves; this would include permissive upbringing, too much affluence, or some family pathology. A second grouping of hypotheses is sympathetic to the student, finding him a victim of or a crusader against some external circumstance. This would include the war in Vietnam, the deterioration in the quality of life and the problems of civil rights. And finally, Halleck has a group of neutral hypotheses, which include impersonal processes such as increased technology, mass media, and reliance on scientism. Halleck believes the neutral hypotheses are the most persuasive in understanding the student unrest.

Other recent writings have made an even more sweeping examination of the entire Zeitgeist and tried to describe youth in general from a broad overview of our times. Rovit (1968) has written a very scholarly piece on "the contemporary apocalyptic image" in which he traces the history of the metaphor of the Apocalypse, and tries to relate it to the development of the newer revolutionary or radical thinking. He suggests, in language appropriately dramatic for the theme he is exploring, that we may very well be on the brink of a brand new epistemology—a new technique and concept of rationality which may build on the advances of binary computation, field theory, and games theory and include the irrationalities of extra-sensory perception, mental telepathy, hallucinogenic drugs, and other open-ended, nonteleological modes of understanding. This, of course, does not mean that man and his world have changed in any cardinal, unnatural way. Men will continue to be born, to suffer, and to die. The constants of human experience will remain inevitable and constant. But the dominant metaphor from which man draws his meanings and values may be in the throes of an explosive transformation [pp. 466–467].

Rovit retreats, however, from this apocalyptic metaphor, and ends by saying "the magic of man may after all lie in his capacity to enter into and exit from the metaphors that seek to capture him in rigid definitions. The ideal of polymorphous perversity—an ideal of complete fluidity—can be as inflexible and inhuman as any other absolute [pp. 467–468]."

Keniston (1968), in a more direct effort to identify basic characteristics of today's young radicals, stresses the importance of *style*. He too sees fluidity and flux as a major attribute and believes that the way the younger generation approaches the world reveals more communality than their actual behavior. With the emphasis on change, it is difficult to find common or constant ideologies.

However, Keinston's central thesis—in its way as broad as Rovit's—is that the most important variable influencing the behavior of these young individuals is the threat of violence and their sensitivity to this issue. He believes "the issue of violence is to this generation what the issue of sex was to the Victorian world [p. 242]."

I would like to focus down from that level of broad generalization and touch on the dilemmas inherent in the process of protest itself. To this observer the student protesters reveal an unusual mixture of righteousness and wrongishness. This is exemplified in what I would call paradoxes of protest. I will cite just four. Many more could be found.

Perhaps the most central and prevalent paradox is that in the very effort to uphold their individual freedom the student activists forcibly abridge the freedom of others. It is on one or another variation of this point that university administrators have taken their stand. Almost uniformly, dissent has been permitted without punitive retaliation up to the point where college programs are disrupted or suspended, through acts of violence or coercion.

This point gets to the heart of the philosophy of the new left which is, interestingly enough, now being attacked by some of the social and political commentators whose earlier writings influenced the young activists. Thus, Paul Goodman (1968), the social critic, recently wrote on anarchism as a political framework for today's protesting students. At one point he does say, "The protesting students are anarchists because they are in an historical situation to which anarchism is their only possible response [p. 13]." However, he criticizes both the new left and the hippies because their philosophy ends up in the same kind of power struggle that they are presumably rebelling against.

I saw this dilemma regarding individual freedom acted out on a much smaller stage at one of the colleges I visited in the spring of 1968. Two of the students that I interviewed presented the opposing points of view very clearly. One student, who had sat in on a Dow demonstration, explained that for him it was a symbolic action that he had undergone because of his own personal conscience. He had made a moral judgment on genocide and felt that this was the only way he could express his point of view. All during the actual sit-in, which, incidentally, turned out to be less moral and less symbolic than he had anticipated, he was ambivalent about his action but did not leave for fear of disrupting the effect of the group behavior. The other student who had not sat in pointed out that he felt himself just as much involved in a moral judgment, but that it had been his position to consider the issue of freedom of choice more important than the issue of genocide. He did not want to do anything which would deny that freedom of moral judgment to others in pursuing their own moral conscience. Both students admitted the obvious conflict of moral issues and recognized that other students would decide in whichever direction they felt the moral value to be the greater.

The dilemma inherent in this situation was described in forceful language by Allen Wallis (1967), the president of the University of Rochester, at the time of their Dow demonstration:

> To a community devoted to the life of the mind, carried on through reasoned discourse, persuasion and dialogue, nothing is more repugnant than coercion. Even the use of coercion to prevent coercion is abhorrent to us, not only in any specific instance, but because both reason and experience show the dangers of using coercion to protect freedom. We must recognize, however, that we may find ourselves face to face with the dilemma that through the ages has faced groups devoted to the free and peaceful life. The dilemma is that a small group which is determined to have its view prevail, even at the cost of obstruction and coercion, can guarantee that freedom and peace cannot both prevail. Such a willful group can certainly destroy one or the other temporarily.

Still another paradox is to be found in the intellectual antiintellectualism and the dogmatic antidogmatism. It is perfectly obvious that most of the student activists are, by definition as college students, considerably above average in intelligence. The leaders tend to be the brighter students in the better schools and if they are anything they are articulate.

One of the best examples of both the articulateness and the dogmatism can be found in reading a report of a conference held in August 1967 at the Center for the Study of Democratic Institutions at Santa Barbara. The conference, titled "Students

and Society," was attended by 22 student leaders from universities around the country (Center for the Study of Democratic Institutions, 1968). At various points in the discussion, almost every American institution and ideology came under scathing criticism. One of the participants said, "I believe there is something fundamentally wrong with this country, and the wrong is caused by the institutions of this country. I sincerely believe that the institutions of this country must be destroyed [p. 26]." And a variation of this statement was repeated a number of times during the course of the three-day conference. One of the student participants himself best characterized the doctrinaire nature of this kind of extreme criticism:

> Disruption of constructive dialogue results in intellectual dogmatism. Students, for example, who refuse to form a coalition, except on their own terms, who refuse to compromise at any level, frustrate the dialogue even while they labor under the illusion of communication. The refusal to listen, the intransigent style, the extremist position, the total conviction of one's own righteousness—all characterize the authoritarian personality and the lust for power. These are the very traits which the young find repugnant in adults [p. 41].

He goes on to point out that today's students will have to give way soon to a new generation of students whose ideas will again be different and that the only sensible way to continue a process is to establish a dialogue which permits communication with those who will follow.

A third paradox is that in the rebellion against what the activists see as an authoritarian and unresponsive politicized society they find themselves engaged in all kinds of complex political strategies and tactics. It is this aspect which troubles those student activists who are not part of the very extreme and very active core of the new left. While the Students for a Democratic Society (SDS) has successfully sponsored the major demonstrations of the past year, many of the idealist students with less extreme viewpoints are not in favor of the tactics of the demonstrations. Thus, a recent survey by Barton (1968) on the Columbia crisis shows that, while 51% of the faculty and 58% of the students were for the goals of the demonstration, only 10% of the faculty and 19% of the students supported the tactics.

The last dilemma I want to mention that relates to students is one that is difficult to label. It probably comes under the heading of "no matter what you do you can't win!" And this goes both for the students and the groups and institutions against which they are struggling. On the one hand, the students do want a confrontation. They want something definite and unyielding against which to resist. Today the so-called sincere liberal among the older population is probably, for the militant activist, the most scorned and the most detested of the adult types with whom they deal. As one activist student at a western state college said, "I know who my enemy is. He is the 'sincere liberal.' You talk to him and he agrees with everything you say and then he doesn't do a damn thing." At the same time, of course, if a college president, for example, takes a firm stand, such as Pusey at Harvard or Wallis at Rochester, the students view him as a perfect example of the entrenched establishment.

What happens when the institution provides the kind of environment that most, if not all, of the student body desires? The contrast between the situation at a prestigious eastern university and an equally prestigious eastern institute of technology gives some suggestion of an answer. The disenchantment of the students at the university is not duplicated in the environment of the institute of technology. As a matter of fact the faculty and administration in the institute of technology seem genuinely interested in encouraging the students to be more active and more involved in other than their strictly academic pursuits. At this institution there are no parietal regula-

tions and the student body has a great deal of freedom. Furthermore, the institute, by virtue of its areas of specialization, provides for its students faculty models with whom the students can identify. In fact, the students identify so well with the role of a professional technician that both the faculty and the administration are working very hard to see that the students enlarge their view beyond that of just becoming a competent electrical engineer, biophysicist, or the like.

It is in this kind of climate that the following remarks were made in a final editorial of the outgoing editor of the student newspaper.

> The administration is not guilty of denying students their rights, of suppressing them, or halting their actions. It is guilty of a system far more subtle and hence far less easy to detect or combat than any heavy-handed establishment. The administration has made a second-class partner of the student and especially of the so-called student leaders. But in forming the facade of partnership the students have not realized the consequences of their pact, nor have they been aware of the price they pay. The administration has crucified the students on a cross of responsibility. It has made incompetence (in the narrow, bureaucratic sense of the word) a cardinal sin.

He goes on to say that the newspaper itself has had excellent cooperation from the administration but then interprets this as follows:

> The subtle favors granted—mailing rights through institute mail, briefings by the president from time to time, phone calls on important occasions—all work a subtle, unconscious allegiance to the administration's point of view. Such an allegiance is a more effective censor than any brute coercion.

In talking to the Dean of Students at the institute about the attitudes expressed in this editorial, I was told that he and other members of the administration were somewhat perplexed. His explanation was that the editor was expressing the frustration of the students at not having an issue on which to have a confrontation with the administration. I suspect the editor may have just finished reading Marcuse's (1965) now-famous article on "repressive tolerance."

These four paradoxes, which I have lightly touched on: one, the coercive efforts to uphold freedom; two, the highly intellectual form of the antiintellectualism; three, the political nature of the attack against today's politics; and four, the struggle to find a basis for confrontation, even in the most permissive of environments, are neither new nor of themselves the major variables in this phenomenon of student protest. I have not touched on any of the aspects of student activism which are not a function of the students themselves, but of the situation in which they find themselves and the people with whom they have to deal.

In this latter set of categories, a great deal more is now being written both as it relates to society at large, and to the state of the university in particular. The latter topic, for example, has been addressed in a recent issue of the *American Behavioral Scientist*, which is devoted to "The State of the University: Authority and Change" and includes a number of articles by a group of scholars using the history of the past four years at the University of California at Berkeley as their point of departure (Kruytbosch & Messinger, 1968).

In these articles, and in other recent examinations of the academic institutions, such as that of Jencks and Reisman (1967), the pressure for student participation in university governance is seen as a major force for change on campus. Jencks and Reisman point out that conflict on campus is not new. It was equally widespread at various times in the eighteenth and nineteenth centuries. What is a departure from the older confrontations, they believe, is the challenge to the legitimacy of adult authority. The distrust of the older generation has been the result of massing together, in colleges and high schools, very large numbers of young people whose common social background and generalized feelings of discontent have produced deep distrust of the adult generation.

The size of the student body is one aspect of the present state of the university which was mentioned in my visits around the country by almost everyone as a major source of the present tensions on campus. The growth of the college population in recent years has been phenomenal. By 1970, it will have doubled from the level it had reached in 1960! Another way of looking at it is to note the increasing proportion of 18- to 24-year-olds who are and will be going into our colleges and universities. In 1950, it was approximately 15%; in 1970 it is expected to be around 30%, and projections, tentative as they may be for 1985, indicate 40%. This rate of growth, in the face of an increasing population of 18- to 24-year-olds, makes for a staggering expectation. The effect of this one characteristic alone is extremely significant.

In the first chapter of his book entitled *The Revolt of the Masses*, the Spanish philosopher, Ortega y Gasset (1932), talks about the fact of agglomeration and points out that towns are full of people, houses full of tenants, hotels full of guests, trains full of travelers, cafés full of customers, and so on. He says, "What previously was in general no problem, now begins to be an everyday one, namely to find room." After tracing the impact of that circumstance, Ortega y Gasset ends his book with the following statement:

The youth, as such, has always been considered exempt from doing or having done actions of importance. He has always lived on credit. It was a sort of false right, half ironic, half affectionate, which the no longer young conceded to their juniors. But the astounding thing at present is that these take it as an effective right, precisely in order to claim for themselves all those other rights which only belong to the man who has already done something. Though it may appear incredible, youth has become a *chantage*. We are, in truth, living in a time when this adopts two complementary attitudes—violence and caricature. One way or the other, the purpose is always the same, that the inferior—the man of the crowd—may feel himself exempt from all submission to superiors [p. 189].

It would be easy to dismiss this interpretation by pointing out that it was written some 35 years ago. In fact, immediately after the Berkeley Free Speech Movement (FSM) events in 1964, there was a sufficient positive reaction on that campus and others to the developments of that particular effort so that any misgivings about the extreme nature of the protest were lost in the sympathetic acceptance of the students' struggle against the inefficiencies and inequities in the university structure.

More and more, however, as additional incidents occur on other campuses and as individuals and groups who began in sympathy with the student protests find their own institutions threatened, there is an increasing reaction to the student protest movement. In January 1968, George Kennan (1968), the former ambassador to Russia, wrote a brief commentary in the *New York Times Magazine* called "Rebels Without a Program." It was published the day before I visited one of the eastern private universities and every faculty member and administrator on the campus with whom I spoke that Monday had read the article and was quoting from it. In it Kennan expressed his sympathy with the idealistic roles of the student activists, but he was sharply critical of the means they were using to achieve presumed goals.

The sequence of events in the past year accompanying some of the student protests has increased this kind of reaction. It is interesting to note the point at which each group of sympathetic faculty and older revolutionaries find their unwillingness to continue to support the more extreme student activities. A good example is a law professor, an active advisor to the local SDS chapter at a very liberal midwestern state university, who was appalled that the student activists made a mockery of a moot court trial of the student demonstrators involved in the protest at that university.

At this point, you may well ask what is the direct relevance of all this to clinical psychologists—especially when the author himself was trained as a clinical psychologist? I want to point out that I have deliberately omitted any suggestion that student protest is related to individual pathology, although some of the student activists are undoubtedly acting out certain personal problems. The spread and impact of student protests at the present time make them much more a sociological and a political phenomenon than a psychological one. And yet, one of the most powerful attributes that seems evident now is, in fact, psychological in nature. What seems to underlie much of the force and vitality of these student protests is the sense of drama, the feeling of participation, and the excitement of being caught up in a group experience.

In a very vivid recent description of the FSM at Berkeley, Michael Rossman (1968), who played a prominent role in the 1964 events, described those days as having been "distinguished throughout by a fierce joy." There was a real sense of the theatre. More recently, one of my colleagues at the Center for Advanced Study in the Behavioral Sciences, who had been in Paris during the Paris student riots, emphasized how strongly the student participants felt that they were reenacting revolutionary days. There was a great deal of play acting, and overhanging all the events was the sense of history that this was where revolution had occurred in previous generations. The lecture halls in the Sorbonne were crowded all day and all night and it was a period of feverish and emotional general debate for all (Laslett, 1968). The activists themselves use such description at times. Rossman (1968), in the description of the FSM events mentioned a moment ago, talks about "a theatre of affirmation in joyful disruption; a theatre of social therapy."

Combine this social therapy with the violence of the confrontation and the implicit intent to shake up this society with the romantic expectation that the structure will somehow reorder iself into a more effective network of interrelationships and it would not be too far fetched to compare this with some kind of mass electroshock therapy. The convulsive nature of this kind of therapy is evident in the heat of the confrontation and the demonstration itself. What is not so clear, perhaps, is the subtle way in which this so-called therapeutic process is misinterpreted as being in itself an important and constructive way of life. There is a kind of reversal of figure and ground here. The confrontation itself is viewed as a most meaningful educational experience. The drama, the pseudo-event, all take on more significance than the day-by-day existence against which this is a reaction. Thus, the theatrical becomes reality and reality is dismissed as outmoded.

There is an interesting corollary to this reversal in the world of the theatre itself. Walter Kerr (1968), the well-known drama critic, who seems to be developing misgivings about today's advanced drama, wrote a recent commentary on the "delusion about illusion." He seems to be saying that the effort to make theatre as close to reality as possible and at the same time impress on the audience that everyone on the stage is really acting is a back and forth shuttling of identities which ignores the fact that the audience can never really be convinced of the reality of the play and does not need to be reminded of the reality of the players.

So, too, the student activists are deluding themselves if they believe confrontation is really living while at the same time taking refuge in their role as students. This kind of thinking was exemplified in a comment to me by one of the students at a midwestern university. At the end of a rather long and strong argument by the students in favor of student activism, he came up to say goodbye and said smilingly, "Don't take us too seriously, we're just students."

What all of this suggests is that with everything that is being written today, the major finding about student protests today is that we really have not been able to keep up with the fast-developing events in this process. I suspect that some of you have personal experiences with college students in your own family whose actions and views have left you at least a bit perplexed. In fact, it is just the children of parents in our category—professionals, well educated, liberal, and interested in society—who make up much of the student protest group. Lots of statements are being made about this phenomena, but careful studies of the process of confrontation itself are still very few in number.

In the recent paper in *Science* from the Behavioral Sciences Center, it was pointed out that there were a number of assertions being made about activism which had little or no nationwide data to support them (Abrams et al., 1968). These assertions relate to the numbers of students involved, the causes of the demonstrations, and the manner in which the demonstrations on campus actually proceed. It was suggested in the paper that

these assertions and many others that are now being made, need to be examined in broad perspective, and, in the light of recent events, the dynamics of protest itself need to be examined and understood. How does a handful of students enlist an increasing number of students and faculty in the sequence of events that occur during a student protest? Who stays and who leaves during the sequence of events in a campus crisis? In what way does the response by faculty, by administrators, and by the rest of the student body influence the process?

The entire matter of communication is a key variable. What is the nature of communication during the protest and after? What role do the communication media play in these demonstrations?

There are broad aspects of behavior and social process that need to be examined. If student unrest is a form of social movement, how are students recruited into it? What are some of the underlying value commitments? In what way does protest influence the future of those who participate? [p. 22]

While these and other questions are being addressed in some of the individual studies that have been done and are now being done, this entire phenomenon deserves a much more comprehensive examination, based on fact rather than opinion.

Is there any way of summarizing the present status of student protests? I think not. The situation continues to be extremely fluid. The forces that, on the one hand, are striving to contain student protests and those that are, on the other hand, stimulating new episodes are perhaps more polarized than they were a year ago. But for those university campuses that have not had a serious student protest it all remains somewhat academic until it actually occurs.

Not only are we in a period of rapid social change, but the effects of that change are amplified by the network of almost instantaneous communication that now surrounds the lives of all of us. Within hours after Martin Luther King is assassinated, the psychic shockwave is felt throughout the nation, leaving a frightening aftermath. Today's communication media by their visual and oral impact are undoubtedly influencing behavior. The full extent of that influence has not been evaluated. For example, what is the effect of the fact that among all the other kinds of worlds we live in, this is the world of instant replay. No sooner does something happen than it is predigested and regurgitated by the communication media as a new stimulus on top of the original real event. An example of this kind of instant regurgitation occurred on April 9, 1968, at 11:30 p.m., when the National Broadcasting Company (1968) had a special program entitled, "Ten Days in April." The program recapped the events beginning with President Johnson's announcement that he would not run, and included a review of the Martin Luther King assassination and the subsequent riots.

There is a paradox in that little incident which relates back to the paradoxes of student protest and which brings me to my final point. On the one hand, it is obviously grandiose and slightly premature to broadcast a program on April 9th, even at 11:30 p.m., which is entitled "Ten Days in April" and yet, at the same time, it was not only done but, within the constraints I have just indicated, it was done not too badly.

I would like to suggest that for many of the activist students there is the same grandiosity and impatience and yet within the constraints of what they are attempting they also manage to pull it off to some extent. The basic problem that we all face, however, is that there is a serious discontinuity between what the students believe they are trying to do and what actually seems to be happening.

In an earlier draft of this paper, I wanted to demonstrate another aspect of discontinuity by the very process of my presentation. I intended to give literally two talks simultaneously—a verbal presentation somewhat similar to the one I am giving now, and a visual presentation of a series of slides on a totally different topic, namely, mental health manpower. I was going to end my talk by trying to suggest in a kind of "the medium is the message" approach that this kind of disjunction is the way the student activists view the disparity between what they are told about their college education, and the way they actually see it. The two versions do not relate. It is for them truly a *double talk*.

That was one side of the message I wanted to give in that two-sided presentation. It was not too profound. I wanted to suggest something else, however, which I believe is somewhat less obvious.

In one of the many popularized accounts of the meaning of student activism, Irving Kristol (1965), who is himself a veteran of the old Left, sees these students as bored and totally unenthusiastic with the prospect of moving into a nice neat safe life in our present bureaucratic society. They have no difficulty in coping with the complexities of the organizational state. They are quite competent to deal with the IBM world they despise. They just do not see it as an exciting challenge. And, I think here, with apologies to Marshall McLuhan, "the tedium is the message."

It is too easy either to be sympathetic and supportive of the somewhat romantic idealism of some of the student activists, or, on the other hand, to be sternly reproving of the methods that they are using in their efforts to be heard and responded to. Thus, they are called by one author a "prophetic minority," and, in contrast, "rebels without a program."

What is important in all of this is that these characterizations, positive and negative, result from the fact that student activists are doing more than just being students. And here everyone seems to agree that the current generation of college students is far and away the most competent, the best prepared, and the most dedicated. The student activists are often, although not always, from among the best students in their school. They can do more than they are being asked or allowed to do in their present status as college students.

They can look and listen to two distinct messages and get something out of both. In that sense the theatrical and the real can be mutually supportive rather than disjunctive.

If I may apply today's cliché term "rising expectations" to the student activists themselves, we should expect them to rise to the opportunity of helping us all find a way to be responsive to these seemingly disparate elements and, more importantly, to find some meaningful relationships among them. And this purpose requires a continuing reevaluation of what is said and what is seen, by them and by all the rest of us.

## REFERENCES

Abrams, M. H., et al. 1968. Student protests: A phenomenon for behavioral sciences research. *Science* 161 (3836): 20–23.

Barton, A. H. 1968. *The Columbia crisis: Campus, veterans, and the ghetto.* New York: Bureau of Applied Social Research, Columbia University.

Center for the Study of Democratic Institutions. 1968. Students and society. *Center Occasional Paper,* vol. I, no. 1. Santa Barbara, California.

Goodman, P. 1968. The black flag of anarchism. *New York Times Magazine,* July 14, pp. 10–12.

Halleck, S. L. 1968. Hypotheses of student unrest. Address to American Association for Higher Education, March 4, Chicago, Illinois.

Jencks, C., and Reisman, D. 1967. The war between the generations. *The Record* 69 (1): 1–21.

Keniston, K. 1968. Youth, change, and violence. *The American Scholar* 38:227–245.

Kennan, G. F. 1968. Rebels without a program. *New York Times Magazine,* January 21, pp. 1–4.

Kerr, W. 1968. The delusion about illusion. *New York Times,* July 21, pp. 1–3.

Kristol, I. 1965. What's bugging the students. In *The troubled campus.* Boston: Atlantic.

Kruytbosch, C. E., and Messinger, S. L., eds. 1968. The state of the university: Authority and change. *American Behavioral Scientist* 11 (5): 1–48.

Laslett, P. 1968. The Paris revolt. Informal address at Center for Advanced Study in the Behavioral Sciences, Stanford, California.

Marcuse, H. 1965. Repressive tolerance. In *Critique of pure tolerance,* ed. R. Wolff. New York: Beacon.

National Broadcasting Company. 1968. Special news program, April 9.

Ortega y Gassett, J. 1932. *The revolt of the masses.* New York: Norton.

Rossman, M. 1968. Breakthrough at Berkeley. *The Center Magazine* 1 (4): 40–49.

Rovit, E. 1968. On the contemporary apocalyptic imagination. *The American Scholar,* pp. 453–468.

Sampson, E. E. 1967. Student activism and the decade of protest. In Stirrings out of apathy, ed. E. E. Sampson. *Journal of Social Issues* 23 (3): 1–33.

Wallis, W. A. 1967. Statement before College Cabinet, University of Rochester, Rochester, New York, November 6.

# READING 42

# From the Ashes: A Personal Reaction to the Revolt of Watts

**JIMMIE SHERMAN**

The following article is an example of a reactional biography. Jimmie Sherman describes for us his feelings and motivations before the Watts revolt. The changes he underwent as a result of this revolt—his experiences and insights—can give the reader an understanding of how a person can be affected by his environment and environmental changes.

### QUESTIONS

1. What kind(s) of insight into the problems of minority groups can a reactional biography give the reader?
2. Are answers to discrimination and the problems surrounding this social issue to be found in the realm of psychology? Explain your answer.
3. This biography is reminiscent of the old Horatio Alger stories. Is an environment of poverty and conflict necessarily "bad"? What kinds of advantages can be found in this kind of environment?

## I

The year 1965 marked a change in many people's lives. For some, it was a year of tragedy; for others, it was just a passage of time. But for the people of Watts, it was the year that was. The year that had to be and finally came. It was the year that all patience wore thin, and Watts burned to the ground.

For many people, it marked the beginning of a new day—a new era. An era that was such a long time coming, and a long time cried for. An era in which Watts would start to progress along with other communities in this fast-moving society. Prior to August of that year, Watts, like other ghettos in this land, stood motionless in a world that sped by too fast and too unconcerned to even take notice. While rockets were being launched for Mars and the moon, and the Vietnam situation was taking a new shift, and the budgets were reaching new heights by the day, we of the ghettos went hungry and were dying in filth and poverty.

Crime was as common as unemployment, and need was always present. Young men stole and sold dope, and young ladies went into shoplifting and prostitution, in order to survive. Teenagers hung around on street corners in packs, smoking weed, drinking wine, and fighting, because there was nothing to do and no place to do it in. And the schools? Schools were just institutions that even the teachers cared little about.

When our cries for better schools, better housing, fair employment, a hospital, and better police community relations were ignored, our many frustrations mounted. Then, after a period of years (each year worse than the last) we exploded. It was like a keg of dynamite that only took one match—one incident—to set it off, and any one thing or anybody could have lit the fuse.

When it happened, tempers burst and buildings went up in flames. Cars were smashed and turned over in the street. People crusaded through the night, burning, looting, throwing rocks, bricks, and Molotov cocktails, and screaming, "Burn, baby burn!" Sirens cried out everywhere, speeding from one uprising to another, fire to fire, and casualty to casualty. And for four straight days the city was in a state of shock and confusion.

## II

The facts were there
The dreams were gone
The deadly viper listened on.

I never thought that I would become a writer. I never really believed that I would ever be anything. I only knew that I wanted to be something.

As a child I used to dream of being a great man when I got big. I wanted to be a general, a lawyer, a man who flew those big shiny planes. I wanted to be lots of things —not just one. I even wanted to be President. But sadly enough, dreams withered with time, and age brought me closer to reality—a reality I wanted no part of. I began to notice many things around me— things I did not like, but could do nothing about. I noticed my mother going out to the white folks' houses, scrubbing their floors and serving their food every day. I realized that my father, the man I idolized and imitated, had been cleaning sewers all of his life and getting nowhere. I even heard a white man call him "boy" a couple of times. That really made me mad. It made him mad, too. But what could he do but take it? I noticed the old shacky house we lived in— the cold splintered floors, the torn curtains, the broken chairs we sat in, the pie pans and jelly jars we ate and drank from. I noticed the roaches crawling on the walls, across the floors, and breeding all over the house, and the junk and the trash that piled up and scattered in the yard. And for the first time, I realized that I was in poverty.

Then I discovered that we weren't the only family in that bag. My friends were in bad shape, too. Their parents were also servants, and they were living on beans and and hand me downs, just as we were. And I discovered that being black had something to do with it.

I became angry—very angry. I started to rebel. I rebelled against everybody—parents, teachers, anybody—I didn't care. School no longer meant anything to me, and home was just another place to get away from. I started smoking cigarettes—both kinds, tobacco and marihuana. I drank wine, picked fights, and learned to gamble. I did everything that I possibly could to say, "I don't care."

People tried to talk to me but I didn't want to listen, because they were talking that same old stuff about going to school and being somebody some day. To me, that was just a bunch of bull, and they couldn't tell me nothin'.

The only person who could talk and make me listen was my grandmother, an old lady who needed an ear to fill. We used to talk all the time, for hours, sometimes a whole day. She used to tell me of the old days and of how things were then. She told me of old superstitions that she and people of her day believed, and stories of strange things that happened to her and those she knew. It was just like being there, and she had my undivided attention. After the story or lecture she would conclude with a wise saying. She would say something like: "So that jus' goes t' show yuh, boy—never whip a dawg an' pet a cat," or, "A man ain't free when somethin's ailin' 'em." Finally she would ask, "What's ailin' you today?" And I would tell her. She always had a remedy or a ready-made solution, and her advice was nearly always good.

Immediately after turning seventeen I took her advice and joined the service. I had to get away for a while, because even I knew that I had to change. I spent three years in the army—three years of changing, and three years of learning that a black soldier had it rough and that discrimination was in there too.

When my three years were finally over, I was honorably discharged and ready to take another stab at civilian life. I had decided while I was in that when I got out I would get two jobs, make a lot of money, and go into business for myself. But I was soon disillusioned. I looked all over town for work. I searched the want ads through and through. I phoned places, wrote places, and went for scores of interviews, but no one was hiring. Those who were, weren't hiring Negroes. And those who were hiring Negroes wanted experience. No one wanted a man who had no skills.

### III

"You's a good boy, Sammy Lee,"
Missa Charley said.
Den 'e rubbed an' patted me
Ri' chea on dah head.
I grinned an' showed em all my teeth
An' said, "Y' thank yuh boss."
I kept my feelins down beneath
Dis happy shinin' gloss.

I nevah lakt dat good boy stuff
'Cause I knows what 'e means.
Long as I can mop an' buff
An 'cept a plate of beans,
Long as I say, "Yassm boss,"
An' make lak um in joy,
Wit' dis happy shinin' gloss
Den um a good boy!

Finally I found a job at a downtown clothing factory. I worked as a shipping clerk, making minimum wages. I worked there for two weeks and found that I couldn't save any money, so I quit and found another low-paying job, then another. Within the span of one year (from February 1964 to February 1965) I went from shipping clerk to stock clerk to used car salesman to janitor to unloading potato trucks. Then I weakened and went to the unemployment lines. I had completely given up.

I abandoned all plans for going into business. I started drinking wine and smoking pot again, and hanging around the pool hall all day with other guys who had also given up. I found myself bumming pennies, nickles, and dimes from people passing on the street, not for wine or dope, but for a candy bar or something sweet to spoil my appetite. I felt pretty low. I felt like a dog who had no bone, or a boy who had never graduated to manhood. I felt sorry for myself—very sorry and very ashamed and unnecessary. I felt mistreated, because this country owed me something—the white man owed me equality and should give me a taste of the good life too. And I was stupid enough to sit and wait for it.

I grew weak and weary waiting, and all ambition died with patience. I was destined to live and die as my fathers did before me, in ignorance, filth, and poverty—a "good boy."

### IV

I'm here!
At last, I'm here.
Despite the pain, despite the fear,
I'm here!
Here to meet another soul and chat a while,

At last, I frown, I cry, I smile,
I'm here!
I'm glad, I'm here, despite the bitter
    pain and fear.
The pain feels good—Good I'm here!
Thanks to life and hail to birth,
I cheer!
At last, a life—mother earth,
I'm here!

Then came salvation! It came with the flames of the Watts revolt and changed my life completely.

The revolt had such an impact and so much meaning that it made me start thinking again. I mean seriously thinking. I spent nearly a week after the revolt in my room, thinking and feeling every drop of anger that had built up within me over the years. Each thought made me angry, each thought brought resentment. I was angry about many things. I couldn't understand why I was hungry and couldn't get a decent job, or why I had been ashamed of myself for all these years and ashamed of black. And the main thing I resented and the least I understood was the fact that I was still a slave in the twentieth century.

On my last day in that room I said to myself: My forefathers slaved in the masters' fields. Many black men have fought hard and died in this country's wars to preserve its freedom. Black men have sweated endless hours in the laboratories inventing the "American brand." We have added a new beat to this nation's culture. Our literary contributions have been tremendous, ranging from novels to poetry to the blues. And for this and much more, all we've received in return was the "blues."

After those thoughts, I felt the deepest desire to protest. I felt the need to sing the blues and the compulsion to just say, "God damn that wicked man whose foot's on my neck!"

I wanted to scream it out and let the whole world hear—especially that Southern bigot and that Western politician and the Northern liberal who boasts about the leftovers he gave the maid—I wanted to tell them all that,

This is the home of my fathers.
They helped win this land.
They've conquered the fields of your fathers
With a strong, black helping hand.
In chains, they've suffered sharp pains of a whip
And strenuous work of a slave.
In protest I've cried,
You're hurting my pride
When they've earned and you claim you gave.

This is the home of my fathers.
In all of your wars they have died;
In every battle they've risked their lives,
And for what?—Freedom being denied!
They've toiled and strained with muscle and heart,
Their bodies all covered with sweat,
And with sad weary eyes
They protested the lies
That stated, "We give what you get."
I am the son of my fathers.
I deserve what they never got.
That's a chance to excel
In the things I do well
Without being hanged or shot.
This is the home of my fathers,
Soon it will be of my sons.
I hope by that time
They'll be able to climb
'Cause oppression may lead them to guns!

Instead, I wrote it. I wrote it not only for myself, but for my people as a contribution to the cause. It was the first time I had ever thought of it like that—as a contribution—and it was the beginning of a new outlook. I didn't care about the pains, the fear, the ups and downs in life anymore. I had a job to do and I was ready to accept all of the pains that went with it. I was ready to make a new start.

I wrote more, much more—poems, songs—you name it, I wrote it. My work began to pile up. Soon I had stacks of it, enough pieces to present to anyone, and I was ready to, as my good friend and colleague, William Marshall, might say, "Straighten up the backbone—stick out the jaw bone—throw away the wishbone—and step on it!" I gathered up everything that I had written and hurried down to the State Employment Office, hoping that they could help me find a job as a writer. I showed them my work and they seemed to like it but they couldn't help me. They referred me to the Urban League. I went to the Urban League and they sent me to the NAACP. The NAACP referred me to the *Sentinel* newspaper. So I tried the *Sentinel*. Though they weren't hiring, my trip was not in vain, for they encouraged me to keep trying the different newspapers, even the smaller ones, and to accept anything to start with, even if it was sweeping the floors. They assured me that I was heading in the right direction, and I left happy and full of confidence.

I was in luck. I landed a job selling advertisements for the *Star Review*, a Watts weekly newspaper. The editor was a very understanding person who liked to see young people trying. He knew that I wanted to write and that I had never written a newspaper article before, but he gave me a chance to prove myself. He sent me out on a story, a big story. I was to report on the First Annual Community Beautiful Parade in Watts. I was very excited, and so thankful for the opportunity that I wrote much better than he and I had anticipated. A week later, I was promoted to Business Manager. And two weeks after that, I was appointed Co-Chairman of the Citizens for Good Government Committee. Things were happening fast and I was beginning to get deeply involved in community affairs.

The following month I, along with Mr. George Crawford of Crawford's Men's Store, and a few other merchants up and down 103rd Street, and with the help of Westminster Neighborhood Association, got together and reorganized the Watts Business and Professional Association, and they elected me secretary. Shortly after my twenty-second birthday, I resigned from both the newspaper and the Business Association (in good standing, of course) to have more time to help form the Watts Happening Coffee House. I felt that I would be able to help a few guys like myself, who needed some form of direction. So I pitched in and became the Publicity Director of the Board. While serving on the Board, I met Budd Schulberg, who was down in the area trying to help young writers like me get a start.

He told me of the classes he was teaching, and he said that he would be glad to have me as a member. So I joined. It was an honor to be able to learn from such a great and genuine person as Budd Schulberg. I attended every class.

Then, two months later, there came a tragedy in the family. My grandmother passed on. At her funeral, I learned a fact she had never told me. I learned that in her younger days, while teaching at a little country school in Texas, she wrote a play. I also learned that it was stolen because it had not been protected by copyright. Upon hearing this, I grew angry again, and through my anger I was inspired to write a play—my first play. I wrote it in verse and folk dialect, in memory of her, and filled it with slavery, oppression, protest, and revolt. I built it around two poems: "The Home of My Fathers" which I already quoted, and "Negro History," which goes like this:

> A ship
> A chain
> A distant land
> A whip
> A pain
> A white man's hand
> A sack
> A field
> Of cotton balls
> The only things
> Grandpa recalls.

I called the play "A Ballad from Watts." I took it to Budd Schulberg, and he liked it. He advised me to find a group and have it performed. That was a good idea; I had never thought of it. So I did as Budd said and took it around town to different theatre groups; but everyone was busy doing other plays. It would have been at least two months before any of them could get around to mine, and I couldn't wait. So with the encouragement of Budd Schulberg and William Marshall, I formed my own theatre group—The Theatre of Watts—and produced and directed the play myself.

The following month we performed at

the Watts Summer Festival and were successful. From then on there was no stopping us. We went from UCLA to the Elks Hall, and each time we performed we picked up new members. We grew from a nucleus of sixteen to an organization of forty, and we're still growing. Our main goal is to make Watts the Broadway of the world. And we will do it.

So, if one should ever ask me what I believed in, I would have to say, "I believe in progress through unity, self-help, and determination—this I believe." And it is for this I am fighting. If I were asked the same question before the revolt, I would have answered, "Burn, baby, burn!"

Well, the burning is over, thank God. People are beginning to progress, and there is a lot being done now, though still very much more to be desired.

I don't regret what happened in August—not in the least. My only regret is that it was necessary. I'm letting the oppressor regret the rest. I benefitted from it, opened my eyes, and for once I realize that "I'm here."

> The dead has finally awakened;
> A soul has found its way
> And I'm a writer now!
> Born through flames of August chaos
> Into an era of self-help and progress . . .
> From the ashes, I came,
> And with me, many others. . . .

# READING 43

# Ecology and the Science of Psychology

**S. B. SELLS**
**Institute of Behavioral Research**
**Texas Christian University**

With the present emphasis on laboratory experimentation, the relationship between man and his natural environment is sometimes obscured. S. B. Sells provides us with a good discussion of the validity and necessity of field research and of studying man's behavior in its natural setting. He proposes the use of ecological techniques and suggests that research which does not consider phylogenetic and ecological factors is limited in its meaning.

**QUESTIONS**

1. Does "instinctive drift" exist in man? Try to find some examples.
2. Discuss the problems involved with "artificial and unrealistic experimental situations." Sells states: "The laboratory must be a valid simulation of conditions of the natural setting or it may fail in its primary purpose." Do you agree?
3. Compare Boring's concept of science with the considerations of the present article. What conclusions can you reach?

In the hierachy of life sciences, psychology occupies a place between the biological disciplines — which focus on the structure, development, and functioning of organisms — and the social science disciplines, in which the significant unit of observation is a population group. Psychology, which is both biological and social, takes the molar behavior of the individual in his physical and social setting as its observational unit.

A major concern of the biological and social sciences has long been the nature of the interaction of organisms and populations with the embedding environment, which supports, influences, and determines limits of structure and function for the life that exists within its domain. The generic term representing scientific study of organism-environment interaction is *ecology.*

Revised version of a paper presented at Southwestern Psychological Association, Oklahoma City, Okla., April 8, 1965; the preparation of this paper was supported by Office of Naval Research Contract No. Nonr 3436 (00).

Traditionally, ecology has been recognized as a branch of biology, while the term *human ecology* has been used to designate the investigations, principally by sociologists and geographers, of the distributions of human population groups in relation to material resources, health, social, economic, and cultural patterns. These disciplines have produced significant bodies of knowledge and theory and they have developed distinctive journals, literature, and learned societies.

No such formal development has yet occurred in psychology, although an ecologic emphasis has become pronounced in recent years and may well be gathering enough momentum to crystallize as a major trend in the next decade. If this should happen, however, it will undoubtedly be a protest movement against strongly entrenched traditions which may indeed have themselves evolved as ecologic phenomena in the development of the science.

The discussion will review some significant, converging developments contributing to the ecologic trend in psychology and also some issues and difficulties that must be faced and eventually resolved. This presentation is focused principally on implications of the ecologic emphasis on content and method in psychology.

## ECOLOGY AND THE CONTENT OF PSYCHOLOGY
### PHYLOGENETIC PERSPECTIVE

One generalization that appears to be widely accepted is that the behavior of organisms is rooted in biological development. As a result behavior mechanisms have developed and must be understood in phylogenetic perspective. Even the psychologist who views practical human problems as predominant must acknowledge that a thorough science of psychology embraces the entire range of living species. Indeed, the interdependence of structure and function makes it imperative for the behavioral scientist to understand both the long- and short-term development of the biological structures and systems that determine and are determined by the molar behavior of the organism (Murphy, 1947, 1958).

One distinguished psychologist (Hebb, 1958) has stated a position related to this issue as follows:

> The most pressing problems of behavior are those of mental illness and social conflict . . . The 'pure-science' approach, the development of theoretical understanding, complements the practical approach by providing the only guarantee of better methods in the future. Mental illness involves perception, memory, emotion, thinking; so does the attitude of hostility to other peoples. But we do not fully understand perception, memory, and so on; thus, anything that tells us more about these processes, whether it is the study of the eye-blink in a man or a study of the mating habits of the rat, is a potential addition to our understanding of mental illness or the causes of social conflict.

This argument also implies that the illumination of pressing human problems constitutes a *raison d'être* of experimental and comparative psychology. But this is not necessary. The phylogenetic perspective is intrinsic to the structure of the science of psychology. *Homo sapiens*, as well as every other species, is an emergent member of a complex, dynamic system of living organisms, which reflects systematic continuities, even in the face of observed discontinuities, and in which historical position and relationship provide significant insights concerning structure and function. In this system studies of eye-blink phenomena and mating habits of any species have only the most limited meaning when pursued in isolation, as ends in themselves, but make their greatest potential contributions when related to an overall periodic table of phylogenetically organized and oriented data.

### ADAPTATION

In order to organize the science of behavior phylogenetically, psychological inquiry must take account of the most pervasive characteristic of biological systems, the principle of *adaptation*. Essentially this involves the self-regulating tendency of living organisms to maintain themselves by various means of accommodating or adjusting to changes in the environment. At different levels the principle of adaptation can be observed in the mechanisms of species change, in growth, tissue regeneration, regulation of biological functions, and in molar behavior processes, such as learning and motivation.

In an earlier paper (Sells, 1963a), these phenomena were treated operationally as interactions, which are systematic and adaptive rather than random encounters between inner and outer forces, as for example, Dobzhansky's (1962) account of natural selection, Davis' (1961) description of cold acclimatization, Pribram's (1960) discussion of variable, tunable homeostats, and the more recent literature on the Law of Effect in learning (Kimble, 1961), which are straightforward, deterministic accounts of observed events.

Natural selection occurs when two or more classes of individuals, genotypically distinct in some characteristic, transmit their genes to succeeding generations at different rates and one is better able than the others to survive under prevailing environmental conditions. Purpose is unnecessary to the linkage of the events described. The record of survival and extinction of classes differentially adapted to environmental change, though incomplete and not without problems, supports this conclusion, and the evidence is considered tenable that cumulative change of a magnitude recognized as evolution of "higher" types occurs as progressive adaptive change. Thus, the evolutionary progression of Hominidae, Hominae, Homo, and Homo Sapiens discloses the appearance of new patterns of behavior reflecting the sequential, cumulative effects of complex new organism-environment interactions continually enabled by the development of emergent structures. The occurrence of these causally-linked

events, in which complex consequents follow antecedent change, appears to be as lawful and untainted with hormic implications as any of the phenomena of gravity or thermodynamics.

## THE FEEDBACK MODEL

Adaptive function of an organism also implies the existence of feedback mechanisms. The posture of the organism at any moment is in effect the expression of an intrinsic (and not necessarily consciously experienced) *hypothesis* concerning the nature of the environment. Every response is similarly an *interrogation* of the environment and the resulting feedback provides information (also not necessarily conscious) that enables adaptive response. The existence of biologic and neurophysiological feedback systems is a necessary assumption about adaptive organisms.

The specific nature of the biochemical and bioelectric feedback mechanisms involved in adaptive biologic function and behavior is not yet clear, but this is not essential to the present discussion. However, the argument developed here does depend on the assumptions that such mechanisms are essential components of adaptive organisms and that both biologic functions and molar behavior are controlled by information-processing systems in which anticipation,[1] expectation, posture, or set is one fundamental characteristic, and adjust-

---

[1]The adoption of computer terminology by psychologists has made it possible to discuss *anticipation* and *information* inherent in feedback mechanisms without resorting to anthropomorphic expressions. This is apparent in the substitution by Cofer and Appley (1964) of the *equilibration model* for the *need-reduction model* in their discussion of feedback systems relevant to motivation and in their proposed sensitization (SIM) and anticipation (AIM) mechanisms as proposed models for motivation theory. Other noteworthy developments incorporating or implying feedback concepts include Woodworth's comprehensive law of homogeneity (1938), Hebb's concept of response equivalence (1949), the concept of reinforcement in learning, Piaget's concepts of accommodation and assimilation (Hunt, 1961), Helson's adaptation level theory (1964), the TOTE unit of Miller, Galanter, and Pribram (1960), the Sherifs' (1956) principles of stimulus structure and psychological selectivity in perception, and the information-processing model of motivation presented by Hunt (1963).

ment, based on information-feedback, is another.[2]

These characteristics of adaptive behavior emphasize the importance of the environment with which organims interact in biological and behavioral development and function.

## THE ECOLOGIC NICHE AS CONTEXT

The arguments advanced thus far are the basis for four postulates concerning the strategic role of the *ecologic niche* in the structure of behavior. First, it is recognized that every species and class of living organisms has evolved by adaptation to a particular set of environmental conditions with reference to which its morphologic structures, physiologic systems, and behavior response repertoire are optimally suited. This environmental pattern is defined as the ecologic niche and represents the adaptive match between circumstances and species schema (Hunt, 1961).

Second, these very structures, physiological systems, and repertoires of responses, defined by the ecologic niche, are the characteristics that are strategically relevant to the periodic table of phylogenetically oriented data referred to above. Focusing on behavior, it may be said that the response repertoire represents the *natural* way in which a species "makes its living" in its natural environment.

Third, the differences between species in historical position, critical environment, and related response repertoires all limit the types of cross-species comparisons that may be meaningful and suggest types of comparative studies that many profitably illu-

minate behavior in phylogentic perspective.

And finally, the understanding of behavior requires systematic study of the characteristics of the environmental pattern defining the ecologic niche of each species and the adaptations required by that environment as well as of response processes.

These postulates are the basis for two contextual prescriptions concerning the content of psychology: (1) There is a need for a master plan, corresponding to the periodic table mentioned above, to place psychological research in phylogenetic perspective. Such a schematic analysis could serve as a systematic guide to the definition of empirical information required for a comprehensive science of psychology. Considering the aspirations of psychology as a systematic science, it is sobering to consider the limited range of our knowledge of species outside of rats, chicks, monkeys, college students, military basic trainees, babies, and hospital patients. (2) For every species and class this schematic table should contain a detailed description and quantitative analysis of both the features of the environment defining the ecologic niche and the matching behavior response repertoire.

The conspicuous lack of such normative data is strongly voiced in the following remarks by Roger Barker (1965) in a recent address to the American Psychological Association:

This state of affairs is most surprising in view of the situation in the old, prestigeful sciences which psychology so admires and emulates in other respects. In these sciences, the quest for the phenomena of science as they occur unaltered by the techniques of search and discovery is a central, continuing task; and the development of techniques for identifying entities and signaling processes without altering them (within organisms, within cells, within physical systems, and within machines) is among the sciences' most valued achievements. Handbooks and encyclopedias attest to the success of these efforts. I read, for example, that potassium (K) ranks seventh in order of abundance of elements, and constitutes about 2.59% of the igneous rocks of the earth's crust; that its components are widely distributed in the primary rocks,

---

[2]This interdependence was perhaps most critically appreciated by Ashby (1962) who faced the problem of specification of environmental inputs in his computer model of a brain. Here the rigorous requirements for detailed information demonstrate the inadequacy of the often-cited global expression for interaction, $R = f (I \times E)$, in which R (behavior) is a function (f) of the interaction of organism (I) and environment (E). Not only must the nature of the function term be explicated, but the variables comprising the I and E sets must be specified and measured before such an equation can be realistically useful.

the oceans, the soil, plants, and animals; and that soluble potassium salts are present in all fertile soils. *(Encyclopaedia Britannica, 1962)*. The fact that there is no equivalent information in the literature of scientific psychology (about playing, about laughing, about talking, about being valued and devalued, about conflict, about failure) confronts psychologists with a monumental incompleted task.

The programmatic work of Kinsey and his associates on human sexual behavior (1948, 1953) and of Barker and the staff at the Midwest Psychological Field Station, University of Kansas, on recording units in the "stream of behavior" of children in several locales has demonstrated the importance of ecologic norms for understanding particular problems (1963). For example, Clifford Fawl (1963), a student of Barker's found that when referring to observational records of children's behavior in their natural surrounds, as contrasted with the psychological laboratory, *frustration* occurred rarely, and when it did occur, it did not have the behavioral consequences observed in the laboratory (Barker, 1965). Barker commented on this as follows:

It appears that the earlier experiments (by Lewin, Dembo, and Barker) simulated behavior very well as we defined and prescribed it for subjects (in accordance with our theories); but the experiments did not simulate frustration as life prescribes it for children.

We may wonder about other experimental treatments of segments of behavior and their relations to the occurrence of the designated behaviors in real-life situations.

Another example, from a paper by Gump and Kounin (1960), the former a student of Barker's, illustrates this point further. Gump and Sutton-Smith (1955) investigated the reactions of poorly skilled players when they were put in more or less difficult game positions or roles. For example, in games of "tag," the it-position is more demanding under some rules than others.

As they played the game experimentally, an *it* in the center of a rectangular playing field attempts to tag opponents who run to and from *safe* areas at each end of the rec-

tangle. One variant of the game gives *high power* to the *it* position by permitting the child in that position to "call the turn" when runners may attempt to cross from one safe position to another. Another variant gives *low power* to the *it* by permitting players to run whenever they choose. In one phase of the experiment, slow runners were assigned to high-power *it* positions, and in another, to low-power *it* positions.

The hypotheses, that poorly skilled boys would be more successful in high-power than low-power *it* positions, and that scapegoating of these inept boys would be less frequent in the high-than low-power positions were unequivocally confirmed. However, Gump and Kounin also observed boys in natural, rather than experimental situations, in gyms, playgrounds, and camps, and obtained the following impressions:

(a) poorly skilled boys do not often get involved in games they cannot manage; (b) if they do get involved, they often manage to avoid difficult roles by not trying to win such a position or by quitting if they cannot avoid it; and (c) if they occupy the role and are having trouble, the game often gets so boring to opponents that these opponents let themselves be caught in order to put the game back on a more zestful level.

The experimental game, which was watched by adults, was artificial in that poor competitors were inappropriately placed in skilled positions and in these circumstances no opponent ever let himself be caught. It actually created a highly unusual and, to the children, desperate circumstance, in which interfering adults were intervening agents. Gump and Kounin concluded that "The experiment probably does suggest hypotheses as to why certain games and roles are avoided by inept children, and it shows the extent to which children can scapegoat when conditions are artifically favorable."

A third example may be found in the 1961 report of Keller and Marian Breland, which not only recognized the primary relevance of the ecologically matched behavior response repertoire, but presented evidence of the *prepotency* of such responses over others to which animals were conditioned in the laboratory.

The Brelands, who built a highly successful business on the operant conditioning of animals for commercial exhibits, encountered a number of "disconcerting failures" in which conditioned animals after thousands of reinforcements of specific (ecologically artificial) learned responses, gradually drifted into behaviors entirely different from those which were conditioned.

The direction of this drift was toward what the authors called "instinctive behaviors having to do with the natural food-getting behaviors of the particular species." For example, "dancing chickens" drifted toward persistent scratching behavior, which is a prominent feature of the natural response repertoire of gallinaceous birds in their native habitat; chickens that were conditioned to peck a souvenir toy onto a chute drifted toward hammering them apart, thereby reverting to their natural habit of breaking open seed pods, killing insects, and the like; and the pig who was trained to pick up a coin and carry it to the bank, gradually began to drop it and "root it along the way," thus demonstrating the prepotency of a strongly established food-getting component of the natural repertoire of his species.

It is really providential that the early success of their enterprise resulted in the continuation of many of their "experiments" for a sufficiently long period (far beyond the duration of most laboratory experiments) that the so-called "instinctive drift" could occur. Their scientific insights may be regarded as a handsome repayment to academic science whose "impeccable empiricism" they have extensively exploited.[3]

For the present discussion these studies symbolize a host of experimental analyses of behaviors that occur only in the artificial and unrealistic experimental situations contrived to fit the hypotheses of experimenters who are either ignorant of or indifferent to the conditions of occurrence of those behaviors in their natural settings.

Although the position advocated here favors multivariate field observation and experiment over univariate laboratory experiment as the methods of choice in psychological research, the value of the laboratory as an adjunct to the field research station, to isolate, test, verify, and replicate particular aspects of phenomena observed in natural settings, should not be overlooked. Unfortunately, it has become orthodox policy in many university circles that the laboratory is supreme, that investigation without experimental manipulation of treatments and testing of hypotheses is unworthy of the term research, and that laboratory environments are preferable to natural settings. Unless the laboratory is a valid simulation of the conditions of the natural setting, it may fail in its primary purpose of contributing to the understanding of behavior, even though it may well serve the economic goal of producing more graduates.

## ECOLOGY AND THE METHODS OF PSYCHOLOGY

Acceptance of the ecologic principles discussed above has a number of profound implications for the scientific methods of psychology. In the first place, methods are required that are adapted to the circumstances of the real world in which behavior occurs naturally rather than for the convenience of the scientist. A new generation of field-oriented workers in psychology will be needed to go forth into the world as it is.

However, this world of reality is complicated, often uncontrollable, and frequently intolerant of prying investigators.

---

[3]No disparagement of the experimental method *per se* was intended by the Brelands; nor by the present writer.

[4]Many critics have recently drawn attention to the hollow, unproductive, artificial, and even pointless activities in many animal and so-called experimental laboratories, and urge attention to realistic human problems; see, for example, the papers by Bakan, N. Sanford, and Berg in the March, 1965, issue of the *American Psychologist*.

It operates according to rules of privacy and inviolacy and at a pace that often seems to defy investigative resourcefulness. These are problems that have beset many an unwary investigator and they have long been appreciated. They enable us to understand, if not approve, the advantages of the uncomplicated, traditional, laboratory milieu. Unfortunately the more removed from reality it becomes, the more illusory the science will be.

What is the resolution of the dilemma? First, the need is indicated for vastly greater communication and cooperation between psychology and both the bio- and social-sciences, for the methodology most appropriate to many of the fundamental psychological problems is necessarily interdisciplinary.

## INTERDISCIPLINARY APPROACH

Source data on major parameters of both the physical and social environmental behavioral effects have been compiled and published by oceanographers, climatologists, limnologists, physicists, geologists, geographers, anthropologists, sociologists, and even psychologists, as well as workers in many other disciplines. The following examples are mentioned merely to illustrate the wide range of excellent material available: Tromp's (1963) comprehensive work on medical biometeorology, dealing with weather, climate, and the living organism; environmental and operational data on the Polar Basin and the Arctic Region, in Sater's (1963) report for the Arctic Institute of North America; the effects of unusual environments encountered by men in military and space operations, by Burns, Chambers, and Hendler, psychologists (1963); extensive files on the detailed social, economic, political, legal, judicial, religious, health, familial, educational, scientific, military, and behavioral structure, folkways, and norms of the peoples of the world, coordinated by Murdock, Ford, et al. (Murdock, 1958); and definitive studies of human social structures, social systems, culture, and

social change, in the two volume work edited by Parsons, Shils, Naegele, and Pitts (1961).

Zoologists and other biologists have published extensive material on the behavior of animals in their native habitats. Recent books by Portman (1961) and Etkin (1963) on social behavior and organization of vertebrates illustrate scientific contributions by these colleagues, of value to psychologists.

Recently, the Federation of American Societies for Experimental Biology (Altman and Dittmer, 1964), under Air Force support, published a *Biology Data Book*, for which 470 botanists, zoologists and medical scientists contributed and reviewed data. The Data Book presents authoritative information on the parameters of genetics, reproduction, growth and development, morphology, nutrition and digestion, metabolism, respiration and circulation, blood, biological regulators, environment and survival and other factors for many species of plants, vertebrates, invertebrates and man. While much of the detailed data is of primary interest to biologists, this publication contains much material of psychological interest, such as effects of temperature, shade, and light on growth and survival of many species, effects of exposure to ionizing radiation, estimates of the number of species of plants and animals and taxonomic classifications of living animal species.

The purpose of citing this vast and wide-ranging array of literature is to document the point that the task of compiling a schematic periodic table focused on the environmental niches and behavior repertoires of animal species will receive a large assist from the older sciences that have long ago appreciated its importance. These disciplines have faced and in many cases overcome the difficulties of inaccessibility of observable phenomena, danger, discomfort, and privacy.

## PSYCHOLOGICAL FIELD RESEARCH

A number of field studies, representing a wide range of behavior, support the belief that there are no insuperable obstacles to effective field observations and no lack of ingenuity among investigators convinced of the importance of the approach. The interview procedures of Kinsey and his co-workers (1948-1953) paved the way for others to penetrate the seeming iron curtain of mystery and repression surrounding human sexual behavior. The behavior protocols of Barker and his colleagues (1963) demonstrated that observational techniques need not be confined to the baby's crib or the conference table. Both of these pioneers produced data of acknowledged richness and importance to the structuring of scientific inquiry in psychology.

Zinner (1963), recorded observations of 56 specific behaviors[5] on 90 Airmen, over a period of 25 days, with the help of 98 specially trained Airman observers, in 30 different real-life situations in Basic Training.[6]

In general agreement with a less ambitious observational study of one nine year old boy in two different situations of one day's duration each, by Gump, Schoggen and Redl (1963), Zinner observed a number of dependencies between situations and specific behaviors, for example situations that either facilitated or inhibited smoking or talking in varying degree. Factors extracted from his data were stable over subjects and occasions.

Observation of behavior in its natural setting, without interference or manipulation by the investigator not only frees psychology from insurmountable limitations due to experimental exclusion of complicating, but ecologically highly relevant variables. It also reduces the equally inescapable difficulty of *iatrogenic* influences on results, that is, the built-in effects of the experimenter's hypotheses expressed in his

particular designs and procedures (Kintz et al., 1965). Even simple invertebrates such as planaria have demonstrated such experimenter effects, according to a report by Rosenthal and Halas (1962).

On the other hand, this enthusiasm must be tempered by concern with the real problems of effective field-oriented methods. There is no question that they will raise the cost of psychological research to an awesome degree, for they involve multivariate observation and analysis on a time scale far in excess of present practices and over numbers of subjects, situations, and replications that imply massive organizations for data collection, reduction, and analysis.

In addition there are technical difficulties. The two most important of these are: (1) The problem of recording observations appropriately and completely and of reducing observational protocols to reliable units for quantitative analysis, and (2) the problem of encoding the environment.

## THE PROBLEM OF RECORDING BEHAVIOR

The first problem may look more difficult than it actually is. Zinner's observations were highly reliable. However, the behaviors he observed were selected to be objectively discrete and overt and his observers were carefully trained. Dickman (1963), a student of Barker's, on the other hand, found that naive beginning psychology students agreed poorly on the analysis into units of continuous samples of behavior presented in a motion picture. Still, improvement occurred with practice.

Dickman also pointed out that:

> . . . the "stream of behavior' attains orderliness in the eyes of other humans to the extent that goals and motives are imputed to the behavior. Independent observers of such a behavior continuum demonstrated significant agreement on general patterning and specifically on the points at which units began or ended. They agreed very poorly on identical incidence of units, yet they were able to agree on the general meaning of the sequence.

---

[5] . . . such as using left, right, or both hands, eating, hands in pockets, drinking, holding an object, non-personal rubbing of shoes, brass or windows, writing, urinating, leaning against something, smoking, talking to one person, saying Grace, smiling, and the like . . .

[6] . . . such as Wake up, from lights-on until the subject left the personal area, Personal area involving bunk and footlocker, Latrine, Marching to Messhall for breakfast, Table at breakfast, and so on from 4:45, in the morning until 5:00 in the afternoon . . .

He attributed this paradoxical result to differences of the inclusiveness of goal or behavior perspectives of the judges.

To some extent this problem is reminiscent of the experience of McClelland and his associates (Atkinson, 1958) in their efforts to obtain reliable scoring methods for TAT protocols. However, Barker (1963) has suggested that increased familiarity with observational methods will lead to improvement of these methods.

## THE PROBLEM OF ENCODING THE ENVIRONMENT

The problem of encoding the environment is the big hurdle. However, one program of research on this problem (Sells, 1963a, 1963b) makes it look more viable in the frame of reference of field study than from the perspective of the laboratory. The isolation of laboratory performance from the context of a stream of behavior, which Barker has emphasized, prompts one to think of the environment in discrete, molecular terms, while the real life setting suggests the patterned regularity and coherent structure of the familiar physical and social environment. The physical world consists not of discrete bits of light, heat, moisture, and the like, but of patterned events, with system qualities, in which day-night cycles, months, and seasons have associated with them characteristic temperatures, light, climatic variations, activity patterns, modes of dress, and the like. Similarly, the social world consists of patterned events with system qualities embracing multiple discrete stimuli which typically (except in unusual, extreme conditions) influence behavior, not in isolation, but by virtue of what Sherif and Sherif (1956) have called their *membership character* derived from the qualities of the respective systems. In this frame of reference a given unit may belong to more than one system and function differently in each.

The important work of Hadden and Borgatta (1965) on the factor structures of census characteristics in American cities paves the way to a systematic accounting of fundamental variables in the ecology of urban environments. A number of studies (Findikyan and Sells, 1964, 1965; Sells and Findikyan, 1965; Friedlander, 1965; Pace and Stern, 1958; Stern, 1956; Thistlethwaite, 1959a, 1959b; Astin, 1961, 1962, 1963) have demonstrated the value of multivariate analysis of variables used to measure aspects of the social environment. Such studies are particularly important, for example, in identifying characteristics of organizations, of social climates, of work situations, and of other subsystems of the social environment that may be useful for measurement purposes.

Dependencies between characteristics of situations and behaviors encourage further exploration of environmental determiners of behavior. Until we can assign to environmental variables the proportions of variance in behavior for which they account, our understanding of behavior will be incomplete. When this is accomplished, the goals of an ecologic approach to the science of psychology will have been achieved.

## REFERENCES

Altman, P. L., and Dittmer, D. S. 1964. *Biology data book*. Wright-Patterson Air Force Base, Ohio; Biophysics Laboratory, Aerospace Medical Research Laboratories, USAF. Report No. AMRL-TR-64-100.

Ashby, W. R. 1962. Simulation of a brain. In *Computer applications in the behavioral sciences*, ed. Harold Borko. Englewood Cliffs, N.J.: Prentice-Hall.

Astin, A. W. 1962. An empirical characterization of higher educational institutions. *Journal of Educational Psychology* 53:224–235.

Astin, A. W. 1963. Further validation of the environmental assessment technique. *Journal of Educational Psychology* 54:217–226.

Astin, A. W., and Holland, J. L. 1961. The environmental assessment technique: A way to measure college environments. *Journal of Educational Psychology* 52:308–316.

Atkinson, J. W., ed. 1958. *Motives in fantasy, action, and society: A method of assessment and study*. Princeton, N.J.: Van Nostrand.

Bakan, D. 1965. The mystery-mastery complex in contemporary psychology. *American Psychologist* 20:186–191.

Barker, R. G., ed. 1963. *The stream of behavior.* New York: Appleton-Century-Crofts.

Barker, R. G. 1965. Explorations in ecological psychology. *American Psychologist* 20:1–14.

Berg, Irwin A. 1965. Cultural trends and the task of psychology. *American Psychologist* 20:203–207.

Breland, Keller, and Breland, Marian. 1961. The misbehavior of organisms. *American Psychologist* 16:681–684.

Burns, N. M.; Chambers, R. M.; and Hendler, E. 1963. *Unusual environments and human behavior.* New York: Free Press.

Cofer, C. H., and Appley, M. H. 1964. *Motivation: Theory and research.* New York: Wiley.

Davis, T. R. A. 1961. Chamber acclimatization in man. *Report on studies of physiological effects of cold on man.* Army Medical Research Laboratory, report no. 475.

Dickman, H. R. 1963. The perception of behavioral units. In *The stream of behavior*, ed. Roger G. Barker. New York: Appleton-Century-Crofts.

Dobzhansky, T. 1962. *Mankind evolving.* New Haven: Yale University Press.

Etkin, W., ed. 1963. *Social behavior and organization among vertebrates.* Chicago: University of Chicago Press.

Fawl, C. L. 1963. Disturbances experienced by children in their natural habitats. In *The stream of behavior*, ed. Roger G. Barker, New York: Appleton-Century-Crofts.

Findikyan, N., and Sells, S. B. 1964. *The dimensional structure of campus student organizations.* Technical Report no. 5, contract no. Nonr 3436(00). Texas Christian University, Institute of Behavioral Research.

Findikyan, N., and Sells, S. B. 1965. *The similarity of campus student organizations assessed through a hierarchical grouping procedure.* Technical Report no. 6, contract no. Nonr 3436(00). Texas Christian University, Institute of Behavioral Research.

Friedlander, F. 1965. Behavioral dimensions of traditioned work groups. Unpublished manuscript. China Lake, Calif.: U.S. Naval Ordnance Test Station.

Gump, P. V., and Kounin, J. S. 1960. Issues raised by ecological and "classical" research efforts. *Merrill-Palmer Quarterly* 6:145–152.

Gump, P. V.; Schoggen, P.; and Redl, F. 1963. The behavior of the same child in different milieus. In *The stream of behavior*, ed. Roger G. Barker. New York: Appleton-Century-Crofts.

Gump, P. V., and Sutton-Smith, B. 1955. The "It" role in children's games. *The Group* 17:3–8.

Hadden, J. K., and Borgatta, E. F. 1965. *American cities: Their social characteristics.* Chicago: Rand McNally.

Hebb, D. O. 1949. *The organization of behavior.* New York: Wiley.

Hebb, D. O. 1958. *A textbook of psychology.* Philadelphia: Saunders.

Helson, H. 1964. *Adaption-level theory.* New York: Harper & Row.

Hunt, J. McV. 1961. *Intelligence and experience.* New York: Ronald.

Hunt, J. McV. 1963. Motivation inherent in information processing and action. In *Motivation and social interaction*, ed. O. J. Harvey. New York: Ronald.

Kimble, G. A. 1961. *Hilgard and Marquis' conditioning and learning.* New York: Appleton-Century-Crofts.

Kinsey, A. C.; Pomeroy, W. B.; and Martin, C. E. 1948. *Sexual behavior in the human male.* Philadelphia: Saunders.

Kinsey, A. C.; Pomeroy, W. B.; Martin, C. E.; and Gebhard, F. H. 1953. *Sexual behavior in the human female.* Philadelphia: Saunders.

Kintz, B. L.; Delprato, D. J.; Mettee, D. R.; Persons, C. E.; and Schappe, R. H. 1965. The experimenter effect. *Psychological Bulletin* 63:223–232.

Miller, G. A.; Galanter, E.; and Pribram, K. H. 1960. *Plans and the structure of behavior.* New York: Holt, Rinehart & Winston.

Murdock, George P. 1958. *Outline of world cultures.* New Haven: Human Relations Area Files Press.

Murphy, G. 1947. *Personality: A biosocial approach.* New York: Harper.

Murphy, G. 1958. *Human potentialities.* New York: Basic Books.

Pace, C. R., and Stern, G. G. 1958. An approach to the measurement of psychological characteristics of college environments. *Journal of Educational Psychology* 49:269–277.

Parsons, Talcott; Shils, Edward; Naegele, Kaspar D.; and Pitts, Jesse R. 1961. *Theories of society: Foundations of modern sociological theory.* 2 vols. Glencoe, Ill.: Free Press.

Portmann, A. 1961. *Animals as social beings.* New York: Viking.

Pribram, K. H. 1960. A review of theory of physiological psychology. *Annual Review of Psychology* 11:1–40.

Rosenthal, R., and Halas, E. S. 1962. Experimenter effect in the study of invertebrate behavior. *Psychological Reports* 11:251–256.

Sanford, N. 1965. Will psychologists study human problems? *American Psychologist* 20:192–202.

Sater, J. E. 1963. *The Arctic basin*. Centerville, Md.: Tidewater Publishing.

Sells, S. B. 1963a. An interactionist looks at the environment. *American Psychologist* 18:696–702.

Sells, S. B., ed. 1963b. *Stimulus determinants of behavior*. New York: Ronald.

Sells, S. B., and Findikyan, N. 1965. *Dimensions of organizational structure: A factor-analytic reevaluation of the Hemphill Group Dimensions Description Questionnaire*. Contract no. Nonr 3436(00). Texas Christian University, Institute of Behavioral Research.

Sherif, M., and Sherif, C. W. 1956. *An outline of social psychology*. New York: Harper.

Stern, G. C. 1956. *Activities index, form 156*. Syracuse, N.Y.: Syracuse University, Psychological Research Center.

Thistlethwaite, D. L. 1959a. College environment and the development of talent. *Science* 130:71–76.

Thistlethwaite, D. L. 1959b. College press and student achievement. *Journal of Educational Psychology* 50:183–191.

Tromp, S. W. 1963. *Medical biometerology*. New York: Elsevier Publishing.

Woodworth, R. S. 1938. *Experimental psychology*. New York: Holt, Rinehart & Winston.

Zinner, Leon. 1963. *The consistency of human behavior in various situations: A methodological application of functional ecological psychology*. Unpublished doctoral dissertation, University of Houston.

# READING 44

# The Behavioral Scientist and Social Responsibility: No Place to Hide

**LEONARD KRASNER**

The behavioral sciences are developing techniques to manipulate the physical and psychological environment of man. These techniques can lead to specific changes in behavior. The pressure of society to utilize these techniques is rapidly accelerating, thereby creating a growing concern on the part of the individual. Krasner discusses some of the implications of these developments and looks at the relationship between scientists and social responsibility.

## QUESTIONS

1. Science fiction is filled with possible futures often involving societal control of human behavior. Is this fiction or fact? How is human behavior controlled by the techniques of mass media? How does education control human behavior?

2. Although this article is oriented toward clinical psychology and therapeutic problems, it has much wider application. Discuss how the other areas of psychology have developed techniques and theories governing man's behavior.

3. Throughout this article, Krasner presents many different views of man. Pick out comments representing the viewpoints of behaviorism and phenomenology (cf. Hitt).

4. How aware is "Sam America" of the influences that control his behavior?

In recent years, at least four interacting developments have made a discussion of

Portions of this paper were presented in the symposium on "Social Responsibilities of the Psychologist," at the meetings of the American Psychological Association, Philadelphia, Pa., September 1963. The preparation of this paper was facilitated by support, in part, from Research Grant M-6191 from the National Institute of Mental Health, Public Health Service, through Stanford University and VA Hospital, Palo Alto, Calif.

The author was USPHS Visiting Scholar, Educational Testing Service, Princeton, N. J., 1964-1965.

the social responsibilities of the psychologist of vital importance. The first is the development and refinement of techniques for the avowed purpose of influencing the behavior of other individuals. These techniques have been developed by behavioral scientists, psychotherapists, educators, and others actively engaged in the control of behavior. The techniques have included psychotherapy, operant conditioning, therapeutic community, attitude influence, hypnosis, placebo, brain implantation, drugs, sensory deprivation, teaching machines, programmed instruction, and others. These techniques bring the behavioral scientist closer and closer to being able to manipulate the physical and psychological environment of individuals to bring about specified changes in their behavior.

The second development is the increasing pressure from society to utilize the findings of behavioral scientists in specific situations such as schools, community clinics, advertising, hospitals, and even broader problems of war and peace.

A third development is the increased acknowledgment on the part of some behavioral scientists that as scientific investigations continue at a rapidly accelerating rate the possibilities of modifying behavior increase accordingly. Consequently they express growing concern as to the societal and value implications of such developments. This increasing professional preoccupation is evidenced in research efforts, scholarly papers, symposia, and in activities of scientific organizations. Further, this professional concern is part of broader societal fears, some justified, some not. These fears in the public express themselves in articles in national magazines, in popular books (Gross, 1962; Packard, 1958), and, in extreme form, through attacks on the mental health movement.

The fourth development, partly a reaction to the first three, is the perpetuation in some quarters of old myths and the development of new ones behind which the behavioral scientist, particularly the psychotherapist, may hide, if he so wishes, to avoid taking a fully responsible role in society. In this paper I would like to develop each of these themes more fully and discuss their implications.

First, why is there increasing concern, both professionally and societally, about the social responsibility of the psychologist at this time in history? Although there has always been concern about human behavior control, currently special historical and professional conditions make it especially salient.

The first and obvious association and analogy is with the development of atomic energy and its application in the "bomb," the reaction of the physicists who made it, the great moral struggle, or lack of it, which has racked physics as a profession with mutual recriminations, guilt feelings, accusations, soul-searching, vehement defense and counter-defense. This is still very much alive in our daily papers, magazines, and professional journals. In literature it was best personified in fiction by Snow (1955) in *The New Men*. A possibly over-dramatic analogy is that we are now on the verge of important breakthroughs in the scientific control of human behavior, and that we must be aware of the dangers inherent in our present situation. Psychologists have said this, as have nonpsychologists. This view is most succinctly summed up in the often-cited comment of Oppenheimer (1956) in his talk to the American Psychological Association. "The psychologist can hardly do anything without realizing that for him the acquisition of knowledge opens up the most terrifying prospects of controlling what people do and how they think and how they behave and how they feel."

Hobbs (1959) has expressed the same concern. "Psychological knowledge can bring man increased certitude, dignity and joy, and it can also enslave him. These have within them the seeds of ultimate tragedy or triumph. The stakes seem to be getting even higher, and the rules of the game, embodied in ethics, ever more important" (p. 225).

These general comments about the potentialities of behavior control are probably true and may by themselves be enough to generate concern with the type of problem we are dealing with here. But more needs to be said. Even without the model of the physicist before us, we would have been brought to this point by what seems to be a period of crisis or transition in our profession. We are at a crossroad with respect to our self-image, our role function in society, our training, our research. Whether or not this period also has the characteristics of a "scientific revolution" in which our basic "paradigms" are being overthrown (Kuhn, 1962), only time will tell. A number of factors contribute to this crisis—novel social demands upon us, current types of research investigations, fundamental questioning of our conceptual models, the changing nature of the applied psychologist — especially the clinician — changes in the nature of the doctorate program, relationships between disciplines, and in general the demands of the space age opening up before us. Eric Goldman (1962), the social historian, has pointed out that it is rare for individuals living in a transitional age, an age of crisis and change, to be aware of such changes. Any claim that this is an age of transition will be greeted with a healthy skepticism. The claim does represent a calculated guess, but it seems like a good one.

As we consider the possibilities of the control of human behavior it is within the broader context of an increasingly bewildering control of our external environment—with the development of greater automation, the growth of computer applications, and the general physical mechanization of our society. With the growth of mass communications, mass advertising, the growth of mass ideas, and the overwhelming growth of numbers of people, the individual and individuality are likely to become lost. There is still a growing fear of "conformity," a topic of central concern in the late 1950's, just as "control" may well be the topic of concern in the 1960's.

Another factor on the social scene is the historical recency of large-scale political coercion usually labeled brainwashing—a major phenomenon in controlling individual behavior. Just what brainwashing is, and just how effective it is, are still matters of controversy. For example, Biderman (1962) strongly questions the efficacy of brainwashing on our Korean prisoners. But the word itself is now a popular part of our vocabulary—a word to be applied to any kind of behavior influence with which we do not agree.

Because of the dramatic nature of the topic, behavior control has an extraordinary fascination for newspapers and magazines, as well as in our own professional lives. Examples are *Life's* "Control of the Brain" series, (Coughlan, 1963); *Harper's* "Homemade Utopia"—an article on Skinner (Klaw, 1963); *Commentary's* "The Science of Thought Control" (Fraiberg, 1962), which reviewed Lifton's excellent book on brainwashing; the Biderman-Kincead (1963) debate in the letters column of *Time* magazine. Another example is the two conferences held at the University of California Medical Center on "The Control of the Mind," which centered primarily on potentialities of psychopharmacological agents (Farber & Wilson, 1962; Farber & Wilson, 1963).

To what extent can human behavior be controlled? Obviously, at this point, the most reasonable answer is that, given certain types of situations, certain specific behaviors can probably be strongly influenced. There is a close relationship between how one sees the basic nature of man and how influenceable one feels he ultimately is. A behavioristically oriented investigator would feel that there are probably few limitations to the potentialities of control as the science of behavior advances, primarily because of the importance he attaches to environmental stimuli in influencing behavior. On the other hand, those theorists who see behavior determined by inner dynamics or forces are less likely to see human behavior as controllable.

The arguments for the controllability of behavior come from at least three major sources. First, it derives from the view of psychology as the science of behavior. If we really believe that our profession is a science and that human behavior is lawful, then it follows that as research advances, human behavior becomes more predictable and hence more controllable. Skinner (1953) has argued most eloquently for this point of view. Second, there are a growing number of investigations which can be categorized within the generic term "psychology of behavior influence." These are studies which emphasize stimulus manipulation, learning, conditioning, modeling, hypnosis, psychotherapy, placebos, drugs. Third, there are the real life situations in which our behavior is influenced daily by our interactions with others, by education, by newspapers, by parents, by peers, in effect, by the totality of stimuli to which we are continually being exposed.

Further, the issue of the control of behavior must also be put into a broader time perspective. As behavioral scientists, we can modestly, and truthfully, say at this point that we are still very limited in what we know about the variables that influence behavior change. Traditional psychotherapists are most entitled to make such modest statements. At this point to talk about the control of human behavior with any degree of certainty as to its eventual possibilities sounds grandiose. We all know some of the very practical difficulties in helping just one unhappy individual change his behavior even slightly so that he may find his environment a bit more satisfying. However, if we put our research efforts in the longer context of the age of the earth, the age of man, the age of psychology as a science, then it would seem clear that the scientific information required for effective behavior control will probably be a reality in a relatively short period of time, be it 10, 20, or 100 years.

This point is nicely illustrated in a book by Arthur Clarke (1962) in discussing the hazards of prophecy about potentialties of controlling behavior. He points out how frequently in history would-be prophets, especially the scientists, come to logically inescapable but wrong conclusions when they prophesy something as being impossible to do. He gives a wonderfully apt quotation from a prominent American scientist. "The demonstration that no possible combination of known substances, known forms of machinery and known forms of force can be united in a practical machine by which man shall fly long distances through the air, seems to the writer as complete as it is possible for the demonstration of any fact to be." This statement was published in 1903! Clarke gives a warning: "Even things that are undoubtedly impossible with existing or foreseeable techniques may prove to be easy as a result of new scientific breakthroughs."

A similar view of the potentialities of behavior control has been expressed by Crutchfield (1963).

> But the most striking new factor in the increasing threat to independent thought in a conformist world is the development of far-reaching new psychological methods for behavior control—direct electrical stimulation of the brain, high-speed computer control of man-machine systems, radical manipulation of strange and artificial environments, biochemical control, shaping of behavior through new automated techniques of programmed training —the so-called teaching machines.
>
> All these methods have barely begun to show their remarkable potential—a potential both for destroying independent thinking and for promoting it. Just as there is a race between peaceful and destructive uses of nuclear energy and a race between medical advances which reduce death rate and those which control birth rate, so is there a race between the destructive and constructive use of these radically new techniques of behavior control. And behavior control, we shall presently see, implies thought control.

It is not possible at this point to summarize the growing literature in the psychology of behavior influence in the fields of attitude change, operant conditioning, brain stimulation, drugs, milieu control and therapeutic community, sensory deprivation, hypnosis, psychotherapy, interview control, and brainwashing (Krasner & Ullmann, 1965). There are perhaps no major breakthroughs but rather an accelerated accumulation of basic information relative to the variables which control behavior in a variety of situations. We cannot yet make dramatic statements that behavior can be controlled at will. The omnipotent hypnotist or Svengali must still remain in novels such as *The Manchurian Candidate* (Condon, 1959). But we are making rapid strides in acquiring knowledge of the variables related to how behavior, attitudes, feelings, and knowledge do change.

A recent and interesting development is the growing, albeit grudging, acceptance by many writers and practitioners that psychotherapy is a controlling technique. Here there is still considerable controversy. I emphasize the control problem as it is related to psychotherapy in part because of my own interest in therapy and in part because therapy represents such an important example of the influence process backed by strong societal need and interest.

A clear statement on therapy control is by Rogers (1961) from his book *On Becoming a Person*. "In client centered therapy, we are deeply engaged in the prediction and influencing of behavior. As therapists we institute certain attitudinal conditions, and the client has relatively little voice in the establishment of these conditions." With the growth of these techniques, the demand on the psychologist to contribute his unique knowledge about the influencing of human behavior has increased tremendously in the fields of education (teaching machines as an example), in mental health (psychotherapy), in industry, in the community, and in world affairs.

Just to give one illustration, Vice-President Humphrey when a Senator made several speeches about the need for behavioral scientists to participate more in world and national affairs (1963).

> The behavorial sciences can help us resolve the awesome dilemmas we face.
>
> It is not just the physicist, the chemist, the biologist who can find new answers to the prevention of World War III; it is the psychiatrist, the psychologist, and allied professionals. From all these people we need not only facts, we need questions. We need innovative concepts. We need challenges to cherished dogmas. We need imagination.
>
> I urge you not to relax your individual and collective efforts to see that national decisions are made with the benefit of what we know about people, about human behavior.
>
> There should be a behavioral scientist in the office of Science Advisor to the Secretary of State. Behavioral scientists ought to serve as Science Attachés abroad.

Stanford Ericksen (1963) in the *American Psychologist* points out that:

> Psychologists are part of the dramatic cultural changes that are taking place in the intellectual world and many of these trends are probably just now beginning to gather some degree of momentum. This acceleration force may fractionate psychology but in the meantime, and this I believe is more important, these centrifugal factors have moved us into a position of authority that has disquieting implications for the future.
>
> This all adds up to the uncompromising fact that psychology has now extended itself, for whatever reasons, into the nerve centers of society and we must not separate, in some rationalistic way, our expertness in behavior control from our social responsibility. If we are going to identify these powerful human-control procedures, and we must and will, then we should have the sense of social obligation to go into the community and help implement their proper public use. If, on the other hand, we perform gnome-like duties, unknown and in the Inner Room, then we will become an association of human factor technicians doing our work on prescription from those who may be less sensitive to the human use of human beings.

Ostow's (1959) paper is an example of a psychoanalyst's interpretation of the therapy situation as one of behavior control.

> In all activities in which two or more people are engaged in some relation to each other, a more or less mutual influence prevails. Only

when he is working on the soil, on the earth's resources, and on material things (or on the scientific study of these) is man temporarily not participating in an exchange of influence with another person, though when even these activities are performed in solitude, they usually have an indirect goal determined by the individual's relation to other people. It is possible to follow in the history of civilization accounts of methods and goals of influencing human behavior. These are seen in the areas of group organization such as government, religion, ethics and morality; in areas of personal gratification such as family life and affectionate relations; and in areas of the individual's relation to the group such as commercial activity, teaching, and personal and professional service.

If the therapist is seen as a controller of behavior, then we are directly faced with the third development, concern with the issue of values. With increased recognition of his deep involvement in investigating control of behavior, the psychologist has more and more gone into problems of value, ethics, and controversy about the social implications of control. And here the list of publications is growing, with the Rogers-Skinner (1956) debate of a few years ago setting the way for papers by May (1953), Lowe (1959), Rogers (1955), Hobbs (1959), Patterson (1958), Krasner (1962a), and many others. The broader issues involve conceptions of the nature of man, the role of the psychologist, determinism versus free will, the growing mechanization of man, the role of science, and so forth.

There have been several review articles on the investigation of values including Dukes (1955) and Ehrlich and Wiener (1961). In the latter paper, the authors were particularly interested in the measurement of values in psychotherapeutic settings. One of their comments is relevant here:

> Regardless of the differences in opinion concerning the place of values in therapy, relatively few therapists would not take issue with the assumption that therapists' values get communicated explicitly or implicitly to the patient; and that they also enter in some measure into the initial selection of patients, and decisions about the appropriate time for termination of treatment .... By and large, we were impressed

by the apparent scarcity of empirical efforts in the area. This lack was particularly striking in the light of the persistent recognition and acknowledgement of the functional role of values in psychotherapy by various prominent writers on the psychotherapeutic processes and methods. Ehrlich and Wiener conclude that changes in values and description of values in given situations can be fruitfully, if not simply, investigated via scientific approaches.

The fourth development may be paraphrased by the subtitle of this paper, "No Place to Hide." The behavioral scientist still has plenty of room to hide. Hiding in this instance involves the denial of control potentiality and the perpetuation of a series of myths behind which he can take refuge in denying role responsibility. Most people, perhaps, do not stop to look at the implications of their social roles. The psychologist cannot intelligently avoid this. When I talk about hiding behind myths, I refer not to any one psychologist or to all psychologists but to an abstract psychologist who is to some extent in all of us.

This is not to say that the psychologist is not a person very much interested in his society and the implications of his role. There are behavioral scientists who are interested in politics, in world affairs, who have research and ideas of importance to world problems, who are very much concerned about the implications of atomic testing, who are apt to join various organizations such as SANE, Turn Toward Peace, Scientists on Issues of War and Peace, SPSSI, and the West Coast group, Application of the Behavioral Sciences to the Strategies of Peace, ABSSOP. In these groups the behavioral scientist sees his role as an educated layman who understands human behavior, who tries to think clearly above the emotionalism of the times and who has a deep sense of social responsibility.

There is no lack of social responsibility on the part of psychologists as citizens. They vote, run for office, take part in community and social activities in support of racial integration, civil liberties, and support of the U.N. As professionals they give part of their valuable time to their organizations and to the community; organize research to investigate important phenomena such as prejudice, segregation, fluoridation, and bomb shelters; study problems of war and peace, both over-all strategies and processes of decision making. They are active in formulating and spreading ideas of a better world and are trying to find solutions to our various political, social, and economic dilemmas (Fromm, 1961; Osgood, 1962). They take part in advice to executives, governmental agencies, the Peace Corps, and even the Eleventh Hour. Finally, as psychologists, they have a code of ethics which they take quite seriously.

Given such strong evidence of social responsibility, it would be difficult to make a case out against "the psychologist" as being an irresponsible person. Yet, even in their work on the type of problem under discussion, a case can be made that behavioral scientists are still hiding behind a set of myths, hiding from the larger issue which faces them today—that of the ethical implications of the controllability of human behavior.

I use the term "myth" in line with the Oxford Dictionary definitions, "fictitious or imaginary person or object," and "a purely fictitious narrative usually involving supernatural persons, actions, or events, and embodying some popular idea concerning natural or historical phenomenon. Often used vaguely to include any narrative having fictitious elements."

The myths are concepts out of the past in our quick-changing world. We may refer to cherished concepts of only five or 10 years ago as myths. We make this reference with the certainty that a future generation will look back upon us and say we replaced the older myths with newer ones. Further, I am well aware that each of these myths has been under attack by at least some investigators, but belief in them is held by a considerable portion of our profession. I am

using therapy processes as a major source of these myths because therapy is a prototype of all other behavior influence situations, because it represents the most important of these behavior influences processes, because it is so widespread, and because it is such a fertile ground for mythology.

First is the myth that the therapist is not basically responsible for resultant changes in his patient. Of all the myths to be cited, this will probably be the first to die, if it is not already dead. In its simplest form it attributes change to the patient's desire to grow and to self-actualize. Although they may set the most permissive conditions for this to happen, therapists sometimes strongly deny that they were really involved in this process. This may be called the "look no hands" phenomenon in its attempt to deny control and attendant responsibility.

The recent upsurge in behavioral and learning approaches to psychotherapy has sharply pointed up, to an extent not previously emphasized, the responsibility of the therapist for what he does. By being aware of the variables of behavior change, the therapist is for the first time becoming free to make decisions and to take fuller responsibility. The learning viewpoint allows the therapist to be aware of the consequences of various kinds of behaviors and, in effect, opens up a larger repertoire of potential therapist and patient behaviors (Kanfer, 1965; Krasner, 1962a).

Second is the "myth of mental illness," a phrase popularized by Szasz (1961). This myth, too, is under growing attack. Increasing numbers of articles written by psychologists and psychiatrists put the term "mental illness" in quotation marks or refer to it as "so-called" mental illness. This is nicely illustrated by the statement in the *American Psychologist* on the report of the Joint Commission on Mental Illness and Health by the Board of Directors of the APA (1963).

Although the general tenor of the Commission's recommendations is courageous and imaginative, the conceptual framework within which the problem of mental illness is defined in its report is traditional, and does not take into account recent basic criticism of the medical model of health and illness in its application to disorders of thought and behavior. We support the substance of the Commission's recommendations for the better care of persons traditionally classified as mentally ill, but we anticipate that, in the long run, a different way of conceiving their problems of living may turn out to be more appropriate.

Menninger, as cited in Appleby, Sher, & Cummings (1960), for example, advocates a unitary concept of mental illness.

> Now I not only believe that no such disease as schizophrenia can be clearly defined or identified or proved to exist, but I also hold that there is no such thing as a psychosis or a neurosis. My point is that no one can satisfactorily define these terms in a way which the rest of us can accept so that if we use the terms we involve ourselves in confusion because we are all, or nearly all, talking about different things.
> Most investigators no longer consider schizophrenia a disease entity, an inherited disorder, an expression of a somatic disease or a disorder susceptible to a "specific" somatic treatment.

Menninger's views are almost identical with Szasz's in their call for the elimination of "mental disease" concepts and their replacements by concepts such as normal living and growing.

Historically, the disease model in its day represented a major advance for mankind. Considering unusual or deviant behavior as the result of a disease process was a step forward in contrast to previous notions that unusual behavior represented the work of witches, demons, or even represented criminal behavior. Now most of the current jargon and labels which are so widespread in our society follow from a disease model of abnormal behavior. These include terms such as "mental illness," "emotional illness," "psychopathology," "mental health," "mental hospital," "mental patients," "diagnosis," "prognosis," "psychotherapy," "treatment." Therefore, it follows that in

the psychotherapy situation, we have a person in a sick role labeled a patient, and another person in the role of society's healer, the psychotherapist. The disease model views the specific behavior of an individual as symptomatic of an underlying *disease process*. This point is, of course, of major significance in any discussion of how behavior may be modified. Generally, the disease concept implies that there are internal mediating forces within individuals that are responsible for the observable behavior. These forces are often represented as being unconscious or as having psychodynamic significance. All too frequently illness itself becomes an explanatory concept; an individual behaves a certain way because he is ill, sick. It is far too easy to label as "sick" behaviors of individuals of whom we don't approve. It is paradoxical that society and the psychologists, on the one hand, seek to eliminate sick behavior and, on the other hand, maintain such behavior by sanctioning a societally approved social role labeled "mentally ill" and in many ways reward such a role.

Since the disease model of mental illness is the accepted standard in our society, why is it under growing attack at this time in history? There are, of course, many possible reasons, one of which may well be the growing feeling of frustration regarding many standard techniques based on psychodynamic sickness formulations such as psychoanalysis. Further reasons for the current attacks have grown out of the rapid changes in treatment procedures in mental hospitals, the failure of the traditional organic therapies such as electroshock and lobotomies, and the recent growth of the application of learning theory in new behavior therapies, some derived from Pavlov and Hull (Eysenck, 1960), some derived from Skinner (Krasner, 1962b).

The attacks come, in part, from learning theorists who argue that since all behavior, including deviant behavior, is the result of a lawful series of events in a person's life, then all behaviors are also modifiable by learning procedures. There is no sharp distinction between the laws which govern normal and abnormal behavior except insofar as society labels behavior with these terms. The strongest attack on the disease model, however, comes from a psychiatrist who is not identified with the learning theorists, Thomas Szasz (1961). In a series of papers culminating in his book, *The Myth of Mental Illness*, Szasz would prefer to make emotional problems understandable entirely in terms of social reactions and problems in communication. He is willing to forego a concept of the inner world of man. He feels that the concept of mental illness is unnecessary and misleading since it implies a disease of the brain, and "neurosis" and "psychosis" are clearly not diseases of the brain. He suggests that the phenomena now called "mental illnesses" be looked at afresh, that they be removed from the category of illness, and that they be regarded as the expression of man's struggle with the problems of how he should live. He makes the radical proposal that psychiatry, and implicitly clinical psychology as we know it in this country, be scrapped and be replaced by nonmedical model professions. He argues that psychiatry has nothing to do with medicine. Diseases of the body have no connection with difficulties in living. These difficulties in living may be fully understood in terms of the rules of the game as imposed on individuals by the culture and the misuses of the rules or personal deviations from the rules by the individual. Szasz contends that the future of modern psychiatry lies in the field of values not in the field of medicine.

Others who have attacked this disease model also are Sarbin (1963), from a role learning model, Bandura and Walters (1963), from a social learning view, and Krasner (1963), from a social reinforcement view. Perhaps the strongest comment comes from Pratt (1961). He says "let's put the blatant facts bluntly, psychological disorders are just that. No . . . etymological gyrations argue for anything else. Labels such as 'mental' or 'emotional illness' with a posited biochemical pathogen referent derive from a misapplication of organic disease entity nosology and are theoretically and experimentally untenable, and at face value both semantic and logical absurdities." Pratt in a sarcastically bitter attack on the disease concept calls behavioral scientists guilty of the "crime" of being accessories to mislabeling psychological disorders as mental disease, referring to this as the "major hoax of the 20th century."

The next myth in our series is that of "robotism." This is the portrayal of the behaviorally oriented therapist, the person who advocates the application of learning theory to treatment of the individual or who insists on systematically applying psychological science to societal problems, as one who is cold, impersonal, and mechanical in his approach, as a destroyer of freedom, an enemy of love, a little un-American, and ultimately a menace to society. The picture is of a mechanical robot who *advocates* the control and manipulation of behavior as a good thing in itself. May (1962) expressed this position as follows:

> Now obviously this kind of conditioning approach to psychotherapy means that the patient is conditioned to the goals of the therapist, as the therapist controls the patient, but the therapist also takes no real responsibility for this, because the therapist, himself, is a programmed IBM machine, and one does not need to go into detail to indicate that the full meaning of human freedom and responsibility in any meaningful sense is thereby undermined. I think, not only undermined, but to the extent that if this would be our approach to therapy, freedom would be destroyed.

Herein probably lies the heart of the difference of view. What May says the behaviorist is *advocating*, the behaviorist argues actually *exists*, namely that psychotherapy *is* an influence process. To deny it is to hide from one's real responsibilities. It is neither good nor bad, it *is* the therapy process. To recognize and to be aware of this fact represents freedom and responsibility in its finest sense; to deny it and to hide behind the myth represents a shirking of responsibility and a genuine loss of freedom.

Several other ways of presenting the robot myth may be cited. Urban and Ford (1961) in a provocatively named paper, "Man: A Robot or Pilot," discuss how the image of man which a scientist maintains determines his procedures and his end-products. At one extreme, they cite the view of man as a robot: "Man is often conceived to be an apparatus, albeit an extremely intricate one, who behaves after the fashion of a programmed machine. . . . In this approach, he is conceived as having a behavioral repertoire, built in as a consequence of his innate equipment on the one hand, and the subsequent events of his training on the other." From this point of view, all behavior is situation-determined in the final analysis, and you can control behavior by external manipulation of the stimuli.

In contrast to this is the pilot view. "A contrasting image has viewed consciousness or awareness and the thoughtful self-direction of his behavior as the crucial characteristic of man. He influences situations as much as they influence him. Man is able to perform symbolic operations of higher mental processes. . . . The individual, in short, is being viewed as steering his own behavioral course."

The robot view is also vividly described by Adelson (1960).

> Some psychologists tend to project an image of man as a *tabula rasa* which is to be inscribed with certain dicta and values by a series of properly timed and spaced reinforcements. These psychologists have been chiefly concerned with stimulus response connections and patterns, with resolving whether it is more persuasive to state the pros or cons of an issue first or last and when it is better not to state the cons at all. Their view of man leads naturally to the kind of world Skinner has portrayed in *Walden Two* (1948).

Another group sees man as a thinking, judging, valuing, and creative being. These have been concerned with the principles governing cognitive organization and the conditions necessary for productive thinking. Their view is that "The good life is a process of movement in a direction which the human organism selects when it is inwardly free to move in any direction."

These differing conceptions of man's nature lead one school to suggest means of manipulating man's destiny, the other to search for ways of fostering his growth. The one has, and the other seems not to have, faith in man.

Chein (1962) contends that:

> The contrasting and, among psychologists whose careers are devoted to the advancement of the science, the prevailing image of Man is that of an impotent reactor, with its responses completely determined by two distinct and separate, albeit interacting, sets of factors: (1) the forces impinging on it and (2) its constitution (including in the latter term, for present purposes, momentary physiological states). Response is at all times and at every moment an automatic consequence of the interaction of body and environment. He is implicitly viewed as a robot — a complicatedly constructed and programmed robot, perhaps, but a robot nevertheless.

I have cited these dichotomous views of the nature of man because of the descriptive vividness of the metaphors involved, e.g., pilot or robot, and because they are such clear-cut statements of the "robot myth." The "robot" refers in these instances both to the role of the therapist and the model of man with which he works.

We can state the problem quite baldly; what is man, robot or pilot? The common-sense view would, of course, be that man is both. Urban and Ford (1961) actually conclude that the two views really complement each other, in that each model accounts for a different set of behaviors and each neglects behaviors the other accounts for. This is the easy, logical way out. Others, such as Chein (1962), conclude that only the "man as pilot" view can be acceptable to psychologists.

The view I would argue for is somewhat different. I would conceive of man clearly in the robot end of the continuum. That is, his behavior can be completely determined by outside stimuli. Even if man's behavior is determined by internal mediating events such as awareness, or thinking, or anxiety, or insight, terms which we are all so reluctant to give up because myths die slowly, these events can be manipulated by outside stimuli so that it is these stimuli which basically determine our behavior.

However, there are several important points which may save the day and put man back into the driver's seat where most investigators want him to be. Here are the factors which should help to do it. First, the kind of environmental control which would make man fully a robot does not exist; it is only theoretical. Society is not set up to manipulate systematically man's behavior. Nor is it likely that in the near future there will be experimental studies which will reveal the tremendous complexities of human behavior so that complete social control will be possible. Thus man can and should behave *as if* he were the pilot of his own destiny. He is still free to the extent that there is no systematic societal manipulations of his behavior and to the extent that he behaves as if he were free. Secondly, even with a robot model of man, what is usually lost sight of is that a robot's behavior is determined by human beings. Put differently, man may be a robot but man also programs or controls the input into the machines and, at present, the program works, at best, in probabilistic terms.

Thus to the extent that men can behave in terms of having alternative behaviors available, to that extent they are free. The person who is aware of several alternative behaviors in a given situation and is able to verbalize the consequences of these various behaviors is, for all practical purposes, free to select one of them. He is far freer than the person who believes that his behavior is going to be determined by un-conscious forces within him and consequently acts as if his behavior is determined and he has no responsibility for it.

A major implication of the behavior viewpoint is to increase the responsibility of both therapist and patient, to get them both out from behind the myth that we are not responsible human beings. When we talk in terms of consequences of behavior, then we can see the possibilities inherent in alternative kinds of behaviors. As free individuals in a responsible role in society, we must consider the ethical and value implications of our behavior as a major factor in our decision making.

The robot myth is closely associated with the next myth, the myth of the "word." This is the myth which the psychologist should be least susceptible to, but unfortunately this is not so. This is the myth that the word is the real thing. Stuart Chase (1938) once called it the "tyranny of words." We all should know that a word is really a symbolic representation of some physical object in the environment. But do we?

As an example, a "Society for Humanistic Psychology" has recently been formed. Their announcements (1963) have these curious phrases:

> Humanistic Psychology may be defined as the third main branch of the general field of psychology (the two already in existence being the psychoanalytical and the behavioristic) and as such is primarily concerned with those human capacities and potentialities that have no systematic place, either in positivistic or behavioristic theory or in classical psychoanalytic theory: e.g., love, creativity, self, growth, organism, basic need-gratification, self-actualization, higher values, being, becoming, spontaneity, play, humor, affection, naturalness, warmth, egotranscendence, objectivity, autonomy, responsibility, psychological health, and related concepts.

I feel that, as a behaviorally oriented psychotherapist, I can live without terms such as "ego-transcendence," "being," and "becoming." But I would feel some resentment to find that we are going to lose such words as "love," "creativity," "values," "objectivity," "responsibility," "play," and especially "humor." These are all human behaviors, the dimensions of which are quite specifiable, and they can and should be dealt with by any behavioral scientists.

The statement from the "Humanists" implies that behaviorists, and even psychoanalysts, are not interested in freedom and warmth or humanism, the very attributes that characterize human behavior. I would object to the implication that behaviorally oriented therapists are anti- or nonhumanistic. I would submit that all psychology, even psychoanalysis, irrespective of orientation, is humanistic; for man, and his behavior, is still the center of the universe of behavioral science. To say that only one view of man has a monopoly on "freedom" or "love" is rather unrealistic. But even further, to return to the tyranny of words, what is freedom? Obviously the word "freedom" is good, perhaps in the same way that certain four-letter words are bad.

I am deeply concerned that while we worry about the problems of existence, being, becoming, and growing, the knowledge, information, and techniques of controlling behavior will be established in the real world outside, and our freedom, however defined, will be gone; and, as the crowning blow, we will not be aware of it and we will still think of ourselves as free to exist, to be, to become, to grow, and to self-actualize.

Next is the myth of the existence of an internal force or entity called the "unconscious." The concept of the unconscious is listed as a myth because it has proved to be of little value in advancing the science of psychology. Again this touches on an ancient problem, since the concept itself, of course, goes back far before Freud to the days of the ancient Greeks (Whyte, 1960). The concept has become so fixed a part of our professional and popular thinking that we are prone to fall back on this crutch to explain behavior whenever we may not know the variables which control a specific behavior.

To call the next concept a myth is really to defy fate and the gods, that is, the concept of an internal state labeled "anxiety." In tracing the meaning of the concept of anxiety, I run into puzzlement, frustration, and, consequently, considerable anxiety on the part of investigators. Anxiety means so many things that it means nothing. Do I deny that people feel anxious? As a human individual, poet, lover, of course not; we all can and do have anxieties. As a behavioral scientist, the term is increasingly meaningless in having no clear behavioral referents.

For example, May (1950) gives the following meanings of anxiety: "It is certainly to be agreed that the term 'anxiety' in English often means 'eagerness' ('I am anxious to do something') or a mild form of worry or has other connotations which do not at all do justice to the term 'Angst.' But the German Angst is the word which Freud, Goldstein, and others use for 'anxiety'; and is the common denominator for the term 'anxiety'."

Anxiety is termed a myth because of the potent lure of hypothetical internal states which we must somehow affect to bring about any "real" change in a person. Anxiety is transitory, illusionary, and the Lorelei of our clinical activities.

Psychology has for too long been seduced by the myth of anxiety. Anxiety belongs in poetry and not in an objective description of behavior. We go on measuring the unmeasurable with different instruments which have little relationship to each other and label everything "anxiety," and then wonder why we have such great difficulty in replicating personality correlate experiments. When a concept has such a multitude of meanings, then it has no meaning at all.

We also have the myth of fallibility-infallibility. Both ends of the myth exist. At one end is that of infallibility or omnipotence. There have, of course, been so many denunciations and disavowals of either the scientist as God, or the therapist as omnipotent, by scientists and therapists, that there is no need to point this out as a myth—no one really believes it anymore! The other end of the myth, fallibility, is expressed, in the ultimate of modesty, by "how little we know," and how long it will take to know things definitely, and how powerless we are. One humble psychologist at a symposium on what can psychologists contribute to urgent, present peace problems said, "we can do nothing, we can have no role because our research is still very tentative. However, come back in about ten years, then maybe we can help you."

We move on to the myth of objectivity. It is the belief that the experimentalist is scientifically oriented and objective in his views. He is somewhat cold and aloof and remains in his laboratory above the strife of real life battle. The practitioner, usually the clinical psychologist, is less objective, but is guided by the humanity of helping people. This stereotype of the behavioral scientist is now continually being questioned. For example, a physicist, Reif (1961), points out how the consequences of society's present reward systems determine to a very large extent the very competitive research behavior of the physicist, the types of research he does, his publication battles, and his relationships with his fellow scientists. His analysis would apply equally well to the psychologist-behavioral scientist.

Recent studies on the social psychology of the experiment and the social psychology of psychotherapy by Rosenthal (1963, 1964), Orne (1962), Barber (1962), and Goldstein (1962), among others, are helping to shatter, in one area, what is left of the myth of scientific objectivity. The demonstration of the effects of examiner biases influencing outcomes in research, the effects of the demand characteristics of the research task on subject behavior, and the role of verbal conditioning, modeling, and instructional sets in shaping and determining patient or subject behavior are all evidences of the impossibility of eliminating the investigator or therapist variable in behavior influence situations with humans, whether research or therapy (Krasner & Ullman, 1965). However, it is this very nonobjectivity of the influencer which is the core of the behavior influence situation, and future research must move up one level and be designed to investigate the behavior of this major variable, the investigator.

Finally, one comment about the last of our myths—that we train our graduate students for a realistic, meaningful role in society. Graduate school is the time when the major programming of the future therapist or researcher takes place. How much emphasis is there on the value implications of his behavior, the development and the use of his own behavior in affecting societal goals?

We must use both academic and practicum training to program creativity, not conformity, in our professional "controllers," so that they may give serious, informed thought to what they are doing, the personal and social consequences of their roles as scientists and as behavioral influencers. As psychologists, these roles are inseparable. New myths will develop and students must be trained to cope with them. A clear implication of the recent emphasis on behavioral techniques is that behavior influence and its major subsection, psychotherapy, is teachable. The danger of splitting psychology into "experimenters" and "practitioners" is great. It is a great myth that you can separate the two; practitioners must be rooted in the science of behavior, not in the nether world of obscurity and mythology.

What do we do about this dilemma of behavior control in order to come out from behind our myths? It is far easier to raise questions than to suggest answers. In fact, it is almost certain that we have only scratched the surface of our mythologies, leaving untouched and unseen many which others would clearly see and identify. However, I would sketchily prescribe several bits of behavior possible for behavioral scientists as part of their scientific investigations.

1. Continue and extend work on values. Man's value system, his verbalized conceptions of good, desirable behavior, is a major part of his behavior and can be investigated. Values are *not* outside the realm of science.

2. Continue to develop alternatives to the disease model of deviant behavior.

3. Explore to the fullest, in our ideas and in our research, the potentialities, implications, and the social consequences of our research. Continually point out and focus on these consequences both to the general public as well as to our colleagues. Pure laboratory research in psychology no longer exists. Perhaps that it ever existed may have been one of our best myths.

4. Encourage and continue the efforts of psychologists to use their fantasy or extrapolative powers to design cultures, utopian ideas, solutions of man's basic problems of war, peace and existence. A book such as Skinner's *Walden Two* (1948) and the consequent reactions, abhorrent as some have been, to such a society by individuals, such as Krutch (1954) and Rogers (1961), represent one of the major developments of our time. A better world is conceivable, designable, and arguable. A variation of this is suggested by Gardner Murphy (1958). Murphy describes a concept of

> . . . a museum of the future, a systematic and orderly display of the various potentialities which the future may indeed bring. A study by all the methods of analysis and extrapolation might reveal to us the possible future directions of cosmic and human development. The task would be to fill the gaps and at the same time extrapolate in directions suggested by existing trends for upon this possibility intelligent planning depends. . . . The more serious social science predictions, the Utopias, the science fic-

tion of today, would all occupy alcoves in such a museum.

The more behavioral alternatives available, both on an individual and societal basis, the better will be the choices made by members of our society.

Sir Watson-Watt (1962) nicely summarizes the responsibility of the scientist.

> The ethical responsibility of the scientist, within the definition to which I have chosen to limit the title of scientist, is, I believe, crystal-clear. It is this: In recognition of the privileged and endowed freedom of action he enjoys, he should, after an appraisal that may well be agonizing, declare all the social consequences he may foresee, however dimly, which are even remotely likely to follow the disclosure not only of his own contributions to science but also of those of other scientists within his wide sphere of knowledge and competence. He should outline the social good that he can foresee as resulting from the technological follow-up of "pure" research; he must outline the potential social evil. He will seldom be qualified to make quantitative estimates, but to the best of his ability he should define fields and magnitudes. Nothing less can suffice as partial payment for his privileged tenancy of the Ivory Tower. No plea that he "doesn't understand politics or economics" that, "even if behavorial science be a science (which he doubts) he is even further from understanding it," should be sustained. We must all do our poor best, with the intelligence at our disposal, toward mapping the upward, and marking the downward, slopes on our still long road of social evolution.

We are still avoiding the issue of who will control the controller; rather, we are saying that by focusing on the potentialities of control, we will continue the present system of a multiplicity of controllers, which is a saving grace. There is a difference between investigating control and actual control. The behavioral scientists are investigating influence at all levels in society. The more we know about the potentialities of control, the more we discuss the implications of control, then the less likely any one group in society will become the decision-makers on control. Our real danger lies in secret sources of attempted control whether they be by, as some movies portray, the mad hypnotist, or by clandestine political or social groups which desire deliberately to control or influence others. It is awareness of behavioral contingencies and implications which is so vital a source of protection of freedom (Roe, 1959).

We are at the crossroads in many respects. It is in the area of modifying deviant behavior that the hardest decisions have to be made. They will not be made suddenly but rather in the sum total of little decisions that are being made all the time. Is clinical psychology, or applied behavioral science, to be part of Psychology, or is it to grow into its own discipline, or will it merge with psychiatry, or will it go the way of mysticism, philosophy, religion, or mythology? There is nothing intrinsically wrong with any of these directions, except that the world is already full of physicians, mystics, philosophers, social workers, ministers, artists, and poets. And that is the way it should be. But the world also desperately needs behavioral scientists in the fullest sense of the word, both in their academic and practitioner roles.

## REFERENCES

Adelson, D. 1960. Ethical dilemma. *American Psychologist* 15:269–270.

Appleby, L.; Sher, J. M.; and Cummings, J., eds. 1960. *Chronic schizophrenia*. Glencoe, Ill.: Free Press.

Bandura, A., and Walters, R. H. 1963. *Social learning and personality*. New York: Holt, Rinehart & Winston.

Barber, T. X. 1962. Experimental controls and the phenomena of "hypnosis": A critique of hypnotic research methodology. *Journal of Nervous and Mental Disease* 134:493–505.

Biderman, A. D. 1962. March to calumny. New York: Macmillan.

Biderman, A. D., and Kinkead, E. 1963. The few and the many. Letters to the editor. *Time*, February 1.

Board of Directors, APA. 1963. Statement on report of joint commission on mental illness and health. *American Psychologist* 18:307–308.

Chase, S. 1938. *The tyranny of words*. New York: Harcourt Brace.

Chein, I. 1962. The image of man. *Journal of Social Issues* 18:1–35.

Clarke, A. C. 1962. *Profiles of the future*. New York: Harper.

Condon, R. 1959. *The Manchurian candidate*. New York: McGraw-Hill.

Coughlan, R. 1963. Control of the brain. Parts I and II. *Life*, March 7 and 15.

Crutchfield, R. S. 1963. Independent thought in a conformist world. In *Control of the mind*, pt. 2, ed. S. M. Farber and R. H. L. Wilson. New York: McGraw-Hill.

Dukes, W. F. 1955. Psychological studies of values. *Psychological Bulletin* 52:24–35.

Ehrlich, D., and Wiener, D. N. 1961. The measurement of values in psychotherapeutic settings. *Journal of General Psychology* 64:359–372.

Ericksen, S. C. 1963. Legislation and the academic tradition in psychology. *American Psychologist* 18:101–104.

Eysenck, H. J. 1960. *Behaviour therapy and the neuroses*. Oxford: Pergamon Press.

Farber, S. M., and Wilson, R. H. L., eds. 1962, 1963. *Control of the mind*, pts. 1 and 2. New York: McGraw-Hill.

Fraiberg, Selma. 1962. The science of thought control. *Commentary*, May.

Fromm, E. 1961. *May man prevail*. Garden City, N.Y.: Doubleday.

Goldman, E. 1962. On the social-cultural background of modern America. Lecture, Stanford University, Stanford, Calif.

Goldstein, A. P. 1962. *Therapist-patient expectancies in psychotherapy*. New York: Pergamon Press.

Gross, M. L. 1962. *The brainwatchers*. New York: Random House.

Hobbs, N. 1959. Science and ethical behavior. *American Psychologist* 14:217–225.

Humphrey, H. H. 1963. The behavioral sciences and survival. *American Psychologist* 18:290–294.

Kanfer, F. 1965. Issues and ethics in behavior manipulation. *Psychological Reports* 16:187–196.

Klaw, S. 1963. A psychologist's homemade utopia. *Harper's*, April.

Krasner, L. 1962a. Behavior control and social responsibility. *American Psychologist* 17:199–204.

Krasner, L. 1962b. The therapist as a social reinforcement machine. In *Research in psychotherapy*, vol. 2, ed. H. H. Strupp and L. Luborsky. Washington, D.C.: American Psychological Association.

Krasner, L. 1963. Reinforcement, verbal behavior, and psychotherapy. *American Journal of Orthopsychiatry* 33:601–613.

Krasner, L., and Ullmann, L. P., eds. 1965. *Research in behavior modification*. New York: Holt, Rinehart & Winston.

Krutch, J. W. 1954. *The measure of man*. New York: Bobbs, Merrill.

Kuhn, T. S. 1962. *The structure of scientific revolutions*. Chicago: University of Chicago Press.

Lowe, C. M. 1959. Value orientations: An ethical dilemma. *American Psychologist* 14:687–693.

May, R. 1950. *The meaning of anxiety*. New York: Ronald.

May, R. 1953. Historical and philosophical presuppositions for understanding therapy. In *Psychotherapy: Theory and research*, ed. O. H. Mowrer. New York: Ronald.

May, R. 1962. Discussion on existentialism and current trends in psychology. Conference at Sonoma State College. As reported on KPFA, Berkeley, Calif.

Murphy, G. 1958. *Human potentialities*. New York: Basic Books.

Oppenheimer, J. R. 1956. Analogy in science. *American Psychologist* 11:127–135.

Orne, M. T. 1962. On the social psychology of the psychological experiment. *American Psychologist* 17:776–783.

Osgood, C. E. 1962. *An alternative to war or surrender*. Urbana, Ill.: University of Illinois Press.

Ostow, M. 1959. The control of human behaviour. *International Journal of Psycho-Analysis* 40:273–286.

Packard, V. 1958. *The hidden persuaders*. New York: Pocket Books.

Patterson, C. H. 1958. The place of values in counseling and psychotherapy. *Journal of Counseling Psychology* 5:216–223.

Pratt, S. 1961. Of myths and models, an agonizing reappraisal. Paper presented at the annual meetings of the American Psychological Association, New York.

Reif, F. 1961. The competitive world of the pure scientist. *Science* 134:1957–1962.

Roe, Anne. 1959. Man's forgotten weapon. *American Psychologist* 14:261–266.

Rogers, C. R. 1955. Persons or science: A philosophical question. *American Psychologist* 10:267–278.

Rogers, C. R. 1961. *On becoming a person*. New York: Houghton Mifflin.

Rogers, C. R., and Skinner, B. F. 1956. Some issues concerning the control of human behavior: A symposium. *Science* 124:1057–1066.

Rosenthal, R. 1963. On the social psychology of the psychological experiment. *American Scientist* 51:268–283.

Rosenthal, R. 1964. Experimenter outcome-orientation and the results of the psychological experiment. *Psychological Bulletin* 61:405–412.

Sarbin, T. 1962. A new model of behavior disorders. Paper presented at VA Hospital, Palo Alto, Calif.

Skinner, B. F. 1948. *Walden two*. New York: Macmillan.

Skinner, B. F. 1953. *Science and human behavior*. New York: Macmillan.

Snow, C. P. 1955. *The new men*. New York: Scribner.

Szasz, T. S. 1961. *The myth of mental illness: Foundations of a theory of personal conduct*. New York: Hoeber-Harper.

Urban, H., and Ford, D. 1961. Man: A robot or pilot. Paper presented at the annual meetings of the American Psychological Association, New York.

Watson-Watt, R. 1962. Observations on the ethical responsibility of the scientist. Address to the ACCRA Assembly.

Whyte, L. L. 1960. *The unconscious before Freud*. New York: Basic Books.

# INDEX

escape, 78
free recall, 273ff.
imitative, 411
inter-problem, 155
Law of Effect in, 442
paired associate, 260ff., 272, 277, 296, 403
paramecia, 51ff.
probe-digit, 269
protozoan, 51ff.
rat, 44
rote, 257ff.
serial, 260
set, 155
single item, 277
verbal, 256, 272, 295
Leary, Timothy, 387
LeeLectronic Trainer, 83
Lesser, G. S., 392
Lester, O. P., 258
Leventhal, H., 394
Levine, R., 183
Levine, Seymour, 110, 134
Levinson, D., 401
Lieberman, A. M., 188
Lilly, J. C., 108
Lindholm, Byron, 111
Lindley, R. H., 143
Lindsley, Ogden R., 67
Lockard, Robert B., 37
Loess, H., 278
Lorenz, K., 43, 45, 125ff.
Lovaas, O. Ivar, 77
Lowe, C. M., 456
LSD, 376ff., 387ff.

McCleary, R. A., 182
McClelland, D. C., 112, 183, 188
McConnell, J., 57, 178
McConnell, R. A., 199
McDougall, W., 107
MacFarlane, J., 419
McGeoch, J. A., 258, 269
McGill Picture Anomaly test, 299
McGinnies, E., 183
McGlothlin, William H., 375
McGraw, M. B., 125
MacLean, P. D., 122
MacLeod, R. B., 4
McNeil, Elton B., 178
McNeill, David, 283
McNemara, H. J., 96
McNiven, Malcolm A., 140
Magendie, François, 16
Maier, N. R. F., 57, 60
Malcolm, N., 4
malingerers, 362ff.
Marcuse, H., 429
marihuana, 375ff., 387
Marquis, D. G., 167
Maslow, Abraham H., 10, 348

May, R., 459
meaningfulness, 264, 323
Mednick, Martha T., 67
memory, 402
immediate, 249
primary, 268ff.
secondary, 272ff.
trace, 256, 278
Menninger, Karl, 13
mental illness, 360ff., 458
mental patients, 369ff.
Merton, Robert K., 16ff.
mescaline, 388
Messinger, S. L., 429
methamphetamine, 378
Meyer, D. R., 107
Miles, W. R., 39
Milgram, Stanley, 400
Miller, George A., 240, 309
Miller, J. G., 181, 185ff.
Miller, Neal E., 106, 140, 167
Mills, Judson, 92
Milner, P., 109
minority groups, 434ff.
molar behavior, 440
Moller, Jean, 31
Money, J., 133
Monkman, J. A., 107
Montgomery, K. C., 107
Moore, Marv, 418
morphine, 386
Morris, D. D., 126
Morton, W. D., 64
mother-surrogate, 109, 133
motivation, 105ff.
Mowrer, O. H., 87
Mueller-Lyre illusion, 181
Müller, Johannes, 16, 169, 175
multiples, 16
Murdock, B. B., Jr., 272ff.
Murdock, George P., 446
Murphy, Gardner, 183, 202, 441, 464
Myro, G., 418
myths, 360ff., 457

Naegele, Kaspar D., 446
narcolepsy, 117
narcotic character, 388
natural selection, 442
neophobia, 41
Nesberg, L. S., 188
Neuringer, Charles, 319
neurotic, 388
Newell, A., 310
Newhall, S. M., 182, 185
Nissen, H. W., 140, 169
Norman, Donald A., 268
nude marathon groups, 344ff.
nudity, 344ff.
Nyswander, Marie, 388